NO LONGER THE PROPERTY OF
BALDWIN PUBLIC LIBRARY

THE LEONARD BERNSTEIN LETTERS

THE
LEONARD
BERNSTEIN
LETTERS

EDITED BY NIGEL SIMEONE

BALDWIN PUBLIC LIBRARY

YALE UNIVERSITY PRESS
NEW HAVEN AND LONDON

Letters by Leonard Bernstein © Amberson Holdings LLC. Used by permission of The Leonard Bernstein Office, Inc.

All other letters are the copyright of their respective owners. All rights, including the right of further reproduction or transmission, are reserved.

Introductory and editorial material copyright © 2013 Nigel Simeone

All rights reserved. This book may not be reproduced in whole or in part, in any form (beyond that copying permitted by Sections 107 and 108 of the U.S. Copyright Law and except by reviewers for the public press) without written permission from the publishers.

For information about this and other Yale University Press publications, please contact:

U.S. Office: sales.press@yale.edu www.yalebooks.com
Europe Office: sales@yaleup.co.uk www.yalebooks.co.uk

Set in Arno Pro by IDSUK (DataConnection) Ltd
Printed in the United States of America

Library of Congress Cataloging-in-publication Data
Bernstein, Leonard, 1918-1990.
  [Correspondence. Selections]
  The Leonard Bernstein letters / edited by Nigel Simeone.
    pages cm
  Includes bibliographical references and index.
  ISBN 978–0–300–17909–5 (hardback)
  1. Bernstein, Leonard, 1918–1990—Correspondence.   2. Musicians—United States—Correspondence.   3. Composers—United States—Correspondence.   4. Conductors (Music)—United States—Correspondence.   I. Simeone, Nigel, 1956– editor.   II. Title.
  ML410.B566A4 2013
  780.92—dc23
  [B]
                                                                  2013033122

A catalogue record for this book is available from the British Library.

10 9 8 7 6 5 4 3 2 1

For
Mark Horowitz,
Lauren Doughty,
and
Jasmine Simeone

Contents

Illustrations

Introduction and Acknowledgments

The Beginning of the Project

In early 2010, just after finishing a book about *West Side Story*, I was in the Performing Arts Reading Room at the Library of Congress, talking to Mark Horowitz about possible future projects. Mark's position as a Senior Music Specialist in the Music Division includes responsibility for the Leonard Bernstein Collection – so he knows this enormous archive better than anyone. In the course of one of our frequent chats, Mark made an apparently straightforward suggestion: "Why don't you do a book of the correspondence?" Those words lodged in my mind and the idea quickly began to take root.

One reason *not* to do the letters was their sheer bulk: many tens of thousands of them, grouped in different series: Personal Correspondence, Writings (which include few but wonderful letters), Fan Mail, and Business Papers – taking up hundreds of linear feet. But the temptation of working with Bernstein's correspondence was far too exciting a challenge to let these statistics – however daunting – get in the way. Betty Comden wrote to Bernstein back in 1950 about how he saved "every scrap of correspondence [. . .] from Koussevitzky's pages on life, music, and your career – to Auntie Clara's hot denunciations of meat" (Letter 301). How right she was. I already knew some of the letters from earlier research, and a trawl through the general correspondence was enough to demonstrate what an engrossing project this could be.

But how best to approach the task? The Bernstein Collection, used in conjunction with others in the Library of Congress, offered an enticing option: to present correspondence both to and from Bernstein. This was also made possible thanks to the efforts of Charlie Harmon at the Leonard Bernstein Office: after Bernstein's death in 1990, Harmon contacted significant people in Bernstein's life requesting photocopies of the letters they had received from him, and these copies were integrated into the folders in the Bernstein Collection. The Library of Congress already had Aaron Copland's and Serge Koussevitzky's papers, and it acquired David Diamond's in the course of my research. I drew up a preliminary selection of letters in early 2010 and set to work on the process of transcription and annotation. By the end of that year, the selection needed major revision – for the best of reasons. At the end of 2010, the Bernstein estate decided that a substantial group of letters sealed after his death should be made available, and added to the Bernstein Collection in the Library of Congress. Many of these "new" letters turned out to be enthralling: personal, funny, and revealing. As work progressed, still more letters came to light (thanks to the generosity of the recipients, or their heirs), and I was in a position to make a final selection – acutely aware, of course, that more Bernstein letters will emerge in the future.

The selection of correspondence in *The Leonard Bernstein Letters* is necessarily a personal choice: there were some very difficult decisions to be made in terms of what to leave out, and there is scope – and more than enough correspondence – for several further volumes. To give just a couple of examples: I have omitted most of the correspondence with his sister Shirley (including a large number of letters, mostly undated, written while she was a student at Mount Holyoke College) and from his brother Burton. A book of Bernstein family letters could make for fascinating reading. Many of them, however, concern family matters, and I had already decided that my principal focus for this book should be on correspondence that told us something about Bernstein himself, and particularly his life as a musician. It is for a similar reason that I have omitted most of the letters from Martha Gellhorn – many of them have little to say about music – though I have included a splendid letter about *West Side Story* and a most revealing one about her marriage to Ernest Hemingway.[1]

Illuminating a Musical Life

Anyone interested in Bernstein has the great advantage of Humphrey Burton's superbly researched and beautifully written biography. Twenty years after its first publication, it remains definitive as well as enthralling, and subsequent writers on Bernstein owe Humphrey Burton a great debt of gratitude. The present book would have been unthinkable without his work, but it sets out to do something different. While Burton quotes from a good deal of correspondence, his main purpose is to tell a life story. In *The Leonard Bernstein Letters* I have aimed to allow the letters mostly to speak for themselves, rather than to be woven into a linear biographical narrative. In addition, a number of letters have emerged or become available since Burton's book was published in 1994.

One of the delights of the Bernstein Collection is its astonishing breadth: there's extensive correspondence not only with those working in music, but also with writers, politicians, film stars, artists, journalists – and long-standing friends

---

[1] Other letters from Gellhorn to Bernstein are to be found in Moorehead 2006, pp. 265, 277–9, 280–2, 290, 292–3, 317–18, 323–4, 351–2, 413–14, 438, and 482–3. The letter about Hemingway is not included in Moorehead 2006.

who offered Bernstein support at times when he needed it. I have tried to reflect something of the range of these friendships. Even so, it is as a gigantic *musical* personality that Bernstein is remembered, and this has been my primary criterion for choosing the letters to include in what is the first published volume devoted to Bernstein's correspondence. In terms of other composers, Bernstein was in very close contact with Aaron Copland from the end of the 1930s onwards, and he also had an extensive correspondence with David Diamond stretching over five decades – a group of letters sometimes marked by tetchiness on Bernstein's part, and by a tendency to over-sensitivity on Diamond's. Such is the volume of the correspondence that I have had to omit letters from other close musical friends such as Paul Bowles and Irving Fine. These deserve to see the light of day in a future publication. In addition to correspondence with composers and performers, I have also aimed to include letters that chart the genesis of Bernstein's compositions. Two of his first big successes were collaborations with Jerome Robbins: a ballet (*Fancy Free*) and a musical (*On the Town*). In the case of *Fancy Free*, much of it was conceived and composed while Robbins and Bernstein were working away from home. As a result, there was detailed discussion by letter. It's frustrating that Robbins' letters to Bernstein about this ballet seem not to have survived. (Bernstein was constantly moving house at the time – and it was just before the arrival on the scene of his assistant, Helen Coates, who ensured that everything thereafter was carefully saved.) However, Bernstein's letters to Robbins constitute a fascinating chronicle of the work's composition. *On the Town* is a very different case: a collaboration where those concerned were working in the same place at the same time. As a result, there is no substantial correspondence about it with any of the collaborators (Bernstein, Robbins, Betty Comden, and Adolph Green) – indeed, in 1945, just after the show had opened on Broadway Comden mentioned in a letter to Bernstein that it was the first time she had written him since 1941.

West Side Story presents a more complex case – partly because it took so long to get started. A fascinating letter from Arthur Laurents, undated, but probably written in April 1949, raises some detailed points responding to what had evidently been a difficult phone conversation with Bernstein. A follow-up letter from Laurents (Letter 283) reveals that Bernstein considered pulling out of the project altogether. In 1955, the collaboration was revived, with greater determination on all sides to see it through. Again, there are some revealing letters, especially one from Robbins in which he responds in detail to Laurents and Bernstein about a draft scenario. Stephen Sondheim joined the creative team just after this, but there is no correspondence with him about the show until the opening night on Broadway (26 September 1957; Letter 402); then, a few weeks later, a marvelous description of the sessions for the original cast recording and the trials and tribulations of the show early in its run. Sondheim and Bernstein were not only in the same town but often in the same room while they were working on *West Side Story*, so the lack of correspondence during its creation shouldn't come as a surprise. That it was a happy creative partnership from the start, we learn from letters sent to other people: Bernstein wrote to his brother Burton in October 1955 that *"Romeo* proceeds apace, with a new young lyricist named Steve Sondheim, who is going to work out wonderfully" (Letter 363). The final stages of *West Side Story* are described by Bernstein in an engrossing series of letters to his wife Felicia, full of interesting details as well as his excitement, frustration, exhaustion, and optimism.

Bernstein's descriptions of his concerts reveal some recurring tensions. He often wrote (without irony) of his "triumphs" on the podium, but his phenomenal public success in the United States, in Europe, and in Israel was often tempered by an underlying frustration: after describing yet another acclaimed performance, Bernstein would sometimes declare that he was going to do less and less conducting, in order to devote time to what really mattered to him – composition.

It was conducting that gave him the opportunity to travel extensively, and Bernstein wrote some memorable letters home describing the places he visited. From being a young man who told his Harvard friends that he wasn't sure whether European travel was for him, he became not only a globe-trotting maestro but also an unusually observant traveler, writing about the sights and sounds of Prague, London, and Paris in the years after the Second World War, of months spent in Italy in 1955, of South America, Japan, and – most touching of all, perhaps – the accounts of his long visit to Israel during the 1948 war.

"Every one I love, I love passionately"[2]

Music was Bernstein's greatest and most constant passion. But his love life was an essential part of his make-up, and his letters allow us to form a fuller picture of an emotional life that was full of twists and turns – neatly summarized by the conductor Marin Alsop in 2010: "Clearly, he was comfortable with being sexual in many different ways and yet he wanted a traditional life, with a wife and children to whom he was devoted. He was a complex, complex man, and complex people have complex personal lives."[3] Intriguing as the letters are from those (usually men) with whom Bernstein had relationships during the 1940s, I have chosen instead to focus on Bernstein's own attitude to his sexuality, and its implications for his career. In correspondence with Copland and David Oppenheim in particular, and in some letters to his sister Shirley and to Diamond, he explores his sexual identity, often revealing a state of confusion and inner conflict. On the one hand, his background inculcated traditional values and relationships – ultimately marriage; on the other, his preferences in the 1940s were usually for men. Once his college studies were over, he began a process of self-exploration with the psychoanalyst he called the

---

[2] Leonard Bernstein to Mark Adams Taylor, quoted in Burton 1994, p. 507.
[3] Dougary 2010.

"Frau" – Marketa Morris. As we can see from their letters, he shared the same analyst with Oppenheim (with whom Bernstein had a close, surely intimate relationship in the early 1940s; their friendship was lifelong).

It's no surprise that Bernstein remained silent on the subject of his sexuality in letters to Koussevitzky – until, that is, he proudly announced his first engagement to Felicia in December 1946, suggesting a picture of his sexuality that was at best incomplete. Bernstein himself was anxious that his sex life might have a damaging impact on his employment prospects, fearing he could have difficulty finding a job as a conductor if it became known that he was gay.

It's worth pausing for a moment to consider the cultural and social context that gave Bernstein such concern about how others might view his sexuality. Many American psychoanalysts in the 1930s and 1940s considered homosexuality to be a mental illness that could respond to "treatment". The research by Alfred Kinsey and others published in 1948 as *Sexual Behavior in the Human Male* (the first "Kinsey Report") attempted to codify degrees of homosexual, heterosexual, and asexual behavior in men with the "Kinsey Scale", aiming to demonstrate that men did not fit into neat and exclusive categories.[4]

There was a predictably violent reaction to Kinsey's findings: among others, J. Edgar Hoover, director of the FBI, was quick to denounce the findings in the pages of *Reader's Digest*: "Man's sense of decency declares what is normal and what is not. Whenever the American people, young or old, come to believe that there is no such thing as right or wrong, normal or abnormal, those who would destroy civilization will applaud a major victory over our way of life."[5] In other words, homosexuality, like communism, was "Un-American". Two years later, in December 1950, the austerely named Senate Committee on Expenditures in the Executive Departments issued a report on the "Employment of Homosexuals and Other Sex Perverts in Government," coming to the hair-raising conclusion that "homosexuals and other sex perverts are not proper persons to be employed in Government for two reasons; first, they are generally unsuitable, and second, they constitute security risks."[6]

Bernstein was not, of course, seeking employment in the government, but he craved acceptance. There's little solid evidence to suggest that conductors were not appointed to particular positions because of their homosexuality in the 1940s and 1950s, though Dimitri Mitropoulos apparently believed he had been

---

[4] Kinsey, Alfred C., Wardell B. Pomeroy, and Clyde E. Martin (1948): *Sexual Behavior in the Human Male*. Philadelphia: W. B. Saunders.

[5] J. Edgar Hoover, contribution to "Must We Change our Sex Standards?", *Reader's Digest*, June 1948, p. 6.

[6] This report is reprinted in Foster, Thomas A., ed. (2013): *Documenting Intimate Matters: Primary Sources for a History of Sexuality in America*. Chicago: University of Chicago Press, pp. 144–7. According to an editorial note (p. 144): "More homosexuals than communists were fired from federal jobs in this period [the 1950s]."

victimized. But several of the most highly regarded figures in the arts were homo-sexuals, not least Aaron Copland, who had, by the mid-1940s, become the most popular and distinctive voice in American classical music. Bernstein, however, aspired to be the music director of a major American orchestra and felt– rightly or wrongly – that he needed to demonstrate he was a conventional, traditional family man. Despite Bernstein's frequent protestations that he craved the more private life of a composer (where his sexuality would not have been an issue), he could never let go of conducting as an essential part of his career.

What he didn't need to worry about as much was the possible impact his sexu-ality might have on his marriage – at least not as far as his chosen partner, Felicia Montealegre, was concerned. She knew what she was committing herself to: just after they married, she wrote: "you are a homosexual and may never change [. . .] I am willing to accept you as you are, without being a martyr or sacrificing myself on the L.B. altar (Letter 320)."

After a shaky start (mainly due to Bernstein's initial tendency to regard marriage as a kind of experiment), the relationship of Leonard and Felicia blossomed – particu-larly after Jamie, the first of their children, was born in 1952. An exceptionally bright child, it's clear from Bernstein's letters home how much he adored her. The same love shines through in Bernstein's comments on all his children (Jamie, Alexander, and Nina); and his absolute devotion to Felicia is apparent in many letters from the early 1950s until the mid-1970s. It was a relationship that had its rocky moments, but only with the crisis of 1976 and their "trial separation" did it threaten to fall apart. At the end of his life, Bernstein joked to Jonathan Cott that "you need love, and that's why I have ten thousand intimate friends which is unfair to them because I can't give any one of them everything".[7] But for a quarter of a century, Felicia was the exception: she was unquestionably the greatest love of his life.

Editorial Method

Original spellings have been preserved (except where stated otherwise), as have ampersands and punctuation in the main texts of letters, though opening saluta-tions have been standardized to be followed by a comma. Names have sometimes been added in square brackets for the sake of clarification. Titles of works that would normally be italicized in a printed text (*West Side Story, Fancy Free, The Age of Anxiety*) have been italicized. In the original letters they appear in a variety of styles – in double quotation marks, in single quotation marks, under-lined, in capital letters, in plain text. For the sake of consistency, I decided to standardize their presentation. Words underlined in letters have been italicized. Dates of letters are presented in a standardized day-month-year format, the form

---

[7] Cott 2013, p. 77.

usually preferred by Bernstein himself. Where a date (or part of a date) is uncertain, or speculative, or deduced from the content of a letter, it is given in square brackets. Addresses have been standardized, and for the sake of avoiding ambiguity, those sent from outside the United States include the country. Those sent from within the United States include the standard two-letter state codes (NY, MA, CA, and so on). In rare cases where a word is unreadable, this has been noted in square brackets. Most letters are presented complete, but where cuts have been made, or where only an extract has been included, these are shown by an ellipsis in square brackets, thus: [. . .]. In many cases the letters speak for themselves, but occasionally clarification or further explanation is necessary, and those letters can have quite extensive notes. I have also included short notes about all the correspondents (at the end of the first letter to or from the person concerned). In the case of a particularly long or complex document such as Bernstein's 1953 affidavit, I thought it useful to include an explanatory note exploring the context in greater detail.

Acknowledgments

My largest debt of gratitude is to Mark Horowitz of the Library of Congress. I am immensely grateful to him for planting the idea for the project in the first place, and for all his subsequent help and advice, his constant support and encouragement, and his friendship. During many visits to the Performing Arts Reading Room of the Library, every single member of the staff I've encountered has been helpful and as done a great deal to make my research easier.

Marie Carter, Vice-President of Licensing and Publishing at the Leonard Bernstein Office, Inc., has been encouraging from the start, and extremely helpful throughout. I am deeply grateful for her patience in answering my numerous queries and the wisdom of her replies, and for allowing me access to newly released correspondence at the earliest possible opportunity.

Mervyn Cooke offered a number of invaluable suggestions after reading an early draft of the text. His wisdom and experience have done much to improve the book.

Sophie Redfern shared the fruits of her own research on Bernstein's early ballets with overwhelming generosity, and also read the text from start to finish with a most careful and discriminating eye. I am enormously grateful to her.

For various acts of kindness – large and small – there are many people I need to thank, including Mark Audus, Peter and Mary Bacon, Stephen Banfield, Adam Binks, Humphrey Burton, Marius Carney, William Crawford, Lauren Doughty, Barry Irving, Libby Jones, Barbara Kelly, John McClure, Dominic McHugh, Richard Marshall, Gary O'Shea, Tom Owen, Robert Pascall, Caroline Rae, Catherine C. Rivers, Reggie and Josephine Simeone, Máire Taylor, John Tyrrell, and, most importantly, my extraordinary wife Jasmine.

The editor and publisher gratefully acknowledge the permission granted to reproduce copyright material in this book. Every effort has been made to trace copyright holders and to obtain their permission for the use of copyright material. The publisher apologizes for any errors or omissions, and would be grateful for any corrections, which will be incorporated in future reprints or editions of this book. For kind permission to quote letters, I thank the following individuals and institutions: The Leonard Bernstein Office, Inc., Ellen Adler, Marin Alsop, the Richard Avedon Foundation, the Britten-Pears Foundation, Humphrey Burton, Victor Cahn, the Aaron Copland Fund for Music, Inc., Christopher Davis (Marc Blitzstein), Sam Elliott (David Diamond) Martin Fischer-Dieskau Cornelia Foss (Lukas Foss), Very Rev. Nicholas Frayling (Walter Hussey), David Grossberg (Alan Jay Lerner), the Barbara Hogensen Agency (Thornton Wilder), Janis Ian, Pat Jaffe (David Oppenheim), Jay Julien (Farley Granger), Caroline Kennedy, Marko Kleiber, Alexandra Laederich (Centre international Nadia et Lili Boulanger), Maureen Lipman, Sandy Matthews (Martha Gellhorn), Michael Merrill (Bette Davis), Laurie Miller, Phyllis Newman (Adolph Green), Tom Oppenheim, Christopher Pennington (Robbins Rights Trust), Shirley Gabis Perle, Eddie Pietzak (Elia Kazan), Menahem Pressler, André Previn, Harold Prince (Saul Chaplin), Sid Ramin, Mary Rodgers, Isabella de Sabata, Gunther Schuller, Anthony and Andrea Schuman, Lady Valerie Solti, Stephen Sondheim, Stockhausen Stiftung für Musik, John Stravinsky, Margaret Styne, the Music Division, Library of Congress, Washington, D.C.; the Beinecke Rare Book and Manuscript Library, Yale University; the New York Public Library for the Performing Arts; and Stanford University Library.

At Yale University Press, my proposal for this book was taken up with the sort of enthusiasm that would warm any writer's heart. When I first presented the project to Robert Baldock and Malcolm Gerratt, their eagerness did much to spur me on, and Malcolm has calmly nurtured the book throughout. Tami Halliday's eagle-eyed reading during the book's final stages was of the greatest assistance. Candida Brazil has overseen the editing of my unwieldy manuscript with kindness and skill. Steve Kent devised the attractive layout and design of the book. Thanks are also due to Lauren Doughty for compiling the index. The text has been improved beyond recognition by the copy-editing of Richard Mason and the proof-reading of Vanessa Mitchell. All its faults, however, are mine.

Nigel Simeone
Rushden, Northamptonshire
June 2013

1

Early Years
1932–41

Leonard Bernstein was born on 25 August 1918, the first child of Jennie and Samuel Bernstein, in Lawrence, Massachusetts, 25 miles north of Boston. He attended the William Lloyd Garrison Elementary School in Roxbury, 35 miles from Lawrence, then, from 1929 to 1935, the prestigious Boston Latin School – founded in 1635. The oldest public school in the United States, its distinguished alumni included five Founding Fathers of the United States (among them Benjamin Franklin), the author Ralph Waldo Emerson, and the Puritan preacher Cotton Mather. The most famous musician to attend Boston Latin School before Bernstein was Arthur Fiedler (1894–1979), conductor of the Boston Pops for half a century. It was here that Bernstein's interest in languages and literature began to flourish, but what already obsessed him as a teenager was music. His first piano lessons (in 1928) were from Frieda Karp, the daughter of a neighbor, who charged $1 an hour for a lesson. Bernstein remembered her as "unbelievably beautiful and exotic looking,"[1] and his musical progress under her tutelage was swift. By 1930, he was taking lessons from Susan Williams at the New England Conservatory of Music, and in 1932 he auditioned with a former pupil of Theodor Leschetizky, Heinrich Gebhard, a distinguished soloist and the most sought-after piano teacher in Boston at the time. Gebhard believed that there was still fundamental technical work to be done, so he suggested Bernstein first take lessons with his assistant, Helen Coates. Bernstein's first communication with Miss Coates – who became his devoted secretary in 1944 until her death in 1989 – is also the earliest letter in this book. She taught him until 1935, when she sent him on to Gebhard, but by then they had become firm and devoted friends. Other friends and contemporaries with whom Bernstein corresponded regularly during his years at Boston Latin School, and later Harvard, included Sid Ramin, Beatrice Gordon, and Mildred Spiegel. Bernstein's letters to Sid Ramin are overflowing with shared enthusiasm for new musical discoveries – and talk of girlfriends – while to Beatrice Gordon he is passionate, self-revealing, and poetic. With very few exceptions, Bernstein's correspondence with Mildred Spiegel (later Mildred

---

[1] Burton 1994, p. 11.

Zucker) has not been made public, but as this book goes to press the Library of Congress anticipates adding these letters to its collection shortly. They document an important and lasting friendship. Descriptions of this correspondence can be found in Appendix Two.

Bernstein mentions difficulties with his father in a number of his letters from the 1930s. A one-page essay written by Bernstein on 11 February 1935 entitled "Father's Books" begins: "My father is a very complicated human being. A man of irregular temperament and unusual convictions, he is a rare combination of the shrewd businessman and ardent religionist." He was also an implacable opponent of Bernstein's pursuit of a career in music, and relations between father and son were often strained. His mother, by contrast, provided a warm, supportive household in which her son's ambitions flourished.

It was while studying music at Harvard University (1935–9) that Bernstein made some of his most important friendships: three of them in 1937. In January that year, he met the conductor Dimitri Mitropoulos, an encounter that left a deep impression on him. Then, as a music counselor at Camp Onota near Pittsfield, Massachusetts in the summer, Bernstein instantly formed a close bond with Adolph Green, who was to give him some of his first paid work (as pianist for The Revuers, nightclub performers of songs and comedy material, including Betty Comden, Green, and Judy Holliday) and who collaborated with him on two Broadway shows (*On The Town* and *Wonderful Town*). Finally, on 14 November, during a chance encounter at a dance recital in New York, Bernstein met Aaron Copland – father figure, confidant, and the closest Bernstein came to having a composition teacher.

Though it was as a pianist that Bernstein first attracted the attention of the local press, he confided to some of his closest friends that his real interest was conducting. In 1936 he wrote to Beatrice Gordon about auditioning to be assistant conductor of Harvard's Pierian Sodality (founded in 1808, and now known as the Harvard–Radcliffe Orchestra); at Camp Onota in 1937 he was photographed for the local paper conducting a group of children. In 1939, during his Senior Year at Harvard, Bernstein appeared for the first time as a composer–conductor (directing his incidental music for a production of Aristophanes' *The Birds*), and he directed Marc Blitzstein's musical *The Cradle Will Rock* from the piano.

After graduating from Harvard, Bernstein was uncertain about his future. He spent the summer of 1939 looking for a job in New York (sharing an apartment with Adolph Green), and explored the possibility of studying conducting at the Juilliard School (but he had missed the deadline). His only realistic option was to audition for the Curtis Institute in Philadelphia – specifically for the conducting class taught by Fritz Reiner – and he was admitted. From 1939 to 1941, he studied with teachers who were all at the top of their respective fields: conducting with Reiner, the piano with Isabelle Venegerova, orchestration with Randall Thompson, counterpoint with Richard Stöhr, and score-reading with Renée Longy Miquelle.

Finding Philadelphia a grim and dirty place, Bernstein would escape to New York for weekends at the slightest opportunity. His years at Curtis were marked by some important firsts, including his earliest professional recordings. These demonstrated his versatility, playing improvised incidental music and song accompaniments for *The Girl with the Two Left Feet* by The Revuers, and recording a Prelude and Fugue by David Diamond (less than five minutes of music about which Bernstein received long, anguished letters from the composer while preparing for the recording). In the summer of 1940 – midway through his studies at Curtis – Bernstein attended the inaugural summer course of the Berkshire Music Center at Tanglewood, to study conducting with the legendary Serge Koussevitzky. Mentor and pupil quickly became friends, and that summer Bernstein conducted the Second Symphony by Randall Thompson. Before the end of his studies in Philadelphia, Bernstein's first musical publication had also appeared in print: his solo piano transcription of Copland's *El Salón México*. He received his conducting diploma from Curtis in May 1941 – not a moment too soon, as he had been desperate to get away from the stifling atmosphere of Philadelphia.

At the first opportunity, Bernstein headed to Boston, where his years of study came full circle: he returned to Harvard to conduct the new incidental music that he had composed for a production of *The Peace* by Aristophanes. With war raging in Europe, it was a poignant choice. Back in January 1941, one of Bernstein's closest friends at Harvard – his room-mate, Al Eisner – had died in his early twenties. Eisner's letters from Hollywood are among the funniest and the most brilliant of all Bernstein's correspondents during his time at Curtis, while there was also a lively correspondence with Kenneth Ehrman, another Harvard friend, with whom Bernstein shared hopes, fears, and doubts about what his future in music might be.

1. Leonard Bernstein to Helen Coates[2]
8 Pleasanton Street, Roxbury, MA
15 October 1932

Dear Miss Coates,

I recently had an interview with Mr. Gebhard at his home. He was very encouraging in his remarks, and referred me to you as a teacher, with an occasional lesson from himself.

---

[2] Helen Coates (1899–1989) was Bernstein's piano teacher from the end of 1932 until 1935, and they became close friends. She kept a maternal eye on her protégé during his student years, and gave up piano teaching to become his secretary in 1944. She remained so until 1989. Her unspoken role in this book is of the greatest importance. It was Miss Coates who assembled and maintained Bernstein's scrapbooks, filed all his correspondence, labeled his photographs, organized his papers, and, as a consequence, did much to arrange the comprehensive documentation of his life that later formed the basis of the Leonard Bernstein Collection in the Library of Congress.

Having talked the matter over at home, I have decided to study with you, taking one lesson every two weeks. Would you please let me know by mail or phone when it would be convenient for you to give me my first lesson?[3]

Hoping to have the pleasure of studying with you soon,

Sincerely yours,

Leonard Bernstein

2. Leonard Bernstein to Sid Ramin[4]

17 Lake Avenue, Sharon, MA

26 June 1933[5]

Dear Sid,

I couldn't possibly write to you on newspaper (which was all the stationery we had in the house). I didn't until, a couple of days ago, I bought a box of stationery. So here I am and I have so darned much to tell you I don't know where to begin. Let's see . . .

First, I don't know if 40 is the right number Walnut Ave, but I'll take a chance. But I've got much more important news. *Turn over and see!*

I bought *Bolero*!!!

Well, well! You see, I didn't know it was arranged for 1 piano, but I happened to see it in Homeyer's window. Of course dad gave me the necessary $0.80 as he is so enthused about the piece. So for the past week it's been nothing but *Bolero*. My mother says I'm boleroing her head off. But am I in heaven! It's all written in French, and it's all repeats. In the original orchestral score, they repeat four times, but I repeat only once – which is enough because it gets boresome on the same instrument all the time, and repeating once takes 10 minutes anyway. And I can't get over it. Of course it doesn't come up to the way the orchestra plays it, but it's marvelous anyway. And the ending! Speaking of cacophony!! Boom! Crash! Discord! Sock! Brrrr-rr!! (down the scale).

---

[3] At the top of this letter Helen Coates has written the date of their first lesson: "Sat. at 1:00 Oct. 22".

[4] Sid Ramin (b. 22 January 1919), American composer, songwriter, arranger, and orchestrator. His credits as a Broadway orchestrator (in collaboration with Irwin Kostal, Robert Ginzler, or Hershy Kay) include *West Side Story* (1957), *Gypsy* (1959), *A Funny Thing Happened on the Way to the Forum* (1962) and *1600 Pennsylvania Avenue* (1976). He won an Academy Award for the new orchestrations he made with Kostal for the film of *West Side Story* (1961) and wrote the original score for *Stiletto* (1969). As a songwriter, Ramin is best known for "Music to Watch Girls By," originally written for a Diet Pepsi commercial, and subsequently widely recorded.

[5] This is the first of several letters sent by Bernstein to Ramin during the summer of 1933. Bernstein turned 15 on 25 August 1933 and Ramin was five months younger. Both had attended the William Lloyd Garrison Elementary School; when Bernstein went to the Boston Latin School (1929–35), Ramin went to Roxbury Memorial High School, but the two remained close. Ramin characterized their lifelong friendship as "a relationship of teacher and student that never changed throughout the years. Lenny was a born teacher; I was a born listener. [. . .] That relationship really was one that lasted until Lenny passed away. Always, it was teacher and student" (quoted in Oja and Shelemay 2009, p. 13).

Well now that I've got that off my chest I feel better. Oh you have got to hear it soon. But my piano is so lousy that one note doesn't play – but it serves the purpose.

I'll write you again soon and tell you a convenient time to come to Sharon, etcetera, and so forth, Amen.

But first write me – immediately – please don't forget. I'm dying to see and hear from you. Answer soon – meanwhile

Lenny

Is waiting.

P.S. I'm starting to teach my mother jazz! Heh! Heh!

P.P.S. I arrived home at 3.00 this A.M. Some time.

P.P.P.S. Write soon. Sincerely, L.B.

3. Leonard Bernstein to Sid Ramin

17 Lake Avenue, Sharon, MA

14 July 1933

Dear Sid,

I'm going to fool you twice. First – I'm not following your pattern on the envelope – you know, the "US" stuff. Know why? You couldn't guess in a million years. The post office complained about your exalted style – and "hope it shall be discontinued in the future." Imagine! So . . . But don't let it worry you.

The second way I'm fooling you is that I *did* hear Fray and Braggiotti[6] Tues. night. Were they swell! I was praying you were listening too. Will we have plenty to try over when you come. I hope it's lousy.

Listen, you probably know that the Chicago Civic Opera is putting on *Aida* – open-air – at Braves Field the 20th of this month. It looks like my father might take me. Wanna come? I'll be in town Mon. to get tickets. So expect a call from me Monday morning and tell me whether or not you're coming so I'll buy you a ticket. It'll be swell – a real big production – so try and come – I'm dying to see you anyway. So be ready Monday to say "Yes".

Gosh, I'm not in a letter-writing mood today, as you can probably see – this letter is a flop. But I'm tired from over-sleep. About 12 hours a night. I'll have to stay up all night tonight to make it up.

Listen, you come to see *Aida* with me, and we'll discuss all about your coming out here – in a week or two, I think.

Well a kid just called for me to go swimming – so I'll close here.

---

[6] Jacques Fray and Mario Braggiotti were a celebrated piano duo. They began their career at Le Bœuf sur le Toit, the Parisian cabaret, and became friends with George Gershwin when he visited Paris in 1928. They first came to New York in 1929 and quickly achieved immense popularity through regular appearances on the radio, and extensive tours of the United States.

Say – write longer letters; that last one was no answer for my 7-page letter.
Write soon.
Expect call Mon.
Regards to all.
Sincerely,
Lenny
P.S. Try to come next Thurs.
P.P.S. Fray & Braggiotti also played *España*.

4. Leonard Bernstein to Sid Ramin
17 Lake Avenue, Sharon, MA
18 July 1933

Dear Sid,

You didn't receive a call from me Mon. morning as we are not going to see *Aida* – that is, my father isn't, so that's where the "we" comes in. That's my whole card. Much as I hate to waste the rest of the card's worth, I have nothing more to write – so I must.

So long,
Lenny
Letter following.

5. Leonard Bernstein to Sid Ramin
[Sharon, MA]
25 July, 11:05 a.m. [1933]

Dear Sid,

I have a letter of letters in store for you (if I can get this pen to write).

There – that's better. I have so much news to write that it would take a telephone book to write it all. So I thought that it's as good an excuse as any to invite you, and you can come any time you want between now and Christmas. Only drop me a card letting me know when so that I can expect you. But make it darn soon. Tomorrow isn't soon enough.

Well, little Lenny has turned chauffeur! In the past week I have driven (in the old Chrysler) some 90 miles. Yesterday I did 60 [miles] an hour to and from Newton on the new road. What a life! My mother calls me "a good driver but a little reckless." But who could resist 60 on that road? We went to Newton to pick out colors for the new home. You should see that place! It's bigger, I think, than the 2-family house I lived in last year. A regular Colonial. It is beautiful.

You know, I'm making $1.00 every day I go in town and work for my father. And do I work! Last week I worked 3 days – $3.00. It's not so bad. So between that and working on these grounds I'm kept pretty busy.

Listen! Guess who's coming out here to visit someone across the street. Phil Saltman, who plays over the radio! You know him. I met his sister at a dance last Sat. night and she told me all about him. Am I excited! By the way, did you hear *Bolero* played by the Goldman Band last Sun. night? "Swunderful".

Now this letter is also going to be very private correspondence. So guard it in your "iron frame". First, you're not the only one who's met a nice girl. There are a couple of girls who keep pestering us, but we don't pay any attention to them. But last night a crowd of us went for a moonlight swim (it was wonderful! – till it began to thunder and lightning) – and I met her – and – well, we're kinda interested in each other. I['ll] let you know of further developments.

Secondly, I'm on a "no cigarette" campaign. I'm trying my darndest not to smoke. But you know the old psychology, "If you want to break one habit you must substitute something else for it." So I'm trying the old pipe. And it seems to be working OK. You know, a pipe is a much healthier smoke than a cigarette – so I hope it works. Did you see Eddie Schnaub? How does he look. Does he speak like a New Yorkite?

Listen, don't answer this letter. Just drop a card, as follows:

Lenny:

Will be out on _____. Sid.

That's all – and come as soon as possible. If you have no way to come, write me first the same and I pick you up in Roxbury coming home from town. Forget not.

So that's that. Make sure you come. That's the main point to this letter.

Expecting you soon,

Lenny

P.S. What to bring? About a week's supply of stockings, handkerchiefs, a couple of shirts, a sweater, bathing suit, tooth-brush, comb, a couple of pair of pants – one old and one new – *and* expect to be talked to death and driven by me up a lamp post.

Heh Heh!

L.B.

See you sooner than soon.

6. Sid Ramin to Leonard Bernstein
Postmark Revere, MA
28 August 1933

Dear Len,

I just heard the *Creole Rhapsody* written by Duke Ellington. It was also played by him and his orchestra. It's written on the same scale as *my* Rhapsody in Blue and you ought to hear the big discords. Wow! It's written in two parts and it has a very pretty melody running throughout. Listen to it. Yes, it's nice. I've *only* heard it about six times.

Syd

P.S. Say, answer my letter!

7. Leonard Bernstein to Sid Ramin

17 Lake Avenue, Sharon, MA

2 September 1933

Dear Sid,

I plead for every pardon in not writing to you before – *but* I can fall back on the old, substantial excuse – no stationery – and I couldn't get any until I went into town yesterday and bought some of Kresge's famous 10¢ 'Evon' stationery. (Can't you recognize it?)

By the way, I heard the Fred Waring version of *Bolero* – and it was sort of heavenly. But too much was cut out.

And to think you used a whole postcard just to inform me of the existence of the *Creole Rhapsody*! Thanks. I haven't heard it yet.

Listen, I'm thinking seriously about meeting you in town. Is this OK?

Time: Wednesday, Sept 6 between 9 and 10 at

Place: my father's office, 48 Wash[ington] St, Boston.

If I'm not there, wait! If you're not, I will. Bring some dough – we'll see a show, have lunch, etc. etc. Please try to make it. I'm counting on it. If you can't, well, just do anyway. It'll be one of the last times I'll see you before I move to Newton. I was in town yesterday and we moved. Is it beautiful in Newton! Our house couldn't be gorgeouser than it is. And guess what!! I'm getting an organ for Newton!!!! Don't ask, now you'll have to come out and visit us.

I haven't written half the things I had in mind, so I'll tell you Wed. morning. Please try to come. I'll be expecting you.

Sincerely,

Lenny.

Come Wed.

P.S. Eddie R[yack][7] just went home. I think he had a nice time.

Please come Wed.

---

[7] Eddie Ryack was a school friend, and co-inventor with Bernstein of Rybernian, the imaginary language they devised.

8. Leonard Bernstein to Sid Ramin

17 Lake Avenue, Sharon, MA
7 September 1933

Dear Sid,

It's just as well you didn't come Wed., because at the last minute my father told me I couldn't go. So that's that. I prayed that my letter wouldn't reach you in time.

Write me by return mail how long you'll be in Revere, and also your new address. We'll be in Sharon until the middle of Oct.

Lenny

P.S. We were in Winthrop the other day but I didn't have time to look you up. (Write soon.) L.

9. Leonard Bernstein to Helen Coates

17 Lake Avenue, Sharon, MA
13 July 1935

Dear Miss Coates,

I was awaiting the opportunity of receiving my Board returns before writing you, and that event has just transpired – with explosive definiteness. Following is the glad news:

English: the highest mark in the school, 90%. That makes me one of the very fractionary percentage of candidates who were allowed to receive 90% or over. (I believe the percent is .1%.)

French: 90%

Physics: one of the highest marks in the school, 70%

History, my nemesis: 60%. Which is excellent considering my heavy doubts and serious lack of knowledge in the field.

All of which makes me an 82% man; and with the fine recommendations I have received, I should be accepted into Harvard. I shan't know until about the end of this month.

Before I forget myself and write an "I" letter, I want to wish you a very pleasant summer. I surmise that you are now basking in the sun-pure, orange-sweet air of California.

My summer has so far been so full I haven't had time to waste. I'm in perfect health, have gained weight, and grown bodily and mentally. But there is more than that. I intend to offer the public another Bernstein operatic production such as *Carmen* last year. We intend to use *Rigoletto* or possibly *Faust*.

I know how interested you are in my friends and associations, and so I feel I must tell you what a wonderful friend I have just made. Last week a girl I know here in Sharon introduced me to another boy she knows. His name is Laurie

Bearson,[8] and he is the epitome of intelligence and artistic sympathy. We became very close friends in the past week. It is as though we were soul-mates; there is a perfect understanding between us. He is intensely interested in dramatic work, and has been doing Sunday night broadcasts for some time. He is four years older than I, but that seems such an insignificant factor when we talk together. Of course there is always an interference; and in this case it is that he is going to New York to work. He left this morning and it feels as though a mountain has collapsed. But we shall correspond regularly.

My Sunday evening broadcasts are finished, and with apparent success as far as "Avol"[9] is concerned. I am to play next week for Mischa Tulin's[10] program. I have begun to do some earnest practicing, and with the help of our mutual friend Mildred [Spiegel], hope to keep it up.

I should love to hear from you in the near future. Write me and tell me how you are enjoying your vacation.

Very sincerely,

Leonard Bernstein

By the way, one of the themes I wrote on the English board was based on genius. Being allowed to draw from unliterary material, I used my musical knowledge, and that probably secured for me my 90 –

L.B.

10. Leonard Bernstein to Beatrice Gordon[11]
9 September 1935

Envelope addressed: "For one in whom I cannot distinguish the Pitti-Sing from the Beatrice."

To Beatrice, on the occasion of the 17th anniversary of her birth.

I.

I sometimes think of you as a Beethoven who frowns;
And wastes his passion, eloquently labored
On clowns.

---

[8] Lawrence Bearson, who later worked as a writer for the Federal Theatre Project of the Works Progress Administration (WPA), c. 1937–9.

[9] AVOL were sponsors of a series of Sunday radio broadcasts on WBZ, Boston in 1935. These gave the young Bernstein some early experience of playing on the radio.

[10] Mischa Tulin (d. 1957) was a Russian pianist and Theremin virtuoso who emigrated to America at the time of the 1917 Russian Revolution. His teachers included Glazunov and Busoni.

[11] Beatrice Gordon (1918–83) lived in Roxbury, MA. She was described by Bernstein as "the love of my life" at the time (Burton 1994, p. 22). She performed in his teenage productions of *Carmen* (1934) – a spoof version, performed in drag (she appeared as Don José opposite Bernstein's Carmen), and as Pitti-Sing in *The Mikado* (1935), a more ambitious staging put on by "The Sharon Players." Burton summarized their relationship as follows: "His attachment to Beatrice Gordon, who sang Don José in matador pants at Sharon, went well beyond music. They were both romantics, enamoured of poetry and words. He called her "Tiger on Brocade" (an early example of his obsession with anagrams) and "Rosebeam" ' (Burton 1994, p. 29).

II.

I sometimes think that you are Palestrina, who measures;
And sets an irrevocable, Bach-like standard
For pleasures.

III.

I one time thought that you were a Godiva – shameless;
Who flaunts her unconventionalities,
Blameless.

IV.

And ofttimes you are Miniver,[12] who mourns each passing day,
Because it carries him from Renaissance
Further away.

V.

I sometimes think of you as Amy Lowell;[13] – "Old Lace" –
Too delicate to touch, and yet to[o] stern
To face.

There are, you see, two youths to every life;
The first, the ten and seven years just past,
In which the phantasies of you engage in strife;
The next, which till your dying day will last,
Will harbor all these phantasies again,
But bring them into concord, free from pain,
To make the complex *you*, sans blush, sans feign . . .

Best of luck!
Leonard Bernstein
Sept 9, 1935

11. Leonard Bernstein to Beatrice Gordon
Eliot G-41, Harvard University, Cambridge, MA
1 October [1936]

Dear Verne,[14]
   Never before in the history of mankind have such great and impossible steps been taken by an individual to improve his native resources and induce foreign ones. I have resolved myself to a year of work & study – imagine, a complete

---

[12] Probably a reference to "Miniver Cheevy" (who "loved the Medici"), by the American poet Edwin Arlington Robinson (1869–1935).
[13] Amy Lowell (1874–1925), American poet who was awarded a Pulitzer Prize posthumously in 1926.
[14] Verne was Beatrice Gordon's middle name.

cutting down of – I shouldn't say complete – I haven't the courage to resolve completely – but cutting out, shall one say, of most social life, of a great deal of outside playing, of innumerable other time-wasters. Diametrically opposed as that realization is to my character, I have little doubt of the results, but there is no harm in hoping. And I am going to practice! For instance, three hours of it tomorrow in the very romantic tower room. Under the expert guidance of my roommate who does everything by systems & budgets, I shall perhaps prosper.

I don't know when I can see Dixon (properly spelled [Harry Ellis?] Dickson) but I think I can next Friday morning.

Among other things [...] there is a quasi-contest here sponsored by the conductor of the Harvard Orchestra (Pierian Sodality to you) for an apt candidate for associate conductor with opportunity to conduct rehearsals & "study conducting with Malcolm Holmes" (Pfui*). Tryouts next week.

Courses? Two in Music – Harmony & historical survey – a complete Shakespeare (perfectly thrilling) and a course in types of Philosophy given by Hosking. Later on, advanced Italian (which means Dante, Tasso, Ariosto, Castiglione etc.) Wonderful?

Write soon, & let me know of your studies.

Affectionately,

Len

*Consult Oxford Dictionary

12. Leonard Bernstein to Beatrice Gordon
Eliot G-41, Harvard University, Cambridge, MA
30 January 1937

Your note, dear Verne, was most charming and thoughtful. In fact it was really a lamb's ear.[15]

I'm so sorry that I couldn't come over sooner or let you know why, whether, or when; but, you see, your note appeared on a scene of great confusion, it being (and still is) exam period, and in the midst of that still greater emotional upheaval of which you have no doubt heard.[16] I must tell you all the details some time. It's the most fascinating, occult, hair-raising fairy story you could conceive of. You know, something one reads or dreams about – not experiences.

My very dear Beatrice, I'm so anxious to see you & will do my very best to be down as soon as I can after the examinations.

---

[15] In some of his letters to Beatrice Gordon, Bernstein signs himself "Lamb's Ear".
[16] A reference to Bernstein's first encounter with Dimitri Mitropoulos in January 1937, which was evidently a torrid occasion.

What are you doing to fill your time? I'm very anxious to hear about your 50-cent pupil. Give him (or her, or it) my very best personal regards and recite to her the following after each lesson:

Some folks think they get a lot
By paying huge recompense;
But I know one who gets the best
By paying fifty cents.

Also, if you have time:

It's a funny thing about strip-girls,
They give you so much, no more;
They never go below a certain point
Except Tuesday which have twenty-four.
(A metrical masterpiece).

Take care, & my love to your mother and all concerned.
From
Leonard
with affectionate January.

13. Leonard Bernstein to Beatrice Gordon
Eliot G-41, Harvard University, Cambridge, MA
28 February 1937

It's a curious thing, Beatrice – I'm being quite frank – or maybe I'm a curious being, I know not which. But I can pass months at a time, blindly busy with the immediacies which engage me, always unconscious of time and space, barred in by momentary emotions and reactions. Then I may chance upon something quite without this fettered up little circle, and be quite startled. That happened to me today, when I saw you. It occurred quite suddenly to me that I hadn't seen you for a very long time, and that I really was interested in seeing you. And it's doubly curious when I think that I *have* been communicating with you, hearing your name mentioned, even occasionally struck by a thought of you; and always taking the thing so amazingly without cerebral deflection. And for no reason – tho your picture has been here on my desk, and tho your hair had collapsed – I remember that here you were, and I hadn't seen you.

All this must sound fairly obviously like the product of dementia, and Lord knows I don't know why I'm writing it. I merely felt a moment ago that I should like to talk to you. I have nothing to say – I'm too tired – yet this. I am suddenly aware of you.

That's all: there's nothing to say.
Good night, Beatrice.

14. Leonard Bernstein to Sid Ramin

Eliot G-41, Harvard University, Cambridge, MA
12 March 1937

Dear Syd,

I'm glad to see that you've decided to study with me. I think you'll get a lot out of it. You see, even if I don't have the professional training that the "Miss Jewels" have, I can give you a comprehensive outlook on harmony – which is the most important of the three – with an eye ever cast in the direction of jazz. What I can give you will always be directly applicable to jazz, and there will be nothing superfluous, and, I hope, nothing neglected.

It seems to me that Fridays at about 3:30 would be ideal; if you can't make it so early perhaps 4:00 would do, but not later. In fact, the earlier the better; if 3:00 it's even better. See if you can't make it next Friday at 3:00. If you can't, drop me a card and we'll make other arrangements. If I don't hear from you, I'll take it that you're coming.

Best of everything,

Len

Incidentally, voici les particuliers of how to get here:

Go to Summer Street Station and walk thru to a Cambridge train. Get off the latter at the last stop – Harvard Square, which is like this:

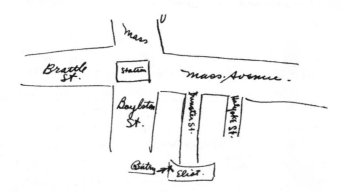

Walk down Dunster Street *as far as you can*; it will take you right in the back door of Eliot House, leading you to a courtyard into which all the entries face. Go to G (gee) entry, walk up to Room 41 (all doors are marked) and knock vigorously. Voilà!

Then I'll either see you next Friday or hear from you sooner.

Good luck,

Len

15. Leonard Bernstein to Helen Coates
Camp Onota, Pittsfield, MA
4 August 1937

Dear Miss Coates,

I hope that you are now fully recovered from your operation. I was so sorry to hear of it, but I'm sure that you are glad to be over & above it by now.

I'm having a splendid time here at camp,[17] though I get very little time for myself. But I guess that a good vacation is as important as work; and I am trying to rearrange my schedule to allow for practice.

I hope that you're enjoying a very pleasant summer. I should love to hear from you.

As always,
Leonard Bernstein

16. Leonard Bernstein to Beatrice Gordon
Eliot G-41, Harvard University, Cambridge, MA
8 September 1937

Beatrice – Dear Beatrice!

Had I known that you were not invited to the party I should have taken definite measures. I understood that you had been asked – I cannot imagine any possible reason for such an oversight. I've argued and argued with my sister, and she cannot possibly find any reason for forgetting you. She just did, as any child of her age is apt to do, and as she did forget some other people. So please forgive her. But I cannot understand why you didn't come up after I had asked you.

At any rate, let's pass over it – there's not much to be done now.

I expected to see you in Sharon, but today you suddenly disappeared. Sunday I was busy with my horde of guests from N.Y – Monday & Tuesday were horrible holidays, & when I finally sought you Tuesday evening, lo! you had awayed to the movies. I did want very much to see you – there would have been much to say.

I'm really very happy over your new (or is it already old?) job, & I wish you all success in it.

As for me, I shall spend until the opening of Harvard College gently fed sleep by a rosebeam.

I do hope to see you soon.

My best to all at home.

Take care of yourself.

Lamb's Ear

---

[17] On 31 July 1937, a few days before writing this letter, Bernstein had been musical director for a Camp Onota production of Gilbert and Sullivan's *The Pirates of Penzance*, with Adolph Green as the Pirate King. The first known photograph of Bernstein as a conductor – conducting the Camp Onota Rhythm Band – also dates from the summer of 1937.

17. Leonard Bernstein to Beatrice Gordon
Eliot G-41, Harvard University, Cambridge, MA
[9 September 1937]

Rosebeam:
        Still the years go on,
        And still you're two weeks behind me –
        Perhaps as years go on
        You will really catch up and find me;

        But until you do
        May Fortune be our brother;
        And may we in joy march thru the years
        Two weeks apart from each other.

        And one more little wish:
        (For me as well as you) –
        May nothing but those two little weeks
        Ever come between us two.

        Lamb's Ear

    N.B.1: I make up, you notice, for your omitting to send me the customary poem by addressing the gist of the above trivial, tho very sincere, masterpiece to the both of us.
    N.B.2: Lose not another minute before reading Gabriele D'Annunzio's *The Flame of Life*. Quick! It's incredible.
    Happiest of Birthdays!

18. Leonard Bernstein to Mildred Spiegel[18]
[October 1937]
Announcement for a concert at the Sanders Theatre, Cambridge, in which Bernstein played the Ravel Piano Concerto with the State Symphony Orchestra, amended by Bernstein:

---

[18] Mildred Spiegel (b. 1916), American pianist. One of Bernstein's closest friends in the 1930s and early 1940s, she became his regular partner on two pianos and they were both pupils of Heinrich Gebhard. Bernstein wrote his Piano Trio for Spiegel's Madison Trio (active from 1935 to about 1940). Its members were Mildred Spiegel (piano), Dorothy Rosenberg (violin), and Sarah Kruskall (cello). According to the violist Raphael Hillyer (1914–2010), Spiegel also played the Piano Trio with him (violin) and Jesse Ehrlich (cello) at Harvard in about 1939 (see Derrick Wang: Raphael Hillyer Interview, http://isites.harvard.edu/icb/icb.do?keyword=bernstein). In 1951, Spiegel married Zevi Harry Zucker (1921–2012).

THE ~~STATE~~ *Boston* SYMPHONY ORCHESTRA

~~ALEXANDER THIEDE~~ — Conductor

serge koussevitzky

announces

LEONARD BERNSTEIN

(Artist-Pupil of Heinrich Gebhard)

SOLOIST

in the

RAVEL PIANO CONCERTO

Sympho. 2nd Performance in Boston

AT S~~ANDE~~RS THEATRE, CAMBRIDGE

SUNDAY, OCTOBER 31st, 1937, at 8 P. M.

This au 1 go on !

19. Dimitri Mitropoulos[19] to Leonard Bernstein

Minneapolis, MN

5 February 1938

My dear, dear boy,

Believe me, your letter touched me very deeply. I never forget you. I was only really very busy, all this past year and now just the same. But now I feel you more near and that gives me more courage to write you.

Then, dear friend, is that so, is that true, that you believe so much in me? Have I really failed to you, have I really left you a void after our last meeting? This thought makes me crazy, and so happy that I dare not believe it. Nobody else has ever written me such a thing! In any way even, that you thought to write it makes me happy.

Dear boy, if you only could know how alone I am, all my life is a complete devotion to my art. Beyond this I am living like an ascetic.

There are many people probably who love me and are my friend, but it fails me, this unique one to whom I can believe with all my heart and soul. I am so full of the necessity to give my love, I am so full of love, that I am always spending it to every human being. Your letter was really a great gift for me and I thank you, thank you so much for this your unexpected gift.

Now let me tell you what I am thinking about your last interest on modern American dance music. I can't say I know it well, but in any way I advise you to be careful and don't forget that even the American dance music is always a dance form and that this kind of music form is not the most interesting and useful form to exercise oneself on it. I feel sorry if the most part of your composing is devoted to such a poor form of music. Of course I agree that we may release

---

[19] Dimitri Mitropoulos (1896–1960), Greek conductor. Bernstein first encountered him in January 1937 and the two immediately became very close. At some time in the late 1930s they almost certainly became involved in a relationship.

from time to time doing easy and light things, to amuse ourselves, but not too much. We must train ourselves to [do] difficult things, to surpass ourselves, not to leave even a moment of your life without to be anxious to do it. In any way, to avoid to sleep too much on a very soft bed! I hope you will understand me. I had the impression that you are a very deep feeling boy and I hope that this your last sympathy with dance music is momentary. Perhaps you needed to relax, but excuse me in your age you don't need to relax before [you] have done your duty towards your art. If it is only for a pleasure, good, but not too much. We must keep ourselves as pure as possible.

Now tell me dear boy, do you wish to spend some holidays (about a week for instance if you can be free) and come to me here. I am inviting you in any way and I shall take care of *all your expenses*. Will you?

I shall be very happy if there was a possibility to see you again.

With all my sincerest sympathy.

Yours,

D. Mitropoulos[20]

20. Leonard Bernstein to Aaron Copland[21]
Eliot E-51, Harvard University, Cambridge, MA
[received 22 March 1938]

God damn it, Aaron,

Why practice Chopin Mazurkas? Why practice even the Copland *Variations*? The week has made me so sick, Aaron, that I can't breathe any more. The whole superfluousness of art shows up at a time like this, and the whole futility of spending your life in it. I take it seriously – seriously enough to want to be with it constantly till the day I die. But why? With millions of people going mad – madder every day because of a most mad man strutting across borders – with

---

[20] Some of Mitropoulos' spelling has been silently corrected.
[21] Aaron Copland (1900–90), American composer whose music, and whose friendship, wisdom, and advice, made the deepest impression on Bernstein. Always regarded by Bernstein as his most important musical mentor, Copland's admiration for Bernstein was more nuanced: he had the highest regard for him as a conductor but sometimes expressed reservations about his compositions. From the start of Bernstein's career, Copland gave him the fullest support. On 17 March 1940, he wrote the following recommendation to Mrs Grant for Bernstein to be admitted to Koussevitzky's conducting class at Tanglewood: "In my opinion, Mr. Bernstein is an extraordinarily gifted young musician. I have seldom met his equal for sheer musicianship. His musical memory is remarkable, and so is his ability to sight-read both scores and piano music. He is besides a first-rate pianist. He possesses the type of temperament which I believe is particularly sympathetic to Dr. Koussevitzky. His practical experience as a conductor is very slight, but he has had a year's training at the Curtis Institute under Fritz Reiner. Randall Thompson told me that Mr. Reiner considered Bernstein one of the best students he had ever had. Needless to say, I think it important that Bernstein gain an individual seance with Dr. Koussevitzky when the proper moment arrives. I'd appreciate it if that could be arranged."

every element that we thought had refined human living and made what we called civilization being actively forgotten, deliberately thrown back like railroad tracks when you look hard enough at them – what chance is there? Art is more than ever now proved entertainment – people, we thought, were ready, after two thousand years of refining Christianity, to look for entertainment as such; to look for things that come out of the category of vital necessity! And so we were willing to spend our lives creating that entertainment. Aaron, it's not feasible; it's a damned dirty disappointment.

Then came the climax of the week. Cara Verson – whoever she is; to me she looks like an enlarged porcupine – had advertised for weeks that she was going to give in the Jordan Hall here, a whole program of modern music. I was all excited; it was unprecedented, and very courageous of her in this dead city, etc., etc. And I put so much hope in that damned concert. It came: and I find it difficult to talk about it. It was a tremendous program – Malipiero, Kodály, Hindemith – and – joy of joys! – the Copland *Variations*.[22] That, I guess, was the premiere in Boston. Well, to get to the point, I don't know whether you knew it was going to be played here, but if you did, how did you allow it?

In short, she gave really no performance at all. I can stand a bad performance, but not *no* performance. She began the thing wrong, played about two measures, skipped some variations, got lost again, skipped about 5 pages, played a few measures out of tempo – entirely without any discernment, without any idea of rhythm – and kept this up (playing little measures from choice variations) until she reached the coda. Then she played about half of it and called it a day. I was purple – I wish I could let you know how incredibly bad it was. It was the work of an imbecile. I left then and broke dishes in the Georgian cafeteria.

Do you see what that farce meant, Aaron? The few people that were there thought she was wonderful – such a *touch!* (!!!) They tried to look intellectually intelligent about the music when the whole performance was one of bafflement! The one little chance that this little town gets to hear some modern piano stuff – (nobody dares to do it at a recital) – we find instead the complete distortion of the whole art, a perversion of these people's attitude when we need every resource to show them the right thing, correctly done. And where did this foul woman get press notices for her folder? Aaron, find that woman and have her put away. She's fatal.

Excuse this outburst, Aaron, but the whole concatenation of rotten, destructive things has made me very angry and disappointed. At Harvard the situation is aggravated by these horrible musical dolls who infest the place. I find it almost impossible to stand. Thank God for you. Our last hope is in the work you are doing.

Leonard Bernstein

---

[22] A work Bernstein knew very well. He had played to Copland when they first met, on 14 November 1937 – Copland's birthday.

21. Aaron Copland to Leonard Bernstein

Hotel Empire, Broadway at 63rd Street, New York, NY
23 March 1938

Dear Leonard,

What a letter! What an "outburst"! Hwat a boy! It completely spoiled my break-fast. But it couldn't spoil the weather, so thank Marx for that. The sun has been shining in a way to defy all wars and dictators, and there's nothing to be done about it.

That "female" you tell of [Cara Verson]. I've never seen her, but I had reports of her at a time when she played the *Variations* here, which I studiously avoided attending. I see that did no good, since she continues to "play" them. But what can a poor composer do? I know of know way of stopping her once the piece is published, do you? Think what people do to the three B's etc. and nothing can be done about *that*. As for your general "disappointment" in Art, Man and Life I can only advise perspective, perspective, and yet more perspective. This is only 1938. Man has a long time to go. Art is quite young. Life has its own dialectic. Aren't you always curious to see what tomorrow will bring?

Of course, I understand exactly how you feel. At 21, in Paris, with Dada thumbing its nose at art, I had a spell of extreme disgust with all things human. What's the use – it can't last, and it didn't last. The next day comes, there are jobs to do, problems to solve, and one gets gradually inured to things. At my advanced age (37) I can't even take a letter like yours completely seriously. But I'm glad you wrote it, if only to let off steam. Write some more!

Now it's definite that I'm not due to be up in Boston. I've been bought off with the promise of a performance at the coming Berkshire Festival. (Don't mention this around, will you.) I'm vaguely thinking of a trip to England in May. Sir Adrian Boult is to conduct my *Salón México* at the I.S.C.M. Festival in June, and previously on the BBC on April 20th; also here when he conducts the NBC orchestra in May. I hope you're coming to New York soon. I always enjoy seeing you.

Always,
Aaron

22. Aaron Copland to Leonard Bernstein

Box 15, Princeton, NJ
Sat. [April 1938]

Dear Leonard,

I've come out to Princeton for a few weeks to try to finish that book[23] by June. It's lovely here – reminds me of my spring in Cambridge (unfortunately Cambridge is 5 hrs from N.Y. and this only 1 hr.).

---

[23] Presumably Copland's *What to Listen for in Music* which was published in 1939.

I got your Minn[eapolis] card. Wish I could hear more about your trip.

I had a letter from the WPA[24] orchestra in Boston the other day saying they had programmed my *Dance Symphony* for Apr 26 at Sanders Theatre. If you have time to go will you write me your impressions of the performance? And send me any reviews that appear? (Don't forget – it's an early work!)

How are you in general? Is Bennington decided upon? I haven't seen Norman Lloyd[25] since I talked with Davis, but I'll mention you to him when I do.

Any chance of your being at the Berkshire Fest. this year? I'm vaguely tempted to go. By the way, Adrian Boult is supposedly broadcasting my Mexican piece on May 14th over NBC at 10 p.m.

Remember me to Davis,

Yours,

Aaron

23. Dimitri Mitropoulos to Leonard Bernstein
Minneapolis Symphony Orchestra, Minneapolis, MN
4 May 1938

My dear, dear boy,

Yes, you are right to be worried about me. I couldn't answer your first letter; you were asking me too much. If you remember, you wished to know more about me; but I think it is better that you look at me as you wish to – put at me your own imagination, your ideal. Who knows? – otherwise you would be disappointed. And, dear boy, I need your appreciation, your respect, your love! It is of great importance in my life. I should be happy to see you again before I leave. I am beginning the rehearsals in New York the 24th. The concert is the 28th of May, and I leave the 8th of June. May I ask a small picture of you to be my companion on my Europe trip?

With affection,

D. Mitropoulos

24. Dimitri Mitropoulos to Leonard Bernstein
The Biltmore, at Grand Central Terminal, New York, NY
7 June 1938

Dearest friend,

Thank you! I was so unhappy this last time! But now everything is again all right. I was so stupid to think that you didn't care so much about me. Wasn't I stupid?

---

[24] The Works Progress Administration.
[25] Copland's mention of Bennington is presumably a reference to Bennington College in Vermont. Norman Lloyd (b. 1914), American actor, a member of the Mercury Theatre founded by Orson Welles and John Houseman.

Your picture is so good, I like it, God bless you!

You see, my dear boy, sometimes I am so sad, and I need so few, just a little to be happy, and this little sometimes nobody gives me, it seems to avoid me.

Can you imagine for a moment, I thought I lost your love, and then, I was asked me, perhaps I am not right to ask anything, to expect anything, from anybody, that my destiny is to be alone with myself and my art.

But you my dear friend, tell me, it is not so, I am something for you, yes . . . don't forget me.

Goodbye dear,

Dimitri

25. Leonard Bernstein to Aaron Copland

Eliot E-51, Harvard University, Cambridge, MA

[received 20 October 1938]

Dear Aaron,

It's going to be hard to keep this from being a fan letter. The concert was gorgeous – even the Dvořák.[26] I still don't sleep much from the pounding of:

in my head.[27] In any event, it's a secure feeling to know we have a master in America. I mean that too (don't pooh-pooh). I sat aghast at the solid sureness of that construction of yours. Timed to perfection. Not an extra beat. Just long enough for its material. Orchestral handling plus. Invention superb. And yet, with all that technique, it was a perfect rollercoaster ride. And it's not the exhaustible kind of cleverness (like Françaix, or his ilk).

I want seriously to have the chance to study with you soon. My heart's in it. Never have I come across anyone capable of such immediate absorption of musical material, possessing at the same time a fine critical sense *with* the ability to put that criticism into words successfully. This is not rot. The little demonstration you gave with those early things of mine proved it to me conclusively.

Saw the Group Theatre bunch today and they all asked for and about you. [Clifford] Odets,[28] true to form, thinks the *Salón México* "light", also Mozart except

---

[26] Koussevitzky conducted the Boston Symphony Orchestra on 14 and 15 October in a programme that included Copland's *El Salón México*, Mozart's Divertimento K287, and Dvořák's "New World" Symphony.

[27] Copland's *El Salón México*.

[28] Clifford Odets (1906–63), American playwright and screenwriter. He was a founding member of the Group Theatre.

the G minor Symphony. That angers me terrifically. I wish these people could see that a composer is just as *serious* when he writes a work, even if the piece is not defeatist (that Worker word again) and Weltschmerzy and misanthropic and long. Light piece, indeed. I tremble when I think of producing something like the *Salón*.

Casting is a wretched business.[29] It's slow but sure. And so tiring. (What word from the Marc [Blitzstein]?) But I think we'll have a fine show.

Let me hear soon. As Dame Fortune said to you backstage last Saturday night, "On to bigger & nobler things."

Always,

Lenny

P.S. I hope you're really haunted by:

Maybe not *convincing*, but maybe *haunting*.

26. Aaron Copland to Leonard Bernstein

International Society for Contemporary Music, United States Section, New York, NY

[October or November 1938]

Dear Lenny,

Of course you're crazy! I'm sorry if you felt a "strained feeling" that Saturday. The moral being – you mustn't be so sensitive. I remember Victor [Kraft] was acting strangely and I was embarrassed at not being able to invite you to the ballet[30] – but that's nothing to have "omens" about. Anyhow – remember this – I feel much too friendly and sympathetic to you for anything I can possibly imagine making our relations "strained".

As a peace offering, I'm sending you a copy of the *Second Hurricane*[31] which is just out.

Affectionately,

Aaron

---

[29] For Bernstein's Harvard production of Blitzstein's *The Cradle Will Rock*.
[30] Probably *Billy the Kid*, first performed on 16 October 1938.
[31] The piano–vocal score of *The Second Hurricane* was first published by C. C. Birchard of Boston in 1938.

27. Leonard Bernstein to Aaron Copland

Eliot E-51, Harvard University, Cambridge, MA
[received 19 November 1938]

Dear Aaron,

In the midst of ten million other things I'm writing a thesis for honors. I think it's interesting – certainly it is potentially interesting. The subject is Nationalism in American music – presumably a nonentity but on the whole a vital problem. We've talked about it once or twice. You said, "don't worry – just write it – it will come out American."

The thesis tries to show how the stuff that the old boys turned out (Chadwick, Converse, Shepherd, Gilbert, MacD[owell], Cadman etc.) failed utterly to develop an American style or school or music at all, because their material (Negro, American Indian, etc.) was not common – the old problem of America the melting pot. Having ruthlessly revealed the invalidity of an Indian tune surrounded by Teutonic development, etc., I will try to show that there is something American in the newer music, which relies not on folk material, but on a native spirit (like your music, and maybe Harris' & Sessions' – I don't know), or which relies on a new American form, like Blitzstein's. Whether this is tenable or not, it is my thesis and I'm sticking to it.

Now how to go about it? It means going through recent American things, finding those that sound, for some reason, American, and translate that American sound into musical terms. I feel convinced that there is such a thing, or else why is it that the *Variations* sound fresh and vital and not stale and European and dry?

This is where you can help, if you would. What music of what other composers in America would support my point, and where can I get hold of it? Would the music of Harris? or Ives? or Schuman? or Piston? or [Nicolai] Berezowsky? You see, I know and hear so little American stuff. This is my great opportunity to get to know it well, and find out something about it. I feel more and more that there's something to all this, and that it can be told in terms. I'll be infinitely thankful for any suggestions.

Again, thousands thanks for the *Second Hurricane* – it's just swell.

Always,
Lenny

28. Leonard Bernstein to Kenneth Ehrman[32]
Eliot E-51, Harvard University, Cambridge, MA
6 December 1938

It's wonderful, Ken, the way you lack enthusiasm when it's more or less expected of you. Hello. A dull thud – that's the way your letter read. 500th crossing, and all that – trip is really as can be expected.

But it was very good to hear from you, all wrapped up in your mauve-lined Parisian envelope. [. . .]

Everything is almost O.K. You ask after the *Advocate*[33] competition – I won. I am now proud possessor of all manner of records. As for the *Birds* – I won that too, and am busy as a bee on the composition and orchestration thereof. As for courses, I am fuguing and advance orchestrating and thesising, and another half next half (what am I saying). [Tillman] Merritt hates me, but Mother loves me. [Walter] Piston doubts me, but Copland encourages me. I hate the Harvard Music Department. You can quote that. You can even print it if you want. I hate it because it is stupid & highschoolish and "disciplinary" and prim and foolish and academic and stolid and fussy. I want to go home.[34] [. . .]

Toujours –

Bernstein

29. Aaron Copland to Leonard Bernstein
Hotel Empire, Broadway at 63rd Street, New York, NY
7 December 1938

Dear Lenny,

I know I'm late in answering but I've been swamped with things to do and your letter asked so many questions!

Aren't you coming down to N.Y. during Christmas holydays? And since it would be so much better to do this *viva voce* than by letter, could it wait till then for my grandfatherly advice?

---

[32] Kenneth Ehrman was a friend of Bernstein's in Eliot House at Harvard. He graduated in 1938 and Bernstein corresponded with him regularly during his own senior year at Harvard and his time at the Curtis Institute. Ehrman recalled one of his earliest encounters with Bernstein in a letter to Humphrey Burton dated 23 October 1991 (copy in the Library of Congress): "He had been playing the piano in the Eliot House Common Room after dinner, and it was a beautiful warm spring night and we walked around Cambridge for several hours. He was talking non stop about his plans – the composing, playing, writing, teaching (he never mentioned conducting in those days, at least to me). About the [. . .] musical world, and how he would be such a big part of it. Suddenly he stopped, looked at me and said, 'Who do I think I am, everybody?' "

[33] *The Harvard Advocate* is Harvard's undergraduate journal of poetry, fiction, art, and criticism.

[34] This is part of a longer letter, but its main interest is Bernstein's scathing attack on the Harvard Music Department.

You sound as if you were very much on the right track anyhow both as to ideas and composers' names. Don't make the mistake of thinking that *just* because a Gilbert used Negro material, there was therefore nothing American about it. There's always the chance it might have an "American" quality despite its material. Also, don't try to prove *too* much. Composing in this country is still pretty young no matter how you look at it.

Good luck and let's hear if you're coming down.

Consider yourself missed.

A.

30. Leonard Bernstein to Kenneth Ehrman
Eliot E-51, Harvard University, Cambridge, MA
17 January 1939

Dear Kenuel,

I had a mad inspiration to write you several days ago when the enclosed suddenly popped up in one of my pockets. But put it off again and again I did, and so it was after all your letter which evoked this little opus. Mad Shirley tells me that our Stark ("Watch that boy") played the lead in the school production of *Tovarich* some time ago, and walked off with the public-speaking prize. Are we proud!

Life has been going on, as it has a way of doing. Just a series of minor catastrophes of varying kinds. Most noteworthy: I left a valuable manuscript of Copland's plus another printed piece of his plus a valuable manuscript book of mine plus a valuable fountain pen plus *all my thesis notes* over which I had theoretically slaved (!) in New York on the train coming back from that City of Sin. The infallible New Haven Railroad is unable to find these things, which means that I must start my thesis all over again at double speed, and type this letter, faut d'un stylo, and be generally upset at having lost Aaron's manuscript for him. He of course took it as only he could take it – with a philosophical phrase. Good old Aaron: if it had been anyone else but he I should long ago have gone into voluntary exile.

Aaron, by the way, could never understand my lack of desire for going abroad. In his day, says he, there was never a composer who would not insist on Paris first. I have always been inclined to pooh-pooh the idea, on the grounds that a composer can go through his "Paris" period here in America as well as abroad. But lately little ideas have been creeping around in the brain. The thought of Paree attracts me mightily these days. And your letter has set me off on another gush. It would be wonderful, I am convinced. Of course, a great deal depends on funds. But there's always the possibility of a fellowship (please Goddy Woddy); and then my father almost bowled me over last night with the statement that he would be responsible for me for one more year after college to the extent of the equivalent of what it takes to keep me in college one year. I may go abroad with it if I choose (sounds impossible to me), or to a music school.

I still don't know whether to take him seriously or not. But that added to a fellowship would be simply de trop, as Mary Boland says.

You see, Ken, the sudden surge toward la vie transatlantique is due, I suppose, to an equally sudden horror of what is to come here next year. I planned for a while on a few months in Mexico. It would be swell, but, in the final analysis, pretty unconstructive. I also toyed with the idea of California (I'm still a C————iac[35]) for a year or so. But I know all the while that I am not yet prepared to settle down somewhere and write music. I still have so much to study. In America there is but one person I am interested in working with after college, and that's Aaron. Now (how mathematical this discussion is) working with Aaron involves being in New York. Maybe it's just that I've recently returned therefrom and had a bellyful, but more and more I do not want to go there – at least not yet. The people of the "artistic world" that I encountered on this last trip revolt me in every way. I have been made sick by the depravity of the Greenwich Villagers, the totally degenerate homosexuals, the equally degenerate heterosexuals, the foolish and destructive attitudes, and the frantic attempts to preserve the atmosphere of postwar bohemianism. Oh, there are some who are all right, of course. They are far and few enough, God knows. And the thing I am really afraid of is that I could so easily fall prey to that sort of thing. You may remember my chief weakness – my love for people. I need them all the time – every moment. It's something that perhaps you cannot understand: but I cannot spend one day alone without becoming utterly depressed. Any people will do. It's a terrible fault. And in New York, the people who would fill that place with me would inevitably be those wretched people who haunt the Village Vanguard by night, and each other's studios by day, and act positively in only one way – as a destructive and retarding force in their societies. This, by the way, is not bitter or dramatic in any way. But it is this great horror of taking my place with these people, and becoming an "artist" that half kills me. There are two rebuttals, of course. One, you should say that I ought to be strong enough to resist all this; but sometimes I am much afraid that it wouldn't take too much effort on my part before I would be like them. I always absorb my surroundings – but to a degree! Second rebuttal: Paris holds the same kind of crowd and the same lack of healthy art. Well that's for you to tell me. I don't know. Let me know the lowdown soon. I am thinking very seriously now of going abroad.

Strange how I miss you. Perhaps I'm not so "universal" or promiscuous as I thought. You were very important to me last year. So steadying for me; and you helped me over many a rough place without perhaps knowing it. No, the afterthought is not after all, "He meant well. Good old Ken."

The Birds comes along slowly and unsteadily. The whole score is finished but the Finale. The chorus doesn't show up for rehearsals. The orchestra is still being slowly assembled. But it's fun.

---

[35] Presumably "Californiac".

The [*Harvard*] *Advocate* has a new Board, all Socialites. So the new Music Editor is a Socialite. No more records for little Lenny.

I have already reset the ribbon on this machine twice, which means that this is a very long and probably silly letter, and I ought to stop.

My best to Aunt Mattie, whom etc., and to all the Messings, Truebloods, Bluebloods, Peggrams, etc. that you come across.

Happy skiing.

Always,

Len

[...]

31. Dimitri Mitropoulos to Leonard Bernstein

Minneapolis Symphony Orchestra, Minneapolis, MN
18 February 1939

My dearest friend,

At last a letter from you. I was completely despaired and beginning to think that you completely forgot me. For a while I thought it was because I sent you by mistake a letter without signing it, and that you were offended; but fortunately your letter came to prevent my disappointment.

I am very happy to hear that you are working hard, but I am sorry to see that you neglect your piano, which could be a great help to your career.[36] I see you too come to the position now to have problems: musical, artistic, social and spiritual – and the worst of all, sexual. Unfortunately I am too far away to help – to give you good advice. But I hope you are a clever boy and that you realize the great responsibility toward yourself, its importance. As far as the conditions of my personal life are concerned, actually, I must tell you that neither my life nor my Weltanschauung has undergone any change; but it has improved, I think, in wisdom and in self-concentration.

May I tell you an agreeable thing. I am invited to conduct the Boston orchestra in the middle of next January for two weeks. I look forward to have some moments again in your inspiring and friendly company.

With my best wishes,

D. Mitropoulos

---

[36] Mitropoulos specialized in directing concertos from the keyboard, notably Prokofiev's Piano Concerto No. 3.

32. Aaron Copland to Leonard Bernstein
Hotel Empire, Broadway at 63rd Street, New York, NY
[April 1939]

Dear Lenny,

I've been meaning to write and tell you what a swell host you make and how pleasant in retrospect my little "week-end" was, and now it has to be accompanied by this regretful letter from La Holm[37] which of course spoils my effect. But don't fret – something *must* turn up sooner or later.

When I got back here I learned that *Quiet City* has been cancelled. The Group [Theatre] wasn't satisfied so my career in the theatre has been a flop – obviously. Nothing left to do but write a Piano Sonata.[38] Or perhaps something special called "The Beach at Revere" or "The Birches at Sharon".

Well anyway – I hope something will drive you to N.Y. soon. D[imitri] M[itropoulos]'s Greek concert, or the World's Fair, or my ballet or sumpin!

Best to you,

A

33. Leonard Bernstein to Kenneth Ehrman
Eliot E-51, Harvard University, Cambridge, MA
April [1939]

Great & Good Kenneth,

To think!

a) No fellowship

b) No job at Mills College this summer. They're reducing their staff, and cutting out the production end entirely, reserving only [for] educational.

c) I'm dead on my feet. I just handed in the thesis, having stayed up all night, and I'm just beginning to recover. I have [no] control over myself, so excuse typing, et al.

d) No prospects for the summer or next year. Maybe a job with a dancer next year. Maybe a job on *Modern Music*. Maybe Mexico this summer. Maybe Sharon (God forbid!) Maybe anything. The prospect is lousy. Any suggestions?

e) Everybody's lousy. People are always getting divorces from nice people like An or being impotent with nice girls or flunking exams or vomiting over the European situation. And for God's sake keep out of Greece and concentration camps. Of all times to be where you are![39]

---

[37] Hanya Holm (1893–1992), German-born American choreographer and dance educator.
[38] Copland did so. His Piano Sonata was composed between 1939 and 1941. The earliest sketches date from about June 1939, shortly after he sent this letter.
[39] Ehrman was living in Paris at the time, on his way to Italy and Greece.

f) I never recovered the lost thesis notes. (This is irrelevant.) (But so's Margaret.[40] I told [David] Prall[41] about that particular fetish and he beamed all over.)

g) *The Birds* finally comes off next week.[42] It should be good.

God, Ken, it's a dull and wretched state I'm in. No practicing, no composing, no plans, no money, no ideas. Static. Tired all over. I'll be all right tomorrow. I've met a wonderful girl. I'm about to have a sex life again. That's encouraging.

Have a swell trip, and be careful. [. . .]

I long for California, and the peaches and ladyfingers and artichokes. I long for so many things. Why can't I stop this silly wailing. Really, I'm just tired.

Again, be careful, stay alive, write. With devotion, affection, greetings, warmth, cordiality, sincerity, verytrulyness, blessings,

Lenny

34. Adolph Green[43] to Leonard Bernstein
Hotel Astor, Times Square, New York, NY
[27 May 1939]

Dollink Lennie,

First of all – good luck with *The Cradle* tonight.[44] I hope Blitzstein is there. He told me about it, & I was going to come up, but I can't get Saturday off. You see, I'm working every night except Monday & Tuesday. We started on April 6th or so doing Saturday Shows, just about the time I was planning to come up for your Aristophanes.[45]

---

[40] Margaret Prall, David Prall's wife.
[41] David Prall (1886–1940), professor of aesthetics at Harvard whose teaching had a profound influence on Bernstein.
[42] *The Birds* was first performed on 21 April 1939.
[43] Adolph Green (1914–2002), American lyricist, playwright, and scriptwriter whose writing partnership with Betty Comden produced several successful Broadway shows including *On the Town* and *Wonderful Town*, both with Bernstein. In Hollywood, Comden and Green's greatest successes were at MGM, notably *Singin' in the Rain*. Green first met Bernstein at Camp Onota in the summer of 1937, where Bernstein put on a production of Gilbert and Sullivan's *Pirates of Penzance* and Green sang the part of the Pirate King. They instantly became firm friends through a shared passion for music, and within a couple of years Bernstein was playing the piano for Comden and Green's comedy troupe, The Revuers.
[44] Bernstein's production of *The Cradle Will Rock* opened on 27 May 1939. The *Harvard Crimson* (23 May 1939) announced the event as follows: "The Student Union will present Marc Blitzstein's opera *The Cradle Will Rock* at Sanders Theatre, Saturday evening at eight-thirty o'clock. The production is under the direction of Leonard Bernstein '39, and Arthur Szathmary, 2G. This Student Union presentation will be the first Boston production of Blitzstein's proletarian music drama. Featured in the cast are Donald Davidson, '39, William Whitcraft, '39, Rupert Pole, '40, and Myron Simons, '40, all of Eliot House. The piano, which furnishes all the music, will be played by Bernstein."
[45] The production of *The Birds* with Bernstein's incidental music.

Lennish, I'm doing famously. So help me. Its all – quotes – like a dream – unquotes. Exciting as hell. But I'm not in the dough yet. We've been signed by the Wm. Morris Agency but they haven't found us any good spots yet. And there's Radio & Television yet & everything and all in the offing. Nothing materialized. But, Gott zei dank, I'm making a little salary. I've lost about 25 pounds, so I'm no longer rolly-polly-Adolph, just a flabby Adolph.

It all began about 2½ months ago, when we did a guest booking for an Actors' Party at Café Society. Herman Shumlin & Arthur Kober & others were there & they went nuts about us. So since then everything happened. Publicity – all kinds – *New Yorker, N.Y. Times, Post, Journal-American,* [*The New*] *Masses,* [...] [*Daily*] *Worker,* all over. Everyone in theatre has been to see us. And composers – ay, ay – Blitzstein, Copland, Paul Bowles, Jerry Moross, etc., etc. They're swell people, too. By the way, I gypped a Satie composition from Bowles' house for you.

So enough of this self-indulgent bloating.

I would like, is it possible, to hitch-hike up to Boston on Monday & stay for a day or so. Hmmm? Is it possible? With me, I would have a young boy, Julian Claman,[46] a nice charming lad, who is our lighting man at the Vanguard.[47] Would that be possible? If so, send a telegram to A. Green, 835 Riverside Drive. If not, also send a telegram. You can send it collect *if you want to*. Heh, Heh, Heh.

Listen, are you coming to the City this summer? Will you have a place to live? If not, I've found a terrific 2-room also with kitchen apt. – with 3 beds – to be sub-letted for the summer. It's got swell furnishings, it's got a phonograph-radio, it's got a good Grand Piano, it's large, comfortable, on 55th St near 6th Ave, and Julian and I want to take it. With 3 of us at about $50 a month, it would amount to $3.50 a week each. We'll talk about it.

So let me know about Monday.

Give my love to S[hirley] B[ernstein].

Give my love to Blitzstein if he's there.

Adolph

P.S. Lenny, my love, I love you.

Copland told me your Aristophanes music was a remarkably fine work.

Christ, what an incoherent letter. Forgive, forgive.

P.S. I've seen Weil[48] once in the last 6 months. Is my heart bleeding? Not precisely.

---

[46] Julian Claman (1918–69) sometimes appeared with The Revuers and became a writer and playwright. His 1955 play, *A Quiet Place*, starred Tyrone Power, but closed out of town, before reaching Broadway. The title and title song (sung by Power in the show) were taken from *Trouble in Tahiti*. In 1953, Claman married the actress Marian Seldes; they divorced in 1961.

[47] Claman has written in the margin: "Tentative love, Julian".

[48] Probably Robert Weil, mentioned in Letter 538.

35. Leonard Bernstein to Aaron Copland
17 Lake Avenue, Sharon, MA
26 June 1939

Aaron,

Patiently I have waited. The rains have come and gone. The sun, the moon, have seen another cycle. Millennia have elapsed. I have graduated with honors. I have been to all kinds of class days, commencements, baccalaureate services. I have grown old. And no word about cabins. Have you investigated? Are there cabins? Are they good cabins? Are they in America? Have you forgotten me? Is there something wrong? Do you hesitate? These, and other thoughts, as Kipling would say, are my constant companions.

I am madly trying to recover my lost ergs. According to laws of nature they must be conserved somewhere, but I'm having a time finding where. I frequently stand up only to fall down. I sleep very easily (a bad sign for one who has always slept not too well). I have subtle little pains in my back. I have become positively hypochondriac. I live in waiting to hear from you. Please – before I rot in the provinces, let me know the outcome. At the above address.

Letter from Blitzstein says that he likes Yaddo [artists' community] again and is about to convince himself that he ought to get to work.

I have ideas for a piano and fiddle sonata, but I can't work on them here. I have begun to practice again. It is a strange feeling. Fingers slowly begin to move again.

For God's sake, Harvard, I got an A in that Government exam!

Tired, and so to bed, silently, alone.

I wait with renewed vigor . . .

Lenny

There is talk among some people I know of a cabin for me or us or two cabins for us in Scituate, Mass. (on the South Shore) – very nice. Promise of seclusion. Would you be interested? Cheap . . .

Say, I thought you were leaving the Empire on May 30?

36. Leonard Bernstein to Kenneth Ehrman
61 East 9th Street, New York, NY
13 July 1939

Cher Kenuel,

I know it's been overlong, and I've been lax, and I deserve one thing and another, but so much has happened – all relatively unimportant – that I've saved it all up to this minute.

A. I've graduated with a bang. An incredible A in the Government course, and a cum laude. A great class day skit which I performed to a roaring crowd through a mike, and got in some parting cracks [. . .] at the old school and its officials.

B. The inevitable letdown. Bringing us to

C. What now? So I came to New York, where I've subletted an apartment with two friends of mine in the nightclub entertainment business. Here I am trying to establish that most horrible of words *contacts* (insurance man's term). I have made a few, but can as yet report no results. All kinds of troubles with the union. You have to belong, and they won't take you because they have more unemployed than they can take care of, so they are charging an outrageous price for admission.

D. I'll stay yet awhile, and see what happens. If nothing, well. But oh for something! Any old kind of job that would pay a living wage. You see, I still don't really know quite what I want to do. Conduct, compose, piano, produce, arrange, etc. I'm all of these and none of them. The Big Boys here (and thank God they're rooting for me) have it all decided that I am to become America's Great Conductor. They need an Apostle for their music. Or else they want to keep a rival composer out of the field. At any rate, they've been fine to me, and there is even talk of a scholarship at Juilliard in the fall. But nothing happens here until it happens, so only waiting. They also wait who serve the meat.

E. How are you? Al [Eisner] and Austin, as you have probably heard, are in Hollywood. Al has this incredible job at $50 per with MGM, and Austin is living with him or on him.

F. Complaints about the piano playing here may mean our eviction. That would be at least interesting.

God bless you, son, and my best to all the lads. Flights of angels wherever you may be, Greece or Naziland or Turkey. Write write away and right rite away. I hope maybe some day to see you, you vagrant wretch.

Alaways,

Lenny

37. Leonard Bernstein to Aaron Copland

61 East 9th Street, New York, NY

30 July 1939

Astral Aaron,

I. Many blessings for the Stadium tickets. I'll see that they're used.

II. Last night I almost wrote you a very desperate letter. I was desperate. Having to do with those in the songwriting industry is no fun. And no success. I now know what it is to be rebuffed by the Beeg Ceety. But today I'm more cheerful. Probably because I've forgotten about songwriting. The crowning disappointment, though, was when I went up to the Juilliard School to see about conducting fellowship, and found I was a month too late for application. Can something be done? Or do I turn in desperation to the possibility of Curtis?

III. I saw Rolf Kaltenborn today, and he says I should see Davidson Taylor about employment.[49] You can do me a *great* favor by writing Taylor a letter about me right away so that I can see him soon, loaded down with press clippings & scores (?). Please write him – it means much to me – and can you let me know as soon as you've written him so that I can plan an attack? Thanks, thanks.

IV. I saw *The City* and it's a knockout. The opening is too long. But the NYC sequence is swell. And the music all one could ask for.[50]

V. [...] You've been wonderful and terribly helpful, and I'm more bewildered than ever. I think in the last analysis, it's all up to me. [...]

Ever,

Lenny

Please – about Taylor. I'm so in need of a job – especially psychologically. Write me soon.

L

38. Leonard Bernstein to Aaron Copland

[New York, NY]
9 August 1939

Dear Aaron,

Many thanks for all endeavors. You've been superb. I spoke with Davidson Taylor and he held out little hope, but I felt hopeful for the first time. He was the first interview I've had in NYC where I wasn't greeted by a patronizing attitude. He says he'll try and see what can be done, but oh! *Experience!* Where does one buy or rent radio experience. You have to start somewhere.

[Roy] Harris was very nice. He is writing Hutcheson[51] at Chautauqua about me, and may be able to get me in. He also speaks very seriously about my changing my name. Something Anglosaxon like Roy Harris, no doubt. He thinks I might thereby ride in on the crest of the wave of reaction against the foreign artist craze, which reaction he thinks is due for the next twenty years. Mind, he is not referring to the Jewish question (!).

I saw Reiner at the Stadium last night (bless you for the tickets), and he was matteroffact. Then I mentioned the aspiration towards conducting, he threw up

---

[49] Davidson Taylor worked as musical supervisor for the CBS radio network at the time. It was one of several positions he held in the company. In 1938, Taylor had been the executive producer of Orson Welles' *The War of the Worlds*. He later became a vice president at CBS.

[50] Made for the 1939 New York World's Fair, *The City* is a documentary film notable for its close integration of spoken narration (written by Lewis Mumford), cinematography (by Ralph Steiner and Willard Van Dyke), and Copland's score. This score led directly to Copland's invitation to work in Hollywood the following year on *Our Town*.

[51] Ernest Hutcheson (1871–1951) was an Australian pianist and composer. He was President of the Juilliard School, and Director of the Chautauqua School of Music at the Chautauqua Institution, in western New York State. In 1925, Hutcheson had arranged for Gershwin to be given secluded accommodation at the Chatauqua Institution so that he could complete the Concerto in F.

his hands and yelled BAD! But write to Curtis, says he, and he'll give me an examination at the end of September. Purely routine. He asked me to tell you, by the way, that it is very urgent that he have the score of the *Outdoor Overture* immediately. Address: Westport, Conn.

All else is the same. O tempora.

Write soon. The address is still 61 E 9[th Street], and will be probably for another week. Then – shux.

Best,

Lenny

39. Leonard Bernstein to Aaron Copland
17 Lake Avenue, Sharon, MA
29 August 1939

Aaron,

Two momentous things.

a) I've just finished the *Salón México* reduction – it's fine.

b) I've just finished my Hebrew song for mezzo-sop. and ork. I think it's my best score so far (not much choice). It was tremendous fun.

Under separate cover, as they say, I'm sending the *Lamentation* for your dictum. Please look at it sort of carefully – it actually means much to me. Of course, no one will ever sing it – it's too hard, and who wants to learn all those funny words? Eventually the song will become one of a group, or a movement of a symphony for voice and orch., or the opening of a cantata or opera, unless you give a very bad verdict.

I'm not sending the *Saloon*, as you couldn't read my hasty script, anyway.

Your card was forwarded to me days after you sent it. I'm awfully sorry to have left NYC. Can't we see each other soon?

Best,

Lenny

My best to [Benjamin] Britten.[52] Did he get his Concerto (?) back?[53]

No jobs. No future.[54]

---

[52] Britten came to America in April 1939, staying until April 1942 when he returned to England. He first met Copland at the 1938 ISCM Festival in London (where Copland's *El Salón México* and Britten's *Variations on a Theme of Frank Bridge* were performed in the same concert); "Britten thought *El Salón* 'really beautiful and exhilarating' and the 'brightest piece in the festival,' while Copland admired 'the technical adroitness and wizardry' of the *Variations*" (Pollack 1999, p. 72). Copland spent a weekend with Britten after the festival, and a warm friendship developed during Britten's time in the United States. On 17 June 1950, Pears and Britten gave the world premiere of the first set of Copland's *Old American Songs* at the Aldeburgh Festival, and subsequently made the first recording for HMV. For Britten's links with Bernstein see note to Letter 87.

[53] Britten and Pears spent six weeks of the summer at Woodstock, NY, as neighbors of Copland's; they left Woodstock a few days before Bernstein wrote this letter. The "Concerto" was Britten's Violin Concerto, which he worked on throughout the summer and completed at the end of September.

[54] Bernstein spent the summer of 1939 in New York, looking for a job, without success. But it was a productive stay: there was a grand piano in the apartment and he spent a good deal of time playing

40. Aaron Copland to Leonard Bernstein
Woodstock, NY
30 August [1939]

Dear L,

I sent off the paper to Curtis [the] day after it got here – with a heated recommendation at the bottom.

When there was no answer to my card I assumed you had left NY. I actually did broadcast again at the Stadium.

Nice that you've been able to finish pieces in these troublous times. (I haven't been able to do much more than read newspapers). If you sent the *Lamentation* by express, it's waiting for me over in W. Hurley. I'll try to write you about it, tho I hate writing "critiques" – much prefer telling you viva voce! (Things one says with a glance look so awful on paper!)

Try to make an ink copy of the *Saloon* as I'm keen to see what you've done.

Are you going back to NY during Sept? If so, maybe you could stop off here on your way down. It's only 60 miles from Albany – down the river. (It's even nearer Poughkeepsie – if there's any way of going there directly from Boston.) Anyway keep it in mind and keep me posted with where you are.

B. Britten left Woodstock a week ago. He never mentioned anything about his Concerto coming back. He was all flustrated about the war news when he left.

I've been reading about the phenomenal success of the Vanguard children.[55] Nice!

Met a friend of yours at the Stadium last time – a pupil of Prall's about to leave for Mexico – an athletics scholar – name Szatmary (?) or something like that.[56] Also exchanged words with young Kaltenborn about you.

Glad you took me out to Sharon that day. Now I can visualize where you are.

Amitiés.

Aaron

---

and composing, as well as enjoying evenings with Green and the other members of The Revuers, including Judy Holliday and Betty Comden. Most importantly, Bernstein was starting to think seriously for the first time about a conducting career, and getting down in earnest to composition. The Lamentation he sent to Copland did indeed become "a movement of a symphony." In the programme note for the 1944 premiere of the *Jeremiah* Symphony, Bernstein wrote: "In the summer of 1939 I made a sketch for a Lamentation for soprano and orchestra. This sketch lay forgotten for two years, until in the spring of 1942 I began a first movement of a symphony. I then realized that this new movement, and the scherzo that I had planned to follow it, made logical concomitants with the Lamentation. Thus the symphony came into being." Almost forty years later, at a concert for Bernstein's 60th birthday on 25 August 1978, Copland conducted the Lamentation from *Jeremiah*.
[55] Presumably a reference to The Revuers whose regular venue was the Village Vanguard in Greenwich Village.
[56] Arthur Szathmary, who co-directed *The Cradle Will Rock* with Bernstein at Harvard.

41. Helen Coates to Leonard Bernstein

Barbizon Plaza Hotel, New York, NY
14 October 1939

Dear Lenny,

I was very disappointed not to see you while you were home, tho' I appreciate the effort you made. Mother was happy to see you, as always. I phoned your mother Wednesday evening to see what had happened to you, and had a nice talk with her. She seemed quite reassured to hear that I thoroughly approve of your specializing in conducting.

I'm thrilled to know that you got the scholarship at Curtis and hope it will fulfill all your desires for *serious study* this year. I do hope you'll get some lessons with [Rudolf] Serkin, too.

Knowing my passion for details, you'll be prepared for an avalanche of questions about your work, living, etc.

First of all, how are you working out your expenses? Just what does the *scholarship* give you, and did you decide to accept D.M.'s (as I shall call your Minn. friend)[57] offer to finance you this year? I shall, of course, keep this confidential. So where are you living and are you able to practice regularly at Curtis? And what kind of people do you find studying at Curtis? Tell me about the new friends you make.

I came down from Boston last night, and had a little time before I began to teach, so thought I'd answer your welcome card. I'm hoping you'll be coming to New York on one of my weekends here, so we can have a real visit and I can find out how everything is going with you. I'll be here again on *November 4th* and also on *Nov. 25th*. Let me know in *plenty of time* if you are to be in N.Y. on either of those dates.

I know you'll make the most of your time this year, and I do hope you'll live a regular sort of life for the most part and get *plenty of sleep*. You have a wonderful opportunity ahead of you, if you work hard and fulfill the hopes D.M. (and I) have for you.

Do write me soon – a real letter – and answer all my questions. I'm always interested in anything that vitally concerns you.

Mother would want to send you her love with this.

My love and best of wishes for a truly wonderful year – and may the little scores be a real inspiration and a reminder of

Your affectionate friend,

Helen

Sorry I mixed up these pages!

---

[57] Dimitri Mitropoulos.

42. Leonard Bernstein to Helen Coates
408 South 22nd Street, Philadelphia, PA
17 October 1939

Dear Helen,

Thanks for the lovely Barbizon Plaza letter – even without it I know you're with me every inch of the way.

Things couldn't be better. The Institute is surpassing. The staff is perhaps the *only* bureaucratic setup that I have ever seen so helpful and considerate. Randall Thompson (director) is all a director should be, and the staff of teachers (I should say faculty!) is the best.

As to conducting, it looks like a long uphill climb, but I proceed nothing daunted, despite all the venomous attacks I hear on all sides against Mr. Reiner, with whom I am studying. As a matter of fact, in the one class we've had (only 3 students) he was gentle as a lamb. Maybe only lamb's clothing. There are several supplementary courses (students can take the whole curriculum if they wish – it's all open & free) – such as transposition and score-reading, orchestration, etc. The first two are with Madame Miquelle (daughter of Longy) and the third with Thompson. There is also a course in formal analysis with Dr. Stöhr, an incredible old German with walrus mustache & Van Dyke & all. A wonderful man, though given to a high-school-teacher manner.

Ah! The piano! I passed my audition for Serkin, but am not studying with him. First, he's not yet in the country; second, I seem to be *over age* (!). They've tentatively allotted him a chap of 16 & a girl of 13, so that he can *mould* them. At the same time, I had impressed the worthy jury (and am consequently majoring *both* in piano & conducting). So they asked Mme. Vengerova,[58] who, I am told, is the greatest piano teacher in America, better than Serkin a million times, etc., etc. I don't know if she would take me. They decided they couldn't give me to a supplementary teacher. She accepted (hesitantly at first at being second fiddle to Serkin, & having me "palmed off" on her), but since her contract hours were full, they increased her contract & I am now studying with the greatest teacher Curtis offers. As a result of which, the school moved a Steinway grand into my room this morning – just an old Curtis custom – since Madame *insists* I have just that to practice on. It's a dream of a piano. As I say, things couldn't be better.

I work & work & work (practice about 3 to 5 hrs a day), & do nothing else except sleep plenty. No social life – no friend to speak of.

I have accepted D[imitri] M[itropoulos]'s offer. Not in desperation – in joy. My mind has changed drastically – I want nothing more than to have obligations to him.

---

[58] Isabelle Vengerova (1877–1956), pianist and teacher who studied with Theodor Leschetitzky. One of the founding teachers of the Curtis Institute, her pupils included Samuel Barber, Lukas Foss, Gary Graffman, Abbey Simon, Gilbert Kalish, and Jacob Lateiner, as well as Bernstein.

You wanted details – you got them. It's rather nice & easy to write details that are pleasant.

Best of all: I *may* be in NYC on Nov 4 – I'll write later.

Meanwhile write again & much affection from this city of dust & grit & horror.

Always,

Lenny

43. Alfred Eisner[59] to Leonard Bernstein
Metro-Goldwyn-Mayer Pictures, Culver City, CA
[?October 1939]

Lennie,

In haste and I've mislaid your address so it will take longer, so for the love of God answer pronto and even faster if possible. They've dug up a babe named Helen Gilbert who is beautiful enough to make St. Anthony tear his beard in frustrated rage and who also happens to be a magnificent cellist, yes indeed, and I'm doing one for her and I need a little information, to wit: some technical language that might be expected to pass between a teacher of cello and his pupil: you know, bowing, arpeggio, crap like that. Also, technical language that might be expected to pass between a teacher of voice and a pupil: breathing, or what have you. Casting the babe opposite a young baritone they're grooming to replace Nelson Eddy. This will definitely not be shit: the girl's a refugee from Vienna (in the picture) and her old man, a violinist, gets his hands burned with acid even as did the great Feuermann, and the setting is to be the Paris Conservatory (after the escape from Austria) and for chrissake get the dope to me as fast as fast, because if this job turns out as well and gets as much attention as my last you'll have refuge indeed in times of stress and that in style.

And why the hell don't you write to a guy: Too busy. Yeah, sure.

Al

44. Alfred Eisner to Leonard Bernstein
Metro-Goldwyn-Mayer Pictures, Culver City, CA
31 October 1939

Lenny mine,

Not a word did I know, no, not a soupçon, of thy good fortune until but three days gone when I walked into Aaron [Copland] outside my office door (like the

---

[59] Alfred (Al) Eisner was Bernstein's room-mate in Eliot House at Harvard. After graduation, he went to Hollywood, where he worked as a scriptwriter at MGM. He died from a brain tumor on 4 January 1941, in his early twenties. The third of Bernstein's *Seven Anniversaries* is entitled "In Memoriam: Alfred Eisner (Jan. 4, 1941)".

Raven). He lost no time in acquainting me with the vagaries of my sainted room-mate. Liebchen, you cannot imagine what being put au courant of your goings and comings did to this brassed over heart, this spirit worn thin in the wasteland. The doubtful privilege of three thousand miles gives me the right to vicarious thrills, and second hand glowings. I was, and am, so goddamned glad for you. Aaron tells me you went to town on a competitive exam, which makes it even better. Baby, look down dat lonesome road: do you see the shining city, the purple hill? If I am over sentimental and Tom Wolfish, forgive me; it's because I miss you so hellishly much. Yes, that vaunted individualist, that brave soul: Eisner, pines. It would be a boon indeed in his young life to pass a quip once again with you. Ah, Steinbern, would I could climb again on those collines de autre fois, crunch through les neiges d'antan, eheu, eheu, miserere mihi (does miserere take the dative?) But 'twont be so very long: I return to God's country as soon after the 19 December as is humanly possible, to remain for a month and then once again must I take the flinted trail back and earn those golden objects which, it is my fond hope, will give me a measure of independence next year.

Intelligence note: Pratiner celebrates his nuptials shortly. A bitch name of June Herbert. Excuse: If he marries her maybe he can take her for granted and get some work done. R.I.P.

Interruption Goddammit. Some damn fool wants me to collaborate on a picture that will offset *Mr. Smith Goes To Washington*. In the kishkas I'll give him.

My personal little river flows along. I finished the script about the cellist to much critical acclaim, which is probably all the attention the damn thing will ever get. A wonderful job, but too much this, not enough that, etc. I don't care. If the acclaim will get me $300 per *week* that is sufficient, thank you. And I think I'll get it. Jesus, what a laugh. Well, I'm worth 300 as much as some of these mockies are woith 1500. Note silly manifestation of conscience.

Political note: purged myself from the Party. Recent events, coupled with tortured casuistry of *Daily Worker* did for me.

Not much else in the way of news. I languish most of the time. This job is absolutely the snappiest snap ever invented by the mind of man. One of the boys has produced a chess set and now no one even talks about working. Before that it was all day crap games. I see a lot of pictures in private projection booths and shit like that. I seldom go on the stages anymore. I don't feel particularly well. Climate seems to be enervating. I sleep a lot, read some, work a little. Don't get around much anymore. The testament of a man in exile. [...]

What of Ken [Ehrman]? Did he join the French Foreign Legion or something?

Again and toujours, write.

De profundis

Al

45. Betty Comden[60] to Leonard Bernstein
29 West 65th Street, New York, NY
1 February 1940

Dear Lennie,

Just a line to let you know, you darling, that we all miss you – but that we are glad your work for the moment is not being interrupted by the intrusion of anybody's two left feet.[61] To get to the sordid facts – the machine is still in a state of collapse – necessitating the checkup up of every inch of wiring in the place. This little investigation will take at least another week or so – and we have chalked it up to a stroke of "Revuers luck". The phrase is much talked of nowadays.

I'll keep writing and who knows, some time this year we may get the old opera recorded yet. We've added some new music and attendant stuff, but nothing too frightening. Oh – *Pursuit of Happiness* on Feb. 18.[62]

Are you coming in at all? – business or no? Again, I miss you. The house is an empty shell, reverberating with your memory.

Betty

46. Betty Comden to Leonard Bernstein
29 West 65th Street, New York, NY
9 February 1940

Lennie dear,

All is not lost – well, not quite all. We have set a date for the recording – February 24 and 25 – but is that convenient for you? It is more likely that this time The Revuers and not the machine will break down – but I, personally, am sticking to my cod-liver oil – and hoping that all will go well. Also – do you think you might be able to come on Friday – the 23rd? – It's been so

---

[60] Betty Comden (1917–2006), American lyricist, writer, and performer, the writing partner of Adolph Green for numerous successful Broadway shows and Hollywood films. Bernstein came to know Comden in 1939 through Green, when both of them were members of The Revuers. Bernstein made one of his first recordings with The Revuers in March 1940 (*The Girl with the Two Left Feet*), and they subsequently collaborated on two Broadway triumphs: *On The Town* and *Wonderful Town*. Betty Comden was to remain a lifelong friend. Like Green, she was passionate about serious music, and was as interested in Bernstein's conducting and his concert compositions as she was in his work for Broadway.

[61] A reference to *The Girl with the Two Left Feet* by The Revuers, with improvised music by Bernstein. A proposed recording is the subject of Comden's letter.

[62] *The Pursuit of Happiness* was a CBS radio show broadcast for one season (1939–40; 30 episodes in all). Directed by Norman Corwin and Brewster Morgan, and hosted by Burgess Meredith, it was aired immediately after the Sunday afternoon broadcast from the New York Philharmonic. The Revuers appeared in two episodes, on 12 November 1939 and 18 February 1940.

long, and also there may be some new music, and vigorous rehearsal would be a great idea.

Listen – if you can bear it – on the 18th to *The Pursuit* (*of Happiness*) – and write to me as soon as you get this – or wire – about your coming to New York. Will the 24, 25 & 26 fit into the Bernstein schedule?

Wish you very much love from Betty – and the other bright young people.

47. Leonard Bernstein to Kenneth Ehrman
408 South 22nd Street, Philadelphia, PA
[20 February 1940]

O never-to-be-forgotten one!

The only news I've had from you is the one solitary fact that a letter you sent to me this summer was returned to you, address unknown. I live from moment to moment in expectancy of your return, capture by the Germans, or some such rot. Why don't you let a fellow who remembers a brown bag that sags to the ground, & will never forget Mr. Bowie? (If there are *New Yorkers* in Paris, cf. Thurber cartoon of recent date captioned "Every day is Arbor Day to Mr. –")

Things are progressing at a great rate here. I can almost play the piano again, was the only student to get an A in conducting from Reiner, have had pieces broadcast, am receiving ghastly label of Pennsylvania composer. You would like our director, Randall Thompson, one of U. of Calif.

So is Margaret.[63]

Kenneth, believe me, I perish to see you. I get these fits from time to time – it was studying Brahms' Third for Reiner tonight that did it. Please, I beg, write endless letters, or better still, come home. I don't know whether to envy you, or be perplexed, or simply be angry: once in a while la moutarde me monte au nez. From what I can gather, you're doing nothing in France. And all these Hearst papers in America.

Next year looks wonderful for me. Great things are brewing, & I can't say anything now. But, as you've already guessed, it's mostly the fault of Dimitri. A most blessworthy man.

Are you married? Do you still like music? Have you read Spengler? (I am now). Is tertiary syphilis curable? (Jot that down, Miss Wilson). Is Gordon still Messing? Is Bob still Wernick?[64] Tell all to yr still truest –

Love that transcendeth death,
Lenny

---

[63] Probably Margaret Prall.
[64] Gordon Messing and Robert Wernick were friends from Harvard.

48. Betty Comden to Leonard Bernstein

[New York, NY]
1 March 1940

Lennie dear,

There's little left to say by this time. If your patience has not worn too thin (I'm suffering too, you know – it's not us if I'm enjoying all this, you know) – whether next weekend is divinely free for you – and whether you could possibly come in on Friday – even if it is late. There has been such a lapse of time since we last battled through that score – and some new to learn (!!!). The more time we have for it the better. Yes – I know April is far off and we needn't rush into this blindly, but Lennie – the age of miracles is not yet dead – we may yet make those there new records *March 9th and 10th.*

I listened last Sunday – and your music was by far the most distinguished on the program, no matter what you may say. Hearing your name gave me a warm glow.

Write me Len – and if you're free, come anyway. It has been *much* too long, too long.

Love,

B

49. Betty Comden to Leonard Bernstein

[New York, NY]
6 March 1940

Lennie!!!!

You didn't like *Grapes of Wrath*!!!! But no matter – it alters not the "us" that stands triumphant and invulnerable above all petty differences. I don't care if you didn't like *Winter Carnival.* Come to dinner Friday anyway, and I shall try to break bread with you without a hard word about the Joads. Come at six-ish? We have an appointment with that unmentionable recording outfit at *eleven* – Saturday morning. That leaves us Friday evening to run over what is now a rusty better-forgotten memory to us all. In fact, it probably leaves us the whole weekend if I know Musicraft. But no, this time they said "positively".[65]

All the news is exciting about you, Lenny. Mme Miquelle said you were only *talented*?

Till Friday,

Betty

---

[65] The Revuers and Bernstein did record *The Girl with the Two Left Feet* for Musicraft in March 1940. This was Bernstein's first commercial recording. He plays an improvised score between accompanying the songs performed by The Revuers. This delightful recording was released on CD by Pearl in the set *Leonard Bernstein – Wunderkind* (GEMS 0005).

50. Leonard Bernstein to David Diamond[66]

408 South 22nd Street, Philadelphia, PA

18 April 1940

Dear David,

Forgive me if I emote. Today has been horrible, and I have been missing you strangely. April is the cruelest month. I received a wire from Dimitri that knocked my world completely to hell. I have had queer forebodings about the next year affair in Minneapolis all along – and you, sympathetic to the super-normal, can certainly understand them. Today saw their manifestation. I quote from Western Union:

"Don't leave your class for next season – some real difficulties here because of my engagement in N.Y. and one month of orchestra tour and some guest conductors – it is not wise to stop studying for a doubtful season for you here – am very awfully sorry. Dimitri."

Now take a breath & put yourself here with me at 408 [South 22nd Street]. I have been staggering & pale green all day, fighting with my lifeblood that wants to stop coursing.

What happens to one's Weltanschauung when the curtains fall together again? When one has been living & working according to a quasi-divine plan,

---

[66] David Diamond (1915–2005), American composer. He quickly became one of Bernstein's closest friends, though their friendship was often stormy and disputatious. Their correspondence over almost half a century is extremely lively, and sometimes volatile. Bernstein provided financial assistance for Diamond from time to time, while Diamond was an enthusiastic supporter of Bernstein's own compositions. Diamond studied with Bernard Rogers at the Eastman School, with Roger Sessions, and with Nadia Boulanger. Bernstein performed several of Diamond's major works and recorded the Fourth Symphony for Columbia in 1958. Diamond recalled his first encounter with Bernstein in an interview with Paul Remington for *Cosmik Debris* (No. 21, February 1997):

I had heard about him from Aaron Copland and Marc Blitzstein. They told me about this extraordinary pianist that was at Harvard studying with Walter Piston, Edward Burlingame Hill and Randall Thompson. And, one weekend I was going up the stairs to thank Koussevitzky for such a wonderful performance after a Boston Symphony concert. They performed Ravel's Left Hand Piano Concerto. Of course, he knew I had known Ravel, so he was so pleased that I came back and that I was so moved by the performance of the work. And there at the top of the stairs was this very good-looking young man. I remember he was looking down at me. He said, "I know you!" I said, "Who are you?" He said, "I'm Leonard Bernstein." I evidently reacted to that, and he said, "and you're David Diamond!" He said, "You must come out to the Curtis sometime and spend a weekend with me there." He had enrolled in the Curtis Institute and had a full scholarship there. So, I got him to record some of my Preludes and Fugues. It was the first professional recording he had made. . . . I would go out to visit him almost every other weekend. I helped him with his counterpoint, I remember. . . . He was still a conducting student of Fritz Reiner's while at the Curtis Institute. He was composing at that time and had written theater music while he was at Harvard. But, he was working on a clarinet sonata, or maybe it was a violin and piano sonata that became a clarinet sonata. I didn't know him at all as a composer. But, he was a phenomenal pianist. From an orchestral score, he read through my

setting aside certainties and doubts into one category that depends from the arm of a world-force – succumbing to élan vital – letting oneself be driven by a reversed future? And suddenly all the bases, the category itself – the whole reason for doing all this is wiped out – an instant – equivalent to a career. Time recedes. The instant equals the career. All of Time is upon me now; I can hardly bear it.

Don't think I am carrying on, please. The prospect of next year, prefaced by a summer in the Koussevitzky class, was for me the one, single motive of my activity now; every move, every note studied, project rejected, person loved, hope ignored, was a direct preparation for next year. From the scores I chose to study to the sexual life which I have abandoned – all.

It is as hard to write this as it must have been for Dimitri to send the wire.

This is all meaningless to you: but I have to think to someone else in order to arrive at any conclusions. I'm much clearer now – I think I know what I shall write Dimitri.

After all, I could still go as pianist, unless he is really regretting a hasty decision. And again the possibility of 2 seasons hence is not removed. One must have faith & be able to make these efforts at adjustment. One day to another is one adjustment to another. So please say nothing of this to anyone. I had to think aloud to you: somehow the rapport I feel with you is uncanny.

I received yr. letter & music today just before the telegram. You will understand that I have not had a moment of open mind to look at your music. I'll do it now.

Write to me, & flights of angels attend yr Kouss [Koussevitzky] reading. I love you.

Lenny

51. Leonard Bernstein to David Diamond
408 South 22nd Street, Philadelphia, PA
23 April 1940

Dear David,

Matters are worse, & more complex. It all came out, in a letter from D[imitri] M[itropoulos] this morning that it's the union that put the monkey wrench in

---

1st Symphony that way. He just knocked me out as a musician. He was just phenomenal. And so, as the years went on, he saw that I was being performed a great deal. Then he made that amazing debut with the New York Philharmonic, substituting very quickly for Bruno Walter. Then, suddenly, he was on the map as a conductor. Then he was given the City Center Orchestra, which was an orchestra that was put together for him. He wasn't paid a salary, but that orchestra that he built up had marvelous programs. The second year he had that orchestra he did my 2nd Symphony, after he had heard Koussevitzky do it. Then, almost every other year he would perform a work of mine. And then he began to compose a lot. But, I guess I was the only one of the friends that felt he was a gifted composer. Copland didn't think he really had it as a composer. He thought he was very good for Broadway, but he didn't care for his composing. He didn't like *Jeremiah* whatsoever. Now, I thought *Jeremiah* was extraordinary.

the works. All sorts of complicated things involving firing and hiring & local talent as opposed to imported same etc. etc. The maestro will be in NYC around the 15th so I'm going to delay returning to Boston til after that. Ergo, no need to hang around Boston. I'll try to get in touch with you in the Beeg City.

Please don't think those thoughts re Dimitri. He's no false promiser. He has an integrity that is sans pareil. He's simply up against a strong machine. I too have heard the story of the Woltmann $1000 affair (minus the ten-dollar bill aspect), & I'm inclined to believe it.[67] He does things like that, & has faith in Woltmann. The man is incredible that way.

It's difficult for me even to think about our relationship (yours & mine, I mean), harder to discuss it. I too must be very careful for many reasons, all of which I will burden you with when I see you in New York.

God bless Rochester.

And you.

Lenny

I hope you will send me programs & reviews. Even if they don't make sense. It will fortify your presence here. Alles gutes to alle Guten, especially Roy.

52. Alfred Eisner to Leonard Bernstein
Metro-Goldwyn-Mayer Pictures, Culver City, CA
10 June [1940]

Bernsteinell,

Returned in triumph from San Francisco to be promptly assigned to a western for Beery[68] which is directly responsible for the half dozen heads I've bitten off in the past week. All very sad and making me want all kinds of out, preferably Mexico. Great exodus to Mex. from here and the Eisner feet itch *à faire peur*. If I could get a few bobs ahead I could do a little thinking with guts about such things – but good broke.

Mad about Frisco: a city of character, albeit some hilly. I walked up the California St hill and so have reason to be bitter. Squandered sixty bucks in four days and not a solitary sou regretted. Ate expansively if expensively – and some-times not so expensively. Stumbled on a place on Front St. where you eat for two bits, and second helpings yet; as yet no ptomaine. Really, if such phrases as "feeling, character, spirit" have any meaning when applied to cities, Frisco is all of that. I called Ken (your letter didn't reach me until return) and Ehrman *mère* took a deep breath and *drove* – quelle talker. Ken, it appears, is supposed to have taken ship at Marseilles last week, but in his last letter home (some months before) he had hinted darkly at joining the ambulance service and hanging

---

[67] In 1940, Mitropoulos conducted *The Coliseum at Night* by Frederick Woltmann.
[68] The actor Wallace Beery (1885–1949).

around for the duration. So Mrs. Ehrman didn't know and wouldn't I come out? All in all great time containing proper ingredients of culture, gastronomy, debauchery and lechery – and how is your sex life.

No, not married. Lived for a couple of weeks with a would-be actress in a house (small) in the hills with all of God's California spread like a burned over rug outside the bedroom window. Temperaments clashed and I'm back in an apartment which looks, fittingly enough, like a monastery. Actress, so help me God, had a glass eye and came from Brooklyn. And the most luscious body ever I rubbed against. Something, mon vieux, to see that eye come out. No, I didn't fuck her in the eye socket, although I imagine the procedure would have had a tang.

Otherwise, but little. I may hit *story* again soon. They're making up their flighty little minds now. Been writing quite some. Started my first novel. The "To Own The World" epic I worked on will be released soon under the title *We Who Are Young*.[69] Has been sneaked and reactions very whoopsifying. (Glossary: Whoops – to puke, to vomit under strong emotional stress due to violent nausea, colloq.) Remember when your head is being held, only about 20% of the clotted pool about your feet is my fault.

Would like very much to get out and away, but the studio has a viselike grip about my economic balls. The prospect is not encouraging: you look about you and realize that literary New York has descended *en masse* on Hollywood demanding bread and butter. Even that old die-hard, Maltz,[70] is in town looking for a job and, incidentally, not getting it. They're letting them out in droves and starvation marches with banners along Hollywood Blvd. Heard of a writer last week who was reduced to living in a house with a view on only one side and no swimming pool. Poor lamb. I get around quite a bit now and think nothing of going to parties where you put ashes in the drinks of Dorothy Parker or Sinclair Lewis etc. etc. Everybody is out here. Sometimes you actually tell yourself you're having an exciting time of it. I intend to get out in the fall. I'll have some dollars five hundred, and we'll see.

Distressing about your next year crumbling about your hapless head. But methinks next year is going to crumble about everybody's hapless head and plans and dreams and whims and hopes and lives will be all one lovely goulash thanks to the Stukas. Some guy I know out here leaves next week for France and the volunteer ambulance service. Wanted me to go along. I laughed for the first time in weeks.

And so at the coming of the great noon tide my phone rings and a producer wants to talk to me about a scene for Beery that even Beery can't play, and I am suddenly sick with the thought of talking about it. Weep for me lost among the lost and write.

Al

---

[69] *We Who Are Young* was released on 19 July 1940. Produced by Seymour Nebenzal, the cast included Lana Turner in one of her first major Hollywood roles.

[70] Albert Maltz (1908–85), author and screenwriter, one of the "Hollywood Ten" blacklisted in 1947 for refusing to answer questions from the House Un-American Activities Committee.

53. Leonard Bernstein to David Diamond

86 Park Avenue, Newton, MA
[14 June 1940]

Dear David,

Terribly sorry about that bit of automatic watercolor – it was God trying to express himself. As I remember it, the chief substance thereof was simply the cheerful fact that I had sat waiting by the phone from day to day, so to speak, and to this moment have had no word from D[imitri] M[itropoulos]. A strange silence, which is difficult for me to understand. It cannot be that the thing is over. I wrote him several days ago asking *why* and as yet have no answer. I'm sure that when I feel there's something wrong or misunderstood that I'm not simply making excuses to myself. These things simply cannot present themselves, naked and unexplained; the human quality would then become utterly cheap, like the stationery I'm writing you on.

As things go, however, I shall be in New York next week, probably from Wednesday to Saturday, for a television job with The Revuers. There's a sizeable reward, and I can well use it this summer. The Berkshire people have agreed to pay half my living expenses as well as the scholarship, and this job, I think, will just make up the rest. Ergo, if you're anywhere around the city next week, perhaps you might call me. I'll be staying at 29 W 65; the name is Comden; the phone is Trafalgar 7–9719, I think.

Renée Miquelle tells me of your piece, which she liked, & of doing the Village with you. Was it fun? She is terribly upset about France, more than all of us, because her home town & mother are involved. A ghastly business.

It was Heaven when Aaron came to Boston.

I want an reste, I've been working intermittently on my Violin Sonata, which I like, & which you probably won't, I'm afraid. These labors, Catiline, what with learning new scores & practising *Tombeau de Couperin* & assorted small subjects, & trying to see all the people I should when I have no real desire to, and trying to awake from a general depression, have all kept me fairly tied up. La vie marche. La mort approche. La naissance reste.

I really regret not having seen you – I wanted to – and perhaps you'll have some reason to be in the City next week. I hope so. Write me there if you can't come.

Best always.
Lenny

54. Betty Comden to Leonard Bernstein

[New York, NY]
Wednesday, 26 June [1940]

Dear Lenny,

Enclosed please find an impressive looking letter – and my love. I'm glad New Hampshire was on hand to welcome you and it sounds nice up there. You may or may not know that we all crashed Leonard Lyons' column in an item about Aaron [Copland] being the distinguished page-turner at the telecast.[71] Adolph has spoken to Aaron and he is amused and amazed – and not the least bit angry.

There is a slight lull. Judy [Holliday] is away. The rest of us are doing some work and hoping that by the end of the week we'll be able to take a day or two off too. A dull letter, I know – but I'll write soon again – and I hope I'll have something to *enclose* as well.

Love,

B

Do you want those lovely slacks? – and jacket?

55. Leonard Bernstein to Renée Longy Miquelle[72]
Hanover, NH
1 July 1940

Chère Mme,

Lunch is calling, and I have but a moment to write – the television venture being over, I am safely ensconced in this charming but dull college town with the Silvermans[73] (or should it be Silvermen?) and working, actually. I see nobody, but lead a quiet, useful and pleasant existence. I've already learned Beethoven's 4th and *Scheherazade*. Starting Copland's *Music for the Theatre* today. Practicing. Composing. The fiddle Sonata almost prêt. Leaving for the Cranwell School, Lenox (my next address: please write) on the 5th, probably. Aaron told me that I might have to conduct Randall Thompson's Symph. (No. 2, naturellement) the first week, since that's when Randy will be there. Kouss, in searching around for the person to do it, suddenly said to Copland (so goes the tale) "*your* Bernstein!" I don't know.

---

[71] This telecast was a "special" from NBC's experimental studio, featuring The Revuers. Bernstein was the pianist and Copland turned the pages (see Burton 1994, p. 72). In Lyons' article, Bernstein is described only as "the accompanist": "Saturday Night, when The Revuers appeared on NBC's full-hour television program, the unbilled stranger who turned the pages for the accompanist was Aaron Copland, the noted American composer" (*New York Post*, 25 June 1940).

[72] Renée Longy Miquelle (1897–1979), French-born pianist, theorist, and teacher. She moved to the United States when her father, Georges Longy, became principal oboist of the Boston Symphony Orchestra. Her first teaching post was at the Longy School of Music, which her father founded in 1915. Subsequently, she taught at the Curtis Institute (where she was Bernstein's score-reading teacher), then at the Peabody Conservatory in Baltimore, the University of Miami, and the Juilliard School in New York. Her other pupils included the pianist Jacob Lateiner, cellist Leonard Rose, and several members of the New York Philharmonic including flutist Julius Baker and oboist Harold Gomberg.

[73] Raphael Silverman, later known as Raphael Hillyer (1914–2010), was a graduate student at Harvard where he often performed with Bernstein. He led the orchestra in the 1939 production of *The Birds* with Bernstein's incidental music. After a spell in the Boston Symphony Orchestra as a violinist, Hillyer switched to the viola in 1946 and became a founding member of the Juilliard String Quartet, with which he played for 23 years. He was the dedicatee of Bernstein's Violin Sonata, referred to in this letter.

Nothing to do but pray. And perk up about the abroad situation. It's getting exciting now; Russia, it seems, is going to have a lot to say about what Germany does, soon, and forcibly. Again, we can only pray. [. . .]

Lenny

56. Betty Comden to Leonard Bernstein
17 July 1940

Lenny dear,

Kouss may have been impressed by your conducting – but his feelings cannot compare with mine. I'm thrilled at the thoughts of your concerts and I absolutely will make it my business to get up to see you somehow this summer. But actually conducting! And after all that silly fretting over whether or not you'd memorize *Scheherazade* in time. [. . .] It's wonderful about the conducting and the summer sounds magnificent for you. [. . .]

57. Leonard Bernstein to Kenneth Ehrman
17 Lake Avenue, Sharon, MA
[August 1940]

Ken,

I was very desolated that your visit was so short – it hit me afterwards that I hadn't really seen you outside of some small talk & some big talk forced in somewhere to give your return significance. I wanted so to reestablish us again – & then you left. I find you, thank God (?) very much the same Ken, the most pleasant article to be with I've ever encountered, cool, and unimpressed by most superficial things, more impressed than he will admit by the basicker things. I was touched by your reaction to the hundreds of busy little Tanglewood bees: if it caused the slightest stirring up in yr creative being, I feel a Messiah, indirectly. Hast du ein eingiges Wort geschrieben? Is Palo Alto? Does your family intrigue you any more? You should keep away from it. It's a kind of monstrosity anyway, as you will admit – but you can't live in a sideshow.

Come east, where I can see you often.

Tanglewood was a complete success. Where did you leave? – yes, at the Bach, which was done standing up & [Putnam] Aldrich playing the harpsichord. The performance was an ode to Viola Wasterlain. *Scheherazade* was wonderfully exciting, despite some bad slips from the solos, & there followed the Haydn *Symphonie concertante*, the Brahms *Haydn Variations*, Copland's *Outdoor Overture* (at the Allies Benefit!), & a performance I wish you could have seen & heard of Stravinsky's *Histoire du Soldat* with my own words (local color) served up as a surprise for Koussie on his terrace at a tea he gave for the school. A hit. Kouss is greatly impressed wants me to study with him in Boston this winter, if he can get an orchestra for me to work with. I'll know in a few weeks. Write, & spare no gory details. I'm with you til the plane wheels flaming to the Japanese (Chinese, I suppose it shd be) soil –

Len

58. Leonard Bernstein to Aaron Copland
17 Lake Avenue, Sharon, MA
[August or early September 1940]

Aaron, foremost of men,

Where are you? And if so, why no word? You said you'd write, according to Green. Not seeing you is something of a shock, you understand. The summer was a revelation in that regard. Neither of us (I hope) tired of the other (I had feared you might) and I came, in fact, to depend in many ways on you. I've never felt about anyone before as I do about you. Completely at ease, & always comforted with you. This is not a love letter, but I'm quite mad about you.

Might Yaddo on Sept. 7 & 8 be interesting?[74] Are you planning to go? I was thinking of upping to Lenox next week or so to see the Kouss. Perhaps I could combine both. Write fast & let me hear. Best to Victor.

Love,

Lenny

P.S. I've finished the Fiddle Sonata, &, by God, there's something about the ending that's wonderful – almost mature. I want you to see the whole thing now – I like it better.

59. Leonard Bernstein to Serge Koussevitzky[75]
17 Lake Avenue, Sharon, MA
[before 5 September 1940]

Dear Dr. Koussevitzky,

Words are a remote enough medium of expression for any musician, but it is especially difficult for me to find words for this letter. Let it be brief.

---

[74] A weekend of the Yaddo Music Festival comprising four concerts of contemporary American music given at the Yaddo artists' community in Saratoga Springs, NY. The programme for the weekend was printed in *The New York Times* on 7 September 1940 and listed works by (among others) Paul Bowles, Henry Cowell, Paul Creston, David Diamond, Roy Harris, Mary Howe, Charles Ives, Gail Kubik, Otto Luening, Paul Pisk, and Quincy Porter.

[75] Serge Koussevitzky (1874–1951), Russian-born conductor who served as Music Director of the Boston Symphony Orchestra from 1924 to 1949. Along with Copland, Koussevitzky was one of Bernstein's most important mentors, initially through conducting classes at Tanglewood, then as an enthusiastic promoter of Bernstein's career as a conductor, pianist, and a composer of "serious" music: he strongly disapproved of Bernstein's activities as a Broadway composer, and this may well be one of the reasons why, after *On the Town*, Bernstein wrote no Broadway shows until after Koussevitzky's death.

This summer to me was beauty – beauty in work, and strength of purpose, and cooperation. I am full of humility and gratitude for having shared so richly in it. These last six weeks have been the happiest and most productive of my life. I have been able, for the first time, to concentrate completely on my main purpose, with a glorious freedom from personal problems.

It was a renaissance for me – a rehabilitation of the twisted and undefined Weltanschauung with which I came to you.

For your creative energy, your instinct for truth, your incredible incorporation of teacher and artist, I give humble thanks. Seeing in you my own concepts matured is a challenge to me which I hope to fulfill in your great spirit.

I am now at home, resting with my family. I hope to be in Lenox within the next few weeks, and I should very much like to see you and talk with you. Can you let me know when this would be best for you?

Please give my very warm greetings to Madame Koussevitzky, and to Miss Naumoff.

In devotion, and in gratitude,
Leonard Bernstein

60. Serge Koussevitzky to Leonard Bernstein
Lenox, MA
5 September 1940

Dear Leonard,

Thank you for your letter.

Nothing could have made me happier than to know that your work this summer has really given you beauty and strength and a better understanding of the gifts with which nature has endowed you.

I shall be glad to see you sometime during the middle of this month, let us say Tuesday, the 17th, or Wednesday, the 18th, – and I shall look forward to your coming to Lenox.

My best wishes are with you always.
Serge Koussevitzky

61. Leonard Bernstein to Serge Koussevitzky
86 Park Avenue, Newton, MA
30 September 1940

Dear Dr. Koussevitzky,

As I sit and wait for the outcome of your plan, in a kind of Proustian twilight state between knowing and not knowing, between sleeping and waking – in the midst of all this I have had an inspiring idea. It would have to have – and I pray it will have – your support.

I have met one or two of the people who have been conducting small orches-tras in Greater Boston, and I have been singularly unimpressed – or rather, singularly *im*pressed with their lack of equipment. It occurred to me that if they can get orchestras of young people, perhaps I could. And with your support, almost certainly.

If you are unable to establish connections with the representatives of Backward Boston, don't you think it would be wise for me to attempt the organization of a young orchestra? I am sure there are many instrumentalists in Boston who would be glad of orchestral experience; if you liked the idea, we might even establish it as a kind of training orchestra for the Boston Symphony. If these young people knew you were behind it, I am sure they would rally to the cause.

The problem for me is to make contact with these people. Again, if you could speak to the men of your orchestra, they might be willing to send their pupils to this orchestra. I realize the responsibility I would be shouldering, but I do it only under the influence of your spirit which still hovers around me. I could then work with an orchestra (which would derive great benefit from their association with you) and still be here to work with you this season. Please don't think me presumptuous; I am just making a great effort to be practical.

Please try to get some rest before the season. I am sorry to intrude on your privacy even with this letter; but I am made bold by my recent reading of Nietzsche, who teaches me that I must be somewhat bolder if I, like his Zarathustra, shall ever face "the great Noon-Tide."

In eternal devotion,

Leonard

Warmest greetings to Madame Koussevitzky and Miss Naumoff.

62. Leonard Bernstein to David Diamond

2122 Walnut Street, Philadelphia, PA

11 October 1940

Dear David,

I am (O wrest the power from the powerful) in Philly. Nay, living here. There has been a commotion in the diplomatic heavens[76] and I, O fearful pawn, was set with a sharp click in Rittenhouse Square. I'll tell you all anon.

---

[76] Presumably, the "commotion" was Fritz Reiner's furious reaction to Koussevitzky's suggestion that Bernstein should study with him in Boston rather than with Reiner.

Which means that I shan't be in Boston when you are. God bless the Sat. night concert, & have a good burlesque show.

I'd be incredibly happy to do the NMQR recordings. I *am* "serious" about it, and very flattered that you should still want me to do it. So write, & set some dates, voice the stipulations, & I'll pop out as from a pigeon-hole. Mais l'important, que tu m'écrives, et cela bientôt.

Lenny

63. Leonard Bernstein to Kenneth Ehrman
2122 Walnut Street, Philadelphia, PA
15 October 1940

Cher Kenneth,

Incredible that you put up with what you put up with what you put up (with?). Everything that constitutes a means of improvement for you is at your disposal, except, apparently, the initial desire. That's available, to, at a reasonable fee. You're not lazy. Why don't you investigate?

I couldn't imagine what you were doing at Lafayette, Ind., but I wrote you there, & no response. Of course, I wrote you again at Palo Alto (first sending it to Box 817, Palo Alto, 'steada Menlo Park). By the way, did you know there was Menlo Park, New Jersey?

But having forgotten what I said to you in that Odyssean letter, I may be guilty of repeating myself. En tous cas, comme tu aperçois, sans doute, ci-haut (that sounds wrong) I am in Philly. I don't know; I never asked to be here. Something makes it inevitable. I may have told you that Kouss had great plans for me which involved my staying in Boston but they were given the K.O. by the Hon. Curtis Institute, which objected strenuously at (read: to) student-swiping, & vowed to discontinue all relationship with Kouss & his school if I didn't return. Matter of ethics, don't you know, setting a precedent, don't you know, etc. Reiner was furious. He had seen me referred to in printed items as Kouss' pupil – no mention of *him* (antecedents again; means Reiner). So me voici, & lucky to be, O misery me, ta da ta da. But I've got a magnificent room with a double bed & massive mahogany furniture, & the school is doing almost all the supporting. Therefore, easier. Therefore, out goes Mexico, & Kouss, & you, & Cambridge, & California. Nothing left for you to do but come here. Please try; there are some things you might profit by that you haven't yet seen. By "here" I mean East, not Philly: I'm in this city only because Koussie realized that he'd be losing an A-1 customer in Mrs. Bok if he didn't kowtow. So I became a fearful pawn ([Edna St Vincent] Millay) in the hands of wily diplomats. Write me very soon.

I to my naked spinet in your corner.

Lenny the pawn, & Penny the prawn,
   and Henny the lawn, & Jenny the spawn, & Renny the griswoldforlawn.

64. Alfred Eisner to Leonard Bernstein

Metro-Goldwyn-Mayer Pictures, Culver City, CA
[?October 1940]

Lennie, old mole,

I have just finished reading Hemingway's new novel from the galley proofs and am still a little breathless.[77] A master stroke managing to get hold of those proofs, involving larceny of some proportion. But she's a novel, old gum drop, a book of infinite insight and agony and the soul of a man hovering halo fashion over the brow of his body while he kills with cold savagery. Writing that positively *gooses* you! Hemingway saw Spain cameo-clear; and his book is just two years – two? Four! – too late and its anger will cause not a ripple in the hysteria of warmaking. 'Twill be just a good novel by Hemingway about something out of ancient history. The people who will realize what it is he is saying will already know, and there it will end.

Where have you been, old sausagefoot? Aeons have whirled their course since that card from Tanglewood. Not a word. I suppose by this late date you have a devoted slave in the Kouss. I thought as much. Indirect word of you from Austin, who described you as "forging ahead" and deciding with some acumen, I think, that he (A.) and Kenneth needed a kick in the pants. Back at Curtis? What? All the days crammed to the brim that I must know about. Successes. Quiff. Friends. Plans. Already written, in the writing, to be written. Prospects. Aaron. On and on, and I want to hear about it all. So to it, Rosinante, to the road again; get thee pants and write me a letter that will consume at least a morning of MGM's time in the reading. Trust me to kill the afternoon.

I won't even mention the draft. It's just too goddamn funny to even talk about. One thing: what are you going to do? Me, I can't wait until the army makes a man of me. Can't decide between the air force and fighting my war toying with some secretary's breasts. Simply *can't* decide. We live in parlous times, halvah, old boy, very. Dies irae, dies illa, solvet saeclum in favilla. But yes.

Hattie arrives in some two weeks to take over not only my care and feeding but also the not inconsiderable job of delivering me from the financial toils. I make enough money for three men, and am a pauper, yea, I sit among the ashes and for garments sackcloth. I'm tooting madly about looking at houses. To date, nothing I like. *Must* find something within the week.

Of my tenuous existence, trivia. The Eisner soul grows small and curls inward like the anemone to confess that he has ghosted two (I must be very

---

[77] Hemingway's *For Whom the Bell Tolls* was published in October 1940. It is likely that Eisner's letter was written shortly before then. The draft mentioned later in Eisner's letter was the Selective Training and Service Act, which came into force on 16 September 1940, the first peacetime conscription in American history.

tired or something) jobs for a quickie studio, for the gain of silver.[78] One, a mouse called *Thirty Boys and a Girl* (subtitle: The Gangfuck) has just been finished. Shooting time: six days. Budget: 10 grand. So you can imagine. No, you can't imagine. But the banks honor their checks, if you worry them into giving it to you. Working here at Metro with a couple of German Jew writers whose English is even worse than their script which is negligible. We communicate in mangled French, English and German. Nice people though: one an outspoken anarchist. All for the assassination of L.B. Mayer (after the expiration of his contract, of course). The other is a gourmet who drags me about to restaurants of stature and flies into tantrums if the béarnaise sauce is not up to his idea of sauce béarnaise. One night he insisted on going to the kitchen and bawling out the chef. I was sure he was going to get a meat cleaver in his head. Nip and tuck there for a minute.

Taking a course in the novel given by the League of American Writers school here, more as discipline to make me sit down more often to an already started novel, than in the hope of learning anything. Some very wacky people in that class: I expect murder before the month is out. And River[79] (*The Torguts*) to have nervous prostration. Also a new story of mine will appear in *The Clipper*, a literary monthly put out by the League pretending to some excellence. Be in excellent company anyway: Dreiser, Meyer Levin, Belfrage, others. I think every writer in America is either here or on his way. You meet them all.

Intended coming home this month, but Mother Metro like the python has me in her coils. In the spring. Letter from Ann and Nathan today: they desire word of you. And remember, it's *Keats*. So heavyhearted, I go home to my cell and it's another day. Write, sluggard, hear the voice crying in the wilderness and write.

Con brio,
Al

65. David Diamond to Leonard Bernstein
Yaddo, Saratoga Springs, NY
29 October 1940

Dear Lenny,
Henry Cowell[80] forwarded your little "critique" to me, asking me to get some definite plan worked out for the recording. Naturally, I don't feel the way you do

---

[78] Much of this sentence has been deleted and retyped.
[79] Walter Leslie River (1902–81), American novelist and screenwriter.
[80] Henry Cowell (1897–1965), American composer and founder of the periodical *New Music* for which Diamond's piece was being recorded.

about the 3rd fugue and neither do I approve of a series of preludes. If I had wanted that, I would have written them without the fugues. And Lenny, perhaps your kind of musicianly temperament will be the kind that succeeds best because it turns hot and cold easiest, but in the long run you will find your own way of treating music (the way John Kirkpatrick does by the way, but instead of saying "dull", he says, "quasi-baroque") to be the merest surface glazing. It seems incredible to me, that in this short time, you can already pronounce so dark a verdict on the several fugues, when I'm sure, knowing your high-pressure endocrine system, that you could hardly have spent much concentrated effort on them since Cowell got the music back to you. I can only say that I believe in the 3rd Prelude and Fugue whole, that if the fugue to you seems dull, it is like X telling me much of the *Art of Fugue* and the *Great Fugue* is dry and paper-music. The art of counterpoint is a true art. It has to be realized before one can say things pro or con. And to realize the 16th century masters, much of late Bach and Beethoven, the Stravinsky of *Persephone* and the *Symphonie de Psaumes*, the fugue from Bartók's *Music for Strings, Percussion and Celesta*, we must first know the notes so well, the line so accurately and the nuances so perfectly and rightly proportioned, we should be able to reconstruct the works ourselves. You will say, but I am no sixteenth century master, Bach, Beethoven, Stravinsky, or Bartók – but my aims and purposes are the same, my deep compassion for the past the same and my belief in the future the same. Lots of Reger may be dull, but not this baby. I've learned when to stop the machine in time of crisis! When you employ the word *dull* to the 3rd fugue, you are simply failing to unmask the secret character behind the piece.

As Cowell seems very pressed, I promised I would write at once ill or not. I've been in bed over a week with a serious streptococcus infection. This is really my first day up. But back to the recording: no, I don't OK the prelude idea – sounds too easy à la Bernstein. The original plan is the one I hold to. If you feel the matter much too taxing to go through because the fugue is dull, just write and tell Cowell so. I'm getting more and more used to this kind of thing. There are fewer and fewer kindred spirits left each year. By the time this war is over, there will be none. If you take yourself by both your shoulders, for a change, work the notes carefully, you'll find the fugue will grow quite rapidly inside of you. Let me know what you decide. And if you go ahead, I'll send you $2 with which to make a test recording for me as I will not be able to come to NY. Make it in Philadelphia at a reliable recording place and send it to me, and I'll write right back about tempo etc. All good things ever, and let Cowell know at once what you've decided.

David

66. Leonard Bernstein to David Diamond
2122 Walnut Street, Philadelphia, PA
[after 29 October 1940]

Dear David,

I was shocked by your letter. I'm afraid you misunderstood. I intended no criticism of the music *per se*, but simply referred to the probable reaction of a record audience. I suggested that the 3rd fugue, unpianistic and unrelieved as it is, might be an unfortunate choice with which to introduce yourself via recording. If you want it, then certainly I will be glad to do it.[81]

But why the maleure? I understand that you've been ill, and down, and probably out, and kind of out of the world, but, Lord, David, – "too easy à la Bernstein" – "take yourself by your shoulders for a change", etc. etc. And I thought you knew me better than to intimate that I would make superficial dicta about music. Believe me, I know what the fugue is worth. I can list for you all the fine points – your achievements in it. But there are "stains"; your second stretto, for instance, is anticlimactic because it is a four-measure stretto, whereas the preceding one was a *one*-measure stretto. This is especially true of a subject in unrelieved half-notes. Again, you speak of nuances to be mastered thoroughly – but you haven't *one* in the piece except the opening *ff*! From my point of view there must be a dynamic growth – involving especially a drop to *piano* in the 17th measure, to rise to the final climactic stretto, & possibly the same thing again (modified) before the second stretto. Write me what you think of this. And is ♩ = 63 strictly to be maintained throughout?

I shall make a test record as soon as possible & send it to you. Let me know about the above very soon. And please keep well, & somewhat happier.

Best,

Lenny

67. David Diamond to Leonard Bernstein
Yaddo, Saratoga Springs, NY
5 November 1940

Dear Lennie,

I am happy that you have decided upon the fugue too. As I look over the letter you sent to Mr. Cowell, it is true that you were thinking of recording purposes, but all the same *that* word is there thus: "The third prelude is good but the fugue is *dull*. . ." etc. – and to me that still pertains to the music, recording

---

[81] Bernstein's first solo recording, made for New Music Recordings in January 1941, was of David Diamond's Prelude and Fugue No. 3. The tetchy correspondence about it was symptomatic of many of the letters Bernstein and Diamond exchanged over the next half century.

or not. I won't argue the point further, for we seem to be beyond that now. Furthermore, I think you should have realized by now that I'm pretty stupid on consideration to be given the purely commercial aspects of music. Where public relations are concerned I simply don't function nor want to. And whether one makes the right start in recording works by choosing the best to represent the composer on discs doesn't interest me either since no one cares how a composer is introduced or in what order. It's the music that counts in the long run. Where Aaron for example should have made his bow on discs with say, *Music for the Theater* or *Hear Ye, Hear Ye*, he made it with the *Piano Variations* and *Vitebsk* and that would seem wrong but nevertheless that is how he began and it makes no difference to anyone. People still hate the *Variations* and eat up the *Salón México*, alors? So don't worry your pretty head about the introduction part of it; "c'est la musique qui compte" as [Nadia] Boulanger always said to me when I would pose such questions as you have brought up. Truly, dear Lennie, I don't care a double fuck for anything dehors de la musique. You know that, why worry about it, no one else does, time takes care of all the necessary sifting out.

Now about the music: I don't agree about the drop to a *piano* at the 17th measure, lawsy no! After the full strong half note pulse with accents and the general *ff*, it would only appear as an affectation! I should have right in the first measure put *sempre* after the *ff*. It should be *ff* throughout and always a quarter to 63 with the natural push forward towards 70 circa which happens by itself. It must be very sustained, very bold, the notes will provide the necessary *espressivo* I believe. The chord quality at measure 17 is sufficient to stir emotionally anyone capable of being touched by the chord without changing the dynamics. You mistake my meaning of the word, nuance; it does not mean dynamics – I'd rather it meant conception and feeling for the natural flow and modulation of the whole musical line, *chiaro*? I'm not worried in the least, I know you'll do a beauty of a job. And if you can keep a secret, a venture is afoot which will mean much for both of us if it works out with Victor. I enclose $2 for the test recording and as soon as I've heard it, I shall let you know my feelings.

Why let us start a series of polemics? You say I should know you by now, I can hardly agree with that. You never allowed me to, ever. I tried in so many ways to know you better, looked forward to seeing you in NY, but you didn't come last spring, came to Tanglewood to see you but got a cold shoulder [...] At Yaddo [...] I was simply hurt by the strain you forced to exist in not being open enough about your true feelings. It would have been far better to have said, "David, understand that there can be no physical relationship between us, therefore I'd rather not stay with you tonight." [...] It's all right though now. Nothing matters much right now.

Always,
David

68. Aaron Copland to Leonard Bernstein
Hotel Empire, Broadway at 63rd Street, New York, NY
6 November [1940]

Dear LLLLLLL,

Your latest burned the end of my fingers. The next one will probably burn up en route. All I can say is that you've made rapid progress. All that's missing is for you to fall in love with a hermaphroditic goat . . . or sumpin'.

I vaguely remember the Mr. Nelson you mentioned. It was two years ago on the way to France. It was his great moment – just at the age when the world seems too too wonderful, and he [was] sought after by all the most desirable creatures, a different bed every night, etc., etc. That type is the worst after the first fresh glow of youth is gone. All his stories are rot, of course.

The enclosure by D[avid] D[iamond] is also sumpin! The less said the better. There is a frighteningly dumb and humorless streak in the boy.

I'm up to my neck in fussing over the new loft. V[ictor Kraft]'s dark room is sumptuous, but all my things are strewn to the four corners of the joint. It's awful – I'll never move again.

Don't forget to listen in on Sat. at 9:35.[82]

Love,

A

69. Harold Shapero[83] to Leonard Bernstein
"XI–?–1940" [November 1940]

Dear heart,

You're full of shit. You're full of shit because you're exuberant, and exuberance is not especially welcome at this moment. The world and I don't need exuberance, what we need is revolution. Especially the world. Especially me. Especially me. And the world too.

First, I have to say, and not with any obligation, but with sincere co-jubilation, that I'm glad for you and all the successes you mentioned. I'm glad for every every weentzy one of 'em. You're doing the right things in a big way. (Funny, that's what you always told me.) And you're making money too. 'Sis dir gut!

Walter[84] thinks Diamond stinks, and what's good enough for Walter is good enough for me. It's always been a mystery to me (on the basis of the stuff I've

---

[82] The first performance of the Suite from *Billy the Kid* was broadcast on Saturday, 9 November 1940, by the NBC Symphony Orchestra under William Steinberg.
[83] Harold Shapero (1920–2013), American composer. A near contemporary of Bernstein's at Harvard (Shapero graduated in 1941), he subsequently taught at Brandeis University for 37 years. Bernstein recorded Shapero's *Symphony for Classical Orchestra* in 1953.
[84] Walter Piston (1894–1976), American composer and teacher who taught both Shapero and Bernstein at Harvard.

seen, and I've seen enough to get an indication) how the hell Diamond's gotten as far as he's gotten. Honest to God, Lenny dear, David Diamond is a bust as far as I'm concerned. For his own sake I hope he's better than I think he is.

Tell me about how Charlie Demuth was a tragic figger.[85] I don't really know his biography. Nobody seems to.

What was your draft number? 8000[86] I hope I hope I hope.

I saw a Georges Rouault show at Boston's hoi polloi Institute of Modern Art. The guy's a great, awfully great, painter, even though he believes in God, and is fanatic about it. To be corny, the sheer magic of the man's textures (great gobs of paint) and the magic of the man's facility for expressionism, Jeez, terrific.

The curious tone at the beginning of this letter wasn't for nothing. I will now list mes calamités:

1) Do you remember the slow movement of the quartet? Well Walter, and finally I, agreed that it stunk. So, with Walter egging me on I kept going. It still stunk. It has now been thrown away.

2) I had to copy my Overture (why, I don't know) and as I copied I got an awful feeling. You, Bernstein, don't realize how silly and false that piece is.[87]

3) I started a fast quartet movement that was gonna be great stuff. I took a look at it two weeks ago: the sterilest, lousiest, beatest, etc.

4) Since I passed in my thesis title one (1) day late the Committee on Honors of Harvard Univ. has refused to let me write a thesis. So: I can't get honors. So: I can't get a fellowship.[88] So: I have not written a note (except harmony & strict cpt. exercises) for a month and I'm not going to for at least a year. Probably more. So: I'm enrolling in the Museum School after graduation and I'm gonna learn how to paint & draw. At least if I can't use my head I can use my hands.

---

[85] Charles Demuth (1883–1935), American artist whose friends included the poet William Carlos Williams, the artist Marsden Hartley, and the photographer Alfred Stieglitz. He bequeathed many of his paintings to Georgia O'Keeffe. A childhood illness left Demuth with a pronounced limp for the rest of his life, and his health was always precarious. According to Robert Hughes: "Demuth was not a flaming queen, in fact he was rather a discreet gay, but if he could not place his deepest sexual predilections in the open, he could still make art from them" (Robert Hughes, *American Visions: The Epic History of Art in America*, New York: Knopf, 1997, p. 380).

[86] Probably a reference to the draft papers drawn up in Washington, D.C. in 1940, which had the numbers 1 to 7,836 printed on them.

[87] Shapero is being hard on himself here. The *Nine-Minute Overture* won the American Prix de Rome in 1941. His success was reported in the *Harvard Crimson* on 9 June 1941: "Harold S. Shapero '41 of Newton has won the annual Prix de Rome in Music, it was announced yesterday by Howard Barlow, conductor of the Columbia Symphony Orchestra. The work, *A Nine-Minute Overture*, was played during Barlow's regular Sunday afternoon radio program. Instead of the customary privilege of studying at the American Academy in Rome, Shapero will receive $1,000 outright. Recently awarded the Knight Prize for composition by the Music Department, Shapero is the first Harvard undergraduate to win the Prix de Rome. The winning piece is his first attempt at writing for orchestra."

[88] The award of the Prix de Rome and Harvard's George Arthur Knight Prize (for composition) enabled Shapero to study with Nadia Boulanger after graduation.

5) I'm in love with a New Yorker who's in love with someone else. And I fell in love with her because she said things like "Jeez, this guy's (me) got the terrificest vocabulary, all the way from A to Beat."

6) I could go on forever, I got millions of 'em.

Goodbye, be good, have a Scotch on me.

Sonny

70. Alfred Eisner to Leonard Bernstein

Metro-Goldwyn-Mayer Pictures, Culver City, CA

[?1940]

Dear Lennie, mon vieux, mon vieux,

At long last opportunity offers itself to look up from this verdammter desk and inform the friends de ma jeunesse that I am definitely not dead. Have been working day and night and night and day on a yarn scheduled for Bob Montgomery having to do with the Jack the Ripper slashings and a guy who achieves a change of personality as a result of suspicion accidentally falling his way: a very choice assignment and the first story I have anything to do with that excited me at all. Picture to be produced by one [Seymour] Nebenzal, a refugee cinemateer who did *M* and *Mayerling* among others. A very intelligent gimmick and we have an orgy making ourselves understood in mangled English, French and German. Believe it or not, progress manifests. Neby is of the old German school of thought that reasons something like this: if I can work 20 hours a day, why, please tell me why you can't work 15? So you work 15 or better. I whacked out an 85 page treatment in exactly four days and nights, severing myself from all matters earthly and living the life of a hermit, yea, a veritable anchorite. Maybe this one will pay off. Please God.

Item: have a new car, a most spectacular 1933 Plymouth convertible coupe that is doing its very able best to bleed me to death. To date: new brake re-line, clutch plates, oil filter, new floormat, motor tuneup – and I've had the car only about a month. Really, it's in grand shape and a swell buy and I drive it all over hell and gone desertward, seaward, and mountainward. Eisner discovering California. However, I borrowed dough from the studio to pay for the car and they nick me every week for a payment, bills, expenses, so for a change I'm eternally broke. But I live, and not too badly. At long last beginning to make friends, good people, and I don't go as batty from loneliness as I did. Getting quite a lot of work done of all descriptions. Have a new girl: a rabbi's daughter, praise Gawd. Hi-ho-methusalem, etc. Fucks like a jackrabbit, and cooks wonderful goulash, a duality of accomplishment not nearly as unimportant as it sounds.

Of else, but little. Time and tide and flux. Much rain: the Pacific in perpendicular lines, hills washing down, flood. California. Write of yourself and that without delay.

Ewig,

Al

71. Aaron Copland to Leonard Bernstein
Hotel Empire, Broadway at 63rd Street, New York, NY
Friday [?1940]

Dear Pupil,

What terrifying letters you write: fit for the flames is what they are. Just imagine how much you would have to pay to retrieve such a letter forty years from now when you are conductor of the Philharmonic. Well it all comes from the recklessness of youth, that's what it is. Of course I don't mean that you mustn't write such letters (to me, that is), but I mustn't forget to burn them.

You were right about the chuckle – but it was a very sympathetic one. Actually, when I opened your letter I was worried that something had gone wrong. If it's any consolation, things like that incident can sometimes turn out very wrong indeed. (That's Lecture No. VI.) However, I reluctantly admit that they sometimes turn out very well. You takes yer chances – but I'm not sure you're in the proper mood. Anyway, I should have liked to have taken the first train down there to investigate the "situation", but I controlled myself. [. . .]

I'm a little busy with the new loft – fixing it up, etc. When are you going to find a pretext for another visit. The last one made a deep impression.

Regards to the blue hat. But be careful!

A

72. Aaron Copland to Leonard Bernstein
Hotel Empire, Broadway at 63rd Street, New York, NY
Fri [Autumn 1940]

Dear L,

Glad you're settled OK. I'll remember the invitation!

Nothing new here – except Virgil was made critic of the *Tribune* which is positively flabbergastious.[89]

Saw Paul Bowles. He says he is going to Phillie for 2 weeks when *12th Night* goes there, which should be in another few weeks. So look him up. Added 2 more ink pages to the Sonata.

[Robert] Weatherly[90] came over to try out *Quiet City*. He played it OK but it still should be changed.

I'm lecturing in Boston on Dec 12. Will you be there then or is that too soon for Xmas Holydays?

I dream about you frequently.

A

---

[89] Virgil Thomson (1896–1989) began writing for the *New York Herald Tribune* in 1940.
[90] Robert Weatherly (1921–2005) was a student at Juilliard when Copland sent this letter. He later became principal trumpet of the St. Louis Symphony Orchestra.

73. Leonard Bernstein to Aaron Copland
2122 Walnut Street, Philadelphia, PA
[?December 1940]

Dear Aaron,

Chi[cago] is vergangen! Wieder zu Hause, & a little bit glad to get back to even a semi-normal life. All-night vigils both ways on Chicago trains are not my speed. But the week was fine. Thompson A-1, expenses almost nil, much opera, rehearsals & performances, ballet. [. . .] I missed *Billy* [*the Kid*] by a week. The Kurt Weill was really exciting. *Rosenkavalier* is puffed up, but has extraordinarily beautiful passages. Reiner is a genius. Music is a hard profession. All this have I gleaned, O richer I, from a week in Chicago! [. . .]

To work aussitôt que possible on the *Saloon*. I reel at the thought of royalties. (Isn't that split, by the way, another typical gesture?) I accept $25 of course, beggars can't etcetera, but should they know about the royalties? If not I'll shut up. Am I being a pig in taking them (assuming there will be any?).

I'm afraid I'll still be in Philly on the 12th, but my love to Koussy
& to you,
Lenny
[. . .]

74. Leonard Bernstein to Aaron Copland
2122 Walnut Street, Philadelphia, PA
10 December 1940

Dear Aaron,

Shipped off the *Saloon* to you today to dispose of at your convenience to Heinsheimer (sorry, but I'd lost the Boo[sey] & Haw[kes] address). Hope it's good enough. Look especially at the rather turgid & theatrical *ossia* at the end of the slow middle section, & if it gives pain simply cross it out. I did it only because there had to be some theatrical interest at that point (which is, I'm afraid, a bit dull even in the orch.) Don't take it too hard.

I'm desolated that I can't be in Boston with you, but I'll ring up en passant through NYC.

At a cute performance of *Bohème* tonight I ran upon my painter friend Zeil (recall?) who, it seems, has been sick with a housemaid's knee variety of arthritis. Gruesome. I am to see him this week. I quail; I suspect syphilis.

How do you do these days? It seems aeons since I heard from you. Literally. Write soon, very.

Love,
Lenny
Volevi dire, bella come un tramonto . . .[91] very nice libretto.

---

[91] A quotation from *La Bohème*.

75. Aaron Copland to Leonard Bernstein
Hotel Empire, Broadway at 63rd Street, New York, NY
Mon. [16 December 1940]

Dear Lennypenny,

I suppose we'll be crossing letters. But anyway –

The piece came and I've been sweating my whatchacallits off ever since trying to put it in shape. Your idea of a manuscript "ready for the printer" is to weep. I'm preparing one of my best lectures for you on said subject. But when are you coming through?? We need a couple of hours to talk over several points. What I'm doing now is mostly crossing the T's and dotting the I's. But I don't want to hand it over the Heins[heimer] until I've seen you.

Was up Boston way and saw that screwball Shapero. Also met John Lessard[92] there, who turns out to be as nice as his Piano Sonata.

Plan to stay over a day or two so that I can get a good look at you.

It just occurs to me – *of course* you'll be coming for Dimitri's debut on Thursday.[93] Or do I err? [...] If I guess right, let's have supper zusammen, just to start things properly.

A

76. Leonard Bernstein to Aaron Copland
[Philadelphia, PA]
[December 1940]

Aaron Excelsus,

No, our letters didn't cross, because I couldn't decide whether to cut the President's (Mrs. Bok's) Christmas Party on Friday night, plus a class or two, to be in New York Thurs. night. Lord knows I would have loved to. I had planned so hard on it. But I've been persuaded, & duties is duties, and I must stay. I'll be in NYC Saturday afternoon, probably around 2 or 3 o'clock. I'll call immediately (if not OK let me know like mad) – we can operate on *Saloon* on Saturday & I can hear Dimitri on Sunday, & be home Monday. Damn the Christmas Party anyway.

You sadden me infinitely about the *Saloon*. I thought I had it done. Heinsheimer has been clamoring. I tremble at the thought of your lecture. See you Sat.

Love,
Lenny

---

[92] John Lessard (1920–2003), American composer.
[93] Mitropoulos made his debut with the New York Philharmonic on Thursday, 19 December 1940.

77. Kiki Speyer[94] to Leonard Bernstein

Wednesday [?December 1940 or January 1941]

Mon pauvre petit chou,

I was so sorry to receive such a sad letter from you – and I wish I could come to Philly for a few days to cheer you up. However this is impossible as I have very recently come back from New York. I went with the B.S.O. and had a simply wonderful time. I saw your sweet friend Dimitri (what a marvelous person). Also Aaron, Chasins, Hindemith, Szigeti etc. I was wined and dined to my heart's content and came back to Boston no longer quite so depressed. Friend Stresemann[95] I also saw quite often!!

What a shame you are unable to go off on a "toot". You need it, Leonard dear, and I mean it seriously when I say that you drive yourself too hard. At least if you keep yourself as busy as you did in Tanglewood and here when you were on "vacation". Do be careful – you've had one bad cold and now la grippe est everywhere, so button up your stunning new overcoat!

There is little news – concerts, rehearsal, lessons and practising keep me fairly well occupied. A few dates sprinkled in add zest – yet like you I am sad, and, my pet, it is the war. I think of it so often although to what avail??

Kouss is on vacation for three weeks in the Berkshires. He had a cold (yours no doubt!!) and felt rotten in New York. His Shostakovitch had a marvelous ovation in Carnegie.[96] Even I was so thrilled when I heard it – the chills ran up and down my spine! And Haydn . . .

Words of sympathy come to my pen with difficulty but be advised that I fully realize your loss.[97] I often think of you and hope that we will see you soon. Mother sends her love and a big kiss. Dad and André also send their best.

Love,
Kiki

78. Leonard Bernstein to Aaron Copland

Hotel Empire, Broadway at 63rd Street, New York, NY
8:45 p.m. [January 1941]

Aaron,

I don't know quite what I'm saying – but just a word to tell you I didn't elope or get killed last night – just drunk. In fact, I slept in the Empire from 7:00 to 10:00. Didn't you get a message to call me?

---

[94] Kiki [Jacqueline] Speyer was the daughter of Louis Speyer, who had played under Pierre Monteux in the premiere of Stravinsky's *Sacre du printemps* and was the cor anglais player of the Boston Symphony from 1919 until 1965.

[95] Possibly Wolfgang Stresemann, then a young conductor.

[96] Koussevitzky conducted Shostakovich's Fifth Symphony with the Boston Symphony in Carnegie Hall in November 1940 and again in January 1941. The November concert also included a Haydn symphony.

[97] Possibly a reference to the death of Alfred Eisner.

I missed the funeral & spent all day chez les Eisner.[98] I am at the moment a half-crazed mystic. Forgive last night's disappearance act.

Expecting you in Philly. Write exactly when.

Love,

Lenny

79. Aaron Copland to Leonard Bernstein
Hotel Empire, Broadway at 63rd Street, New York, NY
Tuesday [January 1941]

Dear L,

All terribly dramatic wasn't it? I felt so sorry that your vacashe turned out so hectic. I'll be curious to hear the full story of the last night and day (I got a message to call 511 – Mr. Green – never dreaming you were there – and I just waited too late before taking the pain to call.

I'll be down on Monday. I'll take the one o'clock train. Will you be home after 2:30? If so we can have an hour together before I start my duties: Around 3:30 at the Free Library, at 5 for interviews, and at 7 for dinner at the Art Alliance. (Ain't it awful.) I won't be staying over – so may I use your room as a place to change in?

Heinsheimer says the proofs of *El Salón* are being sent me – so I may bring them with me if there are any changes needed.

I feel even closer to you after all that's happened.

Love,

A

80. Leonard Bernstein to Helen Coates
[10 January 1941]

Dear Helen,

Forgive me for not writing sooner – I have been in a messy state of mind. Last Saturday I lost one of my closest friends – Alfred Eisner. I'm sure you remember him as my roommate for two years. A malignant tumor on the brain – and it was all over. Just as he was about to reach the top – with the world before him, wonderful jobs in his hands, and 24 years old. I've been completely numb ever since: something seems to die in you, & refuses to accept a fact as cruel and unjust as that. Coming so soon after the death of David Prall, it makes me very leery of world values – so much so that at the present I find it difficult to consider anything important.

Please write soon – I know you will understand the brevity of this letter.

Love,

Lenny

---

[98] Alfred Eisner died on 4 January 1941.

81. Helen Coates to Leonard Bernstein
66 The Fenway, Boston, MA
13 January 1941

Lenny dear,

I found your letter here less than an hour ago but I'm so shocked over the death of your close friend, Alfred Eisner, that I must write you at once. My heart goes out to you in the tragic loss of your very good friend, and I grieve to think that such a brilliant young person should be taken from this world. Tho I never met him, I, of course, do remember him as your roommate, and often heard you speak of him. And then when we had dinner together in New York in late November, you went on that evening to the hospital to see him. I never thought to inquire of him afterward as at the time you thought he had some sort of a throat infection, nothing serious.

Death is appalling enough at any time (except in the cases of very old people or those who are seriously incapacitated) but at your age the death of anyone so close to you strikes a particularly hard blow. I feel the keenest sympathy for you, for I had so many experiences, beginning when I was just a little older than you, that just knocked all support from under me and very nearly disillusioned me completely. All sense of values goes, and as you say, you "find it difficult to consider anything important." There's nothing very encouraging I can say to you at such a time. Each one has to battle his own way thru the fog and find something to hold on to. I can tell you this however: that, as one gets older, the blows from any tragic experience seem to strike a little less deeply. I suppose one's senses are not quite so keen, and one's emotional nature not so easily unbalanced.

It is cruel that you have lost two such wonderful friends in so short a time. Last week in N.Y. I saw a friend from the west whom I hadn't seen for 10 years – and discovered to my amazement that he and his twin brother (whom I did not see that day) were old and very good friends of David Prall. Robert and Frederick Schlick (from Portland, Oregon) graduated from the Univ. of California and studied there with David Prall. They were very good friends – often went together to Carmel to stay with other friends. Later when the twins were in Paris and David Prall was at Oxford, he went over to stay with them in Paris. I'd like so much to have you and the Schlick twins know each other. (Their mother and my mother are very old friends, and were friends before I was born.) Frederick is a playwright. He's had one play produced on Broadway a number of years ago,[99] and he's been writing for Paramount. Robert is a poet and has a very unique plan about his life's work.[100]

---

[99] Frederick Schlick's *Bloodstream* ran on Broadway in 1932 for less than a month.
[100] Robert Schlick was a gay poet who married the London-born artist and illustrator Pamela Bianco in 1930.

If you and I can hit upon another weekend in N.Y. this winter (they are there just for 4 months) I'll arrange to have you meet them (they're just 35).

Phila. must have seemed particularly gloomy after such a tragic personal experience. Somehow, I hate to have you come so close to tragedy. I'd like to protect you from such heartbreaks and disillusionment. But, unfortunately, no matter how fond we are of another, we cannot do that for anyone. The only solace I've ever found when the world looked so black I didn't see how I'd ever go on, was *work* and *more work*, and – *the passing of time* which somehow eases the keen edge of suffering.

Write me soon.

Much love,

Helen

82. Leonard Bernstein to Aaron Copland

2122 Walnut Street, Philadelphia, PA

[January 1941]

Aaron, best of all,

Please don't think of me as a fool – I was just knocked out by the death of my friend: I didn't quite know what I was doing. I tried to get you on your return from Allentown, but apparently you didn't revisit the loft or the hotel.

I'm back, and suffering. I can't tell you how numb I feel. As if part of me had died, refusing to accept the fact. The phenomenon of music on the brain, which has always been with me (you know that) has stopped. I have no tune to sing. My head feels like dry, brown, cracking wood. I took a piano lesson tonight, & having nothing to play, did the *Variations*,[101] badly, & Vengerova didn't like them. Thursday night will be good. Strange – they seem like a different piece now. I see them more in formal outline.

How was the Whittemore & Lowe affair?[102]

I'm sending a pseudo-bill to Boosey.

Let me know when you arrive in Philly.

Heard Serkin in dull Reger tonight.

Saw my 16-yr-old girl[103] – I don't know.

Much love, & apology,

Lenny

P.S. Just got yr. letter – of course I'll be on hand after 2.30 Monday. Just taxi up to the door. And you can change or anything else you want to do here (I can't decide whether to come to NYC Sunday next).

---

[101] Copland's *Piano Variations*.

[102] The two-piano duo Arthur Whittemore and Jack Lowe gave a recital at Town Hall, New York. It was reviewed by Howard Taubman (*The New York Times*), who mentions that the concert included an unspecified work by Copland.

[103] Probably a reference to Shirley Gabis, who was born in 1924.

83. Oliver Smith[104] to Leonard Bernstein

7 Middagh Street, Brooklyn, NY
6 February 1941

Dear Leonard,

The Stravinsky last Saturday was very swell; I want you to know how much I appreciated it, as well as the tremendous concert a week earlier. I would have written sooner, but I have been in the process of moving. I am now living in Brooklyn Heights, which is the nicest part of the city. It seems completely dominated by the bridge, the river with the endless chain of boats, and nice old streets, very quiet and full of nostalgia. I don't know why I sound so dopey. Perhaps it's because I'm freezing in this new house which is marvellous. Auden, Geo. Davis, Gypsy Rose Lee, Benj. Brittle[105] live here. Miss Lee has since vacated. I think perhaps Paul and Jane [Bowles] will move in. I have two rooms, no furniture, and lots of nice drawings on the walls, a Picasso, several Bérards, a Chirico, and a Smith. Downstairs are empty rooms with rat holes, an enormous piano – I think you would sound very well on it – and books. The atmosphere is completely surrealist. I enjoyed meeting you very much, and I hope I will see you again some time.

Sincerely,
Oliver Smith

84. Leonard Bernstein to Aaron Copland

2122 Walnut Street, Philadelphia, PA
6 February 1941

Dear A,

There's a good chance of my doing *Quiet City* at a *private* concert here on Feb. 20. I want very much to do it. (Orch. from Curtis.) How much wd. we have to pay, if any? Could I get the parts & score before Feb. 18? Trumpet part sooner? Please make it go thru –

Lenny
Write writeaway

---

[104] Oliver Smith (1918–94) was a designer and producer whose brilliant sets were an important part almost all Bernstein's theatrical works, including *Fancy Free, On The Town, Facsimile, Candide, West Side Story*, and *Mass*. This letter appears to be their earliest contact. The house at 7 Middagh Street, where Smith was living at the time, was an old brownstone that was home to a remarkable group of creative artists in 1941. It was owned by George Davis, and among the residents were W. H. Auden, Britten ("Brittle"), Peter Pears, Louis MacNeice, Carson McCullers and – shortly after Smith wrote – Paul and Jane Bowles. Britten and Pears stayed for just a few months, finding the atmosphere too Bohemian.

[105] A humorous reference to Benjamin Britten.

85. Aaron Copland to Leonard Bernstein
Hotel Empire, Broadway at 63rd Street,
New York, NY
Friday
[February 1941]

Dear L,

Heinsheimer says you can have *Quiet City*. Write to him direct. I forgot to ask him whether there would be any charge. The proofs of the score are to be ready Monday. I have a sort of a trumpet part I could let you have. OK?

Just finished *Billy*!! Mills was a big help.

El Saloon is being held up on account of they say they want a picture on the cover.

Outdoor Overture is being done today in Manchester by the London Philharmonic – Germans permitting.

I *still* think on you lada dia.

See you Thursday.

A

"Unless love is love is love love?" Paul Frederic Bowles.

86. Leonard Bernstein to Kenneth Ehrman
2122 Walnut Street, Philadelphia, PA
13 February 1941

Ken,

What's happened to you? You have a most unnerving way of dropping out of people's lives. If you live, reply!

There's much to write, but I'm taking no chances with disappearers. Reply, reply, softly, and with brittle brads.[106]

I've just earned a small but cozy nest-egg & am thinking *O so seriously* of an exotic trip in May – Mexico or Cuba, or maybe Palo Alto. Why don't you come with me? Please. Almost anywhere you say. Costa Rica. Guatemala. Reply, reply, gravely and with Jesuit joy.

I can't make myself say any more until I hear from you, embodied and calm.

A more than ludicrous transition, but I take it you've been informed of the wretched and tragic death of Al Eisner. Not another word about it. You understand.

Please write immediately if you can. And keep that trip seriously in mind.

Always the best,

Lenny

---

[106] Small wire nails or prickly spikes. Bernstein is referring to a phrase in William Francis Hooker's *The Prairie Schooner* (1918): "For hours a kindly bullwhacker helped me pluck the sharp and brittle brads from my back."

87. Benjamin Britten[107] to Leonard Bernstein

7 Middagh Street, Brooklyn, NY
28 April 1941

Dear Lenny,

Please forgive the lateness of this – but I have been working all days & nights for the last three weeks on the score of the operetta[108] & I haven't had a moment for letters.

I was very, very pleased that you liked the Sinf[onia] da Req[uiem].[109] Judging by your remarks you certainly "got" what I wrote, & it was extremely nice of you to take the trouble to write & say so. I am sure that it's the "best so far" – and as it's the last, that is as it should be. I might argue with you about one or two of your remarks about my earlier masterpieces – but may be there is something in what you say. The only thing is, may be those particular vices are less vicious than some others I can think of – such as inhibitions, sterility, self-conscious ideas of originality – but we won't go into that now!

How are you? I saw you were conducting on the radio on Saturday – how did it go? When do you come to New York? I shall be around until June 1st or there-abouts. Give me a call when you get here. How are your chamber concerts going? As you probably know, the Bowlesesses departed for Mexico.

The operetta is chaotic. [Max] Goberman is not doing it – Hugh Ross has taken it over – & although he has the right mentality for training choruses (entre nous) he is not so hot on orchestras. However – we shall see.

Thank you again for your note. You ask how the others liked the symphony – all the ones I respect were pleased – including Aaron, Chávez, Colin [McPhee], Lincoln [Kirstein] et. all –

    Best of luck,
    Yours ever,
    Benjy B

---

[107] Benjamin Britten (1913–76), English composer, already established as one of the most brilliant figures in British music by the time he went to the USA in April 1939. It was in America that Britten wrote his first work for the stage, the operetta Paul Bunyan. Bernstein conducted several of his works: the American premiere of Peter Grimes at Tanglewood in 1946; the Spring Symphony (in 1963) and the Sinfonia da Requiem (in 1968) with the New York Philharmonic; and in April 1976, the US premiere of Britten's Suite on English Folk Tunes: A Time there Was with the New York Philharmonic. Bernstein included the Four Sea Interludes in his final concert, with the Boston Symphony Orchestra at Tanglewood, on 19 August 1990.

[108] Paul Bunyan, first performed at Columbia University on 5 May 1941.

[109] The world premiere of the Sinfonia da Requiem took place in Carnegie Hall on 29 March 1941, with John Barbirolli conducting the New York Philharmonic.

88. Leonard Bernstein to Shirley Gabis[110]
86 Park Avenue, Newton, MA
[May 1941]

Hello, you Galatea!

Time out (2 minutes) from orchestrating music for a Harvard production of *The Peace* of Aristophanes (a new headache I've contracted). My hand is numb from writing score; & to make matters worse, I bruised my metacarpal (!) playing baseball this afternoon. All of which makes good for concerto-playing the 25th! To say nothing of Scriabine-playing the 17th. And conducting the *Peace* music the 23rd & 24th. Life, dear one, is hectic plus – I really need your steadying hand on mine now. It's amazing to look back & see that it really was a steadying hand. Phenomenal effect for an adolescent Galatea to have! But then, you're you.

Of course Bill [Saputelli][111] has told you of our Atlantic City escapade (mostly gabbing with Curtisites). And now you're doing algebra, & going to Ivy Balls [. . .] & putting your hair up and down according to your escort, & eating chez Saputelli, – I've completely left your mind. See? I told you so.

But make an effort anyway, & write me all – a bright moment of letter-opening in all this muddle of a bustle. And darling, take care of yourself.

All my love, to split with Rae.[112]

Lenny.

Isn't it daring to do *The Peace* at a time like this? I love it – the music is good too.[113]

---

[110] Shirley Gabis (b. 1924), American pianist. She became Bernstein's closest friend at the Curtis Institute and the two remained friends until his death. She later became Shirley Rhoads, then Shirley Perle when she married the composer and Berg scholar George Perle. The first of Bernstein's *Thirteen Anniversaries*, dated July 1981, is entitled "For Shirley Gabis Rhoads Perle (b. April 7, 1924)."
[111] William Saputelli (1916–2001) was a friend of Bernstein's at the Curtis Institute. A cellist, he joined the Philadelphia Orchestra in 1952 and remained with it until 1988.
[112] Rae was Shirley Gabis' mother.
[113] "Playgoer" in the *Harvard Crimson* (23 May 1941) reported: "The play is by Aristophanes and three thousand years old, but the production to be offered at Sanders tonight and tomorrow by the Student Union Theatre is as timely as the latest headline, and as diverting as the brightest Broadway revue. Even in dress rehearsal disarray (which is when we caught it) *Peace* gave every indication of being the most stimulating theatrical event around Cambridge this season. Of course, the plot – the attempt of a group of Athenians to bring Peace back to their city – is a natural for Student Union parallel-parable making, but even the most ardent Bundle for Britain will hardly object to swallowing this socially-significant pill, sugar-coated as it is with distinctively modern music by Leonard Bernstein, clever lyrics by William Abrahams, a colorful abstract set by Howard Turner and John Holabird, and a cast that is not merely capable but alive. And all of these elements have been brought together skillfully and with a refreshing lack of pretension by director Robert Nichols. There are, to be sure, flaws; but what this Student Union Theatre group may lack in slickness, it more than makes up for in spontaneity. These people are obviously having a good time, and their enthusiasm communicates itself to the audience. They are immeasurably helped by the Aristophanic tradition which is one of rowdy fun, rather than self-conscious artiness, and within the limits of the tradition this

89. Leonard Bernstein to Shirley Gabis

86 Park Avenue, Newton, MA
[after 25 May 1941]

Sweets,

It's all over & I breathe again. Quel week! The Greek show brought the house down both nights & my score was universally beloved. But at the price of awaking on Concerto day with a fine feverish cold. Hence the concerti were under par, but very exciting. Good reviews, too. Vital, vastly impressive, etc. But could have been perfect but for that damned fever.

Now I'm home nursing this lovely cold, sort of good-for-nothing & let down. No trip for me, I think – I'll spend the dough on records, raquets & phonographs. God, it's good to be home.

When do you graduate? Or do you?

Miquelle came for the concert – in fact she's dropping round this afternoon, as one might expect.

All kinds of congrats to Mel & Dot. May they grow fine grapes together.

Nothing now 'til Tanglewood; & I plan to go up next week to [. . .] see Kouss. Will you be up this summer?

I think I'll write an orchestral piece.

Have you read Henry James? Read *The Turn of the Screw*, one of 2 stories in a book called *The Two Magics*.

Write soon.

Love,

Lenny

---

company is almost wholly successful. The production lasts little over an hour, the admission is sensibly low, and anyone should have fun. For those who don't, there is always the advice of the concluding couplet in the conga finale: 'If you don't like venery, Get thee to a nennery.' " The music for the Conga was reused by Bernstein in *Wonderful Town*. Another section, the "Sacrificial March," became the chase music in *On the Town* (see Massey 2009, pp. 80 and 81).

2

First Successes:
From Tanglewood to *On the Town*
1941–4

After receiving his diploma in conducting from the Curtis Institute in May 1941, Bernstein went to Harvard to conduct his incidental music for *The Peace* before spending the summer at Tanglewood, where his conducting was widely admired, especially a performance of William Schuman's *American Festival Overture*. Bernstein then fled to Key West at the southern tip of Florida, to escape a complicated romantic entanglement (with Kiki Speyer) and to compose. It was a productive stay: he started the Clarinet Sonata and an unfinished ballet called *Conch Town* that was to provide a rich harvest of musical ideas for subsequent works, including *Fancy Free* and *West Side Story*. After Key West, Bernstein returned to Boston in need of a job. He set up a studio to teach piano and musical analysis in December 1941, but attracted depressingly few pupils. The year 1942 saw some early successes: the first performance of the Clarinet Sonata in April (by David Glazer and Bernstein) and, the following month, Bernstein conducted Copland's *Second Hurricane* (subtitled a "play-opera for high schools") in Boston, repeating it a month later. Throughout this time he received constant encouragement from Copland, from Renée Longy Miquelle, and from Betty Comden. To earn a living, Bernstein took a job at a music publisher (part of Warner Bros.), working as an assistant and occasional arranger, often under the name Lenny Amber.

In the summer of 1942, Bernstein met David Oppenheim at Tanglewood. He was a young clarinetist studying at the Eastman School of Music, and the two quickly became very close. The correspondence between them in 1943 is often absorbing, with letters that are by turns passionate, funny, full of career worries (and, in Oppenheim's case, his military service) and musical questions, above all because of Oppenheim's performances of the Clarinet Sonata. Though David Glazer had given the premiere, it was Oppenheim who introduced the work in New York and who made the first recording (both with Bernstein at the piano), and he appears as its dedicatee on the first edition. Oppenheim and Bernstein also shared a fascination with psychoanalysis and the interpretation of dreams – they went to the same therapist (Marketa Morris, "The Frau") and had similar obsessions. While the correspondence with Copland is warm, funny, and loving, with some entertaining anecdotes from Copland in Hollywood and musical news of the East Coast from Bernstein, it is with Oppenheim that Bernstein shared some of his innermost thoughts.

The year 1943 was a crucial one for every aspect of Bernstein's career: in February he played Copland's Piano Sonata in New York, and in March he made his New York conducting debut (Paul Bowles' *The Wind Remains*). Bernstein played his own music too: a performance of the Clarinet Sonata with Oppenheim led quickly to its recording and publication. Adolph Green's long letter to Bernstein in September 1943 paints a funny and richly detailed portrait of Hollywood viewed through the eyes of a native New Yorker who seemingly finds himself in a weird and alien country.

The end of 1943 brought the most spectacular successes: in September he became Assistant Conductor of the New York Philharmonic – his first conducting appointment. Such a junior position usually involves quite menial tasks, but in Bernstein's case good fortune struck two months into the job. On 14 November 1943, Bruno Walter was due to conduct the Sunday Philharmonic concert at Carnegie Hall, but his sudden indisposition meant that Bernstein had to take over. The result (broadcast nationally on the radio) was a triumph – and a major news story: the front page of the next day's *New York Times* was dominated by news of the war in Europe and the Pacific, but it also reported Bernstein's debut under the headline: "Young Aide Leads Philharmonic. Steps In When Bruno Walter Is Ill". Two months later, on 28 January 1944, Bernstein conducted the world premiere of his *Jeremiah* Symphony No. 1 in Pittsburgh – at the invitation of his old conducting teacher Fritz Reiner.

At the same time Bernstein was hard at work on the ballet *Fancy Free*. Because Jerome Robbins and Bernstein were both away from New York for weeks on end while the ballet was being written, this is one of the very few Bernstein collaborations where musical matters are discussed in considerable detail by letter: those from Robbins to Bernstein have not survived, but the letters from Bernstein to Robbins are a fascinating chronicle of work in progress. On 18 April 1944, *Fancy Free* triumphed at the Metropolitan Opera House. Bernstein's first collaboration with Robbins was instantly acclaimed – the headline of John Martin's review in the *New York Times* (19 April) read: "Ballet by Robbins Called Smash Hit". Of the score, Martin wrote: "The music by Leonard Bernstein utilizes jazz in about the same proportion that Robbins' choreography does. It is not in the least self-conscious about it, but takes it as it comes. It is a fine score, humorous, inventive and musically interesting. Indeed the whole ballet, performance included, is just exactly ten degrees north of terrific." Robbins and Bernstein turned at once to their next collaboration – a Broadway show, with Bernstein's old friends Comden and Green brought in to write the book and lyrics. With the support of the vastly experienced George Abbott as director, the result was another huge success: *On the Town* opened at Broadway's Adelphi Theatre on 28 December 1944 to rave reviews. But Bernstein's brilliant achievement with his first musical brought conflicts too: Koussevitzky was already uneasy about Bernstein's balancing act between conducting and composing, and he lost no time telling his protégé that writing for Broadway was a waste of his talents. The criticism hit home: Bernstein did not write another musical until after Koussevitzky's death in 1951.

90. Leonard Bernstein to Renée Longy Miquelle
Cranwell School, Lenox, MA
15 July 1941

Chère Renée,

Tanglewood again – and as wonderful as ever. It never fails to impress me – as much each morning as the first time I set foot here. The *esprit de corps* just got going (I conducted my first rehearsal this morning – the Billy Schuman [*American Festival*] Overture!) I was supposed to open the series last Friday night with Billy's piece, but I had to go back to Boston to receive my award *and conduct The Esplanade!* Had you heard? I did the *Meistersinger* prelude – 22,000 people! Très exciting. I would have let you know, but it was all in such an unsettled state & I wasn't sure until very shortly before the concert. So Billy is this weekend (Friday night), & he's coming up for the performance – Kouss liked the rehearsal today, but insisted that I looked like un Moulin qui va avec le vent.

First tragedy of the season – Gundersen[1] (1st fiddle, BSO) died last night. Heart failure. Great sorrow.

If you haven't heard of this tragedy, hold your seat. This is really heartbreaking, I shall simply state it and not say another word. M. [Gaston] Dufresne[2] has an assistant here – Miss Kathryn Wolf. Don't ask me another thing about it, I'm completely nonplussed.

Any hope? Any news from La Bok?[3] How's Claude[4] & regards from Shanelian. Rest, & really summerize.

Bien à toi,

Lenny

---

[1] Robert Gundersen (1895–1941).
[2] Gaston Dufresne taught solfège and played double bass in the Boston Symphony Orchestra. Presumably Bernstein was hoping to find work for Renée Longy Miquelle at Tanglewood.
[3] Mary Louise Curtis Bok, founder of the Curtis Institute.
[4] Miquelle's son.

91. Leonard Bernstein to Shirley Gabis
Cranwell School, Lenox, MA
[after 15 August 1941]

Dear Gabe, babe,

I'm limp. I've just written Alvin.[5] Quel effort! I just took off a morning, & canceled everything at Tanglewood, & stayed home, & wrote letters. Otherwise impossible. Life here is hectic – but hectic. Tremendous successes in conducting the past two weeks: I did William Schuman's *American Festival Overture*, & it knocked everyone for a bingo.[6] Really brought it down. And last week,[7] I did Lambert's *Rio Grande*, with chorus, &c. Très brilliant, & terrific hit. This week I'm stuck with the Brahms B♭ Concerto,[8] but it's only an interregnum of rest. Ain't you never coming up?

Just heard from the Quashens,[9] & they'll be here Thursday. With Anna Sokolov.

Whatsamatter with you? Are you a step child?

God, I pity you in Philly! I'd perish, personally. You, of course, are of hardier stock!

I got my questionnaire.

Love to Rae – & let's hear.

Love,

Lenny

92. Samuel Barber[10] to Leonard Bernstein
The Hermit, Pocono Lake Preserve, PA
24 August 1941

Dear Leonard,

I suppose the Berkshire performance was one of the most exciting evenings of my life: nevertheless in retrospect I felt as if I had returned from a political convention in which there were nine thousand people too many. It narrows

---

[5] Probably Alvin Ross, an artist friend.

[6] The composer himself was among those "knocked for a bingo." Schuman wrote in his diary: "A most remarkable performance – Bernstein should develop into the first sensational American conductor. He has everything. Koussevitzky so excited by Bernstein performance – he walked up to the stage & kissed us both in public!" (Swayne 2011, p. 120).

[7] Bernstein conducted *The Rio Grande* at Tanglewood on 15 August 1941.

[8] The soloist in the Brahms Piano Concerto No. 2 was Carlos Moseley, later the Managing Director of the New York Philharmonic.

[9] Probably the family of Ben Quashen who studied with Hindemith at Tanglewood.

[10] Samuel Barber (1910–81), American composer. Bernstein was never particularly enthusiastic about Barber's music, nor did they get on in later life. Bernstein recorded the Violin Concerto (with Isaac Stern) and the Adagio for Strings. A performance of the *Second Essay* from 1959 was published on CD in *Bernstein Live* (New York Philharmonic NYP2003).

down to individuals, and in the end I cannot remember many of them. But I should like to continue the brief acquaintance you and I began there.

I hope the army will not get you – there are too few conductors who can beat legato (even in Lambert); anyone can hurl *sfs* at brass instruments. I shall be here and in New York the next few weeks, and could put you up either place. Life in the woods here is rather solitary but pleasant and it is only 3 hours by train from New York. Is there any chance of seeing you in either place?

Let me know. One meets few people who promise something in their own right or as friends. We might become the latter.

Best greetings and luck.

Yours, not misanthropically,

really très bien disposé.

Sam Barber

93. Samuel Barber to Leonard Bernstein

The Hermit, Pocono Lake Preserve, PA

Monday [25 August or 1 September 1941]

Dear Leonard,

Curious, our letters crossed. I wrote you c/o Berkshire Music Centre. Why don't you stop in here? Are you driving? I can put you up anyway for three or four days, but cannot say definitely for longer, as my plans are uncertain after the middle of next week. But I may very possibly stay on here. The only hotels are very dull and expensive (Buck-Hill, Sky-Top) but life here in the woods is quiet and pleasant. I've no servant, at present, but we eat in a nearby dining camp. The woods are beautiful, it is about 2,000 ft high (certainly higher than Bethlehem, a vile place) and I, who am also allergic to rag-weed (not cats) rarely remember sneezing here at all, except from the cold – the nights are very cool. If you come, bring some books and music – there is nothing much to do except swim or tennis, if you like. But I think you might like it, and I should enjoy having you.

You can get me by phone by calling Pocono Lake Preserve and they page me (1/2 hour wait for you) or telegraph. One drives here by Port Jarvis, Stroudsberg, Pocono Pines. Train is more complicated. I am afraid you would have to come from New York (3 hrs) on the Delaware & Lackawanna to Pocono Summit, where I could meet you. Bring your most decrepit clothes, it is just backwoods.

[Gian Carlo] Menotti and a poet are here at present, working feverishly on the translation of his new opera, but they are departing at the end of this week, probably Sunday, after which I'm alone. There is always room, anyway. Do come.

Best greetings,

Sam Barber

P.S. Sorry not to be able to recommend a place to stay here, but there is really nothing very attractive that I know. S.

94. Leonard Bernstein to Serge Koussevitzky
17 Lake Avenue, Sharon, MA
[August or September 1941]

Dear Dr. Koussevitzky,

Again it is my privilege to be able to thank you for another summer of glorious and inspiring study. I feel humble and grateful in the face of the added responsibility that comes with each new advance in my work.

I am rather in doubt as to how to continue that advance now. As you know, I have already received a questionnaire from the army; and, as far as I know, I am perfectly eligible, except for a siege of asthma and hay fever that I am now undergoing. It is therefore difficult to formulate any winter plans; for I cannot be given a responsible position while there is the probability of my being suddenly taken away from it by the army. Secondly, my formal schooling, I believe, is reasonably complete, embracing nineteen years and three diplomas! And, in general, once in the army I should have to forget completely about my work, and begin all over again, God willing, in some uncertain future year.

In the light of world events, however, I want *least* of all to shirk my responsibility to my country; and I therefore wonder if I might be of service to the U.S.O.,[11] where I could simultaneously serve national defense, and remain in my field of endeavor. Do you agree with this attitude? I am registered, of course, in Philadelphia (Local Board no. 9, in the Land Title Building). Please let me know how you feel about this question, as I want to do the right thing morally and practically; and I feel that I can rely completely on your guidance.

In devotion and gratitude,
Leonard Bernstein

95. Leonard Bernstein to Shirley Gabis
Tamiami Champion (East Coast) New York–Palm Beach–Miami [on board train]
"August something or other" [1941]

Dear Chipmunk,

I passed Philly last night, but the train didn't stop long enough for me to phone. Besides, you were probably in Hanover, unless I miss my guess.

The secret is that I'm on my way to Key West for at least a week of escape.

---

[11] The United Service Organization, which provided (and still provides) entertainment for United States troops.

(Do they have NYA[12] orchs in Key West?) Key West for a rest, the rest can be guessed, the pest to be blest, the best for a guest, a rest in Key West. And maybe a stealthy boat trip over to Havana on the side. All alone. No one to phone. Sounds like fone, no?

I hope the Tanglewood evils have blown over, and all is in clover. 'Twas all so freaky with Kiki. And all so bleaky. And cheeky.

I'll write you again, with a better pen. The train sways madly, so I write so badly. My love to Rae, & all the rest; I'm on my way to old Key West. (For a much-needed rest.) Have you ever seen a letter that naturally rhymed better?

Four hours of sleep in a small coach seat, you arise in a heap unable to eat.

Much love to Rae

And to Shirley Ga–

(Bis-mark-Antony-and Cleopatra-with asps on her breast – Oh Mother Nature – I'm coming!)

Lenny

96. Betty Comden to Leonard Bernstein
Summit Lodge, Fort Thomas, KY
9 September 1941

Dear Lennie,

We have a slight business proposition: we have to have our music rearranged. That is, we have arrangements of our numbers, but there are many changes that have been made since, and the music is all marked up and hard to follow. Also the stuff is for 17 pieces, and we want it arranged for 9. Also the music belongs to NBC. In a word – will you please get in touch with us at Judy's (write to her – Judith Tuvim,[13] 226 West 58th St) and tell us whether or not you would undertake the job. There are about eight numbers that need such treatment. Could you figure out a price and quote it to us? And also tell us when you can come into New York to talk about it – and about how long it would take. We will be back in N.Y. on Sept 19, so if you can write us here before the 18, do that. Otherwise wait till the 22nd and write to Judy in the city.

By the way – we're in Kentucky! – right across the river from Cincinnati! – and we're doing well! – and hope you are the same!

With much love,

The Revuers

---

[12] The National Youth Administration (NYA) was originally set up under the New Deal as part of the WPA. It organized educational and cultural opportunities for Americans between the ages of 16 and 25, including the establishment of orchestras for young musicians.

[13] Judith Tuvim was the real name of Judy Holliday.

P.S. This is terribly important to us, Lennie, because the bad orchestrations make our work much harder – so please write and inform us as soon as you can. Again, thanks.

97. Leonard Bernstein to Kenneth Ehrman
17 Lake Avenue, Sharon, MA
17 September 1941

Dear Ken,

God it's been years. Are you still around? One said you were in the army; one said in Hearst; one said in sin. I have much eagerness to see you. Really. Write me now.

I've just returned from Key West, brown & asthmatic – a new factor in my life, all bound up with September & hay fever. Ghastly – no sleep.

Definite career-point reached – thru with school for good; but plans from now on very vague. I'm off to see Koussie this weekend to discuss same. Perhaps some NYA[14] orch., if possible. I need an orch. so badly – know of any?

I've always had a great yearning to live in San Francisco, as you know. Do you think me mad to have the idea of going, Horatio-Alger-like[15] to S.F & climb there? Is it untapped & fertile? How old is Monteux (hm!)? Diable que je suis! But I consider it well & seriously. How's the NYA there?

Of course, all this is thought of with no consideration of/for the Draft, by which I have already been *questioned*. And you? Please write to Sharon & let me know all –

Love,
Lenny

98. Betty Comden to Leonard Bernstein
15 October 1941

Dear, dear Lenny,

The news about the army is terrific! I am so very happy for you. Now you can go ahead and make the plans you want to make, instead of having that hopeless feeling. I send my love and my very best wishes to you.

I am also sending, under very separate cover, the music. Hoping you will still have time.[16] Write and tell me if you have. We would never have waited so long had our plans been more definite. But things have been sort of vague and ghastly.

---

[14] The National Youth Administration. See note to Letter 95.
[15] Horatio Alger (1832–99) was the author of numerous rags-to-riches tales for children. He travelled to California to gather material for his stories.
[16] Presumably the music for songs by The Revuers referred to in Letter 96.

I have tried to explain some of this battered road map as best I can. My suggestion is that you look through it all first – just the piano parts and the attendant remarks on yellow paper – and see if it makes sense. If *anything* at all seems puzzling, please, please ask – by phone or any way – because it would be foolish to go ahead with any mistakes. Will you be in town at all? That of course would be perfect – an hour or so with you once you have looked over the stuff would clear up any questions I am sure.

Could you drop me a line as soon as you get the stuff? Just so I'll know where it is.

Much love –

Many thanks –

Betty.

The Banshees is the most complicated.

99. Leonard Bernstein to Aaron Copland
17 Lake Avenue, Sharon, MA
[Autumn 1941]

Aaron Copland!

You didn't get my letter from Key West? Clearly addressed to the American Consul in Lima, & you should have coincided, according to the itinerary with same. A long and passionate epistle it was, too, and full of Key West Weltschmerz. Now there's so much to tell that you should know already.

1. I went to K[ey] W[est] to get away from people, & Kiki [Speyer] who came back to Sharon with us, & I went back to Lenox with her, & to see Kouss, who was yachting, so I fled south. Hot & lovely & wonderful down there. Beautiful & tragic, & how I longed for you! I never thought it possible to miss anyone so.

2. All the while suffering wretchedly from asthmatic hay fever, & returned home with same to face –

3. The draft situation. Kouss had written an imploring letter to Mrs. Bok in Philly about it, but that was all rendered unnecessary by my complete rejection in Boston by the Medical Advisory Board! God, I have a lucky star! Not so much the asthma, either (tho that was the legal excuse) as the fact that the particular doctor who examined me insisted on preserving the cultural foundations of the USA, not killing all the musicians. And so I am in class IV! Go, attend to your career, said the great M.D., and that will be yr greatest service. Osanna in excelsis!

4. Since then in Boston, or rather Sharon, except for a spell in NYC where who should I meet in a shady 8th Street bar but [blanked out][17] with

---

[17] In some of Bernstein's letters to Copland, names were blanked out at a later date.

whom now very friendly & sentimental! God, the curves of life! And all in secret, too!

5. Have been directly under Kouss' wing for the past month. He keeps me on a string re: some surprise which never seems to come thru. But I'm very happy because he wants me to play with him (concertos, yours possibly), and –

6. There's a great possibility of a guest appearance with the New York NYA Orch now that Mahler's out. Looks very good indeed, due to a good thick letter from Kouss and

7. I'm probably going to play the Chávez concerto with him (Chávez) when he is guest in Boston in February! Isn't that terrific? It just happened & everything is settled but the contract from the management.

8. Tomorrow night Mozart & Ravel concertos in New Bedford, of all places, with Fiedler and the Boston NYA. A slow beginning, this.

9. Then to NYC to confer with Stanley Stevens about the NYA possibility. Pray for me in Rio [. . .].

10. So much to tell you – God! This week most theatrical, since the Evans company is in town with *Macbeth* & I met them all thru Alex Courtnay who was the charming boy in the Tanglewood box office last summer, & now he's in *Macbeth*, & in my heart, & Evans is coming to my Fiedler rehearsal tomorrow, & it's all so mixed up because

11. I confessed all, like a ghoul, to Kiki, explaining the whole summer fiasco, & now it's all normal again, & she wants to marry me anyway, and accept the double life, or try for my recovery. And Alex blows in on all this! It's such a confused week! But all my weeks are, as you well know. Why can't you be here, & tell me what I should know in such cases? Aaron, I miss you so that I could scream. Write long and hard & soon. There's much more to tell, but I forget, & I must be up early in the morning. I'm waiting for your answer already, so please –

Love, love,

Lenny

On second thoughts, there's more.

12. Delighted at yr great success in the south. Can't wait to hear the 3rd mov't of the Sonata. Have a nice, robust sex life in Rio.

13. A great to do about Kouss doing Billy Schuman's 3rd Symph. K[ouss] was sehr disappointed, & wanted to call it off, & called me in for advice, & I made him do it all, with great cuts which Billy sanctioned wholeheartedly, & it was a great success & now Kouss adores the work. Ach, Gott, my life is full of Kouss & Kiki and Kiki & Kouss & Kiki & Kiki and Kouss & Alex & Olga and Ted and memories of you.

How do you like my manuscript pen? Look [illustrates with the first four notes of Beethoven's Fifth Symphony]

100. Aaron Copland to Leonard Bernstein
The Francis Marion Hotel, Charleston, SC
13 December [1941]

Lenny, Lenny Lenny!

Just as I was about to arrive back home by air we were grounded in Charleston! I'll be home ingloriously by train tomorrow. South America is all over now – but I think it was worth it. I saw more than 60 composers and looked at their stuff – I made about 25 public appearances as lecturer, performer, or on the air. I played the Piano Sonata in B[uenos] A[ires], Rio, and Havana. But most fun was conducting in Santiago de Chile. Musically speaking, i.e. the rest can wait! . . .

Of course I got your letter in Rio and it certainly sounded 100% like you. Hecticness personified. But now I feel all out of touch again and wish you would write me to the Empire and bring me up to date.

Is there any chance of your coming down the week that Mitrop[oulos] does the *Statements*?[18] (I'm assuming that Mitrop. is still planning to do them.)

I haven't any news much – spent 3 weeks in Rio which is all it's cracked up to be – was very palsy-walsy with Villa-Lobos and [Francisco] Mignone – had very good Portuguese lessons (took your advice) – stopped off for a day in Belém where there is an incredible fort[19] and zoo, stopped off in Trinidad and saw Rudi who is stationed there – spent 10 days in Havana which is wonderful as always (renewed acquaintance with the younger set) – and now I'm in Charleston, South Carolina.

It's all been quite wonderful – but I'm glad to be back – and keen keen keen to see you.

Love,
Aaron

101. Leonard Bernstein to Aaron Copland
295 Huntington Avenue, Boston, MA
[late 1941 or early 1942]

Aaron, Liebchen,

Won't you come to Boston for *Quiet City*, which sends its quiet message to all loving Boston hearts this Fri & Sat? Also the Harris 3rd [Symphony]. Oh I know you've heard it before, but what a good excuse it provides! Are you too busy? No.

---

[18] Mitropoulos conducted the world premiere of Copland's *Statements* with the New York Philharmonic on 7 January 1942.

[19] Presumably the fortified Belém Tower.

I never thought it possible to miss one person so thoroughly as I have you. And if you come – please come – won't you bring a copy of the Buenos Aires Sonata? My studio hungers for your blessing.

Love,
Lenny

102. Kiki Speyer to Leonard Bernstein
37 Addington Road, Brookline, MA
[late 1941 or early 1942]

Dear Leonard,

My message of wishing good fortune and happiness is long overdue for your new venture. I didn't feel the need to tell you in so many words – hoping you might feel them even when they were left unsaid. I realize, however, that perhaps now is a good time to tell you that I feel with all my heart that your success is near – and your studio[20] is the first step toward it. It won't fail if you have a little patience, for faith in your tremendous gifts exists in many hearts.

This letter may seem strange to you – but I sensed sadness and a little feeling of defeat in seeing you the other day. You have much to give – but don't be too generous, even to the "first pupil" – same for the rest that are to come.

Your past successes have perhaps been easier – this one will be really worthwhile for the comfort you will receive and the certain peace for which I think you are searching.

I've never told you that I've always felt you were a grand person with such a beautiful mind! You'll be a great musician and the best conductor ever – just you watch and see – you need help from yourself only.

Yours,
Kiki
P.S. That has killed the bad taste . . . so chalk it up as your first fan letter.

103. Judy Holliday[21] to Leonard Bernstein
[?early 1942]

Dear Lenny,

I'm sorry not to have written you in such a long time but many upsetting things have been happening. This morning, after a long siege of distemper, the

[20] Bernstein opened a studio for teaching the piano and musical analysis at 295 Huntington Avenue, Boston, in December 1941.
[21] Judy Holliday (1921–65), American actress. Born Judy Tuvim, she was a member of The Revuers. She later married David Oppenheim. One of her greatest Broadway successes was her Tony-winning performance as Ella in *Bells are Ringing*, written by Comden and Green with music by Jule Styne and choreography by Jerome Robbins.

dog died. It seems weak to be sad and weepy over a dog's death – as many people have assured me – when so many worse things are happening in the world, but after all it's just a question of relative importance, or something. What am I saying. I do feel completely lousy. Well, other things too are coming to a close I'm afraid. Nothing has been said yet between Eddie and me, but she becomes more unhappy every day, and as much as I try to bring things back to where they were, I only succeed in resenting her more for suffering because of me.

Excuse me Lenny. When things are all right I can write amusing letters. Just now I can't even achieve a coherent sentence. The strain of the past few weeks has told on me in the form of a hugely swollen cheek – from wisdom tooth. [. . .]

About Adolph [Green] I've had to tell him a few things about you which may not be strictly the truth. You ought to know about it.

As of course you know, he's crazy about you and he felt rotten that this business with Lizzie [Reitell][22] should have implicated you in any way. You probably didn't, as I didn't, know the extent to which she went in describing her feelings for you. She threw it in his face that she was very much in love with you and had spent every moment with you in Boston. Naturally the whole thing has been preying on his mind. He was very shocked when I told him I had told you something about the way Lizzie felt and he wanted to keep you out of it. But he worried nevertheless about how you felt about Lizzie. I suppose it was a mixture of being hurt himself and not wanting you to be hurt by Lizzie, and not wanting your friendship to be hurt. However, I told him that you not only were not in the least bit in love with Lizzie but that the idea of any contact with her horrified you. Maybe I shouldn't have stretched the truth quite so much but it gratified and consoled him to hear it so much that I wasn't sorry I had put it so strongly. I just felt that you ought to know what I've been up to. I think it would probably be just as well if you never brought up the subject, which you wouldn't want to anyhow. The thing seems well ironed out now and Adolph has succeeded in making a sort of monster out of Lizzie for his own calm, and since it's helping him to get over the hurt, it seems just as well.

If you can make anything out of this letter, write me and tell me. I would love to see you. We're leaving the Park Central next Tuesday and Adolph said something about going up and joining you. If he does, don't tell him I messed about in this, please, because I suppose I shouldn't have.

Write me soon though I don't deserve it, and have a successful time.

Much love,

Judy

---

[22] Lizzie (Elizabeth) Reitell (1921–2001) was Adolph Green's first wife. She later had an affair with Dylan Thomas in the last months of his life.

104. Leonard Bernstein to Shirley Gabis

295 Huntington Avenue, Boston, MA
[?early 1942]

Dear Gabeling,

Thanks, thanks, thanks. And I really didn't mean to cause a furore about the ankle, which, by the way, is prospering beautifully. It's now mauve.

I want to send you a thankyou present. Don't shriek – I don't usually, but now I do. Something in the Brillo price range. What do you want? Halvah? Defense stamps?

Of course there's really no use in trying to apologize away the situation that arose in Phil[adelphia], like going to the opera with A[dolph] and a slight Liz session. You understand & know. I worry greatly about the Adolph-Liz marriage.[23] From what she says, it won't work much longer. God – what a blow to Adolph that will be! I spent the whole night trying to change her mind. Did Adolph mention anything to you?

Write soon, work hard, & give my best to all who hate me.

Love, & to Rae,

Lenny

105. Leonard Bernstein to Aaron Copland

[early 1942]

Aaron darling,

I had the feeling (silly but que faire?) of having perpetuated a misdemeanor. Lousy have I felt about it since, tho I know you understand. Or do you? The last days, nay moments, of Hyatt, ere the fateful return of the Vanishing Virginian. You must know. The V[anishing] V[irginian] returned, 4:00 a.m. Sat. morning, & called & I shall see him tonight, & it won't be easy to take all that barrage of Boston brashness after the dulcet quietness of Dick [Hyatt]. And so the answer is still to be found – I'm still searching. Which is as it should be, 23 years & everything, & a late start, considered.

Dick H. is convinced that nothing matters to me but Copland. I gave him a chronological recital of you last night. He was thrilled, & his extravagant remark is almost completely true. When everything is said & done & over, I guess the core of the whole thing will still be Aaron, & there's nothing to be done about it.

I want an *Hurricane*, much talk & activity is afoot for a second performance, probably in Sanders Theatre, & possibly for Russian Relief. At this moment I am waiting for the phone on same. Collier is really excited this time about the publicity & anything can happen. Pray. Any news from [Alfred] Wallenstein?

---

[23] They married in 1941, but as Bernstein gloomily predicted, it didn't last.

I want you to have this *Monitor* review, as an example of the worst possible tripe by a fuckfool who obviously didn't attend the performance. Note especially the Gertie Stein paragraph.

Take care of Jean & advise him right. He's had more than his share of trouble already.

When do you leave for the Hills?

Aaron, Aaron, Aaron. My God.

L

106. Leonard Bernstein to Aaron Copland
[before 21 April 1942]

Aaronchen, Liebchen,

How I was furious and raging at this little frustration! I did not spend Wednesday night *beim* studio, & found your wire only upon returning the next morning. What to do? My head spins crazily. Cleveland! He's been out of Cleveland for ages now.[24] And at that moment came the second wire. The shame, and disappointment of it all!

It would have been wonderful to see you. God, yes. On our first beautiful spring day. And we would have walked in all Boston's parks and spoken long, quietly & with the heart. Such gab. Can't you come anyway? We must have a session on that Copland youth opera, you know. The master's interpretation. Hell, I miss you so.

Voici le printemps, et moi sans amour.

Life has only just stopped being hectic. Since I've seen you last I have sped through a series of great triumphs involving a heavy social life, and all ending in complete nothingness. I've turned down jobs, gotten into a row with Paul Lukas, who was all ready to wire Hollywood to give me a job (big talker), miffed a good chance with Irving Caesar, etc. I should have come to NYC this year, dammit. Even Kouss has shown his usual cooling process – not a word all month about playing with the BSO. I suppose I haven't approached his model for me sufficiently. I haven't changed my name, or learned to schmoos, or become a dignified continental. The hell with it.

Et voici le printemps, et moi sans amour. But wait.

Lovely letter from David, who seems to be supported by one Aaron Sapiro, & has won Stravinsky's heart. Very mysteriously interested in my summer plans, but can't divulge why.

We must also meet to plan *our* course – or is it still on?

---

[24] Probably a reference to Artur Rodzinski, who was Music Director of the Cleveland Orchestra from 1933 to 1943, when he moved to the New York Philharmonic.

What a year. It's hard to keep calling it transitional & let it go at that. Nothing happening but the Institute Concerts, & the happy prospect of the *2nd Hurricane*. I've been dying to give a Sonata recital, including yours, & Schumann, & Scriabin, & Scarlatti, & I can't find anyone to rent me the hall. God dammit. But I'm learning the Sonata (3rd mov't is a bone in the throat), & I'm working very hard on my Key West piece, which ought to turn into a ballet.[25]

Sorry you saw [David] Glazer. You weren't supposed to know that the Clarinet Sonata was being done![26] Direct defiance of your orders. But, hell, I've got to hear it. You will condone, won't you?

Do write, or come to Boston. Love to everyone & kiss Jean[27] for me. (The worst part of all that wire business was that I *was* free on Thursday from noon on!)

Much love, & Goddammit,

Lenny

107. Leonard Bernstein to Aaron Copland

[Boston, MA]

[early 1942]

Dear Mr. Copland, dear Aaron,

A more sober word today. Shirley is sending you the reviews – all good, and one even *interesting*. I hope she remembers to get the *Monitor* this afternoon.

I'm rather serious suddenly about making that piano reduction of *Billy* [*the Kid*]. It would be a "suite from the suite", maybe using a connecting motive & only a few numbers. The orch. suite is terrific in performance, but I think all that return of slow music at the end is a bit letting-down after the excitement of the

---

[25] A reference to *Conch Town*, which Bernstein almost completed in a version for two pianos and percussion, but never finished. He later harvested it for several works including *Fancy Free* (the "Danzón") and *West Side Story* ("America").

[26] The first performance of Bernstein's Clarinet Sonata was given at the Institute of Modern Art in Boston on 21 April 1942 by David Glazer, with Bernstein at the piano, in a concert promoted by Young American Musicians. A lukewarm review by Winthrop P. Tryon in the next day's *Christian Science Monitor* described it as "well-constructed in general, and in particular, too, as far as the mere music went. Whether it was inevitably an ensemble composition for wind and keyboard instruments might be questioned. Both the clarinet and the piano have plenty of business allotted to them, and both chime together all right, if for its own sake chiming counts greatly. But the problem of treatment of two qualities of sound seemed more or less ignored. The music turned out to be abstract in a way not usually intended in studies of the sort. But, for all anybody knows, that may be one of the very purposes of Young American Musicians, to get things free of the old tracks."

[27] Probably Jean Middleton, who was a pianist and a composition pupil of Arthur Berger's, and one of Bernstein's longer romantic relationships during the 1940s.

middle. It occurred to me that the suite would be a real killer if it ended with the macabre dance, in C major:

Are you shocked? Of course it's too late now, but the piano suite could well do that. (My writing suddenly looks just like yours.)

Aaron – this is important. I was at the Peabody Playhouse this morning trying to sell the *2nd Hurricane*. They'll let me know, they say, after discussing it with the big shots. *You must* send a letter of recommendation for me (they're wary about whom they entrust their kids to), saying that I'm the ideal one to do it, that I've had all this experience, am Koussy's prize, etc. etc. Can handle children, etc. I didn't think I'd have to sell myself, but so it seems. Write *as soon as possible* to:

Miss Hyek, Peabody Playhouse, 357 Charles Street, Boston.

Make it good. It means much for both of us, I hope. I'm so sleepy. And rather useless. But there's a certain *élan vital* left, pretty latent now. I love Jean [Middleton],

And you.

Lenny

108. Aaron Copland to Leonard Bernstein
Hotel Empire, Broadway at 63rd Street, New York, NY
26 May 1942

Lensky,

I loved having your letter, even though, as you guessed, the first paragraph about "misdemeanors" was completely unnecessary. Silly is a better word for it. You could talk till doomsday but I could never hope to make competition with the D[ick] H[yatt]s of this world, in my own mind, I mean. You've convinced me that I have my little niche (*big* niche, really), and on my own "acceptance" theory, that's what I accept. As Edwin [Denby] so prettily puts it in this number of *M[odern] M[usic]*: "It is the thrill of needing, not the delight of having." But in accordance with the theory, I'm right ready to always be on either side of Edwin's comma. If this is too much literature, it's your own doings, so there!

I'm still talking about you and the *Hurricane*. Kouss was here – and we spent all Sunday afternoon together raving about one Leonard. You ought to be very proud – quietly proud – to have two such supports. Just as I am quietly certain that if you hang on it is bound to end someplace good. In the meantime I called Wallenstein and of course he was all set with rehearsals, assistants, etc., – which is not so good.

I'm off to Stockbridge on Monday. I'm hunting frantically for a cook-houseworker. I've had a few nibbles – but haven't taken anyone on. All the young uns are seemingly in the Navy. This will have to be solved by Monday, come what may.

Just to give you my plans: I'll be down to NY of the 11th for the broadcast of the S[econd] H[urricane] and down again on the 17th for conducting the *Outdoor Overture* with the Goldman Band. When you know your own plans better we can fix up a time for a quiet interlude for us both in the Boikshires.

Kouss was fighting mad about the Festival, but anyhow I think we'll have a school. He says it's all to be decided tomorrow (Wed.)

Since I got back I've had an offer of a ballet commission from the Monte Carlo company, but we are still dickering about a subject. If it should work out, I'll have to do it fast in June. All this is just as you prophesized, but keep it under your hat.

I can't seem to connect with Jean. I'm always out or he's always out. Donald [Fuller] says he wants J. to live with him in NY this summer. He (DF) played me 1st movement of his Symphony. Terribly complicated it is.

Did you see the *Times* and our joint letter?[28] What say.

Good bye and be good. If I said what I felt the paper would melt. (Poetry).

A

109. Leonard Bernstein to Aaron Copland
Sharon, MA
[8 June 1942]

Aaron darling,

The second *Second Hurricane* is over,[29] and I am a limp rag drying out in the Sharon sun. And a lovely sun it is. The performance was, as I guess you know, carried out with piano only, and it was apparently even more successful than the

---

[28] On 24 May 1942, *The New York Times* published a letter signed by 11 composers (Aaron Copland, Arthur Berger, Edward T. Cone, Henry Cowell, David Diamond, Anis Fuleihan, Alexei Haieff, Frederick Jacobi, J. B. Middleton, Harold Morris, and William Schuman) who had been performed in a concert of works chosen by members of the Music Critics Circle. The letter was a furious protest against Olin Downes' scathing review of this event. A short extract gives a flavor of the composers' mood: "Mr. Downes does not hesitate to lambaste savagely and hold up to ridicule ten of the twelve works carefully selected in the first place by their original performers, and chosen in the second place for rehearing by his own fellow-critics. This leaves Mr. Downes in a position of lonely grandeur from which he can survey the stupidity of every one concerned but himself. Perhaps we American composers are as puerile-minded as Mr. Downes gloatingly proclaims, but we are not so half-witted as to be led into a discussion of the merits of our compositions with the pontifically minded Mr. Downes. Others may do so if they care to. We shall continue to write our compositions, they will continue to be played, and Mr. Downes will, no doubt, continue to survey the field from his isolated post."

[29] After conducting a successful performance of *The Second Hurricane* under the auspices of the Institute of Modern Art in Boston on 21 May 1942 (attended by Copland), Bernstein conducted a second performance on 5 June at the Sanders Theatre in Cambridge, MA.

first. No reviews, naturally, unfortunately. We covered all expenses, doing it all on our own. We did our own publicity, management, printing, etc, & came out better than the Institute of Modern Art has, with all its fancy pretensions. And so this is a brief but lovely period of smug nose-thumbing at the decaying aristocracy. WCOP here gave a whole day to plugging the thing, & I had an interview during which I gave quite a lecture on your history. And Boston is all agog and all aware. What a team! *You write 'em, kid, & I'll do 'em.*

And now a month intervenes before the Koussevitzky Memorial Foundation, Inc. (sic!) takes over. I suppose you know that setup – it's staggering. There are five big shots: [Howard] Hanson (why?), Olin Downes (God!) [Gregor] Piatigorsky (I guess he has money connections), [Richard] Burgin & Kouss selbst. And private money. Quite a boy, ce Serge-ci.

During this month I would like to make a visit with you. When? And seriously, do you suppose I could live in your house this summer? I'd adore it. Think it through, from the points of view of the *exec. & admin. depts*. Have you an extra room? Did you get a cook? Is it gorgeous & quiet up there? I miss you terribly.

Did you see me publicly announced as a two-fold assistant in the *Times*? I'm rather glad of that announcement. It gives me dignity.

Renée [Longy Miquelle] told me of her Dallas idea & your rather discouraging reply. I think however that this might really be something. Jacques Singer, the draftee, was very young too. There *is* a precedent. And what an opportunity! Perhaps Kouss should write a letter. God, I want an orch. Can you help?

Much love – & write to 295 Hunt[ington Avenue] now. [. . .]

Lenny

Try this one on your piano:

Si ces seize cent soixante six sensus-ci sont sur son sein sans susser son sang, sûrement ces seize cent soixante six sensus-ci seront sans succès, c'est sûr.

It looks like no local broadcast. Maybe later.

What of Downes' retort in yesterday's *Times*? Sort of leaves the whole thing back where it started.[30]

110. Leonard Bernstein to Aaron Copland
40 Charlton Street, New York, NY
[?June 1942]

Dear Aaron Copland, Earth-Scorcher, Location-Adorner,

Charming, charming to get your letter. I know I've been remiss, as they say in elegant diction, but so have you, and I've been moving, for a change. Look! This

---

[30] Downes' response to the protest letter by Copland and others appeared in *The New York Times* on 7 June 1942, under the title "Critic's Duty. Further Examination of Reaction to Circle Concerts of American Works." Downes wrote a lengthy and exhaustively argued defense of his position.

is my fourth address this year, and a few more are coming up soon. I can hardly keep track of myself. I find myself getting off the subway at 23rd instead of Houston, which is now my locale (and not a bad one, either, if you like that sort of thing). It's always very difficult when you move so much: you have to spend all your time making sure that someone who wants to get in touch with you has found the correct forwarding address, which they haven't, of course, since the Chelsea is so remiss, as they say, about giving out forwarding addresses. For instance, Henry Simon, who wants me to do the piano parts of the operas for his new book on operas (and for $2500 yet!) had to get in touch with me via Sharon! Today I was back there complaining away in a loud bitter voice and found to my astonishment a dozen or so letters that had never been forwarded. And yours among them, just so as not to bore you. And a letter from Edwin Franko Goldman saying that there would be a rehearsal of the Band *yesterday* – I tell you, it's infuriating. Oh yes, I forgot: I'm conducting the *Outdoor Overture* with the Goldman Band June 19 in Prospect Park and June 20th in Central Park. It's good fun seeing the old notes again; though I'm completely nonplussed by all the fancy instruments, their incomprehensible arrangement on the page, and especially on the stage. And I must memorize the damn thing, since your lovely big manuscript score won't fit on the bandstand. All in all quite a job. Goldman, in fact, had asked me to be his assistant this summer, and then pulled a long face, saying that the budget would not allow an assistant. Sounds like a typical Bernstein, doesn't it?

To make sure that you'll keep reading this, I'll start a new paragraph. It must be a strain.

Who(m) do you think called me up the other day from his house in Westport?[31] And he wants to do my Symphony in Pittsburgh next fall, and he loves it, and he wants me to conduct a program anyway, and maybe to do the Symph myself! Lovely lovely news. But he is most anxious for a fourth movement, insists it's all too sad and defeatist. Same criticism my father had; which raises Pop in my estimation no end. I really haven't the time or energy for a fourth movement. I seem to have had my little say as far as that piece is concerned, and I want to get on with something else. And parts have to be made. Real young composer tsurus.[32] Apropos of which, I saw Marion Bauer[33] t'other day, and she insists on a young composers' committee meeting for next season, of which I shall be one. Feels sort of like a composer. But my real function, I find, is to be the middle-man between all the pairs of antagonists and antipathetic little cliques here. They're all my friends, and hence none of them is really my friend. I go around justifying Berger to Schuman, and Schuman to Bowles, and Thomson to Schuman and Bowles to Diamond, and I'm always having

---

[31] Fritz Reiner.
[32] A Yiddish word (sometimes spelt "tsuris") for trouble or difficulty.
[33] Marion Bauer was a leading figure in the League of Composers.

dinner with all of them but none of them ever has dinner with any other one of them. Good Lord, I'm lucid and articulate tonight! Must be the invigorating air (of the *Outdoor Overture*, I mean, not, certainly, of Charlton Street).

It just looks as though I'll never see you. Though, b'God, if that Simon job comes through (and there's a competition factor, with old Szirmay)[34] I'll take the dough and fly to Mexico to see you. Nothing can stop me, once there is dough. Really, Aaron, I don't understand how and why I get along at all with you away so long. And here's what I mean:

The Frau-sessions have borne some fruit.[35] Little green fruit, of course, but fruit. The main thing being that I can't kid myself any more. Kid myself, that is, into thinking that I have a closeness with someone when it is all really wishful thinking, or induced, or imagined, or escape from being alone with myself, etc. And so, one by one, all the old relationships tend to fall away; and I find that I'm not at all interested in seeing anybody – really – whereas I used to run and see anybody at the drop of a hat. This all makes the trouble harder, of course; since I still hate being alone, and yet don't want anyone in particular. And that's where you come in; cause you're the only one that persists and persists, come hell or high water. And I love you and miss you as much as I did the first month I knew you, and always will. Believe that, Earth-Scorcher, it's so real. And then this wish for closeness always manifests itself in a sexual desire, the more promiscuous the better – giving rise to experiences like being taken (by Pfb [Bowles], of course) to a Bain Turc (or is it Turque?) and seeking out the 8th Street bars again. But I'm not attracted any more to any one I find there, and it's just as horrible as if I hadn't gone at all. One of those unpleasant stages forward.

I'm living, of all places, in a high school! I have a whole school to myself; but I really live in the apartment atop the Little Red Schoolhouse High School in the Village. It's quite nice, but I shall have to move again in July when the real tenant returns (a lovely lady who is unfortunately in love with me) and then my troubles start over again. The Staten Island venture seems to grow more dismal all the time. It's so complicated without a city apartment, and I'll have to have one of those. I won't trouble you with that problem: it involves too much Bowles.

David Diamond is going to study the piano with me! And don't let him kid you into that "outdone me" stuff; the soldier (what a boy!) would rather have come with me, but DD had done all the *work*, and the soldier was afraid of a scene. As it turned out, he came to my room the next night, full of love and amusement.

One final experience – and then we close, with love to Victor.[36] Last night I resolved to stay home for a change and cook my own dinner and study. Which I

---

[34] Albert Sirmay. See note to Letter 395.

[35] "The Frau" was Bernstein's nickname for his psychoanalyst, Marketa Morris.

[36] Victor Kraft, "the most important romantic relationship of [Copland's] life" (Pollack 1999, p. 239).

did; but just as I had begun to work, there was a blackout. I went up on the roof to see it all (I have a marvelous roof) and found a young soldier there, in the blackout, who, it turns out, lives with the housekeeper downstairs. Sure enough, he knew me, had attended my concerts, worshipped me; and there was fun. *Until* the lights went on; and he turned out to be so fat that I could hardly stand it; and now I'm in a Bernsteinian pickle, with an adoring fatman and no wish to see him and life in a high school is hard. Moral: if you need sex, don't go searching everywhere – look in your own back yard. Which does *not* necessarily apply to you! All kinds of love, and write soon.

    L

111. Leonard Bernstein to Renée Longy Miquelle
c/o Welsh, Box 411, Lenox, MA
11 July 1942

Dear R,

I heard tell that Baudex had called you. Qu'est-ce qui est arrivé? By this time, something must have happened. If not, you had better come out and replace K[athryn] W[olf] by brute force.

Tanglewood is all different this year. Not half the spirit or the excitement of previous seasons. And I, as Aaron put it, have been "kicked out upstairs". Because I have been elevated to "assistant" I never get a chance with the orchestra, since all the time is taken up with the conductors' preparation for their concert. I am doing jackal's work – but that's great experience for one who is too easily a lion.

Walter [Hendl][37] is apparently in a bad state. His mother seems a real problem, and he doesn't appear to be able to concentrate on his work. He is terribly worried about his concert on Saturday.

So – he is in a bad state, you are in a bad state, I am in a bad state. Let's get together and form a secessionary State Confederacy!

And I've been rather stupidly ill all week with a bad stomach. Ça va mieux maintenant, mais il me faut s'endormir. I can't be well except when I'm *too* busy. Remember a certain *Hurricane*?

Write & tell me all.

Love

    L

Thanks for the "Philadelphia Story" – I gave it to all those interested.

---

[37] Walter Hendl (1917–2007), American conductor who studied at the Curtis Institute with Fritz Reiner, and at Tanglewood with Koussevitzky (when he met Bernstein). He was Music Director of the Dallas Symphony Orchestra 1949–58 and in 1958 became Associate Conductor to Fritz Reiner at the Chicago Symphony. From 1964 to 1972 he was Director of the Eastman School of Music.

112. Leonard Bernstein to David Oppenheim[38]
158 West 58th Street, New York, NY
postmark 22 September 1942

Are you dead?[39]

113. Leonard Bernstein to David Diamond
295 Huntington Avenue, Boston, MA
[September–October 1942][40]

David,

Thank you, thank you, thank you. For so many things. For housing me. For leading me straight into the arms of a great and quiet and radiant joy. For making one sacrifice after another. For the burst of temper, which showed that you still had enough feeling & respect for me to worry about my weaknesses. For being such a remarkable host. For showing me at last what a terrific talent you have. That I now know, & understand.

And for every one of those things, there is a corresponding apology. None of which I need itemize. You're really very tolerant, and you know very well what you know.

Shirley is very, very fond of you, despite her first confusion. And that's an indication of something phenomenal.

---

[38] David Oppenheim (1922–2007), American clarinetist, record producer, television producer, and academic administrator. Oppenheim and Bernstein were extremely close friends in the 1940s, and remained on very affectionate terms for the rest of Bernstein's life. They first met at Tanglewood in 1942. Oppenheim appears as the dedicatee on the 1943 publication of Bernstein's Clarinet Sonata and he made the first recording of the work with Bernstein in 1943 for Hargail Records. In 1948 he married Judy Holliday, who had worked with Bernstein as a fellow member of The Revuers (Oppenheim and Holliday divorced in 1957). He was hired by Goddard Lieberson to work for Columbia Masterworks and served as director of the label from 1950 to 1959, producing recordings by artists such as Bruno Walter and George Szell, before moving to television, first at PBS and then at CBS as a producer of arts documentaries, several of which involved Bernstein, the most famous of which was probably *Inside Pop: The Rock Revolution* in which Bernstein discussed the Beatles, the Monkees, Bob Dylan, and Janis Ian whose "Society's Child" became a hit after being featured in the broadcast (see Letters 527 and 533). In 1969, Oppenheim began the last and most successful part of his career when he became Dean of the School of Arts at New York University. According to his obituary in *The New York Times* (3 December 2007), he "transformed NYU's arts programs into a major institution" and among his enduring achievements was to secure a huge donation from the Tisch brothers that enabled NYU to build its Tisch School of Arts. He retired from the University in 1991.
[39] With this pithy, three-word postcard, written in pencil, Bernstein re-established contact with David Oppenheim, a few weeks after meeting him for the first time at Tanglewood.
[40] From the mention of the Broadway revival of *Porgy and Bess* (13 September–2 October) it is possible to date this letter. Bernstein's reference to Diamond's "terrific talent" was probably the result of seeing some orchestral works, including the First Symphony that Diamond recalled Bernstein playing from the full score; it had been given its premiere by Mitropoulos and the New York Philharmonic on 21 December 1941.

Paul du Pont[41] has his clothes, & I hope to see *Porgy* this week. [...]
Bless you – & please write.
Lenny

114. Leonard Bernstein to Renée Longy Miquelle
158 West 58th Street, New York, NY
postmark 22 October 1942

Dear R,

I think something may be breaking (if the union doesn't make complications). Next Wednesday night, Oct 28 at 10:30, CBS, I'm conducting a show called *The Man Behind the Gun*.[42] It will be swell fun, & 50 dollars, & if I'm good it's a steady job! Pray for me and listen (music by Diamond).

Love,
Lenny

115. Leonard Bernstein to Renée Longy Miquelle
Advanced Music Corporation, RCA Building, Rockefeller Center, New York, NY
postmark 8 December 1942

My dear Madame Miquelle (!)

Just wanted you to see my gorgeous new official stationery. Here I sit, at a desk, important as a bookworm, at $25 a week, doing little or nothing, waiting until the great bosses decide what my function here should be. This is the great musical industry of Warner Brothers Pictures, and is called the Music Publishers' Holding Company (impressive, n'est-ce pas?) and includes four publishers, Harms, Remick, Witmark, and Advanced, where I am. It's all très délassé et doux, and I must be here from 10 to 5:30, just being around en causant, fumant, causant, etc. And I have my pupils come here for their coaching. In fact, Bobby is coming here in an hour to play my pieces for me. He's broadcasting them today. It's great fun.

And then the Riobamba Club opens Thursday,[43] and I've written the title song, "The Riobamba" which will be plugged and plugged, and may even be a success, if

---

[41] Paul du Pont was the costume designer for the 1942 revival of *Porgy and Bess*.
[42] According to John Dunning (Dunning 1998, pp. 430–1), *The Man Behind the Gun* was a war drama series broadcast from 7 October 1942 until 4 March 1944. The show's regular music staff included Bernard Herrmann and Nathan Van Cleave, and the writers included the young Arthur Laurents. David Diamond's incidental music for the program was apparently first used on 14 October 1942 (the show's second episode) conducted by Herrmann (see Kimberling 1987, p. 127).
[43] The Riobamba Club, at 151 East 57th Street, opened on 10 December 1942, a glittering social event reported at length in the *New York Evening Post* the following day. This makes no mention of Bernstein's contribution, but the singer Jane Froman topped the bill and may well have introduced Bernstein's "Riobamba" on this occasion.

you keep your fingers crossed.[44] That keeps me plenty busy with rehearsals. This song is all that is left of the once hopeful Key West Piece [*Conch Town*], but I think it makes a better popular song. And speaking of such matters, I finished orchestrating the first movement of *Jeremiah*, and it's being copied, and I have no time to devote to the second movement, but I swear it will be done, if only as a gift to you.[45]

And tomorrow night I do Aaron's two-piano piece[46] with him in Town Hall. And that has me tied up in knots. I wish you could be there to hear it. Don't you think I'm really very lucky, for a young Boston yokel only three months in New York?

I'm flabbergasted at the fire in Boston,[47] and I'm told that Bob Lubell's sister was a victim. It's too shocking to believe. Anyone else we know?

Take care of yourself. And don't write Edys [Merrill] [a] card, and leave me in the cold! I know I deserve such treatment, but be merciful, and come to NYC soon.

Much love,

Lenny

116. Samuel Barber to Leonard Bernstein
166 East 96th Street, New York, NY
[?1942]

Dear Leonard,

Awfully busy with unimportant things, Curtis opening etc., firing Filipinos, looking for a little house in the country to run off to. I can imagine what you are going through with the draft question: ever since I've heard that any use of musical gifts in the army or U.S.O. is discouraged, I'm all for getting out of it – at least for the present. With some imagination you ought to be able to develop an impassioned asthmatic wheeze which would send them rolling. Let me know what happens. Was Koussevitzky of any real help?

When are you coming down to New York? I've told no-one that I am back, and it is very pleasant. It was raining very hard on my terrace; I spent the morning in bed – there was a Baudelaire on the shelf and I sank into a lazy stupor and felt as sinful as if I were 16 again. The Filipino came in with new headlines

---

[44] The most lasting success this tune had was as the "Danzón" in *Fancy Free*.

[45] The reason for the "gift" was that Miquelle had lent Bernstein the Steinway on which he composed *Jeremiah*. A month later – as a sign of how grateful he was to her, and of how much he valued their friendship – Bernstein gave Miquelle the complete autograph short score of *Jeremiah* (inscribed on the first page "To Renée with love & gratitude, Lenny, Jan. 5 1943"). This was returned to Bernstein after Miquelle's death in 1979. In a note to Helen Coates concerning the manuscript, Bernstein wrote: "HC – This is very precious – the entire symphony in *final* sketch! I had no idea where it was all these years, but of course I had given it to Renée in thanks for her having loaned me her Steinway on which the symphony was composed (52nd St.). I am so happy to have it back."

[46] *Danzón cubano.*

[47] The fire at Boston's Cocoanut Grove nightclub on 28 November 1942, which killed almost 500 people.

about the Russian war. I felt worthless but happy. The next time I shall have a box of chocolates! Interesting life, eh? Now the sun is out again, damn it.

Best to you,

Sam B.

117. Leonard Bernstein to David Oppenheim

15 West 52nd Street, New York, NY

postmark 16 December 1942

Dear D,

Very comforting to know that you exist. Of course come down to the city before Draftuary the first.[48] Let me know when. Above is my new address, apartment extraordinaire: the rest is PL-5-2966. Thanks for the letter.

Best always,

Lenny

118. Leonard Bernstein to David Oppenheim

15 West 52nd Street, New York, NY

postmark 15 January 1943

Dave,

It appears that WNYC wants the Clarinet Sonata on their Festival of American Music sometime between 12 and 22 [February]. Could you possibly do it, via a Lincoln's Birthday week or some such device? Probably not, but I'd love it if you could, needless to say. Otherwise I shall have to get a NY guy, maybe Eric Simon with whom I'm rehearsing these days. Even he would be second choice, obviously. You're the top 5/8 man in these parts [and you] know it.

In the latter regrettable case, you'd have to send the score so that it can be used, or copied, and more scores made. Depending, in turn, on when you plan to do it in Rochester, if you still do. Do you? You see, I tend to lose track of your vibrations when you don't write.

And if you "can't write" as you put it, at least write saying you can't write.

Let me know Jack's[49] address, the story of the Sonata, and what leprechauns (or have they become gremlins by now?) are goading you through these tough days.

Love,

L

---

48 In other words, the date for Oppenheim to join the army.

49 "Jack" is mentioned in several of the Bernstein–Oppenheim letters. He is probably the composer Jacob (Jack) Avshalomoff (1919–2013), who studied with Bernard Rogers at the Eastman School and was a classmate of Oppenheim's.

I tripped across Whitman again yesterday.

I hope you trip too.

Read the Calamus poems again – they may have a new angle these realistic days.[50]

119. Leonard Bernstein to David Oppenheim

15 West 52nd Street, New York, NY

[before 19 January 1943]

Dear D,

In the first place, that Complexion Soap with Lanolin, Macy's 15 cakes for something or other, is *not* the same as our soap, which is clearly labeled "Lightfoot's", and far superior.

In the second place, I have two more pupils and have become violently busy.

The score (a beautiful job of quasi-legible gray ink) was two days late. I was all for jumping off Harvard Bridge when I heard the New England bitchvoice of Elizabeth Allen saying "It's an inflexible ryule! I'm afraid I cahwn't accept it. Good-bah." At which moment [...] Alex Thiede, a prominent Boston semi-conductor (really semi-Boston too, being a good guy) who called influential folk, explained how wars made trains late and unpredictable (lucky if they're going in the right direction), & the thing is now before the board of trustees, who must decide if they can abrogate the rule relating to deadlines, and suffer the score to enter the contest. (There being such a plethora of American talent on the boards, of course, that they can afford, the bastards, to be snooty about what scores they accept, the idiots, when the issue is a day's lateness, the lice.)

It is to be prayed for, and keened over. I charge you to organize a wake in Rochester, with Wing-of-Angel Avshalomoff as chief crier and you as bartender.

This empty prattle is induced by the extraordinary emptiness and prattledom of this office, where I still have nothing to do, and grow weary just pretending to be absorbed. For the last hour it has been the London *Times* Crossword Puzzle – something you'd go mad about. I must admit I'm writing a song, stolen heartlessly from the Double Concerto of Brahms. Mighty purty. Has to have words about love, and I'm stymied. Me, primus amoris filius! It's my last vestige of self-consciousness in the matter, being afraid I'll reveal too much. I'm sorry to hound you, but I love you very much. You will, of course, destroy this letter. Unless you some day give up the clarinet in favor of blackmail.

The office grows gradually madder, each songwriter fighting for the phonograph to demonstrate his latest horror. There's a new one about to be

---

[50] The "Calamus poems" are a group of poems in Walt Whitman's *Leaves of Grass* that celebrate "the manly love of comrades." They are Whitman's clearest published declaration of his ideas about homosexual love.

plugged – a real nightmare – called "Each Time I Puff On My Cigarette". Watch for it, if only in order to avoid it.

If you think your mad dreams about mixed up sexes are confusing, listen to this little job of mine that I cooked up in Boston last weekend. I was due at a small legendary village on Long Island to give a lecture. I arrived at a completely deserted little station – *end of the line* – called Arnold Park. (Related, among more obvious things, to Ozone Park, on my way to Rockaway, where I lectured this autumn.)[51] No one was there to meet me, but I waited a few minutes and was suddenly confronted by the most gorgeous girl imaginable, and she loved me and I loved her. At which point some dope called up to inquire about a rehearsal. I enclose 2 & 9 for a complete interpretation by Zolar Oppenheim. It is understood that this coupon puts me under no obligation whatsoever.

Bless you for all the yeoman work you did last weekend. I could never have done it without you [...] especially the last five pages of the Scherzo,[52] which came out very strangely primitive. Also interestin'. And my best to Jack who was truly noble.

And to you – ça va sans dire.

Lenny

120. David Oppenheim to Leonard Bernstein
19 January 1943

Dear Len,

Of course I'll come down to N.Y.C.! Did you think I'd let an outsider play it? I can be down any time between the 14th and the 22nd. On the 13th is our "big dance" and of course I have to go, duty calls. I like dancing but not "big dances". Maybe this time will be different. You see I'm working on dozens of theories about myself, all more or less inspired by the writing of our friend Karen Horney.[53] And I've really had some results. Tell you about the whole business in N.Y.C.

I've been working hard since I saw you last. I'm at school at 7:30 a.m. and leave at 5:30. And I average 3 hrs a night of reading etc. Sunday is a field day for work. And I feel fine for it. The important thing to me is that I want to do it. None of the horrible neurotic impatience of yesteryear. If my progress in self-analysis keeps up I will be a new man and better, one day.

I didn't get your letter or your card until yesterday. The fuel ration board thought we could heat the joint [for] a month with the amt. of oil we ordinarily use for a week. So now I have a room in a small "hotel" (8 people live here). It is atop

---

[51] Related, too, to Arnold Park, Rochester, where Oppenheim lived until December 1942.

[52] Almost certainly a reference to Oppenheim's help with copying sections of Bernstein's *Jeremiah Symphony*, and specifically the end of the Scherzo ("Profanation").

[53] Karen Horney (1885–1952), German psychoanalyst who settled in the United States. Her book *The Neurotic Personality of Our Time* (1937) was a bestseller.

Rochester's best restaurant and it is warm, private and *alone*. I can really be by myself now more than ever. It is not a neurotic compulsion either. I just have enuf to do and enuf to think about so that I don't need anyone. Pardon the digression.

My address is: 33 Chestnut, c/o Belvedere Hotel.

I really had no idea (?why) you would write me. If you keep writing I'm sure I will. I am going to have a lot to tell you I think. So –

When I do come to N.Y.C. I want a couple of appointments with the Frau if possible – for the purpose of seeing if I am on the right track.

Seeing mother was terrible. A tight-stomached unrelaxed experience full of hate or something very strong and uncomfortable. Good that it was short. That phase of my life is still unilluminated – a few ideas but not much evidence. Wish I understood it. I'm sure it is significant. [...]

A plague on Lizzy Allen, and bless Alex T[hiede]. They had damn well better accept the score or I will personally pluck Liz's pubic hairs out one by one with ice tongs.

We are all "dovening"[54] for you here at Rabbi Hanson's[55] Schule.

I have had no repercussions, at least not negative ones, about anything that happened in N.Y Lenny. None, do you hear me – none. I never felt better, see.

Today I rendered at the console – piano exam – McHose[56] – Head of department decided to wean me on Haydn symphonies. So my first score reading at the pianoforte begins. Hope I am up to it. I dazzled him with a Haydn sonata – worked up a fever pitch in 7 days. Also I am to learn accompaniments to clarinet repertoire (pronounced repertwa with a little soft palate thrown in). An excellent idea. Horn players learn horn accompaniments etc. So when we teach we can drown out our little aspiring bastards – if there is a piano in our attic.

You can contact Jack c/o Eastman School of Music. I can't recall his home address now.

I am in a strange relation to Mad now – very complex and to be told about in detail with you in N.Y.C. and incidentally, I refuse to copy a note or draw a single line in N.Y. Understand!!! I have a copying pen and some ink and I practice on every orchestration paper I turn in. I am doing lots better. You would be proud, Leannish.

How is Edys?[57] My best to her. In the short time I knew her I became very attached to her.

It was awfully good hearing from you, son.

Dave

---

[54] Praying (from Yiddish).
[55] A reference to Howard Hanson, Director of the Eastman School.
[56] Allen McHose (1902–86) was chair of the Theory Department at the Eastman School.
[57] Edys Merrill, with whom Bernstein shared an apartment. She was the dedicatee of *I Hate Music! 5 Kid Songs*, and she had inspired the title: when Bernstein's playing became too much for her, she would go round the apartment singing "I hate music! But I like to sing – La dee da da dee."

[Musical quotation enclosed on a slip of manuscript paper]:
What is this? – been on my mind for weeks.

121. Leonard Bernstein to David Oppenheim
15 West 52nd Street, New York, NY
[before 14 February 1943]

"Dear Len – Terrible and wonderful things have happened to me since I saw you in NY."

Me too. And almost the identical symptoms, for the identical length of time. Fantastic. More about it in a separate letter.

Thanks, anyway, for the case history. I was getting worried. The Frau has heard it all.

The 6/8 theme (the "lousy theme") is, i'faith, from a Mendelssohn Trio, I think. Check on it. D minor probably.[58]

And *will* you be in NY for the 14th? Just say it, so I'll know.

And did you take the 6 Pieces back to the Northwoods? [...] They are nowhere to be found. Are you copying them? Is the Cl. Sonata being copied? Sorry to trouble you with these worldly problems now, but they're *reality* aren't they?

The Frau says she now has a superficial report from the Rohrschach (first time I ever wrote it) test, but that the main, detailed job lies ahead. She says that it's full of revealing and fascinating ideas and facts. She is drawing up a paper for you – prefers not to write you – so you must come down and hear about it.

I can never tell you on paper what I went through yesterday. It was the most formidable day of my life. I'll wait till you come. Bless you in your emotional trials. Best to Mad.

And love to you,
L

122. Leonard Bernstein to David Oppenheim
15 West 52nd Street, New York, NY
[early 1943]

Dave,

This is one of those letters that the OPA[59] or WXQR[60] would list as "non-essential". But I'm all full of strange mixed feelings, and you've been elected to

---

[58] Though Oppenheim wrote this theme out in 6/8 and C major, it is in 3/4 and A major, and comes from the first movement of Mendelssohn's D minor Piano Trio.
[59] The Office of Price Administration, a regulatory authority that could control prices and ration scarce supplies. The OPA banned "non-essential driving" in 1943 to save gasoline.
[60] WXQR is a classical radio station in New York City, on air since 1939.

receive them, willy-nilly. Brace up, boy, they're wild! All having to do with petty ridiculousnesses (!) like having had to sit with a fuming but empty lyric writer named Eddie DeLange, while he burst his stolid head trying to get a lyric to the tune I stole from the [Brahms] Double Concerto. He finally came through with a little horror called "Exactly As You Left Me" (That's How I'll Beee When You Retoin), which nauseated me so that I tore homeward to find a little peace & do a little work, only to find that the apartment had been invaded by a small army of plumbers, wreckers, carpenters, et al, who have orders to remodel the apartment, break down walls, rip out waterpipes, put in walls, put in doors, etc., for a whole week, without any warning. Christ. The noise. The dirt. The lack of walls. And of water. It's a panic. All of which leaves with only one resort – to write a non-essential letter to Uncle Dave, and get some Peace by Proxy.

> *Are you serene?*
> Do you feel jittery when walls fall around you?
> Do you get peevish when you see the bathtub on its side?
> *Take* Oppenheim's *Little Love Tablets.*
> Delicious to chew slowly!
> Nibble your Neuroses away!

But tonight is better. I played a wow concert at the Stage Door Canteen,[61] and they screamed for more, and I gave autographs, and was fêted by three Australian airmen who represent a fresh, new beauty in the world. I wish you could have talked with them, heard their eternal-young speech, seen them getting drunk on milk. All with a tranquil and unconscious bravery that surpasses heroism – they leave for the raiding-grounds tomorrow.

Be good to yourself: work hard, stay healthy, and God, man, keep away from that Army – wonderful Dave.

L

123. Aaron Copland to Leonard Bernstein
Samuel Goldwyn Studios, Los Angeles, CA
[February 1943]

L–P–,[62]

Now I'm in *your* class. I have a desk, a phone, stationery, – even a Steinway baby grand. The metamorphosis is awful sudden. Actually I'm back on the old lot near the big gas tank where I wrote *Our Town.* Everyone seems very pleased

---

[61] The basement café of the 44th Street Theatre, demolished in 1945 (the last show to run there was *On the Town*).
[62] "Lenny-Penny" or "Lennypenny", a nickname Copland occasionally used in letters to Bernstein (see, for example, Letter 75).

to have me around – even including the Big Boss, Goldwyn himself. I may even be writing some songs with Ira Gershwin as lyricist. (All subject to change, of course.)[63]

Anyway, I'm here. Holy Wood is surprisingly the same as when I was here almost 3 years ago – outwardly, I mean. There are even the same extraordinary young men with wavy hair and impeccable complexions who used to be on Hollywood Blvd – still around. I wonder how they escaped the Army. And there's plenty of the Army too. Well, it's a fantastic city.

I'm not settled yet – just in a hotel. So maybe it's a little early to invite you for a weekend or a year. I must say it's relaxing to get away from N.Y. – even tho my conscience pains me no end when I think of all my skipped responsibilities.

I hope you're writing me voluminously. But don't forget who your real pal is ——> ME

124. Aaron Copland to Leonard Bernstein
Samuel Goldwyn Studios, Hollywood, CA
13 February 1943

Dear Lensky,

The blow has fallen, they are not letting me go back to NY for the concert. I'm naturally disappointed as hell, but I got myself into this jam so I might as well take it like a man (if possible). I don't know what Kenneth Klein, Heinsheimer and Saidenberg will decide to do – maybe call off the whole show, but if not I've suggested you play the Sonata instead of me. You'll probably be hearing from them, and if you can't wait, call Heinsheimer. In the meantime I feel like something between a heel and a fraud. However, it's interesting to know what a bad conscience feels like for a change. I suppose way in the back of my little head I had been trusting to my usual good luck to get me out of this mess. Nice to think that Dave [Oppenheim] is arriving in time for the concert. Nice also to think about you "walking streets" because Hollywood Blvd is a continual temptation which is bloody hard to resist. I'm still not settled in a place of my own, nor have I looked up anyone except Jerry Moross.

Well, there's nothing for me to do but sit and wait for the dawn of the 18th.[64]

As always, you slave,

Me

---

[63] Copland was in Hollywood to write the score for *The North Star*. The cast included Anne Baxter, Dana Andrews, Walter Huston, Erich von Stroheim, Farley Granger, and Walter Brennan, and it was directed by William Wyler. Copland's extensive score includes songs with lyrics by Ira Gershwin.
[64] The Town Hall Music Forum in New York devoted to Copland took place on 17 February 1943. Bernstein played Copland's Piano Sonata, and Daniel Saidenberg conducted *Music for the Theatre* and the first performance of *Music for the Movies*.

125. Leonard Bernstein to David Oppenheim
15 West 52nd Street, New York, NY
[February 1943]

Dear D,

Just received word from WNYC[65] that the date is definitely set for Sunday afternoon, Feb. 21, from 6:30 to 7:00 p.m. I get the full half-hour, to boot, so that I can do, or have done, the 6 Piano Pieces.[66] It ought to be good fun, and I'd like to have the whole thing on records for all time.

Why don't you come down for the whole week from Sunday the 14th to Sunday the 21st? That would seem to work well – assuming, of course, that you have some sort of vacation then. The Copland Forum will take place in Town Hall on Wednesday of that week, and you surely want to hear that. Aaron is supposed to play his Sonata; but he has just left for Hollywood to do the Lillian Hellman picture,[67] and it's possible he won't be able to be back for the forum, in which case I would play the Sonata, which would also be fun. *Music for the Theatre* is to be done as well, Saidenberg conducting, me on piano.

A Rochester composer named Burnall Phillips just called, and is coming over this afternoon to spiel me his works. Do you know him? He seems like a nice guy.

Where are your letters? Must I give two to your one?

Love,

Lenny

126. Leonard Bernstein to Renée Longy Miquelle
15 West 52nd Street, New York, NY
20 February 1943

Chère Madame,

As you may have read in the New York papers, I have suddenly made a totally unexpected Town Hall début. Aaron was to have played his Sonata at the Music Forum at Town Hall last Wed., but couldn't escape the clutches of Sam Goldwyn in Hollywood. I was asked at the last minute, and practiced madly for a day, bought a suit of tails, played the Sonata, very successfully, answered questions with "adroit wit" (*N.Y. Post*), and got lovely reviews. "Superbly interpreted"

---

[65] WNYC is a public radio station in New York City, on air since 1924.
[66] Bernstein originally conceived a group of six pieces, but by the time of publication by Witmark in 1944, he had added "Dedication to Aaron Copland" to make *Seven Anniversaries*.
[67] *The North Star* was based on a story by Lillian Hellman, with a screenplay by her. It was made by Samuel Goldwyn at the request of President Franklin D. Roosevelt to help boost support for America's alliance with the Soviet Union against Germany. The "North Star" of the title is a farming collective in Ukraine, a community whose life is shattered by a brutal Nazi occupation.

(*Herald-Trib.*), "great facility and remarkably complete understanding" (*Sun*). And *P.M.*[68] was great: "L.B. played the Sonata with all the devotion and skill the composer himself was unable to bring to it." And Virgil Thomson, on the stage, publicly acclaimed me. What a début! Especially since I had to play it all over again at the end of the program. I wish you could have been there. It was really exciting. And the second time was much better than the first, which was full of errors. But then, no time to practice, no right notes. Vengerova insists that I send La Bok a program and clippings!

Wonderful that you have a job – but terrible that it's so dull. Tell me more. And try to get to NYC (impossible) Sunday, the 21st, at 6:30. Clarinet Sonata & 6 pieces for piano. And write me.

Love,

L

127. Aaron Copland to Leonard Bernstein
Samuel Goldwyn Studios, Los Angeles, CA
Sunday [21 February 1943]

Dear Lensky,

As far as I can judge Wed.'s concert seems to have been a real triumph for you. You apparently were the Rob't Shaw of the occasion! Why even Minna Lederman was won over. What surprised me more than the "superb" perform-ance of the Sonata was the report of how good you were in the forum. The new Movie Suite seems to have been put completely in the shade. What's it really like?

I think Heinsheimer was appalled at the criticisms. They certainly were stin-keroos. But then what can one expect from Noel Strauss or J[erome] Bohm. (Of course Virgil's sending Bohm to both the *Danzón* concert and Wed.'s event, knowing in advance he was giving me the ax – while sending P[aul] B[owles] to cover his own concert – is purest bitchery. Well, anyhow, now you see what it's like – being a composer, I mean.)

Of course, what really interests me is what went on at 15 W 52 *after* the Wittenbergs! I want a play by play description. You're a pretty smart fellow. (Where was D[avid] O[ppenheim] all this time? As soon as I dropped the phone I regretted not having asked.)

Hollywood is dull dull dull. I've written a guerrilla song that everyone says is good (32 meas[ures]! Oh no – it's 36!!) – even Mr. Sam Goldwyn. Wish you could have seen us playing the Internationale to him in his office – (He said: It's a "steering" tune.)

---

[68] *P.M.* was a short-lived left-leaning newspaper published in New York between 1940 and 1948.

You deserve some kind of medal – but I'd rather wait till I can pin it on myself. Anyway, I'm proud of you.

Love,

Me

P.S. Just heard the Strav. Symphony on the air.[69]

128. Leonard Bernstein to David Oppenheim

New York, NY

postmark 25 February 1943

Dave,

Excuse this ridiculous card[70] long enough to be warned that at risk of life, limb & name, I have succeeded in getting the Cl. Sonata on the League program Mar. 14. Don't fail now.

Love,

L

129. David Oppenheim to Leonard Bernstein

[Rochester, NY]

2 March 1943

Dear Len,

When I got back from N.Y. I played the Sonata records[71] for Rogers[72] and showed him the piano pieces (which I took quite by accident). He was impressed but screamed Copland all thru your last movement – 5/8 etc.

Rogers: "Did he study with Copland?"

Me: "No, but they are very close friends."

R: "Is he that way – you know – Copland isn't normal. Is *he* normal?"

Me: "Perfectly."

We talked for about an hour. I gathered that he thinks Copland distant and impossible to get to know if you aren't his type. He cited his own case of 15 yrs acquaintanceship without any familiarity at all. He also thinks C.'s music

---

[69] The NBC Symphony Orchestra conducted by Leopold Stokowski gave a broadcast performance of Stravinsky's *Symphony in C* on 21 February 1943. Bernstein's reply ended with a plea for Copland to put in a word for him, and his reaction to Stravinsky's symphony: "Can anything be done about me? Do they need Sonata-players in Hollywood? I heard Igor's symphony too. What a fine first mov't! A little long, but so good. Main criticism: sounds too much like Harold Shapero. I just live for the moment when you pin that medal on me. I love you. L."

[70] The card depicts three "Skyscrapers of New York City" (the Empire State Building, the Rockefeller Center – where the Advanced Music Corporation had its address – and the Chrysler Building).

[71] A recording of the radio broadcast given by Oppenheim and Bernstein on 21 February.

[72] Bernard Rogers (1893–1968) was a composition pupil of Nadia Boulanger and Ernest Bloch. He taught at the Eastman School during Oppenheim's time as a student there.

intellectual and unlyrical and believes Aaron hasn't fulfilled the promise he showed 10 yrs ago. R[ogers] admires Aaron's fight for music in Amer. and has general positiveness and seemed apologetic but firm in his criticism. Insists no bitterness exists. Thinks the L[eague] of C[omposers] a narrowing element. Thinks Harris is awkward & not at all graceful. Thinks Boulanger not what she is cracked up to be. He studied wit h her for three months – with Bloch for three years.

He is a good guy tho – I like him. The comp. students around here idolize him & his music. I haven't heard enough to say.

Dream No. 89625436 – I dreamt of cigarettes in sugar bowls filled with sugar. [. . .] I heard or read a story about a guy who fucked his secretary: "He put a cigarette in her monkey (vagina) to make it smoke."

Interpretation – maybe my cigarette phobia finds here its genesis. I jumped 3 feet off the chair when I had it. It seemed right. I haven't had time to see if it had any effect on me yet. [. . .]

Your letter was your most optimistic utterance to date and a good thing. Sounds wonderful. With the progress I have been making I think I will be able to be just as optimistic before long. Many things must happen first tho. Incidentally, K[aren] H[orney]'s *Neurotic Personality of Our Time* is a fine book for you – better than the other two I believe. Read it!

1. The clarinet is better than ever.

2. I am working harder & better than ever.

3. I feel better than ever.

4. I miss you.

Love,

Dave

Don't get the impression Rogers doesn't like C[opland] because I don't think that is true.

Hello to E[dys] M[errill].

130. Leonard Bernstein to David Oppenheim
New York, NY
postmark 5 March 1943

My Dear Mr. Oppenheim,

Listening to the recording of the Clarinet Sonata, I am more and more impressed and moved by your performance. Especially the "high, controlled" part of the last movement. It is, in all seriousness, some of the finest, flutiest playing I've ever heard. Bless you. Those records are giving you quite a reputation in the Big City.

As to Lukas Foss, I have already asked him about sending you his Konzert, but he has only one copy and has to hold on to it. Perhaps you can see it while you're here. Are you coming, I ask again, at the risk of being an utter bore.

I had a lovely surprise the other day, which you will please keep a dead secret. I was called into the Arthur Judson office by Bruno Zirato (manager of the Philharmonic), who told me that Rodzinski[73] is very interested in me, and wants me to hang around all Philharmonic rehearsals etc., next year, and finally conduct a concert. I had no idea he even remembered me, but apparently he does, very clearly. Some Brahms performance or other at Tanglewood.

I had a terrific night last night. I had my "attack" again at *Shadow of a Doubt*[74] and thought I was going insane. All of which provoked some stunning analysis, and had me sitting up late, putting on cards all the elements of the story of my life. I think I'm pulling it all together now, and will soon have a working basis for active self-analysis. It's a good, active sign.

But why these attacks of panic and insanity-implications? Is it the state of nerves under analysis? I have been this way since you left. It is as though a layer of skin had been removed, figuratively, so that each little emotion, resentment, etc., inflicts a real registering of panic, instead of the customary vague heart-throb. It's a kind of crystallization of all psychic processes. I'm unprotected, and have been laid bare, baby. I think perhaps it signifies progress, somehow or other. It is Joe Id's way of informing me what's really going on. And the root of the whole thing is definitely lack of aggressiveness, out of fear, fear of being active, hostile, retaliative. It's all fairly clear now.

I believe in your cigarette analysis. It sounds quite right. Keep up the mental life, keep sending those lovely senseless picture postals, and I miss you too.

Love,

L

131. Leonard Bernstein to Aaron Copland
15 West 52nd Street, New York, NY
[late February or early March 1943]

Dearest Aaron,

Now that it's all died down, and everyone has written you all the details, including Edwin Denby & [Kenneth] Klein & [Minna] Lederman (she came back & spoke to me – endlessly!) – I would like to add only that it was a real experience to feel that I really *had* redeemed the Sonata; that I played it marvelously, full of errors through lack of preparation (and nervousness), that it was

---

[73] Artur Rodzinski (1892–1958), Polish conductor who was appointed Music Director of the New York Philharmonic, 1943–7. Bernstein became the orchestra's Assistant Conductor in September 1943 (see Letter 152).

[74] *Shadow of a Doubt* was directed by Alfred Hitchcock with a screenplay co-written by Thornton Wilder. It was released in January 1943.

thrilling to see & hear Virgil [Thomson] so impressed with it, to have Jim Fassett call up & tell me how he had always disliked it, and now loved it – to have such a lovely accidental début, such good reviews – and especially to hear Virgil say that I seemed to be composing it as I played it. That's always my feeling with your notes, my love. It's in the books. There's much more to say, but I must wait til Dave Oppenheim leaves (he's sitting here reading *Serenade*[75] right now. Am I a masochist!) He came down to do the Clar. Sonata – which was lovely. I also did the Six Pieces, & the piece I wrote at your house in Stockbridge (now called *Dedication to Aaron Copland*)[76] and a new one-minute clar & piano affair called *Extension of a Theme by Adolph Green*.[77] I have it all on five records, for you to hear – ah, but when?

And I've seen Victor [Kraft], & talked with him for the first time, & I've been confusing him & Dave [Oppenheim] in my deep down mind. What's it mean?

And I was swamped by Ted Colombo in a bar, & *that* was *interestin*.

And life is most peculiar. What are you doing?

Love, love, love,

Your slave,

L

132. Aaron Copland to Leonard Bernstein
Samuel Goldwyn Studios, Los Angeles, CA
Sunday [March 1943]

Dear Disciple,

What a letter! I had a wonderful time with it – better than any novel. But now I want to read the next chapter. Thing that surprises me most – you always look and act so conscious that I can't imagine the inner psyche doing its own imaginings. It made me wonder if I too had an inner psyche doing funny things without my knowing it. But I guess it's just envy – sounds like so much more fun. The identification of D[avid] & V[ictor] seems so natural – the part that seems curious is that you should want to be me. (I'm so glad you're not!) I always want you to be you, so that I can go on feeling about you the way I do. *Please* write the next sequel soon.

---

[75] *Serenade* by James M. Cain. A few years later, Bernstein contemplated a musical setting of this novel. See Letters 262–265.

[76] Collectively these pieces – the *Six Anniversaries* and "Dedication to Aaron Copland" – became the *Seven Anniversaries*, published in 1944.

[77] This short piece was subsequently orchestrated as "Variation 2 (Waltz)" in *Fancy Free* (1944); the ballet is dedicated to Adolph Green. I am grateful to Sophie Redfern for helping to clarify this, and for showing me the relevant pages in the sketches for *Fancy Free*. These include sketch pages for clarinet and piano headed "Extension by Leonard Bernstein" (in Green's hand) "of a theme by Adolph Green" (in Bernstein's hand).

I've got a little grey home in the west now. It's tiny but cute. A sun porch, a big piano, a eucalyptus tree, some new books – everything except a companion. It's better than living in a hotel room as I had been – but still I'm not like that Louisiana tree – and standing alone in the Hollywood desert gets oppressive at times. Any suggestions?

Bumped into guess who in the blvd – Jesse Ehrlich[78] and wife. We are all going to hear the W. Coast premiere of the Sonata tomorrow night. (Any report as to how J. Sykes performed it?) J & J are settled here during the period when Warner's are filming the army show. They seem to have living with them a delicate young negro boy from Katherine Dunham's dance group. Nice looking kid. (Did I say anything?)

I heard Roy [Harris]'s 5th Symph broadcast yesterday. Decided my chapter on him[79] was triply just. What a pity – with all that good material he can't pull it all together and make it go places. Still, the personality is so strong that it may make up for the lack of intellectual grasp of the material. I'd be surer of this if he didn't repeat himself so much in general mood and formulas. His music shows no signs whatever of reactions to outward events. Well, you know all this.

(By the way, as your "only" musical influence, I'd like to know what the influence consists of – in one or twenty sentences.)

I've been here four weeks now and accomplished practically nothing. Most of the time goes in gab fests. Shooting starts tomorrow and lasts 2 months. I'm doing a 2 minute Russian peasant dance with Lichine as choreographer. It's practically impossible at this stage to figure out what the whole thing will add up to, musically speaking. [. . .]

If only you had experience in pictures we could bring you out to conduct. I've tried them – they won't take a guy who has never before done a picture. So there. Now will you come to Hollywood?

Love you too,
Me

133. Leonard Bernstein to Aaron Copland
15 West 52nd Street, New York, NY
[14 March 1943]

Dear A,

I haven't heard from you yet, and by all precedents you don't deserve a letter. But I have some confessing to do; and after all, I can't betray you without letting you know!

---

[78] The cellist Jesse Ehrlich was one of Bernstein's friends from Harvard (he played the cello in the orchestra for *The Birds*), and he was a roommate at Tanglewood in 1940.

[79] Copland wrote about Harris in *Our New Music* (1941).

First, I betrayed you by playing the Clarinet Sonata today at the League Concert (Library)[80] instead of the Six Pieces, as you had wished. I felt the need to present my first League composition as a piece with a slightly larger form than just six germs for large pieces, and the Sonata does approach, at least, a big form. Besides, it was more fun than playing alone, and – biggest point – it provided a lovely excuse for having D[avid] O[ppenheim] come down. So you will forgive me, won't you? Amusing part, of course, is the great secret twixt Marion Bauer & me, since neither she nor any "committee" ever saw the Sonata first; but she trusted me, &, as it turned out, liked it, & didn't think the 1st movement was Hindy[81] at all!

The reviews aren't out yet. Paul [Bowles] covered it for the *Tribune*; & Virgil's article today on the French approach to music is something of a masterpiece.

I've betrayed you further by deciding to urge Victor to go to Hollywood. It's so hard for him to get his mind on a goal & set about reaching it. And here he piles up hate on resentment for analysis. In L.A. he might lose that, & under your aegis, even try it. He'd be so much happier there than torturing himself here (and getting drunk, & forgetting the simplest obligations & duties). And especially *you* would be so much happier. So why not? We've played squash together somewhat, & I know him better, & thus decided on betrayal. As for my feelings, I can be awful controlled sometimes. I'm a good disciple, no, my love?

Saw *Lady in the Dark* tonight,[82] & loved it, especially seeing it with D[avid] O[ppenheim] who is consulting the Frau madly these days. It is, as you say, slick – over-slick – but I'm no critic, being an analysand (!).

Thanks so much for the Lincoln piece:[83] it looks marvelous, & I wish the Kostelanetz ban was off it. I love you. And, oh, I resented Lukas [Foss] telling me that he'd got one too. Crazy frankness, but that's the sort of irrational habit analysis gets me into. Out with the resentments, Bernstein!

I finished a fifth *Kid* song, completing the cycle,[84] & it's beautiful, if a little on the Copland side. I have to make a change to the "Indian" one, & it will be done: everyone loves them.

---

[80] According to Paul Bowles' review published on 15 March 1943 in the *New York Herald Tribune*, the League of Composers Concert at New York Public Library on 14 March included the *Pastoral* for viola and piano by Elliott Carter, a String Quartet by Vincent Persichetti, songs by Beatrice Laufer, Lukas Foss' Duo for cello and piano, a group of songs by Van Vactor, Wilde, Bacon, Bricker, and John Cage, and Bernstein's Clarinet Sonata.

[81] Paul Hindemith (1895–1963), German composer and violist. He emigrated to the United Status in 1940, returning to Europe in 1953.

[82] *Lady in the Dark* ran on Broadway in 1941–2, and returned there in February 1943 with Gertrude Lawrence reprising her starring role as Liza Elliott.

[83] Copland's *Lincoln Portrait*.

[84] *I Hate Music! A Cycle of 5 Kid Songs.*

Have I told you how things have been popping? Like Herman Starr placed *our* Brahms song in a Warner Bros picture? (Don't worry, you'll get the 10%!) And how there's a possibility for me to be ass't conductor of the Goldman Band this summer? And that I've had a *nibble* in Hollywood, but I don't like it so good, so I'm waiting still. And how I've been offered a teaching job for next season at the Little Red Schoolhouse? And that Rodzinski wrote me, asking me what my plans were for next year; and I hear from the Judson office that he wants me to conduct a Philharmonic concert? Have I told you? Cause I'd hate to repeat myself.

Write me of the progress & the Hollywood life, & Jesse & June [Ehrlich] (give them my love) and I hear you have a Hauserish[85] cook, and I hope V[ictor] comes out soon to cheer you up, & I only wish it could be me.

All my love,

L

P.S. Just got the *Tribune* – have a review! Hindy not mentioned![86] I love you.

134. Aaron Copland to Leonard Bernstein

Samuel Goldwyn Studios, Los Angeles, CA

25 March 1943

Queridissimo L–P,

I think of you every day, particularly when I don't write to you. It seems a long time since I last did – tho for no special reason. Life goes on placidly enough out here. With my little songs and choruses written there's nothing much to do but leisurely visit the shooting on the back lot – see the daily rushes the next day – and generally keep Mr. Goldwyn happy.

Best news of the week was a wire from Kouss telling me he had managed to get Kostie[87] to unban the Lincoln piece. He's doing 7 performances – isn't that wonderful? I'll be listening to the broadcast from Boston on the 10th. Maybe

---

[85] Probably a reference to Caspar Hauser (1812–33), the mysterious German youth of reputedly noble origin who inspired a poem by Verlaine and is mentioned by Herman Melville in *Billy Budd* and by Hans Christian Andersen in *Beauty of Form and Beauty of Mind*, as well as being the subject of Jakob Wassermann's 1908 novel *Caspar Hauser oder Die Trägheit des Herzens*.

[86] Paul Bowles wrote in his review that the Clarinet Sonata "had something which is at a premium in contemporary music: meaty, logical harmony. It was also alive, tough, and integrated. The idiom was a happy combination of elements from both east and west of the Rhine, but only indirectly from that far away. There were stronger hints of what goes on north and south of the Rio Grande, these perhaps more directly via Copland. Through most of this (the andante seemed less real) ran a quite personal element: a tender, sharp, singing quality which would appear to be Mr. Bernstein's most effective means of making himself articulate. The work was expertly performed by David Oppenheim, with the composer at the piano."

[87] André Kostelanetz (1901–80), the Russian-born American conductor who had commissioned Copland's *Lincoln Portrait* and had exclusive performance rights at the time.

you'll write me the impression in a concert hall, and what Kouss does to it. (Why, oh why, am I in Hollywood??)

So – you played the Clar[inet] Sonata! It's still full of Hindemith, because I say so. (And don't forget who sat next to D[avid] O[ppenheim] at the Lenox Town Hall and practically arranged the original performance.) I want to hear about your writing a song that has no Copland, no Hindemith, no Strauss, no Bloch, no Milhaud and no Bartók. Then I'll talk to you.

The mysterious check enclosed is for ½ the royalties I collected for the 1 piano *Salón*. They sold 250 copies (a suspiciously round number) and I get 8¾¢ on each copy. So you get 4 ⅜¢ on each copy. Of course, the point is to prick your conscience so that I collect 10% on the Brahms song, which should amount to 20,000,000,000,000,000.00. In the meantime spend the 10.94 in good health!

Tickled to hear about the Rodzinski letter you got. He also wrote me – but I'm not saying nothin' – mostly because you repeat everything you hear (you also leave letters lying about.) Also tickled that you "resented" my sending Lukas a score. That's fine – shows you really care about me. Also tickled with your Goldman possibility. Hollywood nibble, and Red school house "job". However, don't forget you're a conductor waiting for an orchestra.

Did I tell you about the hero of our picture? Just 17 and doing his first film – Farley Granger by name. Sensitive as a flower. It would be very easy for somebody to do a *Death in Venice* on him.

Stravinsky invited me to dinner! Cordial as could be. Made me big compliments about *Rodeo*, of all things. [George] Antheil[88] was there and we played the *Symphony in C* in the Stokowski version, with Strav. singing all the tempi as they should have been. He's coming to N.Y. so you'll probably meet him.

You're a good disciple – but an angelic love –

Me

135. Leonard Bernstein to Renée Longy Miquelle

Advanced Music Corporation, RCA Building, Rockefeller Center, New York, NY
postmark 29 March 1943

Dear Renée,

Desolé that I didn't get a chance to see you after all. I had to catch such an early train the next morning that it seemed really silly to go all the way out to Rosl[indale] that night, especially after I'd been invited to start at the

---

[88] George Antheil (1900–59), American composer whose career began in Europe as an experimental composer of works inspired by technology (*Airplane Sonata*, *Ballet méchanique*). In Paris he met the likes of Erik Satie, Ezra Pound, James Joyce, Virgil Thomson, and Ernest Hemingway. He went to Hollywood in 1936 and subsequently worked regularly as a film composer while continuing to write concert works.

Copley-Plaza with Bill Schuman (just around the corner from your fabrique – you should have dropped in for a rye). Anyway, I'm desolé.

These days are all full of the Museum of Modern Art & the Bowles opera (which goes on tomorrow night, & is really a mess) and the Marquis[e] de la Casafuerte, & much talking in French & pidgin Spanish. I'm also conducting Revueltas' *Homage a Garcia Lorca* – my first conducting in NYC[89] – & my orchestra is wretched – really dumb trombone & oboe & harp – and no amount of shrieking helps – and there's no time for rehearsal, & they hammer up scenery during the rehearsal – and it's a mess. It will probably end up either a *fiasco* or a *succès fou* – & the Marquise Yvonne is probably going "in jail", as she says, because she put an ad in the *Times*, and it's forbidden by the Museum Charter. Shades of a former opera and a former Museum. Rather the same caliber of people – rather more neurotic – the same bungling and disorganization. Virgil is largely the bungler (destroy this letter!) and the director is wacky. Anyway, it's an orchestra.

Rumors float around like crazy. That Rodzinsky plans for me to do 2 weeks with the Philharmonic next year! That I may get the Goldman Band this summer (assistant, of course). Etcetera. Nothing *real* to report. Finished the "Kid Songs" & they're universally loved. I want you to hear them. They may be published; & I've had an offer to publish the Clarinet Sonata.

Well, now you tell me. And soon.

Much love.

L

136. Leonard Bernstein to David Oppenheim

Advanced Music Corporation, RCA Building, Rockefeller Center, New York, NY
postmark 29 March 1943

Dave,

Whwhwhwhwheeeeere have you been? Pas un mot. Have you had a post-NYC reaction? That would seem rather silly. Let's have a sign of life.

Days and nights are full of the Bowles opera: rehearsals – and rehearsals – and a really wretched orch – stupid & unmusical people – some of them Philharmonic, too, and *not* fired by Rodzinski – and we do need you! I'm exhausted.

---

[89] Bernstein's New York conducting debut took place the day after he wrote this letter. On 30 March 1943 he conducted the premiere of Paul Bowles' one-act zarzuela *The Wind Remains* (after Lorca) at the Museum of Modern Art. The choreography was by Merce Cunningham, and the sets were designed by Oliver Smith. At the same event he conducted *Homenaje a Federico García Lorca* (1936) by Silvestre Revueltas.

I've had an offer to publish the Clarinet Sonata. Something called the Hargail Press or something. They publish recorder music & heard your performance, & want to print it. Do I have your consent?

What happens in Rochester? When is the army?

Love, as usual,

Lenny

Some hours later, I still have the feeling for writing to you. Things that were left unsaid:

Like: Indolence in correspondence will not be tolerated. I, no. 1 indolent in correspondence, expect prompt remission.

Item: Had a glorious long talk with Shirley last night – I'm sure it bore lovely fruit – she is growing up like crazy. And sends you her warmest, no doubt.

Like: What is Jack's address, so we can send him a reward of some sort?

Or: How was Detroit and mother? Did you have enough money? Was the meeting bleak or short enough to be gay. How are your post-New York, post-neurotic neuroses?

Item: What has happened to your resolution to study? And investigate scores? What goes with Mad. (to whom my best).

(Seizing on anything for paper)

The other unsaid things are almost unsayable things. Be good, unconfused, hardworking, and write me everything you feel.

Again,

L

137. Leonard Bernstein to David Oppenheim
[after 30 March 1943]

Dear Dave,

Given any situation at all that I happen to fall into, it inevitably becomes involved. I told you of this here Hargail Music Co. that wants very much to publish the Sonata (the owner heard us do it at the Library). He makes me an excellent offer, and moreover wants to issue a commercial recording simultaneously! (Of course, with you & me as soloists.) All that is quite wonderful, provides a lovely pretext for another visit to NYC, and would once and for all finish this Clarinet Sonata business.

The thing gets involved, tho. I had to report this as a matter of course and courtesy, to Warner Bros., and now they're all excited about it (stupid competitive instincts). They say they can do so much more with it – that a small outfit like Hargail could never sell what they could, etc. And at that moment, Frank [Campbell-] Watson, who works as editor in the "standard" dep't, as they call their *classical* dep't, came in, said he had just been up to Eastman, and had heard great things about the Sonata from Fennell![90] Now I'm up a tree; and have to show them the score, & play the records. I personally trust the Hargail man more, and am especially attracted by the idea of an authentic recording, with you on the clarinet. At any rate, send me the score *immediately*, really immediately, insured, etc, since this must all be done fast. (You do have it, don't you?)

It is also important to know exactly when you may be called by the army, so that we can make this recording, if we do, before you go (that dreaded moment).

Let me know all this very soon.

The Bowles, etc. concert was a knockout, with a real whopperoo of a rave review from Virgil (picture and all) and other lovely ones. I'm exhausted now, and trying to recover.

A pupil is zooming up the stairs – so addio – and be very good & send the manuscript presto.

I love you, as usual –

L

138. Leonard Bernstein to Aaron Copland
[after 30 March 1943]

Aaron, my love,

The Third Serenade[91] reached actuality and by some miracle or other, was a success. Paul's music is, I think, universally loved, tho what it has to do with that fantastic slop of words I shall never know. Paul's OK. He should be in Hollywood – can't you get him there? – doing scores for things like the *Human Comedy*. Stothart, indeed![92]

Poisonally, I came off very well. The *Times* was lovely, & the enclosed whopperoo from Voigil is about the best yet.[93] I feel good – and tired. Those last few days of trying to get an opera & concertstück together in no time at all were

---

[90] Frederick Fennell (1914–2004), American conductor who studied with Koussevitzky at Tanglewood in 1942 when he was a classmate of Bernstein, Lukas Foss, and Walter Hendl. Fennell later made numerous recordings for Mercury with the Eastman Wind Ensemble.

[91] The "Third Serenade" was presented by the Museum of Modern Art; it was one of five "Serenades of rare music ancient and modern on alternate Tuesday evenings beginning March 2, 1943," so-called because they were modeled on the concerts given by *La Sérénade* in Paris before the outbreak of the Second World War, which had been organized by the Marquise Yvonne de Casa Fuerte, co-organizer of the Museum of Modern Art "Serenades" with Virgil Thomson.

[92] Herbert Stothart (1885–1949), American composer and arranger who spent the last 20 years of his life working for MGM. His credits included *A Night at the Opera* for the Marx Brothers, *The Wizard of Oz* for which his background score won an Oscar, and *Mrs. Miniver*, which Bowles himself described in an article for *Modern Music* (November–December 1942) as "the regular, overstuffed, plush tonality of Hollywood."

[93] This is less surprising given that Virgil Thomson was one of the organizers of the concert. But he did single out Bernstein for praise, describing his conducting as "superb and musicianly."

terrific. I was exhausted *before* the concert, and ready for the Bellevue *after* it, but after that Askew party – ay! All night affair, and I very drunk, and Constance[94] lovingly making me play all night, which I did – she's fun – and Diamond being an uninvited unwelcome guest, & really *getting* it from Constance, and being dramatic, and V[ictor] very drunk, and everyone missing you, and I found a new boyfriend [...] (married, Goddam) [...] the one who sang Paul's opera. Looks a bit serious, but not to worry. My French has picked up enormously, what with the Marquise [de Casa Fuerte], & Mme Alphand, and my new friendy-wendy, Prince George Chavchavadze.[95] All very confusing, & I still love D[avid] O[ppenheim]. What to do? I know, marry my new girlfriend – she's lovely – my dentist's daughter.[96]

A thing called Hargail Music Co., run by a Harold Newman, which publishes recorder music (!) wants to publish my Clarinet Sonata! *And* make a record of it – commercially. Sounds good. And Schirmer's may bite at the Kid Songs[97] [*I Hate Music!*]. Life is full and empty by turns – the latter mostly cause you're away.

Bless you for the pretty *Saloon* check. It's lovely.

I'm going to the *Lincoln Portrait* this weekend. Kouss says it's your masterpiece. He's swimming in ecstasy. My love to Farley Granger. Can you fix us up? Write soon. I love you.

L

139. Leonard Bernstein to Aaron Copland
The Park Savoy, 158 West 58th Street, New York, NY[98]
[after 3 April 1943]

Dear A,

Just a few words a propos of the *Lincoln Portrait* performance. (Look at the stationery I discovered – remember?)

I suppose everyone has written you all about it. How Will Geer[99] completely disregarded your foreword in the score, and drawled away in a pseudo-Lincolnesque

---

94 Constance Askew (1895–1984) was a generous patron of artists, writers, and musicians, including Virgil Thomson. She was married to the art dealer Kirk Askew. John Houseman described her as "a New England woman of means, of broad cultural experience and striking beauty." The arresting portrait of her by Pavel Tchelitchew (1938) now hangs in the Wadsworth Athenaeum in Hartford, CT.

95 George Chavchavadze (1904–62), Russian pianist.

96 Rhoda Saletan.

97 The songs were published by Witmark.

98 This is the address on the headed paper, but by the time he wrote this letter Bernstein was living at 15 West 52nd Street.

99 Will Geer (1902–78), American actor and activist. Following his university studies in Botany, Geer began his acting career in the late 1920s. In 1934, he joined the Communist Party and toured

performance that was truly embarrassing. (He made up to look a little like Abe, and sat on this chair like the Lincoln Memorial in Washington. I'm told the whole thing was Koussie's idea, which is certainly plausible.)

Kouss didn't do as well by it as I had expected. The opening was too agitated because he divided his beats – there was no feeling of tranquility and space. He missed a few cues (or passed them up), like "disen*thrall* ourselves"; and usually simply waited for the end of a speech, & then played music. But the sum total was good – the impression was very exciting, & the audience was charmed. Why must you be in Hollywood? Although after the parade of bowing composers (Billy & Barber) it was very distinguished of you not to be present – sort of specialness, you know.[100]

It's a fine piece, my love, despite all the repetition, and Vernon Duke's verdict that it's "just 20th Century Fox". He's insufferable anyway.

Mad party at Arthur Berger's last night – Jean [Middleton] & Victor [Kraft] & Paul [Bowles] & Virgil [Thomson] & David [Diamond], etc., etc., etc., oh, & Colin [McPhee] & Paul Morrison. David was drunk & cutting up, & being dramatic again. I left with Paul Morrison, & it was like old times (remember the Boston incident?) Jean was pretty dramatic too, & left early. What a good world to stay away from! And I'm confused as ever, what with my new friend, and my new girl-friend, whom I am afraid to involve unfairly, and Edys'[101] & my decision to part company, which raises all sorts of problems, like which one of us is to move; and if she does whom should I get to share the rent here – since I ought to but can't afford to live alone. It popped into my mind that Victor might be a sensible idea for it, if he wants to stay here (in N.Y.), but, as he says, can't stand the loft alone. What do you think? Is it crazy as hell? Of course I realize it would be the talk of the town. But that's such fun – makes such good memoirs, as you would say.

Just finished Gide's memoirs, by the way (*If I Die*) – & had an excellent time thinking of you. I miss you like my right arm.

Write me more than you do –

Love,

L

---

government work camps with Woody Guthrie and Burl Ives as well as working as a classical actor. He appeared regularly as a member of The Group Theatre at its summer home in Pine Brook Country Club, Nichols, CT. Blacklisted in the 1950s for his refusal to testify before the House Un-American Activities Committee, he renewed his interest in botany, setting up the Theatrum Botanicum, an outdoor theater for blacklisted actors with a garden in which every plant mentioned by Shakespeare was grown. Geer later achieved fame as Grandpa Zebulon Walton in *The Waltons*. At his deathbed, Geer's family sang Woody Guthrie's *This Land is Your Land* and recited poetry by Robert Frost. His ashes were buried in his own Shakespeare Garden.

[100] Koussevitzky performed Copland's *Lincoln Portrait* several times in March and April 1943 in Boston and New York. At Carnegie Hall on 3 April it appeared on the same program as Schuman's *A Free Song* and Barber's *Essay for Orchestra No. 1* ("Billy & Barber"), with Beethoven's Fifth Symphony in the second half.

[101] Edys Merrill.

140. Aaron Copland to Leonard Bernstein

[Los Angeles, CA]
11 April 1943

Dear Honeychile,

There are two letters of yours here that are still "unanswered". I'm beginning to lose contact with your every thought. I have a sense of your having had a great triumph out of the Bowles opus,[102] followed by a kind of let-down which is natural enough, complicated by several new personal adventures, new boy and girl friends, who are nothing but names to me. Hadn't you better expand a bit? So's I know where I am.

V[ictor] wrote a full description of the Askew party that is a classic of its kind. Bill Schuman wrote a description of the Bowles opus that tore it to shreds. Anyway I get the impression I know just what it was like. After your own description of Koussie's *Lincoln* [*Portrait*] I heard it on the air yesterday at Ira Gershwin's house, surrounded by Harold Arlen, Harry Warren, Yip Harburg, Earl Robinson, Arthur Kober and other noted worthies. (Get the company I'm in!) Of course I didn't approve of Geer's way of doing it, but more than that, why did Kouss take the middle part so fast?? It made it seem superficial. It lacked charm and bite done that way. What we need is *Amurkian* conductors. In the meantime, however, I'll take Kouss.

I don't know what to write you about because nothing much has happened out here. I've been to a couple of musicians' parties for Sanromá[103] and P[aul] Whiteman. I've stopped going to the studio in the mornings because there's nothing to do. The picture is growing each day, but I have no over-all idea of what it's like yet. Next week I do a short dance sequence with Lichine. But nothing of background music as yet. I dawdle a lot, and fuss with themes of my own, and the unfinished 1st mov't of the violin piece, and argue with Mr. Goldwyn. And that's about it.

Spent an evening with G. Antheil[104] who played me his 2nd, 3rd and 4th Symphonies. They're hard to describe. He's in a Mahler–Shostakovich period, and everything comes out of there in great unwashed gobs of sound that billow you about until it's all over and you're not sure what you heard. Some of it is very effective, and it all has a typical Antheil drive, but somehow when it's all over, one doesn't give a damn. That's the sort of thing that's hard to tell a composer.

I read a lot, mostly to make up for the lack of any warm relationships here. I get a great sense of luxury out of buying all the books I want. I spend whole nights in book stores making up my mind. Victor is sending me a two volume affair[105]

---

[102] *The Wind Remains.*
[103] The pianist Jesús María Sanromá (1902–84).
[104] See note 87 to Letter 134.
[105] Probably the two-volume edition of Havelock Ellis' *Studies in the Psychology of Sex* published by Random House in 1940.

that had to be ordered via Dr. Safford. Do you remember my telling you about it? I originally spied it in a store in Rio, and now I've tracked it down. I'll save it for you.

This is the end of my tenth week. I have ten more to go, and then a big question mark. It would be a much more exciting life if you were here.

Love and all,

A

P.S. Monday. Just had word that V[ictor] is driving out. [Margaret] Bourke-White is coming to take stills.

141. David Oppenheim to Leonard Bernstein
17 April 1943

Dear Len,

"Publishing-pains" indeed. Seems to me like the worst publishing pains a piece could have is no publishing at all. And you wound up with not one, but two publishers, get the biggest plus the tempting part of the smaller publisher's offer – recording – and you can say P[ublishing] P[ains]. Nonsense, Bernstein, nonsense. At any rate I'll be down in NYC next Friday nite. May I stay with you or will there be complications. Also I will be there until May 2nd. OK? Better be!

Sunday a.m. is awfully soon for the recording in as much as I am just recovering from a two day sojourn at the Hospital where I was treated for flu & an infection on my face. If you can with ease and safety stall it off for a few days so much the better except that I never get any work done in N.Y. anyhow.

Five years with W[arner] B[ros.] is a long time m'boy. Are you sure you want that. Would that tie you up. Could you travel, conduct etc. I suppose the decision has already been made & I am just making things harder. Sorry, but somehow I hate to see you do it.

I see you have learned to spell Rorschach.[106] I'm glad about the new seriousness. Soon I'll see you & we can talk about it. I'm very anxious to see you.

Gene Shamalter, the guy who wanted to see me in N.Y. but couldn't & who wrote me at your place was here this week. As I suspected, he is as I suspected. Remember. But complete, never felt otherwise. He is alternately resigned and unhappy about it, wants to renounce sex altogether. A most sensitive chap too.

1. I've slept with Mad.

2. Army day is in May I think.

3. I'm 21 now.

Love,

Dave

---

[106] Bernstein often spelt it "Rohrschach"; Oppenheim's "Rorschach" is correct.

142. Leonard Bernstein to Aaron Copland
15 West 52nd Street, New York, NY
[April 1943]

Aaron darling,

Since I never hear from you any more, I suppose I'll have to write, & wring a letter from you. May I burden you with my many little present conflicts?

First, though, I think it's great that V[ictor] is finally going west. He needs it, you need it, I need it; and the best, of course, is that he made a decision at all. Treat him right now – get him going as a man. He's really such a foetus! (Look who's talking!)

Viz: the little Hargail Music Co. (mostly recorder music) wanted to publish the Clarinet Sonata. Out of professional courtesy I showed it first to Warner's, & they knocked me over by loving it, & insisting on publishing it. I was down-hearted, since Hargail wanted to make a commercial recording of it. Now Hargail is offering me all sorts of fantastic royalty rates if I'll give it to them, & says that they will make the recording anyway! A labor of love, if I ever heard one. But Warner's points out that they, as a large firm (Witmark will be the publisher) can do so much more for it than can a little thing like Hargail. What you do think? Matters are now suspended by a hair.

Viz (2): Warner's presented me with a five year contract! I'm taking it to a lawyer today to find out what it says. It looks like my life that I'm signing away. But it adds to my little old salary a substantial weekly advance on future mythical royalties, which increases each year. What do you think?

Viz (3): I've got to move, and there's the biggest problem. I want the sort of apartment I can't afford alone. And I have a wonderful guy to live with – which is quite a story. He's [. . .][107] the big, beautiful, brilliant 20-yr-old [. . .] & I want to help him (but how can a poet earn a living?) I really want desperately to help him – although I have doubts about whether he can stick it out. [. . .] The Frau won't hear of it. I have to be alone, & suffer, & break through the pain of loneliness, even if it means living the summer in a hot place, which is unbearable in New York. God, I'm perplexed! What do you think?

Viz (4): – a possibility of giving a recital in Town Hall next month for the Little Red Schoolhouse,[108] which is mad but exciting, and I don't know if I should do it. I do get diffused. And Jacoby really wants me bad in his new night

---

[107] Name blacked out.

[108] On 18 May 1943, Bernstein took part in an evening presented by The Little Red Schoolhouse (a fund-raiser to buy scientific equipment for the progressive school in Greenwich Village) at Town Hall, with Virgil Thomson as master of ceremonies and Bernstein as commentator and pianist, to "illustrate the influence of folk music and jazz on the contemporary composer." Bernstein illustrated his points by playing his piano transcription of Copland's *El Salón México*. The event was reviewed by Paul Bowles in the *New York Herald Tribune* on 19 May 1943.

club (the Blue Angel), & wants to build me, etc., comme impresario. And I had another nice letter from Rodzinski. Am I diffused?

So I should talk about Victor, yet!

Please write, my love – I miss you like mad.

Ewig, ewig, ohne End!

L

143. Aaron Copland to Leonard Bernstein
Samuel Goldwyn Studios, Los Angeles, CA
29 April 1943

Darlingest L.P.

I know you're probably feeling awfully neglected, or maybe you're all absorbed in your new friend and have forgotten all about me.

Anyway, from my angle – not hearing from me doesn't mean a thing. I got tied up writing a Russian number for Lichine's choreography. It was the last of the pre-recorded stuff – and now I don't have much to do but wait around until they finish shooting the picture, which looks as if it would be around June 15th. Of course, I get ideas and whole sections while waiting. I wonder what it will all add up to. [. . .]

V[ictor] arrived in Posh[109] (now renamed Poshalopy) yesterday, so a new chapter in my Hollywood life begins. He seemed pleased with my house, my office, my secretary, etc. And I'm very pleased to have him here.

He brought reports of your signing the Warner's contract. Is it true? I wish I could have read it. I was out on the Warner lot the other night watching Adolph Deutsch scoring a picture with an orchestra of 80. When I think how you could fit in over there I get noivous.

Is the Clarinet Sonata being published?

And are you alone – like the Frau wants?

I never heard the sequel to your last letter which was full of problems.

By the way, that book I once wrote you [about] arrived – and it contains the most wonderful Glossary of specialized slang you have ever seen or ever can hope to see. I can't wait to show it to you. The rest of the book is H. Ellis' case histories brought up to date – and I recognize a little bit of you in each of the 300 cases![110]

How are you? That is, hello. And what's the summer look like? All signs point to me being out here until August 1st. After that I hope Mexico or New Mexico. Wouldn't it be lovely if we could somehow connect up sometime somewhere.

---

[109] Copland's nickname for his car.
[110] In Letter 140, Copland called it a "two volume affair".

Tell Pfb [Bowles], if you see him, that his M[odern] M[usic] phrase about "harp vomit" has become famous among Hollywood orchestrators. I met a number of them at a party the other night – they're my principal public out here. Seems that Max Steiner's wife is a harpist – which they say explains the featuring.

Margaret Bourke-White is on the lot, photographing us. We just carried out the "scorched earth" policy on the back lot set – and boy did we make a mess of that. Beautiful set. Farley Granger gets more simpatico every day. I've promised him the *Saloon* records. Do you think that will do it??

Still I love *you*.

A

144. Leonard Bernstein to Renée Longy Miquelle
Hotel Chelsea, New York, NY
14 May 1943,

Chère Renée,

Ce sont des jours tellement français, ces jours-ci. Je viens de lire Gide en français. Je vais jouer tous les dimanches-soirs chez "Le Bleu Angel", un nouveau club en quelque sorte Parisien (comme l'ancien *Bœuf sur le Toit*, ou le *Ruban Bleu*); le clique des Concerts *Sérénades* (ton amie la Marquise, etc.); mon monde semble aujourd'hui tout à fait français. Et alors, que faire? Rien que d'écrire un mot à la première Française de toutes Françaises. Tu me crois enivré? C'est point l'ivresse – c'est l'amitié.

La cause immédiate de cette lettre, c'est Mme Claude Alphand, chanteuse extraordinaire au *Blue Angel*.[111] Chaque fois qu'elle chante "Les Moules

---

[111] The Blue Angel was a nightclub founded by Herbert Jacoby. An article in *Time* magazine from 26 April 1943 – just a couple of weeks before Bernstein wrote this letter to Renée Longy – evokes Claude Alphand's singing at the club:

> The De Gaullist movement has found its loveliest voice. She sang last week at a new Manhattan cabaret, the Blue Angel, opened by balding, long-nosed, toothy Herbert Jacoby, ex-secretary to France's imprisoned ex-Premier Leon Blum. Chic as a Paris bandbox, its jet-black walls garnished with white lilies and orchids, the Blue Angel gave off more than a suggestion of the smarter mortuaries. But it ceased to be funereal when a swarm of De Gaullist refugees and friends produced an opening-night crush of such confusion that New York Daily News Columnist Danton Walker, for one of the few times in his professional life, was presented with his own check.
> Many of the throng went especially to hear Claude Alphand sing. She is a beautiful, blonde, rather waxwork-like Frenchwoman who accompanies her balladry on the guitar. Rated by many as the best French chanteuse since Yvette Guilbert and Lucienne Boyer, she sings with a feline throatiness and great stylistic elegance. Her favorite song is: Prenez le temps d'aimer [...] – Alphand's delivery of such sentiments makes her worth $750 a week to the Blue Angel's Jacoby.
> Mme. Alphand has only recently turned professional. Before the war she was prominent in Paris society; she is the wife of Hervé Alphand, former Treasury attaché of the Vichy Government in Washington. Her father, Robert Raynaud, founded La Dépêche Marocaine, the first French daily newspaper in Morocco. When the Alphands arrived in the US three years ago, Hervé Alphand said: "In France now there are only two things to do: to work and to be silent. I have come here to work and to be silent." But he did not stay silent long. Less than a

marinières" ou "La Belle Journée" ou "Tu m'as voulu, tu m'as eu",[112] je me souviens violentement de "Mon Mari est bien malade".[113]

Qu'est-ce que tu fait ces jours? Pas encore l'assembly-line, j'espère! En tous cas, je serai à Boston la semaine prochaine, et j'insiste de te revoir. Notre ancien ami, L'Institut de l'Art Moderne (zut) m'a invité à jouer la-haut le jeudi soir. Eh bien, quelques dollars, et un voyage payé à Boston! Mais quelle existence! Le mardi, j'ai un lecture-recital très important à Town Hall; le mercredi, j'ai un lecture à L'Art Alliance à Philly!!!! Et le jeudi à Boston! Je reserve toutes les nouvelles pour ton oreille, pas ton oeil . . . .

Lenny.

Et voilà celui qui a gagné le Prix Paderewski! Gardner Read! *Effrayant.*[114]

145. Leonard Bernstein to Serge Koussevitzky
Hotel Chelsea, New York, NY
29 May 1943

Dear Doctor,

Every once in a while I am appalled at the idea that I never see you – and I feel that I must write you, or talk to you, if for no other reason than my constant warmth of affection for you. No matter how much time elapses without seeing

---

year after his arrival, he announced his disagreement with Vichy policy, resigned, went to England where he joined the De Gaullist fighting forces.

Mme. Alphand had to find a way to earn her living. Her friends had long admired her repertory of some 200 salty popular songs. Helped by a group of them (Lady Mendl, Henry Bernstein, Elsa Maxwell), she began appearing at a French hangout called Le Petit Palais. Among Manhattan's Francophile intelligentsia, her nostalgic music was sensational. Manhattan's Liberty Music Shop issued an album of Alphand recordings, quickly sold 1,000 copies.

Today, though Manhattan's swankest pub-crawlers flock to hear her, Mme. Alphand is already tired of professional life. Says she, with a Gallic shrug: "If I am not to sing, then I must sew, I must make hats or something." But she admits that she is not doing badly in the new world, says: "Heaven was very charming to me."

[112] Three popular French *chansons*.

[113] A French folk song.

[114] Bernstein's original French text is included out of interest. The following is an English translation:

Everything is so French these days. I've just read Gide in French. I go to play every Sunday evening at The Blue Angel, a new club of a Parisian sort (like the old Ox on the Roof, or the Blue Ribbon); the clique of the Serenade Concerts (your friend the Marquise, etc.); my world seems these days to be completely French. So what to do about it? Nothing but to write a word to the first Frenchwoman among all Frenchwomen. D'you think I'm drunk? It's not drunkenness at all – it's friendship.

The immediate cause of this letter is Mme Claude Alphand, the extraordinary singer at The Blue Angel. Each time she sings "Les Moules marinières" or "La Belle Journée" or "Tu m'as voulu, tu m'as eu," I am forcefully reminded of "Mon Mari est bien malade."

What are you doing these days? Not still the assembly line, I hope! In any case, I will be in Boston next week and I insist on seeing you again. Our old friend, the Institute of Modern Art (damn!) has invited me to play up there on Thursday evening. Well, it's a few dollars and a trip

you, you are always with me, guiding my work, providing the standards by which I measure my progress in our art. And today I feel simply that I must communicate with you, out of love and friendship – that is all.

Reading your letter to the [New York] Times[115] made me think of the wonderful Tanglewood days when we discussed your wonderful plan together. I became inspired all over again; and I was very happy to find that the general reaction to your idea is so favorable and understanding. But who can resist an idea at once so bold and so simple?

Of course I am desolated that there is no Tanglewood this year for the first time in many a year. The summer holds no attraction for me. I am searching for a little farmhouse on Staten Island, where I can be alone and work during the summer months. What are you planning to do? I have heard reports that you may go West! That would be a grand idea, if the traveling were not too difficult. There is nothing on earth quite like the Far West of our country.

As for me, I am still in an undecided state. I hear rumors, all the time, about my coming connection with the Philharmonic – sometimes they reach crazily exaggerated proportions – but I have still had no definite word from Rodzinski. But I am used to this kind of delay – it is rather typical of my life. The one moment I still anticipate eagerly next year is my conducting my symphony with the Boston orchestra. That will be a *real* moment!

Meanwhile, I go on doing my horrible chores for Warner Brothers in order to live. It is dull beyond belief, and takes much too much time; but I feel that somehow better things must be coming for me.

I have given up my apartment, and live temporarily at the Chelsea Hotel, until I find my summer house. Please let me hear from you and Olga, for it may be a long time until I see you again.

Warmest greetings to Olga, and to you, the same love and sincerity,
Leonard

---

to Boston paid for! But what an existence! On the Tuesday, I've a very important lecture-recital at Town Hall; and on the Wednesday, a lecture at the Art Alliance in Philly!!!! And Thursday it's Boston! I'll keep all the news for your ears, not your eyes . . . .
Lenny.
And look who has won the Paderewski Prize! Gardner Read! *Frightful.*

[115] Koussevitzky's letter to *The New York Times* published on 16 May 1943 was headed "Justice to Composers," and was a plea to support creative musicians: "What is being done for the composer of our day? [. . .] It is time to wake up to our responsibility toward the composer and to repay the debt long standing that we owe him. [. . .] We musicians must be first to stand by the composer because we owe him most. We have ripened to this consciousness. Therefore I say the time is ripe to act." He goes on to propose the setting up of a fund to support the work of composers, initially by a donation of $1 from each professional performing musician in the country. This would, he argues, "go a long way toward establishing a composers' fund. A far-reaching and wise plan must be worked out for a proper distribution of the fund [. . .] For that purpose an organizing committee must be formed without delay. Whatever action we take now will lay the groundwork for the impelling and just cause of the composer. Embracing that cause, we shall ascend to new heights, we shall gain in confidence, in self-esteem and in fortitude."

146. Aaron Copland to Leonard Bernstein
"about 30 miles outside Hollywood"
3 June 1943

L P (you dawg),

Don't worry, I haven't lost my job. It's just that we are on location – about 30 miles outside Hollywood, in heavenly rolling hills, dotted with cattle. Pure William Bonney[116] country. I come out each day with about 250 people. They are about to film 2 of my songs, only the sun won't stay out as it's supposed to in Cal[ifornia] – so 250 people sit around at old Goldwyn's expense – and I get a chance to write the letter I've been thinking for weeks on end.

We're on the 4th month of the picture's shooting and still no end in sight. My contract, which was to have ended on June 19th, will have to be continued indefinitely or there'll be no score. As things stand now, I can't imagine being free of the place until Aug 1–15. Because so far there *is* no score, except for a few songs and a dance number. Isn't it amazing? Most composers get 2–3 weeks to write their music. And look at me, sitting pretty in my 18th week!

The really good thing would be if I could tell you I'd been working on the side all that time. But I ain't! Hollywood affects me as it does everybody else – not creative country . . . (except when you're paid).

Of course, you're a villain and a wretch for letting weeks and weeks go by with nary a word. And your letter – tho I ate it up – was scrappy. I put it all down to the evil genii of the Chelsea Hotel. Watch out for those guys. You can listen, but don't touch.

D[avid] D[iamond] sent a triumphant paragraph of how he had outdone you one Sat. night. It gave me visions of a promiscuity "sans bornes", and I tremble for you. I expect to return and find nothing but a pulpy dismembered jellyfish. Awful!

I went up to Oakland (Cal!) last weekend and delivered me of a lecture at Mills College and spent some charming hours with the Milhauds and saw much of Sandy Jones. I even played the Piano Sonata. I can't tell you what a nice person Darius is. He played me the opening page of *Bolivar*, and presented me with a manuscript of his Lily Pons songs. I wish something could be done about getting his bigger works put on more regularly. Another job for young conductors!

Read a biography of Hart Crane by Horton. Very touching book. Did you ever read it? Also I've been reading Latin-American poetry, my first Lorca plays, more Henry Miller, the Fausset Whitman biography, and good old Hindy's[117] *Unterweisung* in translation.

---

[116] Billy the Kid.
[117] Hindemith's.

V[ictor] was busy with M. Bourke-White when she was here and is now "recovering". Looks quite "Hollywood".

Tell Pf [Bowles] I have his letter and will answer soon.

Antonio writes wild letters from Mexico. Why can't we all meet at Chávez's Festival of Modern Music Oct 22–29? Simple idea, what?

Lead the good life.

Always your viejo,

A

147. Aaron Copland to Leonard Bernstein
Samuel Goldwyn Studios, Los Angeles, CA
3 July 1943

Lenny-Pen,

You write the most wonderful letters – just the kind I love to get: the "I miss you I adore you" kind, the while sailors and marines flit through the background in a general atmosphere of moral decay.

Well, the fact is I miss you too, and there aren't any sailors in the background either. In fact, there isn't anybody – because V[ictor] has gone to Mexico, and I've been alone for a week. So the scene is set for a wonderful reunion – the only hitch being that you'd have to come here. How about it? How about just hopping [on] a plane and coming here for two weeks or two months or whatever. I know it's a wild idea – but it's fun to contemplate. I have a tiny house with a concert grand that fills it up completely. There's a little porch where one sunbathes, and a big eucalyptus tree that covers all. With a whirlwind like you around the neighbors will suffer, but that's their lookout. I even have a small kitchen where you could demonstrate the culinary art. And it's never hot – just pleasantly warm. Oh yes, and it wouldn't cost you anything once you got here (just a minor detail!) and of course you'd write reams of music, – and good music, it being my house. What do you say.

The idea is probably full of complications for you. Your draft board, your job, your frau, your things, your etc., etc. I dread thinking about the fit of confused brainstorms this letter will bring on. But I just can't resist the temptation of suggesting the whole thing and living in hopes for a couple of days. Maybe you'd better wire me collect as soon as you know anything. The two week plan couldn't be so complicated, could it? Anyhow, even if nothing comes of it, I've had the pleasure of asking you, and it makes me feel less of a wretch in abandoning you all these many months.

Truth is I'll probably be stuck here until Sept. 1st. That's why V decided to go. There wasn't much for him to do here, and it looked as if he would just be hanging around, and not even get his trip to Mexico in. So I encouraged him to make the break though it was as hard as getting caramel out of your teeth.

The picture is now in the cutting stage. In another week or two they'll be dropping it in my lap and screaming for the music in a hurry. In the meantime I finished the first movement of the Violin Sonata, and started a ballet for Martha Graham.[118] And when Hollywood is over I am still hoping to fly to Mexico for a short stay before coming home.

I had Virgil out to dinner the other night and he gave me a few details of the winter music temporada. He also launched into a full scale attack on all psychoanalysts that took me by surprise. He says all that deep down stuff is better left unstirred. He sees no harm in talking about yourself for a few months, but insists that the new science never cured anybody. It also seemed to annoy him that it cost so much in most cases. What sayest thou?

You wanna hear what's fun? Stokie wrote and asked to see the *Short Symphony*! Just ten years after abandoning the performance the first time. David says he won't play it anyhow, but I was amused to think he hadn't forgotten it.[119] Did you happen to hear that [Alexander] Smallens version of *Rodeo* at the Stadium? I suspect it was murder.

I know you want me to be amazed at your successes as composer but nothing that happens to you can ever surprise me. Isn't that too bad. Least of all your triumphs as composer. But I am pleased that Reiner wants you to conduct in Pittsburgh. Koussie will be jealous that he didn't get you first. Maybe you can start a career as our first native guest conductor.

Whatever "news" I had I must have written to D[avid] D[iamond] who must have told it all to you, so I won't make the mistake of repeating myself. How I would like to sit in on one of those "piano" lessons. They must be the most original lesson periods given anywhere.

Well, anyway, if you are coming here, no need to go on. Let me know sumpin' *soon*.

Love,

Me

P.S. My home address is 8663 Holloway Plaza Drive. Tel. Crestview 1-0432. Just in case I miss you at the airport!

148. Leonard Bernstein to David Oppenheim
40 Charlton Street, New York, NY
postmark 12 July 1943

Dear Dave,

Here I am with two letters from you, and not the faintest idea of what's going on inside that newly militarized brain of yours. Is it all censorable? Or haven't

---

[118] This became *Appalachian Spring*.

[119] Stokowski conducted the America premiere of Copland's notoriously difficult *Short Symphony* with the NBC Symphony Orchestra on 9 January 1944 (though according to Copland himself it was an "extremely inadequate reading").

you collected your *real feelings* (big chord)? It's good to know that you've been classified as a musician, which seems to augur well for your future life-span. Does your uniform fit you? Have you got a weird little snapshot? How much vibrato do you apply to the sax?

I suddenly find myself with a lovely call for an Army physical tomorrow night. God knows what will happen. I sometimes have a strong wish to go and get it over with and be calm and unresponsible. Then I see how easy that way out of a mess is, and the old realities, like career, and so on, crop up, and I want to stay as far away from it as I can.

My plans now call for two more Goldman Band concerts this month, finishing up Warner Bros. chores, a visit to Kouss in Lenox, to make plans for a performance of my symphony in the fall, then to Boston to conduct a pair of cute concerts with the 25 or so first-desks of the Boston Symphony (very good chance, and all modern pieces) and then to light out to Hollywood for a month of rest with Aaron, then perhaps to Mexico for a very short visit, then back here to become assistant to Rodzinsky. This is, of course, all the ideal way, and probably none of it will pan out, as it depends first of all on what the Army physical turns out to decide, then on whether I get a job collaborating on a book with Henry Simon, which I have been promised, and which would net me several thousand bucks over the summer, and finally on whether Rodzinsky ever makes up his mind. I found out, by the way, who the other two conductors are that Rodzinsky has asked to be his assistants – Max Goberman and Danny Saidenberg. What a trio we would make! But no real competition, you'll admit. Or won't you?

Reiner has set the date for my conducting of my symphony in Pittsburgh – probably some time in January. It's to be a three-ring circus for Bernstein – I'm to solo in the Beethoven Triple Concerto, then to conduct my (our) *Jeremiah* (which seems more beautiful every time I correct another page of score) and then to finish up the program conducting some big work. Isn't that fun? And it really doesn't sound like Reiner to allow all that, does it? Wish you were around to take the clarinet solos. When Kouss heard that Reiner loved the piece so much he got all pepped up again, and asked me to come and play it for him again (his reaction last time was tired, you may recall, and there were so many people in the room, etc.). Truth is, it takes him a while to grasp a piece, as he himself will admit: so this time when I play it for him in Lenox it ought to be a real hit. He wants me to do that same sort of three-ring circus in Boston.

Apropos of which, I've run into conductor trouble about the first performances. Reiner demanded that his January date be the first (first performance), and I had to consent. Then when I had breakfast with Kouss at the St Regis the other day (!) he was a bit hurt and put out, as you can imagine, and ruefully suggested that he had a November date in mind for me. What an act. But he's still awfully sweet. It occurs to me now and then that with my idiotic way of handling these situations I may well wind up without either performance. It would be typical Bernstein. At the moment everything is passably under control. And Warner's is starting to make me the parts etc. (you know, they took the symphony) so maybe we'll have a piece yet. The Clarinet Sonata should be out any week now. As for the records, who knows the mysterious ways of Petrillo.[120]

I feel good that I solved the double acrostic puzzle in the *Times* this morning. And I wrote a new song called "The Nicest Time of Year".[121]

Mrs. Landeck has come back, bringing another married woman with her, and I am stranded here in sin with both of them, since I can't find another apartment, and anyway it seems silly to take one at this mixed up point. It creates quite an interesting triangle.

I had the final Frau session, and left with conflicting feelings of regret and relief. She'll be back in September, and believe me, I really welcome the breathing spell. But there's no denying that she's done wonders, or at least somebody has. I can almost look at the problem now as a problem instead of as a Fascist enemy ready to strike. I have some amazingly tranquil moments. I almost married Rhoda [Saletan] last night; but stopped when I saw Judy [Holliday], and decided to marry *her*. What do you hear from Mad?

And what in Heaven's name happened during those ten days in the psychopathic ward? It must be a luscious tale. Sit down when you're bored some evening (are you ever bored?) and put it all down on a piece of stationery. There's no postage necessary, after all.

Yes, Avshalomoff came to see me at my last Goldman Band concert, and we had a fine time. We saw each other again at David Diamond's. He's a good boy, and very sincere, and I wonder if he writes good music too. That would be almost too much.

Love, and write me the ganze Geschichte.

L

What means all that nonsense in your address? It's the most fantastic one to date.[122]

---

[120] James Petrillo (1892–1984), the powerful leader of the American Federation of Musicians. In July 1942, Petrillo imposed a ban on American musicians making commercial recordings for major American companies because of a dispute over royalty payments. The union settled with Decca and Capitol in October 1943, and with RCA and Columbia in November 1944. During the strike, Petrillo had to authorize the release of new recordings.

[121] An autograph sketch and a fair copy of *The Nicest Time of Year* (both with a slightly different title, "The Nicest Time of Day") are in the Leonard Bernstein Collection. The tune was used for "Lucky To Be Me" ("What a day, Fortune smiled and came my way," etc.) in *On the Town*. But, as indicated in this letter, it was composed as a single song a year before Bernstein started working on the show. My thanks to Sophie Redfern for drawing my attention to this manuscript.

[122] The envelope is addressed to "Pvt. David Oppenheim, A.S.N. 12208749, 1633rd S.V., Brk. 130, Co. A, Camp Grant, Illinois."

149. Leonard Bernstein to Aaron Copland

40 Charlton Street, NNNYYYCCC [New York, NY]
[July 1943]

Dear and Wonderful Aaron,

When I got your insidious invitation to go west I dismissed it immediately as a real wacky idea. As time goes by I find it becoming more and more a real possibility. The only thing is that I couldn't possibly come now, especially since I want very much to conduct that little concert in Boston. I did write you about it, didn't I? It's a pair of concerts in a little series whipped up by the first desks and associates of the BSO, to relieve the monotony. I've been asked to conduct and if possible play the piano at the same time. I plan to do the *Création du Monde*, thank God, the *Dumbarton Oaks* (in *two* rehearsals, forgive me) and a suite from PFB's [Paul Bowles'] opera. It seems to me that I could stick around here for the rest of July, finish up my chores at Warner's, do another Goldman Band pair (*Outdoor Overture* again, and Billy's [Schuman's] *Newsreel*), spend a few days with Kouss in Lenox, play him the Symph again, go to Boston, do the concert, and streak out like a wild one for Hollywood. Does that sound reasonable or not? Very simple. And then Mexico in September where we could meet Pfb who is dying to go there in September, and then home to become, God willing, an assistant conductor of the Philharmonic. Sort of a nice way to become 25 years old. Is it still possible with you, or has V. suddenly come home to roost? Of course I completely disregard the situation of his absence that makes my visit possible; I don't usually go in for being 2nd fiddle, but with you it looks good. (Or on you.) I'm all for it.

Of course a lot of this depends on whether that job that Henry Simon has offered me comes through or not. Remember? The book on opera he's writing, and I'm to do the musical part of it, for 2 or 3 thousand bucks. Which would make the trip feasible. I ought to know in a few days.

And the other catch is that I've received another call for an Army physical on Monday night. If my asthma is anything then like it is at this moment, they'll toss me out on my ear. I've really got it bad today, suddenly. Maybe unconscious preparation for the exam, as any analysand would say.

Had the final Frau session today, which is rather thought-provoking about what has been accomplished. Answer: much. The rest is up to me now, as you might imagine. And God knows what evil deterrent influences may befall me in sinful California. But come what may, I'm ready to try.

Found out who the other two conductors are who have been asked for assistantships by Rodzinsky. Guess. Max Goberman and Danny Saidenberg. What a trio we'd make – Saidenberg, Bernstein and Goberman, the three prides of Goebbels. No competition though, really, you must admit.

Had breakfast with Kouss yesterday at the St. Regis. Lovely time, he's a lovely man, it's a lovely hotel. He asked me up to Lenox for a few days, admitting that he hadn't really heard the Symphony very well when I played it to him in Boston, since there were so many people in the room, and he was tired. I think Reiner's enthusiasm kind of pepped him up. You were right about the jealousy though (you're always right). He was a little hurt that Fritz had copped the first performance. Added rather ruefully, "Well I have planned a date for you in November (when I told him that Reiner's date was in January) but I suppose now we'll have to make it for the second half of the season." What an act. We'll see. I have a feeling I'm getting into a deep well full of hot water with this first performance racket. I really don't quite know how to handle the boys. But just think how well I'll understand someday when some young composer from Podunkville won't know how to handle me!

Went to a long cocktail party last night with Pfb [Paul Bowles], home of Paul Peters and Herr von Auw!!! Occasion: triumphant return to these parts of one [John] LaTouche. Great to-do. It went on all night, mostly me and Touche and Paul, and wound up at Peter Monro Jacks' (horrid) and we finally left Touche there in his four o'clock cups. He's a terror if there ever was one. I sort of like him in a weird way, especially when he's sentimental in that mountebank manner. It's a wonderful aggressiveness.

Just thought: what will happen to poor David's piano lessons if I leave?

My asthma is really kicking up. I'm going to bed, [words blanked out] and creep guiltily back to some semblance of normalcy.

Morton Gould completely ruined *Billy the Kid* at the Stadium last week, to say nothing of *Newsreel*, which isn't so hot to begin with, to say nothing of Roy's *Ode to Truth*, which – well, I can't even describe it, except as an eternal measure of turdlike notes that will never be counted out. It's a piece with his three tricks in it, and it does make a very unpleasant sound. What else? Seems like I've given out with a lot of news. I'll have nothing to say when I arrive. Write me right away, and tell me you approve of my little plans.

I love you, as if I had to point *that* out!

L

The *Salon* cover is awful pretty.

150. Aaron Copland to Leonard Bernstein
Samuel Goldwyn Studios, Los Angeles, CA
16 July 1943

Dear Second Fiddle Black Magic,

Too bad, too bad – this was the perfect moment for you to come to Hollywood. I dread to think what life will be like in August. I may not have a house by then – it's only a sub-let and my lady threatens to come back "sometime in August". Houses are scarcer than Filipinos out here, and *they've* practically disappeared. I will be doubled up with notes – right in the midst of it in August – with hardly a moment to eat, no less take care of a bombshell like thou. (There's an hour's worth of music to be written – I just finished calculating it. Where will all those notes come from, I wonder?)

On the other hand, I saw the announcements of the Boston concerts – it all looks quite impressive and naturally you're right to be staying and conducting. So of course come in August if you still think it's insidiously attractive – but consider yourself warned that you may have to sleep on park benches, and converse with a guy that has noten indigestion. Whatever you decide to do, you'd better make reservations now, because trains and planes are full-up. As you point out, the Army may step in and end this little pipe dream.

I was surprised you had a "final session" with the Frau. In my innocence I thought those things went on for years. You mean you're done? Finished? How extraordinario.

And exactly, may I ask, what is an assistantship to Rodzinsky? Is anything guaranteed? Or even promised? I'd like to know what's really up the old boy's sleeve. His monkey business with American composers in Cleveland makes me suspicious of the purity of his motives. But don't forget to neglect to mention my reaction to him.

Heinsheimer says that Reiner has programmed the *Salón* with the Philharmonic for Aug. 8th. Did you have a hand in that?

Spent an awful pleasant evening with Jesse and June [Ehrlich] in their little house perched precariously on top of a Hollywood mountain. They're so gentle and "different" – sort of poetic people. They had a soldier guest for me, who kept spewing venom at Irving Berlin all evening. Oh yes, and I met Leonard Posner out here. Remember him? He played that there violin piece of yours on WNYC. And also I met a guy who says he knows you – pretty cute looking too. A Mr. Pole. He was in the Army, but they let him out after 4 months – lung trouble. Anyway, that's what he says. Oh yeah, and I had dinner with Gail Kubik[123] in a uniform. Quite a lot of boyish charm despite the bald head. And the Van Eycks – Ruth and Goetz (renamed Peter for the movies) have parties all the time. Harold Clurman came out and made me less lonely. (You lush thing you.) And thus and so.

Love

---

[123] Gail Kubik (1914–84), American composer who studied at Harvard with Walter Piston and with Nadia Boulanger. During the Second World War he was Music Director of the Motion Picture Bureau of the Office of War Information.

151. Leonard Bernstein to Serge Koussevitzky
17 Lake Avenue, Sharon, MA
[August 1943]

Dear Dr. Koussevitzky,

An amazing thing has happened! Thursday night I was deferred for all time from the army. As you know, my recent siege of asthmatic hay fever had caused me to be sent for reexamination to the Medical Advisory Board, where I fell into the hands of one Dr. Wesselhoeft, who is in charge. He is a firm believer in the British policy of leaving as intact as possible the cultural foundations of our country, even – or rather, especially – in time of war. He was therefore *happy* to disqualify me on medical grounds; and put me in Class IV, where, he assured me, "nothing can interfere with your career."

I am therefore free to pursue my work through its next channel, whatever that may be; and I am happy to say that because of the spirit of the Medical Board, I feel no guilt whatsoever at my deferment.

Devotedly as always,

Leonard

152. Leonard Bernstein to Serge Koussevitzky
Hotel Chelsea, New York, NY
[September 1943]

Dear Serge Alexandrovich,

How I would love to be with you now to share my great joy with you! I am still so excited I can hardly write this letter. Everything seems to be going so well.

I finally had my talk with [Arthur] Judson and [Bruno] Zirato this morning. They were very nice indeed, and extremely authoritative. I realized immediately that they had the situation in hand, and that I was simply being told their terms, not asked my own. All of which was perfectly all right with me, since I feel so strongly about doing this job, and doing it as well as possible, that I would probably, in my enthusiasm, accept if there were no salary at all.

The first thing is that there is apparently to be no contract at all. As Zirato pointed out, he doesn't believe in them, and never had one with, for instance, [Mishel] Piastro. I am to receive $125 a week. I realize that this is not tremendous, and that there are only 28 weeks in the season. But I am very contented with it, especially insofar as my publishers have raised my weekly royalty advance to $50 a week, which will continue all year. I simply felt that until I have proved myself to the Philharmonic and to the public, I have no real right to make any demands. On the other hand, the absence of a contract has its advantages, because I can be free for the summer, or for any occasion that may arise. It makes finances a little bit unsure, of course, but believe me, I am very happy in spite of that. I hope you can understand the situation in which I found myself; in fact I am *sure* that you will understand it. I simply could not ask $12,000 or any other sum for a job which thousands of conductors in this country would gladly pay to have. Once I have shown that I am of real value to the Society, then there is time enough for me to make demands. I am perfectly willing to seem naïve now; as long as I know myself that I am seeming naïve. The main thing is to do my job; if I can do that well enough, and if I can bear all the huge responsibilities that come with it, the rest will come by itself, I am sure. Believe me, I tried very hard to feel like Koussevitzky while I was in the Judson office, but I was only Leonard Bernstein, and I had to act as I did. Don't you think it is for the best?

And in the middle of all this, I only have to look at your picture in my room, and I am perfectly contented, knowing that there is one supreme friend that I have, who will understand whatever I do, mistakes included. I hope to see you very soon; meanwhile take good care of your health, and know that my love is with you always.

Leonard

153. Fritz Reiner[124] to Leonard Bernstein
Rambleside, Westport, CT
4 September 1943

My dear Leonard,

Needless to say that I am very happy about the news![125] It is a great chance and I do not doubt for one moment that you are going to make the best of it. You have the talent and the tenacity to put it over. I hope that the years spent at the Curtis with me will bear fruit.

As to your appearance in Pittsburgh on Jan. 28 & 30th, you will feel relieved to know that you are not expected to play the Triple or any other concerto. You will only conduct your Symphony and another work at the end of the program about which I would like to have your suggestions. Also – please let me know the name of the lady who is to sing the Symphony in Boston with you. Maybe we could use her also in Pittsburgh.

I shall be at the Hampshire House from Tuesday the 7th until Thursday the 9th in case that you want to get in touch with me.

Heartiest congratulations once more, in which Mrs. Reiner joins me.

Sincerely yours,

Fritz Reiner

---

[124] Fritz Reiner (1888–1963), Hungarian-born conductor, and Bernstein's teacher at the Curtis Institute. One of the most inspiring (and feared) conductors working in America, Reiner was Music Director of the Pittsburgh Symphony Orchestra (1938–48), conducted regularly at the Metropolitan Opera, and became Music Director of the Chicago Symphony Orchestra in 1953.

[125] Bernstein's appointment as Assistant Conductor of the New York Philharmonic.

154. Adolph Green to Leonard Bernstein

[Hollywood, CA]
[September 1943]

Dollink Leonard,

I'm writing, I'm writing, I can't believe it. My pen is tracing figures on paper, making bold, masculine markings indicative of a strong character and a willful mind plus creative ability, yet with a strange strain of tenderness withal and a slight indication of liver trouble.

Forgive me for not writing sooner. As always was the case with the Revuers, we have been through parlous times. I'll give you a brief resumé.

The day we arrived, our agent, Kurt Frings, told us that *Duffy's Tavern*[126] was off. The varied producers had quarreled – but, said Kurt, this was a good thing because now we were free to receive really good offers. We opened at the New Trocadero & were sensational, so sensational that the owner let us go after 4 weeks because he figured that now that he was doing a landslide business, it would continue so without us. At this point we realized that no movie company wanted us. Too smart, they said. First M.G.M. turned us down. Then everybody else turned us down all the way down the line, including dinky little Universal, who screen-tested us and said we stank. We were in despair. Then – our agent Kurt Frings (who, by the way, is a sensational agent, plus a Viennese gentleman) got us an audition at 20th Century Fox, right on the lot. It seems that 20th was the one company that hadn't caught us at the Trocadero. Oh God, we said, an audition, how horrible. We went to the audition. First, in walked high and mighty Lew Schreiber, Darryl Zanuck's chief assistant. We trembled. Then all the producers and directors – Lubitsch,[127] Schambitsch,[128] Perlberg,[129] LeBaron[130] etc., etc. And finally the great Darryl himself in simple slacks & polo shirt. We started doing our numbers. For four numbers no one smiled. We noticed that a number of them wanted to laugh, but had to stifle it, because Zanuck didn't look happy or pleased. Then suddenly it happened. D.Z. grinned. HE GRINNED!! Then he chuckled. CHUCKLED!! From that second on we were in. Everybody there roared & rolled & clutched their sides with helpless laughter. We did number after number & they screamed. That very day we were signed for a super-duper all-dancing all-technicolor, all-Alice Faye[131] picture

---

[126] *Duffy's Tavern* was a popular radio comedy show that ran from 1941 to 1951 and often featured guest stars.

[127] Ernst Lubitsch.

[128] Possibly a name invented by Adolph Green for this list.

[129] William Perlberg.

[130] William LeBaron, the producer who went on to make *Greenwich Village*.

[131] The eventual star of *Greenwich Village* was Carmen Miranda. Adolph Green, Betty Comden, Judy Holliday, and Alvin Hammer all appeared in the film.

with a minimum guarantee of 6 weeks at a very fine figure indeed. The picture doesn't start till the middle of October, & we don't quite know what we're doing till then. Maybe a two or three week engagement at the Mark Hopkins[132] in San Francisco.

The picture by the way is called *Greenwich Village*, and we're going to do *Bazooka* in it, plus a new spot which should be something stupid about the Vie de Bohème of Greenwich Village. We'll have to build it around a song by Nacio Herb Brown – in march tempo – sample lyrics as follows (lyrics *not* by us):

> It's all for art's sake
> It really is
> Whatever we do we really do
> For art's sake.
> There's that lady there
> A very mysterious gypsy
> But honest folks,
> She's really from Poughkeepsie.

Plus another undetermined spot, plus parts in the picture itself. All in all, the set-up looks very good for us.

Hollywood is the weirdest country in the world. I'm only afraid you would love it here. One day Aaron [Copland] & I were envisioning the way you might take to it – a mad swirl of parties and gatherings, with you the life of the [party]. Then you awakening in the morning with a hangover – or fluff on your lungs, a fly on your tongue, etc., etc. – and filled with remorse. "My God, I'm not getting any work done – Oh God, what the hell am I doing – it's fantastic, I'm not accomplishing anything. Oh, my God!"

Of course, I should not talk. Almost everyone I've ever known is out here and everyone is rich as Croesus, and life for me has been that self-same swirl – not terribly mad but the liquor and the thick steaks flow. It's a terribly unreal life out here, if you're with prosperous people who've decided you're a comer & sort of take you up. At first your conscience bothers you that these swimming pools & groaning boards exist while the whole world is starving and dying, & generally tightening its belt. After a while, you relax & enjoy it. After that, you suddenly become horribly bored with it. It's really meaningless & stupid & everyone out here is bored & screaming for some kind of diversion. You see the movie people out here never exchange anything resembling ideas. Most of them are stupid to begin with & impossibly spoiled by all their money, & the more intelligent minority are just *afraid* to exchange any intelligent remarks. Nothing is secret out here, and even the most casual statement might drift back to the wrong

---

[132] The *Top of the Mark* cocktail lounge at the Mark Hopkins Hotel.

person, & shit, you just mustn't offend anybody. The first thing you know, you'll be out on your ear. A good friend of mine is a movie director, Frank Tuttle. He is prosperous now & back in the dough, through having discovered & put across LADD: an Alan. But he was black-listed for almost 4 years because of having openly expressed sympathy for the Loyalist cause back in 1937.

I'll write more about H–wood later. Oy, I've seen so many movie faces and know them all, all the sad little extras & bit players. As a matter of fact, I've scared the hell out of a lot of people with my well-stocked memory.

Incidentally, Tuttle took us out to visit Charlie Chaplin last Sunday. Quelle disappointment! Charlie is now a fattish, ageing man, and he insists on being the life of the party. He was bounding around all afternoon, clowning, grimacing, putting on native Balinese and Hindu phonograph records & dancing madly to them. This sounds charming, I know, & had you been there we might have had some fun with it – but somehow Chaplin was a little more frightening than amusing, mainly I think because there was more of an air of desperation than joie de vi[vr]e in his cutting up. The guy just didn't look cute and I kept thinking, "Who does this mincing fat-necked little fellow think he is, imitating Charlie Chaplin?"

I've seen Uncle Aaron a few times since I've been here. He's been working furiously finishing up his film[133] – and the scoring was completed last night. Aaron let me come to the studio to watch. They had only five small scenes to complete, but the music sounded fine. There's an especially cute little theme for Walter Brennan who seems to be portraying a crusty, lovable old peasant.[134] It's sort of a cross between a Slavonic dance & Schumann's "Jolly Farmer". Anyway, that's the mood.

The orchestra that recorded the score was largely made up of the Warner Bros. musicians' crew and I never saw musicians as excited & enthusiastic over anything as they were over Aaron's score. It was just miraculous to them after all the Steiner–Korngold crap they've been playing. Imagine a composer who not only does not have the hero & heroine do their big kiss to the accompaniment of surging strings, & bl-w-l-anging harps in great Straussian release, but cuts out the music entirely at that point.

Do you see Billy Schuman? Give him & Frankie my love & tell him that I have seen much of his old friend & co-partner, Frankie Loesser, plus his wife. Loesser, it seems, is an old admirer of ours, a hysterical admirer, in fact, and he & his wife have been most generous to us – many dinners, parties, etc. He is a typical Hollywood case – horribly prosperous and a back-slapping one of the boys. He is a very nice guy, though, and really talented at writing lyrics. His new movie *Thank Your Lucky Stars* has some very nice stuff in it, which he wrote

---

[133] *The North Star.*
[134] Brennan plays the part of the pig-farmer Karp in the film.

with Arthur Schwartz, and any song he touches these days is a sure hit. But a typical example of Hollywood in what he said about Billy Schuman. If you repeat this to Billy I will loathe you to my dying day. I was having a nice conversation with him the first time I met him. Here is a man, I said to myself, who hasn't gone Hollywood. Then I mentioned Billy – "Yeah, he's a swell guy", says Loesser, "but you know Adolph, where the hell is he today? That long-haired stuff doesn't get you anywhere. O.K. he's teaching & turning out that symphony stuff & he's got a wonderful wife & a home in Westchester – but what the hell, he's going to end up on the shit end of the stick. He ain't on that gravy train, Adolph. There's no dough on the Icky express" etc., etc. –

For great Horowitz' sake don't tell this to Billy. It just might get back to Frankie L. And besides Loesser really loves him. He was just giving out with the Hollywood jive that only strong men don't succumb to the lure of.

Loesser told me a cute story of him & Billy when young. Loesser is quite a small guy about 5 foot 4. One day he & Billy were walking down a street. Suddenly, out of the clear blue sky Billy turned to Frank & said, "What the hell, I'm bigger than you", and proceeded to wallop the shit out of him.

Enough of all this crap!

All the Revuers are fine, Betty [Comden] is ecstatically happy. Lizzie [Reitell][135] is here on a 16 day leave. Little Alvin [Hammer] is soon sending for his wife & child. Judy [Holliday] is this moment on her way to New York for 2 weeks. Why don't you call her at mama's around Monday. SU-7-6229. She'll be able to tell you in detail of what's been going on.

Write me everything that's been happening to you, at once, do you hear, at once!!!!!!!!!

I'll write you more later.

I think I've been pretty happy here so far, and I look staggeringly better than I have my whole life.

I have a grizzly feeling that we've really got a future in this place, Lord help me, even if we do just do one picture, we won't be back in town before January.

So please write!

Love

Shrdlu

P.S. I hate people who go to Hollywood.

P.P.S. Heard about your appointment with the Philharmonic. Nice goin' kid. Congrats & all that. But strictly between us, where's all that long-haired stuff going to get you? You don't want to end up on the shit end of the stick. You'd better get on that gravy train, son. But nice goin' kid.

Write, write write.

I love you

---

[135] Elizabeth Reitell, Adolph Green's first wife.

I miss you.

Regards to everybody.

What happened to your draft board?

Paul Bowles?

David Diamond?

Your love life?

Your Boston concerts?

Warner Bros?

Rhoda Saletan?

Your symphony? Reiner? Koussevitzky?

See, it's wonderful about the Philharmonic. It's thrilling!! It's marvelous!! I can't wait for the Copland festival!!

Have you seen Jesse Ehrlich[136] & weib? His wife is *not* the big fat colored woman you dreamt of. [...]

We have a wonderful apartment here. It's more of a house than an apartment. 6 rooms, 2 baths, 3 radios, piano, bamboo liquor bar, roof terrace. We got it by a sheer miracle, because you know the housing conditions here are impossible. Viola Essen & her mother found it for us etc. etc. There's an extra bed waiting for you. Come out!!

Love,

Adolph

155. Randall Thompson[137] to Leonard Bernstein
Division of Music, University of Virginia, Charlottesville, VA
16 September 1943

Dear Leonard,

After many years of hard work – under grueling taskmasters; in the face of tyrannies, rivalries, pedantries, rebuffs – there came to the young musician a first-class opportunity worthy of his powers. Notwithstanding a mercurial temperament which was wont to raise him into the Empyrean at moments and drag him, at others, into a deep and brooding melancholy, historians are

---

[136] See note 77 to Letter 132.

[137] Randall Thompson (1899–1984), American composer. He taught Bernstein orchestration at the Curtis Institute. Thompson's Second Symphony was one of the works Bernstein conducted during his first year at Tanglewood (1940), and he remained extremely fond of the piece, playing it in 1959 and 1968 in New York Philharmonic concerts, and recording it for Columbia Records in 1968. An undated note in Bernstein's hand (a draft reply to the Thompson scholar Byron McGilvray) reads as follows: "Randall was a real friend, right from the beginning. At Curtis we shared the joys of both orchestration (which I studied with him) and the London *Times* crossword puzzle, of which we were both secret fans. Beyond this, we shared a common conviction that Curtis should be reconceived, & turned from a conservatory-factory into a real place of learning. (We were both academically orientated, as Harvard men should be.) Randall did not exactly succeed in this, and we both left together (as we had entered together), he as dismissed director, and I with my diploma."

generally agreed that this sharp upswing in his musical career brought him, inwardly, a steady and deep feeling of satisfaction, security and happiness. And they are equally agreed that this feeling was fully matched by what his many (and varied) friends felt on hearing of his new appointment. Not the most eminent nor yet the least devoted among them is known to have been

His ever sincerely,
Randall Thompson

156. Leonard Bernstein to Aaron Copland

Philharmonic-Symphony Society of New York, Steinway Building, New York, NY
Friday [?September 1943]

My Dear Mr. Copland,
    I'm saving all my talk for your very own personal ears; but I just wanted to show you this super-authentic stationery with its *free* stamped envelope. Ah, the life of an assistant conductor.
    It all seems to be working out beautifully. Rodzinsky, of all things, turns out to be a fine gentleman.
    I'm off to dinner with Kouss (we've already spoken very seriously of reviving your *Ode!*)
    Then the weekend with Bill Schuman & Frankie who is *pregnant as hell*!
    But all this is mere substitute for the real thing – the week of Oct 4 is all yours (except that it's the first week of the Philharmonic season). I can't wait. Speed the day.
    I love you.
    L
    Lost my temper with D[avid] D[iamond] t'other night, & left him in a rage in a bar. That's just *one* delicious bit of gossip, a sample of the horrors in store for you. Hurry, hurry, hurry.

157. Leonard Bernstein to David Oppenheim

Philharmonic-Symphony Society of New York, Steinway Building, New York, NY
5 October 1943

Dear David,
    I just ran across, in moving, your ink copy of a little known piece of mine called "Two" which set all kind of memories, delicious and otherwise, in motion. I have a tremendous desire to see you again. Is there any possibility? Where are you? (I'm taking a chance on your last address, as of last summer.) Why did

your fertile crop of letters from the army suddenly stop? You never answered mine, you know; or did you never receive it?

So much has happened since our last contact that it is impossible even to begin to deliver information. Life has been marvelous, hectic, and unreally beautiful since my fantastic appointment, of which you must have read somewhere. It was a real shock to me, since I had had no inkling of it, beyond a rumor that I might become one of *three* assistants. *And* I had never met Rodzinski (who turns out to be a swell and honest guy). The position is unprecedented for one such as me, and a really historic step in terms of other young conductors. But I must see you to tell you, as the Frau says, "what is really going on."

I have a fine large apartment *in* Carnegie Hall (address: Carnegie Hall, Apt 803, NYC) from which I can literally walk on to the stage. It's quite beautiful, and I'm having a very quaint experience furnishing it, and it has an extra bed for you, and my *own* bathroom & kitchenette. If you are within 100 miles of New York at any time, please let me know, & come to town. In fact, let me know where you are in any case.

The day before my appointment was revealed to me, I was rejected might and main by the army for asthma.

Aaron returns next week. Write, & spend your furloughs here.

Love,

Lenny

158. Leonard Bernstein to Renée Longy Miquelle

Philharmonic-Symphony Society of New York, Steinway Building, New York, NY

9 October 1943

Dear [musical notation: D-A-E, i.e. Re-La-Mi],

Well, the opening is over, with a bang-up reception at the St. Regis & your nice letters to both of us, and I a great hit with Mrs. Lytel [Lytle] Hull, & Myrna Loy was there, & Frank Sinatra (who Oscar Levant says is the image of *me*) and Bruno Walter & Fabien Sevitzky & Marshall Field & and & and & and. You would have loved it. The concert was less exciting than the reception but maybe it will all pick up soon.

The other news is that Steinway has just moved a piano into my room. The same color as yours, same shape & size, & they're standing together now side by side like two beautiful horses in the meadow. But one is more in tune than the other (guess which?). Now – what is the action to be taken on *Baby* Steinway? Or will I have *Babies* Steinway? Do let me know.[138]

---

[138] "*Baby* Steinway" is the piano Renée Longy Miquelle had loaned Bernstein on which he composed the *Jeremiah* Symphony. See note 45 to Letter 115.

What the hell is Edgewood Road [Longy's address in Baltimore, Maryland]? Liberty 6510 sounds like Boston. Is it fun? Any nice people – are you branded a Jew-lover yet? Any good students? When do you come to NYC?

These and many other things, write, and make no bones about it.

Love

Lenny

My job is marvelous – 29 hours a day.

159. Leonard Bernstein to Renée Longy Miquelle

Philharmonic-Symphony Society of New York, Steinway Building, New York, NY

15 October 1943

Dear R,

A lovely series of illegible postals have been arriving daily. You say nothing about your work, your students, your milieu. Is it bearable?

As to the furniture, sure I could use it: especially did you say, a chest of drawers or a bureau? Or is that French for desk? The bench sounds swell: the desk is not essential, but could be useful, I suppose. Could it be used as a chest of drawers? That's what's really on my mind – my shirts are all in suitcases. Would it be easy to ship? In storage? In NYC?

The "dame merveilleuse" is writing you today and sending the first payment.

Glad you saw Randall. He's lovely.

I haven't actually conducted yet. Monday the 18th is the first time, & I will do readings of Diamond's 2nd Symph., Haieff's Symph.,[139] & Charles Mills' Symph.[140] And probably all the Chaikovsky rehearsals too.

Yes, we often rehearse on Saturdays. The orchestra is already greatly improved, & Rodzinski is a fine guy, & a very conscientious (if not always over-profound) conductor. Secrecy, please.

Let me know how it goes. I'm very happy. Very. Aaron is back, & all is right again. The *North Star* (his movie) is fine enough, & I've been fighting with Oscar Levant again. I may get a commission to do a ballet for the Ballet Theatre![141]

As I say, let me know . . .

Love,

L

---

[139] Alexei Haieff (1914–94), American composer.

[140] Charles Mills (1914–82), American composer who played in jazz bands from the age of 17. He was commissioned by Mitropoulos to compose a work for the New York Philharmonic in 1951. His output includes six symphonies, and some of his compositions involve jazz groups.

[141] Bernstein did get the commission, and the result was *Fancy Free*.

160. Leonard Bernstein to David Oppenheim
Philharmonic-Symphony Society of New York, Steinway Building, New York, NY, Carnegie Hall 803
postmark 22 October 1943

Dear Dave,

Delighted to hear you sounding much the same (it's even fun to hear you're still neurotic). But it's not so nice to hear that you're so unsettled. Why can't the army discover you and use you properly? It seems a shame that you should languish this way in what you call the plague state.

I'm in a big hurry – as always these days – since the JOB is all-consuming. It's quite glorious & exciting, & I wish you were here to be in on it a little bit.

My best to Mad, & love to you –

L

Keep out of those suicidal depths.

The recording depends on Petrillo's release.[142]

The Sonata is off the press today. Slight delay because of editor's sickness. Will send you a copy.

I guess Detroit is off on both our sides.

Also, Frauistically speaking, I have never been better.

Why don't you communicate with her directly?

Address: Marketa Morris, 562 W. 113th St NYC.[143]

161. Renée Longy Miquelle to Leonard Bernstein
3901 Edgewood Road, Baltimore, MD
Lundi soir [?October 1943]

Darling Spookietchka!

It's such fun getting a really happy-sounding letter, for yours actually exudes happiness and in turn I am truly heureuse for you.

But after these many years you certainly should have learned to read my so called illegible handwriting . . . after all it's not baritone clefs.

I wrote you a postal this morning; I guess I knew you were conducting then. Your letter which I just found this minute confirms that "je ne sais quoi" which I felt earlier in the day.

What have you been fighting with Oscar – "again" you say – didn't know you did before. By the way, if Sinatra looks anything like the picture I saw of him

---

[142] During the "Petrillo Ban" of 1942–4, even a small company such as Hargail Records had to obtain a release from James Petrillo of the Associated Federation of Musicians before a recording could be issued.

[143] The identity of the "Frau" was shrouded in mystery until the emergence of this letter in 2013. For Marketa Morris' letters to Bernstein, see Letters 197, 256, 260, and 261.

in *Time* magazine, Oscar L. is completely "dingo" to say the two of you look alike.

Now on a "terestrial digression" (or is it terrestrial? poor French me don't know) – those odd pieces of furniture are in storage in Philly. They very likely could be picked up by some moving truck, as a fill-in load and brought to you. A bureau is French for *desk*. It's a flat top desk, mahogany finish, with three drawers on the right hand side and another shallower one across the knee-hole [...] The bench you sat on when you had those cotelettes de veau à la crème, and sat on it many another time afterwards. Sorry the bureau does not happen to be une commode, ni un chiffonier. When I go to Philly, I shall check up on all these things and let you know what there is. If you still want it, well and good.

So you have "abandoned" our baby Steinway . . . a fine unpaternal person you've become.

If I say nothing about my work, students and milieu it's because there is nothing to relate about it. Work? Same as before, interesting to some extent, the students fair (ni lard, ni cochon, honest, conscientious, not at all exciting). Milieu? non existent as yet; although it looks as though it might become so, fairly soon.

Have not been branded a Jewess or a Jew-lover yet, although am sharing the apartment of the mother of a former Curtis pupil and they are Jews. Edgewood Road is a bit like the Newtons, but a more recent development; suburbanish. It's a bit far from town, and certainly adds up to an expensive transportation item, let alone the expense of energy (from 50 to 60 minutes to, and same from . . .) Am biding my time, and looking around for something closer to things.

Saw Lester Englander last Friday (he has a job here as cantor, you know, and he comes down every week). He told me that Leo Luskin is back in Philly . . . wonder if he is as literal as ever.

I must stop this so to have it in the mail for the one and only collection around these parts.

My love to Aaron when you see him.

To you . . . beaucoup d'affection.

R.

162. Leonard Bernstein to David Oppenheim
Carnegie Hall 803, New York, NY
postmark 4 November 1943

Dear Dave,

Item: You should receive any day one (1) copy of the Bernstein–Oppenheim Clarinet Sonata, prepaid, and with my love.

Item: You owe the Frau exactly $26.00, plus $10.00 for the Rohrschach job.

Item: You're very slow on answering letters.

Things are fine, O.K, progressing rapidly.
Let me hear from you.
Love,
L

163. Leonard Bernstein to David Oppenheim

Carnegie Hall 803, New York, NY
postmark 9 November 1943

Dave,
Thinking of you daily, I sometimes get the thought that you are desperately needed by symphonic organizations. Isn't there some sort of honorable discharge that would fit your case? Isn't a "line" (and a livelihood) one of your big needs?
Love,
L
Did you get the Licorice Stücke?[144]

164. Leonard Bernstein to Jerome Robbins[145]

Philharmonic-Symphony Society of New York, Steinway Building, New York, NY
Tuesday [late 1943]

Dear Jerry,
I've been a stinker not to have written sooner, but I guess you know what has been going on with this baby. I have hardly breathed in the last two weeks. Nothing but reporters & photographers, & calls & mail & rehearsals, & I'm conducting this week (listen on Sunday!), & my scores pile up mercilessly. My Symphony parts lie uncorrected, & my – *our* – ballet lives only in the head – only one scene on paper. But *it is* on paper (not legible, but I'll make it so as soon as I can).[146] That should cheer you. Fear not: somehow I'll get it done, though it's a fancy challenge.
The scene that's almost done is from the Entrance of Girl I through to the Entrance of Girl II, & the Pas de Deux. Everyone seems to be quite mad about it – I hope you will be. Of course it's all only 3 or 4 minutes – but that leaves only 16 more!! God, what a race with destiny!

---

[144] i.e. the Clarinet Sonata.
[145] Jerome Robbins (1918–98), American dancer, choreographer, and director. A temperamental and intensely demanding genius, he was without doubt the person who forged the most productive creative relationship with Bernstein: their first collaboration was the ballet *Fancy Free*, followed by *On the Town*, *Facsimile*, *West Side Story*, and *Dybbuk*.
[146] Bernstein is discussing the earliest stages of his work on *Fancy Free*. Progress on the score is documented in several further letters. See Letters 165, 166, 169, 170, 171, and 172.

I now to my naked bed to regain all those vanished ergs. All success to you &
I really will do my best.

Love

L

By the way, I have written a musical double-take when the sailor sees Girl #2
– has that ever been done before? And the rhythm of your pas de deux is something startling – hard at first, but oh so danceable with the pelvis!

165. Leonard Bernstein to Jerome Robbins

Sunday [December 1943][147]

Dear Jerry,

This to announce that I've really finished numbers III & IV. I'm not quite
sure about the exact timing, but I have a bit of a suggestion. What do you think
of the idea of having a *part* of a regular commercial song sung (by the bartender,
or the jukebox, or something) during the pause from the exit of the 2 sailors
with Girl #1 to the entrance of Girl #2? You see, the *pas de deux* between you &
Girl #2 is based on a popular song style, but rather a complicated variation of
same; and I think it might also have a bit more (a lot more) meaning if the song
– a part of it – had already been heard in a purely nonchalant, commercial way.
It might also prove to be a success song – which would help the ballet's career,
& yours, & mine. And it would also provide an increased suspense – during a
welcome lull. And add time–weight to the whole work.

I realize that there are all sorts of handicaps, like paying a singer (what
about bartender?) – or getting sound equipment for a jukebox. What do
you think? The song itself is very blue, intimate, sexy and naive, but unusual
formally.

I'm really doing my best to have it ready in time. It's a battle, but everything's
a battle that ever turns out to be good.

Ran across Agnes de Mille last night, & she's really rooting for you & the
ballet. Contract is signed, I've received initial payment. (I've been rooked out of
all bounds, but I don't care.)

Good success to your tour and let me hear soon. Be good.

Love,

L

---

[147] I am most grateful to Sophie Redfern for establishing the chronology of the undated letters from
Bernstein to Robbins about *Fancy Free*. She has kindly provided the following information: the
contract for the ballet (mentioned in Letter 165) is dated 17 November 1943; the "song" described
in Letter 165 was the precursor to the "radio" mentioned in Letter 166, as can be seen in Bernstein's
sketches for the ballet.

166. Leonard Bernstein to Jerome Robbins
Philharmonic-Symphony Society of New York, Steinway Building, New York, NY
[December 1943]

Dear Jerry,

Your description of the state of the Ballet Theatre sounds gruesome. Don't take it too seriously, and get some sleep. (I should talk.)

I've sent the prints of III & IV off to you. I finally got them in ink: but I still am not satisfied with the end of III. It will have to be changed eventually, but it won't make it too hard for you, will it?

I'm working on the second (relaxed) section. I think finally I've got the idea. It's rather suspended in feeling, with little interruptions of staccato rhythms punctuating slow woodwind phrases. Also, the little dotted tune in No. III ("Much faster") will be introduced in this section, as a kind of hot pants feeling. So, you will have, in general, a slow, slightly tense, slightly serious section, but lyrical, perfumed by these little rhythmic urgings in the balls.

I know you can do fine with it. Does it fit with your plans. (It's all thematically related to the opening dance.) Incidentally, I'm stretching the opening dance a little by adding a little section of about 15 seconds. It makes the form more telling.

I've also decided to give the piano quite a solo role. It grows more & more important all the time (it never remains alone for more than a few measures); and seems to be the auditory key to the ballet – since a piano gives the feeling of percussion, brazenness, hardness, brightness, honky-tonkness, clarity, and intimacy. Don't you agree? How does a solo piano sound at the Met?

I heed heartily your pleas for simplicity. The score actually is very simple – only the rhythms have to be concentrated upon like fury. There's no simplifying the rhythms – they're there, & they're the essence & basis of the whole score – but the notes will be very easy. I think it can be done. We can only pray. Nay, I know it can be done.

We'll be good. If we worry enough, it's got to be a smash. Wish you were back in N.Y. It would all go much faster.

About that radio. It's a problem. You see, the song on which IV is based cannot under any circumstances come just before the pas de deux on the radio. The song itself and its completion in IV must be separated (preferably by the transition before it). Can we have the song sung at the end of III (the radio having been turned on during III, as indicated in the print), and proceed directly to the transition? I mistakenly indicated the Radio *after* the transition, which is just where I *don't* want it. It seems simple enough. Is it OK?

No completed Variations yet. Soon, soon. Grace of God, Moses, & The Società Filharmonica. I'm to meet Toscanini on New Year's Day, & I'm being very Italian these days. Bless you, & write.

Love,
Lenny

167. Shirley Gabis to Leonard Bernstein
[?January 1944]

Dear Lenny,

Will you be a sweet boy and send me Adolph's address in Cal.? have a sudden yen to write to him. I heard the Clarinet Sonata on records and feel moved to give you the following criticism – unasked for though it may be – as an honest human being and a conscientious composer it would seem that you should not be satisfied with your music until it has a little bit of the real Lenny in it – and not just a rehash of Hindemith and Copland.[148]

Of course I haven't the vaguest idea of what has happened to the real Lenny and even if he exists any more.

But if you would only be your own severest critic and not let anything you write go out for public consumption until you are sure way down deep that what you have written is truly worthy of you and that is music that is really music and not trash.

My god Lenny why don't you listen to a few Beethoven quartettes – and perhaps you will find in them the true meaning of artistic integrity.

I hope I don't seem too harsh – but it makes me sore as hell that there is perhaps something deep down inside you that is honest, sincere, and good that the you outside ignores. And Lenny, believe me when I tell you that although you are headed for a brilliant career, it will never be a great one. Your driving ambition to be the most versatile creature on earth will kill any possibility of you becoming a truly great artist in any one of the talents you possess.

Think hard, Lenny, bore way down deep into yourself and find there the courage to be honest. Is your mission in life to be the greatest of all dilettantes??

If you have a real contribution to make Lenny, you must find out now what it is. Concentrate and work and make it a great thing – and don't write clarinet sonatas that make any serious musician think you an utter fool – it's not fair to yourself because you're not really an utter fool.

And I say again, listen to lots of late Beethoven, play the sonatas often. Understanding Beethoven can teach you more about the things you must learn than anyone can possibly tell you.

---

[148] Shirley Gabis Perle wrote about this letter on 26 January 2013 (by email): "I remember writing that letter (what nerve), but who knew, as his father famously said, that he would become Leonard Bernstein. His response came on a post card that I didn't save – he was very annoyed by my criticism. [...] I don't suppose I could have written it if it were not for the depth of the connection between us – a connection that remained throughout our lives. I subsequently played the Philadelphia premiere of the Sonata with Stanley Drucker – to make restitution? The piece, after all, does have Lenny's vitality and charm – I was obviously a stickler for profundity in my youth."

Of course there is no reason why anything I think should impress you greatly, and when I tell you that at present I have little respect for you as a person and an artist, you can think "she's a little fool" and with perfect right – but Lenny, despite all I still have a vague sentimental attachment for you, and remember good things about you that seem completely lost now – and I do wish the very best for you, and sincerely hope that somehow, some way, those good things in you might aid you in becoming something truly worthwhile.

And please send Adolph's address for which I thank you in advance.
Shirley
P.S. Good luck for Pittsburgh.

168. Leonard Bernstein to Serge Koussevitzky
Hotel Schenley, Pittsburgh, PA
[28 January 1944]

Dear Serge Alexandrovitch,

Here I am, finally, in Pittsburgh. I am excited beyond words at hearing my symphony. I must say that to me it sounds just as I thought it would. The orchestra is rough, but in a way like the Tanglewood orchestra – full of spirit, young, and cooperative to a great degree. I am having a marvelous experience here. Even the scherzo is *almost* perfectly played – but for a real performance we must wait for the Boston performance. I have had to make surprisingly few changes. And the *Firebird* is a real, fiery, Tanglewood performance.

Have you been reading about the mess in New York since I left? They phoned me here Monday to return for the Tuesday rehearsal, but it was impossible. Then Byrnes [Harold Byrns] rehearsed *Rosenkavalier,* and made a mess of it; so it came off the program – and Hans [William] Steinberg will conduct. I derive great satisfaction from it all – it feels wonderful to have the Philharmonic really dependent on me.

Jennie Tourel is here, and sends love and kisses. She sings the symphony like an angel. It's really heartbreaking.

Reiner is being very kind and helpful. He sends you his warmest greetings; and he suggests that the greatest triumph over Mr. Rodzinski would be to bring the symphony to New York with the *Boston Symphony Orchestra*!! (He specifically asked me to tell you this!)

My love to you; and keep well until I see you again.
Love to Olga.
Lenushka

169. Leonard Bernstein to Jerome Robbins

Philharmonic-Symphony Society of New York, Steinway Building, New York, NY
[early 1944]

Dear Jerry,

II is finished, and should reach you very soon. It's much shorter than we had hoped, but it doesn't sustain. It's difficult to be bored for a long time on stage, & not bore the audience too. (This is *musical* talk again.) At any rate, it provides all the chances you need for pantomime, gum, drinks, or peanuts. And it is constructed so that it can be easily changed around to suit your timing. When you get it, cross out the last measure (unfinished) of page 10, & proceed to page 11. You will notice that II is really part of I. I think the connection to III is a knockout. I changed my mind from dying out of II to a recurrence at the end of it of the excited opening material, giving the feeling of Let's *Do Something!!* And at the least expected moment the girl arrives. I think you'll agree when you hear it. I don't think that the introducing of "Much faster" in II will hurt: when it appears in III it's all different. I'd like to cut a few measures of it, tho', in III; and have changed the tempo mark to "Somewhat faster." God I wish you were here. It's so hard to write about these things. Be good, though, & happy, & like the stuff as much as I do.

Love,

L

(There's a phrase most Aaron-like in II – I hope you don't mind. It's so pretty I can't remove it.)

170. Leonard Bernstein to Jerome Robbins

Philharmonic-Symphony Society of New York, Steinway Building, New York, NY
[early 1944]

Dear Jerry,

It's awfully hard for us to keep up with each other. I've had a flood of special deliveries that appall me. Jerry – *everything* has gone out to you from #1 to #4 inclusive! Why don't you have it? And I sent two copies for you, keeping three, but apparently [J. Alden] Talbot kept one en route. Henceforth I'll send three – one for Talbot.

I'll do everything possible to get recordings to you pronto. It's next to impossible to find the time, but I'll do my best. I can certainly sympathize about the pianist; it's hard to play anyway, apart from the special jazzy style. Wait till he tries number I!

Keep up the spirit. It's gonna be fine. And I'm in the thick of the Variations. And actually with ideas. *And* please like #II!

Love,

Lenny

171. Leonard Bernstein to Jerome Robbins

Philharmonic-Symphony Society of New York, Steinway Building, New York, NY

[28 February 1944]

Dear Jerry,

Slow, slow, but sure. Number 5 is done and being shipped. It's true enough connective tissue, à la movies, and ought to come off. It's more or less all development of the competition motive, with some of the music of Girl #1 to use (during the rotation) for the conspiring of the two girls.

The pauses at the beginning indicate nabbing the exiting pas-de-deux couple, and indecision about the situation. (Rotation.) Then the competition comes in earnest, developing, through a scherzo-like section to a "dancy" section, by which time I imagine them on the dance floor! In the last measure a snare drum rolls, fortissimo, continuing beyond the music as a lead-in to the first variation (à la circus). I think it works.

My only worry is that it may all be too short (don't forget the repeat! It lasts about 2 minutes). If you need more build up, let me know. I'm leaving tonight (Feb. 28) for Montreal, Canada, where I conduct the Montreal Symphony. I stay until Mon. 8th. Write me at *The Hotel Windsor*, Montreal.

At last, it begins to take shape. I can't wait to finish it. I plan to begin orchestrating in Montreal. Has it occurred to you (as it has to lots of composers, etc., for whom I've played it) that this could be a wow for two pianos alone (with maybe percussion?). It would save much time, rehearsal worries, difficulty of performance, and so on. Billy Schuman thinks it's a natural, & predicts that the orchestration will be very difficult. I only *suggest* this – you can throw it out of the window. But let me know.

I've just spoken to Hurok. The dates are settled – April 18, 22, 24. We'll talk about rehearsal schedules later. I hope it will be orchestrated in time! Pray for me.

These are hectic times. When I return from Montreal I have three concerts with the Philharmonic, including my symphony (alas, no broadcast!). Then, boom, the ballet. I'll be a wreck, but I hope a happy one.

And you take care of yourself too. We need one healthy guy in this project.

Love,

Lenny

There's much more, of course. To answer your letter:

1) I'm making the rhythms as simple as I can. The music more or less depends on them, and they can't be scored any more simply. It has to be – and I think it's all feasible enough. (A word for *two pianos!*)

2) I love your description of #1. It surely can be played a little more slowly, if you need it. I raced it in recording.

3) About the two extra bars on page 6: if you need them, OK; but it makes awful music. Maybe we can straighten it out in N.Y. at the last minute.

4) About the ending of #2: Throw it out. It's not necessary, and I see your point. It's very easily fixed; and I used it at the beginning of #5, where it works much better. Do you want the revised ending immediately?

5) I don't see how #3's beginning can be extended. Is it *absolutely* necessary? It gets so dull. If worse comes to worse, OK; but try to avoid it.

6) In "much faster" (changed to "somewhat faster") it's perfectly OK to extend those contrapuntal bars. Just double them. And a slower pace is OK.

7) On the pas-de-deux, repeat anything you want. (But use the extra bar as it was used at the beginning.)

8) On Variation 2 (which turned out very pretty, and as Aaron says, "dancy") the feeling is mostly sweet plus cocky. Your idea, I think. And change the last chord (it's too sour). The left hand should be:

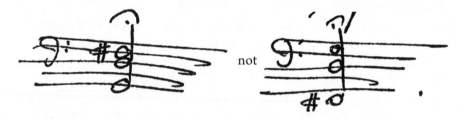

This chord represents a sort of ballet-ish *bow* (or male equivalent of curtsey).

There remains only your variation, which I'm saving for last, the Lindy hop & fight (oy!) and the gag finale. Not too bad. I hope to have it. I hope!! I hope!!!! Again, pray, & be good in the bad West.

Love again

L

172. Leonard Bernstein to Jerome Robbins
New York, NY
Saturday [11 March 1944]

Dear Jerry,

Just a fast one. I've been in Canada for almost two weeks conducting the Montreal Symphony Orch., and returned to find a batch of wires, letters, etc. from you which I have *yet* to untangle. Your last is the one from British Columbia (hello, fellow-Canadian!).

I must dash to conduct a concert at West Point tonight. It's a fearfully frantic year, & I'm almost crazy. But the ballet comes along fine. Have you received No. 5? I hope it's O.K. And I brought the Finale (everything up to the final gag, including a wow Boogie Dance) to the blueprint today.

Didn't you receive my letter to Los Angeles? Judging from your writing, you didn't; and that was a long one, full of discussion. I hope it catches up with you. I told you then that it was OK to cut the end of #2 – you're absolutely right. I'm enclosing the new ending (beginning as if the first measure of p. 12).

(I posed in that letter the problem of whether it might be better to use 2 pianos & percussion, only. It's wild, and only a suggestion.)

Now – Variation 2. I swear to you, Jerry – it's not melancholy at all – not a whit! It must have been played ridiculously. It's whimsical, *very dancy*, a little poignant in the harmony, full of a lyrical jazziness. The main thing is *sweet* and *sympathetic*. The last chord represents a gracious ballet *bow*.

These things are really impossible to discuss like this. For God's sake, get home! I need you!

I'll record the new stuff as soon as I can, but I haven't a minute now for days. Bear with me.

Love,

L

Love to Mitropoulos, if you see him.

173. Aaron Copland to Leonard Bernstein
988 Memorial Drive, Cambridge, MA[149]
Tuesday [25 April 1944]

Dear El Bee,

Got your Friday note today. Poor thing – you don't even know my address – 988 Memorial Drive Cambridge. (Tel. – for you – Kirkland 3042).

I'm tickled about all the excitement, but wish it didn't mean Boston gets a measly two days of you, instead of two weeks. Now that *Rodeo* and *Fancy Free*

---

[149] Copland was a visiting lecturer at Harvard University in 1944.

are hopelessly married,[150] I'd better watch out that people don't say my new one[151] shows Bernstein influences! It's amusing to ruminate on where it will all end – but right now it makes a question mark as big as your piano.

I wrote to Phillie for the *Our Town* parts. Hope they arrive in time!

You must have all the Cambridge news from Helen Coates, so I won't repeat. Our Sanders Theatre concert is tonight.[152] Irving Fine plays the *Danzón* [*cubano*] fine. Apparently all Cambridge Society plans to attend in force.

V[ictor] wired from Miami. He should be in these parts in about five days. (Remember him?)

Be a good boy – take care of yourself – and don't forget your one and only begetter.

A

Give my best to Jerry [Robbins]. He's a sweetheart.

174. Joseph Szigeti[153] to Leonard Bernstein
Palos Verdes Estates, CA
16 May 1944

Dear Bernstein (if you'll allow a grandfather to drop the "Mister"!)

Thanks for your letter to which a hurried reply as my wife's *eye* blood-vessels have been burned by a criminally negligent doctor who gave her infra-red and other "rayons" for her *hand* arthritis! He didn't shield her eyes and she is now suffering untold torture (she was taken to LA to a specialist & will be away for at least 48 hrs).

As I played Mozart A major, Tartini, Prokof[iev] & Chausson in Chicago in *March* my program had to avoid these works, naturally! Your programs will have Beeth[oven] the first night[154] and Mozart D major No. IV with Bartók's

---

[150] A week before Copland sent this letter, *Fancy Free* had its triumphant first performance on 18 April 1944, by Ballet Theatre at the Metropolitan Opera House, conducted by Bernstein. The Ballet Russe de Monte Carlo season at City Center in April 1944 included Copland's *Rodeo*. As for the two ballets being "hopelessly married," they were often mentioned together in press reports.

[151] Copland's "new one" was his "Ballet for Martha," the work that became *Appalachian Spring*. The sketches are dated "June 1943–June 1944, Hollywood, New York, Cambridge." It was first performed on 30 October 1944.

[152] This concert took place on 25 April 1944. The program included works by Walter Piston (Violin Sonata and Piano Trio) and Copland (Piano Sonata played by the composer, Violin Sonata, and *Danzón cubano* played by Copland and Irving Fine).

[153] Joseph Szigeti (1892–1973), Hungarian violinist, pioneer of twentieth-century repertoire, and a friend of Bela Bartók: Szigeti is dedicatee of the First Rhapsody and the *Contrasts* (with Benny Goodman).

[154] 4 July 1944, Bernstein's Ravinia debut. Reviewing the concert in the *Chicago Daily Tribune* (5 July 1944), Claudia Cassidy commented that Szigeti "had an off night, almost as if gremlins rode malevolently on his usually silken bow," but that "the eye and ear inevitably gravitated to the slight young figure on the podium [. . .] A fascinating fellow, this Bernstein, dynamic, emotional, yet under complete control."

Rhapsody No. I (dedicated to me) (9½ min.) the second night,[155] with which choice I feel sure you'd be "d'accord". The Bartók record is no longer on sale but some of our mutual friends are sure to have it (John Hammond's wife? Goddard Lieberson? perhaps Serly? or the boys at Record Collectors Exchange?)

If we can't get a *cimbalom* player who can follow your beat (gypsies often cannot!) we'll have to give the cimbalom part to a piano (with paper fixing between strings). Kuyper or the personnel manager should enquire at Blue Danube Restaurant in Chicago (the pianist there is Harmati) about cimbalom.

Looking forward to our working together.

Very cordially yrs,

Joseph Szigeti

175. Aaron Copland to Leonard Bernstein
Department of Music, Harvard University, Cambridge, MA
20 May 1944

Dear Lensky,

I think I solved the *Our Town* problem. It repeats the waltz as you like, and removes entirely the "ties that bind" section. Some fancy juggling of tonalities on the way, of course. Heinsheimer says he will copy a set of parts "special" if you intend to do it three or four times. OK? And how soon would the part have to be ready for the Stadium, if that's to be the first one?

I'll never forget that face of yours in Reuben's.[156] I've never seen you look so sad. Why you wouldn't even look me in the eye! What on earth were you thinking at that moment??? And the contrast with everyone else seeming so pleased and happy. And me worrying about my lost organ (the voice, I mean). You seemed in a mood to make the most out of any disapproving remark I let drop in your direction. Aren't you idiotical – you know very well I have you hopelessly under my skin. But I'll always watch you like a hawk – that goes without saying.

How does the dinner seem in retrospect – I mean aside from your personal feelings.

You see you owe me a letter.

Alles – but *alles*

A

---

[155] 8 July 1944. Szigeti was evidently back on good form. Though Claudia Cassidy in the *Chicago Daily Tribune* (9 July 1944) noted that the Bartók suffered from "obvious skimpiness of rehearsal," she praised Szigeti's Mozart: "played with his usual patrician serenity and with a special grace and verve for the Rondo, and the orchestra had a touch of the Mozart fire that warms rather than consumes. Mr. Bernstein conducted quietly and carefully, getting his effects more simply than before, but with no less ardor. He has what it takes to learn as he goes along."
[156] Probably Reuben's restaurant and deli at 6 East 58th Street in New York.

176. Harold Newman to Leonard Bernstein
Hargail Records, 299 Madison Avenue, New York, NY
1 June 1944

Dear Lenny,

Here's the long promised royalty statement.[157] Am I supposed to charge for any of the sets sent out for you? I don't know. [annotation by Helen Coates: (No – all gratis)]

Sorry, AmMus refused permission re the K[oussevitzky] Concerto[158] – it is reserved for Koussevitzky.

Glad Lukas is appearing with you at the Stadium.[159]

Good luck,

Harold

177. Herschel, Janice, and Lois Levit[160] to Leonard Bernstein
Camden (*sob*), NJ (*sob*)
3 July 1944

Dear Lennie of the Lenapés,[161]

My tongue hung low and drippy over your program for this week at Ravinia Pk. Oi!!! We noted, with a certain degree of pride, that information as seen in the NY *Times*. How marvelous that your symphony can be heard again – but where do I come in? I have yet to hear it, really. If it is at all possible, please send us a copy of any decent recording you've made of it. Do you think you'll ever do it in Philly? Conduct your symphony, I mean. At any rate, you'd better send the recording or I'll get Lois' boy friend after you. *Then* what will you do?

---

[157] Written on a royalty statement for sales from January to May 1944 of the Hargail Records discs (set MW-501) of Bernstein's Clarinet Sonata. A total of 457 copies sold in that period, with a royalty of 4¢ per set, making a total of $18.28. An annotation by Helen Coates at the top of the page reads: "Thanks for statement. Send royalty to D[avid] Opp[enheim], P.F.C. 12208749, 413th Infantry, Camp Carson, Colo[rado], U.S. Army." Sales of this recording seem to have been livelier than those of the sheet music: a royalty statement from M. Witmark for the three months ending 25 November 1944 lists sales of a mere nine copies of the Clarinet Sonata.

[158] Koussevitzky's own Concerto for Double Bass, Op. 3.

[159] Lukas Foss appeared with Bernstein at the New York Philharmonic's Lewisohn Stadium concerts on 14 July 1944, conducting Ravel's Piano Concerto in G major, with Bernstein as the soloist – probably the first of their many appearances together in New York.

[160] Herschel and Janice Levit (and their daughter Lois) became friends of Bernstein while he was studying at the Curtis Institute in Philadelphia – they were introduced in 1940 by Renée Longy Miquelle. The Levits lived near Bernstein's student rooms and he became a regular visitor (often calling round to take a bath). It was in the Levits' apartment on South 22nd Street that Bernstein finished his piano arrangement of *El Salón México*. Humphrey Burton reports that Bernstein said their upright piano was "just right," "like a Mexican bar room piano" (Burton 1994, p. 84).

[161] A reference to the Lenni Lenape tribe of American Indians who lived along the banks of the Delaware River in Pennsylvania.

Mitropoulos conducted the first two weeks at The Dell – we heard [Arthur] Rubinstein do the Brahms B♭ – as an encore he played the Rhapsodie in B minor, some encore! He & Mitropoulos were pretty terrific. Dimitri made a big hit with his playing & conducting of the Prokofieff 3rd. Tonight we hear [Nathan] Milstein do a couple of jobs: the Mendelssohn & the Lalo.

Will you be back with the Philharmonic in the fall or are you going to free-lance? It certainly would be great if you can get to the Academy to do your symphony.

Best wishes,

Herschel & Janice & Lois

P.S. Dear Lennie, Incidentally, for the summer we are at the address on the back envelope. The house is strictly from modern, as a matter of fact Herschel calls it the "Museum of Modern Art" for short.[162] If you get the chance come visit us – there's a Steinway and you can have your own room & bath. Let us know when. J

178. Leonard Bernstein to Serge Koussevitzky
33 West 67th Street, New York, NY
26 July 1944

Dear Serge Alexandrovich,

I am sending you, with my love and deepest congratulations, a few notes on your birthday, which form a small sketch for the piece I hope soon to have for you. Life is so complicated and busy not that I cannot set any really definite date when I expect the composition to be finished, but I am trying to make it as quickly as possible without sacrificing any quality: – I want this to be as fine as I can make it, since it is for you, who represent quality itself to me.

Please accept this little sketch now, and let us hope it grows into a composi-tion worthy of your greatness.[163]

---

[162] The address (noted in pencil by Bernstein on the first page of this letter) was 628 Stetson Rd, Elkins Park, PA, and it is indeed "modern" – in fact it's a magnificent house designed in 1940 by Louis Kahn for his friend Jesse Oser.

[163] The sketch enclosed with this letter is inscribed "A happy birthday and many more glorious years for Serge Alexandrovich: with love, Lenushka, N.Y.C, July 26, 1944." It is an early version of what became, with very small modifications, the start of the *Age of Anxiety* Symphony. The tempo marking is *Andante contemplativo* (changed to *Lento moderato* in the Symphony), otherwise the music is largely the same apart from minor changes; no instrumentation is given – in the Symphony it is played by two clarinets. It is interesting to find this idea so fully formed in Bernstein's mind as early as 1944: W. H. Auden's poem *The Age of Anxiety* – the inspiration for the work as a whole – was not published until July 1947, three years after this sketch. The eventual work was not only first performed by the Boston Symphony Orchestra conducted by Koussevitzky (on 8 April 1949), but dedicated "To Serge Koussevitzky, in tribute".

Shirley joins me in wishing you long life and happiness.
Devotedly,
Leonard

179. Leonard Bernstein to Serge Koussevitzky
2074 Watsonia Terrace, Hollywood, CA
[August 1944]

Dear Serge Alexandrovich,

Here in Hollywood one sometimes loses perspective on symphonic music; the commercial aspects are so important to everyone here – and the quality is reserved for the mediocre. So it is a great pleasure to contemplate my program with the Boston Symphony – it is a thought like a spring in the desert.

If the entire first half is to consist of the Brahms [First] Piano Concerto, I thought that the second half might offer *Verklärte Nacht* of Schoenberg (this is Schoenberg's anniversary year), followed by a suite from my ballet *Fancy Free*. This seemed well rounded to me, and my ballet suite (about 15 minutes) might make a good closing piece.[164]

---

[164] In the end, the concert, given on 24 and 25 November 1944, consisted of just two works: Brahms' First Piano Concerto with Jesús María Sanromá as the soloist, and Shostakovich's Fifth Symphony.

If you feel that *Fancy Free* should come after intermission, then the program could close with a more usual fin-de-concert piece like the *Firebird*.

Don't you think there should be a short overture, or the equivalent – perhaps Mozart – before the Brahms? Or perhaps the radio requirements prevent this?

What I should really like is to have ready the composition I am planning for you – but I guess I just can't be finished in time. Did you receive the little birthday sketch I sent you?[165]

I hope these program ideas are satisfactory. I would be so grateful for any advice you would give me on this concert. I'm very excited about it, and I want it to be good.

I think of you every day, and send you my love –

Lenushka

180. Sid Ramin to Leonard Bernstein

Headquarters, 84th Inf. Div., Special Service Office,[166] A.P.O. 84, c/o Postmaster, New York

10 September 1944

Dear Len,

Just a note to let you know that I'm leaving for overseas shortly.

In the past, I've been able to tell you where I was and a bit about what I was doing, but the following address makes that a little difficult; however, I can tell you that I'm able to get to New York very frequently – so there's your clue.

I was home on furlough and heard some of your recordings – the side dedicated to Shirley brought back some wonderful memories and the William Schuman bit delighted me.[167] By the way, I saw a copy of *I Hate Music* (Five Pieces for Children) displayed very prominently in a large music store in St. Louis.

Since mail is being censored, I find it hard to write to the folks at home – they're thirsting for news and I'd like to tell them what's happening but I can't.

My pleasures are very simple now and eating at a nice restaurant or club and seeing a musical is just about the ultimate in enjoyment for me at this stage in the

---

[165] See Letter 178.

[166] Ramin served as a Corporal (20120408) in the 84th Infantry Division. From the end of August 1944, the 84th started to arrive at Camp Kilmer in New Jersey, in preparation for departure to Europe. The Division sailed on 20 September 1944 and arrived in England for training on 1 October, landing on Omaha Beach in Normandy a month later, before taking part in the Ardennes Offensive (the Battle of the Bulge). Sidney N. Ramin of Roxbury, Mass., is listed in the *Roster of Officers and Enlisted Men, 84th Infantry Division, European Theatre of Operations – World War II* (Viking Press, 1946). During his time in the Army (in which Ramin was in Special Services), he also found time to arrange the music and conduct the orchestra in a revue called *It's All Yours*, performed at the Stadt Theater in Heidelberg and in Paris (personal communication from Sid Ramin).

[167] Two of the *Seven Anniversaries*.

game. Yesterday I saw *One Touch of Venus* for the second time, ate at the Kungsholm and had a couple of drinks at a good bar – it all made for a pleasant day. The dance routines (Agnes de Mille) in *Venus* impressed me tremendously – but, then again, maybe four years in the army have warped my sense of what's good and what isn't. I expect to be in New York again several times and would like to see you for a minute if you're available and have a minute.

Mail is important in the life of a soldier whether he be overseas or in this country. Overseas, though, the importance of mail cannot be overemphasized and getting a letter from you will mean very much to me.

Each day must be exciting and busy for you and I often think of the contrast between an average day now as compared to the days when we could ramble through the park in Roxbury and while away the hours.

How are your folks? Do you ever run into Harold Shapero?

Best always,

Sid

181. Leonard Bernstein to Aaron Copland
33 West 67th Street, New York, NY
[received 28 September 1944]

Dearest, wonderful A,

I'm a dawg, a dawg, a dawg not to have done this before. You can always check on me because your last letter was a birthday letter one full month ago. But I've reread it so many times, because it brings back something that you think everything is O.K. without, and then suddenly you find it isn't at all, and somehow something's got to be done about the Aaron Copland side of one's life,[168] which is always turning out to be a major side. If that sentence makes sense, especially in Tepoztlan, you're a genius. Just a new way, of course, this being the 57936th letter I've written you, of saying that I adore you.

For the rest, I'm back in town, with problems, being busy, all of which is boring old fluff for you by now. One realistic chimera is that I've got to move by Saturday (Three Days) and I have no apartment. I have thought of temporizing in your loft, for maybe a week or so, if Helen (Coates) still can't find me a place;[169] but I hesitate to ask, and maybe I will find one. I spend the weekends in Detroit now (horreur) conducting broadcasts of the Detroit Symphony (three). Next week is in Boston with the Ballet, so I'm really running out on Helen and leaving the whole problem to her. I'm looking at a really wonderful place on East

---

[168] When Bernstein wrote this letter he was hard at work with *On the Town*, but the need to do something about the "Aaron Copland side" of his life and career was ever-present.
[169] An indication of the growing importance of Helen Coates in managing Bernstein's domestic affairs, as well as the difficulties of finding an apartment in New York City.

57th (Kostelanetz' building), but it's a cooperative and you have to buy it for $5000 and then pay $175 a month upkeep, and then the Board of Directors has to vote on me, and decide whether I look rich enough and dependable enough and presentable enough to be accepted. They've looked into forty references besides my bank balance, and I resent it and stand for it only because it's such a dream of an apartment and I can play music there and I want to live in it.

The show [*On the Town*] is a wild monster now which doesn't let me sleep or eat or anything; in fact the world seems to be composed of the show the show the show, and little else, except a *Verklärte Nacht* or a Schumann symphony here and there. Maybe it will be a great hit, and maybe it will lay the great *egg* of all time. It's an enormous gamble.

You're sweet to dedicate the *Our Town* piece to me; I could do with a dedication or two in these grim loveless days.

God how I wish I were with you. How long do you plan to stay? Forever? Indefinitely? It can't be. At least come back for the opening of the show, which will be, with the grace of God, and if we get George Abbott to direct which looks likely, around Christmas time. And please write a lot, and find me someone nice to bring home as a present, and write a great piece, and give my love to Victor, and I had lunch with P[aul] Bowles and [Yvonne de la] Casafuerte today and got drunk. Bless you, I love you.

L

182. Aaron Copland to Leonard Bernstein
Tepoztlan, Morelos, Mexico
9 October 1944

Dear Dawg,

You're in the delightful position of getting a letter from me without having to answer it, because I'm coming home before you can safely get one here. I have just two more weeks in Tepoztlan (till the 23rd), then to Mexico City for two days, and then I fly to Washington (the 25th). Martha Graham is supposedly doing a ballet of mine that week-end.[170] No one has seen any public announcement of the event – nor have I – but [Harold] Spivacke keeps writing it will take place, so I go on faith. I ought to be back in my hole on 63rd St by Oct. 30th or Nov. 1st. Then we can turn on the "AC side of your life", whatever that is.

In retrospect the summer seems frightfully short. I never got settled until August, and didn't get a piano until the middle of the month. Also, I've been alone a lot of the time. V[ictor] has been away a good deal, doing odd jobs or

---

[170] The first performance of *Appalachian Spring* took place in the Coolidge Auditorium at the Library of Congress on Monday, 30 October 1944.

seeing odd females up in Mexico DF. I find I don't particularly thrive on solitude. So, altho the setting was perfect, inspiration has been spurty. I guess I'd better come home.

Sometimes Mexico seems too much to bear. In Sept. the rain got out of hand, and it poured like hell for three weeks. Then we had a small cyclone that sounded very big in our valley. Then suddenly the water works of the town, being all above ground, goes kaput. Then comes the news of a minor rebellion two miles away and the government sends troops. Then the cook announces the horrifying news that eggs have just gone up to 4 cents apiece. Then suddenly the sun comes out, there's water in the excusado, the troops go away, the eggs go down to 3½ cents and Mexico seems like heaven on earth. It's a peculiar country.

I'm tickled pink that the show isn't going to come off until Christmas.[171] That means I can hang around the theatre during rehearsal period, than which I adore nothing better – as you know. I hope you found a perfect place to live in, but *not* in the Far East 50s. (Too far away.)

Till velly soon.

Love,

A

183. Leonard Bernstein to Philip Marcuse[172]
40 West 55th Street, New York, NY
25 October 1944

Dear Phil,

Thanks very much for your recent letter, and for the Shostakovich[173] records. The latter arrived yesterday, but I have not yet had the chance to hear them yet. I'm curious to hear how it all sounds, even to the thumping of my irrepressible foot. Who knows, hearing this thumping on the record may cure me of that bad habit. Anyway, it will be good for me to hear just how it sounds to the radio audience. [...]

The show[174] goes into rehearsal in early November, and I'm working night and day to have the score ready by then.

Please give my thanks to the person who made the recording, and, again, my thanks to you for sending them to me.

Sincerely yours,

Lenny Bernstein

---

[171] *On the Town* opened at Broadway's Adelphi Theatre on 28 December 1944.

[172] This was one of the earliest contacts between Bernstein and his Detroit friends Philip and Barbara Marcuse. In the 1950s, the Marcuses provided a kind of model of stability for the newly married Bernsteins, and offered them warmth, advice, and support.

[173] Probably a broadcast of Shostakovich's Fifth Symphony, which Bernstein conducted in Detroit during the 1944–5 season.

[174] *On the Town.*

184. Philip Marcuse to Leonard Bernstein
Stockwell & Marcuse Advertising, 2026 National Bank Building, Detroit, MI
26 December 1944

Dear Leonard,

Here's hoping that *On the Town* will be a tremendous success. I read *Variety*'s preliminary review of it, and I gather that it was damned good even though the reviewer didn't know how to say it.

Although we haven't communicated for a couple of months, I have been following your progress and enjoying your radio appearances. We saw *Fancy Free* two weeks ago and found it truly terrific. So did everyone else.

We look forward to seeing you in New York three weeks hence, and once again, our best wishes for your newest musical triumph.

Sincerely,
Phil Marcuse

185. David Oppenheim to Leonard Bernstein
Germany
27 December 1944

Are You Happy???

Do You Stay Awake Nights??

Would your autobiography be entitled: "My Life as a Mole" or – "Digging my way thru Europe"??

Do you fall flat on your face when someone whistles [. . .] Have a *crush* on screaming music? Burpgunitis etc. etc.??

Try Bernstein's Little Battle Pills – Delicious to chew slowly.

Nibble your neurosis away!!![175]

N.B. For adventurers only – my ass!!

I've been watching *N[ew] Y[ork]er* and no *On The Town* yet. [. . .] Do I get score & book over here? And are you gonna write?

A letter I wrote to you to California came back – you had moved and not left a forwarding address.

Now – what are you doing – how is Marketa [Morris]? Adolph [Green], Judy [Holliday], Betty [Comden] – I'd sure like to have Judy here to line my foxhole.[176] She is 20th Century Foxing?? I saw a bad picture of her in a movie magazine some time ago.

Will you conduct the N.Y. orch this year? Or is Art[177] still mad?

Love,
Dave

---

[175] This recalls a much earlier Bernstein letter to Oppenheim (see Letter 122).
[176] Oppenheim and Judy Holliday were married in 1948.
[177] Artur Rodzinski.

3

Conquering Europe and Israel
1945–9

The post-war years saw Bernstein's conducting career flourish, not only in the United States but also as the first American-born conductor to develop an extremely successful career in Europe. His letters home from London, Prague, Paris, and elsewhere are fascinating evocations of great cities recovering from war. These were also the years during which Bernstein composed some of his most serious orchestral scores: *Facsimile* – a ballet with Jerome Robbins – and *The Age of Anxiety* Symphony, composed for Serge Koussevitzky and the Boston Symphony. Despite the encouragement of George Abbott and Betty Comden, Bernstein did not immediately follow up the Broadway success of *On the Town*. Koussevitzky, an inspiration as well as a mentor, gave Bernstein regular opportunities to work with the Boston Symphony Orchestra, but their master–pupil relationship was not without its difficulties, as the tense exchange of letters in December 1946 reveals: Koussevitzky objected strongly to Bernstein's proposal to program his own music in concerts with the orchestra, and Bernstein's only option was capitulation, in order to restore amicable relations. The Koussevitzky connection was not only important personally but also professionally. *The Age of Anxiety* was commissioned by Koussevitzky, who conducted its first performance on 8 April 1949. But it was Bernstein who gave the first American performance of Britten's *Peter Grimes* on 6 August 1946, and on 2 December 1949 the world premiere of Messiaen's *Turangalîla-Symphonie* (a work to which he never returned after the first three performances) – both of which were commissioned by the Koussevitzky Music Foundation in memory of Natalie Koussevitzky. Bernstein also conducted the first European performance of Copland's Third Symphony, another Koussevitzky Foundation commission, in Prague on 25 May 1947. In other words, Bernstein's reputation for playing large-scale works that were recently composed was nurtured to a significant extent on repertoire that Koussevitzky had commissioned.

In February 1946, at a party given by the Chilean pianist Claudio Arrau, Bernstein met Felicia Montealegre. In the course of the year they grew ever closer – a relationship Bernstein chronicled in his letters to Helen Coates – and at the end of December the couple were engaged in Hollywood. Though the engagement was broken off in September the following year, they were eventually married four years later, in September 1951 – a union that both parties entered into in the full knowledge of its potential difficulties, the most significant being Bernstein's sexuality. Something of his turmoil about this is revealed in letters from Marketa Morris (the "Frau"), whom he consulted from the early 1940s onwards, and Renée Nell, another psychoanalyst Bernstein consulted in the later 1940s.

Bernstein's visits to Israel were to become a central part of his career, and they did much to define his Jewish identity. His letters from 1948 to his mother and sister, to Koussevitzky, and to Copland reveal something of the profound impact the country and its people had on Bernstein, the warmth and passion of his commitment to the Israel Philharmonic Orchestra, and the joy he drew from the experience of working with these musicians. For Bernstein, conducting always had to be "fun" – in other words a genuinely rewarding experience – if it was to be worth doing at all, especially when he could never find enough time for composition. In the Israel Philharmonic he found an orchestra with which he was usually at his happiest, even when – as on his 1948 visit – he was confronted with an astonishingly punishing schedule, and concerts that were often interrupted by bombing raids; he was there, after all, during the Arab–Israeli war. On 14 May 1948, David Ben-Gurion had declared the establishment of a Jewish state to be called the State of Israel. War broke out the next day, and was at its height when Bernstein arrived to work with an orchestra that was not only a cultural symbol, but a potent national one as well.

186. Leonard Bernstein to Renée Longy Miquelle
40 West 55th Street, New York, NY
3 January 1945

Dear Renée,

How sweet of you to remember, and send me the Michelangelo. I adore it. I hope it was you, because it contained no card, no greeting of any sort, and I am at a loss as to what occasion it represents. New Years? Christmas? Some obscure but meaningful anniversary? The opening of the show? Paul Bowles' birthday?

Well, the show [*On the Town*] has opened and is a phenomenal hit, in spite of all. The reviews are fantastic raves, especially the *Times* and *PM*, and the *Hollywood Reporter*, which called it the greatest musical ever produced! It's thrilling, and I would be a rich man, except that whatever money I get goes back to Uncle Samovitch for taxes. But it's nice to feel that you've earned a stupendous sum, even if you hold it only for a week.

Now I am bleary with a throat infection, and a general let-down collapse, and struggling to get back into my beard (long-hair) and study Brahms' First for Pittsburgh next week. It will be fun to be back there, and this time with a whole program including *Fancy Free*, the Ravel Concerto, *Euryanthe* and Brahms' First.

I stretch long and loud, yawn, smile, toss my mangy curls, and close with love, to get back to the *Partitur*.[1] Let me hear how everything goes with you. When do you come around again?

Love, and thanks again.

Lenny

Spookietchka

187. George Abbott[2] to Leonard Bernstein
The Town House, Los Angeles, CA
20 February 1945

Dear Lennie,

According to the calendar you must now be back in New York where I shall not arrive for another five weeks, by which time you will probably be waving your baton in some distant city.

I hope soon, however, that we shall all find ourselves together again discussing *life* and *integration*.

I'll postpone that for the moment and take up the subject of opera. I have constituted myself an authority on the subject because I don't like opera; also I have seen very few operas. I find myself moved by the sheer beauty of the sound that assails me, and occasionally by the visual effect, but never by the story. I cannot get from it the feeling of being carried away (to quote from a recent musical comedy hit). Plays, movies, symphonies, novels seem to me to be artistic wholes. Operas seem magnificent anachronisms. So, when I talk of opera, in re [my] interest, I am talking about a new form which does not now exist: I am talking about something which I expect you to create. It will have integration all right, but it will be unhampered by tradition, it will use picture techniques, top dancing or any other feature that adds up to excitement – and it will ruthlessly eliminate the *ridiculous*.

As far as *On The Town* is concerned, please don't let yourself be distressed by minor criticism from some of your pals. It is a wonderful score – a bit too profligate perhaps, too many fresh melodies thrown in where developments of existing ones would have done. That, however, was not your fault – except

---

[1] The German word for an orchestral score.

[2] George Abbott (1887–1995), American theater director, producer, and writer, who also had a successful career in Hollywood. By the time he collaborated with Bernstein, Robbins, Comden, and Green – all making their Broadway debuts – in *On the Town* in 1944, Abbott had already had decades of experience: first as an actor (his debut was as Second Yeoman in the 1915 revival of Gilbert and Sullivan's *Yeomen of the Guard*), then as a writer, producer, and director. His earlier Broadway musicals included *On Your Toes* (1936; book), *The Boys from Syracuse* (1938; book, producer, and director), and *Pal Joey* (1940; producer and director).

as you share the responsibility for an original structure that wasn't very practical – but the result of changes done in a hurry. The final result may not have accorded with the ideal upon which it was based, but it is good. And, what is more, you should feel proud that you have proved yourself so adaptable. Had you been the inflexible type, you could have gummed the whole works. In my opinion you should congratulate yourself that you have had the experience and learned so much of practical theatre matters without going through a disaster to pay for it.

I read *Self-Analysis*[3] on the train. I gave myself the works. But I'm afraid my subconscious is an almost empty cellar. The book more reposes in the hands of one whose subconscious is boiling away. [. . .] We were on the train coming out and there's a fellow who not only needs it, but who knows he needs it. We deduced that he hated his mother – we also staged *King Lear* – it was quite a pleasant trip.

Kiss & Tell[4] is going to be a good picture. Everything is going substantially as I would have it.

The only flaw in my California life is that I have strained a muscle in my side and have to give up tennis for a few days. Since tennis is practically the rock upon which my local life is founded, I am very sulky about the matter.

Give my best to Betty [Comden] and Adolph [Green] when you see them. I wish I were there. But I soon will be.

Yours, as always,

George

188. Leonard Bernstein to Helen Coates
The Windsor [Hotel], Montreal, Canada
28 February 1945

Dear Helen,

Could you reserve two tickets for Arthur Rubinstein (for *On the Town*, natch) for Friday eve., March 9th. And *prepaid*, please. He's a swell guy. The concerts are great.

Love,

L

---

[3] *Self-Analysis* by Karen Horney, first published in 1942.
[4] *Kiss and Tell* was a 1945 comedy starring Shirley Temple as the American teenager Corliss Archer. It was based on the Broadway play of the same name (both were written by F. Hugh Herbert, 1897–1958). The stage play had been produced and directed by George Abbott: it opened at the Biltmore Theatre on 17 March 1943 and ran for a total of 956 performances, closing on 23 June 1945.

189. Betty Comden to Leonard Bernstein
29 April 1945

Dear Lenny,

This must be the first letter I have written you since those apologetic little notes of Revuer days, airily explaining why no check was enclosed – yet. No – a quiet nine piece orchestration is not what is on my mind right now. I'm spoiled forever by the sound of thirty pieces anyway.

We've been meeting with Paul [Feigay], we've been meeting with Oliver [Smith] – we've been meeting with George [Abbott] – and the last has been, needless to say, the most fun of all. And the history of these meetings is briefly this, some of which you know already: We had originally intended to get an idea and do a show with George, leaving one for P[aul] and O[liver] Inc. for some other time. But in the mean time through Bill we were approached with the idea of *The Greeks Had a Word for It* – made into a musical about the twenties, and involving Gypsy R. Lee. After the reading of the play, which is good, we realized that it is not typical of the twenties at all – it was just done at that time – so why bother with it? Better to make up out of whole cloth and our fevered brains – a story of our own, using the twenties as a background. Much as we wanted to ignore the whole thing and concentrate on something for G.A. we couldn't help being intrigued by the period, its color and significance – and against our will got some ideas. These were enthusiastically received by everyone, and they seemed eager to plunge at once. Extremely un-anxious to face as much terrifying vagueness as we had been subjected to before, and dying to do something – anything – with George, we said we would do the thing only if he were involved. We told George all about it, and he got really excited about what we've worked out so far – has met with the Fitelson Gang, and it looks as though something will work out – a co-producing venture plus, of course, George's directorship. Being a very smart man, and not liking the idea of a "star" type deal (possibly involving 10% of the show – and I mean Gypsy of course), and not liking the idea of having to write a show "around" anyone – George doesn't think Miss Lee is essential to the show, but thinks we should get to work and write it, and if there's a part for her, fine, and if not – fine again.

Things are hardly in what you would call a definite state just yet, but we have, naturally, been talking about someone who might be equipped to knock out a coupla tunes to go along with all this – and your name just happened to come up. Not having talked to you, Lenny, since our "opera" meeting, I have no real idea what you are planning. But word filtered down to us from Bill and Shirley, that you like the idea, but (this from the latter) that you didn't feel too keen about working with Feigay and Smith again. As you can see from the above we had a qualm or two ourselves. But now George is in the picture, very much so. And we are sort of stimulated by the prospect. Having him makes all the difference in the world.

I am not going to send you a card saying "I will / will not do the show" – and expect you to underline and return. But we would so love to hear from you, since talking to you is impossible for another week. Musically of course the show has terrific possibilities – and the period and theme are surprisingly significant plus allowing for lots of beauty and general appeal, as well.[5] It would be wonderful to do this show with you, Lenny – of that we are sure. Please write.

Much love,

Betty

190. Izso (Isadore) Glickstein[6] to Leonard Bernstein

7 May 1945[7]

Dear Leonard,

Please accept my heartfelt thanks for the wonderful gift you sent me. I enjoy immensely playing and singing your finale of *Jeremiah*.[8]

You have brought more dignity to the Jewish people than anyone else I know.

I had breakfast with your father today and he told me you may be at Burton's Bar-Mitzvah. I hope you will.

God bless you!

I. G. Glickstein

191. Jerome Robbins to Leonard Bernstein

13 May 1945

Dear Lenny,

It was rather nice seeing you the other night at Al and Dick's.[9] What with your letter and our chance meeting, I thought that maybe (as you said) we could get "that

---

[5] The show became *Billion Dollar Baby*. Bernstein wasn't able to write the score, so Comden and Green turned to Morton Gould. The choreography was by Jerome Robbins, Oliver Smith designed the sets, and Max Goberman was the musical director – all of them later involved in *West Side Story* – and George Abbott directed. It ran for 220 performances, from 21 December 1945 to 29 June 1946.

[6] Izso G. Glickstein (1891–1947) was the Russian-born cantor at Temple Mishkan Tefila, where Bernstein had his formative musical experiences. He described Glickstein as "a fabulous cantor who was a great musician and a beautiful man, very tall, very majestic [. . .] and he had a tenor voice of such sweetness and such richness" (Burton 1994, p. 8). Glickstein was indeed an outstanding cantor, as can be heard on his recordings of "Baroish Hashonu" and "Yaale tachnunenu miarev," made for Victor in 1925 (Victor 68710).

[7] Dated "7-5-1945," so possibly 5 July 1945.

[8] Bernstein must have sent Glickstein the arrangement of "Lamentation" for voice and piano or organ version (adapted by F. Campbell-Watson), published by Harms in 1945.

[9] A restaurant that was a favorite with the *On the Town* company.

old show out of our heads" and do some work. However I have just finished reading the interviews in *Dance Magazine*.[10] Have you seen them? Well, in yours, you talk about the trilogy idea based on *Fancy Free*, even mentioning *Bye Bye Jackie*[11] by name and describing the material. And somehow, Leonard, it all sounds like your idea, and to boot my name isn't even connected with my own registered play.[12]

Now it all might be the fault of the interviewer, and if it is, too bad, because it makes you appear to be dishonest. But if it is something you did yourself, it is a low, dirty trick – and I wouldn't try it again. Fortunately the majority of people in the dance world already know about *Bye Bye Jackie* and the Theatre Guild and others have read it, so that if and when it's done, it won't seem that you have supplied my material and ideas.

I don't like writing a letter like this. But I thought it best we get straightened out on things like this. We are well suited to work together as far [as] talents are concerned, and it would be good if we could manage to do some more ballets. But this kind of business is not a good gesture either as a friend or business associate. So let's have no more of it.

Sincerely,

Jerry

192. Leonard Bernstein to Shirley Bernstein
Mexico City, Mexico
24 June 1945

Queridisima Hermanita,

I'll be home very soon. I leave tomorrow. I love this place madly, but I can't wait to get back. I go to Hollywood tomorrow, where [Irving] Rapper has

---

[10] Francis A. Coleman, "Composer Teams with Choreographer," *Dance Magazine* (May 1945), pp. 12–13.

[11] *Bye Bye Jackie*, subtitled a "ballet play," was written by Robbins in 1944 and was proposed to several composers including Aaron Copland (see Pollack 1999, p. 486) and Paul Bowles, as well as Bernstein (Burton 1994, p. 140). In an interview by Anna Kisselgoff for *The New York Times* (29 May 1994), Robbins recalled the project, intended as a way of explaining the background of one of the sailors in *Fancy Free*: "It was about Jackie, a boy living in Brooklyn, who's getting letters from his brother in some foreign place . . . The kids on the block begin horsing around, and Jackie can't take it. He sees that everyone in the background he's caught in is going off. So he enlists in the Navy, and his girlfriend says, Bye-bye, Jackie. It was a mood piece that went in and out of reality." Robbins explained that the work was never choreographed because Bernstein didn't want to write the score. Their next collaboration was *Facsimile*, in 1946.

[12] Robbins' irritation is understandable. Coleman's interview with Bernstein includes the following remarks: "For some time, Leonard Bernstein has considered the composition of a trilogy of ballets to be built around *Fancy Free*. Mr. Bernstein explains that the trilogy would consist of three one-act ballets with a connecting link in the story which would enable them to be presented as a complete evening's entertainment. The opening work, to be called *Bye, Bye Jackie*, is to furnish a picture of adolescence, in a Brooklyn setting, of tender and emotional quality. *Fancy Free* would become 'something akin to the scherzo movement of a symphony', and carry the story of the ballet through its middle section. Following it, the third work, yet to be planned, is to furnish the fitting climax to this vignette of American life."

arranged a dinner for me which includes my following fans, believe it or not: Bette Davis, Cary Grant, Van Johnson, Ethel Barrymore, Judy Garland, Dana Andrews, *and others*. Want to join me there?

Mü la dü,

Ladüm

Bought you a *fantastic* opal!

193. Bette Davis[13] to Leonard Bernstein

River Bottom, [Glendale, CA]

[late June 1945]

Leonard,

This is to say hello, that I will be listening Sunday, and any other time I know you will be on the air – to say I hope so very much – opportunity will often present itself so I can see you again, and to say – you and your music came along when I needed them desperately. I had hit a new low, and since being exposed to your mighty talents, I am on high – there is probably nothing in the world so encouraging for the future of the world as a super talent in someone – it is the only true inspiration and help in believing the world is really worthwhile. I feel privileged to have spent an evening with you – and thank you so much for playing for me when I know you didn't feel like it. It is an evening I will always remember with the most enormous pleasure. It is hard to have all this *said* to one, I know that. Thus the *written* expression of my delight at meeting you.

Irving[14] has very nicely been willing to be messenger boy for me – wish I were my own messenger boy and could be there to *see* you conduct. You won't mind if I become a 1945 version of Madame von Meck, as regards you.[15] There are some changes in the script already. We have seen each other – that is not according to style – and financially there is no similarity. The only resemblance:

1. I am older.
2. I adore your music.
3. I like you.

Bye for now.

Bette

---

[13] Bette Davis (1908–89), American actress, and an idol of Bernstein's. As her delightful letters demonstrate, their admiration was mutual.

[14] Irving Rapper (1898–1999), British-born film director. He was friend of Bernstein's and director of several of Bette Davis' most important films, including *Now Voyager* (1942), *The Corn is Green* (1945), and *Deception* (1946).

[15] Nadezhda von Meck (1831–94), Tchaikovsky's great patron who stipulated that they should never meet. Coincidentally, one of the reasons Bernstein visited Hollywood in the summer of 1945, en route to San Francisco, was to discuss a possible role in a film to be directed by Irving Rapper: a biopic in which Bernstein would play Tchaikovsky opposite Greta Garbo as Madame von Meck (see Burton 1994, p. 142).

P.S. If you ever have time, send me an autographed photograph, would you: "A real fan I am – Leonard Bernstein."[16]

194. Bette Davis to Leonard Bernstein

River Bottom, [Glendale, CA]
[after 1 July 1945]

Dear Piotr,

That is not the right spelling – but you get the idea. Your wire I adored. A letter I wrote you for Irving to take to you in San Francisco is still waiting for him to pick up – he went a day too early. When I have recovered it, will send it on.

I am in bed with a cold, and loved my hour with you and your music from San Francisco. Only one thought: if they have you must they inflict upon us Mr. S.[17] – a duller violinist never lived in my opinion. If you disagree we will talk about that later. The rubles I am saving up to bring in person. Anyway you were very sweet to wire – I so hope I see you soon. Your *Fancy Free* music is – well – it is Bernstein, and musically I can give you no greater compliment in my opinion. My letter written a few days ago still goes – the Baroness Von Davis adores your music and likes you – till later.

Bette.

I sent your stockings off to be framed today. We created great gossip, all because you asked me to sit beside you at the party while you were playing. Such simple basic people the Hollywood person is. I am flattered – hope you are – all jealousy and I don't blame them. Will drink a toast to you every Wednesday night, in memory of the Wednesday last week when I first heard you play – I am only furious about one thing, that all the time you were here last summer I didn't have the chance to meet you – it is so silly.

Bye again.

B

---

[16] Bette Davis received the signed photograph she had requested and sent a telegram on 14 August 1945: "Please forgive delay in acknowledging photograph. Madame von Meck is very grateful and loves it. Bette."

[17] Evidently, Bette Davis wasn't a fan of Joseph Szigeti, who appeared with Bernstein at a Summer Promenade concert of the San Francisco Symphony on 1 July 1945. Szigeti played the Mendelssohn Violin Concerto and the program also included a suite from *Fancy Free* and Shostakovich's Fifth Symphony.

195. Bette Davis to Leonard Bernstein
[Summer 1945]

Dear Lennie,

Irving and I are working together. The set – so Irving says – is very like your apartment.[18] If so how you must love it. I was most happy to contribute for your composer – and hope his career proves to be all you feel it is.

Read about you so very often in the *New York Times* – my bible of New York – and it is so wonderful to know that your triumphs continue. It must be a great satisfaction to you. Your Madame Von Meck – me – is very proud – only feels slighted that no requests for funds have been forthcoming – can't I get you into my debt somehow? You are not living up to your predecessor – he was much more helpless. Thank you for your message about my marriage.

That was as far as I got last week. In the meantime, I banged my head on the windshield and was away for a couple of days, but a hard Yankee head is able to take it, thank god. Our picture progresses very well today – maybe my head was injured after all – anyway my best to you Lennie – and here's to our next meeting. It was so nice to hear from you. Love,

B. Von Meck.

Bette

196. David Oppenheim to Leonard Bernstein
7 August 1945

Lensky,

Did I dream that you called me the "laziest guy I know" or did you actually say it? Let me know. Future relations may depend on it. The actual quote was: "Besides your other faults you are the laziest guy I know". My impression is that you merely stated the thing as a fact without anger. A good thing.

The new atomic bomb is the most frightening thing that has happened ever ever.[19] Why am I the only one I know to realize this? The whole future of mankind depends on its future use. Imagine what could happen if a few unscrupulous men were to control the principle. Or what a counter-revolutionary device it is. Or how it makes a war with Russia more possible. And when you figure it is still in its primitive stages.

---

[18] Though the letter is undated, the first paragraph refers to *Deception* (1946). Rapper directed this *film noir* with a cast led by Bette Davis, Paul Henried, and Claude Rains. It tells the tempestuous story of Christine (Davis) and her stormy relationship with a composer (Rains) and a cellist (Henried). Erich Wolfgang Korngold wrote the Cello Concerto by "Hollenius" performed at the film's climax.

[19] This letter was written the day after the bombing of Hiroshima on 6 August 1945, and two days before the bombing of Nagasaki on 9 August.

Of course the good it can do should not be underestimated, & really referring to the principle of atomic power, not the bomb. Men are knocking at
the portals of heaven (you may quote me).

When mother said there was a call from Montreal this morning I was a bit
scared that something was the matter. I'm glad you called though. After you left
Monday I felt very blue. Hearing you cheered me up. [. . .] I hope to hell you do
get out to Frisco. My time would be so limited. You might have to meet me
someplace to make it all worthwhile. We'll see later.

I have started *The Well of Loneliness*[20] but I have little patience for anything
just now, being worn out, nervous as a cat and as irritable. Reaction to 30 days
of hard living & no sleep. In fact after you called I had breakfast, read the paper
and went to sleep for 6 more hours.

Mother sends regards to you and to Helen.

I have to stop now before I fidget right off the chair.

Please don't be lonesome. Be happy, serene and effective & write!

Love,

Dave

197. Marketa Morris[21] to Leonard Bernstein
Country Club House, Tannersville, NY
21 August [1945][22]

My dear Lenny,

I just read an article about the possibility of your going to Hollywood. Shall
I congratulate you?

It seems that your decision of not continuing with our work is now a definite
one – so that a few words of mine won't disturb your decision. Of course I would
like to get some information about your trip to Mexico, your plans for the next
future and last [but] not least how you feel mentally!

---

[20] The famous lesbian novel by Radclyffe Hall, first published in 1928, which had been the subject
of an obscenity trial in England and legal challenges in the United States.

[21] Marketa Morris (1889–1965) was a psychoanalyst, known to Bernstein and his closest friends as
the "Frau". A brief article announcing her death appeared in *The New York Times* on 26 May 1965:
"Milwaukee, May 25. Mrs. Marketa Theiner Morris, a psychoanalyst who practiced in New York
from 1942 to 1958, died here Sunday at the age of 76. She was the wife of Prof. Rudolph E. Morris
of Marquette University. Mrs. Morris, who taught child psychology to teachers in Prague from 1936
to 1938, practiced here for six years until her retirement in 1964." The letters from Marketa Morris
to Bernstein provide some insights into Bernstein's innermost thoughts from the psychoanalyst he
consulted most regularly in the 1940s, including comments on his dreams and on his sexuality. It is
apparent from the letters that while Morris saw Bernstein on a number of occasions, she was frustrated by his schedule, which made it impossible for him to see her on a regular basis.

[22] There is no year on this letter, but it can be securely dated 1945: not only did Bernstein spend
some time in Hollywood that year, but on 15 August 1945, a few days before it was written, the
Japanese surrender ended the Second World War in the Pacific, the "Peace" to which Morris refers.

If you feel that writing or talking to me could still influence you and that you are sort of uncomfortable or afraid of it – skip it please and let's wait.

Not only am I personally interested but I also would like to have your report for my records. But – I am repeating – *only* if it *doesn't interfere with your emotions*.

I am enclosing something which might interest you.

How do you feel about the Peace?

Sincerely yours,

Marketa M.

To the 5 of September: Tannersville N.Y., Country Club House.

198. Leonard Bernstein to Aaron Copland
New Hotel Jefferson, St. Louis, MO
Saturday [1 September 1945]

Aaron darling,

Well, the monstrous experiment of juxtaposing you and Chávez turned out to be just that – a monstrous experiment – but such fun! [...] Everyone loves your piece – and, strangely, the *Sinfonia India* was a big hit. One of those Bernstein surprises.

I love you & miss you – and here are the reviews. It gets lonely: won't you send a slight letter? Too many people & dinners & dullards here. Nice – but what happens after midnight.

See you velly soon.

Love

L

I'm here til next Sunday (9th).

199. Leonard Bernstein to Aaron Copland
New Hotel Jefferson, St. Louis, MO
Thurs [September 1945]

My darling A,

[...] I wish you were here. How about dropping in on me suddenly, like a visit? I have a suite, and it's not far. We'd really have a vacation. I've banged my head around over these programs for Paris (I hope it's still on) and come up with these:

I.

Schuman: Prayer

V. Thomson: Five Portraits

Barber: Violin Concerto

—

Bernstein: Jeremiah

Gershwin: Am[erican] in Paris

II.
Piston: Concerto
Harris: Symph no. 3
Blitzstein: Freedom Slop[23]
—

Randall Thompson: Scherzo from Symph II
Sessions: Adagio from Symph
Copland: Lincoln or Billy

That seems to take care of everybody (except D[avid] D[iamond]), and the programs are a little long, but not too much so. And boy, they're hard! Most of the pieces are short, no? I don't think either program is over an hour and a half. What do you think? Couldn't I play the Ravel Concerto on the European program, and your Piano Sonata on the chamber music?

I offer no cheery word on the subject of your father, since I know you're the best one in the world at that.[24] But I hope you're better, and back in stride: I refuse to take *arthritis* seriously in you! It doesn't go at all.

I love you, and hope you'll write soon, if you don't drop around personally; my love to Victor & Ted.

L

The St. Louis Jazz Society is taking me on a tour of old Southern jazz haunts tonight!

200. David Oppenheim to Leonard Bernstein
19 September 1945

Dear Len,

I read in the paper and Shirl tells me that you are up to the neck in auditions. How does it look? Many vacancies to fill? How does your clarinet section shape up? If I were to get out could you hire me for next season or can't you fire a man merely because you have someone else you would rather have play in his place? What does 1st clarinet pay in your orch? Naturally that is the prime consideration. Gotta compare your offer with dozens of others. If I am not let out in time and Local 66 doesn't reinstate me, we will have union trouble.

All the above assuming you don't run in to a great virtuoso of the licorice stüchel to replace hypothetical me. Don't!

---

[23] i.e. *Freedom Morning*, composed in 1943.
[24] Copland's father, Harris Copland, died in 1945 (see Pollack 1999, p. 15).

I've been getting down to L.A. to my Aunt Pauline's for some quiet outdoor weekends, complete [with] charcoal broiled breakfast – eggs, bacon et al.

My cousin Judy is here now. She is the one (do you remember) who introduced herself and a hundred other kids to you as my cousin in Detroit. Wonderful charming 15 yr old colt – the only girl cousin on mother's side of the family – my pet. She saw you at the Berkshire concert this year.

Nothing much to say. I'm grand, as Shirl puts it, except for the old army disease, lackanookie. And not a thing to do about it here. Well, can't keep me in for ever. Congress would raise too big a stink.

Love,

Dave

Seymour's address?

201. David Oppenheim to Leonard Bernstein

United States Army

20 September 1945

Boy, are you lucky – the second letter from me in as many days. But I just got your note. And it was so good hearing from you that I just had to write.

I had no idea that your season was just 12 weeks. I did imagine though that the wages would be low, being paid by the city etc. Too bad you got going so late. Still, 12 weeks is a short season and it kills the season for a musician. I can see where it is hard getting the right players. What is the net result now? How do you stock up and can you whip them into something that satisfies you and that can play modern things? I think you can.

Here is my setup. Quite a while ago it was announced that men with 45 points up to May 12th and/or 50 up to Sept 2nd would not be sent overseas. I had 47 on the first count, 52 on the second. OK.

Today an order came out restricting to the camp area all men with between 45 and 59 points. These men (me) will be shipped someplace by the 24th – Monday (this being Thursday). So almost by the time you receive this I will be entrained for my new station. What, what, what for, or why for, I don't know. Maybe training cadre for new recruits or processing cadre for dischargees. I wish I knew. I don't, but I'll let you know along with my new address. Pray that I am shipped a few thousand miles *East*.

I was supposed to go to Frisco, Sunday through Thursday, for some kind of parade, but now it is off. I was planning to wire you tonight for Seymour's address.

After a month, a good month too, of feeling in contact and in tune and in love with Mad, I suddenly find myself out of contact. I wish I understood why. It has happened before, but without much reason, that has to do with thinking and dreaming too much about her. I don't know why this should have the effect it did, if it did. But that is the way it is. Here, away from you all, your memories remain clear and bright for a while, then suddenly dim and it leaves me very much alone. But I am stronger now than ever and I don't feel unduly depressed. *I miss you all, and it all.*

I haven't slept well either. I sleep, yes. But not the timeless death sleep I used to sleep. When I wake up now I am aware of every hour, the full 8. The way it used to be, I felt as though I had just closed my eyes when I got up. Now it is like I feel when I am sleeping with someone, e.g., slightly conscious because of the fear of rolling too much and waking them up. And I dream now too. At my aunt Pauline I practically floated off the couch two nights in a row. And who was the lucky girl? Aunt Pauline. Aren't I awful though.

I'm looking for a score to *Daphnis*. Can you help without troubling too much.

Don't pills help your sleeping? Or don't you want to try that? When the season or the rehearsals begin you will be better. Meanwhile try doing one thing at a time, forgetting the rest and stop having emotional orgasms. Why you have done all you can, that is enough. Forget it and go to sleep, relax, play some game etc. Really, Lensky, you may be the world's best musician, but you need some looking after – and some common sense. After all what is *really* important. You, or whatever it is you are beating your head against the wall about?

And don't dare say I don't understand how much I don't understand how much it means to have the right kind of players etc. But a little horse sense, or you won't be conducting anything after 40. You'll have ulcers, diabetes, angina and coronary thrombosis etc. etc. etc. Christ man. Take it easy. Do I have to desert to see that you do?

Tell Shirley I'll write her soon. And hello to Helen please.

Love,

Dave

202. Mildred Spiegel to Leonard Bernstein

[Boston, MA]

25 September 1945

Dear Pete,[25]

I was asked by an organization in Boston to write to you for them. The United Order of True Sisters (in existence for 70 years and founded to benefit crippled children) would like to know if you could play for them – from 30 to 45 minutes – at a luncheon and meeting at the Copley Plaza – Tuesday afternoon, Jan. 29th. They want to pay you $200 plus all expenses. It is to be their biggest affair of the season and they naturally want a big attraction to help them

---

[25] Mildred Spiegel's pet-name for Bernstein.

raise a lot of money. They maintain rooms in the Children's Hospital and work in conjunction with the Harvard Commission on infantile paralysis.

Of course I told them about the busy year you have ahead of you, etc., and that the date might conflict, etc., but I'd write you anyway.

I am in no way connected with this group so please don't feel that a refusal would in any way affect me personally – just do as you like about it. If you can make it, they'd like lighter stuff – some Chopin, your Liszt Rhapsodie, some boogie-woogie and you can talk too if you don't want to play all the time.

I know you're terribly busy these days, so have Helen drop me a note so that I can tell them your answer.

Things are getting gradually better all the time – had my first Hershey bar in years today – also had lunch with Re La Mi.[26]

Gonna see your ballet again next week – the same night as *Undertow* and *The Gift of the Magi* – Lukas conducts.

[...]

Best of luck for the orchestra. I know it will be a brilliant yearrrr. Will hear you in February. Take care of yourself and get some sleep some time.

Much love to you and Helen from
Mildred

203. Joseph Szigeti to Leonard Bernstein
Palos Verdes Estates, CA
1 October 1945
[Telegram]

Just learned with shock of Bartók's death.[27] Would it be possible for us to give part of your program pair December 31 January 1 or failing that January 21, 22nd as Bartók memorial with one orchestral work and the Portrait in D major and Rhapsody #1 dedicated to me. Naturally no fee involved. These two works take only 19 minutes together. Am doing Berg memorial with Metropolis [Mitropoulos] General Motors December 30. Rhapsody which we played at Ravinia would have first New York performance.

Joseph Szigeti

204. David Oppenheim to Leonard Bernstein
4 October 1945

Dear Len,

Just a few interestin' facts about some interestin' people we know.

---

[26] Renée Longy Miquelle.
[27] Bartók died in New York on 26 September 1945.

I saw Seymour [Meyerson] in Frisco. Both he and the town are fine. I like him very much. We had a good time roller-coasting etc. [...] That we missed you was obvious in the way the conversation kept turning back to you. He is a great guy, Len. An amazing combination of artiness and common everydayness, plus a healthy objective interest in people and things that make him nice to be with.

And the town is wonderful. I like the hills, water, fog, crooked angling streets, cable cars and the variety of good bars and restaurants. Lots of music too. If my aunt weren't here in L.A. I would go to S.F. on these 3 day passes. But I enjoy even more than S.F. a place to stay and vegetate. I hate the eternal search for rooms and walking lonely streets in search of companionship, that goes with being in a big town minus connections. And I could never get there enough to make any lasting ones.

I thought that your *P.M.* interview was swell, esp. the statement on government sponsorship of music and art etc. But tell me more. How would it work out in relation to other private endeavors as regards comparative wages and as to who is used etc. It could be another political football. I am definitely interested in the idea though.

That is all! You don't deserve more.

Love,

Dave

Tell Shirl that I will write, and soon.

Hello Helen!

205. Leonard Bernstein to David Oppenheim
1239 Broadway, New York, NY
postmark 8 October 1945

Dave Dollink,

You dope. I've been delaying writing you in hopes of receiving your new address. Your last letter said you were on your way – and here you are, exactly as before. Anyway, it's a pleasure to have word again.

I'm awfully happy that you and Seymour [Meyerson] hit it off. He's a top-notch kid, and so are you, of course, so it's a natural. I did receive your little recordings, but they wouldn't make [i.e. work] on my machine. Finally (yesterday) I hit on a plan for making them go, and was finally able to distinguish some highly hysterical (or drunk) carrying-on about roller-coasters & trolleys. But you both talk simultanacklach, so most of it is lost to posterity. Excellent spirit, though.

Tonight's my big, big night.[28] I'm a nervous wreck, but the orchestra is so fabulous and excited and young and interested and in tune and precise and enthusiastic, etc., etc., that if it's not a hit tonight I won't understand it. (Aaron's

---

[28] The opening concert of the New York City Symphony season. In *The New York Times* (9 October 1945), Olin Downes waxed enthusiastic: "Leonard Bernstein, with an orchestra materially improved

Outdoor Overture, Shostakovich 1st [Symphony], Brahms 2nd [Symphony].)
And the latter is a joy.

You really ought to hear it. Aaron was at the rehearsal this morning, and
said – "At last we have American Brahms – lyrical, like a popular song." I'm
happy.

I miss you like the devil. So what *is* happening to you? Don't be so vague.

Ewige Liebe,

Lenny.

Your remarks on government subsidy are to the point. It's a matter of recon-
ciling this with the popular interpretation of the "democratic method". I'm
thinking of agitating for a public referendum in NYC. Much love – and if you
come across the article on me in *Collins'* disregard half of it as pure invention.

206. Rosalyn Tureck[29] to Leonard Bernstein

448 Riverside Drive, New York, NY

5 November 1945

Dear Leonard,

At long last, here is your "personality analysis". I cannot take these things
seriously but they are wonderful fun especially since the person who did it does
not know to whom the doodling belongs.

According to the analysis it looks as tho you must face the fact that you definitely fit into the genius category. As far as I am concerned from what I heard in
your conducting the other night, you do.

I hope to see you at the party after my recital on the 12th.

Regards,

Rosalyn

[Enclosed with this letter is the "Personality Profile" for Bernstein:]

This person's character shows a peculiar and great singleness of purpose.
The sex development is practically nil and the personality which might have
started to assert itself at one stage in the man's development has become
completely absorbed by career.

The career is complex. Its division is almost geometric and the line of demar-
cation, very clear. For each phase of the career, there is a well thought-out and
deliberate development. The dark areas indicate the creative and the white areas

---

over that of last season, conducted a concert of exceptional brilliancy last night." The Shostakovich
was a highlight: "For vividness, conviction, imagination we do not expect soon to hear this performance surpassed." Downes also enjoyed the high spirits of what Copland called "American Brahms": it
was "a reading of high excellence. We believe Mr. Bernstein is now in a good place, with an orchestra
of young musicians like himself to work with, and a repertory to mature in. Here is a conductor."
[29] Rosalyn Tureck (1913–2003), American harpsichordist and pianist noted for her Bach playing,
though she made her Carnegie Hall debut playing the Theremin.

the mechanical. The mechanical seems to dominate the subject and he is more curious about the development of it at this stage than he is about his creative development. There is one point about the career, which seems to come early in the middle life, which indicates the great peak of success. The subject will have attained a very happy balance of creation and mechanics.

The sex symbol is interesting in that the line – the only line connecting it and the rest of the personality chart – extends right to the career symbol. This indicates that the subject's development is completely concentrated in his career. His personality symbol shows the same direction. There is no embellishment, no additions to it, there is no sign that any development of self has been accomplished. The sign connecting it with the career is merely two extensions from the sex symbol.

It is interesting to note that, in spite of the fact that the sex symbol is not developed as a physical unit, it is present and the aesthetic aspects of it will be found in this man's career creations later in life.

This man may not be a good mathematician, but he has an excellently organized mind. It is well disciplined as demonstrated by the complete lack of extraneous matter. It is also the mind of a purist.

This man has great ego-maniacal tendencies and will often go to bizarre ends to gain a point. By nature though, he is retiring and socially shy. His great ego, however, serves as a shield against society.

A fruitful creative life is indicated, but an extremely lonely social life will be his lot.

207. Joseph Szigeti to Leonard Bernstein
Palos Verdes Estates, CA
27 October 1945

Dear Lenny,

I am delighted that I have at last succeeded in wresting [Harl] McDonald's[30] permission to play the Bartók pieces with you on March 4th and 5th – that is, a fortnight before my appearance with the Philadelphia Orchestra in Carnegie Hall. I am intensely looking forward to doing the Bartóks with you; you know how much he means to me.

I hope that Elkan Vogel of Philadelphia has already sent you the Bartók *Portrait* Opus Five [No. 1]. It was at Bartók's express wish that I revived this forgotten piece of his in Budapest in 1939. He was present at the rehearsals and of course at the concert too, and admitted that this forgotten youthful work of his still meant a great deal to him. (I think it must have been written around 1905 or 6.)

---

[30] Harl McDonald (1899–1955), general manager of the Philadelphia Orchestra (1939–55) as well as a teacher at the University of Pennsylvania and a composer.

In the score he gave me, he made a few slight retouches which I will show you in December when I am playing in New York with Mitropoulos. He cuts out the two trombones on page 13, and the first harp – i.e. one of the two harps – on page 15.

As to rehearsals, here is my schedule immediately before our concert: February 26th, Baltimore; 27th, Washington; March 1st afternoon, Baltimore, Peabody; March 3d Sunday afternoon, New York City, Frick Museum. So you can dispose of my time, say on Saturday afternoon, March 2d, and Monday and Tuesday morning.

All good wishes, and au revoir in December.

Yours ever,

Jóska

208. Leonard Bernstein to David Oppenheim

1239 Broadway, New York, NY

11 November [1945]

Armistice Day. Ha.

Dollink Dovidl,

I'm a swine. I haven't written a word in almost a month. Which is not to say that I wasn't thrilled at this seeming prelude to a discharge – or is it? And which is not to say that I miss you like crazy, & wish you home, and in my magnificent orchestra. Of course there would be union difficulties, since I don't suppose you're in this local. That's a big headache. Same is true of Jesse Ehrlich, who is getting out next week. I have huge hopes & plans for next season – all my favorite guys in the orchestra, 24 weeks at least, a commercial radio sponsorship, which looks very likely, and a greatly increased Victor recording contract, which I've already got.

Seymour [Meyerson] has *not* been here, but seems to be arriving this week – just when I'm about to leave for a week in your favorite city of Rochester. I'm doing *Jeremiah* there for the first time, with a mezzo soprano named Zelda Goodman, a student at the school. She's sweet, and it ought to be fun. Last week was Cincinnati – great triumph – and this week I had my 3rd pair with my *own* – do you hear? – my own orchestra. They're the best yet. So much love for music makes them sound as no other organization. And I could still use you in it. And how.

I've just returned from a run-through of Adolph & Betty's new show.[31] It's a killer, a beast, and slumps only in regard to the score, which is fine but dullish, like so much Gould.[32] If that boy had an iota of real *personal personality* he'd be the best one around. But, alas.

---

[31] *Billion Dollar Baby* opened on 21 December 1945.

[32] Morton Gould (1913–96), American composer and conductor. Bernstein never had a high opinion of his music.

Be a good guy and don't copy my delay in writing. Aren't you ever coming back –

All my love,

L

209. Renée Longy Miquelle to Leonard Bernstein
814 Cathedral Street, Baltimore, MD
Jour de la Ste Renée, 12 November 1945

Cher P'tit Kietchka,

How to begin ... I don't know! – because last week and now the next few days make my heart very full of you, for many "anniversaries" are now crowding in together with a very pleasant feeling of pride and well-being while basking in and relishing your musical doings.

In two days it will be two years that you had your "big chance" – as they say – and as all of us who know you *knew*, you've kept right on.

I need not gush and certainly do not want to, for my appreciation of your talents and all attendant accessories is more deeply and dignifyingly rooted than that.

However, since it seems a total impossibility to get to you or see you unhurriedly and en "tête à tête amical" I *must* write and tell you how completely satisfying it is to know you, and to find you growing and maturing all the time; even though there is still more to be done and reached.

My second visit to your orchestra rehearsal last Monday pleased me far more than the first, mainly because you did so much that was really beautiful with the Mozart, and what is more you put it across.[33]

You know what my criticism of the last movement's tempo was (even though Helen said to me beamingly that it was a real Koussy clip, therefore marvelous) – I don't agree. Should that be a criticism? Koussy always takes *El Salón* at a more deliberate pace than it is meant, or so I've heard, yet *you* don't play it that way.

Of course we all know what a temptation it is to play faster than necessary or slower in slow movements; but again, Lenny, *you* of all people must not give in

---

[33] The Mozart symphony that Bernstein conducted on this occasion was No. 39 in E flat major K543, a work he performed many times subsequently, and recorded with the New York Philharmonic (1961) and Vienna Philharmonic (1981). Olin Downes reviewing the concert in *The New York Times* (6 November 1945) had some of the same criticisms of this early performance as Longy. He commented that it was played with "vigor and clarity" but that Bernstein "was inclined to drive rather than release song from the instruments." Paul Bowles in the *New York Herald Tribune* was more enthusiastic: "The high point of sonority in last night's concert came with the Mozart Symphony. Here the orchestra showed that it was no longer 'good, considering', but good, period. The audience responded with rounds of applause."

to that sort of thing. Your sense of tempi is usually so completely right, please don't lose your balance and throw us off ours. But, the rest of the Mozart was so good and so very elegant and nicely wrought that it was a real delight to hear.

Why did you not tell me that you are doing *La Création du monde* at your next concert? Lucky I got the N.Y. paper yesterday for the first time in months!! So I'll be at rehearsal next Monday together with a young friend who cannot attend the concerts, since she works from 3 or 4 on till 11 p.m. (Please tell Helen to put me and Geraldine Viti on the list for admittance.)

Somehow, Randall's symphony let me down. I had a more exalted recollection of it . . . very likely because it had been your first conductorial vehicle and I must have been more eyes, heart and anxiety than ears then.

Last night, more nostalgia besieged me . . . you will know why when I tell you I went to see *Of Mice and Men* again. Five years have elapsed; and it is just as new, strong and right as it was. It very likely will be so for many years. Aaron's music is so right for it too. It is a very poignant experience. Thanks for all time Lenny for having introduced me to Aaron's music.

Why did you not warn me and tell me Marc was back and not looking so well? I could not recognize him – a dreadful feeling – only when that marvelous smile of his burst forth did I know who it was . . . Oh! but what infinite sadness in that smile, darling – I was shocked. What's happened?

When are you to conduct in Boston? And where will you be on November 23, 24, 25?

All my love,

Renée

P.S. Please remember to bring your cuff-links to rehearsal on Monday. You know I want to have them engraved.

210. Leonard Bernstein to David Oppenheim
New Hotel Jefferson, St. Louis, MO
postmark 27 November 1945

Dave,

If it weren't for the fact that you'll probably be out of the army and living around the corner from me by the time I return to NYC, I should be all wails and drama at this moment. Such a teaser as last week with you was! It hit me most clearly as the train pulled out of Penn Station, and I realized that we hadn't even said hello. Maybe we'll never really have to say hello again. Wide-eyed idealism.

Have yourself a time in New York, and be very good to Seymour [Meyerson]. You're so good together, and I like to think of you as reciprocally understanding, even complementary. Singly you're vastly superior guys. Together you're practically God. Let me hear from you in this bleak, foggy place, where, of all things, a charming southern thunderstorm is now raging. The streets are very dark and full of lonely faces. The hotel is very bright and full of lonely faces.

Much love,

L

211. Aaron Copland to Leonard Bernstein
Limestone Road, Ridgefield, CT
Tuesday [?4 December 1945]

Muy querido chatito,

Here is your "slight letter". It's being written from the top of a bleak looking ridge on which sits perched a little house in which sits writing little me to you. I've been here since Sunday. Whether I stay the winter or not depends on whether I can get old Posh[34] up and down the garage without falling off the cliff. The main assets to the house are 1) a nice work room with Steinway grand and 2) a lovely view out the Steinway window. But the ground is snow covered and makes me think longingly of Cuba.

I missed Leinsdorf's concert[35] – being here – and couldn't even get the broadcast. But last week I was in Cambridge listening to Fauré for two days[36] – and discussing tangled Tanglewood problems with Judd & Koussie. (Did you know that Rodzinski offered his place for sale in the *Times* – for $40,000? Maybe you'd like to buy it – in which case I could rent a room from you at $6 per week. Otherwise maybe I'd better write to Mrs. MacSomething Furniss for a house.) Kouss empowered me as ass't problem unraveller to invite you on the faculty – *and* – aside from *Grimes* being at his exercise, there is a good possibility – says Kouss – that he will invite you to conduct a Festival concert of your own. Maybe you'd like to dash off the text for a pageant for the Music & Culture people, which also seems to be on Kouss' mind. Well – sounds like a busy summer. (Stravinsky says maybe he'll come, but no definite answer until Jan 15.)

I've tried to imagine what the [*Sinfonia*] *India* and *Salón* sound like juxtaposed – but the mind rebels (Antheil in his book says I composed the *Salón* in the Hollywood-Franklin Hotel, which he recommended to me. How do you like that for hanging on to the skirts of fame?) Anyway St. Louis seems to have accorded the familiar L.B. triumph.

---

[34] Copland's nickname for his car.

[35] Possibly a reference to one of Erich Leinsdorf's concerts with the Cleveland Orchestra on 11 and 13 October 1945, which included *Appalachian Spring*.

[36] At the end of November 1945, the Harvard Music Department put on four days of concerts to celebrate the centenary of Fauré's birth. On 25 November, Copland wrote an article in *The New York Times* previewing what he described as "a shrine for Fauré devotees."

Dave O[ppenheim] came to see me. He's a sweetheart. And so are you – (but for very different reasons).

L[ove],

A

P.S. My phone no. Ridgefield 637 – Ring one three.

P.P.S. Thanks to you I'm now a member of the Baldwin family.

P.P.P.S. I'm writing a Symphony – just in case you forgot.[37]

212. Seymour Meyerson[38] to Leonard Bernstein
Camp John T. Knight, Oakland, CA
5 December 1945

That you, Lennie!

My return to the Oakland Army Base was heralded by the collective "Did you have a good time?" and made official when everyone in our section walked me over to the PX[39] for gooey ice-cream sundaes and lots of cakes.

Flying time was approximately 22 hours, with far too many waits for re-fuelling and what seemed like stupid and pointless conversations between our pilots and the Commanding Officers of the different fields. Navy goes in for a helluva lot of tradition which makes Army routine seem much more sensible simply by contrast.

At any rate, Dave [Oppenheim] and I have solved our transportation problem, and will probably return the same way. [...]

The night Helen [Coates] invited me to see *Der Rosenkavalier* with her at the Met, we had dinner at the Damascus Gardens, a small Armenian restaurant on 32nd Street. The conversation as we ate was highly personal, and I tried to avoid a good many of her questions. The thing that continually surprised me was not how much she knew about your sex life (in itself kind of "shocking") but how she accepted it, and sought to discover what satisfactory arrangements could be made for you in order to [be] assured that your career would not suffer. You can imagine how perplexed and embarrassed I felt, but since she was so frank I thought it was all right to listen, and also to see just how far her knowledge ran. The greatest shock for her was the idea that you would one day marry and have a family. The slightest mention of this idea caused her to tremble. I was very

---

[37] Copland was working on his Third Symphony.

[38] Seymour Meyerson was a close friend of Bernstein and of David Oppenheim, but otherwise he remains a mystery. He is *not* the same Seymour Meyerson who served in the Army Signals Corps, became a scientist specializing in mass spectrometry (and also co-authored a booklet called *Folk Dancing for Fun*, which helped pay his way through university). I am most grateful to this Seymour Meyerson for taking the time to explain that he wasn't the one who knew Bernstein.

[39] An abbreviation for "post exchange," a type of store operated at US Army bases, which in turn generates income to support recreation, sports, and entertainment.

much caught by the look in her eyes, that expression which inferred an end to her way of life with you, should some "other" woman enter your life. Maybe that's why she can afford to be so tolerant towards your perversity?

Seeing David this coming Saturday. Do you think February will really come?
Much love,
Seymour

213. Leonard Bernstein to David Oppenheim
1239 Broadway, New York, NY
postmark 18 December 1945

Dovidl,

Nu? The last I heard was from Seymour – that he was in doubt as to whether you ever reached camp by 8:00 a.m. after your bout with a stray damozel in a S.F. apartment. Watch it, baby: no point in fucking up your chances for immediate discharge. And I hear you are now being groomed for Wall Street.

I am collapsed at the moment with a tough concert tonight,[40] and very little energy. Christmas will be nothing but sleep, eat and you know. My sun lamp helps somewhat.

St. Louis was a joy. What a *La Mer*! And an immaculate 5th Brandenburg.
Great love to you.
Come back.
L

214. Leonard Bernstein to Renée Longy Miquelle
Ridgefield, CT
postmark 31 December 1945

Dear Rélami,

Your invitation came just a little bit too late for me to change my commitments. Funny you should have asked me and Aaron, because here I am at his sweet snowbound little country house, one hour from New York, and without that slightest indication that New York exists even one hundred miles from here. Anyway it was sweet as hell of you to ask us, and I hope you have a real good rest. To say nothing of a very happy and prosperous Nouvelle Année.

What do you think of our friend Hendl?[41] Were you there by any chance? I was out of town conducting, unfortunately, and missed the excitement, but I'm sure it was swell.

---

[40] It was an unusual program, including Beethoven's Op. 131 String Quartet arranged by Mitropoulos for string orchestra, Ravel's *Shéhérazade* (with Jennie Tourel as the soloist) and *Alborada del gracioso*.
[41] Walter Hendl was Rodzinski's 28-year-old assistant at the New York Philharmonic. When Rodzinski was taken ill, Hendl took the concert on 8 December (the Overture and Scherzo from

When does Claude get back?

Aaron sends his best, and I my love.

Spook

215. Leonard Bernstein to David Oppenheim

1239 Broadway, New York, NY

postmark 19 January 1946

Dear Davrelink,

There's a limit to this silence routine. You *are* supposed to be out, you know. And then comes word from Seymour [Meyerson] that you're very much *in*, and that he's just seen you in your new layout. What, may I ask, is giving? What is the Hotel Vanderbilt?[42] Was your letter written from there implying that you lived there? Are you still dully employed in financeering? Of course I wouldn't dream of anyone else's playing the Klarinetten piece – but I've had to assign it tentatively to Hoffman, since you said you'd be out in January and here it is almost February. Tell all, and very quickly since time wastes fast, and anyway I miss hearing from you.

Your letter was wonderful but so N![43] I couldn't answer sooner because I've been tearing around the globe again – but now it's serious. Let me know.

I've been in Rochester a second time (playing the piano too) and seeing no sign of orchestral resentment. Who told you that anyway? They love you there, and your licorice[44] teacher even expected you might play E♭ on our tour in March. On the other hand Bill Schuman loved you too. (You really impressed him, you charm-monger.) But Juilliard is overcrowded to the bursting point. What will you do? Tell all, my love.

Love, my love,

L

I leave Wednesday for Cincinnati, so write immediately. My love to Seymour & San Fran.

Mendelssohn's *Midsummer Night's Dream*, Schubert's "Great" C major Symphony, and Rachmaninov's Second Piano Concerto) at very short notice. On 9 December 1945, *The New York Times* reported that Hendl's debut "offered a striking parallel to that of Leonard Bernstein, who first attracted wide attention, when at the last moment he was called upon to conduct the Philharmonic."

[42] The Hotel Vanderbilt in San Francisco was used by the Army's Officer Pay Section, where Oppenheim was working.

[43] It's unclear what Bernstein means by "so N".

[44] Clarinet.

216. Jerome Robbins to Leonard Bernstein

Late Monday night [21 January 1946][45]

Len,

It was a really wonderful concert tonight. I'd never heard you really play anything but *Fancy* and *Town* – & the Bach was quite an exciting experience. Then the Stravinsky was new to me – & God! What an experience. 3 Bravos for that alone. I rode along on the *Don Juan* nicely anticipating the Variations – & then I sat & chuckled & gurgled & beamed & nodded & emphasized & had a wonderful time. They sounded marvelously – & the only complaint was a little something on the encore of Harold's dance, trying to picture him keeping up with it. But it sounded wonderfully unsaddled by dancers.

So thank you for a very special evening of music. Good luck & continuous success.

Jerry

217. Joseph Szigeti to Leonard Bernstein

The King Cotton [Hotel], Greensboro, NC
2 February 1946

Dear Lennie,

I was so sorry not to have been able to call you last week but the only time I had was on the day of your *Symphonie de Psaumes* and I didn't want to bother you *then*! I listened in on Monday and was greatly impressed by your performance.

As to the order of the two Bartók pieces I know it would be more orthodox to play *Portrait* and then *Rhapsody* but I have the inescapable feeling that the reverse order would be more *right*! The sturdy, "typical" Bartók first and then this unexpected "horizontal" piece . . . Especially as it is in a way a "memorial", the transcendent ending of *Portrait* seems more appropriate than the brusque (and not very effective) ending of *Rhapsody*.

In haste, all good things to you!

Yours ever,

Jóska

---

[45] On 21 January, Bernstein conducted the City Symphony Orchestra in Stravinsky's *Symphony of Psalms*, Strauss' *Don Juan*, Bach's Brandenburg Concerto No. 5, and Three Variations from *Fancy Free*.

218. Leonard Bernstein to Carlos Moseley[46]

1239 Broadway, New York, NY
23 February 1946

Dear Carlos,

This Prague thing is very exciting indeed: and if I guess correctly, my profound gratitude is due one Moseley.

The programs have been tentatively settled, & cabled to Prague, as follows:

I.

Schuman – Am. Fest. Overture
Harris – Symph. #3
Gershwin – Rhapsody (Eugene List)

———

Me – Jeremiah Symph.

II.

Randall Thompson – Symph. #2

———

pseudo-Czech group:
Dvořák – Husitska Overture
Bartók – Rhapsody #1, Portrait in D – Szigeti

———

Barber – Essay #1
Copland – El Saloon

I think they're swell programs, and I hope you agree. Will we see each other soon?

When do I go in order to rehearse sufficiently?

Are new injections required?

Do send me details.

Affectionately,

Lenny Bernstein

---

[46] Carlos Moseley (1914–2012) was to have a long association with Bernstein. In 1941, Moseley was the soloist in Brahms' Second Piano Concerto with Bernstein conducting, at Tanglewood. In 1946 he was working at the State Department, promoting American music abroad, the subject of this letter. In 1955 he joined the New York Philharmonic Orchestra, first as press officer, then associate manager in 1959 (in time for the orchestra's tour to Russia), managing director from 1961 to 1970, president from 1970 to 1978, and finally chairman.

219. Paul Feigay[47] to Leonard Bernstein
137–145 West 48th Street, New York, NY
17 April 1946

Dear Mr. Bernstein,

As you know the business of *On The Town* on the road has been very disappointing everywhere in spite of the terrific notices. Up to date we have personally lost over $50,000.00, in getting the show ready for the road and the losses on the road. The first week in Chicago the loss was $6,500.00, and then last week we lost $1,600.00, and that was due to the fact that we did not charge off any but cash bills.

We must appeal to you for help. Full royalties have been paid with the exception of the last few weeks in New York. We ask that royalties be waived retroactive to the opening of the run in Chicago and until such time as we start again operating at a profit and royalties should be paid out of each week's profit up until such payments equal 80% of the royalties due.

Unless we can secure urgent and immediate cooperation from all persons receiving royalties we will be forced to close the run in Chicago immediately, regardless of the fact that business is on the upswing there.

A copy of this has been sent to each person receiving royalties. Please sign the enclosed letter under "agreed to" and return it to me as soon as possible.

Very truly yours,
Paul Feigay

220. Leonard Bernstein to David Oppenheim
Orly Field Airport, Paris, France
postmark 7 May 1946

Dearest Dave (Dearer than Crockett, Diamond, Jones, the King, Glazer),[48]

At this very moment life is a horror. I developed a stiff neck and a stinking cold during my first day in Paris. It would have disappeared, but there's no rest. One spends most of one's days in ATC offices, bureaus, Embassies, and most of

---

[47] Paul Feigay (1918–83), American theater and television producer. Feigay's first Broadway credit was as co-producer with Oliver Smith of *On the Town*, and his subsequent career included producing the television series *Omnibus* with Bernstein in the 1950s. *On the Town* ended its successful Broadway run on 2 February 1946, and the arrival of the tour in Chicago (including Nancy Walker and Adolph Green in the cast) was greeted enthusiastically by Claudia Cassidy in the *Chicago Daily Tribune* in her review published on 2 April. Feigay's letter is an interesting snapshot of the vicissitudes of producing a Broadway show, even one as ostensibly successful as *On the Town*.
[48] David Glazer (1913–2001) had given the first performance of the Clarinet Sonata with Bernstein on 21 April 1942. From 1951 until his retirement he played in the New York Woodwind Quintet.

one's nights driving to and from the airports. The flying racket is grand, but always involves the wrong times of day.

All this notwithstanding, the city is so fantastically beautiful that one cannot but be excited. The French are very depressed, and as they say here, on vive très mal. But my flight to Prague has just been called – so bless you & all my love,

L

221. Leonard Bernstein to Helen Coates
Prague, Czechoslovakia
9 May 1946

Dear Helen,

Things are beginning to pick up. Thank God! So far all the wonderful things Europe holds have offered themselves to me as dim visions, due to the fact that I caught a monstrous cold in Paris on my very first day there, and it's still with me. I've had horrible stiff muscles and aches, and sinus blowups. But now it begins to abate, and I'm beginning to be able to receive all this fabulous wonder.

This is the greatest day in Czech history. As you remember one year ago on May 5th, with Patton's army 20 miles away and the Russians at the East door, the people of Prague made a revolution against the Nazis. They just couldn't wait. The next day they were liberated by the Red Army. So this whole week is festival – the first anniversary of liberty. And are they celebrating, as no American would ever dare to do. Outside in the streets the whole town is dancing – to miked-up records of boogie-woogie and Strauss waltzes! People have come from all the provinces – Moravia, Slovakia – in their heavenly national peasant costumes, and the gaiety is beyond description. This morning there was a great parade and celebration in the huge Masaryk stadium, where generals of all the Allies spoke, including the great Konev, McNarney, and chiefs of staff from France, England, Yugoslavia, etc. It was a super-colossal demonstration, with tanks, planes, and the works. Last night there were fireworks on the Moldau, and up in the great Hradčany Castle. It is the only place on earth to be this week.

Of course, the people look on the Russians as their liberators, but all the Hearst talk of the Red Terror here and the iron grip of Russia is nonsense.[49] The Czechs

---

[49] Bernstein's optimism is heartening, but the situation in Czechoslovakia was volatile, and deteriorated sharply over the next two years. On 26 May 1946, two weeks after Bernstein wrote this letter, the first Czech post-war general election had a voter turnout of 93.9%. The result was a victory for the Communist Party of Czechoslovakia. Edvard Beneš continued as president, and Jan Masaryk, son of the founding father of Czechoslovakia, continued as foreign minister. The Communist Klement Gottwald became prime minister. The Communists controlled only a minority of ministries, but these included some of the most important, notably Information, Finance, and the Interior (including control of the police). Through their position of power in these ministries, the Communists were able to establish a solid base from which to launch the Soviet-backed coup in February 1948, beginning four decades of Communist rule that ended with the Velvet Revolution of 1989.

are free as much as men can be, with joy in their reconstruction. It is rather in Paris where the spirit is way down, where the elections bore no fruit, where everyone is pessimistic and wretched (I think probably as much from guilt at their self-defeat as from *la vie dure*). The Czechs are happy and look to the future. They are the sweetest people on earth, and I'm going to have a marvelous week.

My love goes to everyone – please give it to them, and let this letter go to them all. There's so little time to write. More later.

Love,

L

222. Leonard Bernstein to Shirley Bernstein
Hyde Park Hotel, London, England
9 June 1946

Darling,

It's all a mess. I didn't want to go to England. The plane trip was ghastly and a full day overdue, always stopping to fix the foolish crate. The hotel is dreary beyond description. The food is inedible, what there is of it. The English are very down, except for Victory Day (yesterday) when 10,000,000 people went berserk in London. In an ogrish way. (Why do I always hit the parades?)

And worst of all, I'm stuck with horrible programs. I can't fix them – it's too late. All Ford-Hour stuff, masses of Wagner excerpts, with and without Marjorie Lawrence, and waltzes & polonaises by the score. The one help is *Appalachian Spring*. What a dream of a piece.

I have rarely felt so lonely. I don't really know why, but I react to everything with big, soggy depressions. And H[elen] C[oates] is no help there. How I regret not bringing you instead.

Are you a stage-manager yet? What is the state of your maidenhood? A letter from you would help a lot. Soon, please.

First rehearsal tomorrow morning. First concert the day after. (*Jeremiah*, of course, is out.) If I hold up through this I'll be extremely grateful. My love to all around. And many kisses to you. I miss you terribly.

L

Don't forget to phone my best to the family.

223. Leonard Bernstein to David Oppenheim
Hyde Park Hotel, London, England
postmark 14 June 1946

To the Royal Husbandman,
Builder of the House,
Decorator of the interior,

Defender of the Faith:

GREETING.

This is the dullest yet. Of course, I hit Victory Day again, with parades, illuminations (fireworks to us), and 10,000,000 mad folk releasing their repressions in a "frightfully gay" holiday. Now it's over, and it's still dull. Crowds hanging around Buckingham Palace, waiting for Royalty to appear. The sun came out for twenty minutes today, and everyone is grateful.

I'm not happy. The programs are a mess, and there's nothing I can do to change them. I'm tired, usually depressed, and have little if any clarity of mind. I sleep when I have nothing pressing, and try to ignore the dreariness of this hotel and all of London.

I envy you in the excitement of building up your new home. Let me hear about it. This was the time you *were* going to write, remember?

All my love,

Lenny

224. David Oppenheim to Leonard Bernstein

Tuesday a.m., Intermission

[June 1946]

Lenushka,

This is the time I *did* write. Remember!

The news here is good. We have had much success in your absence. Felicia [Montealegre] has a lead role in *Swan Song*, the Ben Hecht–C. MacArthur affair and seems to be doing well in it considering she's a nervophysical wreck and can't swallow food any more, what with 3 days notice on her role. But H[elen] Hayes came up to her dressing room to tell her how much she liked her (I was there) and how much she liked her clothes – so I guess she will live on that for a while. I didn't even know it was Hayes until she had gone. She calls herself Mrs. MacArthur.[50] Who am I to know? She's not a girl any more.

As for your favorite schizophrenic (looks wrong) he has played for Laszlo H[alasz][51] & will continue to do so for the duration of next season. I signed something or other Monday. You must have primed Fallioni like crazy. He welcomed me into his office like a lost brother–old sweetheart combined – gave

---

[50] The famous actress Helen Hayes (1900–93), who was married to Charles MacArthur. Something of a legend in the American theater, she is one of a select group to have won an Emmy, an Oscar, a Grammy, and a Tony. She had two Broadway theaters named after her. In 1955 the former Fulton Theatre was renamed the Helen Hayes Theatre; after that was demolished in 1982, the nearby Little Theatre was renamed in her honor.

[51] Laszlo Halasz (1905–2001) was the first Music Director of New York City Opera, from 1943 to 1951. He then became Recording Director for Remington Records, as well as a conducting teacher at the Peabody Conservatory and Eastman School of Music.

me the parts to about seven operas – told me to call him "when ready & if I needed advice."

At the audition I played *Carmen* & *Traviata* & *Butterfly*. I wasn't great – but I was OK, I guess. After I had played the *Traviata* solo (which I loathe) Laszlo said there was no question about my tone now for some notes. Then the beginning and about 3 pages of Butterballs[52] & I'm sticking to him like glue thru a million Puccini rubatos.

He then conceded that I had "mastered the instrument. Have you the courage to play 1st?" To which I replied modestly – with much Frauentruth – that I didn't have the courage to play anything else. So he said to Fallioni – "Good boy" – & that's it.

Fallioni says over again "I think this will make Lenny very happy, eh."

The house I live in now, not mine to own. We accept each other, with all our faults.

I have made a down payment of $5.00 on a small 5′6″ porcelain bathtub which when I raise the sufficient capital – $13.00 – I will install in my bathroom.

Cheer up friend Lenny. Soon you will be back with those who love you and in the [. . .] Berkshires. Not long from now. We miss you and I miss you.

Love,
Dave
Best to Helen

225. Leonard Bernstein to Shirley Bernstein
Hyde Park Hotel, London, England
17 June 1946

Darling,

Your letter came this morning "bringing hope & cheer." As a matter of fact, I've been feeling infinitely better since writing you last, when skies were really greymalkin. I had my *Lōondonshein* début yesterday, and apparently it was a huge success, though the *Times* critic is still back in 1905, worrying about the question of a baton or no baton. Incredible country. The state of music is a shambles, the programs are embarrassing, the standard of performance abysmal.

I am constantly saying, if you were only here! What fun all this nonsense would be! I saw *three* shambles in a row that would have thrown you. First, a concert conducted by a wildman named de Sabata, who makes Mitrop[oulos] look like a sissy. He beats his head and jumps in the air & the bloody British public screams in delight. Then, the theatre: *The First Gentleman* with wonderful

---

[52] i.e. *Madama Butterfly*.

Robert Morley & heavenly Wendy Hiller, but a play to make one wince (long scenes of dying in childbirth), and the British public screams. Then, the ballet. That was the end. Three ballets in a row at Covent Garden, one more lamentable than the last. And corn! And no imagination, and the audience screamed. So much for the British public.

Peter Lawrence is here, to be followed by the whole crowd. Wait til Nora Kaye gets brought here by two liveried footmen! That will be the take [talk] of the season.

God, I should have brought you. I miss you [. . .] and love you so much. But, as you say, you're here with me, and people often catch me giggling to myself, when I am making Rybernian conversation with you on the latest British idiocy.

[. . .]

All my love – be well – and somehow that Schirmer deal smells bad. I hope it all works out.

If Kouss lets me, I may stay on here till July 4th to conduct opening night *Fancy Free* at Covent Garden. I'll let you know.

Bless you,

L

226. Leonard Bernstein to Serge Koussevitzky
Hyde Park Hotel, London, England
22 June 1946

Dearest Serge Alexandrovich,

I have wanted to write you every day since your generous permission to stay an extra week in England arrived by cable – but I have not been able because I *could* not decide to stay and give up even one week of Tanglewood. You know so well what that paradise means to me – there are only six weeks in all, and every one is so important. Besides, I did not want to upset your plans if anything depended on me in the first week. But two things have finally made me take the decision to stay. First, I have had a serious throat infection this week, and had to cancel one concert (Leinsdorf substituted for me!) – and I need a week's rest in the countryside to get strong and well again for the great work this summer.

The second reason is that I am to make records here on July 1st,[53] and since that is so important, I suppose I must remain, and then conduct my ballet on the 4th. But I promise, when I return I will feel healthier, and be able to work harder; and I *will* take the *first* plane after July 4th!

My concerts are all over here, and they have been very successful, although the programs could not be materially altered. For example, last night was my

---

[53] The recording session on 1 July 1946 was for Ravel's G major Piano Concerto, in Bernstein's dual capacity as soloist and conductor, made with the Philharmonia Orchestra.

final concert, in sold-out Albert Hall (over 5,000 people in the audience) – but the program! Handel's *Water Music,* Grieg's Piano Concerto (with a bad pianist named Eileen Joyce) and Tchaikovsky's Fifth. At least I had a chance to play a major symphony, and it was a great experience to play the Fifth for the first time. Some people in the audience came back and told me that it was better than *Nikisch!* (That, of course, meant it was in the Koussevitzky tradition, but not so good.) Isn't it strange how in this small world all the lines of history and destiny come around eventually in perfect circles? I think that gives me more hope than anything else.

Appalachian Spring has had a great success here. I have played it also in the provinces, where they love it, almost more than in London! But the greatest joke is that the *Times* called me [a] "real Wagnerian conductor" after my *Tristan* and *Götterdämmerung* with Marjorie Lawrence! I had never done *Götterdämmerung* before, and my whole Wagner repertoire has been almost nothing! So much for the critics.

My greatest love to you, and all my blessings for the greatest Tanglewood season so far, and for many, many more. I cannot wait until I join you there.

Devotedly,
Leonard
Kisses for Olga

227. Leonard Bernstein to David Oppenheim
Hyde Park Hotel, London, England
postmark 24 June 1946

Dear Solo Cl[arine]t,
Felicitations and bravo, and all the best for the best of seasons with the best of orchestras under the – what am I saying? I'm very happy. Don't rub it in about Fabbioni. Everything's impartial as a chessmatch. Can I help it if we're both white knights?

And kiss Felicia from me. I think it's swell, but I hear *Swan Song* isn't so swell. Does it last? And what of Gloucester?[54] I wish I could see her in it.

As for bathtubs, I could put two of yours into the one I have here, but I'd give anything to be in yours instead. England has begun to pall. I gave my final concert last night (great success) to a sold-out Albert Hall. Tchai[kovsky]'s 5th. Quite an experience, first time.

I've just come through a strep throat. Canceled one concert. Penicillin worked miracles. Now I'm off to Glyndebourne for the week, to see Britten, &

---

[54] Felicia was appearing at the Bass Rocks Summer Theatre in Gloucester, MA.

the rehearsals of his new opera *The Rape of Lucrece*,[55] and to rest in the country. Maybe a side jaunt to Brighton (beim-sea).

Then back here to record the old Ravel Concerto, with crack boys (including [Reginald] Kell, Brahan,[56] etc.).

Then to conduct opening night of the Ballet Theatre *Fancy Free* July 4th. Then home. (Kouss has sent special permission to let me miss first week in Tanglewood, which I loathe to do. But no can help. (*British ink! Diluted shit!*)[57] When do you go up? Where will you live? Is it all set with the Union? I hope you haven't forgotten (or delayed) to act on that.

Also (not also, but *also*, Deutsch) I will be joining you in the Boiks [Berkshires] around July 8th. I shall miss that opening week terribly. To say nothing of missing you. But hold on. I'm coming.

I've been to a Sadler's Wells party tonight. What a bloody bore. And I've had a siege of singing "Barney Google"[58] with big Andrews Sisters codas.

. . . with his goo, goo, googly eyes –
I mean –
Goo– goo– goo– gle– y–
eye. . . . .s!!!
All my love,
L

228. Felicia Montealegre[59] to Leonard Bernstein
[Summer 1946]

Lennie dear!

I'm in the middle of a rehearsal – I'll try my best to talk to you between cues – my God what a life! I don't get time to eat any more. I'm playing Raina in *Arms and the Man* which we will open with the first of July [. . .]

---

[55] Britten's *Rape of Lucretia* was first performed at Glyndebourne on 12 July 1946.

[56] Presumably Bernstein means Dennis Brain, principal horn of the Philharmonia Orchestra.

[57] The ink has become progressively fainter on the page and here Bernstein refills his pen.

[58] The song "Barney Google (with the Goo-Goo-Googly Eyes)" by Billy Rose and Con Conrad.

[59] Bernstein first met Felicia Montealegre Cohn (1922–78) in February 1946, at a party given by Claudio Arrau after he had played the Brahms D minor Piano Concerto with Bernstein conducting the New York City Symphony. Felicia was not only a beautiful and gifted actress, but had been a piano pupil of Arrau's. During the autumn of 1946 she and Bernstein saw each other regularly and grew increasingly close. Bernstein took Felicia with him to Hollywood in December, and it was there that their engagement was celebrated by a party. Leonard Lyons reported in his "Times Square Tattle" (*The New York Times*, 8 January 1947): "This is how Leonard Bernstein's engagement to Felicia Montealegre, the Chilean actress, was announced: Lester Cowan, producer of *The Beckoning Fair One* in which Bernstein will costar, conduct and compose the musical score, gave a hoe-down for them at his ranch. Sinatra sang, Gene Kelly danced and John Garfield donned boxing gloves. Then came a song written by Ann Ronell, author of 'Willow Weep for Me', 'Big Bad Wolf', etc. The tune was a blending of Haydn's 'Surprise' Symphony, Mendelssohn's Wedding March and Bernstein's

I was so happy to receive your "note" – I was just a little hurt at your not saying good bye – you see dear, even though I know you are terribly busy and "confused" I still halfheartedly hope you'll remember my existence without me forever reminding you.

Are you happy in London – do you like it? I hope you finally caught up with your sleep, that you're rested and enjoying everything as much as you can. [. . .]

When I see you again (I wonder how long it'll be before I do) I must have a long talk with you. I've been thinking (*actually!*) and there's a lot – but a lot – I want to say. I'll probably have to get Helen Coates to make an appointment for me – but I intend to have my say! Oh darling, you can be *so* silly sometimes – life isn't that serious, honest it isn't! I know I shouldn't take some things too seriously, specially where you are concerned, as for example I haven't even looked at another man since I met you (well, perhaps one or two – but that's all!) and I'm not exactly beating my head against the wall – I'm training myself just beautifully, but I must confess that it's rather difficult sometimes!

I never found out how long you were to stay in England. Do you think you might find time to write me again – a postcard maybe? I'll be leaving for Gloucester on the 17th – the address is: Bass Rocks Summer Theatre, Gloucester, Mass.

Goodbye darling – please be good and by the way, why don't you marry Helen off to a retired English Colonel who'll take her off to live in Sussex – well, it's a good idea anyway!

Pip pip, old boy. I do love you rather. A kiss to you with a whiff of K.Y.!
[Felicia]

229. Felicia Montealegre to Leonard Bernstein
[Summer 1946]

Darling!

It's nearly three but I can't go to sleep – I'm feeling particularly lonely tonight; it's rather dreadful getting home late after the show, opening the door, putting

---

Fancy Free, On the Town and *Jeremiah*. The lyrics ended with the announcement: 'This party has been staged, Because they got engaged. Len & Felicia, Are now officia–lly Two.' " In the summer of 1947, Felicia spent time with the Bernstein clan at Tanglewood, and Humphrey Burton wrote of the tensions: "Felicia came to Tanglewood for two long spells that summer [. . .] Life was not easy for her despite her official status as Leonard's fiancée. There was rivalry with Shirley, ostensibly about such mundane matters as who should sit next to Leonard at meals. Helen Coates was also fighting to maintain her old position. Felicia said later that her self-confidence was undermined as Leonard constantly found fault with her" (Burton 1994, p. 166). By September 1947, the couple had decided to call off the engagement and the *Journal-American* on 11 September reported that "Leonard Bernstein's matrimonial plans have been cancelled." Four years later, on 12 August 1951, the Associated Press announced the couple's second engagement, made by Mrs. Serge Koussevitzky at a supper for the faculty of the Berkshire Music Center at Tanglewood, where Bernstein had been teaching and conducting during the summer. This time, the engagement was followed by their marriage a month later, on 9 September 1951.

on the light and being faced with the most acute aloneness – but then as you once remarked, New York is full of people like me (no consolation at all!).

I should be very happy – and, of course, there are moments when I am. This job has been a wonderful stroke of luck for me, and a grand beginning.[60] It's such a satisfaction to be actually *working* and not just studying and preparing – you know – it's feeling that you belong at last to the "something" you were striving for.

I miss you so much. I wonder why an ocean in between should make such a difference but somehow it does – there's something so irrevocable about it. I talked to Shirley today and I was told you had postponed your return – well, at least it means you're staying for something worthwhile. I felt so badly when I heard how miserable and disappointed you were.[61] Cheer up my love and think of Tanglewood, you'll be happy there I know!

It's hot as hell – mierda! mierda! David [Oppenheim] was here this after-noon – his usual wonderful refreshing self – I was soundly kissed in your name, merci monsieur! Twas nice . . . The same to you – many of them, with love.

Felicia

230. Samuel Barber to Leonard Bernstein
Capricorn, Mount Kisco, NY
[August 1946]

Dear Lenny,
I return the Berlioz with thanks. It is all I had to wear in Boston. Whether it was due to *Peter Grimes*, the Benedictine or the very pleasant evening I spent with you, I do not know: but on arriving at 625 Park, clutching the Berlioz, I allowed the taxi to drive off with tuxedo, diamond studs et al, and nothing has been returned. Perhaps I should wear khaki after all.

Enclosed also my favorite critic which will be good for your ego, especially two "wiederums".

Sam

231. Leonard Bernstein to Barbara Marcuse
"Wednesday, but which one?" [4 September 1946]

My dear Barbara and ménage,
Nothing, absolutely nothing, could please me more than a shot at Charlevoix [northern Michigan] the Beautiful. But Charlevoix the Unattainable it must be.

---

[60] During the summer of 1946, Felicia performed in the Broadway production of *Swan Song* by Charles MacArthur and Ben Hecht at the Booth Theatre.
[61] A reference to Bernstein's unhappiness during his visit to London in June 1946.

The Six Weeks were over, true, leaving a gray and bewildered and *Grimes*-weary Bernstein to plunge headlong into a new ballet for production this fall. (Ballet Theatre, of course, and J. Robbins). Roughly two weeks of mad note-jostling, and it's not finished yet, and tomorrow it's back to the fiery furnace (32 West 10th St., by the way, a 4-flight walk-up! The times!) and on to opening night in two weeks.[62] So that's me at the moment, as usual, and goodbye to all this autumnal glory in the Berkshires, and even to the chance of seeing you. But don't you ever come to New York? You really must, you know. A few mad hours by plane, that's all. And I do miss you – there always arrives that moment when I recall the quiet security I sometimes borrowed from the Marcuse "set-up". Alas.

Shirley is "between shows", as they say. Dave [Oppenheim] is on the verge of becoming 1st clarinet in my orchestra; England was ghastly; Tanglewood was hectic but rewarding; I have *four weeks* with the Boston Symphony this winter; and I never said that S[hostakovich]'s 9th was a bore. Tell Phil to take his favorite mag and send it back to Russia.

All my love,

Lenny (Hruba) Nonadjustable

I think I'm going to Palestine, Vienna, Paris, and maybe (shh!) Russia in the spring!

Blessings on Ann and small Ph.[63]

232. Leonard Bernstein to Serge Koussevitzky
32 West 10th Street, New York, NY
6 October 1946

Dearest Serge Alexandrovich,

It sometimes seems that the courage necessary for living simply and clearly in this world is all but a superhuman quality. This has been a week of shadows and misunderstandings which has left me tired and not a little depressed. There has been this incredible muddle, to begin with, over the appearance of my orchestra in Boston. Everyone involved has apparently used subterfuge in one sense or another, leaving me exposed and guilty of an offense I have never committed. I have finally extracted a promise from Miss Canterbury, which she assured me would be put into writing to you, me, and Mr. [George] Judd, that all mention of my name would henceforth be left out of all her publicity. She will also enclose a slip in her program material stating that I will not appear in November. They are trying to negotiate for another conductor (possibly Stokowski). In any case, it will be a mess; but I am rid of it, I think. I have written

---

[62] The new Bernstein-Robbins ballet *Facsimile* was first performed on 24 October 1946 at the Broadway Theatre, New York, by Ballet Theatre, with Bernstein conducting.
[63] Philip and Barbara Marcuse's children, Ann and Philip.

to Adams, stating that I will not appear in Boston. What more can I do? The Canterbury woman has been promising since August that she will cancel the engagement, only to proceed with publicity and newspaper advertising behind our backs. Her excuse is that her own Board of Directors will not allow her to break the engagement, no matter how much she *personally* would like to.

Well, *enfin*, whom does one trust in this world? I don't know what to believe of all these commercial people; but when you told me that *you* had doubted *me*, I was really grief-stricken. If there is no trust between us, dearest Serge Alexandrovich, there is no trust in the world! I believe with all my heart in our bond and in our beautiful relationship; and I am sure that you do. Something so strongly based and real in its love cannot be injured by the meddling of these meaningless interferers!

To make things even sadder, I have had a miserable weekend with poor David Diamond, who has more or less cracked up emotionally. He has always been subject to hysterical actions, but this time it was a real collapse, brought on by the death of a girl who was very dear to him. I truly think that we shall have to convince him to have proper treatment and care in a qualified psychiatric hospital; otherwise there is only a bad end ahead for this talented and affectionate boy who has lost control of his emotional processes.

Let us talk about happier things. I have been trying to revise our Boston programs to include the Bartók work; but the only place where it will fit would be along with the Mahler. Also, since Ruth Posselt must play in New York also, we cannot bring either the Bartók or Mahler to New York. Is it definite that Ruth plays in New York? If so, the programs might look like this:

Boston and New York
I.   Gluck – Alceste
      Stravinsky – Le Sacre
      Schubert – [Symphony] #7
II.   Bernstein – Facsimile (ballet)
      (or an American overture)
      Hindemith – [Violin] Concerto (Posselt)
      Beethoven – [Symphony] #7
Boston only
III. Bartók – Music for strings, etc.
      Mahler – [Symphony] #7

Bartók and Mahler is a very heavy combination, I think, and our old plan of a Mozart Symphony with the Mahler is certainly better; but this was the only place I could find for the Bartók. What do you think? I would also leave my ballet flexible until we can hear it performed this month. I have been looking through the Mahler score, which has marvelous things in it, and is also very long. (I have not been able to find out the exact timing.) I would still love to do it, if you wish. Would it be interesting to give the *Shostakovich #7*?

The concerts here are going marvelously, and it is only this great activity, and all this heavenly music that keeps me going through a week such as I have had. We did the Mozart "Linz" Symphony last night, which more than atoned for the agonies of the weekend. It *is* a marvel! Perhaps I can do that with the Mahler?

I wait to hear from you, with my love and faith strong and intact as always.

Devotedly,

Leonard

233. Leonard Bernstein to Solomon Braslavsky[64]
New York, NY
10 October 1946

Dear Professor,

I have been suddenly inspired to write you a note (if you can pardon the lack of "a propos"). Having listened through a Kol Nidre service, and again the next day to a Yom Kippur service in a completely different kind of synagogue, I have come to realize what a debt I really owe to you – personally – for the marvelous music at Mishkan Tefila services. They surpass any that I have ever heard; and the memories I have of them are so bright, strong, and dear, that I shall probably never be able to estimate the real influence those sounds exerted on me. And please tell Cantor Glickstein that he is still my favorite cantor.

All good luck,

Leonard Bernstein[65]

234. Solomon Braslavsky to Leonard Bernstein
133 Elm Hill Avenue, Roxbury, MA
16 October 1946

Dear Lennie,

I don't know how to thank you for your letter. After all, a note of praise from your pen means much not only for myself, but for the entire Mishkan Tefila. I,

---

[64] Solomon Braslavsky (1887–1975) was born in Ukraine and studied in Vienna, where he was subsequently appointed professor at the Jewish Theological Seminary and conducted Jewish choirs and orchestras before moving to Boston to become Director of Music at Temple Mishkan Tefila in 1928 (see Sarna 2009, p. 39, for details of Braslavsky's early career). Bernstein was overwhelmed by the music he heard at Temple Mishkan Tefila, and wrote to Braslavsky in 1973 that he would "never forget the tremendous influence you and your music made on me when I was a youngster."

[65] The text of this letter is taken from the version published in the *Jewish Advocate* on 17 October 1946, p. 6.

therefore, hope you will not scold me for making your letter public in the *Jewish Advocate*.[66]

A propos (no lack of it on my side) the services at Mishkan Tefila. Another great musician attended our services the first day of Rosh Hashonoh, Dr. [Hugo] Leichentritt. He, too, never heard as beautiful a musical setting as here. [. . .] We, of course, know the reason, but why discussed here? I wish I could say it to the "group" in New York who condemn [Salomon] Sulzer, [Louis] Lewandovsky and others, and are advocating Gretchaninoff (!), Dessau, Milhaud, etc., as proponents of *real* Jewish music. They would not even mention my name in the *Manuals*.

I am trying to clear my decks for November 13 at Symphony Hall. I should like very much to show you my Symphony or, at least, the four short items of Synagogal music which are published now by the McLaughlin and Reilly Society.[67] Will you be able to find a half hour for me during your stay in Boston? I hope, yes.

Many thanks and best wishes for a real happy and successful New Year, with great achievements,

S. Braslavsky

235. Paul Wittgenstein[68] to Leonard Bernstein

310 Riverside Drive, New York, NY

16 October 1946

Dear Mr. Bernstein,

I wanted to say "good-bye" and "thank you" after the concert yesterday.[69] But when Beethoven and the tremendous applause was finished and I wanted to go to the stage and see you, I found the door closed.

---

[66] Braslavsky wasted no time doing so: the letter appeared in the *Jewish Advocate* on 17 October 1946, just a week after Bernstein wrote to Braslavsky.

[67] The Preface for this publication was written by Hugo Leichentritt, who pointed out the similarities between Hebrew sacred music and Gregorian chant, and writes that "Mr. Braslavsky's arrangement is distinguished by a close acquaintance with the peculiar style of this old religious music, and by the skill and beauty of its harmonic treatment." A review by Jules Wolfers appeared in the *Jewish Advocate* (25 September 1947): "Four extremely interesting Hebrew chants arranged for four part mixed voices and organ [. . .] have recently been published by McLaughlin and Reilly, Boston. That a Catholic publishing house is the medium through which these chants are issued is in itself indicative of the all-over worth of this music. The day is past when Jewish music was of interest only to Jews. [. . .] For Jewish choirs and choral groups their chants are obviously a must. In addition, any person interested in Jewish music will probably wish to acquire this set. Publication of four traditional Jewish chants by a firm named McLaughlin and Reilly must make some sort of publishing history. This is a commendable and heart-warming gesture."

[68] Paul Wittgenstein (1887–1961), Austrian-born pianist who commissioned a number of important new works for piano left hand after he lost his right arm during the First World War. The composers he commissioned included Britten, Hindemith, Korngold, Prokofiev, Franz Schmidt, Richard Strauss, and Alexandre Tansman. The most famous Wittgenstein commission was Ravel's Piano Concerto for the Left Hand, the subject of this letter.

[69] Wittgenstein performed the Ravel concerto with Bernstein conducting the New York City Symphony on 14 and 15 October, in a program that also included Ravel's *Le Tombeau de Couperin*

I can only repeat what I have already said: the Ravel concerto is almost as difficult for the orchestra as it is for the soloist, and a success depends upon the conductor as well as upon me, therefore should be divided 50 and 50! I know this out of experience and appreciate with thanks what you have been doing.

The performance of the concerto on Monday was, I think, really excellent! Please let the fact that it wasn't quite as good on Tuesday not spoil your remembering of it!

Don't reply to this letter.

Sincerely & friendly,

Yours,

Paul Wittgenstein

236. Leonard Bernstein to Serge Koussevitzky

32 West 10th Street, New York, NY

[25 October 1946][70]

Dearest Serge Alexandrovich,

I don't know quite how to say this, but I am in the position of having to come to Boston. We have tried everything – Reiner, Stokowski, [José] Iturbi (lesser names they do not accept) – [Manuel] Rosenthal (they never heard of him) – Morton Gould (he is what they call "box-office poison" in Boston) – everything has failed. We even concocted an idea to send a concert of operatic excerpts with our friend [Laszlo] Halasz, but he would do it only if I took over *Onegin*, which I am not up to at this moment. It would be disastrous to do *Onegin* without sufficient preparation; and knowing the situation at the Center as I do, I cannot accept that responsibility. Especially since the premiere is scheduled for the very next night after the Boston visit!

I know that you will understand, better than anyone on earth, what my situation is, and what my obligations are. There is no alternative left; and I do it with a heavy heart, I assure you. I can only hope that the entire incident will be soon forgotten; for it has been the most difficult moment of my short

and Beethoven's *Eroica* Symphony. Olin Downes, reviewing the Monday performance in *The New York Times* (15 October) praised Wittgenstein's playing: "in a most authoritative way, he interpreted the music ... He has a singing tone as well as five fingers with well-nigh the virtuosity of ten, and he is a colorist who understands not only the piano part but every detail of the orchestration. Mr. Bernstein, conducting, supplied a spirited accompaniment and both men acknowledged the long applause."

[70] Though this letter is undated, it must have been written on 25 October 1946, the day after the "ballet premiere" that Bernstein mentions (the first performance of *Facsimile*). The concert to which the letter refers was given by the New York City Symphony on a visit to Boston on 13 November 1946. Though Bernstein had included the *Enigma Variations* in his New York programme on 11 November, the *Christian Science Monitor* announced the change to Dvořák's Second [Seventh] Symphony in a short article published on 12 November.

career.[71] The last thing in the world I ever expected to do was to do something against your wish; and here Fate has plunged me into this *impasse*.

I think I mentioned the proposed program to you:

Purcell – Fantasy on One Note
Walton – Portsmouth Point Overture
Britten – Violin Concerto

———

Elgar – Enigma Variations

I have thought of substituting Dvořák's Second Symphony for the Elgar (I did it here this week, and fell in love with it.) If you have any objection to this, or to any other piece on the program, please let me know, and I will change it immediately.

All the reports of your performance of Aaron's Symphony are superb. I regret so much that I could not hear an actual performance; but the rehearsal that I did hear was a great experience.

I had my ballet premiere last night, and all the reactions seem very favorable for the score. I think it would make a nice little concert piece; and I look forward with so much eagerness to hearing it with the Boston Symphony. It will be a real joy for me.

Again, dear Serge Alexandrovich, I know you will be sympathetic to my predicament with the City Symphony; and please, please forgive me for ever having caused such an unpleasant experience for you.

In all devotion,
Leonard

237. Lukas Foss[72] to Leonard Bernstein
Symphony Hall, Boston, MA
9 November 1946

Dear Lenny,

I received your invitation to participate in the B'nai B'rith contest. I am eager to do so. The only unperformed piece I have is *Song of Anguish*. Even though my

---

[71] It's difficult to see what Koussevitzky's problem was with Bernstein bringing his own New York City Symphony to Boston, but clearly the whole episode distressed Bernstein. Relations between the two continued to deteriorate in the last weeks of 1946.

[72] Lukas Foss (1922–2009), German-born American composer, conductor, and pianist. Foss' friendship with Bernstein lasted fifty years, from the time of their first meeting at Tanglewood in 1940 until Bernstein's death in 1990. He consistently supported Bernstein's compositions and often appeared as the piano soloist in *The Age of Anxiety*. He conducted the first performance of the *Symphonic Dances from West Side Story*.

neoclassic friends prefer my later biblical venture, I agree with Aaron who felt that *Song of Anguish* is as good as anything I've done. I would love to see you and perhaps Tod Duncan (who has learned the part) premiere it in March, but there is one difficulty concerning my entering it in the contest: it lasts 18 minutes instead of the demanded 15. May I enter it anyway?

Good luck with your Boston concert on the 13th. I am unfortunately in Baltimore on that day. But I have already bought tickets for *Facsimile* on the 18th. The best to Helen.

As always,

Lukas

P.S. As I now approach the mature age of 25 this contest is one of very few I can still have a crack at. It's funny not to be "too young" anymore but "too old" for many of these things. No more prodigy stuff. Actually I feel good about it.

L. F.

238. Leonard Bernstein to Shirley Bernstein

22220 Saticoy Street, Canoga Park, CA

7 December 1946

Mine deeoah,

Mine God! and Dine God! and I miss you terribly. This would, as usual, be your meat. But Felicia is really working out. It's a little early to tell anything, but I sense a possible future. How can I tell you in a letter? It must mostly wait. But I can send you signposts, sort of, as we go along.

This week has been Coma-week. Doing zero, absolutely. When the sun is out it's divine; otherwise freezaukūdū. Many fireplaces and scotch, and our own bungalow make it the luxury of all time. Beautiful horses (and can Felicia outride me!), and a pool, when possible.

I've gotten a great idea on the picture and Lester seems sold on it. If it works it will be sensational – a Hollywood *first* – and a really significant vehicle for my debut. The writers are dopes – but this has nothing to do with them.

Two recurrent refrains, which I shall not repeat, dominate this letter: *I miss you*, and *Any signs of a job*? I pray for you. I'm sure you'd do marvelously out here, if we could get you a test. I'm sort of working on it.

I hear *If The Shoe* is a fiasco,[73] goody two-shoes.

Adolph, Betty & Adolph are doing fine, looking great, and send you love. They say Elizabeth Taylor at MGM is your type, but you're prettier.

Write me great gobs of stuff. We're taking a little Ford convertible to Mexico next week. Wish you could come. Shit.

---

[73] It certainly was. *If The Shoe Fits* (with a score by David Raksin) opened on Broadway on 5 December 1946 and closed after just twenty-one performances.

Sunday there's a party here. Dinah Shore & George Montgomery & Buddy Rogers & Billy Wilder & Ad. & Betty & Ad., and so many more. Then Sunday night Rapper is threatening one with Gregory Peck & Lana [Turner] and everything. But that's all. I do nothing but rest. I'm tant fort and grand.

Mü la dü! and Felicia sends hers & will write soon. I miss you horribly. Mü la dü,

Ladim

239. Leonard Bernstein to Helen Coates
12 December 1946

Dear H,

Things are beginning to move again. These last two weeks have really done wonders; I have rarely felt so rested. Felicia and I have just returned from a little side trip through Tijuana, Mexico and Palm Springs – and it was a gorgeous little interlude. The desert is just perfect now, and the mountains beat everything. We ride and sleep and eat and gain weight and become brown.

As I say, things are beginning to move again. I've had an idea which may make this picture[74] a phenomenal thing for Hollywood. It would involve me in four ways – composer, conductor, actor and writer. (I've already done a little writing on the screen play.) In other words, really my picture. If it's to be done at all, it must be begun now, while I'm here, so that there's a musical basis before I leave. Then I can finish it in June, assuming that the Soviet invitation doesn't go through, which I expect will be the case. Even if I have to dash back for two weeks after Tanglewood for final touches or retouches, it would be worth it. Financially it would be more than worth it, and artistically it will be a great satisfaction. I am beginning negotiations now, and hope to complete them soon. Of course, I will call Kouss first and try to avoid another hitch with him. I think you would be very excited about this idea.

As to the *Facsimile*, I hope to have the ending in a very few days, along with program notes. When I send it, get it to [Arnold] Arnstein, and tell him to make parts. The cost should be stood by Harms, who would have to have scores & parts in their rental library anyway. (They have to pay *some* copyist. And they'll rook me for it in the end, as usual. Ah well, the way of the world.) Cowan, by the way, has an idea on my publisher problem. We'll see.

Felicia and I grow closer all the time. She's an angel, and a wonderful companion. I shouldn't be surprised if it worked out beautifully in the end.

Love,

L

---

[74] This refers to a project that was never realized. Bernstein is referring to the proposed film *The Beckoning Fair One* in which he was to co-star and for which he was to compose and conduct the score (see Letters 228 and 238).

240. Leonard Bernstein to Helen Coates

22220 Saticoy Street, Canoga Park, CA
22 December 1946

Dear H,

Life moves on apace. I'm toying with the notion of becoming engaged to Felicia. No marriage yet – she must stay here and do a movie contract, and I must travel. We think of it for June, and it's an exciting and somewhat confusing prospect, as you must imagine. But it's good – I know that, and there's no harm in trying. The pursuit of happiness, you know, is one of our few human rights. Listen to Winchell Sunday night. If I decide, he will probably announce it.

Your notes on the *Facsimile* ending are exactly right. The new ending replaces the old ballet ending after the long pause. I've sent it out, and I think it's good. I spoke to Kouss the other day, and he has me in circles. He wants me to marry immediately, he says movies are fine, "but not now", whatever "now" is, and he doesn't want me to play *Facsimile*! This after many calls & wires to Burk, and head-splitting figuring on broadcasts. I don't know what to say to him in argument – he's so self-contradictory. What a difficult relationship!

[John N.] Burk[75] told me you had a cold. Do watch out; everyone in the East seems to have one, Kouss, Blum, etc. Always on vacation one gets a cold! I have so far been spared. The climate makes me sleepy, but the horses and much sleep make up for it. I am now just ripe for a *real* vacation – just beginning to be relaxed. Well – perfection never did exist anywhere.

On the movie – don't worry. I won't sign any contract until after I return. Negotiations are proceeding now, and I'm composing a little, and having story conferences – but that's all. I don't think it would hurt my conducting career, and it seems like my old friend "fun".

[...]

I'll call you from Cincinnati (next week already!) Meanwhile get well and rested. Have you been able to see your *friend* at all during your rest-month?

Love,

L

241. Serge Koussevitzky to Leonard Bernstein

Boston Symphony Orchestra, Symphony Hall, Boston, MA
23 December 1946

Dear Leonard,

My last talk over the telephone with you left a very disturbing impression. And these are the reasons:

---

[75] Program annotator for the Boston Symphony Orchestra.

Speaking of your programs you stubbornly insisted on the performance of your own composition, even for the broadcast. Do you realize that you are invited as a guest conductor, to show your capacity as interpreter of great musical works? May I ask you: do you think that your composition is worthy of the Boston Symphony Orchestra and the Boston organization? Can it be placed on the same level as Beethoven, Schubert, Brahms, Stravinsky, Prokofieff, Bartók or Copland? . . . You may answer my question saying that I often perform also works of lesser value and scope. But you must not forget that I am the permanent conductor, that I stand at the head of this organization to further and develop the musical culture of this country, and, therefore, have the obligation to help young composers. Thus, my responsibilities are very different from yours, or other guest conductors.

I also want you to know my reaction to your "assurance" that Thor Johnson was invited as conductor of the Cincinnati Orchestra, following your recommendation. Do you believe that the Directors of an old musical organization, such as the Cincinnati Symphony Orchestra, would be so naïve, to consider the recommendation of even a very influential lady in the choice of a permanent conductor? Or do you believe that your influence is so great in this country that a word from you would be enough to bring about immediate decisions? If so you are profoundly mistaken. The Trustees of the Cincinnati Orchestra were exceptionally thoughtful and serious regarding this question. I do not want to go into details now, but can tell you that the engagement of Thor Johnson had nothing to do with your recommendation.

I am writing in this direct manner because I consider it superfluous to talk to you as if you were a "spoiled child". You are fully grown up and have to realize that you are responsible for every word you say and all of your actions, especially responsible on account of your gifts and the position you are beginning to occupy.

Think it over, and I hope you will understand the motive which dictates this letter.

Yours,

Serge Koussevitzky

242. Leonard Bernstein to Serge Koussevitzky
Canoga Park, CA
27 December 1946

Dear Serge Alexandrovich,

I have been deeply grieved all day on account of your last letter. I immediately sent you a telegram, trying to explain the misunderstanding, but I canceled it, realizing that it was not a thorough clarification. I must write you instead, because of my love for you, and my need for you to understand.

Why do these misunderstandings happen? Is there an evil element in my nature that makes me do and say immoral things? Is it that I say one thing and mean another? Or is it that communication between two people who are as close to each other is so difficult? If so, then life is too difficult; something is missing in the human constitution.

You must realize that I never meant to suggest that Thor's appointment had anything to do with my recommendation. I was simply reporting an interesting coincidence – that I had been discussing him with Mrs. Wyman a short time before. And I was so happy to hear that it had come true! But certainly not through *my* efforts.

And you know I am happy to play only what you suggest and approve in my Boston concerts. Whenever I conduct in Boston I am conducting for *you*, deep inside, and whatever I may do well is a tribute to you. My main concern is to make you proud of me, and justified in all your efforts for me. So when you asked me suddenly on the phone to take off my own piece, I was surprised, and merely questioned, why? Certainly I believe in my music, or else I would not have written it – not on a level with Beethoven and Bartók, naturally, but in its own smaller terms. But if you feel it is wrong to play it, I will certainly follow what you say, and gladly.

I have had a very difficult year trying to adjust myself to the conventions of my profession. The réclame means absolutely nothing to me – in fact, it only complicates further my already complicated life. Managers, agents, public charm, the terrifying sense of competition in other conductors – the whole desperate race with time would be worth nothing if it were not for the magical joy of music itself. And this joy is bound up tightly with you, who are my only "spiritus genitor". That is why I become so depressed when misunderstandings come between us.

Forgive me, and
Believe me,
Leonard

243. Leonard Bernstein to Serge Koussevitzky
Montgomery, OH
2 January 1947

Dear Serge Alexandrovich,

In my excitement about answering your last letter I completely forgot to tell you the most exciting news of all – that I have become engaged to a wonderful girl from South America named Felicia Montealegre. We plan to be married in June, when I return from Europe. I am very happy, and I hope you will be.

This news seems to have leaked out into the papers already[76] – and I did want to be the first to tell you, before you might read it. But this has been impossible, since I have been stranded for five days all over the Southwest due to bad flying weather. My plane kept stopping and stopping; so I spent one night in Texas, another in Arkansas, another sitting up on bad trains, and so on. But I am finally here in Cincinnati, tired but happy, and I have had my first two rehearsals today. The orchestra needs a great deal of work, but they respond well, and I hope for an exciting concert.

I am staying with friends who have a wonderful big farm where I can rest a day or two before going to Chicago. Everyone here seems very satisfied with Thor [Johnson]'s appointment, including most of the orchestra men. It was a wonderful move on their part, and a difficult one to make because of the natural opposition to the appointment of a young American. It took courage, and I am sure Thor's success will justify the appointment in every way.[77]

244. Farley Granger[78] to Leonard Bernstein
Friday, 3 [January] 1947

Dear Lenny,

I just received your very sweet letter. It was wonderful to hear from you. Lenny, we all miss you very much. Ethel and Saul[79] talk of you all the time and last night we played the *Jeremiah* twice, after which we decided to build you a city.

I am so glad we became friends, and I hope I see a lot more of you, though it seems no one gets that privilege for long.

Felicia told us about your horrible New Year's. I wish you could have stayed. We all had such a wonderful time.

I am having dinner with Felicia tonight. She is a great girl, and I'm sure loves you very much.

---

[76] The Associated Press broke the news of the engagement in Hollywood on 31 December 1946 and it was quickly reported by the East Coast press.

[77] Thor Johnson (1913–75) was appointed Music Director of the Cincinnati Symphony Orchestra in 1947, announced as the youngest native-born American conductor to lead a major American orchestra. He remained in Cincinnati for eleven years. During his tenure of the orchestra he conducted the premieres of 120 American and European works, many of which he had commissioned.

[78] Farley Granger (1925–2011), American actor best known for his roles in two Alfred Hitchcock films: *Rope* and *Strangers on a Train*. His first Hollywood appearance had been as Damian Simonov in *The North Star* (he met Aaron Copland during the filming). According to Granger's memoirs (*Include Me Out*), he subsequently had a two-night fling with Bernstein in the late 1940s.

[79] Ethel Schwartz and Saul Chaplin were married at the time. They divorced in 1949.

Your letter was late because it went to the studio first.

Lenny thank you for being so kind, and please write when you can.

Rurally yours,

Farley

245. Leonore Goldstein[80] to Leonard Bernstein
1141 Hampton Park Drive, Richmond Heights, MO
30 January 1947

Dear Leonard,

There are three reasons which impel me to send these lines to you – and I don't know which to name first – yes – I think I do – it's your engagement to be married.

Mrs. [Kate] Ratcliffe confirmed what I had read in the *Times*. I am never certain when such items appear in the daily press, but I do *believe* Mrs. Ratcliffe so here are the very heartiest good wishes for your, and your sweetheart's, happiness – and may it continue to the end of time. I know she is lovely or you would not have chosen her.

Thanks over and over for the fine *Leonore III* Overture. I sat here along with my best concert concentration and listened reverently and so admiringly for your really wonderful Beethoven VIIth. No one could have conducted it better: it was a delight and I wish I could have joined the Providence audience in applauding.

I fear I shall not hear the next radio concert on Tuesday, for I shall be with relatives in New York and Heaven only knows what my granddaughter has planned for that evening.

Will you conduct the Bostonians in New York? If so, I simply *must* get into the hall – but how? I know the concerts are sold out. Has the conductor enough influence to melt Mr. Judd's icy heart and have him sell me a seat anywhere in the Hall? I shall be in New York from Feb 3 to Feb 17th and I am hoping that your New York concerts come during these dates.

That you should be conducting that great orchestra for a month is a real triumph – and you – a youngster – under thirty.

My thanks for the pleasure you gave last Tuesday, and much love from

Leonore III

---

[80] Leonore Goldstein (1875–1971) was on the Board of Directors of the St. Louis Symphony for over sixty-five years. Bernstein often called her "Leonore III" after Beethoven's overture. She was the wife of Dr. Max Goldstein, founder of the Central Institute of the Deaf in St. Louis.

246. Felicia Montealegre to Leonard Bernstein

[Hollywood, CA]

Thursday night, 6 February [1947]

Lenny, my darling, my darling!

First of all, today is my birthday – I am a quarter of a century old, a very frightening fact! It is also a year ago that I sat at your feet, a little drunk but terribly exhilarated at the Arraus'. All day I've been wanting to telephone you and it took a lot of self control not to do so – it seemed rather silly. However . . .

Just came back from the Kellys [Gene and Betsy] where I saw – yes – *Of Mice & Men* – I feel drained and weak, it's so *great*! It's difficult to believe that it came out of Hollywood. I kept thinking of you all through it and listening attentively to Aaron's fabulous score, and remembering the things you had mentioned and loved.

The biggest thing that has happened to me since you left is the most beautiful, warm, affectionate black cocker spaniel puppy in the world who is at this moment biting at my pen while I write. She's mine, my very own! I bought her a week ago having fallen in love at first sight (pedigree papers and all for $35). Stanley Donen[81] christened her Nebish, which she isn't at all but the name stuck. I didn't know whether I'd be able to keep her at first (as a matter of fact it still isn't certain). I've gone through tortures because of David, who I am convinced now is verging on insanity. He decided to cross Joanie who was with me when I bought her and loved the idea of a puppy; he reacted in such a strange way and in a Captain Bligh fashion, told me I must "get rid of her" cause she would interfere with his *work!* She's been such a good girl though (of course I'm constantly taking her out) and I haven't found anyone who'll take care of her for me until my life is settled – he hasn't brought the subject up again, but I'm living with a Damocles' sword precariously swinging over my head. I refuse to give her up – we've become inseparable. You'd love her – everybody does (except David of course). A propos, I could talk to you about him for hours – he really worries me. I think he's quite sick.

Oh sweetie – your concert! I finally heard it last Tuesday. It's useless to even try to tell you how magnificent it was – j'étais tellement fière de toi! I'm dying to hear the next – it's so frustrating to know you've already played it and we don't hear it till next week!

Stanley gave me a party at his apartment last night – I didn't know it was for me until midnight when for no apparent reason the lights were turned off and in comes Gene with a lighted cake which Betsy baked herself, and everybody

---

[81] Stanley Donen (b. 1924), American director of some of the most famous Hollywood musicals. His credits include *On the Town, Singin' in the Rain,* and *It's Always Fair Weather.*

singing the "happy, happy". I fought back the usual tears but could have bawled for hours – aren't they wonderful? Tonight Joan had a special dinner for me – just us and Adolph [Green] and Allyn [Ann McLerie] – with another cake and more candles to blow and wishes granted. It was sweet, but I could have felt more cheerful. Sometimes I miss you so much I actually feel sick to my stomach.

Your father gave me the surprise of my life – such a nice affectionate letter – I just loved him for it.

Thank you for the check. The great Montealegre career is at a complete standstill – I am seriously contemplating going back, defeated but healthy! The only trouble is though that I won't get a job in New York either! Oh *shit*.

I will have you know for further reference that I have a learner's permit and will have a license next week. I drive alone all over the place, up hill and down dale, heavy traffic and all – and I'm *great*! So there!!

What's with you? You never really tell me how you feel – is that so difficult? I don't believe it. Are you still terribly worried and depressed about things, or have you decided not to think about it at all. I keep wondering about you and wishing I could be with you – you always sound so happy and communicative over the telephone, but unfortunately your letters leave me "con gusto a poco!" I know, you warned me.

When are you due back in New York – please write me soon, this place is bad enough without your making things worse.

My love to your family – of course it's good to be home again. I rather envy you. Where's Shirley and what are her plans?

Boss darling – good night – much much love and many many kisses.

Fely

247. Bette Davis to Leonard Bernstein
Butternut, Sugar Hill, Franconia, NH
[?February 1947][82]

Lennie,

How really thoughtful of you to write me about my attempt to be a pianist in *Deception*. From you it meant very much, as you can imagine. You were conducting in Boston the other day – and here I am with my project sitting not far away – and unable to come down and hear you. I would have so much loved it. You are doing wonderful things and I am always somewhere else. I read about it though and always the things said are complimentary – and of course I think that is as it should be. Your signed photograph is now on my wall – and a proud

---

[82] This letter is undated, but must date from early 1947. Bernstein had a four-week guest engagement with the Boston Symphony Orchestra in February 1947, and Bette Davis was pregnant at the time: her daughter Barbara was born on 1 May 1947.

possession. It is really exciting about the baby – and so unbelievable to me – but at this point there is definite evidence so I must believe it.

Really so many thanks for your letter – I beamed for days.

Love,

Bette

248. Leonard Bernstein to Helen Coates
Rochester, NY
26 February 1947[83]

Dear H,

I. Testimonial for [Menahem] Pressler: *A genuine pianistic poet.*
II. The Palestine program, as I recall, is:
Schumann #2
Jeremiah
Ravel Concerto.
III. Brussels: Everything seems to be by Aaron or me! I would like to divide the program into three parts, for instance:
Movies: Copland (both suites) appr. 20 min.
Ballet: Fancy Free (appr. 25 min.)
Theatre: Gershwin–Bennett Porgy (appr. 14´)
This would make a nice program, but short (roughly an hour). If satisfactory, this should be it. Otherwise I'll have to cast about for another ballet & play *On the Town* with *Porgy. Undertow* is a possibility, but I don't like it. Furthermore, to be really representative about American film music, I *should* play something like the *Spellbound* score,[84] but I can't stand that kind of Hollywood stuff. Which leaves only Aaron, which precludes a Copland ballet. Would you explain all this to the man and get his reaction?
IV. The PCA[85] business is cleared. All is set for March 25th, I believe.
V. Diamond. I think someone should be put in charge of a fund – not us: we've had our share. Won't Margaret do it? Or, if not, Olga or Mrs. Hirschman. I think musicians should be tapped first; Rodzinsky, Szell, Monteux, Kouss, Dimitri, also Smallens etc. – all the conductors who have ever played D's music. Also composers: Alec Wilder, Hanson, Goddard Lieberson, etc., etc. I think *chief* contributor should be Alice Berezowsky.[86] I'm serious: she started it.

---

[83] Place and date added by Helen Coates.
[84] The score for *Spellbound* was composed by Miklós Rózsa.
[85] Progressive Citizens of America. In Bernstein's FBI file, an Office Memorandum dated 2 March 1949, to the Director from D. A. Ladd, indicates (p. 10) that "Buffalo informant [redacted] advised that on March 25, 1947, Bernstein had been the principal speaker at a meeting of the Progressive Citizens of America in Buffalo, New York."
[86] Alice Berezowsky was a friend of Koussevitzky, wife of the composer Nicolai Berezowsky, and author of the book *Duet With Nicky* (1943).

VI. We are staying overnight in or around Vassar after the concert, leaving next day for Providence. I could go back to N.Y. with you if you can get me a flight to Prov[idence] next day. Although it makes a lot of extra traveling. Don't you think it's simpler to stay over?

Love,

L

249. Adolph Green to Leonard Bernstein
[Hollywood, CA]
[February 1947]

Dollink Lennie,

What is there to say?

You are brilliant, brash, you (28) – I am fat, old (49 ½)[87] and feeble. In short, what is there to say?

Betty & I are Hollywood successes, it seems. *Good News* is about to go before the camera, causing a minor revolution at M.G.M. No picture has ever before been done there without 4 years of preparation, 15 scripts, etc., etc.

Now we are grappling with the horns of an Arthur Freed dilemma. We've been offered a second picture, at mightily increased salaries, and a plum it is by M.G.M. standards: a G-R-E-E-A-A-T-T SCREEN CREDIT. *Easter Holiday*[88] – with J. Garland, G. Kelly, F. Sinatra, K. Grayson.[89] All songs by Irving Berlin & we would have to work with Irving B. – naturally we won't stay in Hollywood but Freed has told us that he can arrange for us to write the bulk of it in N.Y. We are therefore tempted.

Maybe we'll write this thing & be finished just in time for us to write a big, successful show together next winter.

Glad that I didn't marry A.A.[90] out here – double, double doubts – but *away with them!!*

I feel completely sure now that I want to marry her, and I'm very anxious to get back and do it.[91]

Will you be around at the end of March? We'll make it then. You must be on hand.

---

[87] Adolph Green was 32 at the time of writing this letter (b. 2 December 1914).

[88] Evidently, this was a working title for *Easter Parade*, released in 1948. Comden and Green were not involved.

[89] *Easter Parade*, with a score by Irving Berlin, starred Judy Garland and Fred Astaire. Gene Kelly, Frank Sinatra, and Kathryn Grayson were not in the film.

[90] Allyn Ann McLerie (b. 1926), Canadian-born actress. Her Broadway debut was in Kurt Weill's *One Touch of Venus* (1943), and she performed in the ensemble of *On the Town* before replacing Sono Osato as Ivy Smith.

[91] Adolph Green married Allyn Ann McLerie on 21 March 1947. They divorced in 1953 and she married the actor George Gaynes the same year.

Love to everyone,

Adolph

There's an item in the Sunday *Times* about the Hammerstein Rodgers show *Allegro*. Rodgers says "it will combine dance, music and drama as an integrated unit".[92]

About time too. It's an unprecedented notion, very daring, never before attempted – Ahhhh! – shit, fuck, balls!!!

P.S. I love you.

Our associate producer, one Roger Edens,[93] is a great fan of yours, but very displeased with your Boston program. He complains about that Beethoven & Schubert junk and feels it's ruining your career to have to play it. I'm just passing along this opinion for what it's worth. Stick to the moderns, he says.

250. Leonard Bernstein to Renée Longy Miquelle
Lehigh Valley Railroad [on board train]
3 March 1947

Chère Re-La-Mi [written in musical notation: D-A-E, i.e. Re-La-Mi],

Thinking of you on this ghastly train (ghastly pen!), even to the point of recalling your address. So many things made me think of you – a man from Baltimore next to me at lunch, *Homemade pies* on the menu; Claude's appearance backstage in Symphony Hall – etc. etc.[94]

I'm beginning a week's tour with the Rochester orch. and I'm up to my neck in penicillin. Overtired, I guess, and inevitable consequences. I'll live.

Will I see you before I go to Europe April 9th?

Love,

Spooky

---

[92] Lewis Funke: "News and Gossip Gathered on the Rialto," *The New York Times*, 16 February 1947. Concerning *Allegro*, Funke wrote that although Rodgers and Hammerstein were "standing guard over it like a couple of Fort Knox sentries, Mr. Rodgers admitted the other afternoon that it would be a departure from the conventional. In a mood of convivial candor he even breathed, 'experimental', and said it would combine dance, drama and music as an integrated unit – something the avant garde has been talking about for a long time."

[93] Roger Edens (1905–70) was a composer and producer in Hollywood, an important member of Arthur Freed's team at MGM. Edens is perhaps best known for nurturing the talent of the young Judy Garland (they became lifelong friends). He was Associate Producer on a string of successful MGM musicals. Comden and Green's greatest Hollywood success was *Singin' In The Rain* (1952), for which they wrote both the story and the screenplay. Most of the songs were by Freed and Nacio Herb Brown, but the new song for which Comden and Green wrote lyrics was "Moses Supposes," with music by Roger Edens.

[94] In spring 1947, Bernstein was listed as a member of the Renée Longy Miquelle anniversary committee, set up to celebrate her 50th birthday. It is a sign of how widely admired she was that the members of the committee included Samuel Barber, Olin Downes, Gian-Carlo Menotti, Fritz Reiner, and Randall Thompson. Its aim was to encourage donations from friends, colleagues, and former pupils to pay the outstanding mortgage on her cottage on Cape Cod to "insure her future security" in honor of her "long-standing devotion to the profession."

251. Sid Ramin to Leonard Bernstein

32 West 53rd Street, New York, NY
[March 1947]

Dear Lenny,

Just a note to congratulate you on your engagement and to wish you continued happiness and success. I guess I ought to apologize for not using your "secret" phone number and letting you know how I'm making out, but I guess you know me by now.

Incidentally, your engagement came as quite a surprise (I don't know why it should) and now you've got me thinking about whether I ought to be next.[95]

The recordings I was so proud of several months ago, and wanted you to hear, have since lost a lot of the original appeal (as far as my wanting to play them for people). I guess that's a good sign, although I still think there are some good spots worth listening.

However, if I have to bring some recording to use as an excuse to see you and your new phonograph, I think I can manage to pick a few better ones, twenty or thirty!!

Really, Lenny, I'd like to see you and ask a bit of advice in regards to quite a few things that are popping here; also keep you posted on what the past year and a half in N.Y. has held for me. And then, of course, I'd like to see you without having the meet through lots of people, for a change. So . . .

Of course, I don't know where this letter will find you, but when you get back to N.Y. (if you're away right now), how about a letter and an appointment?[96]

Best regards to everyone,
Sid

252. Leonard Bernstein to Serge Koussevitzky

Park Hotel, Tel Aviv, Israel
25 April 1947

Dear Serge Alexandrovich,

If you ever wanted to be involved in a historical moment, this is it.[97] The people are remarkable; life goes on in spite of bombs, police, everything. There is a strength and devotion in these people that is formidable. They will never let

---

[95] Sid Ramin married Gloria Breit on 9 January 1949.

[96] Note in Helen Coates' hand: "Tried to call him but he was in Boston."

[97] April 1947 was a crucial time in the history of Palestine, soon to become Israel. On 2 April the British government referred the problem of the future of Palestine to the United Nations, and on 13 May the UN appointed a Special Committee to examine the question of Palestine.

their land be taken from them; they will die first. And the country is beautiful beyond description. It is a real tropical vacation for me, with the wonderful Mediterranean and the sweet, warm spring.

The orchestra is fine, and I am having a great success. [Charles] Munch has just finished his weeks here, and we finally met: he came to my rehearsal this morning, and was so excited that he wants to arrange a big concert for me in Paris. Tant mieux.

I miss you, and can't wait to return to Tanglewood. Please don't be worried about me; the bombs fly, but the newspapers exaggerate.

My love to Olga, and to you my deepest devotion,
Leonard

253. Leonard Bernstein to Aaron Copland
Hotel Castiglione, Paris, France
27 May 1947

Old Charmer!

It's done. Fait. The Symphony's[98] been heard. Two days ago in Prague.

First I must say it's a wonderful work. Coming to know it so much better I find in it new lights and shades – and new faults. Sweetie, the end is a sin. You've got to change. Stop the presses! We must talk – about the whole last movement, in fact.

The reactions were mixed. Too long, said some. Too eclectic, said Shostakovich (he should talk!). It lacks a real Adagio, said Kubelík. Not up my street, said Wee Willie Walton. And everyone found Chaikovsky's Fifth in it, which only proves their inanity. I haven't seen the press yet, but I think it will be good. It just wasn't a wow, that's all; it was solid, it was serious. The orchestra was exhausted (end of the festival), and the rehearsals were nightmares. (We had six!) But at the concerts they played marvelously. Even to catching our private rubatos in the third movement

which, by the way, is my favorite part. That's the real inspiration – the real Aaronchen. I could make out fine *anti* cases for mov'ts I & II (and of course IV) but not III. That's my personal wow.

By the way, I do it awfully well, and I'd love to do it in the States. Maybe Tangle[wood] – well, maybe the City Center.

---

[98] Bernstein conducted the European premiere of Copland's Third Symphony with the Czech Philharmonic Orchestra on 25 May 1947, at the Prague Spring Festival.

There is much to say. Letters are impossible. But won't you write me and tell about May and Harvard and the Virgil [Thomson] Opera and where you are and Koussie and Victor [Kraft] and everyone? And D[avid] D[iamond]?

If you write me to Holland I'll be sure to get it. I'm there June 8–13. Write now, and they'll hold it for me. G. de Koos, Noordeinde 62A, Den Haag, Holland.

Palestine was a real thrill. More later. Will you be in NYC for my stadium week?

Love, Love,

L

254. Aaron Copland to Leonard Bernstein
Mexico, D.F.
4 June 1947

Young Charmer!

Just received your forwarded Paris letter and I'm dashing a hasty reply on the chance that it will reach you in Holland. It was fun to read the various reactions to the Symph – including your own. I've decided that it's a tough job to write an almost 40 min. piece which is perfect throughout. That's about all I'll concede for the moment! You were an angel to struggle with rehearsals at the tail-end of a Festival. The part of your letter I liked best, of course, was your saying you'd like to do it zum States.

Didn't I tell you I was coming to Mexico to conduct the Symph myself? I've had 3 rehearsals already and the concert is still 2 weeks away. My main trouble is giving cues for entrances. Well, anyhow it's very good experience and I'm getting a kick out of it. (Kouss said to me before I left "If you ruin *my* Symph I vil keel you.")[99]

All my N.Y. news is probably stale for you by now. Virgil's opera[100] was original-looking on the stage – no one has ever seen anything quite like it. But I thought there was more music in *Four Saints* [*in Three Acts*]. It's as if a new musical idea hadn't occurred to him in 10 years. The prosody, as per usual, is superb – but then it's easy to have good prosody if you have nothing else on your mind (I'm quoting myself).

D[avid] D[iamond] looked much improved when last I saw him. I suppose Helen Kates told you of our financial crisis which was solved until August.

Bob Shaw did a bee-utiful job with my new chorus.[101] Most people seemed to like it, but the press was only mildly interested. I can't imagine how you'll

---

[99] Koussevitzky had commissioned Copland's Third Symphony, and gave the first performance in Boston on 18 October 1946.
[100] Thomson's *The Mother of Us All* was first performed on 7 May 1947 at Columbia University. The cast included Teresa Stich-Randall as Henrietta, her operatic debut.
[101] *In the Beginning* was first performed on 2 May 1947 at Harvard Memorial Chapel by the Collegiate Chorale, conducted by Robert Shaw.

react to it. Any ho you won't have to conduct it – since there's nothing but voices. (I decided that Bob's conducting technique derives from the football cheerleader. Or did you say that already?)

I was in Cuba the night you played the Symph in Prague. Mexico seems so naively serious by comparison. I see *Jeremiah* on display here in the record shops. Chávez spoke of asking you to come to conduct a week in August. Did he wire you? And just before getting your letter I was talking about you (I seem to be always talking about you!) with de Spirito[102] and Carrington[103] at lunch. You'll be glad to hear that San Juan de Letran still thrives and that I live one block away.

I'll be at the Stadium concerts. And thanks Gawd for Tanglewood so's we can talk – finally. I've lectures all prepared for you about your City Center programs – completely disinterested since I leave for Brazil on August 14. Your ex-mentor sends you an abrazo muy fuerte –

A.

255. Lena Horne[104] to Leonard Bernstein
16 July 1947

Dear Leonard Bernstein,

I would very much like to have you as my guest at a party at Jerome Robbins' home, 421 Park Ave., on Thursday night July 24th from 8:00 to 1:00 (corner of 56th Street).[105]

---

[102] Romolo de Spirito (sometimes given as "di Spirito"), a tenor who specialized in the performance of music by American composers. In his New York debut recital (27 February 1944) he included songs by Paul Bowles, David Diamond, and Virgil Thomson.

[103] Carrington Welch, who was Romolo de Spirito's regular accompanist.

[104] The legendary singer and actress Lena Horne (1917–2010) was closely involved in the civil rights movement. She fought institutional racism in Hollywood in the 1940s (her scenes were customarily shot so that they could be removed for distribution to states in the South), she refused to sing for segregated audiences of troops, and she worked with Eleanor Roosevelt to pass anti-lynching laws. She was named as a Communist sympathizer – along with the likes of Bernstein, Marc Blitzstein, Aaron Copland, Judy Holliday, Langston Hughes, Burl Ives, Zero Mostel, Dorothy Parker, Pete Seeger, and Artie Shaw – in the infamous *Red Channels: The Report of Communist Influence in Radio and Television* (1950), and she was blacklisted by Hollywood. After her death in 2010, the president of the NAACP – America's oldest and largest civil rights organization – described Horne as "an outstanding, groundbreaking entertainer and a staunch civil rights activist who stood on the side of justice and equality. Lena Horne won the hearts of millions of Americans of all backgrounds as a glamorous and graceful actress and singer. She broke many color barriers and fought valiantly to bring down the institutionalized racism that plagues our society and prevents all Americans from an equal opportunity to pursue the American dream."

[105] This may have been the occasion referred to by the television personality Ed Sullivan – "at the very least a facilitator, if not an informant, for the FBI and the House Un-American Activities Committee" (Vaill 2007, p. 171) – when he put pressure on Jerome Robbins in 1950 to disclose "the names of people who had been at a cause party for Soviet–American friendship he'd allowed the singer Lena Horne to give at his apartment" (Vaill 2007, p. 172). At that point Robbins did not name names, though he did so when he testified in public to the HUAC in May 1953.

We will share delightful drinks and entertainment for the benefit of the fighting veterans organization, United Negro and Allied Veterans of America.[106]

Yours sincerely,

Lena Horne

256. Marketa Morris to Leonard Bernstein

Continental House, Stamford, NY

23 July 1947

Lenny,

Your letter stirred up lots of problems.

To go into them adequately would require an elaborate paper – and that does not agree with my vacations. I try a compromise. I have to be honest in the first place. Honest and short means usually: it hurts! I have to rely on your perspicacity and your English to translate my thoughts into a good, nice, considerate English. Will you?

I don't think that our work will be finished in five months. But there is even some risk of your feeling worse after this period since many problems may have come into the open without finding a solution.

Under the given circumstances I would want to start only if you are taking the responsibility for such a possible outcome.

Of course there is a chance that we may come to some essential clarification. No way to deny it. It's fifty fifty – and you have to know it.

In your dreams there is confusion, you are not able to go where you have to go: two *simultaneous engagements* or dates and so on. You are seeing Felicia and the day she leaves you *have* to see a boy.

The same old pattern. You can't give up. Very eager to resume analysis but the queer fish resistance is as big a fish as your drive to get well.

If you could give up Europe for the solution of your problems, you would have solved quite some of them and we had the most promising start. But would I make it a condition, which, I have to confess was very tempting – I am sure it wouldn't work out, since you would use it against me, that is, against our work.

I don't quite understand your dream involving your parents. What does Rochester mean? Did you intend to leave alone by plane (which you missed!). Could it indicate that it is a "force majeur" and not your own incapacity that you can't separate yourself from them. Being inside still a child as you say (giving up childhood).

---

[106] This was one of many organizations supporting African-American causes that came under suspicion from the government. FBI records reveal that the United Negro and Allied Veterans of America was described by US Attorney General Tom Clark on 4 December 1947 as "subversive and among the affiliates and committees of the Communist Party, U.S.A. which seeks to alter the form of government of the United States by unconstitutional means."

You are toying around with the possibility of being a dull and uninteresting talent – or losing your place in the score (Koussevitzky).

Remember that you wanted to challenge people and find out whether they would still love you.

It's all very sketchy, I know. But I still hope that you can pick out something of help for you.

I did intend to go to Tanglewood, indeed, but it did not materialize.

I had an interesting letter from George today who himself is going to the Berkshires.

Lenny, I hope very much that you understand what I really want to convey to you! Do you?

I am back in town between the 5–10th of Sept.

Sincerely.

M

257. Richard Adams Romney ("Twig")[107] to Leonard Bernstein
34 Beekman Place, New York, NY
25 July 1947

My dear Lenny,

I can't resist writing you, even though I know that the mood I am in should prompt me to be still. I feel sad – and alone in the way only a neurotic can feel alone.

The idea of living with someone else came crashing down around my knees last night just as hurriedly as it had spent itself in the sky the day before. The thought of having to be responsible to an irresponsible degree for someone else's living condition makes me balk like I have heard men do just before they take a wife. Living in this little box has a security that is that of a desperate grasping squeeze . . . I'm reminded of the Steig drawing of the man in the box who thinks "people are no damn good"! I tripped over a stone yesterday. This

---

[107] Richard Adams Romney (1918–2009) was often known to his friends as "Twig". A collection of letters to him from Bernstein, Christopher Isherwood, Osbert Sitwell, Pavel Tchelitchew, John Van Druten, and others is to be found in Yale University Library (Beinecke Library, Gen Mss 462). Romney's obituary published in the *Albany Times Union* (19 July 2009) includes the following information: "Richard Adams Romney, born July 15, 1918 in Salt Lake City, Utah, died in Troy, N.Y. on July 15, 2009. Mr. Romney had been a resident of the Van Rensselaer Manor since September 2001 where he received wonderful care and made many friends. A veteran of the US Coast Guard, he served in the North Sea, receiving an honorable discharge in 1944. Mr. Romney was a resident of Manhattan's Upper East Side from 1945 to 1997 where he worked in the real estate and insurance industries. From 1950 to 1954, he was a gallery assistant at the Betty Parsons Gallery, Manhattan, the first home of artists like Ellsworth Kelly, Jackson Pollock, and Mark Rothko. He was the original owner of Pollock's *Number 3, 1949*. The great relationship of his life was that with the American heiress and supporter of the arts, Alice De Lamar. Their correspondence for half a century resides in the Beinecke at Yale. There are no surviving family members."

was it: the nearer my time came to report to the VA[108] for my chance for psycho-analytical treatment, the more tense I noticed myself to be. I translated it as a natural resistance – for certainly, beyond the chance of talking about myself, hashing over my imaginary reflections, and being an "actress", there is a deep conviction that my locked doors must not be opened. The fear of falling with my faults is funny – for I believe that by uncovering one recovers, yet recognition has not healed me of the failings lately (like Christian Science, for instance, has led me to believe). Why, when one sees an error of premise doesn't that seeing dispel its tenacity? Is it the old self-authority commanding "thus far and no farther"?

Well, I sweat through the interview, with the best manners I could muster – by that I mean without personal messiness, and found I have to go through another interview – also not an MD or Psychiatrist – which will determine whether I am in worth[y] condition to take the time of the Psychiatrist. Then it is probable that psychiatric survey and not psycho-analytical treatment will be granted. So – with all my resistance to being analysed, I am depressingly disappointed that a possibility of being treated is quite improbable. Another contradiction! Perhaps I should take a part-time job and see if I can earn my analysis – even on through my school-time-days to come. (The analyst Bruce Knight is arranging for me to see is named Berkeley – and lives near you on 11th Street, I believe. Have you ever heard of her? I wish she wasn't a her.)

Helen wrote me a lovely thank you card – and it delighted me a good deal. She mentioned your great success with *Appalachian Spring* – but I knew of it the day before by my own conviction. I went into Liberty and listened to the Koussevitzky recordings and was disappointed at his interpretation. There is a lovely excitement in the way you play the "saddle" part – is it Part III? – Koussy rushes it, instead of syncopating it – and the way you end it is moving. Oh, butch, you're wonderful!

This morning's book list from Holliday advertises Auden's new thing along with a new one of Edith Sitwell's. When I get round to send you [*The Age of*] *Anxiety* I will also include *The Shadow of Cain* which the book store insists "reflects more directly the tragic impact of contemporary events on an acutely sensitive and perceptive nature." Then they add, "In their likeness and unlikeness, these two books are an absorbing study."

I have been to Lewisohn [Stadium] twice this week. Hans Schwieger is the poorest conductor I have ever heard with a first rate orchestra. He conducts as if he were leading a hofbrau band.[...] The Philharmonic must realize that many people take to concerts in the summer because of the outdoor "tranquility", and it is their initiation to the best music – therefore they could increase their winter

---

[108] The United States Department of Veterans Affairs. Romney had served as a Coast Guard in the Second World War.

subscription lists with new enthusiasts, but there is a vital danger in sandwiching the very best with the slip-shod. Evidently you set the standard for their summer concerts extremely high. I have heard from many diversified tastes that your concerts were electric. Mr. Schwieger has been a sad let-down.

Do I sound mean, Pappie. Hating people again?

You set me such a fine example of living with other people, I am more aware than ever of my anti-social side. Please don't let my untidy sick mind bore you away from me (I want you to feel a teensy bit responsible so that you won't give me up as unworthy of your good affection). You've touched me deeply – honestly you have.

I'm going to close – hoping you can scribble a card when you're squatting in that hammock. Kisses to Helen. (Gobbles to you.)

Twig

Tell Helen to get *The Gallery*[109] from her lending library (it's already out of stock).

Why don't you try a tone poem of *Anxiety*?[110] The four themes – their inter-relationship, pairing-off drama – etc. might make a good thing. And you could do it! Name it *The Wanderer In Greenwood* after me (forgive that!) [. . .]

258. Richard Adams Romney ("Twig") to Leonard Bernstein
34 Beekman Place, New York, NY
29 July 1947

Dear Lenny,

Forgive all of the overheatedness in my past letters, but know it is only because I know you don't want me to be sillily overboard that I ask your forgiveness. You made me very very happy in those few days, and I have had to try to know what it was about your example and good heart that made me wish I could get right against you.

Here is a snap of me taken on the wharf of Hamilton, Bermuda that I hope you will look at when you forget what I look like. I think it quite good.

What do you think of the *Anxiety* idea? There is so much musical-subtlety in it, and those various metres brought about by the different roads the couples

---

[109] *The Gallery* by John Horne Burns (1916–53) was published in the summer of 1947 and acclaimed by the likes of Gore Vidal, Edmund Wilson, and John Dos Passos. Burns, a Harvard graduate, served as a US intelligence officer in North Africa and Italy during the war, and his book is one of the first to explore gay life in the army.

[110] This letter indicates that the suggestion for using Auden's *The Age of Anxiety* as an inspiration came initially from Romney, who developed his idea in the letter of 29 July 1947. Romney sent Bernstein a copy of the poem very soon after it was first published in July 1947. In Bernstein's reply of 1 August he thanks Romney for the books, but after that there is no mention of *The Age of Anxiety* in his letters to Romney until May 1950.

take and their differing means of transportation, to say nothing of the moods, and the separateness that becomes oneness under alcohol and/or libidinal urges. You mentioned it being good ballet material, yes, but I think, first, it should be composed as music by itself and therefore protect it from being too obvious program music, and then if some clever choreographer can put the musical composition to work, with what added quality good music may give to the themes and material, well and good.[111] I would rather have "it" in the concert hall, where it can be less "handled" than in the ballet school where many talents brush it up. It's too good a thing for many hands.

I am beginning to suffer more for lack of occupation, but until the VA makes some kind of a decision regarding their award of psycho treatment, I don't think I can obligate my time just yet. Do I ring self-excused and lazy? Hummm. If the VA vetoes treatment, I am determined to work it out on my own but taking temporary work during my school days, and immediately before school begins.

The *Tribune* had a high compliment of your first night.[112] I wish I could have seen and heard the performance. I read it at a friend's house – and will get you a copy if you weren't able to grab it in Pittsfield.

Speaking of my friend, she is Anne Gibson Clark – and she is toying with the idea of going home to Grand Rapids to pick up her convertible, and then taking me to Tanglewood one week-end to hear some more music. What you do think of that?

Kiss Helen for me and tell her I will write her the letter I want to, in answer to her friendly card, very soon. She couldn't have been kinder to me and I thank her every time I think of her – which is every day.

Lots of love,
Twigling

259. Leonard Bernstein to "Twig" Romney
Box 102, Lenox, MA
1 August 1947

Dear Twig, fighting to the last,

This should be five or six letters by now. There are so many things to say, and the super-varied contents of your three letters call for all kinds of discussion. But

---

[111] Romney predicts the early performance history of *The Age of Anxiety* with uncanny accuracy. After its first concert performances in 1949, the work was used for a ballet by Jerome Robbins in 1950.

[112] Presumably a reference to Bernstein's concert at Tanglewood on 27 July 1947 when he conducted the Boston Symphony Orchestra in Mozart's *Magic Flute* Overture, Schubert's "Great" C major Symphony, and Stravinsky's *Rite of Spring*, the first time anyone other than Koussevitzky had conducted the Boston Symphony at Tanglewood. *The New York Times* reported that the concert was attended by 8,500 people and that "Dr Koussevitzky listened from his box in the center of the music shed, and later appeared on the stage to congratulate Mr. Bernstein."

I'm not in my "analyst" mood right now, having an uncomfortable back condition these days, and having just finished a long and difficult lecture. So let me just not be "Pappy" now, and send you my love and thanks for all the three books (which I keep trying to find a minute to crack) and to tell you how often I think of you.

The concerts here have been tops; and mine have given me the utmost satisfaction. The reactions have been marvelous, and Kouss was ecstatic. I wish you could have been here: – can't you get up for my next one on Aug 7th?

I don't quite understand the rise and fall of Bruce Knight. What *really* happened? And have you met Miss Berkeley?

I have to dash off for a diathermy on my poor aching back. Write more and often, and better still, come (though I can't promise you space here for a while) and I love your photograph.

Bless you, and don't let your resistance interfere with going through with the analysis.

All the affection you need –

L

The enclosed sheds much light![113]

260. Marketa Morris to Leonard Bernstein
Continental House, Stamford, NY
28 August 1947

Lenny,

Let me be very brief. I feel in your letter that some part in you expects my support for the cancellation of Palestine! That you dare not to see it, but that you would want to do something completely radical – for your Resurrection!

The only thing you can do: try to feel whether that is what *you* want. Not what I want!

Please call me up after Labor day (or even before) best between 9–12 a.m. [on] 4751 because I would want to arrange for our first session in New York. Will you? It has technical reasons.

I don't quite understand why you were pleased not to feel the necessity to thank me for my time? No obligation for conventional feelings? That's okay? But how about some genuine, warm feeling of gratefulness? Could you imagine?

---

[113] Whatever was "enclosed" has not survived.

In N.Y. I refused to take a brother in law of a patient of mine who wanted to come to St[amford] and have daily sessions by saying: not even if he would pay $25 a session.

I am mentioning it deliberately to show you that it is not only you who has to give up and make sacrifices – but that I am willing as well to do so, if necessary. I even proposed to see you once more, if you would have wished. I understand perfectly that you did not since you were so busy making so important decisions.

We'll talk about it more in N.Y.

Have a nice time – a productive time first of all!

Yours,

Marketa

For the sake of order: I am charging (since last year) $10 a session. We had one in N.Y. and 3 in Stamford.

You had no dream? How come after all these important events?

M

261. Marketa Morris to Leonard Bernstein
562 West 113th Street, New York, NY
[?1947]

Lenny,

I got your dream letter. You know that it is quite impossible to give a written interpretation to a dream – and more so a dream without interpretation.

Why am I living in Brooklyn?

Jimmy's Restaurant in Greenwich V[illage]

Why another cab to go to Brooklyn?

What's about 289?

It's getting dark at four o'clock in the afternoon?

Switches putting on lights *upstairs* and not *downstairs*? What's the difference between up and downstairs in this beautiful, big, expensive house?

What about the two girls blocking the exit from behind your desk?

Write me if you feel like – besides the dreams! F[or] i[nstance] why cannot you relax and just simply *not* compose? Remember, *you had* the idea that adjustment to homosexuality could facilitate heterosexuality! Couldn't adjustment to relaxation constitute a capacity of creative work? Of course not *pretending* to relax only.

Marketa

I could see you Monday at 12 (noon) or at 7 p.m. Tuesday at 11 a.m. OK?

262. James M. Cain[114] to Leonard Bernstein
666 South Carondelet Street, Los Angeles, CA
1 October 1947

Dear Mr. Bernstein,

Two proposals have been made to me, one by a leading playwright and a reputable producer, the other by the most successful operetta composer we have, hooked up with a highly successful librettist, to put *Serenade* on the stage;[115] but I am bound to report that in spite of a high personal regard for all of these various gentlemen, all I could detect in their ideas was the most obvious theatrical claptrap, and accordingly I did my best to discourage them. *Serenade*, unfortunately, as seems to be the case with most of my stories, has problems that don't yield to a socko waltz tune, and I am not sure they yield at all. You, though, might be able to get somewhere with it. I mean, I have followed your work & think it might suit your gifts.

As for my doing your libretto, I can only say I never did one, and have a suspicion that at my age I shouldn't try to learn.[116] The rights, for your information, are in the clear, that is the dramatic rights; I own them, and while the publisher cuts in for 25% of anything paid on account of performances, I make the deal, and naturally would be reasonable. My suggestion would be to get in the market for a poet, or poetess, and I would think that the *New Yorker*, which is in touch with every poet there is, may be of some help, if you were to write them, or better still go in there. Katherine White, I understand, is still with them, and could no doubt think of somebody. After that you are in the lap of chance, but no worse with a *New Yorker* nominee than with me.

---

[114] James M. Cain (1892–1977) was an American writer and journalist whose novels included *The Postman Always Rings Twice* (1934), *Mildred Pierce* (1941) and *Double Indemnity* (1943) as well as *Serenade* (1937). Though Cain disliked the label, he was one of the leading writers of "hardboiled" crime fiction.

[115] The "most successful operetta composer we have" and the "highly successful librettist" who had approached Cain (in 1940) were Sigmund Romberg and Oscar Hammerstein II (see Hoopes 1982, p. 366), so Bernstein had reason to be flattered by Cain's positive response to his request for permission to base an opera on *Serenade*.

[116] This project was reported in *The New York Times* more than a year after the exchange of letters between Bernstein and Cain. On 5 December 1948 an article headed "Opera Projects" stated: "Leonard Bernstein has asked James M. Cain for permission to base an opera on *Serenade*. He also asked Mr. Cain to write the libretto for him. The author declined the job, suggesting the composer was competent to write his own book. He promised, though, that he would give no one else prior operatic rights to the novel before the end of the year. He himself is skeptical about the project, for he wrote his agent, Harold Ober: 'I know that anyone who undertakes any stage work based on this book is letting himself in for a thousand headaches.' It was in April that Mr. Bernstein gained his promise from Mr. Cain. Since the composer–conductor will not be back from Palestine till some time this week, it is not known how far he has gone with his plans." In fact, this project went back to the autumn of 1947, as we see in the correspondence between Cain and Bernstein.

To elucidate the rights thing, which on re-reading doesn't seem wholly clear. A contract leasing you the right to produce an opera based on the book would be one thing, and would be made by me, either with you or with your producer. Royalties paid me would be split with Alfred A. Knopf, Inc., my publisher. Your libretto & score would be another contract, made by producers, publishers, etc., with you and your librettist, lyricist, etc. If I did the book, I would be involved in it, but as I hesitate, that complication most likely won't arise.

I should naturally be delighted if you undertake the job, and wish you all luck with it. It has a *theme*, as the picture people found out, as horrendous as the Motif of Sulphur Yellow Truth in Mencken's concert program; but no doubt you know all about that, and let us hope, what to do with it, or how to get rid of it.[117] Many thanks for your felicitations. The lady,[118] as you may have heard, has yodeled quite a bit of opera herself.

Sincerely,

J. M. Cain

263. Leonard Bernstein to James M. Cain
9 October 1947

Dear Mr. Cain,

Thank you very much for your kind letter of October 1 and for your kind comments about me and my gifts. I am happy to learn that the rights are clear, but to be frank, I am not reconciled to the fact that you would not be able to write the libretto from your work. However, I will follow your suggestion and look about for a collaborator though at this writing I have some ideas myself as to the book and lyrics.

---

[117] The "theme" of *Serenade* referred to in the letters between Cain and Bernstein needs some explanation. In the original novel, the opera singer John Howard Sharp loses his voice, ostensibly as a consequence of the trauma of his gay relationship with a famous conductor. His voice is restored when he falls in love with a young Mexican prostitute. Cain explained his premise in a letter to his old friend (and erstwhile colleague on the *Baltimore Sun*), H. L. Mencken: "The lamentable sounds that issue from a homo's throat when he sings are a matter of personal observation. . . . But the theme demanded the next step, the unwarranted corollary that heavy workouts with a woman would bring out the stud horse high notes" (see Paul Skenazy, *James M. Cain*, New York: Continuum, 1989, p. 54). In the end, Bernstein abandoned his *Serenade* project, but a few years later plans were made for a Broadway musical based on the same story. Louis Calta reported in *The New York Times* on 11 November 1954 that "The musical stage rights to *Serenade*, James M. Cain's earthy and highly successful novel of 1937, have been purchased [. . .] Arthur Laurents [. . .] has agreed to do the adaptation. Shortly the producers hope to announce the composer and lyricist for the musical venture." Stephen Sondheim was auditioned as a potential lyric writer, and Bernstein was asked whether he wanted to compose the score (see his letter of 6 May 1955 to Felicia, Letter 353). This project, too, came to nothing. The 1956 film adaptation of *Serenade*, starring Mario Lanza, differs wildly from Cain's novel.

[118] Cain's new wife, Florence Macbeth, was an opera singer.

Unfortunately, I will not be able to give the matter my entire time immediately although the first act is fully formed in my mind both dramatically and musically. I will be occupied with my conducting here until at least the end of the year and then I have foreign commitments to conduct, which will consume the first months of the coming year. However, then I shall have free time and nothing will delight me more than to concentrate on the work.

At the moment I have no producer and therefore I am proceeding on my own insofar as the work is concerned and what I would like to have from you is the right to dramatize the book for musical purposes until September, 1948, which I believe will give me ample time to finish what I have in mind.

I understand that in the event of our adopting a writer of the book and a lyric writer, we will have to arrange for royalties to be divided, among all of us.

My sincerest thanks for your kindness and encouragement to proceed in the matter and if you will be good enough to send me a little note regarding the rights, I shall be grateful. It is difficult at long range to discuss these matters from a practical standpoint or try to get together on the book and lyrics and on more technical business, but I believe we understand each other thoroughly and I assure you I shall give the matter my sincerest cooperation.

Sincerely yours,

Leonard Bernstein

264. Leonard Bernstein to James M. Cain

32 West 10th Street, New York, NY

8 November 1947

Dear Mr. Cain,

I liked your letter very much, not only because of your encouraging words, but also because it was a real Cain special.

I am not completely convinced that you're not my librettist; but, of course, that has to be your decision. May I hope you will keep thinking about this possibility?

What I would like from you right now is an option on the rights to dramatize the book which would extend to December 31, 1948. I think this would give me enough time to make real inroads into the work. So much of this coming year is to be taken up by conducting engagements, here and abroad, that I feel a good year is necessary. I can let you know fairly soon about the producer arrangements.

If you'll be good enough to send me a note regarding these rights, I shall be very grateful. I am sure then that we can get together via attorney or what-have-you on the more technical business.

Don't you ever come east? I do wish we could have a chance to talk about it. For instance, do you belong to the school that believes in the complete deletion of the theme, as you call it, for operatic purposes, or do you agree with me that it could be handled intelligently and without offense?

Many thanks, and best wishes.

Sincerely,

Leonard Bernstein

265. James M. Cain to Leonard Bernstein
666 South Carondelet Street, Los Angeles, CA
2 December 1947

Dear Mr. Bernstein,

A thousand pardons for not answering your note sooner, and forwarding the reservation requested, but I have been down under the ice winding up a novel, and I know of nothing that claims so much of one's time, and leaves so little juice for anything, except possibly, but not in no way probably, the tying of one's shoes.

The enclosed letter will do it, I think.[119] I haven't consulted lawyers or agents, as they commonly scream for a quid pro quo, as I don't think we are to that stage yet, or that it is even much of a stage, financially speaking, with regard to anything operatic. However, I have had a good many things of the same kind before, and think this will do it, if it covers what you are concerned about.

About the libretto: I try to picture myself pulling this off, but have no faintest notion how to go about it, either to block it out by scenes, or what kind of writing to put in it, or anything. I still think you need a poet, and still think Katherine White of the New Yorker should steer you towards a suitable one. She knows every poet in the world, together with how much he drinks before dinner, whether he does it before breakfast, whether he can write iambic hexameters or free verse, and all relevant things. I used to know her quite pleasantly and think she would like to cooperate on that account, as well as being terrifically impressed by you. No, I have no objection to the damned theme, but think as a practical matter it is the most unsuitable to stage use, though it has been tried now and then with no great objection by the police. I merely think it is unpleasant. But if it were used symbolically, a sort of inverted Faust idea, with addiction to *man* standing for cerebral, cold, and sterile things, and *woman* pulsing with all those hot, life-giving elements, it might do. Personally, I still say you'd do a hell of a sight better to put the time in on Aaron Burr[120] or someone like that. There's a good book out on him, by the way, by Holmes Alexander.

---

[119] Cain attached a formal agreement, reserving for Bernstein the dramatic rights to *Serenade* until 31 December 1948.

[120] Burr was Vice-President of the United States under Thomas Jefferson. In 1804, he challenged Alexander Hamilton (former Secretary to the Treasury) to a duel in which Hamilton was mortally wounded.

Will be in New York, in any event, around 28th or 30th of this month, or shortly thereafter, & will ring you then. Until then, all luck with it, and I confess the greatest curiosity as to what in the name of God you have in mind.

Yours,

J. M. Cain

266. Leonard Bernstein to Helen Coates
Hotel Castiglione, Paris, France
3 May 1948

Dear H,

This is it – le jour de départ to be carried off by the Orient Express into the wilderness of Europe. Nobody knows what will happen. Everyone secretly expects war, but is afraid to say so to himself. It is obvious here that the entire war-plan is being instigated and manufactured in America. There is no need for it – but I have a horrible feeling that America will have its way. God forbid.

These last days in Paris have been pure heaven. I haven't begun to see everyone I wanted to see – but I've spent much time with Ellen [Adler] (who sends you all her love) and François [Valéry] and my wonderful shipboard roommate, and my darling Comtesse Marie-Blanche [de Polignac] (and her big Sunday evening last night to which I took Ellen, and where I sang them the *Bonne Cuisine*) and Nadia [Boulanger] and Otis Bigelow. It's been exciting and warm, & Paris is breathtaking.

The traveling plans became complicated at one point – (Milan to Budapest) – of course – because a train would take me through Yugoslav territory, & no Yugoslav permit is faintly possible. I finally found a way to take a train to Zurich, then fly (the next day) to Prague, then to Budapest. This means a Czech permit, & four hours of waiting around the Czech Consulate, plus many grey & pink and mauve cards for the Russian Zone, where I may still be held. But I've made good friends at the American Embassy and they've helped a lot. At least I'll have a night in Switzerland.

The big news is that I may have *two* concerts in Paris – the other with the Conservatoire (and Neveu) on the 30th! Sudden cancellation. I'll know in a few days. It would make an awful scramble (8 rehearsals in 3 days), but I'm game, if it means a public concert. You know, I suppose, that the Radio concert is again without public.

Well – I'm off to the hinterland, and I'll make every effort to come back.

Love to all & you,

L

267. Leonard Bernstein to Aaron Copland
Milan, Italy
16 May 1948

Dear A,

These should either thrill, amuse or infuriate you. Imagine making an Italian debut with *Appalache*! [i.e. *Appalachian Spring*] I love the one that wonders what a "Balletto per Marta" is, and the one that says it reminds them of American movies, and the one that thinks I'm 6 feet tall.

Anyway, it was a wild success, as was Munich (which was a real international problem), and now on to Budapest. It's all exciting as hell, and I'll write you at length later. My train leaves for Zurich in half an hour.

Love love love,

L

Best to V[ictor] K[raft].

If you don't want to keep these notices, send them to Helen C., please?

268. Leonard Bernstein to Helen Coates
Budapest, Hungary
20 May 1948

Dear H,

They say there hasn't been such a scene in a Budapest concert hall since Toscanini was here. The audience stamped & shouted, & especially for Bartók, which they say has never really been heard until I did it, although it's always being played here. Well – another one under the belt. Everyone is wild with excitement. I've never known what success was before this. [. . .]

The *Times* story on Munich is garbled, but good to see.[121] I think the Tanglewood programs are perfect. I'm eating like a king. Of course, I'm a bit tired and rushed (*three* rehearsals yesterday!) but so happy. Budapest is ugly & beautiful together.

If Shirley wants to join me in Holland or Paris do have her come. Just get her on a plane or something. She seems to need it, and I would love to see her here.

The bobby-soxers tonight beat everything I've ever seen. I'm exhausted. Off to bed; tomorrow on to Vienna. I'm crossing my fingers for *that* one.

Love,

L

What iron curtain? It's only cellophane.

---

[121] A report of the concert appeared in *The New York Times* on 11 May 1948: "at the close of the performance, the audience stood on its feet and applauded [Bernstein] for more than ten minutes in repeated curtain calls, amid a storm of 'bravos'. After the first half dozen bows, Bernstein returned to the podium and with the orchestra, repeated the final portion of the [Ravel] concerto."

269. Leonard Bernstein to Helen Coates
Paris, France
29 May 1948

Dear H,

So much has happened that I don't know where to begin. I didn't write from Vienna since everything is censored from & to that city (all your clippings and notes bore the stamp of the censor!) – and besides I had quite a hectic time. It was the toughest city of all to conquer – a chauvinistic, provincial, nationalistic town, convinced that only Viennese can do anything at all, and that all Americans are fools. There was a mess over the program (I suddenly found myself saddled with a violin soloist) – and the orchestra was exhausted (five different concerts that one week, with 5 conductors and 12 rehearsals!) and besides they were all very antipathetic. It's the first time it ever took me 3 rehearsals to overcome the natural hostility of an orchestra, but we made it! Love & music conquered all; and the concert turned out a great triumph. I had been forewarned that nobody ever goes to concerts any more in Vienna for lack of money (even Bruno Walter's second concert was only half full – for the Mahler!!)[122] – but still I had an almost sold-out house. Of course, the violinist helped – he's been there before. And he turned out to be good, despite the fact that we had to do the Dvořák Concerto! The final trouble was that I had to cancel *Jeremiah* – it would have been impossible in the rehearsals and with such a hostile, exhausted orchestra. It's just as well: the house came down, and, as the manager said, "Ganz Wien in ein' Schlag!"[123] The political situation is a horror: more of that later. I have learned and learned and become very sad. It looks fairly hopeless at the moment.

I was *furious* at the *Times* announcement that I had accepted the C[ity] C[enter]. What crust! How dare they! Mortie [Newbold Morris] should be strung up. What will Palestine think – that I accepted the orchestra just for a gag? It's psychologically horrible for them – and I do hope you'll make it clear to the Palestine people that this story is false. It's the last straw.

---

[122] Bruno Walter conducted Mahler's *Resurrection* Symphony with the Vienna Philharmonic in the Musikverein on 15 May 1948. It's extraordinary to think that this legendary – and marvelous – performance (with Maria Cebotari and Rosette Anday as the soloists) was given to a half-full house. A recording of it has been issued on CD by Sony Japan (SICC 92–3) and others.

[123] "All Vienna in one go," but Bernstein's Viennese debut was also his one and only concert with the Vienna Symphony Orchestra. The program consisted of Schumann's Second Symphony, the Dvořák Violin Concerto (with Gerhard Taschner), and the Ravel G major Piano Concerto with Bernstein directing from the piano. Bernstein's report of an enthusiastic audience may be true, but the concert wasn't a critical success: according to Burton (1994, p. 178), "several Viennese critics disliked Bernstein's conducting style intensely [...] he did not work again with the Vienna Symphony and it was nearly twenty years before he overcame his prejudice and accepted another Viennese conducting engagement."

The orchestra here is angelic. They learned *Jeremiah* in one rehearsal, and are so fast and good and in love with me that I actually cancelled today's rehearsal! First time I ever felt I could dispense with a rehearsal in Europe. Jennie [Tourel] is greater than ever.

I see Ellen [Adler] a lot & she sends her love. François [Valéry] and Nadia [Boulanger] are coming to Holland for my concerts! It just angers me that this second year I still don't have a debut in Paris – after all the ego-building of these triumphs; to do just a broadcast here is an anticlimax. Well, what to do? Paris operates in terms of press agents, and [Charles] Kiesgen is asleep. The Conservatoire concert didn't work out after all – a matter of finance & intrigue with the Radio. It's a shame, but it would have been too hectic anyway.

I've had to call off the Prague concert too [. . .] a wire from Bruno Z[irato] practically threatened excommunication if I went. So it's off. Another shame.

What's this with your Hebrew? Are you studying? I'm terribly impressed. But you should learn to write script, not print! [. . .]

Now that the book contract is signed, I have qualms. The old question – When?

I guess it's just as well for Shirley to stick around in America. She wouldn't be much happier in Holland, though I probably would. (A propos, Vienna paid me in greenbacks, & I travel about with a bulging wallet of 20s and 50s!)

I did write you from Budapest didn't I? I hope so, but if not – it was a tremendous experience, and they asked me to stay on a month, giving daily concerts – and they wouldn't be able to meet the demand! That's how wild the success was. Especially, of all things, the Bartók!

Now, for Philadelphia, damn them. I hardly know what to plan (I'm not in a planning frame of mind). But I *must* play a concerto. Maybe Mendelssohn *Italian*, Ravel Concerto and Shosty #5. Or Mozart *Linz* first. Or Copland 3rd and Beethoven Concerto. Or (maybe this is best) Mendelssohn, *Jeremiah*, and Beethoven Concerto. Yes, this is best. Try & push it.

I guess that brings [me] up to date. I'll write next week from Holland. Give Shirley all my love, & tell her it happens to all of us, and it had a great deal of joy in it, after all; & these things are always made of joy and pain together.

Love,

L

270. Leonard Bernstein to David Oppenheim
Scheveningen, Netherlands
10 June 1948

Dear D,

The sun is out, I'm waiting for horses to be brought, I live like a king, I have screaming audiences and flowers at my concerts, and even a lover. There are a few other facts: the sea outside my window is a wonder; the Dutch word for cunt is kunt; there is a performer here named Cilli Wang; and I've bought you a sweet hand-painted chess-set in Budapest.

I send all my love to you & Judy.

L

271. Leonard Bernstein to "Twig" Romney
Scheveningen, Netherlands
20 June 1948

My dear T,

Well, it's over. The big swing around this beautiful messy continent is at an end and I am swollen with success, lush with living, loving and learning.

Germany and Austria were fabulous, filthy, Nazi, exciting. Budapest was grim and gay. Milano was the greatest. Paris a joy, as ever, and Holland a comfort, where I've soaked up milk and lobsters and sun, and been horseback riding every day. I'm happy, and a little bit drunk, to celebrate the end of the tour. I don't lift an arm until July 1st! (I sail the 22nd for New York, arriving the 29th, when you will probably be leaving.)

No sign of Thad anywhere. He missed a thrilling concert – not just musically, but politically. More anon.

More anon also about the Russian regions. It's not so good, to put it mildly.

Maybe we can have a moment before we leave New York. As they say here, *tis te hopen*.

All the best, dear Twig, and if I don't see you, I hope you will love Europe as much as I have. I have a strange lack of nostalgia for America. I could go on here for ever.

Love,
Lenny

272. Leonard Bernstein to Aaron Copland
c/o Israel Philharmonic Orchestra, Tel Aviv, Israel
29 September 1948

Dear A,

A word to say me voici, and Gott sei Dank, and it's all beautiful beyond words.

Marc [Blitzstein] cheered me up immensely the day after you brought me down so about the *Age of A[nxiety]* – he went into positive fits of joy. Who knows?

How would you like some of the enclosed for a present? It's just for you, it's terribly blond & Swedish, & it will be in America (Philadelphia!) by December. Mmm. It was lovely.

I've already started working like a dog. Thirty-five concerts in the next two months! Somehow in Israel one finds strength for everything.

My suite & garden are a joy. Real Garden-of-Eden stuff: palms, mimosa, cactus, & what a sea! You must try Israel one day.

How's by the movie?

You old bastard, I love you.

L

Everyone awaits the 3rd Symphony with bated breath. Just to take *you* down a bit, *Billy the Kid* was *not* played here, only the Celebration Dance, alone & only, and that had to be repeated. You old encore composer!

273. Leonard Bernstein to "Twig" Romney

Tel Aviv, Israel
20 October 1948

Dear Twig,

I tried hard to call you during my three days in New York last month – between a wonderful Wyoming visit and my flight to Israel. You had gone, of course, that very day. But it's good to have your note, and to know that you are now ensconced in the sheltered halls of old V–a, studying, and, I presume, making love like a beaver.

This is such a beautiful experience that I can hardly write of it. Truly I feel I never want to leave, despite all the tragedy and difficulty. I sit here in this charming city in a blackout, with the fucking Egyptians raising hell to the south, my beloved Jerusalem without water, and in siege. But the concerts go on – dozens of them – never one missed – with huge and cheering audiences – sometimes accompanied by shells and machine guns outside. And Haifa is certainly one of the fabulous beauty-spots on earth. Life is hectic, but pleasant beyond words: the orchestra is the most intelligent and responsive I've known: and I think I've fallen in love.

Add it up: do you blame me for having no nostalgia for the States? This is a most miraculous people with a heroism and devotion I have never before seen. I know: – I visited the front in Jerusalem. I could weep with the inspiration of it. Everyone is young, inspired, beautiful in this new Army, and everyone is truly alive in this new State. So they slander and babble in Paris, but these people will never be downed.

I think of you often and with affection, Twig. I shall be back Dec. 9 or so. But I hear that the Philly Orchestra has cancelled the season! Otherwise – it would be lovely to see you.

All the best,

L

274. Leonard Bernstein to Serge Koussevitzky

Tel Aviv, Israel
29 October 1948

Dear Sergei Alexandrovich,

How to begin? Which of all the glorious facts, faces, actions, ideals, beauties of scenery, nobilities of purpose shall I report? I am simply overcome with this land and its people. I have never so gloried in an army, in simple farmers, in a concert public. I am in perfect health, and very happy – only a little tired from the fantastic schedule we have here: 40 concerts in 60 days, here, in Haifa, in Jerusalem, Rehovoth, and so on. The concerts are a marvelous success, the audiences tremendous and cheering, the greatest being special concerts for soldiers. Never could you imagine so intelligent and cultured and music-loving an army!

And Jerusalem – what shall I say of my beloved Jerusalem, tragic, under constant Arab fire, without water (only a pail a day) – with machine guns outside accompanying our performances of Beethoven symphonies! I have visited the fronts, entered Notre Dame, where we held out a few paces only from Arab–British guns, inspected the strategic heights around the city and the Palmach bases. I have played piano in hospitals for the new wounded of the Negev, and in camps for soldiers and "Kibbutzim" people. I have been decorated with the Jerusalem Defense medal and the Palmach insignia. I have almost grown to be part of all these wonderful people and history-making days. Believe me, it will end well: there is too much faith, spirit, and will to be otherwise.

While in Jerusalem I took a side-trip to a formerly Arab village called Ain-Karem where the captain of the Commandos turned out to be named Moshe Koussevitzky! He tells me he is your nephew, son of your brother, and is a charming, warm person, doing a great and heroic piece of work. I photographed him, and am sending you a print enclosed. I hope this makes you very happy.

I am holding auditions for young conductors next week (I have reason to believe there are real talents here). Our good friend Mrs. Frank Cohen advises me that she wishes to donate a scholarship for an Israeli conducting student at Tanglewood next summer. Would you be willing to accept one, as an active pupil if possible, if we find a very talented one? Do please let me know as soon as you can, so that I can make arrangements while I am still here.[124]

I hope the season goes as wonderfully as always – though I am sure this one will surpass all top standards set before. We all love you and pray for you here,

---

[124] Koussevitzky sent a telegram on 9 November 1948: "Deeply moved your letter authorize you select outstanding student conductor. Heartiest greetings to all and orchestra. Love Serge Koussevitzky."

and all your dear friends send you warmest wishes, including the President Weizmann, our beloved MacDonald [Ambassador James McDonald] (who is doing a fine job), and the members of the orchestra, who wait only for your visit one day.

All my love to you and Olga.

Leonard

I feel that I shall spend more and more time here each year. It makes running around the cities of America seem so unimportant – as if I am not really needed there, while I am really needed here!

By the way, I met Moshe Koussevitzky just next to the spring of John the Baptist!

275. Leonard Bernstein to Aaron Copland
Tel Aviv, Israel
8 November 1948

Dearest A,

Well, we've gone and done it. The [Third] Symphony seems to be a success! Of course we could have used much more rehearsal (our schedule is unbelievable), but after the fourth performance it has begun to sound, and quite magnificent at that. It's really a fantastic piece! I must confess I have made a sizeable cut near the end[125] (after the second performance) and believe me it makes a whole lot of difference. Hope you enjoy the enclosed. Most people loved it (the symph.).

In the midst of all this marvelous history & miracle-land & excitement of life, I have miraculously fallen in love. It's the works; and I can't quite believe that I should have found *all* the things I've wanted rolled into one. It's a hell of an experience – nervewracking & guts-tearing and wonderful.[126] It's changed everything. The Swedish is all yours now.

Hope the picture goes beautifully, & my love to all the nice people in H'wood. I can't wait to hear the B[enny] G[oodman] concerto. (By the way, B.G. here means Ben-Gurion. Strange world, no?)

Much love,

L

Hope very much to be able to do the May 4, but I can't be sure til I get back to the States, which will be early in Dec. Where will you be?

---

[125] Bernstein was never afraid to make cuts in recent pieces, even ones as substantial and significant as Copland's Third Symphony.

[126] This latest love may well have been Yossi Stern, the Hungarian-born Israeli artist (1923–92), who illustrated Letter 276.

276. Leonard Bernstein to Jennie Bernstein

[Israel]
[November 1948]

A wonderful hot day. We left our grand pre-fabricated house, Helen, as you see, in the lead, followed by our friend Katya, m'self and artist Yosi.[127] Driving to Ain-Harod we passed so close to Nazareth that we couldn't resist having lunch there. It's a marvelous town; and while Helen ran around photographing everything and everyone in sight, I had a glorious Arab meal, with kh'umus and t'hina, and a fine Arab lad shined my boots. Bought rosaries (blessed by the church) for various Cath[olic] friends, and headed for Ain-Harod, the largest kibbutz in the land.

Of course, first thing I had to have a horse. The gent in charge, a real kibbutz lion, took me out. I had a sort of Palomino beauty which I soon discovered I couldn't handle. So the lion-gent exchanged horses with me (I took his dray-horse), and it turned out he couldn't handle him either. Then the stable-man was called in, and he didn't do better, and since it became a bore to go only in circles we called it a day and went swimming in a marvelous pool in the middle of nowhere. The best swim-sun-and-air I think I've ever had – or thought I had until I went to Elat, but more of that anon. Meanwhile, there is a concert coming up for all the kibbutznicks of the vicinity, 5000 strong.

Jennie T[ourel] sang like an angel. The audience was, as always, the most attentive and appreciative in the world, although they don't know the conventions of clapping, so that Jennie T. lost an encore or two that had been planned. I finally played ye *Rhapsody in Blue,* and we adjourned to a huge party where we danced and sang and drank and made with the Hora until Godknowswhen A.M. To bed, in a real guest-house (a fantastic achievement for a kibbutz) – then up betimes and on to Acre (old Arab city which Napoleon couldn't take) and with the military governor of Galilee went off to visit an Arab village. The road up to it was, as you can see, a real reducer. Since we were with the governor, whom the Arabs adore and fear, they staged for us what is known as a "Fantasia", with guns going off, music, dancing and nineteen lunches, coffee sessions, etc. Whole lambs are brought, torn to pieces by the host (who never sits with the guests but waits until they are through, then with his pals dives into the leavings. When they are through the women pounce on *their* leavings, then the children, then the dogs. Such is the hierarchy.) Then, already sick with so much food, we proceeded to mount the local camels, who are nasty, haughty, dirty beasts. Jennie T., who will do anything for a photograph, allowed herself to be ruptured on one. Accompanied by the elders of the village (Druses, and splendid figures

---

[127] This letter, describing Bernstein's experiences in Israel, is illustrated on every page by Yossi Stern.

they are) we jolted back to Haifa for a concert – one of the worst I've ever given. Arabic burps punctuated the Mahler, which was worse in Jennie's case than in mine. Next morning a great Oriental dancer named Yardena Cohen[128] performed for us – then quick to Lydda airport for the big climax – the trip to Elat. This is the newly-won spot on the Red Sea, southernmost Negev, across from Aqaba (Transjordan) on the Gulf. A beautiful flight (we were flown by the army in a Dakota with bucket seats) and landed in a wonderful Arizona-like wilderness, dry and windy and awesome. After a marvelous swim in the Red Sea (which is the bluest thing you ever saw) and a hard-tack dinner we drove up into the hills and entertained the soldiers stationed there. Jennie sang Carmen, of course – and this place at night really knocked me out. If you can imagine an intimate desert, where every rock and dune seems familiar, this is it. Yosi and I wandered afterwards for hours through the hills. I never wanted to leave, and did everything to miss the plane the next morning. But no soap: they waited for me. So sadly back to T[el] A[viv], and concerts and parties and god-damned professional life, which is driving me mad. But I leave tomorrow for Holland, and my one nostalgia, besides Jerusalem, will be Elat.

Love, Lenny

277. Leonard Bernstein to Philip Marcuse
Hotel Schenley, Pittsburgh, PA
26 January 1949

Phil,

Many thanks for the clipping. It makes me very angry, and doubly so to think of all the fuss that's made over the Furtwängler & Gieseking business,[129] while no attention at all is paid to this *echt* Fascism in our own cities. How did H[enry]

---

[128] Yardena Cohen (1910–2012), Israeli dancer, choreographer, and teacher. In the 1940s this legendary figure in the dance history of Israel created dance dramas and pageants for kibbutzim. Many of these featured female characters in the Old Testament as the central roles. Cohen opened her Haifa dance studio in 1933 and ran it for the next seventy years. She died on 23 January 2012, at the age of 101.

[129] The "Furtwängler & Gieseking business" is a reference to the banning of Walter Gieseking from a concert tour of the United States at the time Bernstein sent this letter, and of Wilhelm Furtwängler from returning to conduct the Berlin Philharmonic the same month, both because of concerns about their Nazi past. The "*echt* Fascism" that so enraged Bernstein was taking place in Detroit. According to a report in *The New York Times* on 21 January 1949, the Detroit Symphony Orchestra "had been warned by Mr. [Henry] Reichhold that every man would be fired if that were necessary to weed out disloyalty to the conductor [Karl Krueger]." Reichhold, the orchestra's president added: "I think a shake-up and good housecleaning is just what the Detroit orchestra needs." Georges Miquelle, the orchestra's principal cellist (married to Renée Longy Miquelle in 1919; they later divorced) was fired in public by Reichhold during a rehearsal on the grounds that he had apologized to the violinist Erica Morini about the orchestra's poor accompaniment for her – an apology that both Miquelle and Morini denied was ever made.

R[eichhold] ever let himself be quoted in such out-and-out Nazi lines? Have they set the date for burning the library in Cadillac Square?

Much love to you and Babs.

L

278. Renée Nell[130] to Leonard Bernstein
470 West 24th Street, New York, NY
30 January 1949

Dear Lenny,

Thank you for your nice letter and poem to which I have this to answer: "When the real animus and the real anima web, you can get married and take your wife to bed."

Some short remarks on your dream: when you are unconscious ("taking a nap, sleeping"), you find that your rather undifferentiated feeling is playing tricks on you, bringing people into your psychology whom you do not want to have in there. Rather than finding out what these people really want from you, or why they were invited, you get angry at that side of yourself who played the trick on you. You get in touch with that side by hurting it, then you regret. You would know more if you would try to make her understand why you don't want these people anymore. Then, when you do get away from the unwanted collective, you get into an even less desirable one, a very pedestrian collective (street). Being alone now, without anything but yourself, you are eager to make contact with some other side, contact in the usual average pedestrian way – sex – which is the substitute for human relationship. When you find that that is impossible you are caught in some very dull, past aspect of your own bourgeois-side. That shows very nicely why you are so eagerly seeking homosexual contact in reality, it seems the way out or the escape from the fear of being caught in bourgeois patterns, and seems to symbolize the free and non-bourgeois life. They talk about your work in the dream; your fear always seems to be that being a conductor and being set in a profession is the same as being dully married and leading a middle-class life. I am sure it could be that way, but must not be that

---

[130] Renée Nell (1910–94) was a Jungian psychoanalyst. In 1938 she escaped from Berlin to Switzerland where she studied with Carl Jung at the University of Zurich, before moving to the United States and setting up her practice in New York City. A pioneer in work with young offenders, she later established The Country Place in Litchfield, CT, describing it as "a residential community for the psychologically disturbed adult who has more insight than he or she can use, who knows how he or she should act but withdraws from action." Humphrey Burton identifies her as the "Frau" (Burton 1994, p. 108), but the letter from Bernstein to David Oppenheim on 22 October 1943 confirms that the "Frau" was in fact Marketa Morris. Bernstein later became disenchanted with Nell's analysis, writing to his sister Shirley on 26 April 1950: "My feeling is one totally apart from analysis: I want only to cope, and through my own powers, without aid – especially of the indulgent, personal sort that was forthcoming from Miss Nell."

way, and will stop to look to you that way the moment you get some real color into your life; then you can give up to the so-called "colorful life" you are leading.

Freud's definition: Id – subconscious; Ego – conscious; Super-Ego – conscience. Ego is the whole of consciousness. Jung: has the same concept of the Ego, he terms it the center of consciousness, the difference between F[reud] and J[ung] is in the way [the] use and function of the Ego are seen. With F. it is the censor and adaptor to reality. With J. it is understood as the channel for the forces that want to flow from the inside to the outside, and vice versa, it has a consciously screening function and serves the forces of the Self or the unconscious. With F. it is supposed to master them. To F. the Ego is the human being as such, therefore it has a very high value; to J. it is an aspect of the human, subordinated to the Self, which means the unspoiled essence of the human being. The Self is to J. the highest value in a human being. I hope that does not confuse you more.

I wonder if you have enough contact with my way of analysis yet that the long distance dream-interpretation means anything to you. Generally it is difficult to get anything out of such answers in such an early stage of work; later when one is more attuned to each other it is easier. Let me know.

I hope you have a fairly good time, not too many tensions.

Kindly,

Renée

279. Leonard Bernstein to Howard Hoyt[131]

32 West 10th Street, New York, NY

8 February 1949

Dear Howard,

For a period of one year from the date hereof I hereby engage you, and you hereby accept such engagement, to act as my exclusive adviser and representative, to assist me in securing employment and negotiating contracts for my services as a performer in radio, television and motion pictures, as a composer of scores and incidental music for motion pictures, and in negotiating a contract for the production of *Operation Capulet*, a dramatico-musical composition based on *Romeo and Juliet*, for which I am currently composing the score and some of the lyrics.[132] Notwithstanding anything to the contrary herein, it is clearly understood that my services as a conductor are excluded from the scope of this contract.

---

[131] Howard Hoyt was a theatrical agent and manager who had previously worked as Eastern story editor for MGM.

[132] The only known use in Bernstein's papers of *Operation Capulet* as an early title for what became *West Side Story*. Jerome Robbins first put the idea of the show to Bernstein on 6 January 1949. Robbins, Bernstein, and Arthur Laurents met for the first time to discuss the project on 10 January, and a month later Bernstein signed this agreement with Howard Hoyt.

In consideration of the above services, I shall pay you a sum equal to ten percent (10%) of the gross compensation served or received by me in connection with any employment and contracts in the above fields, which contracts are entered into or negotiated for during the terms hereof, and upon extensions, additions, renewals and substitutions of such contracts and employment. Notwithstanding anything to the contrary herein, it is understood that I shall pay you no compensation with respect to my ASCAP royalties.

Very truly yours,

Leonard Bernstein

Accepted and agreed to by Howard Hoyt

280. Leonard Bernstein to Hans Heinsheimer[133]

Hotel Schenley, Pittsburgh, PA

9 February 1949

Dear Hans,

Good news for a change!

a) Kouss has promised, finally and definitely, the premiere of *The Age of Anxiety* for April. Originally it was to be the 22nd and 23rd, but my benefit for Weizmann and Truman on the 23rd interferes. He has promised to find some other week in April.[134] Will you check officially with Leslie Rogers at Symphony Hall?

b) I've just this minute finished scoring the first movement (and, to quote Bill Schuman, is it beautiful!!). I'm mailing it to you, registered, and you can begin extracting at once. I hope to finish the second movement by next week. It's a mad race, and I'm exhausted, but it's challenging: and I hope to have it all scored by the beginning of March. (Please God!)

Please let me know right away how the print comes out: I've been using a Parker 51 pen on it, just as an experiment. If it's no good – I have the other ink with me, and can change.

I've set two Rilke poems for Jennie Tourel (when? I don't know!) and she will do one or both at her March 13th Town Hall recital. I hope to have more of them soon. They make a fine group: "Lovesongs" by Rilke.

And love to you –

Lenny B

---

[133] Hans Heinsheimer (1900–93) was a legendary figure in the world of music publishing. He first worked in the opera department of Universal Edition in Vienna (1923–38), then went to New York to take up a position at Boosey & Hawkes, promoting new works by Copland, Bartók, Stravinsky, and Britten. He was fired by Ralph Hawkes in 1947 for writing his memoirs (*Menagerie in F Sharp*), since Hawkes wanted a worker rather than an author. Heinsheimer was immediately hired by Schirmer, where he worked closely with Bernstein, Samuel Barber, and others.

[134] The first performance was on 8 April 1949.

281. Leonard Bernstein to Helen Coates
Columbus, OH
Valentine's Day [14 February] 1949

Dear H,

This is a blessed day for a tired guy. Quiet and raining here, and peaceful enough to orchestrate like mad (page 67 already!).[135] Concert tonight in Zanesville, O., then return here, and I can work til three tomorrow afternoon, when we leave for Dayton.

[...]

It's been a grim weekend: I've been overtired again, and had the jumps at the concerts. I played a very inferior Mozart Concerto, but the Shost[akovich] was great. Too much farewell party. Also, Reiner has left a trail of hostility against me in the orchestra[136] and around it, which makes it still very difficult to establish *rapport* with the men. It's the first time I've had this problem, and it does remove the element of fun to an alarming degree. (The critic Lissfelt,[137] whom you've no doubt been reading, is one of the Reinerites who is simply basically antagonistic. What a sourpuss!)

I think I'll manage all right on tour, if I can get enough rest. I've set myself a deadline of having the score finished by the time I return to N.Y. for the Rutgers concerts. Let's hope & pray.

Love,

L

Izler Solomon[138] just called & we may have a drink tonight. Tossy S[pivakovsky][139] is here playing Bartók with him.

282. Arthur Laurents[140] to Leonard Bernstein
8227 Lookout Mountain, Hollywood, CA
[?April 1949][141]

Dear Lenny,

I'm sending a copy of this to Jerry [Robbins] so that there won't be any wheels within wheels and we'll all be abreast of what is what.

---

[135] Bernstein was working on his Second Symphony, *The Age of Anxiety*.
[136] The Pittsburgh Symphony Orchestra, with whom Bernstein was conducting a series of concerts. Reiner left as Music Director in 1948.
[137] J. Fred Lissfelt, music critic of the Pittsburgh *Sun-Telegraph*.
[138] Izler Solomon (1910–87), American conductor. He was Music Director of the Columbus Philharmonic Orchestra (1941–9) and the Indianapolis Symphony Orchestra (1956–76).
[139] Tossy Spivakovsky (1906–98), Russian-born violinist whose performances of modern concertos such as those of Bartók, Menotti, and Sessions were particularly admired.
[140] Arthur Laurents (1917–2011), American playwright, screenwriter, and stage director. His Broadway credits included the books for *West Side Story*, *Gypsy*, and *Anyone Can Whistle*, and he directed the original production of *La Cage aux Folles*.
[141] This letter is undated, but the evidence points to some time in April 1949, when Bernstein began to have doubts about the viability of the project that would eventually become *West Side Story*. In

Quite frankly, I was disturbed by our phone conversation Monday night. Unless I seriously misinterpreted you, this is what I understood you to say: You conceive of the show's script as being written in an almost purely poetic style; you have doubts (understandable) whether I can write in that style without forcing; and – most important – if my writing cannot be that poetic, then you would not have complete faith in the project and, therefore, would rather abandon it before spending any actual working time.

It is this last point which I found disturbing. I myself have enormous enthusiasm for and belief in the show. I spent a good deal of time and money in New York talking about it and would not have worked on it there *and* all these weeks here had I not, quite naturally, assumed the thing was settled: we were going to do it. It is difficult to work on something you feel may explode in your face at any moment. But difficult or not, I cannot turn back. I am "in" it, and *want* to be "in" it; I must proceed. True, the possibility of chaos does superimpose an unfortunate level to plow through before working. But I'm working. As Jerry knows too well, I was in a vaguely similar situation myself before – when I first started in analysis, incidentally. But even then, I had spent time on the project and had worked on it, and then pulled out (for reasons, which I now regretfully admit, were erroneous and foolish).

Be that as it may, the phone call brought up several problems I had not realized existed. First, the possibility that, even at this date, you might not do the show. Second – the conception. What I have tried to do is make the scenes between the lovers poetic in contrast to the violence of the world they live in. I do not think the rest should be ultra-realistic but I am doubtful whether I think it should be as poetic as you apparently do. Almost pure poetry is competing with Shakespeare on his own play. I can't stand up to that, the show can't stand up to that, no one today, unfortunately, could stand up to that. That is realistic fact. Plus the fact that I don't completely see the show that way. Also – and this would naturally follow your concept – you conceive, as I do, of the lovers' scenes as being almost completely musical but the others as being almost completely musical, too. I admit I do see less music and certainly "songs". I don't mean this

---

Bernstein's "Excerpts from a West Side Log" (Bernstein 1957, p. 47), he included an entry on 15 April 1949, while conducting in Columbus, Ohio: "Just received the draft of first four scenes. Much good stuff. But this is no way to work. Me on this long conducting tour, Arthur between New York and Hollywood. Maybe we'd better wait until I can find a continuous hunk of time to devote to the project. Obviously this show can't depend on stars, being about kids; and so it will have to live or die by the success of its collaborations; and this remote-control collaboration isn't right. Maybe they can find the right composer who isn't always skipping off to conduct somewhere. It's not fair to them or to the work." Bernstein was plainly uneasy about committing himself and was quoted by Craig Zadan as saying: "I remember receiving about a dozen pages and saying to myself that this is never going to work. [. . .] I had a strong feeling of staleness of the East Side situation and I didn't like the too-angry, too-bitchy, too-vulgar tone of it" (Zadan 1974, p. 15).

as a cut-and-dried rule. As you will see, the last scene in the first act calls for music almost throughout, for example.

Perhaps both you and Jerry disagree with me about the concept: perhaps the difference is merely one of degree (which I fervently hope). I am not adamant or absolute in my feelings; they can be modified. But a musical show (and I see this as a musical show or whatever you want to call it, but *not* as an opera or even a modified opera) is a collaboration. A collaboration calls for compromise. Certainly, I don't ask either of you, any more than you ask me, to compromise to the point where you disbelieve in what the final outcome will be. That is foolish and makes for bad working conditions and, more important, bad work. We all must create as we feel and believe. I would not ask you to write a pop tune any more than I would ask Jerry to create a Berlin Ballet Mécanique. You might be able to do it, but it's doubtful whether it would be very good. So you would have to do *your* conception of a pop tune, and Jerry, his conception of the Ballet Mécanique (which, in his hands, might be very funny, come to think of it). I think we all know each other's work, we all can concede and adjust, and there can be a meeting point.

I don't feel that the current lack of exact agreement is a crisis nor do I mean to provoke one. The only serious point in my mind – and forgive if I repeat this – is the one I have stressed. Namely, we agreed to work on the show, to do it, and now – again, unless I misunderstood – you are unsure whether you will or will not do it – unless the conception is the way you visualize it. This stand leaves me on a high wire and I don't know how to walk a tight rope although I am willing to learn. Mind you, no word, line or scene I've written or will write is sacred. I agree some of it should be more poetic. In the very first scene, for example, I was counting on the initiation-ritual being sung in contrast to the sharp violence of the opening (and thus to set the pattern of the show). You told me on the phone that you did not think there should be any music in the scene (although if you look at the graph you yourself drew up in New York, I'm sure you will find music indicated there). But I wonder if we do not disagree about the quantity as well as the quality of poetic language and the quantity of the music. And those points must, of course, be settled soon.

I'm continuing on the script, whipping the rest of Act One into shape so that I can send it off to you and Jerry by, I hope, the week-end. After you read it, you will be able to judge whether our concepts are so far apart after all. Please let me know – and as soon as you conveniently can. The high wire is awfully thin. I'm still planning, too, on coming to New York sometime toward the end of the second week in May.

Best to you both,
Arthur

283. Arthur Laurents to Leonard Bernstein

8227 Lookout Mountain, Hollywood, CA
[?April 1949]

Dear Lenny,

I'm sorry you've decided not to do the show, sorrier still because of the main reason which led you to drop out. I think I understand. And feeling as you do, your decision is undoubtedly all for the best.

One thing I'd like to make clear – and I trust you will believe me. I did not start out with "a priori prejudices". Rather, I started out with admiration for your work and eagerness to become a friend. Along the line, hostility popped up. But since I felt it from you, just as you say you felt it from me, and made the exact same efforts you did, I can only conclude we were both projecting a little and, possibly, were further impaired by the occasional whispers which are ever present.

It's a pity we had such a short run. However, now that the tension is gone, there is probably a much better chance that we can become friends. I certainly hope so.

Whatever show or venture you embark on next, please know I'll be rooting for you.

Arthur

284. Ellen Adler[142] to Leonard Bernstein

[Paris]
[?Spring 1949]

Dearest little Lennie,

Once I wrote you and never mailed the letter and now I can't even find it. I have heard all about you from Bobby Lewis who was here, and now from Harold[143] who arrived a few days ago. I know that you are writing a musical and that you arrived at 161 West 54[144] with several other talented young men, each of you with agents flanking you, all of which amused my mother greatly.

I am well. By this time I speak French, I look French and I am assimilated into Paris, all of which makes me miss New York the more. I see your friends around from time to time, once [François] Valéry,[145] at a café, who told me he was about to write a play about Noah's ark. Now and again I see Nadia [Boulanger] who

---

[142] Ellen Adler (b. 1927) is the daughter of fabled acting teacher Stella Adler. Ellen's close friends included Marlon Brando and René Leibowitz as well as Bernstein. In 1957 she married David Oppenheim (they divorced in 1976). Ned Rorem was bewitched by her "dizzying black-tiger beauty" (Ned Rorem, *Knowing When To Stop: A Memoir*, New York: Simon and Schuster, 1994, p. 578).
[143] Harold Clurman, Ellen Adler's stepfather.
[144] 161 West 54th Street is an imposing apartment building near the intersection with Seventh Avenue in Manhattan.
[145] François Valéry, son of the poet Paul Valéry.

looks more and more like a Grant Wood[146] and is indeed a lurid creature. And then there is, of course, Marie Blanche[147] always seen sweeping into an enormous automobile, and leaning, almost toppling into the arms of her tall, blonde painter friend. But I suppose Bigelow[148] is the funniest. At first this lad was strictly a right-bank spectacle and very dashing, now he is to be seen in the leftest of left-bank hangouts and always sporting a pair of blue jeans. So there, you see, is the evolution of Paris. I started with the left-bank and shall end up on the right, Bigelow started with the right and was doomed for the left.

I have heard wonderful, wonderful things about your last tour and am happy that everything goes on so very well.

Paris is magical, romantic, perfumed and a city of miracles. A spring such as has never been before is here, and it is quite elegant as only Paris can be, and I am very happy. I think of you often, Lennie. Take care of yourself and give my love to all the people about you such as Helen [Coates], Shirley [Bernstein], D[avid] D[iamond] and A[aron] C[opland]. In fact, everyone but Burtie[149] because he's a kid and I want him to take me flying one day.

And kisses to you,

Ellen

285. Leonard Bernstein to Peter Gradenwitz[150]
1025 Park Avenue, New York, NY
11 May 1949

Dear P,

Just time for a few notes:

1) A great joy to receive *our* book, & many thanks for the sweet dedication.[151]

---

[146] Adler – delightfully – likens Nadia Boulanger's austere appearance to the stern faces in paintings such as Grant Wood's *American Gothic*.

[147] Marie-Blanche de Polignac (1897–1958) was a soprano, pianist, patron of the arts, and heiress to the Lanvin fashion fortune founded by her mother, Jeanne Lanvin. She was an intimate friend of Francis Poulenc, who dedicated several works to her.

[148] Otis Bigelow (1920–2007), actor, dancer, writer, and later theatrical agent, who spent a year in Paris in 1948–9.

[149] Burton Bernstein (b. 1932) is the younger brother of Leonard and Shirley. He studied at Dartmouth College and the Columbia Graduate School of Journalism, and from 1957 to 1992 he was a staff writer for *The New Yorker*. He is the author of a biography of James Thurber as well as books about the Bernstein family (*Family Matters: Sam, Jennie, and the Kids*) and about his elder brother (*Leonard Bernstein: American Original*, with Barbara B. Haws).

[150] Peter Gradenwitz (1910–2001), German-born Israeli musicologist and music critic, and an astute commentator on Bernstein's music and his use of jazz idioms. The two became friends when Bernstein visited Israel in 1948 to conduct the Israel Philharmonic. Gradenwitz wrote extensively on Bernstein and his music, from contemporary reports of Bernstein's Israeli concerts for *The New York Times* to the book *Leonard Bernstein: unendliche Vielfalt eines Musikers* (Zurich: Atlantis Verlag, 1984), published in an English edition in 1987.

[151] Gradenwitz's *The Music of Israel: Its Rise and Growth Through 5000 Years* was published by Norton in 1949 and dedicated "To Leonard Bernstein as a token of friendship and sincere appreciation".

2) *The Age of Anxiety* was a walloping success, & I thought of you often in preparing it.[152] Everyone adored it, which amazed me.[153]

3) Doesn't look so good for you & Tanglewood this summer. I have very little to do with it this year – just a token appearance, and I've taken a farm 45 miles from it! Have you heard from them?

4) I'd love to see the "Bernstein article". The Variations you saw remain about the same.

My love to you & Rosi & the kids, & from Helen – sorry this is too short – I'm rushed with plans for a new show.

Lenny

286. Farley Granger to Leonard Bernstein
8227 Lookout Mountain, Hollywood, CA
15 May 1949

My visible verb, my very Dear,

It's Sunday morning, I am playing *Jeremiah* and loving it, and you very, very much. It was so wonderful talking to you the other night. I am sorry that I woke you again, and Shirley too. I hope so very much she really doesn't dislike me. But I have a feeling we two (Shirley and I) will work out well.

Last night I wore the cuff links you gave me. They are so beautiful, and I thank you always. But the thing with me is that I don't feel that I have to wear something you gave me, to be reminded how much I love you. Because [e]very kind, and happy, and warm thing that happens to me I share with you. You are in the lovely adolescent green of the spring trees, you are in the breath of the warm breeze. You surround me with a rare and God given feeling – called love (you are also making a bit of a poet out of me).

My picture is still going very well and I am most happy in my work. Tell Betty and Adolph that for a night club scene in the picture the studio reproduced the Village Vanguard.[154] I'm getting a kick out of working in the same place the Revuers did.

---

[152] Bernstein worked on his new symphony while in Israel, and the first performance of any part of *The Age of Anxiety* was given there. The "Dirge" was played at a Gala Soirée in aid of the Israel Philharmonic Pension Fund on 28 November 1948 in Tel Aviv. In his notes for this concert, Peter Gradenwitz wrote of "the first performance anywhere of a Dirge for piano and orchestra composed by Leonard Bernstein during the few leisure hours left to him on his crowded Tel-Aviv days and completed in full score just in time for tonight's concert – this is a most expressive song of lament showing the composer's style developed on distinctly novel lines."

[153] The world premiere of *The Age of Anxiety* took place in Boston on 8 April 1949, with the Boston Symphony Orchestra conducted by Serge Koussevitzky, and Bernstein himself playing the solo piano part.

[154] Probably a reference to *Side Street* (released in 1950), a thriller set in New York. Granger's most celebrated film role came the following year when he played Guy Haines in Hitchcock's *Strangers on a Train*.

I was asked if I would like to do a picture in China, a thing called *Rickshaw Boy* which sounds very exciting but will not come into being for a while. How about arranging a few concerts for the Far East.

Saw *Ball Game* again and agree with you, there's a good deal of ham in our boy Gene.[155]

Please thank Helen for me, that was very sweet of her.

Write me as much as you can. I will call again soon, but will not make it a late one next time. You are a wonderful man and I love you.

F

287. Leonard Bernstein to William Schuman[156]
Singing Brook Farm, Charlemont, MA
15 July 1949

Dear Bill,

I love it when excuses pop up for me to write you – it seems the only way we get to communicate these days. There are three such at the moment: and may I preface them with my warmest hello to you & Frankie.

1) I take it you've received a copy of the enclosed from [James] McDonald in Israel. I wish I could say that I'd heard the boy, but I don't recall any such experience, although I do remember hearing good things about him. Of course, I'm all for this Israeli stream into Juilliard on general principles, since Israel is the most musical country I've ever seen, and Juilliard is the best school I know for developing that native talent.

2) At the risk of seeing the Juilliard School turned into a little Tel-Aviv, I make so bold as to propose another Israeli for the student body – a young conductor who is now here at Tanglewood – Elyakum Shapirra – who won a competition over there & was selected to be one of Koussy's chosen "Three". He arrived displaying great musicality, integrity, etc., & a lack of knowledge caused by his years in the Israeli Army. He desperately needs schooling, is wild to go to Juilliard; & I think [Jean] Morel would be marvelous for him. The kid's a natural, but such a primitive! He needs Kulture. It would be a great blessing to him.

---

[155] *Take Me Out to the Ball Game* was a 1949 MGM musical starring Gene Kelly, Frank Sinatra, and Esther Williams.

[156] William Schuman (1910–92), American composer. He formed a dance band while still in high school and was soon collaborating with Frank Loesser, a neighbor who was also at the start of his career (Loesser's first publication, *In Love With A Memory of You*, has music by William Schuman. With typical modesty Schuman later said "Frank Loesser has written hits with Hoagy Carmichael, Burton Lane, Jule Styne and other Hollywood grand dukes, but I have the distinction of having written a flop with him."). Schuman's subsequent career was as one of America's most distinguished symphonists, president of the Juilliard School and Lincoln Center.

3) A strong recommendation for Ralph Berkowitz, whom, I hear, you are considering for an additional post at Schirmer's. A nicer guy you couldn't find, nor a harder-working, or more knowledgeable.

There! Now I can go back to Mann's *Dr. Faustus* which sits particularly well in this divine isolation 40 miles from Tanglewood. I'm at last finding a few days for myself – to read, to sleep: it is a most welcome novelty.

Let me hear from you.

Love,

Lenny

288. Leonard Bernstein to Shirley Bernstein
[Wednesday] 20 July 1949

Main,

No need to voice my reaction to the rumor heard the other day of Alan J. [Lerner]'s plan to do a show with Loewe, nor to the item confirming it in today's *Times*.[157] The bastard. A fine double-x. Destroy this letter.

No word yet from Adolph and Betty and Adolph. I am really irked at the Lerner thing. Rest and think, main foot!

The enclosed came to Tangle for you.

I wormed the Gabe personally each night, but he still drags his arms to the ground. Well, so many of us do, and nobody worries.

It was lovely seeing you for an extra hour at the Shelton, even under such trying conditions.

Farfel's mad, and the world is full of apes. I suppose you're as disappointed in Lerner as I am. Maybe you should have snapped up Michael Dreyfuss.[158]

Loveoah,

Dein

289. Menahem Pressler[159] to Leonard Bernstein
Tel Aviv, Israel
15 August 1949

Dear Mr. Bernstein,

Although much in arrears (for which I am only very little to blame, having had so many appearances and marriage to boot), I still could not deprive myself

---

[157] A story in *The New York Times* on Wednesday, 20 July 1949 reported that Alan Jay Lerner and Fredrick Loewe were "at work on a new musical [...] that is set in the United States in the nineteenth century" (the show that became *Paint Your Wagon*). From Bernstein's angry reaction in this letter, it seems Lerner must have suggested a collaboration. A quarter of a century later these two Harvard graduates did work together on *1600 Pennsylvania Avenue*.

[158] Michael Dreyfuss (1928–60), American actor and director.

[159] The pianist Menahem Pressler (b. 1923) fled Nazi Germany to Palestine. He made his American debut with Eugene Ormandy and the Philadelphia Orchestra in 1947. Olin Downes reviewed their

of the pleasure of writing to you and telling you how much I enjoyed playing your *Anniversaries*.

On the occasion of American Independence Day I was invited to play on the radio an American programme. For this programme I also chose seven of your *Anniversaries*.

All the time (for it is ever fresh in my memory) I wanted to write to you and tell you how much I liked them on account of their quaintness, and rare and thrilling harmonizations so strangely appealing to the senses and the intellect. These dedications are real masterpieces of modern art and I admired them very much.

With my best regards to you and your sister. I am admiringly yours,
Menahem Pressler

290. Olivier Messiaen[160] to Leonard Bernstein
13 Villa du Danube, Paris, France
5 October 1949

Cher Maître et ami,

I hope you have had the time to look carefully and to work on the very difficult score of my *Turangalîla-Symphonie*.[161] Take great care of the dark photocopy that I gave you: it's the only copy that it is possible for your work – if you lose it, that will be a catastrophe! You will have realized that this work is very long (1½ hours) and very difficult for the whole orchestra. You will decide for yourself how many rehearsals are necessary. The work requires, in addition, the presence of 2 soloists: an Onde Martenot solo and a piano solo. The only possible Ondiste is Ginette Martenot. The only possible pianist is Yvonne Loriod.[162] Ginette Martenot is leaving in any case for New York (being invited for a different event) and Boston, and she will be there from 28 October to 1 January. The Boston Symphony Orchestra thus does not need to concern itself with her travel expenses.

Carnegie Hall performance of the Schumann Concerto in *The New York Times*, describing Pressler as "one of the few of the young pianists who consider his instrument the agent of glamorous song and not merely a contraption of wires and keys. This, indeed, was the playing of a free artist." Pressler later achieved renown as pianist of the Beaux Arts Trio. Regarding his relationship with Bernstein, Pressler has written: "I always had a fine relation with Mr. Bernstein. Although he invited me to play with him and the City Center Orchestra to make my debut coming from Israel, Mr. Judson, my manager, insisted that I do it with the Philadelphia Orchestra and Ormandy. But I played his pieces and met him many times in different places, even here in Bloomington. Recently I played his Clarinet Sonata with [Richard] Stoltzman" (email from Menahem Pressler, 12 January 2013).
[160] Olivier Messiaen (1908–92), French composer. His first major international commission was from Koussevitzky, for the *Turangalîla-Symphonie*.
[161] Bernstein conducted the world premiere of Messiaen's *Turangalîla-Symphonie* with the Boston Symphony Orchestra on 2 December 1949.
[162] Yvonne Loriod (1924–2010), French pianist. A pupil of Messiaen at the Paris Conservatoire, she went on to give the first performances of all his major works featuring the piano. In 1961 she became Messiaen's second wife.

On the other hand, the piano solo part of my symphony is of a difficulty such that only Yvonne Loriod can play it with the special techniques that it requires (triple notes, modes, very complex rhythms, birdsong, lightness, power, passion, etc.), and to play it *by heart*. Yvonne Loriod has a matchless technique, she is a composer, she is the best French pianist for ultra-modern music, and finally she is the specialist in my music, having played my piano works for the last seven years in all the great cities of Europe. She has already been working for a year on the piano part of my symphony, and not only does she know it by heart, but she understands the whole orchestral score perfectly. The [piano] part is considerable in the work on account of its difficulty and importance, and no one on earth can play it with such brilliant eloquence.

Moreover, I also think that my presence would be quite useful at the rehearsals, for giving exact tempos, and the balance of timbres. It would be a great joy for me to hear my work.

I therefore ask the Boston Symphony Orchestra:

1. To engage Yvonne Loriod and Ginette Martenot to play the parts for piano solo and Onde solo of my symphony and to send them their contracts (date of the concerts, total fees, etc.)

2. To kindly pay the expenses of Yvonne Loriod and myself for about 25 days – a total of $524.

3. You told me that you would give the *Turangalîla-Symphonie* in the last week of November 1949 in Boston and the first week of December 1949 in New York (Boston Symphony Orchestra). I remind you that this will be the world premiere in Boston, and the second ever performance in New York. Will you be very kind and specify for me the *exact dates* of the two concerts?

4. *The orchestral material of the Turangalîla-Symphonie is ready*. It belongs to my publisher Durand et Cie, 4 place de la Madeleine, Paris (8e). When should Durand send it? And to whom? Would you prefer that I bring it myself?

5. I recommend especially your studying my work. Serge Koussevitzky commissioned it from me in 1944, which is to say that I have worked on it for a long time. Of all my works, it is the most accomplished and the most original. I am 41 years old, and I put into my symphony all my powers of love, of hope, and of research. But I know that you are a brilliant man and that you will conduct it as I feel it.

I await a prompt reply and ask you to believe my feelings of warm admiration.

Olivier Messiaen[163]

---

[163] Written in French; English translation by the editor.

291. Arturo Toscanini[164] to Leonard Bernstein
15 October 1949

My dear Bernstein,

I compared the Victor recording of the Love Scene from Berlioz's *Romeo* with the broadcast and confirmed the fact that the Victor is much faster.

And I confirmed also another fact – namely that every man, no matter the importance of his intelligence, can be from time to time a little stupid. So is the case of the old Toscanini.

Your kind visit and dear letter made me very happy. I felt myself forty years younger.

I hope to see you very soon and it will give me a great amount of pleasure.

Most cordially, believe me, dear Bernstein.

Yours ever,

Arturo Toscanini

292. Leonard Bernstein to Burton Bernstein
New York, NY
1 November 1949

M'nape,

Just spent an evening with Irwin Edman[165] (Dept. Philosophy, Columbia) who made me nostalgic for the shelter of academic life, & made me therefore think of you. Also there was Henry Simon, who submitted our "Conversation" (with Spendoah on Beethoven) to his editors who were mad for it & want more and thought the character of YB (Younger Brother) was a masterstroke.[166] I'll send you a copy as soon as I make some.

I saw your North Country Epic to Hi-lee,[167] and loved it. But I never hear any real news from you, appraisal of your courses, directions you may be finding – all the thousand new things that happen in a freshman year. Come on, a good long one.

---

[164] Arturo Toscanini (1867–1957), Italian conductor, and one of the most celebrated performing musicians of the twentieth century. This letter was sent after Bernstein had visited him and asked about the different speeds in Toscanini's broadcast and studio recordings of Berlioz's *Romeo and Juliet* (see Burton 1994, p. 196).

[165] Irwin Edman (1896–1954), American philosopher.

[166] A reference to the "Imaginary Conversation" subtitled "Why Beethoven?" that was published in Bernstein's *The Joy of Music* (New York: Simon and Schuster, 1959), pp. 21–39, in which "L.B.", "L.P." ("Lyric Poet," described as a "poet's poet from Britain" – Stephen Spender), and "Y.B." ("Younger Brother") converse (see B. Bernstein 1982, pp. 179–80).

[167] A letter to Shirley Bernstein ("Hi-Lee"), presumably a "North Country Epic" since it had been sent from Dartmouth College in Hanover, New Hampshire, where Burton was a student.

As for me, only two weeks or so remain before my season starts, and in them I have yet to finish the Herman piece (Woody, remember?) which is on the home stretch; to do music (incidental) for a production of *Peter Pan* (if they raise all the money); write the book, prepare the Messiaen,[168] read scores & concerti for the season, etc. It's a grind. I've been going to parties – lots of them – a strange new occupation for me. [. . .] Life is very pleasant.

Regina[169] was panned by the morning papers, loved by the afternoon ones. It has a fighting chance. By the way, it was a marvelously exciting opening night.

I await that long letter.

Love,

L

293. Olivier Messiaen to Leonard Bernstein
13 Villa du Danube, Paris, France
6 November 1949

Cher Maître et ami,

Thank you for your fine letter.

You must have been looking at the score of *Turangalîla-Symphonie* and noting that it is a gigantic and very difficult work. I thank you deeply for conducting my work, since I know (having seen you in *The Rite of Spring*) that you will do it in a way that is marvelous and brilliant.

You will understand now that *Turangalîla* is the work of my life. It's why I've been so insistent about it being presented under the best possible conditions.

I have sent to Mr. Judd a very detailed analytical note for the program of *Turangalîla*, asking him to make an English translation.

Furthermore, Mr. Judd has telegraphed me that you will conduct *Turangalîla* 3 times: 2 and 3 December and 7 December. He did not tell me in which cities: I think it's in Boston each time.

There are some difficulties being raised about the arrival of Ginette Martenot and Yvonne Loriod into the USA by the union of orchestral musicians. I have said to them that neither Ginette Martenot nor Yvonne Loriod are orchestral musicians, but that they are playing in *Turangalîla* as soloists. And this must be put on the program and on the posters: *Turangalîla-Symphonie* for piano solo, Onde Martenot solo and large orchestra.

Soloists:

Piano solo: Yvonne Loriod

Onde Martenot solo: Ginette Martenot.

---

[168] Messiaen's *Turangalîla-Symphonie*.
[169] *Regina* is an opera by Marc Blitzstein based on Lillian Hellman's *The Little Foxes*. It opened at the 46th Street Theatre on Broadway on 31 October 1949, the day before Bernstein wrote this letter.

Lukas Foss (who is generosity and kindness personified) agrees with me about this.

The difficulties are thus overcome now.

Yvonne Loriod and I will take the liner *Île de France* on 10 November, disembarking at New York on 16 November in the afternoon. We will meet Ginette Martenot there. I will be attending two concerts (17 and 18 November) when Leopold Stokowski conducts my *Liturgies*, and then we leave at once for Boston.

So, Yvonne Loriod, Ginette Martenot and myself will all three arrive in Boston on 24 November. I will have all the orchestral parts for Turangalîla with me. (You already have the score.) It will be necessary to start the rehearsals on my arrival, owing to the extreme difficulty of the work. Yvonne Loriod knows *Turangalîla* completely by heart. She can thus assist you rehearsing with certain musicians separately. I can do the same (especially with the percussion which is substantial and very difficult). Finally, I am completely at your disposal – as is Yvonne Loriod – to rehearse the work with you at the piano and to demonstrate some of the rhythmic features, tempos, etc. I will attend all the rehearsals and will do everything in my power to be useful to you (balance of timbres, nuances, etc.).

These concerts will be the greatest joy of my career. See you soon! Believe always in my total admiration, my gratitude, and my friendship.

Olivier Messiaen[170]

294. George Abbott to Leonard Bernstein
630 Fifth Avenue, New York, NY
25 November 1949

Dear Lennie,

Just after you left, Bob Fryer[171] came into my office inquiring if I would be interested in doing a musical comedy version of *A Tree Grows in Brooklyn*. As soon as I had a chance to think it over, I was most enthusiastic. It seemed positively inspirational. I am now entering into contracts to do same, and this is to find out if you can take a minute out of your busy life to consider whether you would like to go in on it.

I am going to write the book with Betty Smith.[172] And I am going to try to get your old friend, Jerry Robbins, to do the dance, and beyond that, there are no thoughts at the present moment.

---

[170] Written in French; English translation by the editor.

[171] Robert Fryer (1921–2000), theatrical producer whose first Broadway show was *A Tree Grows in Brooklyn*. He later had a string of successes including *Wonderful Town, Sweet Charity, Chicago*, and *Sweeney Todd*.

[172] Betty Smith (1896–1972) was the author of the novel *A Tree Grows in Brooklyn*. She collaborated with George Abbott on the stage adaptation.

It will be a love story of the married couple rather than a tragic matter, and quite gay, albeit poignant, I hope.

I talked to your secretary today. She told me that you were conducting this afternoon, so I knew I could not reach you by phone.

I thought maybe if you were interested in this we could get Betty and Adolph to do the lyrics.

Let me hear from you as soon as you can tear yourself away from all those woodwinds.[173]

Love,

George

---

[173] According to a note in Helen Coates' hand, Bernstein replied to Abbott by phone on 12 December, turning down the project. The score for *A Tree Grows in Brooklyn* (which ran for 257 performances in 1951) was composed by Arthur Schwartz, with lyrics by Dorothy Fields. Robbins was involved informally (uncredited show-doctoring); the musical director was Max Goberman, whose greatest Broadway successes were *On the Town* and *West Side Story*.

4

Marriage, Passport Problems, and Italy
1950–55

By 1950, Bernstein had decided that he needed Felicia in his life – though he seemed unable to tell her directly: two letters sent from Israel to his sister Shirley suggest that he wanted her to be a kind of intermediary – wooing her back by proxy. Strange as this may seem, it worked, and they were married (after the shortest of second engagements) in September 1951. Extended trips abroad meant that it wasn't only his personal life that was being run by remote control. The production of *Peter Pan*, for which Bernstein wrote delightful incidental music, was in rehearsal while he was in Israel, and Marc Blitzstein took on responsibility for overseeing things – describing them in lively detail to the absentee composer. The now-familiar tensions were building: Bernstein the composer was being sent ideas for a new musical by Betty Comden, while Bernstein the conductor was meeting Wilhelm Furtwängler at the Holland Festival before setting off to other European destinations with his brother and sister. The result is a charming series of letters to Bernstein's parents in August–September 1950. That relationship took an odd turn the following year when "Sam" and "Jennie" became the dysfunctional principals in the one-act opera *Trouble in Tahiti*: writing to Shirley from Mexico in 1951, Bernstein wrote that "the two characters, by the way, have gotten themselves called Sam and Jennie, and I think you'll see why." That same letter raises a serious issue for Bernstein – and many of his friends – in the early 1950s: the "Red Scare" and the witch-hunting activities of Senator Joseph McCarthy and others. Aware that others were already coming under scrutiny, Bernstein says it's time to prepare "our blazing orations now," adding that "I hope I'm as brave as I sound from this distance when it catches up with me."

Meanwhile, there was the more private matter of his marriage to Felicia. Bernstein's letters to friends and family suggest that he regarded the first few months of their life together almost as a kind of social experiment, while an undated letter from Felicia underlines the strength of her love for him, but that she was under no illusions: "you are a homosexual and may never change – you don't admit to the possibility of a double life, but if your peace of mind, your health, your whole nervous system depend on a certain sexual pattern what can you do?" It was the birth of Jamie, their first child, in 1952 which transformed their marriage from a slightly uneasy alliance to something that could endure.

Plans for new projects came and went, some of them fascinating, such as an idea discussed with Blitzstein in 1952 for an opera on the life of Eva (Evita) Perón. But conducting engagements in Europe and Israel were piling up, and finding time for composition was becoming increasingly difficult. In 1953 the U.S. State Department became a significant player in Bernstein's future – and a thorn in his side. These were perilous times for Americans with liberal sympathies, especially those involved in film, theater, radio, television, and music. Bernstein was one of the 151 names in the entertainment industry whose "Communist" associations were chronicled in *Red Channels*, published in June 1950, and he came under suspicion throughout the fifties. While he was never summoned by the House Un-American Activities Committee (Copland, Robbins, and Diamond – among many others – weren't so fortunate), Bernstein was required to provide exhaustive details about his former associations with groups regarded as suspect, to renounce Communism, and to pledge his loyalty to the country – all in order to have his passport renewed. The State Department demanded sworn testimony, and the result is Bernstein's long and grimly absorbing affidavit (Letter 328). He wrote to his brother Burton, and to David Diamond, about the humiliation of this episode, but at least he was able to travel again, and in 1954 and 1955 Bernstein wrote a series of long, warm, and often funny letters to Felicia – including the bizarre tale of the disturbed young man who pursued Bernstein around Italy, threatening to blackmail him. He finished one important new work, the *Serenade* for violin and orchestra, but another was to prove much more intractable: *Candide* was to give Bernstein a lot of trouble, and took years of precious composing time, but he stuck with it. On the domestic front, things were a great deal happier, with Felicia expecting a second baby whose nickname *in utero* was "Fink".

295. Marian MacDowell[1] to Leonard Bernstein
Hillcrest, Peterborough, NH
4 March 1950

Dear Mr. Bernstein,
    I have just written Lukas [Foss] that I could not help feeling a deep personal pride in your programme with the Philharmonic last Sunday. I think Lukas did

---

[1] Marian MacDowell (1857–1956), pianist and widow of the composer Edward MacDowell. Though well into her nineties when she wrote this letter, Mrs. MacDowell remained an indefatigable enthusiast for new music. In 1896 she had bought Hillcrest, a farm in Peterborough, New Hampshire, as a quiet place for her husband, Edward MacDowell, to compose. After his death in 1908, this idyllic location became home to the MacDowell Colony, where composers, writers, and artists could work side by side in peace and quiet. Mrs. MacDowell lived to the age of 98. Colonists, and the works they created at Hillcrest, included Copland (*Billy the Kid*), Virgil Thomson (*The Mother of Us All*), Thornton Wilder (*Our Town*), James Baldwin (*Another Country*), and Du Bose and Dorothy Heywood (*Porgy and Bess*).

his part extraordinarily well, but I don't know when I have been so stirred and excited as I was during the playing of your composition. A splendid piece of work! It came over very well on the radio but I wish I might have been there.[2]

Every now and then I most particularly wish I were not ninety-two for I can't do as many things that I would like to do. As for instance, when you are here, leading the local Philharmonic, I am afraid I dare not take the risk of the fatigue which would be entailed should I attempt to go to the concert.

I am really very well but with too little strength to do the things I want to do. I would beg you to come and see me but I know you are going to be overly busy and I dare not hope for it. All the same I would love to.

I have just one regret – that while Lukas had been a devoted Colonist you should never have been there.[3]

Let me thank you for the very kind letter you wrote me a couple of weeks ago. When I heard you converse in the Green Room of the New York Philharmonic giving an outline of what you had done this season and what you are going to do it seemed incredible.

With every warm good wish and deep admiration.

Most sincerely yours,

Marian MacDowell

296. Marc Blitzstein[4] to Leonard Bernstein
4 East 12th Street, New York, NY
16 April 1950

Lenny dear,

Your casual throwaway phrase: "If you run into trouble on lyrics (in *Peter Pan*), consult Marc – he's my deputy" – has borne all kind of fruit: raw,

---

[2] Mrs. MacDowell is writing to express her enthusiasm for the *Age of Anxiety* Symphony which she had heard broadcast from New York on 26 February 1950.

[3] Bernstein himself spent time at the Colony only after Mrs. MacDowell's death, but his stays in 1962, 1970, and 1972 were all productive, as he recalled in 1987 when accepting the 29th MacDowell medal: "All of those times I was writing works which had, at least in intent, a vastness; which were dealing with subjects of astronomical if not mystical and astrological dimension. The first time was *Kaddish*. The second time was *Mass*. The last time was to write the six lectures that I later gave at Harvard known as the 'Norton Lectures'. This vastness is inherent somehow in this place. The air smells higher here, and sweeter, and closer to the vastness."

[4] Marc Blitzstein (1905–64), American composer: a brilliant and innovative musician and a committed Communist. He met a violent death, murdered by three Portuguese sailors in Martinique. Bernstein's student production of *The Cradle Will Rock* in May 1939 took place less than two years after the famous Broadway opening of the original staging by Orson Welles and John Houseman (recounted in gripping detail in Houseman 1972, pp. 245–9 and 254–78). Bernstein was a dedicated advocate of Blitzstein's music (recording the *Airborne Symphony* twice), as well as a close friend. Blitzstein was godfather to Jamie Bernstein, and the two younger Bernstein children are named after characters in Blitzstein's stage works: Alexander after Alexandra in *Regina*, and Nina after the heroine in *Reuben Reuben*. In 1964, Bernstein led a performance of *The Cradle Will Rock* from the piano as part of the Blitzstein Memorial Concert at Carnegie Hall. The cast included some from the original 1937 production.

ripe, rotten.[5] First, they wanted "Dream With Me" revised to make Wendy virginal but grown-up, intimate but not "commercial", etc. So I re-did it. Then it was decided that what the last few minutes of the play needed was a reprise, not a new song. Scurryings about, searching for a spot to introduce "Dream With Me" before the end; no luck. So "Who Am I?" took its place in the finale, with new lyrics by M.B. More stuff was needed for the mermaids' song, to fill in a spot-in-one – while they changed sets from the Pirate Ship (thirty-one) to the Nursery (now thirty-three). At this moment that set-change is so complicated that even more insert-music-and-lyrics would seem to be required; and so on. At this moment, two days before the first preview, the production seems generically right (if you like *Peter Pan* at all), but specifically right almost nowhere.[6] That will change for the better; the tricks are cute, adding up to what seems a Hippodrome extravaganza. Hershy [Kay] has done a fine brilliant transparent job of orchestration; Trude [Rittmann] remains the best person in the field for "incidentals";[7] Miss Arthur gets curiouser and curiouser, which may even help her performance, if she gets over opening-night jitters. [John] Burrell[8] is sound theatrically, but lacking in inventiveness. Great hulking crises in matters of flying equipment, set-troubles (Alswang[9] is fine but should be pruned down, too many busy gadgets on stage), and musicians'-union bickerings. [Ben] Steinberg[10] is almost (not quite) a loss; he refuses to bang down a beat for the poor unmusical performers. The seat of the trouble, I'm afraid, is Peter Lawrence's ineptitude as a producer; much as I like him personally, he's in a deep-sea fog, or appears to be. Who knows? It will probably turn out to be the hit of the century.

I cabled you re Ballo of Radio-Roma, because I had a radiogram from him, asking me to send *Regina* for consideration at the Venice Festival; and I thought you might talk it up. I hope I didn't shackle you with needless problems during your overworked stay in Italy.

Peter Frye wants to do *Cradle* in Israel this summer – Chamber Theatre in Tel Aviv (Guttmann-Bartov, manager). I'd love it, and I'd love to come. Could I send the score to Helen, with instructions not to release it until everything is settled?

The new opera is nearly half-finished! I seem to be working mightily, but need a couple of weeks' rest badly. One song, lied-like, is the best I've ever

---

[5] Bernstein was conducting in Italy and Israel during the preparations and opening of this revival of *Peter Pan*, for which he had written new songs and incidental music.

[6] The opening night of *Peter Pan* at Broadway's Imperial Theatre was on 24 April 1950.

[7] This letter gives a glimpse into the preparations for Bernstein's score of *Peter Pan*, and the involvement of not only Blitzstein but also Hershy Kay and Trude Rittmann.

[8] John Burrell directed the production.

[9] Ralph Alswang, the set and lighting designer.

[10] Ben Steinberg was the show's conductor.

written. And I have sunk my teeth into a translation of the whole of the *Dreigroschenoper* as a sort of memorial to Kurt [Weill]. Folks (Cheryl [Crawford], Lee Strasburg, Gadg [Elia] Kazan, etc.) are wildly enthusiastic at the seven songs already completed; and it may turn out to be a production.[11]

This has got to stop somewhere. Love. Have you seen Kit?

Marc

297. Leonard Bernstein to Burton Bernstein
Turin, Italy
18 April 1950

Dear Frent,

– Then they lost my tails at the Naples hotel half an hour before the concert (which was at six, & rehearsals had lasted til four, with many chills and fevers and a raw cold hall) and the piano broke down mitten der Ravel in Milano, and every city I come to there's always a mess. But such fun & fury! And big successes, natch. Speaking of natch, they called Schoenberg's *Verklärte Nacht* "Verklärte Natch" in Naples. I have just come to Turin by sheer dint, having been in Milan on Sunday (which is 2 hours from here) but had to go to Rome yesterday for a meeting with [Sol] Hurok & Kouss. So I told the Turin people I'd be late, took a 7 a.m. plane this morning, Rome to Milan, hired a private car in Milan (15,000 lire!!), sped to Turin, arrived at this glad-rags hotel, called the orchestra people – and there's nobody there who knows anything – in fact there's nobody there, & they're all eating & who am I anyway, and "Vabbene, Maestro, vabbenissimo."

Then there was the time the bed fell on grandfather . . .[12]

Loved your letter. You're growing it up, growing it up, Mü la dü. Be sure to be in N.Y. when I arrive mid-July.

Ladümü

298. Leonard Bernstein to Shirley Bernstein
Sharon Hotel, Herzlia on Sea, Israel
26 April 1950

Sweedie,

Without even waiting for cable news of the *Peter Pan* opening, I hasten to write you apropos your letter which I received Monday in Rome. I arrived in Jewland yesterday, a hulk of a once proud ship, ridden with intestinal bugs of some sort. The three weeks in Italy were screaming successes, but a nightmare

---

[11] Blitzstein was clearly already at work in 1950 on his English version of *The Threepenny Opera*. Bernstein conducted the first performance of this in 1952 at Brandeis University in Walthau, Massachusetts, with Lotte Lenya leading the cast and Blitzstein providing narrations.
[12] A reference to James Thurber's short story *The Night the Bed Fell* (1933).

1 Leonard Bernstein at the piano in 1936.

2 Leonard Bernstein conducting Stravinsky's *Soldier's Tale* at Tanglewood in 1940 in a version with Bernstein's own words (see Letter 57). Serge Koussevitzky and his wife Natalie are looking down from the balcony. The inscription reads "For Helen [Coates]: Le commencement de 'L'Histoire d'un élève' – with much love. Lenny, Aug. 1940".

3 The Revuers (left to right): Adolph Green, John Frank, Betty Comden, Alvin Hammer, Judy Holliday, 1940s.

4 Leonard Bernstein, 24 May 1944.

5 Leonard Bernstein in Hollywood with his portable typewriter in 1944.

6 Leonard Bernstein and Lukas Foss in 1944.

7 Leonard Bernstein with Jerome Robbins, Betty Comden and Adolph Green working on *On the Town* in 1944.

8 Leonard Bernstein with Aaron Copland at Bernardsville, NJ, in August 1945.

9 Leonard Bernstein studying the vocal score of Stravinsky's *Oedipus Rex*, a work he conducted with the New York City Symphony in November 1946.

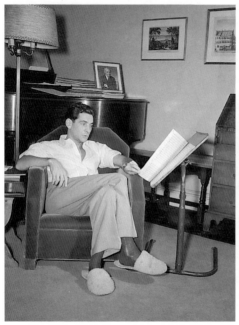

10 Two photographs of Leonard Bernstein in his West 10th Street apartment, c. 1946. The signed photograph on the grand piano is inscribed "To my very dear Lenushka with all my faith, hope and love, Serge Koussevitzky".

11 A series of photographs of Bernstein conducting in Carnegie Hall, c. 1946.

12 Bette Davis in the 1940s.

13 David Diamond c. 1945.

14 James M. Cain, with whom Bernstein corresponded about a proposed setting of Cain's novel *Serenade* in 1947.

15 Serge Koussevitzky with Leonard Bernstein and Lukas Foss, celebrating Koussevitzky's 74th birthday in 1949.

16 Leonard Bernstein with David Oppenheim.

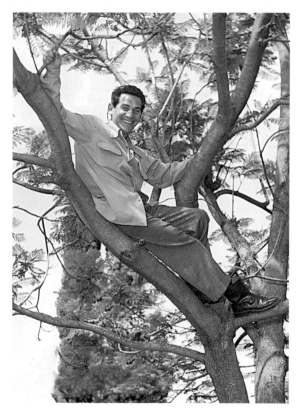

17 Leonard Bernstein at a kibbutz in Israel, festival of Shavuot, 22 May 1950.

18 Martha Gellhorn with Ernest Hemingway at the Stork Club, New York, in 1941.

19 Leonard Bernstein with Stephen Sondheim and Jerome Robbins working on *West Side Story*.

20 Arthur Laurents, Leonard Bernstein and Jerome Robbins being presented with the Key to Washington D.C. by Commissioner Robert E. McLaughlin, 31 August 1957.

22 Felicia Bernstein as Joan in Honegger's *Joan of Arc at the Stake*, 1958.

21 Leonard and Burton Bernstein skiing in 1958.

23 Lukas Foss

24 Sid Ramin, on the back cover of his LP *Love is a Swinging Word* (RCA Victor, released in 1959). To the right of Ramin's photo is an endorsement by Bernstein: "I have known Sid Ramin since we were both thirteen. I was impressed with his great musicality then, and have continued to be more and more impressed ever since. His work with me (and Irv Kostal) on *West Side Story* was invaluable – sensitive, strong, and facile. Long may he wave!"

25 Leonard and Felicia Bernstein with Boris Pasternak, Moscow, 1959.

26 Leonard Bernstein and Aaron Copland with the score of *El Salón México*, c. 1960.

27 Leonard Bernstein at the MacDowell Colony in 1962, working on *Kaddish*.

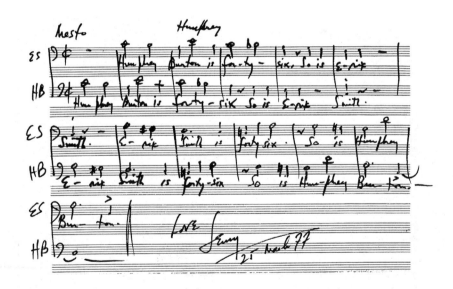

28 Leonard Bernstein: canon written for Humphrey Burton and Erik Smith, 25 March 1977. The text reads: "Humphrey Burton is forty-six, so is Erik Smith. Erik Smith is forty-six, so is Humphrey Burton." Burton recalls the occasion on which it was written: "We dined with LB at the Garrick Club, which is where he produced his composition and we all lustily joined in an impromptu performance, so far as I am aware never repeated".

29 Jacqueline Kennedy with Leonard and Felicia Bernstein and their children Alexander and Jamie at the Theatre De Lys, New York, on 28 June 1965. The occasion was the opening night of *Leonard Bernstein's Theatre Songs*, a revue featuring songs from shows for which Bernstein composed the music.

of impossible schedules, cold rainy weather, and diarrhea. Everyone became my doctor; I used fourteen different medicines indiscriminately and somehow got through. Once in Israel, having two days before my first rehearsal, I decided to avoid Tel-Aviv, and ensconced myself here for two days of quiet & sun and swimming. First, no rooms: so I took one in a house down the road, which is rather nice, but eat, etc. in the hotel. Then – no sun: in fact, a good old New England gale just begun to blow up. I sleep a lot, read a lot (*Male & Female*[13] is more than fascinating, though often in unintelligible prose), and to outgrow this great weakness which follows on these three Italian weeks of superhuman effort. By the way, the A[ge] *of* A[nxiety] brought the house down in Turin, despite a wretchedly nervous and unprepared performance. At the last minute I had to conduct from the piano, since the designated conductor proved incompetent. That is a chore! But at least I know that it can be done, given enough rehearsal, and omitting the famous last piano chord. I shall try the same method here in Israel.

This hotel is most impressive, full of Miami-type rich American Jews, but too small. The food is good, though meat is almost non-existent – which is OK, since I am on a rather lean diet – perföörce. (By the way, Italians are always saying "per forza!" which makes me think of you.) The parents were to come here on Friday next & stay here, but a cable from Dad says the boat is late & they will arrive only Monday, May 1st – so I'll grab their room Friday to Monday, on which day I move into my little house (occupied until then by the Parays).[14] You have heard that [Paul] Paray is finished here, including the American tour, & that Kouss & I will share the tour, with some assistance from [Eleazar de] Carvalho.

But all this is not what is uppermost in my mind – and psyche too. How strange that you should have written just now of Felicia! Ever since I left America she has occupied my thoughts uninterruptedly, and I have come to a fabulously clear realization of what she means – and has always meant – to me. I have loved her, despite all the blocks that have consistently impaired my loving-mechanism, truly & deeply from the first. Lonely on the sea, my thoughts were only of her. Other girls (and/or boys) meant nothing. Even the automatic straining toward general sexuality of the moment – which had always carried a big stick with me, was of no importance. I have been consistently aware of the great companionship of this girl – seen clearly and independent of the damnable tensions that discolored it, the fears melting into thin air. I fret, for the first time in my life, jealousy – a growing resentment of her current affair, and a certain knowledge that D[ick] H[art] was horribly wrong for her. Over all this, a real knowledge that

---

[13] *Male and Female* by Margaret Mead, published in 1949.
[14] The conductor Paul Paray and his wife Yolande. Paray was briefly Music Director of the Israel Philharmonic in 1949–50.

she and I were made for each other, then as now: that we have everything to give each other. Just as right is my feeling that it would have been wrong to marry when we planned in '47, in struggle with the complex tensions of both our young lives then. I would marry her tomorrow, sight unseen, ignorant of all she has lived through these two years or so, willing to learn, insatiably eager to learn.

On the boat I was seized by these feelings – and more: a grave intuition that she was in trouble and needed someone. I prayed it might be me she needed. So strong was this conviction (though I admitted to myself that intuitive deductions are all too easy in mid-Atlantic) that I wrote her a letter explaining my urge. I felt humble writing it, vastly apologetic for the indifferent treatment I had afforded her during her troubled time in California, and in fact all through our "engagement". After mailing it, I was afraid that I had been guilty of bad manners, of possibly trying to disrupt what may have been a good relationship with Hart, of possibly yielding to the impulse of a moment of loneliness. Now I know, weeks later, how sincere and deep the impulse was. I have had no answer, and have thought that my worst fears were justified. Of course I sent it to Washington Place; she may not have gotten it; it may have been intercepted; or she may have reacted only with anger at my interference. How your letter gives me a renewed hope.

I would write all this directly to her, but the unknown fate of my first letter to her gives me pause. I don't mean to use you as a go-between – I know you understand that as deeply as you do my desire to have her know my feelings. So many things become clear when abroad – so many cow-webs [sic] are cleared away: the tongues of dear friends persuading me that she was wrong for me, etc., the psychiatric womb wherein one is safe from the need to cope with sexual adjustment, etc. My feeling is one totally apart from analysis: I want only to cope, and through my own powers, without aid – especially of the indulgent, personal sort that was forthcoming from Miss Nell.

How is Felicia? Did [Eva] Gabor leave, as I hear she might, and did Felicia replace her? Is she still in the show? How does she feel about her career? Is her health OK? These things, of course, I would love to hear directly from her; but if that is not possible, let me hear them from you. I am thrilled that you are close again: that should always be: you have so much for each other.

Only one thing more: last night I dreamed at length that I had found her and solved our problems together. It was a hard dream, but full of richness. And, on awakening, I was desolate at the thousands of miles that still lay between us, and the grayness of doubt and not-knowing. My day-dreams are of her flying to Israel, and our being married in Jerusalem. Renée [Nell], of course, would be the uninvited fairy who would pronounce the curse. Strangely, though, I think she'd be delighted. I was not at all surprised at your news of Renée: I had always seen these things, but had always diminished their importance in the light of her values and of my affection for her. Of course, I have no intention of returning to her, or, I hope, to anyone, if I can begin really to live my life (as I can now) and not only live on the circumference of it. And, willy-nilly, Renée has helped to that point – a point where my world changes from one of abstractions and public-hungry performance to one of reality, a world of creativity, of Montealegre-Cohn, of Spanish & French and travel and rest and love and warmth and intimacy. I've never felt so strongly as these weeks in Italy how through I am with the conductor-performer life (except where it really matters) and how ready I am for inner living, which means composing and Felicia. I'll probably never stop conducting completely, but it will never again be in intensity and emphasis what these last seven years have been.

My interest in *Peter Pan* grows strangely neutral; I feel that the basic defection of Peter Lawrence, and the manifestations thereof in choosing [John] Burrell & [Ben] Steinberg,[15] has (or have?) robbed it, prima facie, of the real life it could have had. If it's a hit, so much the better. But thanks for all your news: and I'm very grateful to Marc. I am shocked by the idea of my name in lights on this show! But these things pass. You are right: I shall never again operate in such a way.

Many thanks for the Mitrop[oulos] profile – I'd love to see the rest (you stopped in mid-paragraph). And the [Wanda] Landowska picture is a gem. Two things were missing from your letter: there was no word of Gabey, and especially no word of Hi-lee [Shirley]. I miss you terribly, and a long letter from you with no personal word in it makes me worry a little: you will please rectify this situation.

Tremendous love, and I await impatiently your reply on all counts. The gale is now over, the sun is out, and I wish you and Felicia were both here.

Lovingly,

L

299. Leonard Bernstein to "Twig" Romney
King David Hotel, Jerusalem, Israel
9 May 1950

Dear Twig,

Your news is good: and I hope your sense of future is as strong and high as that to be found here. Pretty inspiring stuff, and fairly original, I'd say, in a world of passivity and backsliding.

Tonight I give a gala concert here celebrating the 25th anniversary of the Hebrew University. Irony: the University buildings lie in the unspeakably touching view from my window here, across the Old City, but they are unused,

---

[15] See notes 8 and 10 to Letter 296.

unavailable, in Arab hands. Such angering nonsense. But the University functions well in temporary borrowed buildings here, and will celebrate doubly hard tonight.

I am tired, but, as always, goaded on to any amount of activity by the passion in this air. I will be in Holland the first two weeks in July, then flying to America for Tanglewood, then leaving again in mid-August for the Edinburgh Festival. We should be able to see each other there (I shall be in Scotland about Aug 20 to 25): then I return to Holland to finish the Festival. Do let's meet.

The *Age* [*of Anxiety*] is already recorded by Columbia, & should be released in the fall. Glad you like it – I do too.[16]

Till Scotland, then, be good and tranquil. Helen sends a kiss.

L

300. Leonard Bernstein to Hans Heinsheimer
Tel Aviv, Israel
11 May 1950

Dear Hans,

The good news about *Peter Pan* continues to pour in from all sides. What a pleasure. Now to do something really important musically. I can see more and more clearly that the conducting side of my life will diminish rapidly, and the writing side augment. I feel myself less and less a performer. Maybe you'll have a Bernstein catalogue after all. We have to follow our insides, not our externals: was soll'n wir machen? It is a tide.

I was horrified to read about Weill.[17] This must have been a great shock to you. We will all miss him.

Good news about the recordings. How did Goddard [Lieberson] ever agree to a non-Brigitta album?

How is the "plugging" situation?

I was very much pleased with the published songs, but furious at the word-changes in "Peter Peter". They may have been necessary for purposes of the show – but certainly not for general consumption. I find the new lines almost unsingable, awkward and without meaning. Can something be done before more copies are made (if there is a demand)?

The *Age* [*of Anxiety*] was a wild hit in Torino, and a great success here with the musicians, though the public seems a bit puzzled. I have decided that the ending is all wrong (don't scream!). It is only a shame that the recording is

---

[16] This is the only mention of *The Age of Anxiety* in Bernstein's letters to Romney, who had sent Bernstein a copy of Auden's poem when it was first published, with suggestions for its musical treatment (see Letters 257 and 258).

[17] Kurt Weill died on 3 April 1950.

already made and the 2-piano version published. But I am still going to change that Epilogue. After all, Bartók published two endings now and then.

Is it possible that I can see *Peter Pan* before the recording takes place, or is it to be done immediately? I'd love to have something to say about it. But I suppose not.

My best to Nat [Broder]: and thank him for all his efforts. And to you, warm greetings from this marvelous land. I hope we meet somewhere in Europe.

Fondly,

Lenny B

301. Betty Comden to Leonard Bernstein
350 East 69th Street, New York, NY
15 May 1950

Dearest Lenny,

Knowing, as I now do, that you save every scrap of correspondence you get, from Koussevitzky's pages on life, music, and your career – to Auntie Clara's hot denunciations of meat, I write this letter with the full burden of realizing that it must top my incomparable "Musicraft", or "Sam [Paul] Puner" file of a few years back. As if this were not enough, I have the added load of trying to tell you what has been happening these last weeks with you so far away – and successfully bridging the gap of time and miles. Need I add that when I say "I", I am really referring to a certain dark fellow [Adolph Green] as well as myself – although somehow, through some odd trick of fate, it is I, only myself, who is stuck with actually writing the letter. Anyway –

I should begin by saying that the show we all want so much to happen – is not truly an existent entity yet, although we are still working at it, and very hard, too. When you tore off in that hot flush of enthusiasm – we started meeting, and, as you know, met with Jerry [Robbins]. He got interested in the idea – and had some general "feelings" about it – but nothing very specific, and since then – we have met – just ourselves – and a few times with Oliver [Smith]. We talked a great deal about the house on Middagh Street – and the many people who lived there, and what they wanted and how they behaved – and tried like fury to settle on some main characters, and a line of action. What kept happening is that the feeling of the thing kept veering from what we consider one bad extreme to another – either it acquired that "young hopeful" quality of something like *Look, Ma* or *Stage Door* – being about young artistic people trying to "get ahead", or it became about eccentric characters too removed from audience sympathy and identification – too bizarre – too enfant terriblish – too personal. We tried staying in the House for the whole show. We tried getting out of it for most of the show. To arrive at some main story and characters we attempted, finally, a kind of modern *Bohème* – the girl a smart 1950 tramp and the guy a writer or musician, involved in the House – which led us out of the House altogether to thinking of just "a modern love story" – (Does this strike a familiar chord?) – who needs the eccentrics except as background people – let's write that contemporary big relationship story. This ended nowhere – after spending a full day and evening with Oliver. Back to the House idea. We even went to Brooklyn with the boy from Middagh Street himself[18] – and roamed the Brooklyn Heights streets – and saw where the house originally stood – and looked at the breathtaking view of Manhattan – and got all inspired, and came back – and still have not captured what we want on paper. But what has disturbed us particularly is that we get no musical thoughts whatever. We find it hard to think of "number" – the musical expression of what the show should be. We cannot hear it. We sometimes feel it is more a play – and not suited to musical theatre at all. Have you had any time to think of it at all? – and if so, what does it seem to mean to you, musically? All of which brings us to how we wish you had not sailed away before anything could be talked out and either concretized – or discarded. All we have to go on is your parting enthusiasm. That evening should have been followed up by a week of intensive meeting together, but it was impossible. It just feels like no way to work together at all – being so far apart, and not being able really to talk things out. We feel so far removed from what you may be thinking – and even wonder if we have been proceeding at all along the lines that you are. Or are you? We know that outside of being frantically busy you have been sick – but if you have had any fleeting thoughts or impressions about the Idea – or any concretizing of your own feelings about it – please enclose them in return mail.

To add to our situation, we are, as you can tell from the postmark, still in the East – having run into that situation in Hollywood we all thought might happen. Not the right property. We *could* be doing *The Life of Sigmund Romberg* – but as the creators of *Bazooka*[19] we do not feel we could do the subject justice. MGM is out buying us things – but it has dragged on this long, and may a little longer – and what does that do to the date department you may well ask. All we know is – we will do the picture soon.

We want so much for the show to be. We are keeping at it – and in fact have a date to see Jerry about it today or tomorrow. I just felt we had to apprise you of the thoughts we have been having – and also to ask you what has been churning in your head these many weeks. Maybe this will be the first of a series of letters which in a few months will add up to S-H-O-W – a show that will open next spring. Please write – we will again soon. Onwards and upwards!

Much love,

Betty

It's so wonderful about *Peter Pan*!

---

[18] Oliver Smith, who had lived there.
[19] *The Baroness Bazooka* (1942) is a delicious send-up of operetta by Comden and Green.

302. Leonard Bernstein to Shirley Bernstein

Tel Aviv, Israel
19 May 1950

Shalom Shvestoah!

Since I couldn't sleep last night after the concert I have made this a do-nothing day: relaxo profundo on the wonderful beach for three or more hours, followed by relaxo in bed, followed by relaxo with Irwin Shaw's novel. Concert coming up again in an hour and a half – but I want to begin a letter anyway: there is so much to say. Relaxo always brings on tension for me – I'm so unused to any period without release of some sort. I have been engaged in an imaginary life with Felicia, having her by my side on the beach as a shockingly beautiful Yemenite boy passes – inquiring into that automatic little demon who always springs into action at such moments – then testing: if Felicia were there, sharing with me that fantastic instant when the Khamsin is suddenly gone, and a new wind, west from the sea, comes in to cancel the heat with its almost holy approach – and the test works. It's surprising how true some of the old saws out of the analysis book can be: "to establish a good relation to yourself is the prerequisite to any other relation." This self-relation is what I have begun to find: I have discovered the core in myself of human relationship (words, words til now) – the core of a sunburst of quiet energy, and always apropos of Felicia. This, after years of compulsive living, of driving headlong down alleys of blind patterns, dictated by God knows what vibrations – this is a revelation. Not that the demon absents himself: he still pokes me when his occasions arise – the French horn player, the artist in Jerusalem: but the old willingness to follow him, blind to any future, blind to the inner knowledge of the certain ensuing meaninglessness – that is gone. So the demon diminishes.

How can I tell you how touched I was by your letter? You have grown so – you are more than understanding: you understand so many things I didn't say. And you've become articulate in a way I never expected. Your control problem is all too familiar to me – an old Bernstein custom. We can work through it: only it can't be planned, like a Bar-Mitzvah, for a certain date. One day – boom! I feel you're on the road.

I'm happy about Felicia's reaction – especially by the apparent lack of ingrown hostility. We are both in such a strange condition: she with her double-edged sword, I with pure waiting. Waiting is a salutary state for me: heretofore it wasn't possible without tension. But now I feel such a certainty about us – I know there's a real future involving a great comradeship, a house, children, travel, sharing, and such a tenderness as I have rarely felt. I want to comfort her for all her heavy wandering, and to make it right. Only one thing: why does she insist on prolonging the suffering? Is she as sure as you that her present life is not her future? I sure hope she is: – I know from some almighty source that Dick was created for other things. And Felicia is for me, because the thought of her makes me strong enough to deserve her. This is by now repetitious, probably the product of having no contact with her except through you, and I must stop this proxy-relationship. You're a darling, and you have been good and loving in your handling of a delicate position.

Thanks for the idea about Aaron's concerto: I've written him & Dave [Oppenheim], although I suspect Ormandy will get it.

What of Kay Brown? Never a word from her. And what motivates your dark words about Betty & Adolph? You scare me. As for *Tree*[20] I thought Alex North was to do it. I'd hate to be strung up again with a show – that would be too much after last year. What of Charlie Feldman & *Streetcar*?

The parents are furious that you haven't written. Neither has Burtie. What is with that journalistic tycoon? I miss him terribly. The aforesaid parents dash about madly: mother is a regular Marco Polo, & Daddy, in his bungling way, is on top of the world. Helen flies about with seventy friends, busy and protective as ever. Since our housekeeper speaks only French and Bulgarian, Helen has to deal with her in her own mad French, which is mostly a series of those old American whinnies plus endless strings of Oui Oui Oui Oui – replacing the former yes yes yes yes. In French, these strings begin to approximate Rybernian. Weep weep.

It seems I've been here forever & there's still over a month to go. It's partly, I guess, not seeing you (which had become a pleasant lifelong habit) & partly the waiting game with Felicia. I don't feel the same permanence & in-living here that I felt last trip, during the war. Of course there was Azariah [Rapport] then – it all seems so impossible and of a different life. I realize now that he personified for me the war, the incredible bravery of these people, the beauty of their vision. Now, in an American double-breasted plaid – zero.

Give Fel. my dearest love, & tell her not to suffer any longer than absolutely necessary. I treasure the page from *Cue* [Magazine].

Be well; remind Gabey that I exist, & write more often. A letter takes ages (your last took 14 days, what with return for additional postage, etc.). And if Felicia feels she can write – even a line – it would make me so happy!

Bless you, dear Hilee,

L

303. Leonard Bernstein to Aaron Copland
c/o Israel Philharmonic, Tel Aviv, Israel
21 May 1950

Shalom Aaron,

So much time goes by: I don't know you any more – not even through your music, which is not exactly forthcoming. I played your violin sonata with a fine

---

[20] The score for *A Tree Grows in Brooklyn* was eventually written by Arthur Schwartz.

fiddler here the other day, and had a real old-fashioned nostalgic kick. Those faraway days when the C# was holy and the form so surprisingly right. *Where's your music?* God knows we need it. There hasn't been a real exciting American premiere in years.

I fought with Kouss valiantly over the Clarinet Concerto, to no avail. Benny & Tanglewood don't mix in his mind. Shirley had a good idea the other day: to do it with Dave O[ppenheim] at the NY Philh. next Feb. Then someone tells me he read that you've disposed of it to Ormandy. What is the story? I'd love to do it in New York with Dave. Let me know.

What's up? Movies? [Emily] Dickinson? A piano concerto? Eric [Erik][21] & Victor? *You?*

Israel is lovely, weather delightful, concerts fine, [Jascha] Heifetz in top form, Roy Harris 3rd successful, the people gay & forward-looking. I miss you.

Love,

L

304. David Oppenheim to Leonard Bernstein
26 May 1950

Dear Len,

Of course I'd love to do Aaron's piece[22] with you next year. Of course Metro is beckoning with many $s and all kinds of offers, but I guess I'd rather stay our number one clarinettist.

Yesterday, tho', I heard a rather dispiriting rumor that Mitropoulos was promising the piece in the fall with McGinnis[23] but I have no confirmation and it may be untrue. It certainly seems possible though. I'll call Aaron. Meanwhile see if you can set it with the Philharmonic, because even if it is already programmed it will be good for me to be mentioned.

1. House is being plumbed

2. Judy[24] is in Hollywood doing B.Y.[25]

3. Mrs. M. is the only nice person I know

I may tour for a month with a woodwindy quintet this summer, or I may go to Aspen, Colorado, to play at the festival, or both.

---

[21] Erik Johns (1927–2001). He became Copland's secretary in 1948 and they had a romantic relationship. He was later the librettist of *The Tender Land* (under the pseudonym Horace Everett).
[22] The Clarinet Concerto.
[23] Robert McGinnis (1910–76), principal clarinet of the New York Philharmonic from 1948 to 1960. He was succeeded by Stanley Drucker.
[24] Judy Holliday was married to David Oppenheim at the time.
[25] *Born Yesterday*, directed by George Cukor. Judy Holliday won an Academy Award for Best Actress for her portrayal of Emma "Billie" Dawn.

See you in Tanglewood, a weekend, or week middle maybe.
Enjoy,
Dave

305. Leonard Bernstein to Helen Coates
Scheveningen, Netherlands
13 July 1950

Dear H,

End of Round Seven – these concerts are thankfully over, and I leave tonight (earlier schedule, luckily) for New York. I've never been so anxious to get back – not for the country, particularly (I'm always chez-moi anywhere) but for people I desperately miss. The concerts have been gratifying, and the Mahler was a sensation in Amsterdam. I have been weak again, and accepted a week with the Concertgebouw the first days of September (7th & 9th). I thought – as long as I am here anyway until the 2nd I couldn't resist the offer. I had looked forward to it for so long anyway! They are now attacking for me to stay the whole month, and give [Eduard] van Beinum a rest (he is quite tired and ill). But I doubt that I shall.

The *Age* [*of Anxiety*] went well last night. Fine response: van Otterloo is a very intelligent and hard-working guy.[26]

But best of all – only 3 concerts in 2 weeks! And cold, cold air, a grim northern sea, angry clouds – all this is a blessing after months of relentless blue and gold.

I feel much better, though not up to par at all: but I'm prepared for the grind ahead. I hope you've rested, that the Kibbutzim don't prove insufferably hot, and that your trek eastwards proves rewarding. Don't load up with too many 16 x 16 rugs in Damascus!

Tonight I shall hear Furtwängler before the plane.[27] He was at my concert last night, and seemed very happy. A nice man: who can judge?

I am more than depressed by the news: not so much out of anxiety as out of a great disappointment in man – a heavy realization that people really don't want peace, or aren't simple or strong enough simply to decide to have it. It makes all planning seem a little bit ridiculous.

However, we go on. Round Eight . . .

L

---

[26] Bernstein's *Age of Anxiety* was given at the Holland Festival in Scheveningen on 12 July 1950 by the Hague Residentie Orchestra conducted by Willem van Otterloo, with Bernstein at the piano.
[27] On 13 July 1950, Furtwängler conducted the Concertgebouw Orchestra in Beethoven's Symphony No. 1 and *Leonore* No. 3 Overture, and Brahms' Symphony No. 1. The whole concert was broadcast and has been issued on CD by Tahra (Furt 1012–13).

306. Betty Comden and Adolph Green to Leonard Bernstein

M.G.M., Culver City, CA
23 July 1950

Dearest Lenny,

We have delayed writing only to try to find out more definitely just what our dates here will be. Talking to you and hearing you sound so low was not as pleasant as getting your marvelous letter, and we wished we could all have been more close – about our plans, but apparently both you and we are planning on a somewhat later date than September 1. You have taken a couple of more weeks in Holland, and it looks as though we will have to be here until nearly the end of September. Certainly, as far as your staying on in Holland for a rest and vacation goes – if you must, then do it. On the other hand – by that time, we should be winding up here, so if you could come out for those last weeks, we could undoubtedly accomplish something. Feasible? – ou non?

We are still exploding with the desire to do a show. As we wrote you, the Middagh Street opus bore no edible fruit, and we are happy to hear you are not what they call married to same. To make a further stab at an idea, we came out here by train, as you may know – and spent three days closeted with ourselves and our heads – digging – and did get an idea we liked – except that present conditions in this frightened and frightening world seem to have ruined its practicability.

Roughly, it was a post-war theme, capturing, we hoped, some of that Age of Anxiety feeling: Four guys who had been together in the war in the same outfit – pals, they thought never to part – who naturally drifted apart as soon as peace disbanded them – and who try to have a reunion.[28] They had something together during the war – a warmth, a companionship, a sharing, a true friendship – which they try to recapture – but the great "levelling" is not there any more. They are from utterly different walks of life now – maybe an artist, a rich advertising fellow, an elevator man, a stage carpenter. They either meet by accident or plan the evening, and at some point in the night their great comradeship reasserts itself – and although at the end they know they won't ever see each other again, they realize that they had a little glimpse of what life could be – and why should that special kind of togetherness exist only when people have their backs to the wall as in a war or crisis. Or – possibly the story could have been told through one of the protagonists, the guy who has lived on this memory, and for this day, who looks up to the others and has his memory realized, and then sees it finish when they say goodbye.

---

[28] This is very similar to the story and screenplay that Comden and Green wrote for *It's Always Fair Weather* (1955), with a score by André Previn, directed by Stanley Donen and Gene Kelly.

Anyway, this idea interested us and we did a little work on it, but it doesn't seem at all possible now.

Since then we have been up to our earmuffs in this Picture we are writing.[29] But, as stated earlier, we feel if you could come out toward the end, to vacation – at the same time, we might get something done.

Please write, and forgive our delay in answering you.

All our love,

B and A

307. Leonard Bernstein to Sam and Jennie Bernstein
Paris
17 August 1950

Dear Sweet Parents,

We have had a magnificent stay here these few days, in spite of a tough rehearsal schedule, complications with travel accommodations, etc. – plus the fact that we all three arrived so tired after the plane trip. But we've slept a lot (especially Shirley & Burt, who slept through my rehearsals) and feel really happy and well. Paris is of an unbelievable beauty now – cool, invigorating, and dewy; and the fact that so many Parisians are away for the summer kind of leaves the city open & clear for the tourists. We've fallen in love with it again, all over: and Burtie is already an old Parisian, with a beret and all.

Tomorrow we leave for London with the orchestra (by train and boat): we will stay in London two nights, see the shows, do the town – and then proceed to Edinburgh by plane Sunday noon, the 20th. My concerts are the 21st and 23rd: we go to Holland directly on the 24th, and will stay there until September 9th. Why don't you write us there – to the *Kurhaus, Scheveningen, Holland.*

From there we go to Ireland (to this great castle): and Burtie will fly home from Shannon on the 18th, arriving the 19th, while we fly back to Paris, where we will stay til the 24th at the St. James Hotel; then we plan to drive south with Peggy Riley and her husband (wonderful girl) and Harry Kurnitz,[30] the Hollywood writer, arriving in Rome about a month later.

Sounds great, doesn't it? It should be a real rest, fun, and inspiring.

Daddy, hope you're caring for your health: & Mamma, have fun. We wish you were both along! Kisses from us all –

Lenny

I'm writing to Israel about the Apes' refrigerator.

---

[29] The next Comden and Green film to be made was their greatest Hollywood success, *Singin' In The Rain* (1952).

[30] Harry Kurnitz (1908–68), American playwright and screenwriter whose Hollywood credits included *Witness for the Prosecution* and *How to Steal a Million.* He collaborated with Noël Coward on *The Girl Who Came to Supper.* In the 1930s he had also worked as a music critic for the *Philadelphia Record.*

308. Leonard Bernstein to Sam and Jennie Bernstein

London [headed paper of British European Airways]
24 August 1950

Dear Apes,

We've become the most seasoned travelers on the globe by now. At the moment we're sitting at Northolt Airport waiting for our plane to Amsterdam. We left Edinburgh this morning in a blaze of glory (but at 7:00 a.m.!). The final concert last night was a triumph, with a stamping, screaming ovation. I never conducted better. But even more exciting was Scotland itself. We all fell in love with the Scots – a great, friendly, proud people: and Burtie is considering skipping his next term at school to go back there and shoot grouse – to say nothing of Italy and Israel. I think it would be the most wonderful thing for him to visit Israel, don't you?

We're all very well – not a cold in a carload – but a little tired. In Holland for the next two weeks we should gain weight and get a good rest (at least the kids will). The food will be great – and the horses – and the sea. And two weeks in one place – what a joy!

We have had no word from you yet – and we want to know how you are. Don't forget to write us – every bargain has two sides – and we've been writing steadily.

Adolph [Green] may come over to Europe, & we may vacation together with Allyn Ann [McLerie]³¹ and some other friends. It would be such fun (Allyn is dancing here with the Ballet Theatre). We may even take a house in Southern France, after all. I have two whole months free – no dates except Milan in November. Isn't it wonderful?

Write us to Holland – the Kurhaus, Scheveningen.

Love,

Lenny

309. Leonard Bernstein to Sam and Jennie Bernstein

Scheveningen, Netherlands
1 September 1950

Dear Jen & Sam,

My first performance of Beethoven's Ninth was a triumph!³² I have been very worried about this event – the big test in every conductor's life. But it was

---

³¹ See note 88 to Letter 249.
³² Bernstein's first performance of Beethoven's Ninth Symphony was given on 30 August 1950 in the Kurzaal, Scheveningen. It was performed by the Residentie Orchestra of the Hague, the Hague Toonkunstkoor, and the soloists Corry Bijster (soprano), Annie Hermes (contralto), Frans Vroons (tenor), and Willem Ravelli (bass). In the first half, Bernstein doubled as soloist and conductor in the Piano Concerto No. 1. An unsigned review appeared in *De Tijd* on 31 August 1950. The critic was lukewarm about some aspects of the performance, complaining of "sensationalized tempi [. . .] superficiality and lack of nobility in the expression," but the overall impression of Bernstein's Beethoven was "very handsome and very lively, and the applause was exuberant."

so exciting – the solo quartet was the best I've ever heard – the chorus was marvelous – the orchestra never played better. What a tremendous experience it is to do this work! Like tearing your guts out. The public went crazy. Tonight I repeat it. Then tomorrow we are taking a wonderful car to Germany, of all places, for two days. We can get about as far as Cologne, and then come back in time to move to Amsterdam Sunday night. (Monday morning is my first rehearsal there.) Then it's all rest & swimming & sleeping until November!

We're all getting fat on milk and herring and butter and lobster and never felt better. Burtie sleeps at least 12 hours a night, and Shirley about the same. Only old Lenny gets up early to make the money.

I have an interview now – so cheerio for the moment – and we'll write you all about Germany in a few days.

Love & kisses from us all,
Lenny

310. Leonard Bernstein to Sam and Jennie Bernstein
Excelsior Hotel Ernst, Cologne, Germany
2 September 1950

Dear Apes,

We have had a most dramatic day driving a little Skoda (a Czech car loaned us by a friend) into the Rhineland, down the Rhine, through Arnhem, Düsseldorf, and over Hitler's Autobahn to Cologne. We are amazed at the wonderful food, the thriving big city, the luxury of this hotel. It's been raining all day, and Germany looks twice as tragic and ruined and dramatic through the rain. Tomorrow we drive to Bonn – where Beethoven was born – and Belgium and back to Holland – it's all like a wonderful dream for the kids – Burtie is being the mighty American conqueror here – and now we're going to investigate Cologne nightlife. We've just finished a dinner of Wiener Schnitzel which Burtie says ranks with Mrs. Hathaway's.

Write us to Amsterdam – c/o Concertgebouw.

Love,
Lenny

311. Aaron Copland to Leonard Bernstein
American Academy in Rome, Rome, Italy
16 February 1951

Dear Lensk,

Tho' I think of you every day I couldn't figure out where you were in space, until a letter from Helen today tipped me off. I think of you as dashing madly about from one triumph to another, with orchestras vaguely in the background, while here *I* sit in your ex-apt on the Janiculum while Asunta sings your praises. Somehow it all seems as per usual.

I hear you're ditching us at Ta–foot[33] this year. I'll miss you – it was nice to have you put for some weeks of the year. Well you want to do it – so do it.

America seems a million miles away. Rome feels like a haven for some reason – perhaps because we have so little contact with what goes on under the surface here. I haven't been anywhere as yet – just got my Morris-Minor[34] (Moyshe to you) last week – and began at the beginning with the Coliseum at midnight.

Haven't heard a word as to how the Israel Symph. has been received. I'm in Tel Aviv Apr 5 and [Ben-Zion] Orgad is in charge of rounding up 30 composers for me. We are to live together for 5 days in that there Art Colony. And Pesach [Passover] is to be out in a Kibbutzim. If you've got any good advice, send it.

What plans have you for the future? What do you see? What do you know?

Just think – I have a whole Quartet[35] you don't know. I'm writing something that I think will be commissioned, but if not, I'm not writing it. In any case I could only write pretty music in this villa.

Make good concerts.

Love,

A

P.S. Erik sends his best.

P.P.S. V[ictor] is in Brazil – taking jungle pictures, etc.

312. Nadia Boulanger[36] to Leonard Bernstein

36 rue Ballu, Paris, France[37]

19 February 1951

Dear Leonard,

Forgive my silence – you have plunged me into an abyss of perplexity.

---

[33] Tanglewood.

[34] A popular British car, made from 1948 to 1972.

[35] Copland's Piano Quartet was composed in 1950.

[36] Nadia Boulanger (1887–1979), French teacher, conductor, and composer. On 5 December 1974, Bernstein recalled his first meeting with Nadia Boulanger in a letter to Sylvia Vickers: "I first visited Paris after the war (1947?), conducting the Radio Orchestra. I believe it was François Valéry (son of Paul) who took me at that time to the house of Marie-Blanche de Polignac, the beauteous Countess who had the great 'salon' of those years. I believe they were Sunday evenings, and since Marie-Blanche was a charming singer and music-lover (& patron) her salon was filled with the likes of Poulenc and Bérard and Valéry and, I think, Cocteau. It was there that I met Nadia, and have adored her from that day to this. I never studied with her, but I *feel* that I have since everything she said impressed me so profoundly. (Besides, so many composers who are close to me, such as Copland, *did* study with her.) I have almost never returned to Paris without visiting with Nadia, or at least speaking to her on the telephone. She is a super-faithful correspondent and has thus filled in the long gaps between Paris visits, if only with a few always moving lines. [...] She is to this day so terribly aware of time passing, of missed contacts, of the need to be near those we love during every troubled moment. Only last week I had another note from her, in her own shaky but still legible hand, imagine, at her age and in her near-blindness. May she live forever."

[37] Written on the headed writing paper of the Écoles d'art américaines, with Boulanger's personal address printed at the foot of the page.

I like your idea – but to come to N[ew] Y[ork] to play American works superbly played by great conductors – what naïveté and what folly on my part.

I offer you:

1. Cantata: Igor Markévitch (or if you prefer, a cantata by Bach).
2. Ask Copland, Piston and a young unknown American to write a Triptych for the occasion.
3. A group of Monteverdi (I guarantee their effectiveness).
4. Works by my sister.

I need a program within my means because – I am only what I am.

If you only knew how much I am moved by your affection – all so simple and so generous.

Thank you.

Nadia B[38]

313. Leonard Bernstein to Shirley Bernstein
"Privada del etc.", Cuernavaca, Mexico
16 May [1951]

Dear Ape,

So fine to get your last letter: you sound so much better and busier and everything despite the job-problem. Perhaps by now something is a-happen, as they say here? I have never had an answer to my last letter (since our letters cross continually, and you are a stinking correspondent) in which I talked about all other kinds of work from those we know so well. Were you at all reached by this or was it just bilge? What of the Engel sessions?

But it is still wonderful to read a cheerful letter from you, even if it is stuffed with problems about Bob C. and company. I know that one will work out all right: you sound so sensible about it, and self-knowing. It is high time that you could have a relationship with a guy that was not confined necessarily to either heaven or boredom. Just a nice relationship, with warmth and affection and companionship and even passion. And I fully understand the traumatic situation with him and me and D.O. [David Oppenheim] I know you'll lick it. Meanwhile, please, no compromises with Felicia or anyone else. I find myself missing her, though, although, Goddammit, not half so much as I do you.

I wrote Adolph and of course have no answer. What is with his opus? Bob Rossen[39] arrived here again last night and just left for Mexico.[40] He is lonely and restless and beset with all the problems of a martyr and hero without being

---

[38] Written in French; English translation by the editor.
[39] Robert Rossen (1908–66), American film director who won an Academy Award for *All the King's Men* (1949).
[40] Presumably Mexico City, since Bernstein wrote this letter while staying in Cuernavaca, Mexico.

either of them. He is wretchedly lost, having lost Hollywood, and makes braver speeches than he feels. I think he may go back and face the Committee[41] next week. A man like him (only slightly sensitive and bright) can hold up only so long without his work or his family, and the absence of both together leaves him functionless. He talks by turns of settling here with his family, of going to Israel to live, of Rome, of England. He feels finished in the States. It's a mess, and I am very sorry for him. It can also happen to all of us, so we had better start preparing our blazing orations now. Maltz[42] is also living here (Cuernavaca has become a great haven for these poor guys) and regaled us the other night with tales of his lovely year in jail. I lost my dinner. It is utterly incredible that a man of his solemnity and innocuousness and faith in Jeffersonian democracy should be put away with a raft of moonshiners in a West Virginia jail. Dimitryk[43] has certainly made a ghoul of himself: and the boy in the biggest jam right now seems to me to be Garfield.[44] He will wind up in a great perjury mess if he doesn't watch out. It may already be too late. Actually, I suppose, there is nothing to be done when your life and career are attacked but strike back with the truth and go honestly to jail if you have to. This dandling about to save a career can neither save the career no make for self-respect. I hope I'm as brave as I sound from this distance when it catches up with me.

In any case Ross Evans[45] walked in the other day with a six-week old puppy, rescuee of an accident between a boxer and a gloomy Airedale bitch, the pup is a dream, a *Boxdale* (copyright term) and I have named him Machito because he is so macho and he has lovely fleas and will probably wind up on West 55th Street like all the rest, but I love him. The house is bedazzled with pee and shit of all colors, and the whole cycle recommences: Outside! On the paper! Not here! Who's the funniest little Ape? Who's the little Fellowuhss? Well if it isn't the little. . .! I am just at the crisis of deciding whether to return him or brave it through. He is always guilty and doesn't know why he is punished, and I am dienetically re-experiencing a whole lifetime of European hotels and trains and the carpet in the Israel house. Wish you were here.

---

[41] The House Un-American Activities Committee (HUAC), set up in 1938 to investigate subversive activities or Communist links of American citizens.

[42] Albert Maltz (1908–85), American author and screenwriter. One of the Hollywood Ten who were blacklisted in 1947 for alleged involvement with the Communist Party.

[43] Edward Dimitryk [Dmytryk] (1908–99), Canadian-born film director. Another one of the Hollywood Ten.

[44] John Garfield (1913–52), American actor and a friend of Bernstein's who had been among the guests at the party for his engagement to Felicia in 1947. Garfield appeared before HUAC on 23 April 1951 (a few weeks before Bernstein wrote this letter). When he refused to name any names, Garfield's life quickly disintegrated, and a year later, on 21 May 1952, he died of a heart attack at the age of 39.

[45] Ross Evans was Dorothy Parker's secretary and sometime lover.

By the way, might you come? Bob Presnell[46] writes that he is coming after all, probably next week; and that should be pleasant, if I can work with someone around. The show is going great guns,[47] and I keep wishing for you to sing it at, and get the right answers and responses. There are so many aspects of it that only you could understand, libretto-wise as well as musically, and it's a bore to have to figure everything out for myself. The two characters, by the way, have gotten themselves called Sam and Jennie, and I think you'll see why. I have about four and a half scenes sketched out of the seven, and am amazed. It should be roughly finished in a couple of weeks, and then I'll send you a sort of libretto. It's real fun to write music. You may quote. I am ruthlessly turning down offers, still. I finally refused that Harp Concerto commission for Rosenbaum in Philly, and turned down the newly-reforming Detroit Symphony, as well as a three-month stay in Australia. It's much too pleasant just to sit, and sitting here in Cuernavaca is in itself an occupation. I don't know what happens to time here: it gets destroyed, it works on a life of its own, and the days rush by so frighteningly fast that it is tiring only to think of the date. Martha [Gellhorn] and I are talking about a Caribbean jaunt in the fall. But plans in general are hard to make. And it is now time for us to go forth in her jeep to the tennis courts. So bless you and all my love. And write a guy, for cry-eye. Love from Machito, the diarrhetic darling.

X

Tell me more about the Chodorov play. Is it just a play or is there chance for real music? The idea is fine.

Come to think of it, why don't you come down for a visit? Maybe drive with Presnell? It would be free! His address: 126 E 56.

X

314. Felicia Montealegre to Leonard Bernstein
headed paper of the National Broadcasting Company, Inc. [New York, NY] [before 9 August 1951]

Darling!

No word from you – and I *don't* wonder why! Let's let it lie for the nonce – this is hardly a step to take with such great vacillation – someday it may become the most natural and longed for event – if that blissful state of mind should take over (oh happy day!) and I'm still not yet wed, we'll just get on with it and be miserable for ever after!

I miss you terribly – you couldn't have been sweeter or more tender. Both of you helped me so wonderfully through what would have been otherwise a very

---

[46] Robert Presnell (1914–86) was a screenwriter, married to the actress Marsha Hunt (b. 1917). Both were friends of Bernstein, and both were blacklisted in Hollywood during the "Red Scare."
[47] Bernstein was composing *Trouble in Tahiti*.

tough time. I love you for it. However it has made N.Y. seem so grim by comparison – thank God for Hilee [Shirley]!

Rehearsals are ginger-peachy. I have a reading for a play tomorrow – was interviewed for a movie (that old story!) which will be shot here in the East. I had my first real "sortie" with Bert the Card and Claude at Sardi's, ran into the Davids – the Diamond one looking frighteningly thin and peaked and rather cold towards me (judge of my joy!) – had a pleasant lunch with Goddard [Lieberson] (?) –

I feel very well, have had no dire accidents – that is, *yet* – and life goes on in its own plodding way – but I am strangely happy though it could be just an overwhelming sense of relief!

I'm afraid I won't be able to get there for the *Missa*[48] – it breaks my heart, but I just have to take this TV thing seriously.[49] I hope it's going well and that it's a big smasheroo – (just don't bow this time!)

Oh sweetie!

Call me any way – I kiss you long and sweet.

Feloo

P.S. She's not yours – follow me!

315. Leonard Bernstein to Philip Marcuse
127 Wolcott Road, Brookline, MA
5 September 1951

Dear Fil,

Both your letters have lain, screaming for answer, for months, and everything conspires to prevent same. Tanglewood swamped me this summer, and just before the end of the season Felicia and I decided to marry, inducing further activity.

It's wonderful, & I'm deeply happy about the marriage. I've kind of rediscovered this lovely girl, and believe that we will have a fine time of it. The wedding is Sunday the 9th, & we leave straight for California to see her family, then on to Mexico for the winter, returning probably in March or April.

I'm afraid that this will rule out the 9th Symphony in Detroit. I have been so pleased with the idea, & attracted by the notion of another "special" in Detroit, that I have hesitated to write you a yes or a no. But I fear that the no triumphs. This will be a composing year. I may make an exception & do a little festival of 3 weeks at the City Center in N.Y. in the spring, but I've not yet decided. This is a crucial year, & much will be crystallized. I'll be in touch with you throughout.

---

[48] Bernstein conducted Beethoven's *Missa solemnis* at Tanglewood on 9 August, in memory of Serge Koussevitzky who had died in Boston on 4 June 1951.

[49] Felicia was getting regular work in TV drama series. In August 1951 she appeared in "Death Sabre," an episode of *Suspense*, with the young Leslie Nielsen.

Won't you & Babs say some special little prayers for us? Let me hear from you soon, via Helen Coates, 155 E. 96th St., New York.

Much love to both of you.

Lenny

316. Leonard Bernstein to Burton Bernstein
Remount Ranch, Cheyenne, WY
18 September 1951

Baudümü,

Every turn on this ranch makes us think of you. We almost thought of going up to Sheridan, but this took precedence – and it beats everything. We've been here two days & have to leave today and hate to. Such beauty & luxury: & the Knoxes are real pals.

Every day marriage gets better.[50] It may take a lot of days, but I think the big crisis is over. (That took place in Detroit, but Phil & Barbara [Marcuse] were so great, as you know, & they really helped enormously.)

Now get this:

Last night *we went lionhunting.*

We really did. Mountain lions. Didn't find one. But the deer abounded. It's infinitely better than Irish deerstalking. It's civilized. We piled into a Chevvy convertible, top down, in the freezing high air, wrapped in heavy winter clothes & earmuffs and gun in hand. You drive slowly around the hills, shining a strong torch into the trees & rocks and sipping Dewar's White Label. Now there's a plan. It was marvelous, despite the lack of lion, but we did get one shot at a porcupine and missed. All in all, *we went lionhunting.*

Baudümü, be smart at school this year, and be serious and learn and become the wonderful guy you are to become. Can't wait til Xmas.

Felicia loves you & sends a big hug*, & so do I.

Ape-husband-hunter,

Lennuhtt

*She adds *undying* and *passionate.*

317. Leonard Bernstein to Philip and Barbara Marcuse
Humboldt 53, Cuernavaca, Mexico
9 October 1951

Dear Gentle People,

There it is, the address I mean, and now let's have words from you, lots of them. This is not a moment for lots of words from us: it is a moment of getting

---

[50] Felicia and Leonard had been married nine days earlier, on 9 September.

installed in a new house, new life, new everything. The tensions (do you recall this word?) accumulate still, are fought, lived through. Every once in a while a state of comparative ease is reached which promises well for the future. And now we have a glorious grand huge house with a huge garden and a huge pool, and tomorrow there ought to be a huge piano and then there should be some huge work. I am not quite sure what F[elicia] is going to do all winter while I am at the piano, and in my own world, so to speak. But most of that, of course, depends on what security she will manage to find in a marriage contracted in insecurity. We hope and we pray and we wait.

What did you think of the Cadillac idea? Me, I think it's great; and it is a real come-on for me. The Buick is in fine shape (got us here safely, sans accident, sans blowout, sans being pinched).

Let's have a glorious letter!

Love,

Lenny

Felicia adores you both and is as grateful as I am for your presence on earth, and sends her warmest.

318. Leonard Bernstein to Aaron Copland
Humboldt 53, Cuernavaca, Mexico
18 October 1951

Dear Sorelymissed A,

First off, thanks for the delectable wire on the wedding day. If this thankyou is a bit late, fíjate, no más, the enormous automobile trip we have made from Boston to San Francisco (stopping for days at ranches on the way) to L.A. and thence to Cuernavaca. It took about a month; and we are slowly settling now into a glorious house and garden and pool. The piano has arrived, I have written an extra aria for Captain Hook (what shit!) to grace the new road production of *Peter Pan*, and am now starting on the long hard road of writing some real things. I have decided, coute que coute, to finish my little opry [*Trouble in Tahiti*] and then write a few more little opries. There may be some stray notes – like even a piano sonata, and a new idea for an orchestra piece; but the main stem is still that old devil theatre, and I have to see just what my connection with it is.

I still haven't seen the score of the Piano Quartet, and long to. Isn't there something you can do?

Write to me about your life in Boston. Did everything work out well for a house for you and E[rik]? Give him my best, and thank him also for the wire. What word from Victor? Does he find marriage as fascinating as I do (what a word for marriage)? Actually it is the most interesting thing I have ever done, though there are times when one's interest must be that of a person in an audience, or one would go mad. It is full of compensations and rewards, and reveals more to me about myself than anything else ever has, including a spotty array of analysts.

As I say, write, long and lovingly, and give my love to Irving [Fine] and Verna [Fine] and Lukas [Foss] and Tillmange.

Dear old Judgenose, I miss you.

L

319. Leonard Bernstein to Aaron Copland
Humboldt 53, Cuernavaca, Mexico,
14 November 1951

Dearest Aa,

Today is the fourteenth of November, which makes four reasons to write you. 1) that you have just written me; 2) that it's your birthday, whether you like to be reminded or not; 3) that we met on this day about fourteen years ago; and 4) that Bruno Walter celebrated your birthday most spectacularly eight years ago by getting sick.[51] So we owe each other this here Martini on this here day. With all my love.

Also, we bought a phonograph, and there in the same shop was the Clarinet Concerto and the Quartet, on both of which I am therefore now an expert.[52] I am disappointed in the Concerto, and I think it may be a little on account of the performance. I remember it as being so much fun when you struggled with it on the piano (of course everything is more fun when *you* do it on the piano with your apologetic grin), and Benny [Goodman]'s performance is ghastly and student-like, I think. But there is also something that does not quite satisfy about the score, despite its evident beauties. The opening is still ravishing, and I find to my dismay that it is in places less like Satie than like the *Rosenkavalier* trio. Tant mieux, say I, though surprised not a little. Strange, in fact, how many touches of Strauss there are; there is even a slight *Don Quixote* feeling here and there. I still disapprove of the cadenza, finding it cute but arbitrary; but it is the last part that disappoints me because the last part was so much fun. Of all things, the form. Doesn't seem to work.

---

[51] Bruno Walter's illness gave Bernstein the chance to make his spectacular debut with the New York Philharmonic on 14 November 1943.

[52] The first recordings of Copland's Clarinet Concerto (Benny Goodman, Columbia String Orchestra, conducted by Copland) and the Piano Quartet (New York Quartet – Mieczyslaw Horszowski, Alexander Schneider, Milton Katims, and Frank Miller) were released on the same disc by Columbia Records (ML 4421).

But the Quartet, ah, there is another matter. I rejoice particularly in the scherzo, because I think it is the longest sustained piece of continuity you have written in a long time, and it is really continuous, yes, really, and it goes and goes in a remarkably convincing way. I feel rather close to the tonal way in which you are handling tone-rows (I've done it too, here and there); and I find that this movement is a real triumph. The last movement is beautiful too in a way which has already become awfully familiar to Coplandites, so that it is not such a thrill as the second. And the first is lovely, but I never did go for you and fugues, especially here where the opening is so reminiscent of the third Hindemith Quartet. Imagine, Hindemith! Who'da thunk it? But it makes a fine piece, especially for records, because you want to hear it again and again (of course with two or three mambos in between); and I still think you are a marvelous composer.

That's the good news for today, and I seem to have started a piano sonata right in the middle of all my stage-operations, nolens volens, as Kouss used to say.

The lectures look awfully inviting, and I wish I were around. Instead I've got to start thinking up some of my own for the Brandeis festival. Let me know how they come out.

As for T'wood, I am not surprised, though a bit beset by wonderment. Yes, I suppose I'll be coming back, but don't say anything yet: I just *might* have another brainstorm. Sometimes I think I don't really understand about T'wood any more. More of this anon.

Are you really thinking of coming here in May? As far as I know, this house is available then. I think you would love it, though it's very large and expensive (2000 pezozzees a month!) But maybe now that you're rich . . . Let me know. Of course I'd much rather have you around Boston in June to help us out at Brandeis, but I realize that's too much to ask.

So you're a Village weekender, just like all the Harvard boys? I find it very chic, and send Eric [Erik] my best.

Dear Aa, it was a real joy to have your letter and I miss you and hope you will continue to write zillions more like that Piano Quartet.

Much love,

L

320. Felicia Bernstein to Leonard Bernstein
[?late 1951 or 1952]

Darling,

If I seemed sad as you drove away today it was not because I felt in any way deserted but because I was left alone to face myself and this whole bloody mess which is our "connubial" life. I've done a lot of thinking and have decided that it's not such a mess after all.

First: we are not committed to a life sentence – nothing is really irrevocable, not even marriage (though I used to think so).

Second: you are a homosexual and may never change – you don't admit to the possibility of a double life, but if your peace of mind, your health, your whole nervous system depend on a certain sexual pattern what can you do?

Third: I am willing to accept you as you are, without being a martyr or sacrificing myself on the L.B. altar. (I happen to love you very much – this may be a disease and if it is what better cure?) It may be difficult but no more so than the "status quo" which exists now – at the moment you are not yourself and this produces painful barriers and tensions for both of us – let's try and see what happens if you are free to do as you like, but without guilt and confession, please!

As for me – once you are rid of tensions I'm sure my own will disappear. A companionship will grow which probably no one else may be able to offer you. The feelings you have for me will be clearer and easier to express – our marriage is not based on passion but on tenderness and mutual respect. Why not have them?

I know now too that I need to work. It is a very important part of me and I feel incomplete without it. I may want to do something about it soon. I am used to an active life, and then there is that old ego problem.

We may have gotten married too soon and yet we needed to get married and we've not made a mistake. It is good for us even if we suffer now and make each other miserable – we will both grow up some day and be strong and unafraid either together or apart – after all we are both more important as individuals than a "marriage" is.

In any case my dearest darling ape, let's give it a whirl. There'll be crisis (?) from time to time but that doesn't scare me any more. And let's relax in the knowledge that neither of us is perfect and forget about being HUSBAND AND WIFE in such strained capital letters, it's not that awful!

There's a lot else I've got to say but the pill has overpowered me. I'll write again soon. My wish for the week is that you come back guiltless and happy.

F

321. Marc Blitzstein to Leonard and Felicia Bernstein
Ferris Hill Road, New Canaan, CT
19 July 1952

Dear L and F,

Sitting in the kitchen with Cheryl [Crawford] and Ruth [Norman], eating raspberries for breakfast, it comes all over me what a fine time I have been having recently. The *Regina* concert started, really sparked, the sense of well-being; then Brandeis and the *Threepenny* [*Opera*]; then Mina's;[53] then Tanglewood and you-all. Not a great deal of work to show for it; maybe something just as good for me now, and for which I have apparently been hungry: well-being, that says it. It comes over me that for a long time since the Broadway *débâcle* of *Regina* I have been slowly withering on the vine. How one needs these vanity-assuagements!

You are a lovely host-and-hostess, did you know? It goes so smoothly, the guest feels he isn't in the way – that, I suppose, is the stumbling-block of most visits. And if this note betrays a contented kind of stupor, then it does. I have little guilt about it.

Will you let me know about *Trouble* [*in Tahiti*]? What you decided, how it came off, how you feel after the performance. *Reuben* calls, and I return to grappling with it. One small session with [Lotte] Lenya first; then a week-end on [Edward T.] Cone's boat at Water Island; and off to Brigantine and Jo [Davis]'s and the garage. I promise to be more cooperative in the matter of showing you the opera next time.

My love and thanks to Helen. And to you two, you chuckle-birds. Write me simply: care Davis, Brigantine, New Jersey.

Marc

322. Leonard Bernstein to David Diamond
Sunset Farms, Lee, MA
21 July 1952

Dear David,

Reports fly in from all sides that you are really happy at last, and this makes me happy. Apparently Rome has been a joy for you, work-wise and heart-wise; and I cannot resist writing to tell you how glad I am.

Felicia and I live in a constant thrilled expectancy of the child (due at the end of August or so): and it is all an experience to be cherished. Tanglewood proceeds beautifully; the same breathless six weeks. My little opera was a dud at Brandeis, due mostly to the half-baked state in which it found itself at première time; but now the revisions are almost finished, and a new (the true) ending composed; and I look forward to a more reasonable and telling production here at T'wood on 10 August. Then the baby; then a full season in New York

---

[53] Mina Kirstein Curtiss (1896–1985), writer, translator, and biographer of Georges Bizet. Her younger brother was Lincoln Kirstein, one of the most important figures in the development of ballet in the United States.

(imagine!) without a single conducting date: nothing but composing to my heart's content. God, I have waited long for that.

Best to you, & write of your plans and your new works.

Lenny

323. Marc Blitzstein to Leonard Bernstein
Box 74, Brigantine, NJ
15 August 1952

Your letter is full of good spirits. The modest expression of what must have been an enormous satisfaction, in the success of *Trouble in Tahiti*, does you credit. I'm hoping you have copies of the improvements, so I may snag one for my files. And I am happy to see that the Rialto-code-word for the work is not "Trouble" but "Tahiti".

Of course Evita Péron (I can't remember if the accent should fall on the "o")[54] can make a fine operatic subject: her end, of cancer, while young, doesn't fill the picture of tragedy, really seems senseless (except for the saw that "Death is democratic"). But she has glamor, power, evil, and a saint's façade – all qualities which, incidentally (aside from the "good works") characterized Regina Hubbard. That makes me wonder if Lillian [Hellman] is the precisely right librettist. Once the Latin color is snagged, and the expanded picture of power-area registered, will she (L) not find herself treading well-worn paths? Then you could call the opera "The Bigger Foxes" or "The Same Old Part of Another Forest".[55] But I'm happy you've found a subject.[56] Watch out for Fleur Cowles, who has a first-hand interview book on Eva; she may try to claim ownership of what is surely public material. Or, on a second thought, perhaps involve her (Cowles).

Reuben really goes well. More later.

I shall probably be back in town after the first. How is Felicia bearing up these last weeks before the event?[57] My love to her and Helen. And remember, we have a September date to do the records of "3d Opera".

Helen probably told you that Mina's mother died. She might relish a short note. (Mrs. Mina K. Curtiss, Williamsburg, Mass.)

I hug you.

Marc

---

[54] It should be on the "o". Her full name was Eva María Duarte de Perón.

[55] Hellman's plays included *The Little Foxes* and *Another Part of the Forest*.

[56] This project for an opera on Eva Perón came to nothing, but it's clear from this letter that Bernstein was contemplating it within days of her death (on 28 July 1952). The theatrical potential of her story was famously explored quarter of a century later in *Evita* by Andrew Lloyd Webber and Tim Rice.

[57] Jamie Anne Maria Bernstein was born on 9 September 1952.

324. Leonard Bernstein to Solomon Braslavsky
205 West 27th Street, New York, NY
19 September 1952

Dear Brasy,

I want to thank you for *both* your beautiful letters. You are a warm and good soul!

The baby is beautiful beyond works (her English name is *Jamie*), & the mother is just as beautiful. We are slowly getting settled in a new apartment, and should have a wonderful home-like year.

Best to you & your family, and a Happy New Year.

Lenny Bernstein

325. George Abbott to Leonard Bernstein
Hotel Carter, Cleveland, OH
23 April 1953

Dear Lenny,

What a joy it is to work with agreeable people![58] Next time let's put in the contract that any job writers have to submit to a psychiatric test to be sure we get a fairly congenial type. Anyhow Rodgers and Hammerstein would pass the test.

The show is beginning to take form.[59] The scenery never quite works, but it will be when we get where there's a better crew.

Thank you for the wire. Give my love to the beautiful Felicia.

I hope next year doesn't get by without our being together on some exciting effort.

Yours for diminished sevenths.

Love,

George

---

[58] *Wonderful Town* had opened at Broadway's Winter Garden Theatre on 25 February 1953, directed by George Abbott. The show had a book and lyrics by Comden and Green, and a score (composed in four weeks) by Bernstein.

[59] Abbott was directing *Me and Juliet* by Rodgers and Hammerstein, which had a pre-Broadway tryout at the Hanna Theatre in Cleveland.

326. Arthur Miller[60] to Leonard Bernstein

Roxbury, CT
[?June 1953]

Dear Lenny,

I especially appreciated your note because as it happened I was about to go in and shake up the *Crucible* production myself. It is done now. I've removed all the sets, and as much of the fakery as possible, and tried to make it look as much like my work as possible.[61] Some night soon when you are at a loss for what to do I wish you'd go in again and let me know what you think. It is my first try at "directing", and although I could not, under the circumstances, do half of what I would had I started from the beginning, I think you'll get a weird feeling as well as a sense of horror at what production can do to a piece of writing.

I don't know what you do in the summer but if your mind ever turns North give me a call and come up with your wife and baby. We have plenty of room and eat often. I mean it.

Sincerely,
Art Miller

327. Francis Poulenc[62] to Leonard Bernstein

24 July [1953][63]

My dear Bernstein,

I've tried, in vain, to obtain your address in the United States. It's promised to me, but I'm still waiting. So I am sending my letter to Salabert USA (I think, after all, that Schirmer is your publisher). I want to thank you, from the bottom of my heart, for all that you've done for my dear *Mamelles* [*de Tirésias*]! I have received some press cuttings and I know that it went very well. With you I was calm, since

---

[60] Arthur Miller (1915–2005), American playwright. *The Crucible* was widely perceived at the time as an attack on McCarthyism. Miller was summoned to testify before HUAC in June 1956, following a routine request for a passport renewal (a parallel with Bernstein's situation in 1953; see Letter 328). For refusing to name names, Miller was found guilty of contempt of Congress in 1957, a conviction that was reversed a year later.

[61] *The Crucible* opened at the Martin Beck Theatre on 22 January 1953. In June 1953, Miller made several revisions and recast some of the roles. Brooks Atkinson wrote in *The New York Times* (2 July 1953) that in this revised version, "*The Crucible* has acquired a certain human warmth that it lacked amid the shrill excitements of the original version. The hearts of the characters are now closer to the surface than their nerves."

[62] Francis Poulenc (1899–1963), French composer. Bernstein conducted *Les Mamelles de Tirésias* at the Brandeis University Festival of the Creative Arts in June 1953. For Columbia he recorded Poulenc's Concerto for Two Pianos (with Arthur Gold and Robert Fizdale), the *Gloria*, and – as pianist – three songs with Jennie Tourel. Bernstein commissioned Poulenc's *Sept Répons des Ténèbres* for the New York Philharmonic. Shortly after Poulenc's death, Benny Goodman and Bernstein gave the world premiere of the Clarinet Sonata, on 10 April 1963.

[63] Written in French; English translation by the editor.

you played the piece by heart, better than me. As I have a great weakness for this score, you've given me true pleasure, and you have all my gratitude.

At the moment I am composing a big opera based on the *Dialogues des Carmélites* for La Scala. I hope you'll like that too. Let me know when you are coming to France, Danton 52–23, 5 rue de Médicis, Paris.

Until then, I say again thank you, thank you, and I embrace you.

Francis Poulenc

328. Leonard Bernstein: sworn affidavit for passport application[64]
District of Columbia
3 August 1953

Leonard Bernstein, being duly sworn deposes and says:

I am a citizen of the United States and was born on August 25, 1918 at Lawrence, Massachusetts.

---

[64] This lengthy document, a kind of "loyalty oath," is a chilling reminder of its time: McCarthyism was at its height, and thousands of Americans were investigated for alleged Communist sympathies. A number of Bernstein's friends had been ordered to appear before the House Un-American Activities Committee (HUAC). Jerome Robbins testified on 5 May 1953 and named several names (see Vaill 2007, pp. 215–20). Aaron Copland appeared as a witness on 25 May 1953. He wrote a darkly amusing account of his grilling by Senator McCarthy (printed in Copland and Perlis 1992, pp. 193–5): "My impression is that McCarthy had no idea who I was or what I did, other than the fact I was part of the State Department's exchange program at one time . . . It occurred to me . . . as McCarthy entered that it was similar to the entrance of Toscanini – half the battle won before it begins through the power of personality." David Diamond was also summoned by HUAC, and according to Howard Pollack (Pollack 1999, p. 191), a nervous Diamond asked his mentor for advice: "What if I'm asked a question about Lenny?" Copland's sage reply was, "You say what you feel you have to say."

Instead of being called to HUAC (which was well aware of his alleged associations with "subversive" groups), Bernstein endured a different kind of torture: "He was not subpoenaed to appear before HUAC or Senate committees but was instead drawn into living hell in July 1953 by the US State Department's refusal to renew his passport" (Seldes 2009, p. 69). The State Department was entitled to use its regulations to refuse or revoke passport applications if it believed that an applicant had Communist sympathies or associations (a practice halted in 1958, at least in theory, by the Supreme Court's landmark judgment on the right to travel in the case of Rockwell Kent et al. v. John Foster Dulles). Bernstein's sworn affidavit, printed here in its entirety, was a comprehensive document, "a humiliating confession of political sin" according to Seldes (2009, p. 70). It had the desired short-term effect, since he received his renewed passport a few days later, on 12 August 1953.

But this document was to haunt Bernstein for years to come. In 1954 it was presented to the American Legion for its approval, so that Bernstein could be allowed to work in Hollywood to compose the score for *On the Waterfront* (see Seldes 2009, p. 71) – a film directed by Elia Kazan, with a screenplay by Budd Schulberg and including Lee J. Cobb among its stars: all three had named names to HUAC. That all three should have been involved in the creation of a film about the shame and danger of informing is bitterly ironic.

The submission of this affidavit didn't end Bernstein's problems. His declassified FBI files make for absorbing reading (they are available online at vault.fbi.gov/leonard-bernstein) and show not only that he continued to come under suspicion, but that this affidavit was often used as a document that indicated the need for further investigation. In 1954–5 the FBI compiled a report for William F. Tompkins, Assistant Attorney General in charge of the Internal Security Division in Eisenhower's administration. On 1 October 1954, Tompkins wrote to the Director of the FBI with the subject: "Leonard Bernstein. Security Matter – C[ommunist]. Fraud Against Government." The alleged "fraud" was based on apparent contradictions between Bernstein's 1953 affidavit and the information gathered by the FBI about his political affiliations. A memorandum was sent to the New York office by the FBI Director on 12 October with instructions to start an investigation, adding that "this matter should be handled immediately." The reports subsequently sent to Tompkins reveal that informants against Bernstein in the past were recontacted for this investigation. Almost a year later, on 11 August 1955, J. Edgar Hoover wrote to Tompkins that the Bureau had "forwarded additional information for your consideration with regard to a possible violation on the subject's part of the Fraud Against the Government Statutes. It is requested that you advise this Bureau of any decision reached by you relative to this matter." After reviewing this "additional information," Tompkins replied that "the only available evidence linking the subject with the Communist Party is based on hearsay rather than personal knowledge. As such it is insufficient to warrant prosecution of the subject under Title 18, United States Code, Section 1001 [relating to making "materially false, fictitious, or fraudulent statement or representation"] and Section 1541 [relating to fraudulent issue of a passport], for his denial of Communist Party membership or having ever knowingly engaged in activities connected with the Communist Party movement." That investigation was closed in September 1955.

But Bernstein was the subject of other security (rather than fraud) investigations by the FBI between 1951 and 1958, catalogued in an Office Memorandum dated 31 August 1959 from G. H. Scatterday to Alan Belmont (then Assistant Director of the Domestic Intelligence Division). This memorandum also states that "During the security investigation of Bernstein, Washington Field Office reviewed HCUA [House Committee on Un-American Activities] files which were found to be replete with information concerning Bernstein's connection with C[ommunist] P[arty] front organizations."

During the Kennedy years, Bernstein's past was raked over yet again. On 1 September 1961, Hoover wrote to Kenneth O'Donnell, Kennedy's Special Assistant, responding to a request for "name checks concerning eighty individuals in connection with the Advisory Committee on the Arts" and attaching a rehashed summary of the FBI's findings on Bernstein since the 1940s. In 1962 the New York Office of the FBI sent the Washington Field Office a photograph of Bernstein, with a bizarre memorandum headed "*Unsub*: American musician alleged to be a Soviet agent." During the early 1960s, several concerned cranks wrote directly to Hoover, one of the oddest being a nun from the Sisters of St. Joseph in Brooklyn, NY (as with the names of all informants, her name has been redacted in the released Bernstein files). In a letter postmarked 9 March 1963, she wrote: "It has been brought to my attention that Leonard Bernstein, the noted conductor of the new Lincoln Center in New York City, has Communistic tendencies. For this reason I am writing to you with the hope that you will be able to enlighten my Community (two thousand Sisters of St Joseph) and me with the truth. His performances are listed among our very limited number of programs which may be seen. I do not know if the Bureau is permitted to disclose any findings of Mr. Bernstein's past life [...] May God bless you for your wonderful work." J. Edgar Hoover replied personally on 13 March, thanking his correspondent ("My dear Sister") for "the kind sentiments you expressed concerning my efforts as Director of the FBI," explaining that information in FBI files is "confidential and available for official use only pursuant to regulations of the Department of Justice," and ending: "I trust you will not infer either that we do or do not have information regarding Mr. Leonard Bernstein." A note attached to Hoover's reply states that "Leonard Bernstein was placed on the Security Index 5–2–51, and was canceled 3–18–52, when the Prominent Individuals Subdivision of the Security Index was discontinued."

As late as April 1966, when Bernstein applied for his passport to be renewed so that he could go to Vienna to work with the Vienna Philharmonic, an FBI Memorandum recycled much of its earlier material. By 1967, an internal memorandum added Bernstein's support for civil rights organizations to an otherwise familiar summary: "Bernstein has been active in the civil rights movement and in 1965 Harry Bellafonte organized a group of musical and literary artists to take part in the Selma to Montgomery, Alabama, march. Bernstein was one of the artists who made up this delegation." That additional information was communicated to Mrs. Mildred Stegall (aide to President Lyndon B. Johnson) at the White House on 5 March 1968 after she requested a routine security check.

In the available files, two further episodes attracted the FBI's attention. The first, unsurprisingly, was the event held in the Bernstein apartment on 14 January 1970 to raise funds for the legal defence of the Black Panthers. Through off-the-record press briefings and leaks to friendly journalists, the FBI sought to discredit Bernstein and his wife. Ten years later, after some of the FBI files relating to this event had been made available under the Freedom of Information Act, a furious

Bernstein was quoted in *The New York Times* (22 October 1980): "I have substantial evidence now available to all that the F.B.I. conspired to foment hatred and violent dissension among blacks, among Jews and between blacks and Jews. My late wife and I were among many foils used for this purpose, in the context of a so-called 'party' for the Panthers in 1970 which was neither a party nor a 'radical chic' event for the Black Panther Party, but rather a civil liberties meeting for which my wife had generously offered our apartment. The ensuing FBI-inspired harassment ranged from floods of hate letters sent to me over what are now clearly fictitious signatures, thinly-veiled threats couched in anonymous letters to magazines and newspapers, editorial and reportorial diatribes in *The New York Times*, attempts to injure my long-standing relationship with the people of the state of Israel, plus innumerable other dirty tricks. None of these machinations has adversely affected my life or work, but they did cause a good deal of bitter unpleasantness."

The last event covered in the available FBI files is one that shows the organization at its most paranoid. Bernstein's *Mass* was written for the inaugural event of the John F. Kennedy Center in Washington, D.C., on 8 September 1971. On 9 July and on 16 August 1971 memoranda were sent to Charles D. Brennan, then Assistant Director of the Domestic Intelligence Division, with the subject "Proposed plans of antiwar elements to embarrass the United States Government." The second described a "plot by Leonard Bernstein, conductor and composer, to embarrass the President [Nixon] and other Government officials through an antiwar and anti-Government musical composition to be played at the dedication of the Kennedy Center for the Performing Arts [several lines redacted]. The purpose of this action was to embarrass high Government officials, possibly even the President who might be present." It also cited Bernstein's visits to discuss the *Mass* with the priest and peace activist Daniel Berrigan while he was in Danbury Jail (he was on the FBI's 10 Most Wanted list for his anti-Vietnam campaigning). The FBI memorandum of 16 August also describes an attempted visit that was thwarted: "On 7-14-71, Bernstein attempted to visit Berrigan at Danbury but was denied admission by prison officials after consulting Bureau of Prisons in Washington, D.C." On the day of the first performance, 8 September, Brennan received another memorandum (for information only) summarizing the situation and citing a report in *Human Events* that "Bernstein intended to embarrass the President with an antiadministration bombshell," but reminding Brennan that Nixon had already announced he would not be present out of courtesy to Jacqueline Kennedy Onassis, stating that the formal opening "should really be her night." Nixon's views on Bernstein were robustly antagonistic. While he will certainly have known of Bernstein's alleged Communist associations in the past, Nixon also regarded him as a dangerous musical modernist. In a White House memorandum to Bob Haldeman dated 26 January 1970, Nixon offered these thoughts: "As you, of course, know those who are on the modern art and music kick are 95 percent against us anyway. I refer to the recent addicts of Leonard Bernstein and the whole New York crowd. When I compare the horrible monstrosity of Lincoln Center with the Academy of Music in Philadelphia I realize how decadent the modern art and architecture have become. This is what the Kennedy–Shriver crowd believed in and they had every right to encourage this kind of stuff when they were in. But I have no intention whatever of continuing to encourage it now."

One final request for a security "name check" for Mr. and Mrs. Leonard Bernstein was made during the Ford administration, with the FBI submitting the following on 18 November 1974: "Mr. Bernstein, who you advised is a conductor [...] has been the subject of various security-type investigations conducted by the FBI since the early 1950s based on information that he had affiliated with or supported in some manner 15 organizations cited as communistic or subversive. Leonard Bernstein [...] has been active in the civil rights movement. [...]. On May 12, 1971, Leonard Bernstein and his wife hosted a fund-raising party in support of Philip F. Berrigan and five co-defendants charged with conspiring to kidnap Henry Kissinger and blow up heating systems in Federal buildings in Washington, D.C." While this document describes an alleged "conspiracy," it makes no mention of the humiliating defeat suffered by the government when its case failed to secure any convictions on major charges at the trial of the so-called "Harrisburg Seven." Perhaps this isn't such a surprise in the context of Bernstein's FBI file, which for more than twenty years reveals that officials repeated hearsay allegations of his "Communist" associations without ever, it seems, making any serious attempt to discover whether there was a shred of truth in them. The "Red Scare" is generally thought of as a phenomenon of America in the 1950s. Bernstein's FBI files reveal that for the security services, at least, it was still an active issue in the 1970s, with campaigning for civil rights, and against the Vietnam War, being added to lists of "subversive" activities.

I attended Harvard University and was graduated in 1939 with a bachelor of arts degree. While at college I majored in music. Thereafter I attended the Curtis Institute of Music from 1939 until 1941.

After these studies I became assistant to Serge Koussevitzky at the Berkshire Music Center in 1942 and Assistant Conductor of the New York Philharmonic Orchestra in 1943 and 1944. Commencing in 1945, I was Music Director of the New York City Symphony Orchestra for three succeeding years.

In May 1946, I was honored to be selected as the representative of American conductors at the International Festival at Prague and conducted two concerts of American music. I also conducted at Prague again in 1947 as well as in other European cities.

In addition to my work as a conductor and musician I have also composed two symphonies and other musical compositions including the score for several musical shows and two ballets.

I cite the details listed not as a record of achievement, but rather as the briefest kind of summary to indicate that my life and interest have been devoted almost exclusively to the world of music.

The practice of my profession, which is also my livelihood, necessarily entails frequent travel abroad and any restriction on such travel would be a most serious impairment of my right to engage in my chosen profession and an interference with the right to earn a living. Since travel was resumed after the war I have fulfilled engagements in Europe and elsewhere almost every year and my pending application for a passport is for the same purpose.

In connection with engagements to conduct concerts in Brazil, Italy, Israel and at other places I applied to the State Department for a renewal of my passport in April, 1953 but to date the travel document has not yet been issued. I was informally advised that the application is being considered in connection with Regulations of the Department of State having to do with the "Limitation on issuance of passports to persons supporting [the] Communist movement".

Although I have never, to my knowledge, been accused of being a member of the Communist Party, I wish to take advantage of this opportunity to affirm under oath that I am not now nor at any time have ever been a member of the Communist Party or the Communist Political Association. I have never (to paraphrase the language of the Regulation) knowingly engaged in activities which supported the Communist movement under circumstances which would warrant the conclusion that I engaged in such activities as a result of direction, domination or control exercised over me by the Communist movement.

I have not adhered to the so-called Communist Party line or followed it "on a variety of issues and through shifts and changes of that line."

The Regulations referred to are said to have a possible application to my case by reason of the fact that my name has been linked in various ways with a number of organizations which have been denominated as subversive by the Attorney General in connection with the government employee program.

I wish to state generally as to all the organizations involved that my connection, if any, with them has been of a most casual and nebulous character. Almost without exception, their very names are practically unknown by me except in the vaguest kind of way. In fact, in now attempting to recall them and my connection with them, I have had to rely on the memory of my secretary and refer to old scrapbooks, clippings, etc. Needless to say I never knew their real character as they were later denominated by the Attorney General of the United States. I never could claim any exact knowledge as to their objectives or purpose except the humanitarian, benign or cultural one mentioned at the moment I was accosted by some person or scanned the letter or other sugar-coated communication soliciting funds, the use of my name or my services as a musician and conductor.

I wish to emphasize that the name and real purpose of the organizations to which my name became linked through a charitable and well intended impulse, and obviously without the probing deliberation required, are hardly more than a blur in my memory. The link, if any, was on "paper" and not a personal one. Besides my ignorance of their underlying purpose, I have no recollection or knowledge of ever having really *joined* any of them which had a membership roll in the true sense. I do not recall the address of most of them or the years or the city in which they functioned or the names of the officers or principals. I have no knowledge or recollection of ever having attended an organizational meeting of any one of them. It is my general recollection that my name or sponsorship was usually requested in connection with some public function or activity such as a banquet, benefit or concert.

The letter of enticement would frequently excuse me from any personal participation of a non-political character. I did not thereby espouse or intend to espouse the concealed and ulterior purposes of such groups. I did not possess the requisite suspicion and caution to probe the devious and subversive objectives of those by whom I and too many others were innocently exploited. And, needless to state we did not have the facilities to make the proper determination.

Like almost every other person who has achieved some prominence, I have received hundreds and perhaps thousands of letters in the past ten years soliciting my assistance in one form or another for some charitable, cultural or liberal cause which is always made to appear worthwhile and which would appeal to many good Americans. The great majority calling for my services or appearance on a particular date would have to be declined because of prior engagements in this country or abroad. Those asking for the use of my name as a sponsor would usually be accepted on the basis of the prominence of the person soliciting me or the fact that other well known persons, not known by me to be suspect, had previously agreed to the use of their own names. The fallacy of this procedure in evaluating an organization has been demonstrated in too many cases involving others to require elaboration. In the event I did grant the use of my name to an organization, my secretary would usually advise it by telephone or in the letter of acceptance that I could not take part in its activities or undertake any responsibility as a sponsor. The letter of solicitation and my reply usually comprised the entire extent of my connection with or contribution to the organization.

The character of my sponsorship was usually of an innocuous character. In the case of the *American Committee of Yugoslav Relief* I recall it was Quentin Reynolds who asked me to lend my name to a Town Hall American folk song and jazz concert. The *National Negro Congress* asked me to serve on an audition board at a negro talent try-out at Town Hall. It is my recollection that I could not attend. The *American Youth for Democracy* tendered me a dinner and a scroll. I did not attend the dinner and received the scroll in the mail. I assume that this honor was bestowed on me because I had been designated by the United States Junior Chamber of Commerce and others at various times as one of America's "outstanding young men". While I consented to the use of my name on the letter head of the *American Council for a Democratic Greece,* I have no present recollection that I ever attended or participated in its functions or met any of the persons active in it. I have no present recollection of the basis for linking my name with *Action Committee to Free Spain Now* or the *American Committee for Spanish Freedom* but I assume some nominal connection did exist.

I recall that I did permit the use of my name by the *Civil Rights Congress* under the mistaken impression that it was identical with the American Civil Liberties Union. In fact, I only learned of this mistake within the past few days. The only connection with the *Council on African Affairs* I can recall is a small contribution made in response to the representation it would be used to buy food for starving negroes in South Africa.

With respect to the *Joint Anti-Fascist Refugee Committee* I recall being tendered a dinner by the Boston chapter in the latter part of 1944 and attending one or two similar events perhaps in New York or San Francisco. I also believe I made a contribution to a hospital in Mexico City which was being sponsored or assisted by this group.

The *Jefferson School of Social Science* has asked me to lecture on music subjects on several occasions but I do not recall complying with these requests. My secretary recalls I made a small contribution to it. During the war, I recall I had some slight association with the Music Committee of the *National Council of American-Soviet Friendship* which had the support of many outstanding Americans. I recall that my teacher, Dr. Serge Koussevitzky, Conductor of the Boston Symphony Orchestra, was chairman of the Music Committee at the time.

I am advised that my name appears among more than 100 others in a paid advertisement inserted in the March 3, 1945 issue of the *New York Times* advocating support for Representative John M. Coffee's Resolution H.R. 100 which recommended severance of our relations with Spain. Among the other signers were Quentin Reynolds, James Montgomery Flagg, Franklin P. Adams, Hon. Stanley M. Isaacs and the Hon. Joseph E. Davies. The *Veterans of the Abraham Lincoln Brigade* is listed as the organization sponsoring the advertisement. I recall no connection with this organization and believe that Paul Robeson communicated with me about the use of my name on this occasion. I met Mr. Robeson one time while we were both backstage during a concert.

The last occasion on which my name was probably used in what may be described as a controversial setting was in early 1949. The world famous Russian composer Dmitri Shostakovich was expected to arrive in the United States. I recall the *New York Times* music critic solicited outstanding American musicians to sign a cable of greeting. According to the *New York Times* clipping this cable read as follows:

We are delighted to learn of your forthcoming visit to the United States and welcome you as one of the outstanding composers of the world. Music is an international language and your visit will serve to symbolize the bond which music can create among all peoples. We welcome your visit also in the hope that this kind of cultural interchange can aid understanding among our people and thereby make possible an enduring peace.

In this manner, I suspect I became, with other conductors, composers and musicians, a member of the welcoming committee. The arrival of Shostakovich and other musicians was apparently exploited as a propaganda event by means of a conference and formal dinner at the Waldorf Astoria Hotel under the auspices of an organization, which I am informed, is not on the Attorney General's list.

In any event, I did not attend the dinner or the conference and did nothing to promote them either than second a welcome to a fellow composer who came to the United States with the permission of this government.

The controversy which followed the Waldorf Astoria conference in March, 1949 brought unfavorable publicity to myself and others and shortly thereafter my name was included among a list of "prominent people who, wittingly or not, associate themselves with a Communist-front organization and thereby lend it glamor, prestige or the respectability of American liberalism." This article, which appeared in the April 4, 1949 issue of *Life* Magazine convinced me that my name and my good intentions were being improperly exploited by cleverly camouflaged organizations which concealed their true objectives and Communist aims behind a plausible and appealing front. Since that time I have attempted to be most circumspect about permitting the use of my name to organizations in general.

Perhaps one saving grace with respect to my response to organizational appeals is that during the very same period which found me linked to groups later declared subversive, I was also lending my name to activities completely opposed to communism. I have been most active in the cause of Jewish philanthropy and the promotion of Israel as an independent state free from Soviet domination. I have been honored to accept invitations to preach the sermon in Jewish temples in Boston, Chicago and Houston. My religious training and belief would necessarily make me a foe of communism.

I have contributed to the American Red Cross, made radio appeals on its behalf and given concerts in hospitals under its auspices. I made contributions to the Salvation Army, the Boy Scouts of America, the Riverdale Children's Camp, the Al Smith Memorial Hospital Fund, the Harvard Scholarship Fund, the Greenwich House, the National Urban League, the National Federation of Infantile Paralysis, the Irvington House, the United Jewish Appeal, the United Unitarian Appeal, B'Nai B'Rith, American Friends Services Committee, Hebrew Sheltering and Immigrant Aid Society, United World Federalists, National Association for the Advancement of Colored People, Grace Congregational Church, American Friends of Hebrew University, the Y.M.C.A., New York Guild for the Jewish Blind, the Order of the Purple Heart and many others.

I have permitted the use of my name to organizations having no possible Communist-front implications such as The Nation Association, the Planned Parenthood campaign, European Friends of ORT, the Riverside Children's Association, the American Fund for Palestinian Institutions, the Brooklyn Philanthropic League, the Exhibitions of Palestinian Art in America, the American Christian Palestine Committee, the American Red Magen David for Palestine (similar to American Red Cross), American Arts Committee for Palestine, the Hebrew Union College, the United Jewish Appeal (musicians group), Golden Anniversary of the City of New York, the National War Fund, the Serge Koussevitzky Music Foundation and the World Festivals of Friendship, among others.

I have donated my professional services to a number of organizations and for a number of causes. These would include War Bond drives, the National War Fund, the Music Box Canteen, the American Theatre Wing War Service, Veterans' Administration Hospitals, New York Stage Door Canteen and many others. I have participated in hundreds of benefit performances in the past ten years for worthwhile charitable and cultural purposes.

While abroad on previous occasions, I have no reason to believe that my work or activities were a source of possible embarrassment to the government of the United States. Every impression I received, from both the foreign press and other observers, was to the contrary. I had reason to believe sincerely that I was making a small but genuine contribution to international good will and understanding. In this connection, I would like to point out that I have received official and semi-official letters of commendation from members of the Foreign Service of the State Department following my appearances at concerts in

European cities. I have also been invited to return on most occasions. The State Department has asked me on several occasions to submit material of a musical nature for dissemination in connection with its information programs abroad. As recently as July 9, 1952 I acceded to a State Department request for the use of my music from the production of *On the Town* for a Voice of America program. In 1947 I was invited by the State Department to appear on the Austrian section of its International Broadcasting Division and in 1948 I was invited to serve as a visiting lecturer at cultural centers maintained by the State Department in South America.

In retrospect, perhaps the most profound effect made upon my life, philosophy and thoughts was by the celebrated conductor Serge Koussevitzky under whom I studied and who was, among other outstanding achievements, initiator and director of the Berkshire Music Center and the conductor of the Boston Symphony Orchestra from 1924 until several years before his death in 1951. Koussevitzky, already famous, and twice honored by the Czar as early as 1903, left Russia with the advent of Communism and in my close and long time association with him I came to know and share his strong antipathy for Soviet Communism and its evils. While he detested Communism he loved Russia and its people deeply and always looked forward to the day when they could join the people living in a free world.

Most of the events which have been discussed occurred when I was a young man and while I do not desire to take refuge under any claim of immaturity, I was in fact, inexperienced in the realm in which I dabbled. I have, since reaching my majority, voted almost exclusively in New York City where the voter, during this period has had the opportunity to vote for candidates of political parties other than the two major political parties. I have never, during this time, voted for or otherwise supported any candidates except those of the Democratic and Republican parties.

I have in the past spoken out against the inhibitions imposed upon creative artists, particularly composers, under the Soviet regime. I have frequently and publicly stated this viewpoint, in my lectures on 20th-century Operas and Symphonies at Brandeis University at Waltham, Massachusetts, commencing this year. In February 1948 I publicly expressed somewhat the same viewpoint in the Theatre Arts Magazine in which I commented on the proletarianization of Russian art and music. In this statement I referred to the Soviet effort to force its serious composers to write music limited by mass appeal and described one of the resultant products as "dreadful". I added that in the case of the ballet suite in question "the Soviet idea of music for the masses seems to have reached an all time low", and further, "there comes a point beyond which simplicity of thought can become infantile".

In conclusion, I am informed that the United States Supreme Court has stated, in the case of an avowed official of the Communist Party itself, that many organizations have several purposes or objectives, some good and some bad, that persons join such organizations for different purposes and that the evidence of membership to fulfill the bad purpose should be "clear", "unequivocal" and "convincing". What then should be the judgment in a case where membership is practically non-existent, the true purpose is unknown and the connection with the organization is of the most nominal and tenuous character?

I have attempted in the foregoing pages to set forth some of the facts which may be of assistance to the State Department in the consideration of my pass-port application. I express the hope that they may place in better perspective the allegation which has given rise to the long delay in passing upon the problem.

I realize now that I might have made the task of the Passport Division of the State Department an easier one if in 1949, when I came to realize that I had been imposed upon, I had made a public disavowal of the harmful significance which had been attached to the use of my name and prestige by questionable organiza-tions. Unfortunately I did not do so and confined my efforts to advising only my friends and associates of the true situation. I recall that in 1949, in discussing the matter in correspondence with Mr. Edward A. Norman, President of the American Fund for Israel Institutions, that I stated in part as follows:

> Let me state for you and for the record that I am not and never have been a member of the Communist Party, nor have I ever subscribed to communist doctrine or ideology. I have been away from the United States for many months on an extended concert tour, and I have not seen a copy of *Red Channels*,[65] and I do not, therefore, know to what associations or organiza-tions you refer, but I can say unequivocally that I have never belonged or subscribed to any cause which I understood committed me to support of a subversive doctrine, either communist or fascist.
>
> It is possible that, in the turmoil of life to which an artist is subject, and particularly during those days when the necessity of war created many tempo-rary alliances, that I did sponsor activities without closely examining their affiliations. If so, and if any of these have been investigated and found subver-sive by the government of my country, I disown and disavow them completely.

---

[65] *Red Channels: The Report of Communist Influence in Radio and Television* was published by the right-wing magazine *Counterattack* on 22 June 1950, and named 151 actors, writers, musicians, journalists, and others as Communist sympathizers, giving what purported to be details of their affiliations with suspect organizations. Bernstein was included, along with a number of his friends and colleagues such as Marc Blitzstein, Aaron Copland, Olin Downes, Lillian Hellman, Judy Holliday, Lena Horne, John LaTouche, and Arthur Laurents. Eric Barnouw prints a complete list of those named, and describes them as "151 of the most talented and admired people in the industry – mostly writers, directors and performers. They were people who had helped make radio an honored medium, and who were becoming active in television. Many had played a prominent role in wartime radio, and had been articulators of American war aims. In short, it was a roll of honor" (Barnouw 1990, pp. 122 and 124).

I assure you again I have only one allegiance to one flag and to one country, the United States of America, whose democratic form of life I cherish and will defend at any time.

I wish to conclude this affidavit by repeating in the most solemn way the affirmation of loyalty to the United States and opposition to Soviet Communism which I expressed at that time.

Leonard Bernstein

Subscribed and sworn before me this 3rd day of August, 1953.

Maud T. Sauss, Notary Public.

329. Leonard Bernstein to Burton Bernstein

RFD[66] #2, Hillsdale, NY[67]

17 August 1953

Cher Baudümü,

It is hard to know where to write it up on you: are you still in France? Did you get set back by the strikes? Will this letter get to American Express? Are the trains running? These and other questions beset me. But better to write & not reach you than never to write at all.

This morning I am drawing my first breath after a long haul: Brandeis → Stadium → Tanglewood, without interruption. I am dädt. We have changed our plans brilliantly (Feloo's decision): to remain here blessedly until the first of Sept, & loaf & compose and swim. Then I to Brazil on the 5th, alone (Chile wasn't such a good idea after all), then on to Iz [Israel]. Felicia, barring a great starring role, will join me in Iz (maybe with baby) around mid-October, & continue on through Italy with me.

Remember our rehearsed Washington investigation in the Napoleon bar in Boston? Well, it came true. Not a subpoena: but since my passport was not to be seen I finally went down to Washington & had to have a hearing with an ape at the State Department, & *got it*!! The great experience of it all was my lawyer whom I was insanely lucky to get – Jim McInerney,[68] formerly heard of Criminal Investigation in the Dept of Justice – an old Commie-chaser – just the right

---

[66] The Rural Free Delivery Service of the United States Postal Service.

[67] Address added by hand, on the headed writing paper of the Berkshire Music Center, Tanglewood.

[68] James McInerney (1905–63), American lawyer. He joined the FBI in 1935 and was responsible for investigating internal security cases at the Department of Justice during the Second World War. In 1950, he was appointed Assistant Attorney General in charge of the Criminal Division by President Truman. With the change of administration in 1953, McInerney left the Justice Department and returned to private practice in Washington until his death in a car accident in October 1963. His most famous clients were the Kennedy family, for whom he handled many delicate matters.

person to have on my side. And what a great person he is. It was worth the whole ghastly & humiliating experience just to know him, as well as the $3500 fee. Yes, that's what it costs these days to be a free American citizen.

All too depressing, but at least it's settled. I am told that the other things will be cleared as a result: the Committee files, & even *Red Channels*. McI[nerney] knows all these people on first-name terms: he's a great & valuable ally. But it's shameful that one needs such an ally to retain 1st class citizenship.

Where are you & where are you going? Dubrovnik?

Let us hear!?!

Love from all of us.

Ladümü (Lennuht)

330. Leonard Bernstein to David Diamond
RFD #2, Hillsdale, NY
17 August 1953

Dear D,

This is the first moment for a breath in some months now. It has been an uninterrupted madness – the Brandeis festival, the two crazy weeks at the Stadium (recording each night from midnight on after the concert),[69] and boom, Tanglewood. It's over now, & here come a blessed two weeks up here in the hills to loaf & compose & swim. I thought it would never happen. I am off to Brazil on 5 Sept. until the end of the month. Then all of Oct in Israel (why don't you hop over?) – then from Nov 5 on in Italy (Scala, *Florence*, & Rome). Isn't it nice – concerts in Florence too? Felicia will be with me from mid-October on, and we can make up for lost time.

Your letters all sound so ecstatic that I'm beginning to think you should never return to this country. Apparently you have everything you want now (except more performances: and they're coming). Let's hope it sustains: and why shouldn't it?

I have had a to-do in Washington getting my passport renewed. Ghastly & humiliating & expensive experience. But it worked out, largely due to a great lawyer named McInerney; and I can travel. But it's a pretty pass one has come to when one has to suffer so much embarrassment & costliness to retain one's first-class citizenship! I sometimes tremble for my country.

We have had the best Tanglewood summer so far: only a dearth of new works and/or American works. But it has been smooth & highly successful on

---

[69] Bernstein and the New York Stadium Symphony Orchestra recorded four symphonies for American Decca on 22, 24, 26, 29, and 30 June 1953: Beethoven's *Eroica*, Brahms' Fourth, Schumann's Second, and Tchaikovsky's *Pathétique*. A month later, on 28 July, they recorded Dvořák's *New World*.

the academic level. Chávez was here, & a charmer he is. I did Sibelius 4th & stupefied the audience, poor kids, who didn't know what to make of it.

Now these two weeks I have to cram in a violin & orchestra piece & an opera (begin them, at least) – since it will be steady conducting until December. Very hard to know how to balance one's life & work. And you – are you turning exclusively literary? Libretto – and I hope music too.

Best to you and Ciro.[70] It's not long til November.

Love,

Lenny

331. Lillian Hellman to Leonard Bernstein
[?Autumn 1953]

Lennie dear,

This time I think I have it. I don't know, but maybe Voltaire's *Candide*. I think it could make a really wonderful combination of opera – prose – songs. It's so obviously right that I wonder nobody has done it before, or have they? I am very excited by it, but I want to read it two or three times more, think about it, and not decide until – Anyway, please reread it quickly and let me know what you think, if you are free when you come back, etc. I think done right, it could have real style & wit, and great importance. Write quick. Much love to you, Madame, child & Italians.

Lillian

I wouldn't want to do the song lyrics. So if you like the idea – and I still do by the time you write – who would be good? Maybe a good *poet*?

And it would have to be written with kind of doll-like fairy tale scenery.

332. Betty Comden to Leonard Bernstein
350 East 69th Street, New York, NY
26 September 1953

Dearest Lennie,

Your many questions from exotic parts I shall answer in a moment, but I must start with some news which we hope you will like and which might affect your plans – nay, *will*. George A[bbott]. is feverishly anxious to revive *On the Town* – and to do it at once. Both Adolph and I love the idea, and so does Jerry, and George will talk to Oliver about it. The idea, although not worked out at all yet – would be to have the six of us possibly getting all the money ($100,000 George thinks) together among ourselves, so we would own the thing. Ideally, we should

---

[70] Ciro Cuomo was Diamond's Italian secretary-companion who became his devoted friend.

open in January – and George thinks a week of prevues in N.Y. and no out-of-town session. There are of course some workings on it we would all like to do. G.A. for some reason wondered whether we'd write another song for it. I don't think anything that drastic need be done – but of course we can't do this without you – nor would it be any fun to do it without you. I told George I'd write and get your ideas and schedule. This would of course eliminate your going on with your tours to any of those other cities beyond beginning of December. Coincidentally, two nights ago Chris showed the movies he had filmed of the performance of *On the Town* – and they looked simply marvelous and whetted our desire to see the wonderful thing running again. George is sure it will be a smash. We think it will be, too. What do *you* think? Please come home December as planned hmm?

As far as working on other shows in December we are still faced with no Hollywood date in Feb. We have made no, but I mean *no*, show plans – meeting daily though we have been. True, I have been getting settled here with help problems that cripple the creative spirit – but things are straightening out now.

The other questions: Yes, Atkinson on *Carnival* [*in Flanders*][71] was great, and as you know the show has moved to the elephant graveyard along with *Hazel Flagg*.[72] We are still the warmest ticket on B'way[73] – with *Can-Can*[74] breathing hotly on our necks. The performances have been excellent. As for road company, Roz's[75] plans, and the theatre TV deal, we have had three or four meetings since you left, and they have all been as thoroughly unresolved and unsatisfying as the one you attended. Roz won't say if she's staying or going, and we are on the same old tenter-type hooks.

As for other departments, Susanna is back at school – Alan is big and plump. Steve is fine. We had a party last night for Lena [Horne] and Lenny H[ayton], small but musical and late – and I merely stayed up a few minutes longer to give Alan a bottle at 5:45. I could pretend that sleepiness makes me write this way – but you know better – having plowed through the same hieroglyphs on Baker's pudding and other vital topics.

Anyway – isn't it exciting to think of O[n] T[he] T[own] again! And please tell us when to expect you.

Best on the tour, which sounds wonderful – and much, much love.

Bäddim

---

[71] *Carnival in Flanders* was a dismal flop, opening on 8 September and closing four days later. Set in Flanders in 1616, the cast included Dolores Gray and John Raitt. It had music by Jimmy Van Heusen and lyrics by Johnny Burke. The sets were by Oliver Smith.

[72] *Hazel Flagg*, with a score by Jule Styne and lyrics by Bob Hilliard, ran on Broadway from 11 February to 19 September 1953.

[73] *Wonderful Town* began its successful Broadway run of 559 performances on 25 February 1953.

[74] *Can-Can*, with music and lyrics by Cole Porter, opened on 7 May 1953 and ran for 892 performances.

[75] Rosalind Russell (as Ruth Sherwood) was the star of *Wonderful Town*.

333. Felicia Bernstein to Leonard Bernstein
"Monday night 2 a.m."
[September 1953]

Darling,
Your wire was waiting when we got back from several movies last night –
I had spent the whole day having visions of you crashing in the jungle somewhere and the whole *Handful of Dust* bit. Helene, la Belle, has been advised
though by now I'm sure you've received everything – by carrier pigeon if
necessary.

Had dinner with Bob and then went to the Anna Russell opening. She didn't
use any of the material you described and was, I'm afraid, not very funny or
professional (two fs?) We then met Harold C. [Clurman] at Sardi's – the usual
were there. Just took Henry out and he shicked it up.

After seeing you off I came home and spent the day in bed. I felt really sick from
tiredness and I suppose prospective loneliness. I'm going to miss you mine ape.

Yesterday I had Jamie to myself and it was delicious. We went to the park
where she carries on like a soap-box orator and stops traffic with her beauty. I
was proud, Lennuhtt.

Exactly a year ago this minute I started having labor pains – the best thing we
ever did was to get married – you bet – and me laü dü too.

As you can gather by now there is no news *at all*. This is just so you won't
"hacer el ridículo" at Amer. Express.

I kiss you wildly and passionately.
F

334. Felicia Bernstein to Leonard Bernstein
[before 7 January 1954]

My darling,
First of all thank you for the sweetest telegram you ever sent, and which I
received with rather mixed emotions – it's awful to think you'll be away for that
long, it's wonderful you are finally having such a well deserved vacation, it's
terrible that I'm not there (we've never had a joyful relaxed holiday together),
it's good that you'll be on your own and away from me for a while – and that's
how it goes and will always go, I guess, being the ape that I am.

I couldn't write before this – at first, just after you left, I was feeling so numb
I would not have been able to coordinate my thoughts – and then I started
working and had to dedicate *all my time* to it, but I will go into that later.

What I have to say is hard – before I start I want you to accept the possibility
that most of what I say is true. I know that I tend to dwell on things till they get
way out of proportion, but not now.

I was happier in Italy than I have ever been with you – we had fun, we shared everything, we were truly relaxed for once (I am sorry I ever suggested we come home – I needed to see Jamie but I should have waited). Here in New York all the old problems and tensions seemed to be lying in wait – plus the whole Bernstein clan. I love Burt and I love Shirley but they are *your* brother and *your* sister. There is no wall keeping me out, but there is blood and a shared past between you – they are, with Sam & Jennie, your family. I have no family really apart from you and Jamie – and this is all I need. This place is our home – yours and mine – it is beautiful because we have made it so and both our personalities are blended in it – but all of a sudden it becomes so "Bernstein" that I have a hard time keeping in touch with myself, but mostly keeping in touch with you. I can not change this, it is the way things are, but put yourself in my place and admit that it can be a little wearing. You will probably say that all this is a sign of possessiveness – it isn't. My objecting to Jamie being called "Jamela" comes from the same source – it isn't our way of calling her, it is the Bernstein way – something quite foreign to me, something I cannot share in which perhaps does smack a bit of the ghetto to me – it's possible.

Please don't brood about all this – it will explain a little my strange behavior before you left. I was also, may I say, terrified about your flying that day and kept cursing Waldner all through the day and sleepless night!

I have never worked so hard on a show before. I've given it all my time and concentration. We've managed to rewrite the whole thing – it is less obvious and trivial but still dreadfully mediocre. I do have the satisfaction of having created a real character and that has been fun – the director is exciting and between us we've done really good work.

Jamie manages to keep her *joie de vivre* in spite of constant falls, bumps and cracks – however she cannot seem to live without music specially "Sandy the Sandman" and it is driving us all crazy.

Rosalia has arrived and all is well – everything is clean and in its place, the books are right side up, Miss M. likes her. What could be better?

How wonderful that *Medea* triumphed again – it would have been so anticlimactic otherwise.

Dearest, dearest Lennhutt I love you so.

Felicia

Please give me news of Nancy.

335. Leonard Bernstein to Felicia Bernstein
Palace Hotel, St Moritz, Switzerland
7 January 1954

Darling Goody,

When I finally got your letter today it seemed that I had waited for it so long I have already composed it myself. Did you think that I was unaware of all that "bad trouble" you were going through? That arrival home must have been one of the worst, with all things conspiring to exaggerate your feeling of left-outness: first Miss Marx vying with you for the role of mater-familias; then your feeling that Jamie was being presented to me rather than to you; and then all the "clan" business. All at once. Each one of these is soluble and understandable enough by itself, I suppose, but all three at once must have been too much. I don't think it will ever again be like that. This was our first time away and first time returning; it was a crisis (Waldner must have got his dates mixed) and I hope the hard work on the show provided the necessary means of getting through it. I hope you were great in the show, and that all New York is clamoring for you again. I hope Miss Marx has quieted down in her enthusiasm for showing you what she has done for us while we were away (which again is understandable, however irritating it must have been for you). I hope you have been sleeping and having fun and success, and that you have changed the whole dining room into magenta and beaten gold. I hope Jamie can say mama as well as nana now, and that you really understand that you mustn't take it so hard. And I hope you and Shirley and Burtie can exist again on a relaxed level. There is so little I can do to prevent that particular tension: I had missed them both a lot on my long trip (and had not seen Burt for six months), and I was conscious every second we were together that I must not display too much affection or invoke the past overmuch. That was as hard for me as it was for you, and it seems silly to deprive us all of a warm, easy relationship. You wouldn't want that, I know, especially since all tensions between S[hirley] and B[urton] and myself only provoke more tensions between you and me, as well as between you and them. I don't really think it will ever again be so hard as it was this last time, with everything hitting you in the face at once. At least let's hope so, lovely Goody; and please be happy. We have so much to be happy and grateful for: let's both try not to injure it.

Everyone misses you tremendously in Italy, and they all speak of you in tones of hushed wonder. I received some photos of us at the Scala, and people all said: "Molto più bella nella natura." I miss you mightily here: it is a lovely place, though I've had only two days of it (after the last *Medea*), then had to return to Milan yesterday for a fifth *Medea* matinee, which was a glorious farewell, and only late this afternoon have returned here after a long snowy tortuous drive with Maria Ricordi; so, to put it in the old terms, I'm still dead tired. Now I have again two days, and then back to Milan and on to Genoa to catch the boat. Not very much rest in all, but even the slight amount is a boon, and it's glorious to be on skis again, no matter how awkwardly. Tomorrow I shall really make a try at getting better: up to now I've had to be monstrously careful because of the Scala performances; now I can relax and spend more time at it. Nancy is here, looking much better, and skating her head off. I wrote you from Milan about her operation (did you get all those letters with other letters enclosed, a check from your mother, etc.?), and we have run into the whole smart international set, wild mad playboys and playgirls (mostly lonely, once-beautiful women, unhappily married or getting divorced or already divorced, accompanied by huge dogs, and wild queers who are amusing and repulsive, and I seem to be the toast of the bar. That is, for one night, the first, which was bar night – molto dancing and club fun – and no more. It's all too easy not to rest up here, and I'm resting. There also appeared Hakim (Rafael) who went up and down screaming how beautiful you were, and where were you, and why did you ever pick me instead of him. And a pretty blonde named Jenny who will probably turn up in New York. I returned today to find that Ruggiero had broken his arm skiing yesterday. And I became real good friends with von Karajan, whom you would (and will) adore. My first Nazi. Had dinner last night at Fosca Crespi's with Wally, who sends you his dearest love, as does Nancy and Maria Ricordi and Ruggiero (he really does) and Isabel who finally did appear for *Medea* with Letizia Boncompagni and husband, but without Laurence, and all the servitù of the Duomo and all the folks of the Scala. And that's my social news for the night, Marvin.

I've decided to go along with Lillian on *Candide*, imagine, after having written her a letter saying no and tearing it up, I think it will be more feasible than the David piece this spring, and will allow me to do other things as well, like the violin piece, and maybe refurbishing *Peter Pan* for Edwin Lester, who is thinking of doing it with Mary Martin. I'm dying to do David, but for next year. I got lots of ideas, or at least a clearer idea, about the libretto coming over on the plane, and it now looks much more like a big three-act opera with chorus and ballet, which nixes it for this season. I've also decided to give Finzi my general representation in Europe, which was a good decision I think, even if she is always rushing about, because she is young and energetic and will work hard for me, and her assistant Paola is clear-headed for the menial tasks. There is also a lot of talk about London in the winter, and Karajan has asked me to Vienna, etc. So we should have fun next year too. The way it looks now, if you agree, is Europe in May, lit and kiboodle; then Rome (Academy) till Xmas, say; then some real European conducting for two months or so, then home. Almost a year abroad! What do you think? Do you think this plan has any beneficial bearing on paragraph #1 of this letter?

I love you so much, and want you not to worry, ever, or be unhappy, when we must be very happy always. Be good to yourself, and make Liz Arden take away your eye-circles, and help her do it from inside.

All my love,

L

336. Leonard Bernstein to Cheryl Crawford[76]
Vineyard Haven, MA
6 July 1954

Dear Cheryl Crawford,

I received your roundabout request for a short overture to *Tahiti* and have given it some thought. I would love to oblige you, but I can't for several reasons. One, that the opening trio number is itself a prelude and its function in the opera should be just that. Two, that the only material suitable for an overture (outside of writing a whole new special piece) would be the prelude itself, which would cause repetitiousness. Three, I am so rushed in the writing of *Candide* that I couldn't begin to think of writing a special new piece to precede the opera. I am sure you know how it is, when a piece is two years behind you, to attempt to make any sizeable change. I hope the production is going well and I would love to be kept informed of your progress. Can you send me your itinerary? Please give my love to Alice[77] and David[78] and all the cast.

Very sincerely,
Leonard Bernstein

337. Elia Kazan[79] to Leonard Bernstein
Warner Bros Pictures Inc., Burbank, CA
14 July 1954

Illustrious Maestro,

I have sent the letter to Bob Anderson who will send it to his agent who will no doubt despatch the necessary information to the Dearest Maestro at La Scala.

---

[76] Cheryl Crawford (1902–86), American theater producer. Bernstein was to encounter her again two years later when he was working on *West Side Story* (she withdrew before the show opened). In this letter he responds to Crawford's request for an overture to accompany a summer tour of *Trouble in Tahiti*.

[77] Alice Ghostley (1926–2007), American singer and actor. She sang the role of Dinah in *Trouble in Tahiti* on tour, and again when it arrived on Broadway as part of a triple bill called *All In One* (alongside dances by Paul Draper and Tennessee Williams' *27 Wagons Full of Cotton*), described by Brooks Atkinson in *The New York Times* (20 April 1955) as "an evening of superb theatre art."

[78] David Brooks (1915–99), American singer, actor, producer, and director. He directed *Trouble in Tahiti*.

[79] Elia Kazan (1909–2003), American film director and co-founder of the Actors Studio. As a student at Williams College he was known as "Gadget", shortened to "Gadg". His notorious appearance as a "friendly" witness at the HUAC hearings made him very unpopular among his more liberal friends and colleagues, but his gifts were such that Stanley Kubrick called Kazan, "without question, the best director we have in America." Much of this letter is about *On the Waterfront*, for which Bernstein wrote his only score composed specially for Hollywood. The majority of the music had been already been recorded in Hollywood, on 24, 27, and 28 April 1954 (see Burlingame 2003, pp. 130–1). Bernstein's *Symphonic Suite from "On the Waterfront"* was made in 1955 and first performed on 11 August 1955 at Tanglewood. It was dedicated to Alexander Bernstein, who had been born on 7 July.

I am almost through here. And I ought to leave in three weeks. Don't ask me how the picture is. You never know. Everybody always likes the rushes. They don't mean anything. If my basic story is good I guess I'll have a good picture. Certainly my actors are fresh and real. In fact I don't think anybody has ever seen any of them except their mothers and that's the way I like it.[80]

I'm still kind of punchy from my Hoboken episode,[81] but in a punchy way I'm having a lot of fun. I lack some of my usual doggedness and tenacity but I guess it will all come back if I live long enough. In a word, I'm tired.

When I get through with this, I'll come back east and sit out front and enjoy your work. How's it coming? I hope it will be wonderful. When you get all done with it I want to talk with you about a project for us both. My idea, in a sense, is to take a novel and dramatize it entirely as a series of musical numbers with hardly anything in between. You might call it an opera except for the fact that it's not one at all and derives from a much more native source, musical comedy. I'll be starting to think about it.

Betty [Lauren] Bacall misses you. This I know for a fact. What other emotional havoc you brought on out here there is no record of, but she misses you.

Swim a lot. The Pacific is a dirty, cold ocean. You've got the good one there.

Love and kisses,

Gadg

338. Leonard Bernstein to Aaron Copland
Vineyard Haven, MA
29 July 1954

Dear Aa,

I miss you. That's the long and short of it. I don't miss Berlioz or the crowds or the pewpils or the scenery or the meetings on the green furniture of Seranak,[82] or even the hot crowded Monday forums, I miss you, ecco. And Lukas.

I want to hear about things like how the Piano Concerto (yours) went, and the immortal problem of Farrand–Roth, and dirty gossip, and what of next year, and how is *Tender Land* going.

Me, I stay put on this heavenly island, intending never to leave except to Venice for a week in Sept. to conduct my new piece with Isaac [Stern].[83] It's finished, imagine, & all orchestrated except for the finale. Man, I need you

---

[80] Kazan is exaggerating a little, since Marlon Brando and Rod Steiger had appeared in earlier films, but *On the Waterfront* was their first major success; it was a screen debut for Eve Marie Saint.

[81] Some of *On the Waterfront* was filmed in Hoboken, NJ.

[82] Serenak was the home of Serge Koussevitzky in the grounds of Tangleword.

[83] Bernstein's *Serenade after Plato's Symposium* for violin and orchestra.

around for some solid criticism. I could use it. *Candide* crawls along: it's the hardest thing I ever tried, and – you won't believe this – it's very hard trying to be eclectic. I am raising the unwilling ghosts of Hérold and Auber. A new wrinkle.

Love, & write. A big hug to Lukas, & give my best to [Charles] Munch & [Jean] Morel & Olga [Koussevitzky] & all that sort of thing.

As I said, I miss you.

L

P.S. [John La] Touche sends all the best, as does Lillian.

339. Darius Milhaud[84] to Leonard Bernstein

Aspen Institute, Aspen, CO

17 August 1954

Dear Lenny,

I am *overjoyed* at the idea that you will conduct *David* at the Scala[85] – Ghiringhelli[86] hopes very much you can stay until January 13th and from Dec 1st. I will certainly fly to Milano!!

As for the orchestra score that you asked now I really think the *best* would be to have one done at the Library of Congress Kouss Foundation as it costs only 5 cents a page. The orchestra score would not be more than 45 dollars I think and you would have your own score that you could keep.

May be the foundation would be willing to pay for it, otherwise I will be delighted to give it to you as a present and as a proof of my great admiration. Just let me know. The piano score will be soon ready in printing.

Very affectionately,

Milhaud

I *missed* you in Jerusalem. Everything was OK (orchestra, choir, soloist) but George Singer[87] was *horrible*, hysteric and *can't hold a tempo*.[88]

---

[84] Darius Milhaud (1892–1974), French composer whose music, with its elements of polytonality and jazz, appealed strongly to Bernstein. One of Bernstein's first recordings (in November 1945) was of Milhaud's *La Création du Monde*, a work he conducted regularly.

[85] Bernstein was due to conduct the stage premiere of Milhaud's opera *David* at La Scala in January 1955. At short notice, he canceled in order to devote time to *Candide*, and Nino Sanzogno took over conducting duties for *David*.

[86] Antonio Ghiringhelli, *sovrintende* (general manager) of La Scala.

[87] George Singer (1908–80) conducted the world premiere of Milhaud's *David* in Jerusalem on 1 June 1954.

[88] Milhaud was more diplomatic about Singer in his autobiography, *My Happy Life*: "It was George Singer who took on the job of conducting David and he needed all the patience he could muster [. . .] in the end the singers, the Orchestra of the Jerusalem Radio reinforced by the brass from the Police Band, the Jerusalem Radio Chorus and the Students' Choir of the Conservatoire [. . .] gave my work a rousingly ardent reading. It was, after all, their piece" (Milhaud 1995, p. 228).

340. Leonard Bernstein to Frankie and William Schuman
Vineyard Haven, MA
30 August 1954

Dear Frankie and Bill,

Your joint letter gave me much food for thought (and sickroom sympathy) – and, well, you talked yourselves right out of an Italian première.[89] With regret I bowed to your dark warnings, after another look at the score (which I love); and you will be supplanted by the far simpler (and far less interesting) Piston's 4th. Now aren't you sorry to be such Cassandras?

I've finished my *Serenade* (blithely attributed to the authorship of William Schuman in a *Sunday Times* squib a few weeks ago) and it looks awfully pretty on paper, at least. The Italian critics will hate it; but I like it a lot.

The Charaks (?) tell me you are much better, & that they are building you a permanent Vineyard residence. You can't do better than this extraordinary, passionate island. We've loved it this summer. Shall we start making dinner plans *now*? I'll be back from Europe around the 17th.

Love to you all from us all, & be well.

Lenny.

Think of it: I was 36 last Wednesday. As a friend put it, 3 and 6 are 9, which is the cube [*recte* square] of 3; & 3 times 6 are 18, the digits of which add up to 9; and 3 from 6 leaves 3 which is the cube [*recte* square] root of 9. Which means in short, I'm getting old.

341. William Schuman to Leonard Bernstein
241 Elk Avenue, New Rochelle, NY
3 September 1954

Dear Lenny,

Thanks very so much for your note with the terrible news that you have taken my advice and are not performing my 6th [Symphony] in Venice. You can appreciate that it was very difficult advice for me to have given but I feel that it would have been unfair of me to have been less than candid. Until you find an appropriate moment to program the Symphony, I will be nourished by your stated love of it which, as I think you know, means a great deal to me.

I also noticed in the *New York Times* that authorship of your *Serenade* for violin was credited to me. Am I to understand that you are now denying

---

[89] Bernstein originally planned to play Schuman's Sixth Symphony in his Italian concerts.

that I wrote the piece and claiming it for yourself? Naturally, I assumed that you were giving me this work because I am sick and old and so disappointed that you could not perform the 6th. In fact, in my mind, it already took the place of the second favorite composition of my authorship, the first being "The Happy Farmer", and now I am patiently awaiting the first royalty checks from my *Serenade*. Incidentally, if there is an extra copy around, please send it. I am dying to see it.

I am quite well aware that you are now 36 years of age because last Wednesday I tuned in the radio and heard my name followed by the piece of brilliant piano music which I recognized as your anniversary present to me of several years ago. The whole program was devoted to your music and I enjoyed it immensely, the clarinet piece and all (they played the movements out of order). One of these days you simply must take time off and write a great big opera. It is good to know that you will be back the 17th and we look forward to seeing you.

Love to your house from ours.

Bill

P.S. Dictated by phone and signed by Miss Martin so that you will get the note without delay.

342. Leonard Bernstein to Felicia Bernstein
Hotel Bauer-Grünwald, Venice, Italy
11 September 1954

Darling,

I just had a cable from George which said you were having a second hurricane – unbelievable! I tried to get through by phone, but no soap. He assured me everything was OK, but I can't help worrying about it. I'll try and call you from London Monday night. Be safe!

I've missed you terribly – you would love Venice: and it's been a charming week. Ciro [Cuomo] showed me a picture of you that he carries, & I nearly broke down. You're so lovely, & such a *terrific* actress (I just rediscovered this last week at Woodstock) and I love you more than I can tell you.

Isaac [Stern] plays the *Serenade* like an angel – and everyone adores it, Diamond included. If it goes well tomorrow it should be a knockout. The weather is hot & fine, & the Lido is a joy – though there's too little time to enjoy it. (Last night we rehearsed til 2 a.m.!)

I've bought you gorgeous things. I can't wait to show them to you. All my love and a fountain of kisses for Jamie. I pray you're all OK. Love to Allyn.

L

343. Darius Milhaud to Leonard Bernstein
Mills College, Oakland, CA
23 September [1954]

Dearest Lenny,

Lovely to have your letter.

I answer your questions:

1. Cuts. *Not one note.* I know it is a long opera. *But so it is.* 2 hours 50 – we must not lose a *second* between changing scenes.

2. George Singer. *David* is easy to prepare – choirs are easy to sing. Solo parts have no problem. They have in all Italian operas good people to rehearse with. Why take this terrible George Singer, who will prepare all wrong. We need a young conductor from the Scala who teaches choir and soloists notes, solfege, and articulation. Someone who makes *precise work*, and not this frightful hysteric lunatic.

Now if the Scala wanted him absolutely, and wanted to ruin the preparation, and that you will have to rebuild everything, then they should not have ask[ed] me first.

That is my sentiment from the bottom of my heart.

And I admire *you* and have a great affection for *you*.

Darius

344. Leonard Bernstein to Barbara and Philip Marcuse
205 West 57th Street, New York, NY
26 November 1954

Dearest Babs and Fil,

I've let you down terribly, I know, and I'm taking advantage of the fact that today is Thanksgiving, a season of joy and forgiveness and blessing-counting, to try to make reparation. Your nice Mrs. Gilbert phoned some weeks ago with your messages, and I was sorry she had no time to come and visit with us.

I'm taking this time out of the simple family joys (it seems the whole family is here, both sides) to send you our love and greetings. These last months have been overcast with relentlessly gloomy activity. How can activity be gloomy, you ask? It can. We have had big lyricist trouble in *Candide*, and have only now, this minute (two weeks ago, that is) made a final and utter break with Mr. LaTouche. At the point of the break the show was less than half-finished. So, here we are. It should have been finished by end of summer. Nothing wasted of course. I did get off a little 34-minute thing for violin and orch. called *Symposium* which Isaac Stern played like an angel with me at the Venice Festival in September. Didn't read about that in *Variety*, eh? Small wonder. Then, a long stretch of trying to eke out *Candide* with Touche, and not getting much of anywhere. Then the last two weeks of searching desperately for a new lyricist, in vain. But other things interspersed: an article published in the *Atlantic Monthly* (cover piece too, imagine) – did you read it? And last week, no, two weeks, who knows – a TV stint on *Omnibus* that seems to have knocked the national press for a loop. Did you happen to catch it? If not, see last week's *Variety*. I count on that mag as our personal intermediator. Also this week's *Life*, a ghastly inadequate account of the proceedings, but still, *Life* Mag. I haven't appeared in that one since '48, when a glorious picture of me as one of America's 50 leading "Super-Dupes" graced their pages. Then black silence. So this must mean something, a toe in the door.

So then, good news. I have postponed my Scala trip to February instead of leaving Sunday (God!) when I was supposed to. I had royally screwed up my schedule for this season. But now things are straightening out. Lil[ian Hellman] and I have decided to do what I've been screaming for since the beginning: namely to write the lyrics[90] ourselves. It's so natural and right: what were we futzing with Touche for all this time? So now I feel creative and set-up again, and ready for a two-month creative dash; and this time *Candide* will get finished by Feb. 1st, when I leave. I'll be in Milan for three solid months; then all of May in Florence, for that festival; then some concerts with the Israel Orch. in Italy; then the Holland festival in June; then Tanglesberg in July and August; then, Godwilling, the production of *Candide*. Then, maybe a vacation.

Item: among the greater things for which to give thanks on this Thanxgiving Day: we're going to have another baby! Next July. Which is also a problem, because it makes me have to think of cancelling the Holland thing in June, maybe. In any case, not a word: because Felicia won't get any jobs if it is known she is preggy. Isn't it wonderful?

Back now to the family joys. Jamie is beyond any description beautiful and wise: and Felicia is blooming all over in her joyful condition. Did you catch her last night on Kraft Cheese?[91] A bad adaptation of Jane Austen's *Emma*, but she was fabulous in the high comedy style.

There's the news up to this moment. Tune in again, etc. Do you get to New York this ensuing period? Let me hear from you, sooner than you heard from me.

Love from us both.

---

[90] For *Candide*.
[91] Felicia appeared in ten episodes of *Kraft Television Theatre* between 1949 and 1956. *Emma* was broadcast on 24 November 1954, and Felicia played the title role of Emma Woodhouse in a cast that also included Roddy McDowall as Mr. Elton.

Lenny

Looking this over, I am struck by its hectic tone. Are you? But for a change, it's *nice* hectic.

345. Leonard Bernstein to Felicia Bernstein
Grand Hotel Duomo, Milan, Italy
4 February 1955

Darling,

Imagine, I've been here three days and no sign of sinuses or bronchs or the trots or anything. And today, actually, the sun came out, and it was pure spring. It's a joy to be here: deep in rehearsals again – the cast in the afternoon, & the chorus in the morning, and conferences at night with Luchino [Visconti], who is marvelous to work with. I've gotten all steamed up about *Sonnambula*, as with *Medea*, getting wild ideas for cutting & staging and tempi. It's going to be a dream, I think. Luchino has planned a small production, perfect in every stylistic detail, just as I have planned a small orchestra, with emphasis on buoyancy & youth. I wish you could come in time to see it. We open the 19th, & the last one will be around the 25th. Callas is greater than ever. She has shrunk to a pinpoint, & is positively beautiful, even offstage. She has ash-blonde hair, and dresses much better – and sings like a doll. Last night I heard her as Maddalena in *Andrea Chenier*, and she was a divine coquette of 17 or so, completely believable! We had our first reading of *Sonnambula* today, & she made me cry.

I've hunted everywhere for an apartment, but they are all too expensive, or too crowded, or too something. And besides, an apartment is a bore to take care of, whereas at the Duomo I have everything at the touch of a button. So I have decided to stay here, especially since they came down to 5,000 lire a day for this old duplex of ours, which is already reasonable. It's just the same: the same brass bar loose on the stair rug, & hot as hell upstairs, cold downstairs, and all modernistic & hideous – but I've come to love it, & think of it as home, even. Once I unpack, & get a piano & chairs & table & cushions in, it will be OK, & just waiting for you.

I miss you my darling. Everyone asks for you (I saw the Ricordis tonight) & waits for you. Write me all about everything, right away. Isn't it glorious to be free of *Samarkand*?[92] A big kiss to Jamie, and make her say *Daddy* at least once a day.

All my love,

L

---

[92] Felicia appeared opposite Louis Jourdan in the out-of-town tryouts for *Tonight in Samarkand*, a play by Jacques Deval presented in Princeton and Boston. She was not in the cast of the short Broadway run that followed.

346. Leonard Bernstein to Felicia Bernstein

Grand Hotel Duomo, Milan, Italy
11 February 1955

My darling,

I miss you terribly, and love your letters. They carry a whiff of something warm and familiar and joyful. Imagine – after three years: joyful! Is it wonderful: home has always been the spot in which I happened to be: and now it is *a place*, with all that one place connotes. The dining-room one apologizes for, & my studio where you get blind with cigarette smoke; and the two "modern" chairs you hate in the library, and the marvelous sala, and the hall wallpaper you can't stand, and our country bedroom, and the loud canary, and Jamie spreading her presence like a marigold, and the difficulties below-stairs, and Bill with his weather, and all the problems and tensions and joy and noise and quiet. Home. A new experience.

Here all is up in the air. Callas is still abed with her faruncolo, being a real old-fashioned prima donna, suffering, pale, Violetta. Of course we will have to postpone the prima of *Sonnambula*, which was scheduled for the 19th, to I don't know when: and it is a mess, with my having to go to London for the prima of *Wonderful Town* on the 23rd. Very complicated indeed. But pazienza: it will all work out. They love me at the Scala, & do everything to help. I've had some fine rehearsals already, & have fallen for the score, hook, line, etc. It never stales for some reason: fresh & noble & pure.

You won't believe it, but Charlie Roth[93] just arrived, & I'll have to see him tomorrow. God, what a burden he is.

All the Ricordis are waiting for you to come, as is Wally, & Luchino (a doll), and Ghiringhelli & the works. It is fun here, really. You won't be bored. Wally is giving a Ballo in Maschera next Tuesday: that sort of thing. Ghiringhelli sent you a telegram of love on your birthday, & still awaits an answer, kind of hurt & pouting. Do send him one.

I visited the sartoria of the Scala the other day – an incredible experience. On the outskirts of Milan – a huge warehouse with 40,000 costumes, and thousands of new ones constantly being made, all by hand, & such materials & designs & care of work! (I'm going to have tails made for me there!) Ghiringhelli wants to sell about 10,000 of them, since the constant procession of new productions creates a surplus of costumes they cannot house. I promised him I would ask you if you would ask Eaves or Brooks[94] if they'd be interested in buying such a number of really marvelous costumes. Do let me or him know.

---

[93] Charles Roth was "a young conducting student Bernstein taught in 1950 and 1951 at Tanglewood" (Burton 1994, p. 245). Roth was a disturbed individual who threatened to blackmail Bernstein, or to make public Bernstein's letters to him. He is referred to in several letters to Felicia from 1955 as the "Black Fairy".

[94] Eaves and Brooks were the two leading theatrical costume companies in New York.

What is this with *Bourgeois Gentilhomme*? What part? Who How What? It sounds glorious – tell me more. And of course, I want to hear all the news of the opening of *Samarkand*. There must be a lot to tell.

I'm so relieved you've been given the OK by all your MD's. I hope you're blossoming in spite of your kepepelt [cold]. You sounded so strange on the phone: remote & unexcited; and I couldn't decide if it was the kepep or 7:00 a.m. (which was ungodly, but I couldn't help it, as I'd been trying for days, & had to take the call when it got through) or just plain old *abstractness*. I'm planning something with an emerald when you get here (this *must* have something to do with the foregoing) – and Callas is going to wear moonstones in *Sonnambula*, imagine. I'm wandering.

I've never worked so close to a show: really into everything: painting the sets, & spending one hour arguing about the color of the cuff of a sleeve of one costume for one chorus-lady, and kind of co-directing with Luchino, & planning out every second. I'm learning, learning. It's a glorious theatre. Tonight is Nanni's birthday, so a party: & first I'm going with Wally & Luchino to a revue with an incredible sequin-blonde dame who calls herself Dorian Gray. I'm trying to get out of *Bohème* (which is an old production, & therefore a bore for me) & do instead *Traviata* with Callas & Luchino & a fabulous décor de Lila di Nobile (do you know of her?) – but [Victor] de Sabata is supposed to do it, but his heart is bad, & it's therefore indefinite, but how can one be sure, & as you see – it's all very complex.

I hope you can get here in time to see *Sonnambula* at least once: it will be a sweet production, slightly campy, with the stage apron advanced way out, so that Callas sings in the middle of Scala, & sings her last fabulous aria with all the houselights up, & flowers flying from the boxes and – you must see it.

My darling lady, I love you & miss you & wait for your letters with real impatience. Love to everyone, & a big hug & millions of kisses to you & Jamie & Fink.[95]

L

347. Leonard Bernstein to Felicia Bernstein
Grand Hotel Duomo, Milan, Italy
28 February 1955

My Darling,

I am so happy that you got out of that Samarkand affair when you did. Of course, it would have been a different show with you in it, but maybe not with Schneider.[96] As they say here, meno male.

---

[95] Bernstein's pet-name for Alexander before he was born.
[96] *Tonight in Samarkand* was directed by Alan Schneider, whose later Broadway credits included the original (1962) production of Edward Albee's *Who's Afraid of Virginia Woolf?*

I have just had two days of that nameless Milan disease again, fever and bed. No symptoms, no diarrhea, nothing, just fever and bed. It's becoming a bore. Maybe I have something glorious and important like hepatitis. Now begins the Settimana Santa, with dress rehearsals and the whole bit you know so well. I'm not quite up to it, as usual, and I can't seem to memorize the recitativi, but I suppose it will all be fine in the end. I spent three days in London (how I wished you were with me) and it was if anything grayer and colder than Milano, with whipping rain and wind and snow Londonness. The show was a smash,[97] and the Rag[98] was encored, and the people screamed (tears running down, not quite, not in London town) and the press was as good as the London press ever is. The experts forecast a year's run at least.[99] Which would pay for Fink, and save our lives.

The black fairy[100] will not give up. He arrived in Milano, and I bought him lunch and listened to his drivel and sent him home. He wanted to become my assistant, imagine, and co-conduct all tours with me, etc. I told him to knock it off and go back to Vienna. Since then there has been arriving a series of letters, really unbelievable, in which he is threatening me: blackmail, no less! Unless, he says, I make him the world's top conductor ("And when I walk on to the podium, God himself will sing") he will send around copies he has made of all my letters to him in the past, and ruin everybody's lives. The idiot. Of course, there is nothing in any of those letters, nor has there ever been any relationship between us of any kind: but it's still annoying, *aburridisimo*, and all the rest, to think of that ugly little maniac running around making trouble. I've been sending back his letters and *parcels* (whatever they may be) by the ton, unopened. Crazy people always scare me, and especially this one.

Speaking of such things, the Diamonds are here, as is to be expected, and very sweet they are, faithful to the end. They want us to stay with them in Florence, but no.

I don't quite understand about your big trip here with Helena. You mean you would wait until April to come? Que lata! What does Karish say? I know it would be lovely to make the trip with Helena, and I'd love you to, but can't she come earlier too? Your traveling tourist wouldn't make no never-mind. But I hope you don't expect to start with her a pension too! Of course I'll find a nice

[97] The London production of *Wonderful Town* opened on 25 February 1955 at the Prince's Theatre.
[98] "The Wrong-Note Rag".
[99] A slightly optimistic forecast: the London production of *Wonderful Town* did well, but only ran for 207 performances.
[100] "The Black Fairy" was Charles Roth. See note 92 to Bernstein's letter (346) to Felicia of 11 February 1955.

inexpensive place, as soon as you tell me definitely that she's coming and when. I hope you sent an answering cable to Ghiringhelli.

I have to dash off to rehearsal. God, I wish I could have a week of sun and rest. When and where? Please tell me when you will be coming so I can try to promote a week off from the Scala to fit your arrival. Then maybe we can go to Sevilla for Holy Week, or something glorious like that.

I miss Jamie and you terribly. Everyone writes that you are both in the pink, and that helps. But do come in person!

All my love, darling Bubbles.

L

Can Jamie say "Sonnambula" yet?

348. Betty Comden to Leonard Bernstein
350 East 69th Street, New York, NY
17 March 1955

Dearest Leonard,

Shortly after the arrival of your letter, for which many thanks, came photo-stats of the London reviews[101] which cheered us considerably – particularly the one which said our score was full of "toe-tapping tunes" and the one about the cab driver who will soon be whistling his fares home with "Ohio" and the "Wrong Note Rag." We won't rest until some New York cabbie whistles *us* home with "A Million Kids Just Like You etc." For the further popularization of the above and others we have completed a new venture – an album. And it is of this that I am now writing you – in the main, that is.

One Bob Israel, head of Heritage Records called us about making an album – having heard of us from Harold Rome with whom he just made two highly successful albums – one "retrospective" (anyway back to *Pins and Needles*) and the other *Fanny* (also rear-view if you like). Herbie Harris, drummer-boy extraordinaire also urged this lad to get in touch with us. Although cool at first – and seemingly not at all familiar with us – Israel blossomed, after one meeting, into the most hysterically devoted fan we ever had – and after a few rehearsals with a pianist named Milton Greene,[102] and the above mentioned Herb Harris, we cut a platter of some nineteen items one rainy afternoon – and it is about to be released to the unsuspecting public. At least each and every Sadvorousky will buy one apiece.

---

[101] For *Wonderful Town*.
[102] Milton Greene (1913–2000) was a conductor, arranger, and pianist whose most important Broadway credit was as the original conductor of *Fiddler on the Roof*.

Here's what is crammed into a twelve-incher:

On the Town
  New York New York
  Lonely Town
  Taxi Song
  Some other Time
  Carried Away
Billion Dollar Baby
  Bad Timing
  Broadway Blossom
Good News (!?X!?X!!!)
  French Lesson
Two From the Aisle
  If
  How Will He Know
  Catch Our Act at the Met
Peter Pan
  Distant Melody
  Captain Hook's Waltz
  Mysterious Lady
Wonderful Town
  Ohio
  It's Love
  Quiet Girl
  Wrong Note Rag

The last two shows were in the above order – not chronological as all else above – because W[onderful] T[own] was a better ending. You may wonder at our not doing much in the way of *material*-ish things in *WT*. This was so decided because of our burning desire to get the *songs* on records – somehow. Maybe someone might hear one and make a record? It seemed more important than getting the special stuff recorded. This boy is now so excited anyway he wants to make yet *another* album. He is convinced it is a smash. We've heard it and are timidly pleased with it – hoping it will sound to others as good as we blushingly admit it sounds to us. He (Bob) has played it for a few outsiders who echo his enthusiasm. Steve [Kyle] thinks it's terrific.

Here comes the somewhat embarrassing part. Adolph and I would be thrilled and honored if you would write a little something about us for the record jacket. The thing will be called, I believe, simply *Comden and Green* and our pictures will adorn the front. The back is wide open for a paean of praise – say, two–three hundred words long.[103] Gene O'Kelly may say a word or two about us because of his movie connections with our lives – but we more than anything hope you will send us something printable about us – if you can and want to, and have the time to.

Other news – we're in Hollywood two and a half weeks to come up with outline for new picture to write this summer. Hope to write show – maybe. Family all well. Adolph well. Miss you very very much.

Send very very much love,

Betty

349. Leonard Bernstein to Marc Blitzstein
Grand Hotel Duomo, Milan, Italy
20 March 1955

Dear Marc,

You're right to be boiling mad, and I would be too; and you're also right in knowing that *Regina* has never slipped my mind, to put it mildly. It is very hard to get definite word out of these people: there is a kind of compulsion to let things simmer for ages before taking any real step. I don't know if you can feel this ambiente at the Scala; it is such a world of its own, and so convinced that almost nothing else exists or happens on earth, that the time-continuum becomes different from the normal one, and all the time ordinarily allotted to all worldwide decisions is gathered together for Scala purposes only. And this combined with the enormous amount of work and number of hourly problems of work make delays inevitable.

I have brought up the subject on several occasions. Ghiringhelli seems to take it for granted that the work will be done next year, every time I mention it: but it is really up to de Sabata. The latter, a very fine gent, loves the piece, and

---

[103] Bernstein did as Comden requested and wrote a charming tribute for the record jacket:

Ever since we first met, there has been a beloved object in my life called Betty-and-Adolph. This prodigy, apart from being two very dear people, has for many years supplied me with pure, profound laughter, as it has so many others; and it has a way of turning every hearer into a doting fan. But Betty-and-Adolph is not only a thing of laughter. With the years, it has grown in warmth, understanding, theatrical mastery, subtlety and appeal, always making its personal, sweet-sour comment on the follies and lovable sentimentalities of American life. Betty-and-Adolph as performers represent something complete and exquisite. In recent years I have watched them as creators going forward with increasing power, in a fluid state of development that may lead to any number of new forms. It is my belief that this joyous Cerberus will eventually furnish us with what will one day be known as American opera. Nowhere else in America is there to be found this combination of musical instinct and knowledge, theatrical perfection and literate immediacy. It has been my joy to work with them on two shows, and it is my hope to continue forever.

readily quotes and sings from it (especially "Watching my gal watch me", which he performs by heart at the piano) but he has worries about the translation. He has told me that he feels that the "tough" quality of the English has no decent equivalent in Italian; and at the same time he feels that the work will not mean much to the Scala public in the original English. I have suggested a kind of bilingual version, wherein all the Negro parts (not affecting plot: i.e. Chinkypin, spirituals, etc.) could be done in English and the "white" parts in Italian. How does this strike you? With a pick-axe? Each time we discuss this (between acts of *Sonnambula* or other interruptions) he always ends by saying "We must have a long talk about this soon". And that's why I've been delaying writing to you – until there was something definite to write. But I'm writing anyway to tell you that the work is very much on my mind, and that I love you and it. What suggestions do you have? I tried to think of *Regina* in English here, watching *Porgy* having such a big success: but *Porgy* is different, obviously, the story being so apparent and drawn in huge choral strokes. But maybe you feel that *Regina* would work just as well in English. There is also a slight worry about the amount of spoken stuff: the Scala is not well adapted for talk, and the Italians don't understand too well the Opera-Comique idea. Karajan did *Carmen* here in a sort of horrid version of the "talk-version", and it was a large bomb. I don't know what all this adds up to in your mind, but I would love to know soon what you think. I shall try tonight to corner de Sabata (he's been ill) and talk it out. We have had, for example, a tentative date for a month to talk about my Violin *Serenade* which he likes, and haven't yet said a word. You get the picture?

Still, with all this being true, I still apologize for not having written. It has been a wild rush, as you know; and this is now the first breathing spell, now that *Bohème* is finally on (and I alternate operas almost daily). The critics murdered me for *Bohème*, which is natural, since they think they "know" this one; but the public loves it. It's really not a very good production, and I have little to do with the stage, which is ridiculous; but the orch. is divine. The cast is mediocre, the sets likewise, the direction horrid. All this in contrast to *Sonnambula*, which was closely worked out from the beginning by Luchino and me, and shows it. I learn, I learn, all the time.

Now that I have a little time free from rehearsals, etc., I can begin to do the things I have been postponing for six weeks: get *Regina* settled, give some real thought to the problems of *Candide* (which are multitudinous) and all the rest. Let me hear from you about the translation business, and about all the other news that your ire prevented you from sending this time.

It's wonderful to have Felicia here, and we are taking off the next couple of days, probably driving to Florence to see David [Diamond] and Ciro [Cuomo].

Love from us both,

Lenny

350. Leonard Bernstein to Marc Blitzstein
Grand Hotel Duomo, Milan, Italy
28 March 1955

Dearest Marc,

I've been through hell over *Regina*. I am furious and disgusted, and what is worse, helpless. I now understand the run-around I've gotten: and I've spent the better part of three days discussing it with de Sabata. The latter is genuinely thrilled with the music, there is no doubt. But since the score did not supply the full dialogue, he was waiting for the arrival of the libretto before putting to rest his qualms about the subject matter. After reading the libretto, he finds he cannot allow it to be done at the Scala. He says that the public will not accept such a theme: it is too sadistic, cruel (he even doubts whether censors here would pass it, which is nonsense), and non-operatic in nature. The talk of money is not for the Scala, nor is the spectacle of a woman letting her husband die, etc. etc. etc. I talked it all out with him, tried to explain the values of the play, that it was internationally famous and loved,[104] etc. etc. etc. To no avail. I dug up a copy of Ghiringhelli's letter to me last fall saying that it was *definite* for next season: he admitted that there was a misunderstanding. I have one card left to play: that I will take it to Florence for the Maggio [Musicale] next year. That might make him react. And I will talk to them in Florence about it. I am now angry about it, especially after your last letter with all your suggestions and willingness to change and set spoken lines and all the rest.

The worst is that de Sabata admires you so very much, and wants to see everything you've done: and is worried that *Regina* might ruin you here at the outset. Gian-Carlo [Menotti] is here for the *Saint* [*of Bleecker Street*], and while not agreeing with de S. does agree that it is a dangerous work for the Scala public. Screw them, say I, and do it anyway. That's the duty of an opera house, in whatever city.

I'm going to have one last fling with de Sabata on it, and then bring up the subject in Florence.

Dear Marc, I'm sorry. What can I do? *Tahiti* is off in Florence also, through Italian bungling of another sort. And the headlines scare me. And Burtie sends a miserable letter from Puerto Rico. It is all in all a depressing day, and the sun is shining away as though it were really spring.

Much love from us both.

Lenny

---

[104] Blitzstein's *Regina* is based on Lillian Hellman's *The Little Foxes* (1939), an extremely successful play that was made into a film starring Bette Davis in 1941 before Blitzstein adapted it for his opera. Regina was first performed on Broadway on 31 October 1949, conducted by Maurice Abravanel.

351. Elia Kazan to Leonard Bernstein
7 April 1955

Dear Lennie,

I felt terrible about their passing you by.[105] Tiomkin's speech told the whole story. I agree with him.[106] You wrote one of the really original scores and I felt terrible about what happened. Anyway, I hope you feel that you want to do more pictures because I'm going to come at you with another one.

Budd and I really have a very good idea.

I'm going to Greece and Turkey. I'll be back on June 2. Where will you be this summer? I'll be driving around a lot. Where will you be? I'll be headquartered at Box 25, Sandy Hook, Connecticut. I'd like to see you. Let me know your plans.

Love,
Gadg

352. Betty Comden to Leonard Bernstein
350 East 69th Street, New York City, NY
21 April 1955

Dearest Lenny,

A short note about a number of things. First, many many thanks for your beautiful words about us. Second, we are still wildly furious about the stupid Academy and could not hear the next ten minutes of the telecast because of our disappointment. Third, saw *Trouble in Tahiti*'s opening and was re-thrilled, re-inspired, and cried like – like an idiot. It was a triumph.

To get back to the album, one of the things Adolph and I hoped to accomplish with it was getting our *songs* recorded – so that maybe *someone* would hear one and decide to do something with or about it. And that has already happened. Lena H[orne] and Lenny H[ayton] were here at a small gathering – and Adolph brazenly put on the record, and comes "It's Love" both L[ena] and L[enny] got excited and asked about a verse – and getting hold of it – and then at the *Tahiti* opening, there they were and Lena said she's been rehearsing it like mad for nearly a week – and it's great!! Incidentally we'll ship you an album as soon as we have one – in about two weeks.

---

[105] *On the Waterfront* won eight Academy Awards in 1955, including Best Picture, Best Actor (Marlon Brando), Best Supporting Actor (Eve Marie Saint), and Best Director (Kazan). Though Bernstein's score was nominated, it didn't win.
[106] The winner of the Academy Award for Best Score was Dimitri Tiomkin, for *The High and the Mighty*.

As for *Trouble in Tahiti* and my crying – it was beautifully performed by Alice Ghostley, and it is a truly remarkable piece of work – and I had that feeling of closeness, and desire for us to be working with you, and the sadness of the pressure of time, and everything all at once overwhelming me.

The "personal prayer" – your notes about us – is our prayer too. Again, our thank yous.

Love,

Betty

353. Leonard Bernstein to Felicia Bernstein
Via Salaria 366, Rome, Italy
6 May 1955

Darling Bubbles,

Rome is beautiful as I have never seen it: blue blue sky, cool air, and the warm sea, and everything blooming away luxuriantly. I am glad I came; but I miss you here. Perverty it is, of course, as is to be expected, but it is not all so, and I am holding my own very well indeed. I have seen a lot of [Gina] Lollobrigida, a gem of a girl: I went to her singing lesson, and watched her work on her current film, and all with *Serenade* in mind. Remember that one? It's all in the works again, since they fired their Doggyinthewindow composer; Bob Joseph arrived in Milano with Henry Margolies (a charming man, actually, rich and quiet and sensitive) and we have been talking *Serenade*.[107] The indicated combination would be Lolly and Luchino a marvelous combo, and both are very eager about it. I am sure that with the right activity Luchino can get to America. I realize not that Reiner spoke through her ass when she said that Luchino could not be gotten over; she is a big speaker with no authority for one half of what she says. I am sure something will work out. And I would be happy for a postponement of a year on *Candide*: I'd like to have that time to let it cook, and see what should really be done with it. It's wrong the way it is now, that's all I know. The tape has not arrived yet, so I know nothing of the audition sound. I wait every day for word from Lil about May, and I could go to Paris or wherever, but no word from her. Soon it will be too late. I'm a bit sick of the whole thing, and would adore to get going on *Serenade* and the Münch symphony.[108]

I will leave here Saturday to go back to Milano for the opening of the *Saint [of Bleecker Street]*: then I have to go to Geneva, of all places, to rehearse the Israel orch there (13th–15th), then a concert in Trieste (16th–18th), then to

[107] In 1955, the idea of a musical version of James M. Cain's *Serenade* – which had so appealed to Bernstein in 1947 – was explored once again, with Arthur Laurents writing the book. As this letter shows, Bernstein was approached to compose the score.
[108] A very early mention of the work that became the *Kaddish* Symphony.

Florence (19th–22nd) then to Genoa to pick up the Israel gang and make the tour. That's the restful prospect at the moment. I wish you were here to do it all with me. Who's going to writhe out front during my Mozart concerto? But meanwhile I am basking in the Roman sun, and having a sort of social life, and thinking about nothing at all. Lunched with the Roberts yesterday, who sent you dearest love. Tonight cocktail party for me at Ruggiero's followed by dinner at the Chisholms. Thrilling. I spent an afternoon at the American Academy hearing the young music, very exciting indeed. Made me want to compose. Saw a revue, ghastly intellectual type, heard Bricktop, saw La Brignone [Lilla Brignone] act in a bad play of [Curzio] Malaparte, etc. I am sneezy with spring blossoms, but not too much so. The cats are all in the garden (say *that* in six languages) and this is a beautiful house with divine food and comforts and all and all.

I loved both your letters, and ate up every word, and read them over and over. All is as I feared about *Tahiti*. I realized from the notice that the opera had been reduced to a comic aria by Ghostley. You are right in everything you say about it: the same was true this summer in Westport. I am sure that a recording with Ghostley would be ill-advised, despite her talent: because on a record the vocal aspect only is heard, and that won't do for the touching parts. Why won't people realize that it is the touching parts that the opera is about? The rest is only either comment or diversion. I'd love to see you direct it one day. Thanks for not letting them put in the Trio before the office scene: what a cheap amateur notion! The office set simply *has* to be ready, and that's all. I do hope Heinsheimer will not be high-handed again about the recording. If it is done I should conduct it, and only if it is well planned out with the right cast. He's one for getting things on at all costs.

I've just had word that the *Candide* tape has arrived in Milano, so I will hear it shortly.

Please engage a suite for Charlie Roth at Bellevue.[109] I can't wait to break his four-time-fixed nose.

I'm terribly worried about Burtie – no word in over a month, and nothing since my answer to his desperate letter. I wrote him again begging for a word, but nothing. Maybe you should send him a telegram, and insist on some word from him. I really am very troubled about him. Please did [i.e. do] it.

Give my congrats to Marian and Julian (so glad theirs is ugly) and to Pat and Roald.[110] Yesterday a lady told me to rub my left little finger on her nose and then said we were sure to have a boy. No end to the ways of determining sex. Are you bigger and biggering? I hope it's not too hot in NY, and that you stay

[109] Bellevue Hospital in New York is famous for its psychiatric facilities.
[110] Patricia Neal and Roald Dahl. Their first child, Olivia, was born on 20 April 1955. Olivia's tragic death from measles encephalitis seven years later left Dahl "destroyed" according to Patricia Neal. He never spoke of her, but on the twentieth anniversary of her death he dedicated *The BFG* to Olivia's memory.

comfortable through these months. I'm dying to hear about the summer house. Write me care of Finzi, Via Manzoni 5.

Yes I *am* interested in a '52 Jaguar! Is it openable? Let's get it, but make sure someone looks carefully at it to see if it's in good condition, etc. And it really *must* be a convertible, don't you think? Art Stanton was a darling and acted quickly, but I have changed my mind. Too much trouble for too little worth.

I miss you my darling, and long to come home and see what the hell has happened to that little stranger Jamie, and just have a nice long endless booze hour. Keep well and happy, and un sacco di love. Di nuovo,

Lennuhtt.

What do you mean, Shirley quit her job? What will she do instead?

I can't tell you what the light is like at this moment on this terrace. And the birds sing in a glorious way. Luchino sends you dear love.

Thanks for the *Nation* puzz!

354. Leonard Bernstein to Felicia Bernstein
Grand Hotel Duomo, Milan, Italy
10 May 1955

Darling Madrina,

I long for the sight of you, belly and all, and I'll push myself fast through these next three weeks of conductifying to get home fast. Rome was a delight: weather such as I have rarely beheld, and uninterruptedly, day after day. I got a lot of sun and garden-lolling, and got to the sea three times. There was also a great series of parties, nice people, mostly theatre kids, and it's the same all over. We played the snapping 123 game for hours and sang old Rodgers songs, figurati. I saw a lot of Lollo[brigida] and of Henry Margolies and ultimately of Arlene Francis and Marty Gable (the latter I don't like atall atall, but he's also a producer of *Serenade*) and it looks as if things are really cooking for *Serenade* with la Lollobrigida! I had her sing various times, and when she relaxes it is really lovely, though too small a voice for theatre: but she still has a year to train and make the voice grow. And now Luchino is involved as a possible director which would be great with Gina (and also great for the show, I think) and *Candide* can go fly a kite. I am not going to waste another year nohow.

No word at all from Lillian [Hellman] or Ethel [Linder Reiner]: I sat waiting in Rome for a cable which would make me go to Paris, but nothing came, and thank goodness, since I got a bit of a rest. I don't understand what is happening. I began to take the Royal Jelly cure (Queen-bee) and it seems to be doing something: I don't need so much sleep, for example. But it's still too early to tell whether it works or not.

I'm back at the Duomo for two days, just to clean up some items, and then I got to Geneva for a few days (I leave Thursday, stay until Saturday night, when I take a sleeper to Trieste). Address in Geneva: c/o de Toledo, 46 Quai Gustave

Ador. Address in Trieste: Hotel Excelsior (15th, 16th, 17th). From the 18th through the 22nd I'm in Florence (Grand Hotel). The rest Helen has.

I just got the *Candide* tapes (what a mess at the customs!) and I'm off to the Ricordis to hear them. Did I tell you that Maria [Callas] had an operation? You might drop her a note. She's fine now. Address: Corso Porta Nuova 10. Remember?

I have to run: I'll keep writing. Much love to the *kids*, fijate, and a sacco to you.

L

355. Leonard Bernstein to Barbara and Philip Marcuse
[En route from Trieste to Florence, Italy]
headed paper of the Excelsior Palace Hotel, Trieste
18 May 1955

Dearest Marcusi,

Here I sit on a train from Trieste to Florence, at the moment stuck forever in the station of Venice, with apparently no intention of continuing, and I am writing you on stationery from the hotel as you can see, and I am thinking about you very hard. I keep wondering how Phil is (and what he is, now that he has become so fascinating and mysterious with the sort of problems I thought only I had); and I keep hoping you really will show up at Tanglefoot. Felicia has been with me for five weeks (up to about three weeks ago) and I am now doing the last lap by myself. Scala is over (it was a mistake to give 3 months to it: I lost my Milanese glamor) and I am currently doing concerts: last night in Trieste (they loved me in Trieste) and now Florence, and then I pick up the Israel orchestra, which is now touring Europe, and do concerts with them in Genoa, Florence again, Naples, Perugia, Bologna, and finally Milano; and then I go home, having dutifully cancelled Holland as per your instructions, to witness the birth of my · newest human bean. I should be home the first week in June, and the Bean is expected about mid-June, and we go to the Berkshires beginning of July. Of course none of these dates will work out accurately, and it will be a typical Bernstein confusion; but somewhere in it all I hope to find word from you about your summer plans and your combined *stati d'animo*, as we say here. I love you as much as ever and miss you, and hope to see you. I was sorry to have had to turn down the very exciting proposals of Kellman, etc., for a Detroit Festival; but there must be a limit somewhere. I discovered in an old book of Chinese divination that my problem is one of self-limitation, and I am therefore working hard on it (as if I didn't know before out of my own private little Jewish divination what my problem was). Some day, preferably soon, I simply must decide what I'm going to be when I grow up.

Love,
Lenny
Hugs to the kids.

356. Leonard Bernstein to Felicia Bernstein

Grand Hotel, Florence, Italy
23 May 1955

Darling Bubb,

Vera brought me your note, which was another breath of spring in primaveral Florence, as were Jamie's kisses. From Vera's description of Jamie and of her talk I don't know what to expect; apparently she has grown and changed so that I won't recognize her. It's a bit frightening to contemplate: I can't wait to see her again. To say nothing of you. Everyone at the parties and the green rooms is again, as before, stating with certainty that it will be a boy this time. Must mean it will surely be a girl. I'm prepared.

The concerts in Trieste and Florence have both been extraordinary wows, like the great old days. The Prokofieff grows with each performance,[111] and I have been playing a hell of a piano these days, I don't know why. Certainly I haven't practiced. At least now the piano-playing is over, and I now begin to concentrate on the *Serenade* and Isaac [Stern], which is less nerve-wracking, but harder work, because there is a great shortage of rehearsal time with the Jew orchestra. Off to Genoa tomorrow, Sterns in hand. David D[iamond] gave me a charming party last night: he is in fine shape. Titi has been around a lot, and sends you her love, as do all the other Florentines.

You won't believe this, but the black fairy[112] is in again, having covered half the earth from Vienna to New York, he promptly set forth again to Florence, with what money I don't know, and has been beating at the gates to see me (active at T'wood, assistant on the Israel tour, all the old crap) and I have consistently refused to see him. Luckily another pupil of mine, [Piero] Bellugi, has been around, and I got him to take charge of Roth and keep him away from me. According to Bellugi, Roth is madder than ever, and more dangerous. He is now threatening to expose us "all" as communists, the idiot. I am just afraid that he will cause some sort of stink through making a scene, with the consulate here, or somehow. He appeared in my dressing room last night after the concert, and I threw him out, and he left with an air of Well That's It, Now I Do My Worst. I'm really scared both for him and of him. He has no money to get back to the US, and will have to go to the Consulate to be shipped home, and that will cause talk. I alternate between saying Ho-Hum and Jesus-Christ. What a horror he is.

Tremendous news: I've got a kepepelt [cold], at last. I only hope that I hold out these next 10 days. Lillian has been constantly on the phone, and I may have to go to Paris for two days either after Genoa or after Milano on the 3rd. I hope

---

[111] Bernstein programmed Prokofiev's Fifth Symphony for the concert in Florence, along with Mozart's Symphony No. 39 and the Ravel G major Concerto directed from the piano.
[112] Charles Roth. See note 92 to Bernstein's letter of 11 February 1955.

not, I really do. I'm also a bit embarrassed about all this peddling of the script to all these directors – it seems almost everyone in the world has been approached short of the Chinese Theatre, and that does not make good talk. In London she is seeing Rex Harrison and [John] Gielgud and [Garson] Kanin and God knows who else, and in Paris [René] Clair and [Julien] Duvivier and [Jean] Renoir and God knows who else, and for me there is really no work to show that really adds up. It is a situation I don't like at all. I had forgotten what a charm Lil has: speaking to her over the phone reminded me of why one sticks to her through thick: she has a real attractiveness in spite of everything, and a kind of combination of power and helplessness that in a woman is irresistible.

I want to come home! Just think, in addition to coming home to you and Jamie, there will also be Fink – and a Cadillac! The latter is a slight worry – do we have the money? If we do, let's get it, and sell the Olds[mobile] in the fall if we have to. There's always the great idea of the two Nashes!

All my love,

L

Vera says you look glorious!

I spent four hours yesterday looking at emeralds for you, and the only decent one I found cost 21,000,000!!! So, let's wait until Lollobrigida makes us a fortch and then you'll *swim* in emeraldi.

357. Leonard Bernstein to Felicia Bernstein
Hotel Colombia, Genoa, Italy
27 May 1955

Darling,

I am just about to leave Genoa, which was after all great fun, in spite of the exhaustion. I had to rehearse the orch. here for the forthcoming tour, and it was a job and a half, teaching them the *Serenade* and the Berlioz, neither of which they knew, and at a time when they were so tired they could barely read the notes. Then [. . .] the hall was not available for rehearsal, etc. We finally did it, by sheer dint, rehearsal all afternoon the day of the concert, after which I rushed around Genoa looking for a set of chimes, of all things, which Maria [Callas] helped me to find through Ricordi's [. . .] and then there was the concert, and the report is that never before has Genoa seen such a success. Imagine, with my funny modern music and unpopular Berlioz! I had feared for the size of the audience as well as for their applause, and was surprised delightfully on both counts. The papers are raves, and Isaac [Stern] played better than ever, and the orchestra really did miracles, everything considered. Then they just went on to Rome, while I stayed here, thank God, for two days with the Sterns [. . .] A lovely afternoon yesterday at the home of Maria's old parents; today we rented a car and drove to Portofino, but the sun went in bang and we had to come back.

But at least it was a breathing spell. Now on to Bologna, and the rest of the one-night-stands, for six days. *Then home!*

Listen: Lillian, from London, asks that I stop off in Paris for a day en route home, and I really can't refuse; but I worry so that you'll spring the Fink while I'm not looking that I hesitate. Keep me informed every minute about how things look and feel; if OK by you, I'll go to Paris, and be home probably on the 5th or 6th. I can't wait, really I can't; and you can't scare me with Jamie's tantrums. I've been expecting them all along. I'm dying to see her.

I loved your letter, and the Caddylacky sounds like a dream and I wish you were here to hear the *Serenade*. My, how pretty it is. Terrible about Agee:[113] I was prepared for it.

Darling girl, it won't be long now. Please stop yourself up with adhesive tape or corks till I get home!

LOVE

X

358. Aaron Copland to Leonard Bernstein
L'Orangerie, Le Cannet, Alpes-Maritimes, France
17 July 1955

Papa Lensk!

Aren't you both smart! Take a *big* double bow. Hope Felicia and the Knabe are doing fine.[114]

I'm sitting on top of a mountain in a villa overlooking Cannes and the Mediterr[anean]. Picked me a real nice spot (very different from Lago di Garda). It's work in the morning and work in the evening, and the beach in the afternoon (very different from Tanglewood).

Which reminds me – how is the old girl? (Tanglewood). Has anyone noticed anything missing?

After I left you in Rome I conducted in Paris and London. Watch out, I'm gettin' good.

And what, may I ask, has been happening to you? (Did you see the Amer[ican] issue of *The Score*, with 2 articles on Bernstein? If not, they'll tell you.)

Guess who I met in Cannes? – Kiki Speyer and son.

I hear you had to abandon *Canticle* [*of Freedom*] in Hollywood for lack of a chorus. Too bad. Tell Edie to send me Tanglewood school programs. Want to see what you're up to.

Love,

A

---

[113] The writer James Agee died of a heart attack on 16 May 1955.
[114] Alexander Bernstein was born on 7 July 1955.

5

West Side Story
1955–7

It was in the summer and autumn of 1955 that *West Side Story* started to take shape as a viable project. Jerome Robbins, Arthur Laurents, and Bernstein had quietly set the idea to one side since first discussing it in 1949, but quite suddenly it was on again, thanks to the impetus of reports in the news about gang warfare. The story told in Bernstein's 1957 *West Side Log* is that the moment of discovery happened in Hollywood when he had a meeting with Laurents in August 1955, but a letter written to him a month earlier by Laurents suggests that it was more complicated than that. Still, it was the outcome that mattered: a new outline, introducing Puerto Rican immigrants, and, with them, the Latin American musical elements that would be so crucial to the score's colors. As well as refining the plot, a second vital factor was bringing Stephen Sondheim into the project to write the lyrics. Over the next two years, the four collaborators were mostly able to discuss the project in the same place and at the same time – so there's not much correspondence between them about the show – but before they got down to serious work, Robbins responded in detail to the new Laurents–Bernstein outline, giving important clues about how he wanted the show to develop. It was not only as a creative genius that Robbins' role was of such fundamental importance in the evolution of *West Side Story*. On a personal level, he was one of the very few people who could get complete commitment from Bernstein, and who could insist on – and inspire – music of the highest quality. Robbins' letters to Bernstein are often brusque and brutally honest, but the respect they had for each other is unmistakable.

Preparations for the troublesome *Candide* kept Bernstein from devoting himself exclusively to what was still known as "the Romeo show" in mid-1956. And on top of all that, and a busy conducting schedule, there were also television projects. For *Omnibus*, Bernstein's "Introduction to Modern Music" prompted Gunther Schuller to write a long, eloquently argued letter about how to present a balanced account of recent developments in music: he questioned Bernstein's stance on Schoenberg and his complete omission of Webern. (An intriguing sideline: while it's tempting to read too much into the impact of a single letter, can it be a coincidence that a year after Schuller wrote, Webern's *Six Pieces for Orchestra* were included on a Bernstein program with the New York Philharmonic, and in one of the Young People's Concerts?)

While Bernstein was working feverishly on the last stages of *West Side Story*, Felicia took Jamie and Alexander to visit her family in Chile, partly to give him some peace and quiet, and partly to escape what must have been an increasingly intense atmosphere. The consequence is an exchange of letters between Bernstein and Felicia that chronicle the final weeks of composing the show, the rehearsals in New York and Washington, D.C., the changes Bernstein was forced to accept (reluctantly in some cases – but judging from the manuscript evidence of earlier versions of some numbers, the instincts of Robbins, Laurents, and Sondheim were unerringly right), and the euphoria of the first night of the out-of-town try-out at the National Theatre in Washington. Felicia was delighted to hear Bernstein's exciting (and excited) news, and wrote back with plenty of her own, above all some delightful vignettes of the children.

West Side Story opened at Broadway's Winter Garden Theatre on 26 September 1957 – and the day after, Bernstein and Felicia flew to Israel for the inaugural concerts of the Mann Auditorium in Tel Aviv. Bernstein wasn't in New York for the cast recording of *West Side Story*, but Sondheim was, and he sent Bernstein a wonderfully detailed account of the sessions. Parallel to *West Side Story*, there was another major development in Bernstein's career: two weeks before the show opened in Washington, Bernstein signed the contract to become Music Director of the New York Philharmonic: over the next decade, the inevitable consequence of this appointment was a shift in the focus of Bernstein's activities, and it was as a conductor that he would need to concentrate most of his energies. *West Side Story* was a ground-breaking hit, certainly – but it was to be Bernstein's last triumph on Broadway.

359. Arthur Laurents to Leonard Bernstein
Dune Road, Quogue, NY
19 July [1955]

Dear Lenny,

I'm sending a copy of this letter and the enclosed to Jerry. Obviously, it is the barest of skeletons – but it is on the line we worked out and agreed on. And will, I hope, be some sort of basis for all of us to do some thinking on before we meet again.

I don't know whether you've been so busy that you've missed all the juvenile gang war news.[1] Not only is it all over the papers every day, but it is going to be

---

[1] It is worth noting that Laurents wrote this letter more than a month before the meeting between Laurents and Bernstein when they discussed the idea of warring gangs of Puerto Rican and white American teenagers.

[2] Nothing seems to have come of this idea, but Miller writes at length about his observations of gang warfare in Brooklyn during the summer of 1955 in his autobiography *Timebends* (1987), pp. 360–9.

all over the movie screens. Arthur Miller, or so I read, is doing an original drama on the subject for the movies.[2]

By accident, then, we have hit on an idea which is suddenly extremely topical, timely, and just plain hot. For this reason, I hope we can get to serious work on it as early as we planned. But more than that, if there is any way of getting the thing done this season, I hope we can find it. To my way of thinking, it would be perfect timing to present this on Broadway early in the spring. I don't know if it's possible but with all this splurge of interest in the subject, I think we would be missing a big opportunity if we didn't capitalize on it.

Incidentally, I hope you noticed I didn't say "East Side Story".[3] This was because of our mutual feeling that the locale should not be specific or definitely placed in any specific city.

Love to Felicia, your brood and yourself.

Arthur

360. Arthur Laurents to Leonard Bernstein
[Beverly Hills, CA]
Monday [?Summer or Autumn 1955][4]

Dear Leonard,

This, frankly, is an all-out attempt to get you to come out here for a week. And Jerry and I are going to phone you later this week. I would not write this if I did not really think it was important. I wouldn't be staying out here myself, for that matter, no matter how pool-lush the life is. Let me explain.

---

[3] *East Side Story* was one of the several titles for what became *West Side Story*. For years the collaborators called it simply *Romeo*. One short-lived early title was *Operation Capulet* (see Letter 279). A much later title, announced in the press as late as June 1957, was *Gangway!* – an idea that was quickly (and mercifully) abandoned.

[4] This undated letter urges Bernstein to go out to Hollywood (where Laurents, Robbins, and Bernstein all worked at various times in 1955) in order to make progress on *West Side Story*. It's probable that this letter was written before the meeting between Bernstein and Laurents on 25 August 1955 (when Robbins was in New York). But it's also possible – from Laurents' reference to "all the preliminary work that we've all talked about" – that he wrote the letter after the meeting to request a week's visit from Bernstein to consolidate ideas already discussed, especially as Robbins arrived in Hollywood in mid-September to work on the film of *The King and I* (he was clearly in California when Laurents wrote this letter). The meeting on 25 August in Beverly Hills was described by Bernstein: "Had a fine long session with Arthur today, by the pool. (He's here for a movie; I'm conducting at the Hollywood Bowl.) We're fired again by the Romeo notion; only now we have abandoned the whole Jewish–Catholic premise as not very fresh, and have come up with what I think is going to be it: two teen-age gangs as the warring factions, one of them newly-arrived Puerto Ricans, the other self-styled 'Americans.' Suddenly it all springs to life. I hear rhythms and pulses, and – most of all – I can sort of feel the form" (Bernstein 1957, p. 47). However, Laurents had already raised this idea a month earlier, in his letter to Bernstein of 19 July 1955 (Letter 359). The eventual outcome was the radically altered outline that introduced the idea of conflict between white and Puerto Rican gangs (printed in Appendix One) to which Robbins responded on 18 October 1955 (Letter 362).

The Comden–Green–Styne show[5] has bogged down. For many reasons; maybe you know them. Beginning with Leland [Hayward]'s exit, with Jule's [Styne's] productions, with Betty and Adolph's movie work. They don't know how much more work they will have to do on their latest, when they can get back to their show, etc. Furthermore, they spoke to Jerry about doing the lyrics for ours. I understand you spoke to them, about the lyrics. Jerry told them you and I planned to try ourselves. If you and he feel they are right and would like to have them join the project, I am, you know, willing to go along.[6] I don't know how right they are but Jerry seemed to think they could be guided and helped and even pushed – as, he says, they never really have been into doing a good job.

But that is secondary. The point is that Jerry's decks are clear *at this moment* for the spring. He and I have been working very well together. By the end of this week, we should have a pretty good outline to go over with you. His concern about the spring is: Will the show be ready? You know him and how he wants his commitments committed well in advance. If you came out, I am absolutely convinced a) the show would be ready and b) we could convince him that it would be ready and thus he would commit himself for a spring production. He would also take it as an evidence of your faith and more, we could actually wind up all the preliminary work we have all talked about and that is so damn necessary. It would not take more than a week. The fare is inexpensive now and you could stay here. There is plenty of room, he has a man who cooks and cleans (lush life), a big pool (lush life), you and I could work during the day and hash it over with him at night. I admit: no social life. One big party, Jerry says. Unless you make your social life quite late at night or in the afternoons. But what are the words, what can I say to urge you to please come out? None I suppose beyond the fact that I – again – am convinced that the outline would be set and the show would be set for spring. Which is really what we all want. Please think very seriously about all this and then make your reservation to come out Sunday night and start work Monday. One week, that's all.

As for production contracts, that's no part of this really. Except Bob Joseph has really been shooting off his wild mouth rather stupidly, and what he hasn't mucked up, Arnold Weissberger has done, and brilliantly. The plan is now for a collaboration agreement between you, Jerry and me to be drawn up, and *then* proceed from there. But I suppose David Hocker, whom we just spoke to, will or has informed you about all this.

---

[5] *Bells Are Ringing.*
[6] Comden and Green were tentatively considered for *West Side Story*, and during September 1955 they were apparently contemplating taking it on; they were unable to do so because of existing Hollywood commitments. By October 1955, Stephen Sondheim had joined the show's creative team to write the lyrics.

Lenny – again and again: please do come out for the one week. It is terribly important if you want a spring production. I know I do.

My love to Felicia and your brood and, obviously, to you.

Arthur

361. Jack Gottlieb[7] to Leonard Bernstein
806 California Avenue, Urbana, IL
2 October 1955

Dear Lenny,

I saw *It's Always Fair Weather* last night; it was very disappointing. True, there were many funny moments, but they didn't add up. For me it was a slick pastiche without any integration. But more than this, what actually disturbed me was the New York-ese evocation. I should think that after *On the Town* and *Wonderful Town* Comden and Green had had their say on the subject. It seems that this gold mine doesn't exhaust itself for them. Don't they ever have pangs about using the same kind of subject matter? – three soldiers instead of three sailors, the New York stereotypes, etc. Besides repeating themselves, I also felt that at several points they veered dangerously close to *Guys and Dolls*. As for the music – [André] Previn may be a great pianist, but really now!

What this is leading up to is *East Side Story*. If I'm not wrong, this is supposed to be a Bronxite version of *Romeo and Juliet*. The basic idea is novel (as was *Carmen Jones*); so was *Fair Weather*. When I think of what might have really been done with the idea of three war buddies meeting again after ten years – what a truly great drama (*not* musical) could have come out of it. Similarly, *East Side Story* – are you sure this is stuff for a *musical*, and, if it is, are the now familiar gimmicks of the floating crap game, chewing-gum drawl, subway rendezvous (*S[ain]t of Bleak [Bleecker Street]*), etc., ad nauseam, going to be rehashed again? I hope not. Enough metropolitana! Also, don't forget that there are historical connotations involved in *Romeo and Juliet*. When Blacher's version was done at Tanglewood (e.g.) from the historical orientation, how fully could one accept a Negro as Romeo and a white girl as Juliet – even though the whole medium is, to begin with, artificial?

For the past two weeks I have been taking my Doctorate entrance exams – harmonic and formal analysis, ear training and dictation, counterpoint, history, and an English exam and the Miller Analogy Test. I am exhausted! If nothing else, these exams point up how really ill-equipped I am! I still can't write a fugue à la Gedalge; my dictation is abominable. It's quite sickening. Actually, I am nothing

---

[7] Jack Gottlieb (1930–2011), American composer who began work as Bernstein's musical assistant in 1958 and subsequently became publications director of Amberson Enterprises, Bernstein's publishing company.

but an animal in music. I work and respond with emotions; the craft is negligible. One other person is taking the degree with me – Kenneth Gaburo – a Gershwin award winner who has just finished a Fulbright in Italy. He is about 33 and is certainly far advanced in relation to myself. If there were ten of us, I wouldn't mind, but it is so easy to make comparisons when only two are involved. He won the Gershwin award along with James Dalgliesh, who has since died.[8]

It's a good thing that no one else but myself eats my food. I make enough spaghetti for ten people, pot roast like rubber, stuffed pepper like the stones. For anyone else it may be amusing; for me it's just a pain. At least I keep the pots clean – so there's [no] chance of my developing dysentery. If I could only cook – !

Three times a day – morning, noon, night – I journey back and forth to school. That is the extent of my contact with the world. From 8 a.m. to 1 p.m. I keep busy at the desk and piano. I practice about 5 hours every night, plus accompany dance classes 1 hour per day. I knock myself out, so that there will be no time to wallow in self-pity. The only misery comes when I try to fall asleep – it's so damn difficult. I enjoy my students, but, at the same time, I resent their drain upon my time which could be spent composing – preparing lessons, correcting assignments and tests, private coaching sessions; ugh! I'm sorry to say that the main trouble is that my body is in Urbana, Illinois, but my heart and mind are on W. 57th St in Gotham. If there were only someone to talk to –

Love,
Jack

362. Jerome Robbins to Arthur Laurents and Leonard Bernstein
18 October 1955

Dear Arthur and Lenny,
I am dictating this in 15 minutes I have free during lunch, so I'll get right to it. Excuse the directness, but it's the only way I can get this off to you.

It concerns the outline, but before I tell you my objections I want you to know that I think it's a hell of a good job and very much on the right track, and that these differences are incidental to the larger wonderful job you are both doing.[9]

---

[8] In 1954, Kenneth Gaburo and James Dalgliesh were joint winners of the ninth annual George Gershwin Memorial Contest (organized by the B'nai B'rith) for the best orchestral composition by a young American composer.

[9] The outline by Arthur Laurents and Bernstein (see Appendix One) and Robbins' detailed reply in this letter are documents of great importance in the genesis of *West Side Story*. Laurents and Bernstein had evolved the new outline after discussing the project in California in August 1955. Newspaper reports of recent gang violence made them rethink the dramatic outline of a show on which progress had been virtually stalled since Robbins had first proposed the idea in January 1949. Bernstein has written marginal annotations on Robbins' letter that reveal some of his reaction to Robbins' criticisms. These are described in the notes that follow.

I don't agree with the 3 act division. I feel strongly that this negates the time pressure connected with the whole show and mitigates against the tenseness of the story being crammed into 2 or 3 days. Moreover, there's not sufficient material in Act II or III to stand up by themselves. And it's a serious mistake to let the audience out of our grip for 2 intermissions.[10]

Act I, Scene 2. Would like to suggest that the meeting between Romeo and Juliet be more abrupt rather than an observing of each other from a distance at first. In general, suddenness of action is something we should strive for,[11] beginning with the tempo key in which we establish Scene 1. Its violence and excitement should cue us for all our dramatic moments; i.e. the suddenness and horror of the murders at the end of the rumble, the discovery of love, etc. etc.

Act I, Scene 5. You are away off the track with the whole character of Anita. She is the typical downbeat blues torch-bearing 2nd character (Julie of *Showboat*, etc.) and falls into a terrible cliché.[12] The audience will know that somewhere a "my man done left me" blues is coming up for her. Furthermore, this puts the girl above the age limit and experience that the gang should have and completely disturbs the adolescent quality.[13] If she's "an-older-girl-kicked-by-love-before-experiencing-the-worst" (and I'm quoting you) she's much too experienced for the gang, or else is sick, sick, sick to be so attached emotionally and sexually to a younger boy of a teen age gang. I can't put the above strongly enough and at the risk of offending you, Arthur, forget Anita and start writing someone who is either older (like Tante) or younger with the same emotional timber of the rest of the gang.

Act I, Scene 6. The jitterbug dance should finish completely and then start again as an encore with Bernardo entering,[14] otherwise we kill the hand, the dance and the audience's pitch. You might consider the reading of the headlines here because this will tie in with second drugstore scene after murders have been committed. (See later note in Act III, Scene 5.)

Act II, Scene 1. I again object to Anita's downbeat note, the "oh-God-am-I-suffering".[15]

Act II, Scene 2. I wonder about "*children* playing games and marrying themselves". Just as long as it doesn't become cute, coy or silly, okay.

Act II Scene 3. There are extremely wrong things here. First, it's another reprise of the Bernardo-Romeo-Juliet scene of Act I, Scene 2, the first time they all meet: and either the fight scene must be provoked immediately or else we're

---

[10] Marginal note by Bernstein: "good points."
[11] Marginal note by Bernstein: "I thought it *was* sudden."
[12] Marginal note by Bernstein: "True, but maybe a slightly diff[erent] angle."
[13] Marginal note by Bernstein: "How much older?"
[14] Marginal note by Bernstein: "Good point. Both things can happen."
[15] Marginal note by Bernstein: "Not necessarily bad – but avoid cliché!"

boring the audience and stalling.[16] Don't understand why Bernardo doesn't plunge into the scene that follows with his provoking Romeo to a fight. In other words, rather than heightening the following scene, I feel it lessens it and robs it. The only thing I like is the character color of Juliet's strength. I thought the version of Romeo steering someone away from the rumbles was a better idea.

Act III, Scene 2. I am starting to feel we're in serious trouble with the so-called love ballet. (See note on dancers at end.)

Act III, Scene 3. Want to know why Juliet doesn't go with Romeo immediately.[17]

Act III, Scene 5. There are a couple of things I can't adjust here. The boys are jitterbugging to avert suspicion from the police – but what has happened about the death of their beloved Mercutio? In other words, how do you make compatible the effect of the murders on the boys with what you have written?[18] I think this *can* be one, but isn't indicated at all in the outline. Here's where the newspaper headlines, with references to the teen-age gang war and murders could be used. The "hey that's me" effect.

Act III, Scene 6. From the outline I'm inclined to feel that it's all a little too goofy. Juliet becomes Ophelia with the reeds and flowers and is playing a "crazy" scene.[19] I had to read the whole thing a couple of times to find out why Romeo died[20] and I also think it's too right on the head placing it back in the bridal shop.

As for the all-over picture, we're dead unless the audience feels that all the tragedy can and could be averted, that there's *hope* and a wish for escape from that tragedy, and a tension built on that desire. We must always hold out the tantalizing chance of a positive ending. Romeo and Juliet particularly must feel this and be sure of it. It's another reason why I dislike qvetchy Anita so much. Let's not have anyone in the show feel sorry for themselves.[21]

About the dancing. It will never be well incorporated into the show unless some of the principals are dancers. I can see, easily, why Romeo and Juliet must be singers, but Mercutio has to be a dancer, maybe Anita, and for sure some of the prominent gang members, otherwise, if any of the dance sequences do take place over the stage, your principals will move to the side and a terrible separation happens.[22] Practically, it's easier to rehearse with separate units, but with all

---

[16] Marginal note by Bernstein: "True. But there are 2 scenes, so how to achieve the flow like one scene?"
[17] Marginal note by Bernstein: "?"
[18] Marginal note by Bernstein: "Don't see any incompatibility here."
[19] Marginal note by Bernstein: "Why not?"
[20] Marginal note by Bernstein: "True. Maybe he doesn't know – but we know he's doomed."
[21] Marginal note by Bernstein (with a line beside the whole paragraph): "All true."
[22] Marginal note by Bernstein: "Right."

the experience I've had it's by far most beneficial to the unity of the show to have the principals do everything. It's a sorry sight and a back-breaking effort, and usually an unsuccessful one, to build the numbers around some half-assed movements of a principal who can't move. Think it over.

I'm sending this off as fast as possible, so please excuse the abruptness. Let me hear from you both.

Love,

Jerry

363. Leonard Bernstein to Burton Bernstein
205 West 57th Street, New York, NY
29th October 1955

Darling Baudümü,

Here we have been complaining for weeks at having had no word from you, and here today I find a letter you sent immediately, and I am contride, contride. You also sent a pretty photo, which we all thought looked exactly like me, and it does, and we miss you more and more each day. As you say, it's all downhill from here on, and maybe no more than just a nice warm winter in the tropics. But, to judge from the letter to the folks, which they showed us yesterday, you are bored. Are you bored? Is there a promotion coming up for you? And a pay increase?

We just returned from Boston where the *Lark*[23] had its premiere and it seems to be a large hit. Raves, and the audience lapped it up. My music sounded good as hell, with marvelous voices (on tape: and cheap [Kermit] Bloomgarten wouldn't rent good enough equipment, so that it grizzled a bit) but still it sounded pretty. I think there's the kernel of a short Mass there, and I may expand it into one for the Juilliard commission (two birds technique, as of old).[24]

I'm sorry you missed my last *Omnibus* show, On Jazz, and it seems to have had an ecstatic reaction all over the country. Columbia wants to record it, and all the others in a series, and there is serious talk of filming it (and others) for commercial release in theatres. Goodness. Next one coming up in about three weeks, on Bach, about whom I know nothing about whom.

[23] Lillian Hellman's adaptation of Jean Anouilh's *The Lark*, for which Bernstein wrote the incidental music.
[24] According to Jack Gottlieb's note in the score of Bernstein's *Missa Brevis*, it was Robert Shaw who suggested this idea when he attended a performance. In 1988, to mark Shaw's retirement as Music Director of the Atlanta Symphony Orchestra, Bernstein produced the "short Mass" that he had contemplated more than thirty years earlier. See also Letter 365.

Romeo proceeds apace, with a new young lyricist named Steve Sondheim, who is going to work out wonderfully. I still have high hopes of a spring production. No deal reached as yet with Bob Joseph and Co. We may have to give it to other producenicks. I wrote a spic song called "Maria" which may finally bring me to jukeboxes, who knows. And one called "Cool" which will never see a jukebox.

Candide is a certainty for next fall. [Tyrone] Guthrie is signed, and a big rewrite job must take place next late spring and summer. So no T'wood. We're toying with the idea of a huge house in Englewood. Imagine, with a pool and huge grounds. It's one of those monstrosities, but we could make it cheerful and fine. We just may buy it, if we can get it cheaply.

The first Symph of Air concert comes up on the 9th, with Aaron's new *Canticle of Freedom*, and Mahler 2nd. Wish you were here.

So, as you see, life is busier than ever, and everything goes swimmingly except that Felicia just doesn't seem to get work. She is depressed, and I don't blame her. Alexander is a heartthrob, a wonder, and so is Jamie. We long for you. I'm going to try to get to P[uerto] R[ico] for some local research on the Romeo show: any excuse, but I may get away with it. Let's hope. When can you next have a leave?

All our loves; and do write soon, not following my detestable example.

Lennuhtt

364. Marc Blitzstein to Leonard Bernstein
30 December 1955

Dear Lenny,

You have written, and so I answer, although I had planned to do nothing, but let the thing sink into the impassive past. But I am a bum actor; and seeing you both at Eddie Albert's[25] was perhaps too soon. My belligerence to Felicia (poor girl, it wasn't her fault I was left alone with her) *was* Reuben,[26] *was* Bourbon, to the extent I can't remember what I said, but it was probably nonsense – but it was really your outrageous treatment in subjecting me to a private meeting in your drawing-room with the worm Robbins.[27] I have met him at parties, or could; one can't help that. But that it should come from you, who have been over the whole story with me, have once been furious with him ("slap his face" and "my stomach turns at the thought of working with him again" were two of

---

[25] Eddie Albert played Reuben in the original production of Blitzstein's *Reuben Reuben*.

[26] Subtitled an "urban folk opera," *Reuben Reuben* opened in Boston on 10 October 1955 and closed quickly, before reaching Broadway. Blitzstein was still reeling from the disappointment when he wrote this letter.

[27] Blitzstein never forgave Robbins for naming names when he testified to the HUAC.

your phrases),[28] and with the passage of time have let that fury cool and dim and at length yield to other considerations – this is hard to take. I do apologize to Felicia. About you and me – I don't know what to do about our friendship, or my continuing fondness for you. A few more body-blows – put it down to your ego, your thoughtlessness, I don't care – might make any intimacy permanently untenable.

No, I did not send Jamie a gift.[29] Right now, with a sudden unexpected lawsuit against me for "pilfering" *Threepenny Opera*, I was too poor to afford any gifts, including mother, Jo, etc. But she has my love, as does Lex. I don't send cards.

We'll probably meet at Lillian's, New Year's Eve. Let's not get into this talk; I should only become "quarrelsome". Let's let it ride a bit.[30]

Marc

365. Robert Shaw to Leonard Bernstein
Hotel Georgian Terrace, Atlanta, GA
14 February 1956

Dear Lennie,

Please accept my apologies for not contacting you before we left New York concerning your wonderful choruses in *The Lark* and my attempt to program them through the Spring Tours.

In the last few hectic days of rehearsals, I discovered – as I have every season for the past eight years – that the program already was too long, and simply couldn't see my way to getting them installed and rehearsed adequately (which latter was the principal item).

I do think they are absolutely (and variously) captivating and exciting pieces – and I continue to hope that we may be able to perform them in some suite-form in the near future.

Again – many thanks. It was a delight to see you again.

All good wishes,

Bob Shaw

---

[28] This is a fascinating comment; Bernstein's own correspondence contains no remarks about working with Robbins after his HUAC performance, but it would be surprising if Bernstein and Arthur Laurents had not been angered and disappointed by Robbins' conduct. And yet, only a few months before Blitzstein sent this letter, Bernstein and Laurents had got back to serious work on *West Side Story*, and brought Stephen Sondheim into the creative team.

[29] Blitzstein was her godfather.

[30] This was not a lasting rift. As Eric Gordon put it, "Lenny and Felicia Bernstein remained loyal to Marc. They had already made their first child, Jamie, Marc's godchild. Their son Alexander's name is the male form of Alexandra from *Regina*. And their third child they named for Marc's heroine in *Reuben Reuben* – Nina" (Gordon 1989, p. 405).

366. Leonard Bernstein to David Diamond
Vineyard Haven, MA
25 May 1956

Dear Dov,

The news is sad indeed. I had no idea your mother was in so bad a state. Poor Sabina [Diamond's sister] – what that girl has been through, what with one thing and another. And what it must be doing to you – breaking up your household, your work, your peace, and all for such a rush trip home. Mightn't it be possible to bring your mother to you in Italy, and have her spend her last days in all that beauty and quiet, and with you? It would save you so much and keep you together (all of you) – but I suppose that travel is just too much for her now.

I've been searching my brain and my acquaintances for a couple to take your villetta, but in vain. I do hope it all works out well. We must see you of course, when you come, even if only for a bit: so do call us when you arrive, or write us here. The phone is Vineyard Haven 1396.

It's all like a déjà vu. Here we are again, Lillian and us, back at the Vineyard, exactly like two summers ago, with a T'wood leave of absence, but this time with Tyrone Guthrie, who will direct, and incidentally will save the show, I think. Other change: new lyricist, Richard Wilbur, a marvelous young poet who has never written a lyric in his life, and is already doing wonders. I now have hope for *Candide*, for the first time in ages. We go into rehearsal after Labor Day.[31] Meanwhile I am concurrently writing the other show (the Romeo one, with Arthur Laurents and Robbins and a charming gifted boy named Steve Sondheim) and it begins to look like something. Both at once. It's a wild situation, even for me. And, again, concurrently, I must do something about the Boston Symph commission (not a note yet). Plus concerts this summer, in order to support my expanding brood, plus writing TV shows for the fall, plus plus plus. It doesn't look like a relaxing summer, to say the least, but there is much sky and water and air and beauty here, and I love it. I've been here for a week all alone (Felicia follows with brood and company in a few days). It is cold and sunny and bracing, and I am having fun cooking for myself and feeding the furnace and making the fireplaces and watching the late spring come hesitantly forth.

We are all well and send our love to you and Ciro [Cuomo]. Let us hear of your arrival.

Love,

Lenny

---

[31] In December 1956, Diamond played as a violinist in the pit orchestra for Bernstein's *Candide*, though this much-needed paying engagement was interrupted when he was subpoenaed by the HUAC. There's at least one irony in the timing of Diamond's subpoena: *Candide* was partly intended by Hellman and Bernstein as a polemic against HUAC and Joseph McCarthy's Senate hearings.

367. Leonard Bernstein to Aaron Copland
Vineyard Haven, MA
13 June 1956

Dear Aa,

Ah, the pressures. When I think that I have thanked you in my mind for the score of *Tender Land* a hundred times & I have never had a second to write it, I am aghast. I guess I kept thinking I had written, so often had I thought you thanks.

The more I look at the score the more beautiful & special it becomes. And though I still have grave reservations about the libretto (which led you into unavoidable dangers) I find that it has a great theatrical value after all, due largely to the marvelous tonal world created by the music. It has its own *ambiente*, & its own authentic "world", as every work should: & that is the important thing, hoe-downs to the contrary. It's always the work of a master, no denying. So thank you, dear Aa, very much.

Work here on the island goes in five directions, & I hope gets somewhere. Anyway the island is a dream.

Did you know that David D[iamond] is arriving soon?

Are you coming this way, & if so can we have lobsters-in-the-basket all together like a déjà-vu? This whole summer is a kind of déjà-vu, what with *Candide* & Lillian & the same house, – nothing changed. Have fun at T'wood. Best to Jack.

Love,

Lenny

Guess who else is arriving – tomorrow, I think –? Charlie Roth, that gangster maniac. Prends garde. Sauve qui peut.

L

368. Richard Rodgers[32] to Leonard Bernstein
488 Madison Avenue, New York, NY
9 October 1956

Dear Leonard,

We were committed many weeks ago to see Judy Garland this past Sunday night and there was no way to cancel it. However, I have had reports from innumerable people about your performance and the infinitely kind things you had to say about Oscar and me.[33] I am writing to Paul Feigay to see if I can

---

[32] Richard Rodgers (1902–79), American composer, best known for his collaborations with Lorenz Hart and Oscar Hammerstein. These creative partnerships resulted in more than thirty Broadway musicals, including several established classics of the American musical theatre.
[33] The episode of *Omnibus* referred to by Rodgers is "The American Musical Comedy," first broadcast on 7 October 1956.

get a kinescope of the broadcast. I can't tell you what it means to us to have your friendship and enthusiasm.

All fondest to Felicia and you.

As ever,

Dick

369. Leonore Goldstein to Leonard Bernstein
4615 Lindell Boulevard, St. Louis, MO
17 October 1956

Dear Leonard,

I cannot begin to tell you what a glow of pleasure and satisfaction came over me as I read a notice in last evening's *Post Dispatch* over your appointment to the conductorship of the Philharmonic – an avalanche of thoughts came to mind. First, your and Felicia's joy at the great reward for your fine work, Miss Coates' pride that "her boy" had been so honored and also the happiness of your dear parents. Do you realize that you are the very first American to have reached this exalted position, and at such a young age! I am as excited as though you were of my own kith and kin. How I wish myself in Carnegie Hall when you walk on the stage this winter for your first concert as guest, and as the real boss for the next season. What music you will make with that magnificent organization.

Our first concert will be given this week. Harry Farbman[34] will conduct before a group of guests are to appear and then Golschmann[35] remains for 10 weeks until the close of the season.

I have also noted that *Candide* will soon be produced and I am sure that will be another feather in your cap – if it can hold any more.

I must stop – your minutes are scarce but be assured that I share your great honor and congratulate you warmly.

Affectionately,

Leonore III

370. Solomon Braslavsky to Leonard Bernstein
Temple Mishkan Tefila, Boston, MA
18 October 1956

My dear Lenny,

Yesterday I read the good news about your appointment as co-conductor of the New York Philharmonic Orchestra for the next season.

---

[34] Harry Farbman was Associate Conductor of the St Louis Symphony Orchestra.
[35] Vladimir Golschmann was the orchestra's Music Director.

So, you finally made it. Naturally, this is only the beginning. But I am mighty proud of you and everything that happened for two reasons.

First, my prophecy became reality. I always predicted to you, your father and to all of our mutual friends that you will land a big position as conductor. It is true, you are a great composer and you rank high among American composers. But few, if any, of the great composers, past and present, are good conductors, not to speak of great conductors [...] (I remember Arnold Schoenberg conducting Beethoven's 9th Symphony. It was pitiful indeed). *But you are* and you will remain a great composer, but above all you will make history as a great conductor.

The second reason is that you reached your goal by your *own* merits (no string[s], no politics) and with your *own name*. It is neither BERNini, nor STEINkovsky. It is what you always were, what you are and what you always will be.

Congratulations and best wishes for great success. May the Lord bless and keep you in good health and happiness.

With kindest regards to Felicia and the two little geniuses, I hope,
Cordially yours,
Solomon

371. Lukas Foss to Leonard Bernstein
University of California, Los Angeles, CA
25 November 1956

Dear Lenny,

Mailed to you today a full score of my *Psalms*.[36]

This is one time I am really curious to hear what it'll sound like – never had so many instrumental–texture–ideas before. Will you have a chance to glance at it? I wish *Candide* luck and all your other projects – have not yet congratulated you about the N.Y. Philharmonic directorship. My feeling there was mostly "congratulating the Philharmonic".

If N.Y. is going to be that exciting musically we better leave our sunny West and come back.

We will be in N.Y. actually from Jan 14th to February 5th. See you then I hope. Love to Felicia.

Lukas

---

[36] Foss' *Psalms* (for chorus and orchestra) were first performed in May 1957 at the New York Philharmonic in a concert conducted by Dimitri Mitropoulos that also included Kodály's *Psalmus Hungaricus*, Walton's *Belshazzar's Feast*, and the premiere of Nils Viggo Bentzon's *Variazioni brevi*.

372. Stephen Sondheim[37] to Leonard Bernstein

11 East 80th Street, New York, NY

Friday [1956]

Dear Lunnit (sp.?),

You have the distinct privilege of being the first person in these Continental United States to receive correspondence typed on my new and not completely paid-for IBM Electric Typewriter. How about these margins?

Apart from showing off this latest acquisition, I do want to reiterate how much I like the *Candide* music. And, though I was hesitant to say so last evening, I also want to reiterate the offer I made earlier this year – if at any time you want help on the lyrics (or even the music) you need only ask.[38]

See you soon.

Love,

Steve

373. Gunther Schuller[39] to Leonard Bernstein

14 January 1957

Dear Lennie,

Congratulations on your stunning exploration of the why's and wherefore's of modern music on *Omnibus* last Sunday. You are – it goes without

---

[37] Stephen Sondheim (b. 1930), American composer and lyricist. He first met Bernstein in October 1955: according to Bernstein's datebook, Laurents and Sondheim had their first meeting with him on 18 October. Sondheim adds some interesting details: he heard about *West Side Story* from Arthur Laurents at the opening-night party for Ugo Betti's *Isle of Goats* on 4 October, and played for Bernstein the following day, on 5 October: "I auditioned for him without Arthur, and it was the day after the *Isle of Goats* opening. Remember, Lenny and Arthur had to wait for a week till Betty and Adolph knew whether they could get out of *Winter Wonderland* (I think that was the title). I was put on hold for that week, which is when I went to consult Oscar [Hammerstein]. My first official meeting after accepting the job was with Arthur alone, the next with both of them" (Sondheim, personal communication). Bernstein and Sondheim had more than forty meetings between November 1955 and February 1956, and by the time Sondheim celebrated his 26th birthday on 22 March 1956, the score of Act I was starting to take shape – with *Romeo* still as the working title.

[38] Seventeen years later, Sondheim provided more than just help: for the 1973 revival of *Candide*, he wrote several new lyrics including "Life is Happiness Indeed" (a replacement for Bernstein and Parker's "The Venice Gavotte"), "This World," "The Sheep Song," and half of "Auto Da Fe."

[39] Gunther Schuller (b. 1925), American composer, conductor, writer on music, and jazz historian. Two works by Schuller were performed by Mitropoulos in the 1956–7 New York Philharmonic season, and his father Arthur Schuller was a violinist in the orchestra for more than forty years. Bernstein relished the kind of discussion prompted by this letter, and Schuller's enthusiasm may well have encouraged him to program Webern's music. In January 1958, Bernstein included Webern's *Six Pieces* Op. 6 in his Philharmonic concerts, and in December 1965 he conducted Webern's Symphony on the same program as Mahler's Seventh. In 1964 Schuller and Bernstein collaborated on Schuller's *Journey Into Jazz*, composed specially for the *Young People's Concerts*, where it was conducted by the composer and narrated by Bernstein. The following is part of

saying – uniquely qualified for the task. I am very confident that you made many converts with your lucid and detailed explanations which, although of necessity assumed that the viewer knew very little of the composer's vocabulary and method, nevertheless at no point talked down to the audience. How few composers would be able to do this with your naturalness, conciseness and virtuosity!

Having said that much, however, I also felt moved to point out a serious flaw in your delineation, namely an unfortunate intrusion – conscious or subconscious, it is hard to say – of your own personal viewpoint of the subject in the latter half of the program.

After a very *factual* exploration of how atonality developed logically from chromaticism, you allowed your own *qualitative* feelings about Wagnerian heaviness and/or excessive emotionalism creep in to such an extent that it became quite apparent what "camp" you were in. This is all the more a shame since the actual statements you made (juxtaposing the new objectivity of Satie and Hindemith with post-Wagnerian romanticism and expressionism) were mostly valid statements per se – in cold print they would appear quite sound – but the slightly sarcastic coloring & inflection you gave these thoughts made it too obvious which way you wanted the listener to be swayed. In other words, you seemed to momentarily abandon at the crucial point the very "objectivity and clarity" you mentioned so often.

Giving the picture this slant was a little unfair. The further we get into the middle of our century the more objectively we see some of the highly controversial and heated arguments of earlier decades (you indicated this yourself when you said it seems that the two camps were coming closer together, that a kind of synthesis may be in the making). It has thus also become clear that Debussyan chromaticism, which you had in the anti-Wagner camp, is a lot closer to late Wagner than anybody including Debussy was for a long time willing to admit, and that the important works of the Impressionists were to an until recently greatly underestimated extent responsible for not only the

---

Bernstein's spoken introduction to the performance: "These days [...] there is a new movement in American music actually called the 'third stream' which mixes the rivers of jazz with the other rivers that flow down from the high-brow far-out mountain peaks of twelve-tone, or atonal music. Now the leading navigator of this third stream – in fact the man who made up the phrase – is a young man named Gunther Schuller. He is one of those total musicians, like Paul Hindemith [...] only he's American. Mr. Schuller writes music – all kinds of music – conducts it, lectures on it, and plays it. Certainly he owes some of his great talent to his father, a wonderful musician who happens to play in our orchestra. We are very proud of Arthur Schuller. But young Gunther Schuller – still in his thirties – is now the center of a whole group of young composers who look to him as their leader, and champion. And so I thought that the perfect way to begin today's program about jazz in the concert hall would be to play a piece by Gunther Schuller – especially this one particular piece which is an introduction to jazz for young people."

break-through to atonality but the instrumental sound and coloring of early Schönberg and almost all of Webern.

There is not such a big jump, after all, from Debussy's *Jeux* or parts of *Pelléas* to *Parsifal* in one direction, and to *Erwartung* or *Pierrot lunaire* in the other direction, as was first thought to be the case. Is the mysticism of *Pelléas*, the lushness of the *Firebird* really so much closer to the "objectivity & clarity" of Satie than the expressionism of *Pierrot*?

The role of Debussy in this whole development has only lately been correctly assessed. His own explorations into – or *almost* into – the regions of atonality, his experiments with rhythmic counterpoint and irregular rhythms, and above all his concept of the break-up of textures and lines have been only belatedly evaluated, and their important influence on Webern is still all but unappreciated.

That brings me to the subject of Webern. Since most of the young generation of European composers, certainly the important ones, are greatly under his influence (much more so than Schönberg's), omitting him in your portrait of modern music tilts the argument heavily to one side. Mind you, I appreciate the problems involved. It would be hard, on a program directed primarily at a nationwide audience of laymen, to spend time talking about a composer almost totally unknown – even as a name – in America. More than that, if you *had* decided to talk about Webern and objectively place him within the present situation, your whole original point about the "two camps" would have had to go, and from a viewer's or layman's point of view your picture of 2 opposing factions is a much more attractive one. Yet should that have been allowed to govern your decisions? Obviously for the sake of fairness and objectivity, you should have taken the chance of beclouding the issue a little – of making the situation less black & white.

The point about Webern, of course, is that he *was* able to cut his ties with romanticism much more thoroughly than Schönberg or Berg. Schönberg's whole unsuccessful struggle to pour atonal expressionistic ideas into classical forms was avoided from the start by Webern. The "objectivity, clarity & simplicity" which Schönberg couldn't attain (and which you saw only in the music of the other camp) is certainly Webern's most important contribution to contemporary music. What – except neo-classic Stravinsky – could be less verbose, less heavy, less square, less involved with these and any other Wagnerian attributes you care to name than Webern? The trouble is that at this short range we still blame the relative weaknesses & discrepancies of Schönberg's art on the 12-tone system, or on the Wagner-influence, or on Mahler etc., etc. – rather than on Schönberg himself. I am convinced that Schönberg's music, *if* it is "neurotic", "lacking in humor", "subjective" or what have you (and all these points are debatable), it is so because Schönberg's *personality* – and not the 12-tone system or atonality per se – was such as to cause this. He would have written (and did write) the same under another system. What different and opposite musical concepts & styles are possible within atonality or 12-tone is becoming increasingly obvious. By this serious omission, therefore, you failed to present a complete picture of the 12-tone side, and thus slanted the argument considerably in one direction.

In this connection you may be interested in the following account by a composer friend of mine (Boulez) of an evening in Paris 3 or 4 years ago. It was told as proof of the genuineness of Stravinsky's conversion to the serial technique. Stravinsky was in the company of a group of young composers (incl. Boulez, Nono, Stockhausen, etc.) and one old school-chum of the master. They were discussing problems in contemporary music, drinking quite a bit; and Stravinsky, as you know, when he does drink gets very sad & nostalgic. At one point he turned to his old friend and, almost in tears, said (not verbatim, but in effect): "You know, of all of us (meaning himself, Schönberg, Bartók, Hindemith etc.), the only one who went in the right direction was Webern. I've been composing wrong all my life". A pathetic & touching story. It is hard to say whether Stravinsky actually meant *all* of that, but his continuing adoption of 12-tone thinking à la Webern (not Schönberg!!) would seem to indicate that he meant it to be quite an extent, and if he did, what does this do to your "two camps"?

I write you with all this because I like to discuss subjects close to my heart with people I respect & admire. I need not emphasize that I appreciate & admire your absolutely unique combination of abilities. So it is not in the sense of hostile criticism that I write you this letter, but rather in a spirit of friendly discussion.

With best wishes,
Sincerely yours,
Gunther Schuller

P.S. Have a piece about jazz in the Jan 12th issue of *Sat. Review of Literature*. I think it might interest you.

374. Aldous Huxley[40] to Leonard Bernstein
3276 Deronda Drive, Los Angeles, CA
4 April 1957

Dear Mr. Bernstein,

As a very busy man with a large correspondence, I can well understand your annoyance at receiving yet another letter from a perfect stranger. But, at the risk

---

[40] Aldous Huxley (1894–1963), British author of *Point Counter Point* and *Brave New World* who settled in the United States in 1937. One of Huxley's warmest and most enduring friendships in Los Angeles was with Stravinsky.

of being a bore, I am writing to ask if you would be at all interested in reading a dramatic version of my novel *Brave New World*, which I have recently made, with a view to a musical setting. (I envisage the piece as a play with music and dancing, rather than a conventional "musical".) The story calls for a very resourceful composer, who can run the gamut from the primitive dances of the Indian Reservation to the music of the hypothetical future. So I naturally thought of you[41] and am hopefully writing this on the off chance that you may have the time and the inclination to consider such a project.

Yours sincerely,
Aldous Huxley

375. Felicia Bernstein to Leonard Bernstein

[Santiago, Chile]
"Thurs. and Fri." [10–11 July 1957]

Dearest darling Lennuhtt,

It's all most peculiar, wonderful, strange and yet most familiar. There has been a constant stream of friends – about *twenty* at the airport last night – and all day today – exhausting but so heart-warming and nice. I never realized I was loved that much, or that my coming would be such an event – I'm truly overwhelmed by it all! The children are a smash – Jamie has taken over the Alessandri household already – what a delight it is to see all those children together! I'm so sorry that you can't see it too – the squealing, the giggling, the mixture of languages and in the midst of it all Jamie is the queen, the glamorous beautiful imperious pixie and they are at her feet ready for her slightest whim. Alexander spent the afternoon there and the way he and Jamie flung into each other's arms was one of those rare and beautiful moments – they really adore one another.

The trip was a *nightmare*! The Miami bit in spades – it was about 100 degrees, no sign of anybody from the Chilean airline, nobody knew where it was and when we finally found it they didn't know when the plane was leaving – we spent five hours in that fucking airport. The only air-conditioned place was the restaurant where we went twice but couldn't linger because the children got so restless. Anyway we finally were called in and found that part of the seating space was taken up with cargo! The flight itself wasn't bad except between Panama and the next stop we ran into a terrific storm and poor Jamie got sick. [. . .] They both were marvelous though, never cried and were perfect lambs. Alexander once in a while would cry out "vamos a la calle" out of sheer desperation! It's just *too long* – absolutely the end of the world – plus they made more

---

[41] He had already proposed the idea to Stravinsky who rejected it, as did Bernstein. See Joseph 2001, p. 31.

stops than were bargained for so we arrived bedraggled, weary and worn at *midnight* – imagine!!

I think of you constantly and love you more than ever – Jamie talks about you all the time and said yesterday that she must write because poor Daddy was all alone. She looked out the window in the plane and said she saw a map below. [...]

Chita's house is small but adorable with divine food which I've been gobbling up. Yesterday I had a full two course lunch then tea with all the trimmings and then went to Madeleine's for dinner at ten and gorged – it must be something in the air – it's nippy, but clear and sunny.

Following night. Thank you for your darling cable which I got this morning. As you can see there's no chance of writing in the daytime – I took the children to Mamita this morning and they went crazy with the chickens, ducks, rabbits, turkeys, a dog and oranges which they plucked from the trees and ate on the spot. She is the darling of all time – so full of love and goodness, thrilled by the children, supplies them with fresh eggs every day and things that she grows – and she's getting old and sick and it breaks my heart.

About the "girls" I'll tell you in my next – they're marvelous. Madeleine especially has taken a great turn for the better – details later cause I'll never finish.

My darling do write – don't work too hard – tell me how everything is going with the show – if Grace is taking care of you.

As for me I'm bewildered and miss you so that it hurts. I think it's the incredibly depressing distance between us.

I do love you.

Felicia

My love to Helen and the Kats.

376. Leonard Bernstein to Felicia Bernstein
19 July 1957

Darling,

The main news is that I love you and miss you, more than I could ever have known. It's all very well to talk about the salutary effects of periodic separations, and all that; but it's lonely in that big apartment upstairs, and everything looks different without my *people* there. Booze-hour isn't the same with anyone else, sleeping is particularly strange in one of two beds with the other unoccupied. I've managed not to eat alone once so far: that's no problem. But it's different, that's all. In fact, as I've discovered, it's the main difference there can be in living.

But there's little if any time to think about any of the above. The work grinds on, relentlessly, and sleep is a rare blessing. Jerry continues to be – well, Jerry: moody, demanding, hurting. But vastly talented. We start on the book Monday, trepidation in hand; and the score is still not completed. At the moment the Problem is the usual one of the 2nd act ballet, which is finished, and will probably not work at all and be yanked and we'll have to manufacture a new one. It's going to be murder from here on in. My nights are all spent on work, so no fun at all. The only relief is dinner. Once at Ofra's (all goes swimmingly, and Shirley is still in the dark) – once with Lukas [Foss] (who missed you by a day, sends you great love, and was intuitive enough to ask Burtie "Are you in love? You seem dreamy and different.") and once with Steve [Sondheim] and once with Debbie and once with George Schütz and once with [Kenneth] Shermerhorn, etc. etc. And once at the Ricordis. Last weekend was all work. No Stony Point. Maybe this weekend.

Last night was Martha [Gellhorn] night. She finally made it: and we talked in our customary natter for hours. How she loves you and knows you! And how she knows and loves our love (yours and mine). She finds my life ridiculous, of course, but finds me in better shape than ever, all of which she attributes to you, and rightly of course. I was telling her what a marvelous girl you are, how beautiful and bright and witty and wise, and she said: "But how did it take you so long to find out what is perfectly obvious?" Well, I always knew it; I didn't have to find it out; I just suddenly became *aware* of it, found myself able to experience it and share it, and just be plain grateful for it. I'm endlessly lucky in you, and lucky that you've been strong enough to stick out the bad times. You wonderful girl, you, with whom I am recently in love all over again.

I must run: Big Daddy calls. Big hugs & kisses for my two angels – and love to all the family. Write more & lots! You have time, I haven't! Have a glorious time – I kiss you.

L

19 July

Today is Helen's birthday. Do cable her. Grace quit – I have a fine new maid. Greetings to Rosalia & Julia.

377. Leonard Bernstein to Felicia Bernstein
26 July 1957

My darling,

I loved your letter (I guess we've established the usual pattern of crossing letters so that nothing ever gets properly answered) – but it's wonderful just to hear from you – except to hear that you're sick – what a bore. I was afraid that abrupt change in climate might do something like that. And of course it was also only natural that the usual reaction to Chita would set in – too much of a good thing. But you're used to that: don't let it get you down.

I can imagine what a trial it is to be in a place where everything is at a premium – like the old days in Israel – & where medicine is backwuhts and the trunks don't arrive – very Israeli, all that. Don't you dare stop smoking – you're absolutely right!

A propos Israel: I sent a long nagging cable about *Jeanne* [*d'Arc au bûcher*] & just had a letter this morning saying that it's absolutely impossible to get a chorus to prepare it. I'm furious but helpless. There just isn't a chorus that operates in the summer, & they claim they'd need 8 months to learn it, etc. etc. Shit.

So that's out, my darling; but don't let it discourage you from coming to Is. anyway.

Still no word from Buenos Aires!

Milton Goldman has been calling about a part for you in a play version of *Diabolique*. Interested? And Tony Mines called for you today. Gave him your address.

The show – ah, yes. I am depressed with it. All the aspects of the score I like best – the "big", poetic parts – get criticized as "operatic" – & there's a concerted move to chuck them. What's the use? The 24-hour schedule goes on – I am tired & nervous & apey. You wouldn't like me at all these days. *This is the last show I do.* The Philharmonic approved the contract yesterday & all is set. I'm going to be a conductor, after all!

No news on the Burtie–Ofra–Shirley front,

Weather: good – coolish, fair. I don't get to see it much; & my air-conditioned studio saves my life.

Darling I love you & miss you –

L

Dined with Marc last night – sends fondest love.

378. Leonard Bernstein to Felicia Bernstein
Sun a.m. [28 July 1957]

Darling,

Guess where I am – on a plane. Guess my destination – Miami. And as always with any flight involving Miami (as you know too well) there's shit to spare. I was to have left last night: arrived breathless at Idlewild to be told that the flight had been cancelled – only nobody had taken the trouble to inform me of same. No other flights available, except one that would have landed me in Miami at 5 a.m. or so. So back to the Osborne, heckle & peckle, & dinner with Burt, Ofrah, & back to Idlewild this monankûdü, & here I am. Now, to be consistent, there should be nobody to meet me at the airport, the convention is over, forced landing at Palm Beach, or something worthy of the tradition.

Oh, I didn't tell you why I'm going. Columbia Records is having its annual convention, imagine, & it will be fun & games at the Americana Hotel (this year's hotel). I dread it. Home tomorrow, in time (I hope, barring airport Miamisms) for a *run-thru* of Act One! Imagine – already! Where does the time all go to? In a minute it will be August & off to Washington – & people will be looking at *West Side Story* in public, & hearing my poor little mashed-up score. All the things I love most in it are slowly being dropped – too operatic, too this & that. They're all so scared & commercial success means so much to them. To me too, I suppose – but I still insist it can be achieved with pride. I shall keep fighting.

I miss you all terribly – especially you who have come to mean something miraculous to me. You reside at the very core of my life, my darling. I hope your kepepelt [cold] is better, & that the fun goes on. Ofrah bets you won't stick out the two months. She's probably right. But if you come home, what would you find? I'd be no good to you – & you'd hang around the show & get sick of it, & my whining, etc. etc. And then, if I have to go to B[uenos] A[ires] after all – what's the fun without you there? Anyway, don't make any rash decisions yet.

There's Palm Beach down there, looking hot, damp and sunless. We'll be landing soon – & I'll probably drop you a line on Americana stationery, which I am sure is pure gold-leaf.

Bless you my love.

L

Abrazos to all.

Dere Jamie and Alejito:

I love you so mucho!

Dady

379. Leonard Bernstein to Felicia Bernstein

Sat. night, 3 August 1957

Darling,

Two big events:

1) I've gotten out of Buenos Aires! The agent, one Uhlfelder, was here in town, & came to see me, & it's settled, & wow, what a relief. So you can return in peace, & I can see my two angels before Israel – & we can leave from here, after seeing the opening on the 26th, *like a Mensch*. Look: we go to the opening, & then we wait up for the papers, & before you know it it's time for the plane, and Scheu, we're off.

2) I signed the Philharmonic contract. Big moment. Bruno [Zirato] arrived at 10:30 a.m., contract in one hand & a big chilled bottle of Brut in the other, & much emotion (he couldn't write his name for the shaking of his hands) & I'm in – like for life. I made a coup: the lawyers had fallen out so far that the contract was up to 20-odd pages, & growing: & the disputes were growing correspondingly. So I scotched it by tearing up the whole thing, & writing a one-page letter that said I was engaged for such a period for so much money, sincerely

yours. They loved it. Simple, & trusting. We'll settle the details as they come along.

Other events – nothing but the show. We ran through today for the first time, & the problems are many, varied, overwhelming, but we've got a show there, & just possibly a great one. Jerry is behaving (in his own way) & Arthur is doing well. But the work is endless: I never sleep. Everything gets rewritten every day: & that's my life at the moment. And imagine, we open two weeks from Monday.

Some beautiful shots of you & the kids arrived (taken by the hi-fi man at the vineyard – remember) – & they melted me. I miss you so!

I loved your last letter. Did you get mine from Miami?

I hope the trunks are there, & all is in order. My love, & have fun, dear lovely one.

L

380. Igor Markevitch[42] to Leonard Bernstein
L'Aiglerie, Villars-sur-Ollon, Switzerland
3 August 1957

My dearest Lennie,

First of all I want to tell you how delighted I am at the project of *Icare*.[43] I have carefully looked at the dates, and if nothing unexpected happens until then, I will be able to come from Montreal two days before the concert[44] in order to follow the last rehearsals, as you had asked me to do.

This revival is going to be a great event for us. To help you prepare it, I am sending you by the same mail a record which was made during one of my executions. Unfortunately there are whole passages where certain instruments are completely lost, but as one says elegantly: "It is better than a spit in the eye."

Here is a letter that Bartók wrote concerning *Icare* which I am sending you in French:

Cher M. Markevitch, Permettez à un collègue qui n'a pas l'honneur de vous être connu, de vous remercier de votre merveilleux *Icare*. J'ai nécessité du temps pour étudier et comprendre toute la beauté de votre partition, et je pense qu'il faudra beaucoup d'années pour qu'on l'apprecie. Je veux vous dire

---

[42] Igor Markevitch (1912–83), Ukrainian-born conductor and composer.
[43] *Icare* was originally conceived as a ballet for Serge Lifar in 1932, but it was not staged and Markevitch subsequently reworked it as a concert piece.
[44] Bernstein conducted *Icare* with the New York Philharmonic on 10, 11, 12, and 13 April 1958. The performance from 13 April has been released on CD in *Bernstein Live* (New York Philharmonic NYP 2003).

ma conviction, qu'un jour on rendra justice avec sérieux à tout ce que vous apportez. Vous êtes la personnalité la plus frappante de la musique contemporaine, et je me réjouis, Monsieur, de profiter de votre influence. Avec ma respectueuse admiration, Béla Bartók.

The letter is from the autumn 1933, and had neither date nor address, reason for which I didn't answer it. I add, as I already told you, that I didn't know yet the name of Bartók. I would be very pleased if you would send me a word to let me know when you receive the record.

I wish you every possible luck for your new show, my dear Lennie, and I also remind you to keep the promise you made me, to kiss the whole of Israel for me. In the meantime it is Topazia and me who do it with you sending you our most affectionate thoughts.

Yours,

Igor

381. Leonard Bernstein to Felicia Bernstein
"8 Aug already!" [1957]

Darling,

I had a real scare with the news of Asian flu – & when your letter came about how you were all down with it I got scareder. But your cable made me feel better – please be careful! I can't bear the thought of you all sick.

I missed you terribly yesterday. We wrote a new song for Tony that's a killer, & it just wasn't the same not playing it first for you. It's really going to save his character – a driving 2/4 in the great tradition (but of course fucked up by me with 3/4s and what not) – but it gives Tony balls – so that he doesn't emerge as just a euphoric dreamer.

These days have flown so – I don't sleep much; I work every – literally every – second (since I'm doing four jobs on this show – composing, lyric writing, orchestrating, & rehearsing the cast). It's murder, but I'm excited. It may be something extraordinary. We're having our first run thru for *people* on Friday. Please may they dig it! And fíjate, I leave for Washington on Tues. the 13th – so soon, so soon. It's all rushed by like a cyclone.

Of course we're way behind on orchestration etc. – but that's the usual hassle.

How are you? You don't say. Are you fatter from eating? (Me: I'm a bit skinnier.) Do you smoke? (I do, lots.) Have you skied? (I haven't). Do you love me?

Bless you & *be well.*

Love,

L

I adored Jamie's letter, especially the lentils.

382. Felicia Bernstein to Leonard Bernstein

[Santiago, Chile]
"Tues. & Wed." [August 1957]

My own blessed wonderful darling,

I refuse to write about "latas"[45] so I'll skip the whole miserable bit and only tell you that we're on the mend. Jamie has been up for two days and is fine again and Rosalia got up today.

Too incredible! Just got your cable this minute. I suppose there must have been something in the papers about this monstrous epidemic – thank God it wasn't anything worse, just la grippe but in spades. I now read in the paper that it has spread all over the world and that even you may get it – if there is a vaccine handy take it!

I bless the day you couldn't come – I went to Klecky's [i.e. Paul Kletzki's] concert last week and oh Lennuhtt! What a shampepuhls . . . Granted a lot of the musicians were sick, but still! Klecky made "Un grand scandal" – stopped the orchestra in the middle of Beethoven's Fourth and screamed, ranted and then apologized to the audience and started again. We later had dinner at the house of a Canta Maya[46] type lady with the upper echelons of Chilean music, Vincente Salas Via, Juan Orrego etc. and he let them have it! I wanted to crawl under the groaning böwewehd – it was ghastly and embarrassing, said he didn't want to finish out his contract etc, etc. But he's right – like everything else in this insane place it is a hit or miss affair (mostly miss), no musicianship or love of music, no discipline (since they can't be fired) and a devil take it attitude which is hardly conducive to good music. So, with a heavy heart I must say don't did it!

That Catholic priest you made friends with in Washington called Father Woolen is here – we met this afternoon and a charming fellow he is. He adores you and talks about you with enormous respect and enthusiasm. He's been all over South America giving concerts of all sorts – organ recitals, chamber music, piano concertos with different orchestras. Madeleine is in charge of him here (part of her job) and is giving him a small dinner party tomorrow.

Last night I had dinner at an old friend's very old rich family – ancient Milan type mausoleum house – much marble, Aubussons, great food, old retainers and in the midst of all this, a passion for jazz! He's an authority, has a fabulous collection of old and recent records among them your *Omnibus* which he says is

---

[45] A Spanish colloquialism for "annoying things".
[46] Probably a reference to the actress Canta Maya, who appeared in the 1946 film *Bailando en las nubes* (*Dancing in the Clouds*).

the greatest thing to come into his life since the birth of his son – we listened to it in religious silence, eight of us, and it is really so *wonderful*. You can't imagine what hearing your voice did to me – so much of your personality and warmth comes through it and then the clarity of your mind and your articulateness. I was so proud of mine Lennuhtt!

Alexander woke up in the middle of the night and carried on a long telephone conversation with you – he's managed to avoid the flu but has a cold and a cough and can't go out. Jamie is up and about and looks beautiful but is also coughing as is everybody else. Honestly what shit luck. We haven't been able to do a thing or go anywhere – oh well!

I adore your letters and literally live from one to the next – please don't stop or I perish.

Mï laü dü

Tia

Fely

383. Leonard Bernstein to Felicia Bernstein
[New York, NY]
11 August 1957

Dearest Fely,

It's 4:00 a.m. & I've just finished another of those incredible nights (which begin in the early morning) – work & work & work. I'm so sleepless by now I'm punchy. And I'm beginning to miss you *seriously*. And I feel a little bit uncomfortable about you all in that place with no milk and the economy of post-war Germany, & medieval plagues rampant. And then – you POÖAH – the Valparaiso episode, which I just heard about, an accident, yet, and no trunks, & – God, what are you clothing yourselves with? What are you eating? What a ghastly way to have a restful summer! Why not just chuck it all, as soon as you're all well again, and come home? I'm sure the trunks will be here by Xmas. Why feel you *must* stick it out just by way of meeting a challenge, a whatever? You've had a good sound month of what sounds like sheer penance. Basta!

Burtie and Ofra are weeking it up in Stony Point, & Shirley weekends with them and *still knows nothing*! Incredible. We had our run-through for People yesterday, & it was a smash. But I'm worried: there is so much that doesn't work – for me – & I'm sure for [Walter] Kerr & others. But there's a great show there. Darling, think seriously about coming home. I love you & miss you.

L

384. Burton Bernstein to Felicia Bernstein

[early August 1957]

Dearest Feloo,

By far, your last letter was the grimmest single document I've perused since the publication of the famous Abe Miller letters.[47] Even the Abe Miller letters failed in many respects to equal the bathos and pain – nay, the utter desperation – of yours. Needless to say, you have my pity, sympathy and concern; in fact you have everyone's. Now, obviously, all that's left to do is come home, and quickly – even if your trunks haven't arrived in Valparaiso yet. Sergeant, you have done your duty – now get the hell out of there . . . and come back to New York in time for the annual Influenza Festival which is about to begin here any day now. (Chuck [Solomon] claims to have a new vaccine ready in three weeks time.) Really, do what Lennuhtt says and come home. The Chile country is "basheert" by you – I've never heard such a tale of woe. I hope everyone is better by now. Has Alejito gotten it yet?

The news from here is, to say the least, markedly better than your dispatches. Firstnik, *West Side Story* is going to be a large hit and lives up to our highest expectations. Steve even went as far as to say, "It's so good even Felicia will like it." The run-through I saw was before an ideal audience of theatre folk, so one shouldn't really gauge it by audience reaction – but still, it was quite exciting. The strange thing (something I've never experienced before) is that B. Lennuhtt comes off as second best: the show actually is a monster ballet (a jot repetitious in spots) where no one is actually directed but choreographed instead. It's too much of a good thing, if you know what I mean (you know what I mean?). There's so much balletics going on on stage that the music is shunted into second place by the sheer physical force of arms, legs and torsos. But on the whole (and you know how I hate to say this about a run-through from past experience) the show is in frighteningly good condition and looks like a sure thing. I hope that by the time I see it with sets and costumes and everything in Washington next week Jerry will have been convinced that there's too much ballet for the show's own good – or am I being naïve? Anyway, there's very little to fix outside of Lennuhtt's nose . . . So come home already.

[. . .]

---

[47] Abe Miller, born Abraham Malamud, was Sam Bernstein's cousin and he was eventually employed by the Samuel Bernstein Hair Company. Miller and Sam Bernstein "had corresponded over the years, Sam convincing [Abe] that his future lay in the New World" (Burton Bernstein 1982, p. 62). In 1921 he escaped from Korets (Ukraine) via Warsaw, Danzig, and Cuba (where he survived for a year hawking his wares from a wooden box), before eventually arriving in the United States.

The *New Yorker*'s still fun and I got a raise, or did I write you that already? I've really been accepted there as a permanent fixture; the senior editors talk to me in terms of five or ten years from now. Good luck.

I've been doing a lot of flying and I'm well on my way towards getting my private license back. Just a question of time.

So come home. Get well. Abrazos for all.

Mu lau du,

BB

385. Felicia Bernstein to Leonard Bernstein
[Santiago, Chile]
"Monday" [12 August 1957]

My darling,

Tomorrow you're in Washington – with my meager and distorted sense of our capital I see you all rehearsing in a gleaming white Grecian temple with marble steps to spare just across the street from the White House – what I'd give to be there with you, misery and all! After all somebody has to cart in the sandwiches or would I be homing in on weepy Sylvia's domain? By the time this reaches you the sets will be up – with the accompanying gestures. Oliver [Smith] and Jerry [Robbins] won't be speaking. Irene [Sharaff] will arrive (avec la petite Japonaise) and you will keep calling her Gloria. The dancers will find they can't move in their costumes etc. etc. – from way down here it sounds like sheer heaven. But you must be so tired! Who's helping with the orchestration – and why do you always have to do everything yourself? Are you living on dexamils[48] – what else?!

Tony's new song sounds delicious – but can he sing it? I thought you were going to change the name – have you made any cast changes? Someone sent me the pictures of the Sunday Times – it all looks so exciting! Oh Lennuhtt – maybe maybe – I don't dare hope. What theatre, what hotel – nobody tells me these things!

Jamie calls me Tia Fely – what can you do? She is going to an English kindergarten [...] in the mornings. She has an incredible capacity for enjoying herself – at least one member of this safari is having a whale of a good time! As for "muh" I am bored senseless – my friends are all sick in bed, it's been raining and cold, no activities are possible and I ain't got nothing to read! Faut[e] de mieux I'm reading *Mario the Magician* and *Death in Venice*. I miss the *New Yorker* – I read *Time* mag. avidly from cover to cover, even the financial section!

---

[48] Dexamyl was a drug introduced in 1950. It contained amphetamine to elevate mood, and barbiturate to counteract the side effects of the amphetamine.

Your Father Woolen turned out to be a *pest* – plus there's something about a priest who is so unpriestlike which is rather off-putting.

Had a rather Mexican-type afternoon – a dear old maid of ours who lives with Mamita was like everyone else sick with the flu but it developed into pneumonia and there wasn't a hospital bed to be had or an ambulance free in all the city! We finally got a hospital to put in an extra cot in a large room and waited till 10 p.m. for the ambulance – she could have died and there was nothing one could do.

I was asked to give an informal talk on theatre and TV at the Catholic University but it had to be postponed because there were no pupils. I also went to a rehearsal of the Teatro Experimental and the same thing – no director, no leading lady, no nothing! Most frustrating as you can imagine – but, c'est la vie! God, I hope it is nice and warm in Israel (they've had the "Japan 305" there already). I will lie on the beach with [. . .] [Zvi] Haftel and live it up! I hear Sam isn't going – do I hear sighs of relief?

I've just taken my *first* sleepenküdü and I'm beginning to feel a deliciousness – I know that from now on there'll hardly be time for you to brush a tooth but please, please let me know how it goes.

Everyone is thinking of you.

P.S. I love you I love you I love you pshh, pshh, pshh.

386. Leonard Bernstein to Felicia Bernstein
Jefferson Hotel, Washington, D.C.
15 August 1957

Dear Beauty,

Well, look-a me. Back to the nation's capital, & right on the verge. This is Thurs. We open Mon. Everyone's coming, my dear, even [Richard] Nixon and 95 admirals.[49] Senators abounding, & big Washington-hostessy type party afterwards in Lennuhtt's honor. See what you miss by going away. Then next Sunday, which is my birthday, there is the Jewish version – a big party for me, but admission is one Israel bond. All helps the show. We have a 75 thou. advance, & the town is buzzing. Not bad. I have high hopes. I also have a new pen, as you can see, which I adore, because it writes every time, & without a ball-point.

If I sound punchy it's because I am.

Up all night trying to put together an overture of sorts, to carry us through until I do a real good prelude. Orchestra reading all day yesterday – a thrill. We have surprisingly good men, who can really play this terribly difficult stuff (except one or two of them) – the orchestrations have turned out brilliant. I tell

---

[49] *West Side Story* opened at the National Theatre in Washington D.C. on 19 August 1957.

you, this show may yet be worth all the agony. As you can see, I'm excited as hell – oh so different from *Candide.*

Now – how about my plan that you all come home?

Lou Silverstein is getting us (cast, authors, orchestra) all Asian-flu shots – black market, of course – so we won't conk out. I don't know what we do in this show for understudies (we have them – but ...) or for substitutes in the orchestra. If the guitarist gets sick, it takes a week for another to learn the part. Same for all the winds. It's a tough show.

What else is new? The show the show the show ...

I want to see my three Kats!!

Love, Daddy

387. Carol Lawrence[50] to Leonard Bernstein
Washington, D.C.
19 August 1957
[Telegram]

I'm so lucky to be me, to have the privilege of singing your music and to know you. I shall always be a most ardent fan. I thank you for letting me be Maria.

Love,
Carol

388. Felicia Bernstein to Leonard Bernstein
[Santiago, Chile]
"Tues." [20 August 1957]

Sweetness!

Oh joy oh bliss oh rapture. Your cable with the frabgeous news has just arrived – thank you! I'd been desperate for some word all day long. Congratulations to one and all – how happy, how marvelously happy you must be.[51] As for me I'm busting with pride and frustration – of all the moments to miss sharing! Last night I spent the evening looking at my watch and imagining the proceedings – Oh God! How exciting it must have been! Were you very nervous – did you sit through it or pace? Did anyone go to Washington to hold your hand? Is there still a great deal to be done apart from an Overture? Did you get my wire? I was miserable cause I didn't have your address or name of the theatre but your letter arrived in the nick.

---

[50] Carol Lawrence (b. 1932) created the role of Maria in *West Side Story*; 19 August was the date of the opening night in Washington, D.C.

[51] Felicia's letter reacting to the very enthusiastic reception of *West Side Story* in Washington, D.C., was written the day after it had opened at the National Theatre.

Why haven't we left? I sure had a good excuse. Jane Broder cabled about a *Studio One*,[52] rehearsals beginning this week and CBS called me on the telephone no less! But though sorely tempted I just couldn't do it to Chita – she looked so crushed and depressed. I simply had to wait for the sick to get well, the sun to come out and give everyone the chance to show us a good time – the epidemic was such a blow to them all and they felt so guilty and miserable. You will understand I know. Anyway things *are* better. I spent the day in the country which I'd been pining to do since I arrived. It was more beautiful even than I remembered – a glorious jewel of a day, trees blossoming in profusion, lambs grazing, a soft smell of eucalyptus in the air and for the first time I wished desperately that you could see it, because *that* is Chile – the earth, the smells, the snow-covered mountains, the country bread baked in outdoor ovens – all this I will yearn for always just as I don't care if I ever see Santiago again.

Even the orchestra managed to sound like something – the last concert was quite good. *Firebird*, no less, and a [Goffredo] Petrassi piece which I rather liked. Klecki [Kletzki] is good but that's about all I can say for him – pas très grande chose.

Then there are the parties being given and planned and we hope to get to do some skiing this weekend with the children. Their noses have stopped running and they're blooming once more. Alexander is so beautiful and naughty and funny I could eat him! Jamie has become so Chilean it's disconcerting – her Spanish is incredible, full of imagineses de repentes and Por Dioses! They are both really frightfully clever – the Alessandris think Jamie is a genius – God forbid!

Darling, I hope this reaches you for your "Jewish" birthday and that it is a delicious one. I will get you a great present (I wonder where?). In the nonce my boundless love will have to do – and many many kisses of all sorts. I do so long for you.

Tia,

F.

389. Leonard Bernstein to Felicia Bernstein
Jefferson Hotel, Washington, D.C.
23 August 1957

Darling,

It's all too exciting. I never dreamed it could be like this – reviews such as one would write for oneself – the whole town up and doing about the show – the

---

[52] *Studio One* was a long-running television drama series. Felicia appeared in eleven episodes between 1949 and 1956.

delicious long lines at the box office – morale high – dignitaries every night –
the Senate practically in toto – parties – hot newspapers – all the atmosphere of
a mid-season opening – gala-emeralds, furs – the works. Only thing missing –
you. How I longed to have you there & share the excitement! Of course, as they
say, it's only Washington, not New York – don't count chickens. But it sure looks
like a smash, & all our experiments seem to have worked. The book works, the
tragedy works, the ballets shine, the music pulses & soars, & there is at least one
history-making set. It's all too good to be true.

I've just got lunched at the White House – no más. Invited by Sherman
Adams[53] & the whole gang. Again – you should have been there! What a beautiful place – such credenzas, such breakfronts. I really felt "in". Adams & Rabb &
Gen. Snyder – all were talking of nothing but *West Side Story* – I think the whole
government is based on it. Jim Hagerty (Ike's press secretary) turns out to be a
fan of mine! It's all so crazy and unexpected. Even Adams turns out to be an
amateur musician.

Now listen! When are you coming home? I have a constant feeling you're
about to turn up any minute – but look, the time is drawing near. Only 10 days
to Labor Day and the summer's over. What I hope is that you'll be back for the
Philly opening (Monday the 9th) which is our anniversary, for Chrissake – or
even for Jamie's birthday on Sunday. Please try to manage it, huh? Why stick
around that plag[u]ey place, bored as you are, after Labor Day? Let me know
right away when you plan to return, and darling, hurry home. I can't stand not
seeing the children, and I need my girl!

I love you,

L

I'm 39 in 2 days!!

390. Cole Porter[54] to Leonard Bernstein

Los Angeles, CA
23 August 1957
[Telegram]

Dear Lenny,

I hear glowing reports about your new show.[55] All my congratulations to you
and Jerry.

---

[53] Sherman Adams (1899–1986), White House Chief of Staff for President Dwight D. Eisenhower.
[54] Cole Porter (1891–1964), American composer and lyricist. After studying at both Yale and
Harvard, Porter went to Paris where he took orchestration lessons from Charles Koechlin. On his
return to America, Porter became hugely successful on Broadway with shows such as *Anything Goes*
(1934), *Kiss Me, Kate* (1948), and *Can-Can* (1953).
[55] *West Side Story*.

Best,
Cole Porter

391. Felicia Bernstein to Leonard Bernstein
[Santiago, Chile]
"Montag" [Sunday, 25 August and Monday, 26 August 1957]

Dearest Lennuhtt,

And today is the Baroness' birthday and I'm not yet there yet! Like the idiot, fool, ridiculous ass that I am I made a special trip at 2 a.m. to send you a cable, address it to the theatre so you'd be sure to get it – forgetting completely that it is Sunday and probably the only day off you've all had for months!

Anyway, it is sure to be a happy birthday – such reviews! My God! I carry them around with me to read over again in my free moments. How has Arthur taken it all – one of the reviews gave the book to Jerry – oh my! I hear from B[urton] B[ernstein] that there's little to fix apart from your nose.

Next day – why does one ever telephone – such a frustrating five minutes! What do you mean Flora Robson?

Anyway I'm waiting to hear from Pan American – your "new found" success gave me courage and we should be off *in style* a week from tomorrow. Rosalia will follow later by Cinta. My plan is to go straight to Washington (the plane stops there anyway). The children can stay overnight so you can see them and then take a train to New York with Julia. I will have Helen send a suitcase on to Wash[ington] with summer clothes so that I won't need to go to New York at all. How's that for peanuts?

Of course, this last week I've been having a *very good* time – dinner parties galore, lunches in terraces, trips to the country and the mountains – the moment one leaves Santiago it is breathtakingly beautiful! And spring really is here, the trees are abloom, the sun is warm and it is nice – actually *very nice*. I am glad to have stayed on, it would have been too sad to leave with such a memory of misery!

Since there is *nothing* to buy, there will be an enormous lack of regalitos.[56] I've been wracking my brain and everybody else's thinking of an adequate and fun birthday present for you – as yet notensüdü! I almost got you a race-horse cause it was named after me – but then, we lost Alfred Vanderbilt who could have kept it for you. Then, of course, there are copper mines, cattle farms, vineyards etc. and that's no[t] any good.

---

[56] Spanish for "gifts" or "treats".

Darling, next time you hear from me t'will be in my own Flora Robson tones. I'll wire arrival time etc. Please remember *not* to mention my hair which no doubt will look "desperate" after the trip! At the moment Zorina[57] would die of envy, it is so silky and *straight*. I do look awfully well and my *beauty* is toasted to in the chicest circles, my dear!

Listen, please love me still when I get back. I may not be such a raving beauty there but I love *you*.

F

392. Felicia Bernstein to Helen Coates
[Santiago, Chile]
"Tuesday" [27 August 1957]

Dearest Helen,

Bless you for sending me the Washington reviews – I'm still groggy from the impact! Overwhelmingly wonderful. I can only imagine how blissfully happy Lenny must be, bless his heart!

Anyway, the time has come to pack up and leave. I hope to get a Pan American flight the 3rd of Sept which leaves me directly in Washington. I will take the children and Julie with me and Rosalia will take Chita back alone from here. Lenny can then see the children and they can take a train later to New York. Now, if you can send my summer clothes to Washington in a suitcase I can simply stay on with Lenny for a while and dispense with New York entirely. [...]

All this would need to be sent at once though, cause as you know I have nothing but winter clothes with me! I only hope it won't be difficult and a bore for you. I'm sure Ofra would be happy to help – she knows my clothes rather well.

We've been having a very nice time this last week – the weather is heavenly! We took the children to the mountains and they had a marvelous time! They are looking beautiful!

Every one sends love to you and Marie Grace. See you soon.

Love & Kisses,
Felicia

---

[57] Vera Zorina (1917–2003) was the stage name of Brigitta Lieberson, wife of Goddard Lieberson. From 1938 to 1946 she had been married to George Balanchine. Zorina was a dancer and actress who specialized in playing the title role in Honegger's *Jeanne d'Arc au bûcher*.

393. Goddard Lieberson[58] to Leonard Bernstein

headed paper of CBS Television, New York, NY

30 August 1957

Len,

I know you're up to ears in unsolicited praise at this point, but I've found myself so full of this project of yours all this week that I need to let you know what I think of it – if only as a sort of palliative which will allow me to get back into the heart of hackwork, which is my domain right now.

We've glutted the language with so many all-words and non-words that by now a term like "fine" has little meaning. But it has meaning for me, and it's that word which I now find myself stuck with when I think about the way your talent has combined with your material this time.

I mistrust my initial impression a little – I really can't believe that any one thing can be the best thing of its sort in my memory – all I know is the way I felt on Saturday afternoon was very like the experience of *Anne Frank* a couple of seasons ago[59] – I kept telling myself afterwards that there must have been something wrong with me for those three hours – something wrong that enabled the play to work on me the way it did.

I must have been something like a perfect piece of audience on Saturday because I've never known anything in musical theater to do me in the way *West Side Story* did. I'm usually a pain in the neck about those things – thinking all the while, officiously, how it ought to be better done and what I'd see thrown out. But Saturday it just threw me around and that's about the end of it.

People muttered at times about [Gian Carlo] Menotti – in a good way – saying that it's the most moving thing since *The Consul* – all that lobby crap – for me Menotti's always been somewhere over the fence because I don't like his use of language and I don't think the whole thing is comfortable – I never have learned to believe it – I don't know *The Consul*, but the rest of it falls the way I've described – which is a failing in me, I guess, but nonetheless a fact. If it doesn't just happen, then it isn't right.

---

[58] Goddard Lieberson (1911–77), English-born record producer who became president of Columbia Records (1956–71 and 1973–5). After studying composition at the Eastman School, he joined the classical division of Columbia Records. He took a leading role in the introduction of the long-playing record. As well as overseeing important classical recording projects (such as Stravinsky's recordings of his own work), Lieberson also produced many of the most successful Broadway cast recordings, including *West Side Story*, which was recorded a month after this letter, on 29 September 1957 at Columbia's 30th Street Studio.

[59] A stage adaptation of *The Diary of Anne Frank*, by Frances Goodrich and Albert Hackett, opened on Broadway on 5 October 1955 and ran for 717 performances.

I haven't ever seen a production which held together the way yours does – in which the units of work produced by different people fitted so well into a whole – I don't know how it really was. I know you must have had your problems – but none of them show up as scars.

For me, it has terrific power – terrific unity – excellent individual work, though I think the women are by and large better than the men – I can't say enough for Carol Lawrence this time – I've always liked her – and [Chita] Rivera is beautifully inside the work – which I didn't think she'd really be – she doesn't splash out of the production as I figured she might. This probably isn't going to make her, but it's great for the show. I think the men are at least good and will improve for sure – [Larry] Kert particularly. He seemed a little nervous still – but that's like a headcold and can be got rid of.

The amazing thing to me is that everything seems to work so well – with the possible exception of the 2d Act ballet, you never get the half-vision of what was attempted against the way it comes off – I know if you tried to tell somebody why the Balcony Scene works, it'd sound wrong – yet it's the most moving single musical sequence I've seen since the park bench scene in *Carousel* – which I think is a great, great moment.

The Anita–Maria duet is almost on a level with the Balcony Scene for me – just amazing.

I hope Kert gets his first two songs into shape – because they're terrific – "Maria" particularly – and it isn't quite happening – or anyhow, didn't on Saturday.

There's such a fabric there – and such a flow – I wouldn't have believed that it'd be possible on this earth at the end of the first week out of town. I still find it a little tough to be sure about – and yet I know how it was.

For God's sake, change the last five minutes – you don't need to say all that crap, because everything you've been saying since 8:40 has been saying it for you. And much better than any single invention could do, I think.

Lynn, that sponge, cried for ten minutes afterwards and the glue and mascara ran all over the National lobby.

I won't go on – there's nothing duller than praise, when you've had a surfeit of it, I imagine – and you're the last person in the world I'd be caught writing fan mail to – I only had to say, you really did it, man.

Do you know that when you do a work like this you give a boost to everyone who spades around in the same field? It's kind of like knowing that those productive currents and vibrations are still in the air, if you'll only work and reach and not forget.

So, thanks for it.

G

394. William Schuman to Leonard Bernstein
Martha's Vineyard Island, MA
1 September 1957

Dear Lenny,

It's just wonderful news that we hear of the show, and Frankie and I are so happy for you and with you. We send love and all the best for the NY opening where we hope to be present. Excuse this fast note but the sun is out on this beautiful island and I can't afford to miss a minute of these last precious days. We missed you up here and you'll have to arrange next year sans summer rehearsals.

Love from the 4

Schumans

I'm delighted you're doing the 6th [Symphony] – just heard.

395. Albert Sirmay[60] to Leonard Bernstein
Chappell & Co., Inc., New York, NY
11 September 1957

Dear Lenny,

I'm afraid that I'm too repetitious and maybe annoying in expressing so many times my admiration for your score of *West Side Story*. However I do not want to miss to say that it gives me immense satisfaction to read in the article of the *Evening Bulletin* the same words that I used to you on the opening night in Washington and last night in Philadelphia. It was quite a thrill to see my own words "theatrical history" and "milepost" repeated by a professional critic.

Well, my dear Lenny, I didn't need any printed words to make me aware of the greatness of your score. So bear with me and accept again from me my warmest and most enthusiastic congratulations.

Love,

Sirmay

---

[60] Albert Sirmay (1880–1967; originally Szirmai), Hungarian operetta composer who moved to New York in 1926 where he took a job with Chappell & Co., becoming music editor for the likes of Gershwin, Porter, and Jerome Kern. He is credited as the editor of the piano-vocal scores of Rodgers and Hammerstein's musicals: *Allegro, Carousel, Flower Drum Song, The King and I, Me and Juliet, Oklahoma!, Pipe Dream, The Sound of Music,* and *South Pacific*; and he also edited the piano-vocal score of Weill's *Lady in the Dark*. He later became a great Bernstein enthusiast, particularly *West Side Story* in which he invested $500 as one of the show's original backers (see Simeone 2009, pp. 30 and 113).

396. Leonard Bernstein to David Diamond
Warwick Hotel, Philadelphia, PA
12 September 1957

Dear David,

It seems impossible that I haven't written you in all this time – and yet it's true. Six months or so have elapsed since you left – six months of one straight monochromatic labor on this show, which is now thankfully open, and provisionally a smash hit.[61] The three weeks in Washington were phenomenal – sell-outs, raving press & public. Now simile in Philly. It really does my heart good – because this show is my baby, my tragic musical comedy, whatever that is; and if it goes in New York as it has been on the road we will have proved something very big indeed, & maybe changed the face of the American musical theatre.

But the fact remains that I haven't written a letter in all this time – hardly to anyone – and what makes it worse, I have had this news for you for at least two months now that I *will* be doing the 4th Symph – with the Philharmonic next year. I should have let you know long ago – but it's just been impossible to do anything but work on the show. Now I breathe a little – it's on, & going; & it's not all I want, nor will it ever be; but it's good, & I'm proud, & I can write a letter again. I forget the exact date fixed for your Mercury Symph., but it will be in January – with, I am almost positive, a Columbia recording (I've almost talked the Kouss Foundation into it). And Mischa Elman playing Mendelssohn on the same program will insure the public. Only hitch: it won't fit into the Sunday broadcast. What an impossible business, making programs in terms of split minutes! But that's a small sacrifice, especially if we get the recording. I'll be happy to renew acquaintance with it again. 10 years!

The family is home again after a long summer in Chile (I don't know what happened to the summer!) and it's such a joy to be with them again. F & I leave for Israel the 27th (the day after the N.Y. opening of *West Side Story*) & will be there through the month of October. Then home again. Can you make it?

You *were* marvelous in New York, in spite of all the tragic train of events, & I was proud of you. Give my love & Felicia's to Ciro [Cuomo], & many congratulations. Let me hear what you're doing.

Love,
Lenny

---

[61] *West Side Story* opened for try-outs in Washington on 19 August 1957, then in Philadelphia on 10 September, before the Broadway opening on 26 September.

397. Margot Fonteyn[62] to Leonard Bernstein
Hampshire House, New York, NY
24 September 1957

Dear Mr. Bernstein,

Thank you more than I can say for arranging seats for us for *West Side Story* on 3rd October. We are longing to see it and would never have got in without your help. It is so kind of you & I am sure you are overwhelmed with requests.

The Met. Opera House are holding 4 seats should you wish them for tomorrow night. I wish I were dancing, but we are so lazy in the ballet, we only dance now and then!

Yours sincerely,

Margot Arias

398. Renée Longy Miquelle to Leonard Bernstein
24 September 1957

Dearest Spookietchka,

I have been meaning to write you long since but now I can't delay any further since I have

1) to tell you how very much I like *West Side Story*

2) how marvelous it was to see you, talk and reminisce, and

Lastly to wish you the very best Broadway opening and a splendid journey to Israel.

Thank you for being you – for your friendship – you enjoy a very large place in my heart as you know. God speed to both you & Felicia, and all my love.

Relami [Renée]

If you have a recent picture of yourself (not a snapshot) please send it me – sort of a delayed birthday present! The last picture (and only one) I have dates back to Xmas 1945.

Are you giving any exciting new works in Israel? Where can you be addressed there? Till when?

---

[62] Dame Margot Fonteyn de Arias (1919–91), ballet dancer who became *prima ballerina assoluta* of the Royal Ballet, London. She married the Panamanian diplomat Dr. Roberto Arias in 1955, and was appointed a Dame of the British Empire in 1956.

399. Lauren Bacall[63] to Leonard Bernstein

Los Angeles, CA
25 September 1957
[Telegram]

It was worth all the Dexamyl. It's a smash, you're a smash and I'm thrilled for you.
Blessings and love,
Betty

400. Betty Comden, Steven Kyle, and Adolph Green to Leonard Bernstein

New York, NY
26 September 1957
[Telegram]

Dear Lenny,
We can but echo the deathless words of Samuel Hochman: So what's wrong with the hair business? But seriously folks we know tonight will be everything you hoped it to be.
Much love,
Betty, Steve and Adolph

401. Albert Sirmay to Leonard Bernstein

New York, NY
26 September 1957
[Telegram]

Dear Lenny,
For the masterwork which you have created in your score for *West Side Story* my unlimited admiration and my heartfelt wishes for a long-lasting success which you so well deserve with your immense talent.
Albert Sirmay

---

[63] Lauren Bacall (b. 1924, as Betty Joan Perske), American actress. Her idol was Bette Davis and both were friends with Bernstein. Bacall married Humphrey Bogart in 1945. When Bogart became ill in 1956, she wrote a touching letter to Bernstein. ("So sweet of you to take time out to write, and so lovely to hear from you as always. Bogie is coming along, still terribly weak from the treatments and still twenty-five pounds under weight. But in about three weeks it will all be over, thank God, and we can start fattening him up and getting him really well. He's had a time of it but has been saintly throughout.") Bogart died on 14 January 1957. In 1988, Bacall made a memorable appearance at Bernstein's 70th birthday gala at Tanglewood, singing "The Saga of Lenny" (Stephen Sondheim's witty parody of "The Saga of Jenny" by Kurt Weill and Ira Gershwin).

402. Stephen Sondheim to Leonard Bernstein
11 East 80th Street, New York, NY
26 September 1957[64]

Dear Lenny,

You know – only too well – how hard it is for me to show gratitude and affection, much less to commit them to writing. But tonight I feel I must. *West Side Story* means much more to me than a first show, more even than the privilege of collaborating with you and Arthur and Jerry. It marks the beginning of what I hope will be a long and enduring friendship. Friendship is a thing I give and receive rarely, but for what it's worth I want you to know you have it from me always.

I don't think I've ever said to you how fine I think the score is, since I prefer kidding you about the few moments I don't like to praising you for the many I do. *West Side Story* is as big a step forward for you as it is for Jerry or Arthur or even me and, in an odd way, I feel proud of you.

Much as I want to write music, I'm not sure I like the idea of doing another show without you.

I will, of course, and I'll play it for you, and you'll criticize it, and I'll be hostile and sarcastic about your criticism. But I look forward to that criticism and I hope you'll give it freely.

My gratitude and affection, then (in token of which I offer the enclosed unusual portrait of L. Bernstein in a moment away from J. Robbins), and also my best wishes for good luck to our little divertissement. May *West Side Story* mean as much to the theater and to people who see it as it has to us.

Steve

403. Roger L. Stevens[65] to Leonard Bernstein
New York, NY
26 September 1957
[Telegram]

Dear Lenny,

Thanks for your graciousness in remembering the dim dark days when it looked like everything was off. My faith was simple because with so many remarkable tunes the production just had to work.

Roger

---

[64] Sondheim wrote this letter on the day of the Broadway opening of *West Side Story*.

[65] Roger L. Stevens (1910–98), American theater producer and real-estate magnate. Stevens remained loyal to the production of *West Side Story* when Cheryl Crawford withdrew – the "dark days" to which he refers. He later became Chairman of the Kennedy Center for the Performing Arts in Washington, D.C. Stevens was a larger-than-life figure. He was a property developer by profession

404. Stephen Sondheim to Leonard Bernstein
[New York, NY]
23 October 1957

Dear Lenny or Lennie,

I have one of the most unusual and authentic excuses ever proffered for not writing you before this: my electric typewriter blew a fuse. Started to print words like thhhisss, and made interpretation even more difficult than blotted longhand. But I hope this reaches you before you leave for London. Helen tells me that you've been receiving almost none of the mail she's sent you. In a way, I hope it's true, because otherwise my news may be redundant to you.[66]

First of all, your questions about the show[67] could not have arrived at a more opportune time. Ten minutes ago, the phone rang – it was Martin Charnin, informing me that Stephanie Augustine suddenly had to go on for Carol [Lawrence]. This was at four-thirty, so my guess is that something happened to her during the Kaleidoscope (the ballet starts around four-fifteen – by the way, today is matinee day, in case you're hopelessly confused by my incoherence). Charnin couldn't fill me in on the details, since he had to go on for Krupke (the number, not the actor), but I'm going to the show to see how Mrs. Hyman[68] does. [. . .]

On the whole, the cast has been healthier than I expected – a few cases of flu (Al De Sio, who had refused the shot, and whose name outside the theater has been spaced so as to read Aldesio; Charnin, who had received the shot, and one other, whose name escapes me at the moment), a few broken ankles, torn ligaments and sprained wrists (Calin, Roll, Grover Dale, Lynn Ross) [. . .] But there have been no serious crises until today.

I don't know if Helen sent you all the notices, but knowing her maternal instincts, I suspect she omitted Harold Clurman's in *The Nation*. I'm afraid it's

---

and someone who relished the big gesture – none bigger than in 1951, when he led a syndicate to buy the Empire State Building. Stevens gave enthusiastic support to *West Side Story*, and this extended to organizing the opening-night party in New York. His continued involvement resulted in rather a convoluted formula for the original production credits: "Robert E. Griffith and Harold S. Prince (by arrangement with Roger L. Stevens)."

[66] Sondheim's detailed and amusing account of *West Side Story* early in its Broadway run is a mine of information, as is his discussion of the one-day recording session for the Columbia Records cast recording made on Sunday, 29 September 1957. Bernstein was unable to be at the recording as he had flown to Israel for the inaugural concerts in the Frederick Mann auditorium straight after the opening night of *West Side Story*.

[67] The original cast members of *West Side Story* mentioned in this letter played the characters shown in parentheses: Stephanie Augustine (standby for Maria); Lee Becker (Anybodys); Mickey Calin (Riff); Martin Charnin (Big Deal); Grover Dale (Snowboy); Al De Sio (Luis); Larry Kert (Tony); Carol Lawrence (Maria); Eddie Roll (Action); Lynn Ross (Estella).

[68] Stephanie Augustine was married to Joseph Hyman.

the end of Frank Lewis and his ground rules[69] for us, friend, since I'm cancelling my subscription immediately and trust you will do the same. Clurman's was a nasty, personally antagonistic (why? that's the question on a hundred lips; what did you do to him?) piece accusing us of base motives in writing the show. He called it a "phoney" and said we were "intellectuals slumming" for the purpose of making money. The review was framed by statements to the effect that the show would run a year, but no longer. The only personal pan in the review was directed at me, but he obviously was offended by the whole thing.[70] His, however, is the only real blast we got (*Time* and *The New Yorker* weren't great, but they weren't more than ordinarily unkind) [...]

From all indications, however, the show is a smash. We're sold out through February, even though tickets haven't yet been placed on sale beyond December 21st (the extra months are the result of mail orders). The License Commissioner has demanded an investigation of the box office; this, Hal [Prince] assures me, is the sign of a genuine blockbuster – it happened on *My Fair Lady* and *South Pacific*. The question is how long will the situation last. Part of the cause for the unavailability of seats, even at the brokers', is the continual flow of theater parties – every matinee and evening for the next six weeks except for six performances or so. There will be an Actors' Benefit performance November 24th, so jot it down – it should be very exciting. Anyway, Art or no, we'll be making money for a while.

Someone named Ullman (Abe, I believe) at Schirmer's keeps calling me for house seats and telling me apocryphal news of sheet music sales and forthcoming recordings. So far, only one has been out on the market: Jill Corey singing "I Feel Pretty" [...]

Rosemary Clooney has recorded "Tonight", but I haven't heard it yet. So has Vera Lynn, an English thrush, as we say in *Variety*. Sammy Davis wants to do "Cool", "Something's Coming" and "Tonight", but no action yet. Mickey Calin got a recording contract with something called Teen-o-Rama Records (they told him that he'd get his picture in all the teenage fan magazines, so he signed) and is recording "Cool" tomorrow. (He's also gotten numerous movie offers, which should be a surprise to no one.) Incidentally, *Variety* named the Corey version of "Pretty" as one of its weekly best bets (Best Bets, that is). Another one that week was a song by Mary (Rodgers) and Sammy Cahn called "I Love You Whoever You Are".

---

[69] Frank Lewis compiled the cryptic crosswords in *The Nation*. "Ground rules" was the example given by Lewis in a note at the bottom of the puzzle as a potential clue for "lures". Sondheim and Bernstein shared an enthusiasm for fiendish cryptic crosswords.
[70] Harold Clurman's review of *West Side Story* (*The Nation*, 12 October 1957) was a rather bitter attack on the show and its authors, and Sondheim's quotations from the review are exactly as they appear in Clurman's original. The only number he seemed to enjoy was "Gee, Officer Krupke".

As for the cast recording, I was amazed at Goddard [Lieberson]'s efficiency and dispatch, as well as his efforts at maintaining quality. You will probably be displeased with the record for reasons stated below as well as dozens of others, but on the whole I think it's pretty good – at least, by show album standards. It was recorded simultaneously for stereophonic tape (to be released in November as the first show so recorded) and sounds much better than the record. Some of the balancing isn't all it could be, but most of the trouble we had was due to lack of time – time on the record and time in the recording studio. As we had suspected, the amount of music was way overlong. Someone had goofed on the pre-recording timing, claiming that the Balcony Scene (starting with the singing) was 2:40, whereas it turned out to be 5:10. I don't have time to go into all the suggestions for remedying this, but the only one that worked was to cut out the best part – namely, the dialogue. Consequently, to our ears, the scene has been emasculated, going straight from the second chorus to the sung "Goodnight"'s, with four hurried lines spoken over the bridge between. Thus the first "goodnight" has to start on the fifth instead of the second, which ruins it, because the second doesn't fit in with the harmony. It's too bad, but I assure you there was no other way out – at least, none that occurred to us. You are also likely to be disturbed by the following (I tell you these not to ruin your final three weeks before you hear them, but to soften whatever shocks you may get when you're finally back at the Osborne).

FLASH! Hal just called to say that Carol's singing voice gave out at the top of her range, though her low notes and speaking voice remained. She's at the doctor's right now, will probably not go on tonight, but will tomorrow, if all is well. He saw Stephanie from "I Have A Love" on, says that she's okay [...] Jerry wanted to fire her immediately (without giving her a chance to do a whole performance, in effect), but he's in a bad mood anyway – he started his new ballet for the City Center on Monday, and it's apparently not going well.

Drawbacks in the recording, cont'd: A very fast tempo for the prologue, not so much to save time as to make it more interesting. Without the accompanying action, it tended toward monotony. Incidentally, we included street noises and shouts throughout the album, which works very well for the most part, though they tend to drown out the music in The Rumble. 2) Larry [Kert]'s voice on "Something's Coming" gets a little froggy in a few places and he sang the wrong rhythm for "come on, deliver", but it was by far the best of the takes, because the feeling was right. Unfortunately, it was the next to last song recorded and he was very tired, having been at the session for nine hours. His best is "Maria", which was the first number he recorded. 3) Frank Green took Larry's part in The Rumble (shouting "Riff, don't!") and came in about ten bars too late – just before the stabbing – but the orchestra played it so well, that we didn't try another take (it was already the third). Also, they forgot to blow the police whistle at the climax. (By the way, the orchestra was increased to 37 men for the recording.) 4) "America" and "I Feel Pretty" don't sound any better on the record than they do on the stage. 5) A trumpet player goofed badly on the change of key in the final procession. Oddly enough, nobody heard it until it was too late. I was out getting five minutes' sleep during it (I also slept during "America", since the session lasted from 10 a.m. to 1 a.m.). There will be a hundred other subtle and unsubtle goofs that will probably anger you, but the general reaction to the record so far (it came out last Friday – first order being 46,000 copies – is that good?) has been wonderful. *Variety* raved, and Douglas Watt in the *News* gave it a good notice (where he objected to anything, it was to the material, not the recording). The singers were not at their best, Lenny, but they were tired. One thing you ought to like: Goddard insisted that the final chorus of "Krupke" be played very slow with a heavy vaudeville beat. Jerry must have had conniptions. Another sidelight: Irv and Sid[71] put a major cadence at the end of "I Have A Love". I had conniptions, so it was changed back to the relative minor. I presume you didn't want it changed. I certainly didn't.

So all is very cheery at the Winter Garden, although benefit audiences have dampened the general atmosphere. They seem to like the show, though, and word-of-mouth is good. Only in the applause for individual numbers and scenes can that intramural too-many-martinis feeling be noticed. Sometimes the hand for "America" hardly covers the scene change, and sometimes Lee [Becker] has no trouble getting the audience to stop at the end of "Krupke". "Something's Coming" and "The Jet Song" still get weak hands, but the applause at the end of the ballet is constant – or almost so. Benefit audiences don't really get with it till the rumble, and sometimes not until "Krupke". But, as I say, they end up liking the show, so don't worry. I haven't seen a complete performance in two weeks, so I don't know how sloppy they're getting, but Jerry's going to do some rehearsing tomorrow.

I have much more to tell you, but I wanted to send this letter off this afternoon so that it would have a chance to slip in to you between Jewish holidays. I'll write you again, but if I don't stop now – I have to go out – I won't finish it for another four days. Love to Felicia [. . .]

Miss you. Come back on the seventh and no excuses. The groaning board[72] is set up and I've peeked at all the letters.

Love,

Steve

---

[71] Irwin Kostal and Sid Ramin, the orchestrators of *West Side Story*.
[72] This is a phrase that crops up occasionally in Bernstein's correspondence. Traditionally, a "groaning board" was a table weighed down by an abundance of food.

405. Paul Tortelier[73] to Leonard Bernstein
13 October 1957

My dear Leonard,

I regret not to have been able to see you after our last performance of the *Schelomo* [by Bloch]; I wanted so much to thank you again and to tell you "au revoir"!

How is it going now in the formidable Frederick Mann Hall? I often think of you and Isaac [Stern] after the dreamlike days in Israel that we love.

With my son Pascal (10 years old) we are going to hear [Arthur] Rubinstein tomorrow night in his Paris recital; that will be a great joy to hear him again and – perhaps – to talk few minutes with him after the concert.

Well, I must take the coach to the airport now and consequently must leave you quicker than I would like.

My love to Isaac.

Mes hommages à votre charmante femme avec la reconnaissance et amitié de votre

Paul Tortelier

P.S. Also my best remembrance to the orchestra if it is not asking too much.

406. Leonard Bernstein to Aaron Copland
16 November 1957

Dear A,

I tried valiantly to call on your birthday, but no soap. Also yesterday, idem. So, *per forza*, a letter – Happy birthday. Just got back from Izzyland and London, and first thought was – 14 November: there's something terribly familiar about that. Then I realized it was my debut date in 1943, and your birthday (in 1938). (Do you realize that next year on your birthday it will be 20 – twenty – XX – *Twenty* – vingt years we know each other?!!)

And then I realized that I've missed you very much –

As I say, happy birthday

& love

Lenny

---

[73] Paul Tortelier (1914–90), French cellist. He played in Koussevitzky's Boston Symphony Orchestra (1937–40) before embarking on a very successful solo career. Though not a Jew, he was very sympathetic to the State of Israel, and he stayed regularly with his family on a kibbutz.

407. Lukas Foss to Leonard Bernstein
University of California, Los Angeles, CA
22 November 1957

Dear Lenny,

Now that it is official let me again congratulate you and New York and music in America. All I can say is I shall be much more homesick than ever for New York.

My own life almost took a turn which would have made it look a little more like yours (or, let us say, like a provincial version of yours). Thor Johnson is leaving Cincinnati and I was offered his job. Cincinnati is not like New York, but it compares to my present UCLA orchestra much like NY compares to Cincinnati. In fact it would feel heavenly to have a *real* orchestra for a change. Having had considerable repertoire experience over the last 5 years, I was tempted, but finally decided against it. They demanded that I conduct 80 concerts in 28 weeks including pops, junior high, neighborhood concerts, tours etc. Aaron thought I should do it for 2 years – almost changed my mind. I wonder what you would have advised. Felt like giving you a ring, then felt silly. Now the dice have fallen. I am staying here.

I've got a new piece to play for you when I come in January. All my love to Felicia and you, from both of us –

And again: Congrats
Lukas

408. Leonard Bernstein to Goddard Lieberson
21 November 1957

Dear Goddard,

My thanks to you are so overdue by now that your beautiful gift-plant makes it imperative that I rise from my bed of pain to thank you. You did a wonderful job on the W[est] S[ide] S[tory] album. It must have been a hectic session, from all I hear, with split-second decisions to be made all the time – and you did a heroic job.

As to the plant – it is lovely, & we thank you & Brigitte with great warmth.

As to the bed of pain, I'm going to the hospital tomorrow for some check-ups on this ridiculous back of mine, as well as some enforced sleep. S-L-E-E-P, glorious word.

Love, Lenny

409. Joshua Logan[74] to Leonard Bernstein
22 November 1957

Dear Leonard,

West Side Story is one of the most moving events of my theatergoing experience. Your music is such a part of the whole I can't find out where it began or ended. I was just involved & became the slave of all of you from the moment the curtain went up. Thanks for giving us all such a beautiful experience.

Also congratulations on your new job with the Philharmonic.

Best always,

Josh

---

[74] Joshua Logan (1908–88), American theater and film director. Logan's Broadway credits included *Annie Get Your Gun* and *South Pacific*, for which he also co-wrote the book and shared a Pulitzer Prize with Rodgers and Hammerstein. Logan had known Bernstein for several years by the time of *West Side Story*. A telegram from Logan dated 17 November 1955 reads: "Dear Leonard, I know this will be an exciting evening and the more so because of you. Josh Logan" (sent on the opening night of Lillian Hellman's adaptation of Jean Anouilh's *The Lark*, for which Bernstein wrote the incidental music).

6

The New York Philharmonic Years
1958–69

In 1940, Aaron Copland had joked with Bernstein about the time "forty years from now when you are conductor of the Philharmonic." In fact it was just eighteen years later that Bernstein became Music Director of the orchestra, and over the next decade he was to take it on tour all over the world, to make hundreds of recordings, and to give a staggering number of concerts: in 1971 he conducted his 1,000th concert with the Philharmonic, and plenty more followed (his last concerts with the orchestra were in October 1988). In 1958, the press, particularly the *New York Times*, was often critical of playing standards in the orchestra, but Bernstein soon lifted both the morale of the musicians and the quality of their performance. Howard Taubman was chief music critic of the *Times* from 1955 to 1960 and wrote enthusiastically about Bernstein: he warmly welcomed his appointment and was generally positive about his concerts. Taubman's place was taken by Harold Schonberg, who grumbled for years about Bernstein's showmanship and often questioned the value of his musical interpretations. It is sometimes true that a hostile critic can ruin the career of a music director, but Bernstein's popularity was such that even Schonberg's most acidic notices made little impact.

This was the decade where Bernstein had the most regular contact with other composers: commissioning a great deal of new music (something for which he doesn't always get the credit he deserves), arranging events like the celebrations for Aaron Copland's sixtieth birthday at the Philharmonic, encouraging Stravinsky to come and conduct the orchestra, and corresponding with a startling range of composers about their work: the likes of Stockhausen, Xenakis, Feldman, Cage, and Carter, alongside Poulenc, Messiaen, and friends such as Copland, Foss, Diamond, and Bernstein's erstwhile orchestration teacher Randall Thompson.

Tours with the Philharmonic resulted in some remarkable personal encounters, and one of the most memorable came early in Bernstein's tenure, when the orchestra traveled to the Soviet Union in 1959. During this visit he met Boris Pasternak, at a time when the author had been publicly denounced by the Soviet authorities for *Doctor Zhivago*, and a year before his death. For the rest of his life Bernstein would treasure Pasternak's letters – and their meetings at the author's *dacha* and in the green room at one of the concerts. When Bernstein took the orchestra to Japan, Felicia stayed at home, and a long letter he wrote to her is a wonderfully evocative description of the sights and sounds of that country.

Back in the United States, Bernstein was becoming an ever more public figure. Euphoric about the election of President Kennedy in November 1960, he was involved in the ball for Kennedy's Inauguration the following January, and was quite a regular visitor to the White House during the Kennedy years. When the president was assassinated in November 1963, Bernstein was quick to pay tribute to the death of a leader who had become a friend, conducting a televised performance of Mahler's "Resurrection" Symphony. Five years later, when Robert Kennedy was assassinated, it was Jacqueline Kennedy who took care of the funeral arrangements, and she asked Bernstein to be in charge of the music. Her moving letter of thanks is eloquent testimony to the warm friendship between the two of them.

In the 1964–5 season, Bernstein took a sabbatical year in order to compose. He conducted just one concert (of his own music) right at the end of the season, and otherwise limited his activities to four Young People's Concerts. The largest project that presented itself at the start of this year was a new musical based on Thornton Wilder's *The Skin of Our Teeth*, a collaboration with two of Bernstein's best friends, Betty Comden and Adolph Green. By January 1965, this had foundered, and Bernstein wrote to David Diamond about "a dreadful experience, the wounds still smarting. I am suddenly a composer without a project, with half of that golden sabbatical down the drain." The friendship with Comden and Green survived this unhappy episode, but the "golden sabbatical" threatened to produce no new music whatsoever. What saved the day was a commission from Rev. Walter Hussey of Chichester Cathedral on England's south coast for a set of Psalms. Some of the music originally composed for *The Skin of Our Teeth* was quickly recycled in the *Chichester Psalms* (the opening movement and the lyrical theme of the second). The correspondence with Hussey contains no mention of this, but it does show Bernstein laying out his preliminary thoughts about the work in some detail, the decisive moment when he decided that setting the Psalms in Hebrew was something that excited him, and the circumstances of the first British performance on 31 July 1965 – seemingly a rather idyllic visit, at least by Bernstein's standards, with all the family able to travel with him to England. Two weeks before the Chichester performance, these same *Chichester Psalms* had featured as the new work in his only New York Philharmonic concert of the season – a programme that also included the *Serenade* and *The Age of Anxiety*. In short, the sabbatical didn't produce the new Broadway show that was hoped for, but it did result in one of Bernstein's most popular concert works. The *Chichester Psalms* was one of just two substantial pieces to be composed during his years at the Philharmonic – the other was the *Kaddish* Symphony, finished in time for its premiere in Israel in December 1963, but not without a struggle. As the most searching and musically advanced expression of Bernstein's Jewish faith, the work required of him a large emotional investment. The dedication to the memory of President Kennedy was, of course, only added at the last moment, and by the time the symphony was first played in the United States (by the Boston Symphony Orchestra under Charles Munch), Bernstein's friend Marc Blitzstein had also been murdered in Martinique. Bernstein's use of the word "Kaddish" refers to its specific meaning as a prayer of mourning: praising God in spite of personal loss. Thus, Bernstein wrote ruefully to his sister Shirley in January 1964 that "It's an open season on Kaddish, all right. The President. Marc."

Both works from the 1960s were described by Bernstein during his interviews with John Gruen in 1967: "I've written two works in the last 10 years, can you imagine, since I took the Philharmonic, which was at the point when I finished *West Side Story*. Since then I've written two works, neither of them for the theatre [...] one was *Kaddish* and one is the *Chichester Psalms* – they're both biblical in a way. So obviously something keeps making me go back to that book."[1]

In spite of his commitment to the New York Philharmonic, Bernstein continued to work in Europe and Israel, including his first visit to Vienna since 1948. On that occasion he had worked with the Vienna Symphony Orchestra, but now he was conducting concerts and recordings with the Vienna Philharmonic. His relationship with this orchestra was to flourish over the next quarter century, but initially Bernstein was profoundly disturbed by the anti-semitism within it. Georg Solti, another Jewish conductor with extensive experience of working with the orchestra, wrote not to allay Bernstein's concerns, but to counsel a spirit of forgiveness. Solti added that Helmut Wobisch – the former SS man who was the orchestra's manager and one of its trumpeters – was "despite everything [...] probably one of the few trustworthy members of that orchestra." Neither Solti nor Bernstein found it easy to work with the Vienna Philharmonic, despite its fabled past, but both managed to establish a musical relationship that became increasingly close over the years.

Meanwhile the Bernstein family continued to grow: in 1962, Felicia and Leonard's third child, Nina, was born – and, as he had with Jamie and Alexander, Bernstein waxes lyrical and adoring about their new sister. Bernstein himself reached a personal milestone in August 1968: his 50th birthday. One of his oldest friends, Adolph Green – who had known Bernstein since 1937 – wrote a funny, and deeply affectionate letter summarizing what their long friendship meant and, above all, how their first meeting had made such a lasting impact: "What am I wheezily, puffily, floridly trying to tell you??? The simple fact that suddenly there was meaning in my life. I felt *alive*."

---

[1] Bernstein, taped interview with John Gruen, Italy, 1967, transcription online at http://www.leonardbernstein.com/kaddish_commentary.htm (accessed 19 March 2013).

410. Jule Styne[2] to Leonard Bernstein
New York, NY
2 January 1958[3]
[Telegram]

I need a fella who can play in a publisher's office for singers, who can write a ballet and play the dance rehearsals and then orchestrate it, who can write the music for a new musical comedy and then orchestrate it, and who can write a ballet and play for Agnes de Mille and Michael Kidd and Jerome Robbins too, and who can take this ballet and orchestrate it the hard way with the orchestra sitting the wrong way and the horns pointing into the trombone player's ear; who can also do a tour of one night stands, lecture on why the oboe is a double reed instrument, also, what's going on in the world of music in five continents. This fellow must also be able to orchestrate the telephone book; also this fellow must be able to conduct practically every major symphony orchestra in the world like Adolph Green. Besides playing piano in publisher's offices, and writing ballets, this fellow must also be able to have the possibility of becoming the world's most famous conductor and musician and pianist. He must be a member of the union and must be available to open with the Philharmonic January 2, 1958. Do you know of such a fellow? I do. Good luck. Can you cook?
    Jule Styne

411. Jerome Robbins to Leonard Bernstein
154 East 74th Street, New York, NY
[January 1958][4]

Lenny,
    It was a terrific concert!!! I heard it Sunday – I'd been sick all week so missed both rehearsals and the Thursday evening premier[e]. I learned so much about *Sacre* [*du Printemps*] by watching you. *That* certainly ain't no "divertissement". Wow! Boy I hope I can make the stage version have as much stature. Bravo again and again, and also for the Webern which was beautifully played.
    Julius Rudel of NYC Opera called me about staging *Trouble in Tahiti*. Wanted to speak to you about it and couldn't get you today. So will you call me about it?

---

[2] Jule Styne (1905–94), British-born American composer whose Broadway successes included *Gentlemen Prefer Blondes, Bells Are Ringing,* and *Gypsy.*
[3] This telegram was sent the day of Bernstein's Carnegie Hall concert with the New York Philharmonic which included Schumann's *Manfred* Overture, Strauss' *Don Quixote,* the American premiere of Shostakovich's Piano Concerto No. 2 (with Bernstein as soloist), and Ravel's *La Valse.*
[4] The only New York Philharmonic programme in which Bernstein conducted both Stravinsky's *Rite of Spring* and a work by Webern (the *Six Pieces for Orchestra,* Op. 6) was at Carnegie Hall on 16, 17, and 19 January 1958.

Also I would like to talk more about your jazz piece etc. etc. and about ballets, shows, operas etc. So do call.

And again congratulations on the concert. You should be *very* proud. Bask well in all the praise being heaped upon you – you deserve it all.

Love,

Jerry

412. Jerome Robbins to Leonard Bernstein
154 East 74th Street, New York, NY
13 February 1958

Dear Lenny,

It was good to see you last night at the opening. I hope your back feels better. I can't think how a skiing trip is going to help your back any more than it would my leg, but anyway, good luck.

I checked with Edith [Weissmann] this morning. She had returned your call and got as far as the desk as I had reported to you.

I asked you if you had time for any composition because I could use *Fugue with Riffs* as part of a larger piece of yours, in the fashion we had always talked about – you know, some crazy pas de deux perhaps, and enough to make at least a twenty minute work. Maybe there's a possibility of selecting some of the dance music from *On the Town* and adding them to it. What do you think?

Enclosed are two interviews which struck me with as much force and excitement as anything I've read in many, many years. The potential of using this first interview as a basis of an examination of the Beat Generation and their search, pain, drives, ecstasies, depressions and astonished puzzlement could make a wonderful theatre piece.[5] My instinct is to use a protagonist who would answer the questions, but open up all the "meanings" and possibilities of those answers. I'm sure you'll see the immediate places such as "visions", "motorcycle rides", "jazz", "dope", "Paradise", "Heaven", "tremendous", "empty phantoms" and most of all the very very painful last line. I can visualize a lot of these things being episodic experiences which well up and take over the protagonist and leave him with everything inside him and a cool, knowing exterior. In a way these are our

---

[5] Robbins' idea for a theater piece based on the Beat Generation was sparked off by the interviews he enclosed with the letter. The first can be identified from Robbins' quotations: it was given by Jack Kerouac to Mike Wallace and published in the *New York Post* on 21 January 1958, soon after the publication of Kerouac's *On The Road* (Wallace's first question was: "What is the Beat Generation?"); the second was almost certainly another Wallace interview with Beat poet Philip Lamantia. See "Interview with Jack Kerouac: Lowell Author Gives His Version of the Beat Generation," *New York Post*, 21 January 1958, reprinted in Kevin J. Hayes, ed. (2005), *Interviews with Jack Kerouac*. University Press of Mississippi, pp. 3–6.

W[*est*] *S*[*ide*] *S*[*tory*] kids a little older. Do you know any of these Beat people? They're scary, and what's most frightening is that it *isn't* an act or an adopted attitude and façade to deal with life, but a real living thing.

I'd appreciate hearing from you on this as soon as possible. Drop me a note and give me at least your immediate reaction, and if you are interested, when do you think you will be able to have a talk on it.

All the best,

Jerry

413. Lukas Foss to Leonard Bernstein
University of California, Los Angeles, CA
16 March 1958

Cher Lenny,

News just reached me (via Siegfried Hearst) that you want me to do Mozart C major on a program on which you plan to do my Symph. Donnerwetter!!! What a festive occasion that will be for me.[6] You will be amused to know that what *elates* me most is the fact that you schedule my new piece sight unseen. Makes me feel that I have come into my own as composer. Thanks *ever so* much for the confidence implied (that something I put out is worth playing – and this coming from the most "knowing" of musicians). Seems the days of Lukas selling his music at the piano are over and gone. Just played it for a few musicians though, who think that it is my "most"; curious what *you* will say. I finished the score day before yesterday and sent it off to you yesterday.

You will see that it is a virtuoso piece for orchestra, the kind where the difficulty makes for brilliance (I hope). It's no "sight-reading" piece, and a half hour long. Here is hoping you didn't schedule [Stravinsky's] *Agon*, Aaron's *Short Symphony* & Boulez's *Polyphonie X* to go with it. (You could probably pull it off, too.)

The Mozart will be splendid – my favorite slow movement.

How was your skiing trip? It was wonderful having Felicia with us.

Much, much love to both of you.

Lukas

---

[6] The planned program mentioned in this letter took place a year later, in Carnegie Hall on 9, 10, and 11 April 1959. The concerts included Handel's Harpsichord Concerto in F, Mozart's Piano Concerto in C, K467, the first New York performance of *Symphony of Chorales* by Lukas Foss, and Wagner's *Tannhäuser* Overture. Reviewing the concert in *The New York Times* (11 April 1959), Howard Taubman praised Foss' "finely balanced" interpretation of the Handel, in which he played the harpsichord, and enjoyed his stylish Mozart playing that had "elegance, but not at the sacrifice of virility." Foss' *Symphony of Chorales* was a commission by the Koussevitzky Music Foundation. Taubman was largely unimpressed: "The first movement has some brilliance, the second some appealing serenity of mood and the third an attractive pastoral quality. But all of it goes on and on with a meandering garrulity. Agreeable ideas are worried and turned ponderous. It is all reminiscent of a diluted Mahler."

414. Felicia Bernstein to Leonard Bernstein

[New York]

Thurs. night [1 May 1958]

My darling Lennuhtt,

Am dying to hear how it's going – the reports so far sound like a nightmare! I hope that at least your sense of humor has not abandoned you – think of the pastry makers it will all make!

Children are wonderful – I am better – the first days after you left I utterly collapsed. I looked a mottled green with cold sores on my mouth etc. Have nothing sensational to report – just got back from dinner at the Oppenheims with Glen[n] Gould, Eugene Istomin and Vladimir Golschmann. Glen[n] and Gene sat at the piano and loudly and eternally played four hands – sometimes I hate music![7]

Went to the opening of *The First Born*[8] last night – a crasher if there ever was one, a truly abysmal evening! Your "score" is never heard I'm afraid – the girl sings a little snatch of something for no good reason that I could see, and your triumphant finale is utterly drowned in applause since the curtain comes down simultaneously – and there you are!

Have a reservation for the twelfth, will arrive the thirteenth in Lima. The fan mail keeps pouring in – my ego is having a field day!

Please write a few lines – it's unbearably lonely around here without you. Kisses from the three of us and very special love from me,

Felicia

415. Leonard Bernstein to Felicia Bernstein

Hotel Tamanaco, Caracas, Venezuela

2 May 1958

Darling,

Wow, what a three days. First: we're the all time smash. Second, it's all wildly exhausting, but such fun & stimulating. Venezuela is really one of a kind – stinking with money, progressive architecture, happy, low on culture, & lower on education. It's mostly a billionaire top stratum & penniless others. But there is arising a middle class, & they love music, to say the least. I've had two concerts in a magnificent hall called the Aula Magna[9] – sheer perfection with mobile

---

[7] See Letter 416, describing the same evening.

[8] *The Firstborn* by Christopher Fry opened at the Coronet Theatre on 30 April 1958. It included incidental music by Bernstein. The cast was led by Anthony Quayle; it also included Michael Wager, a friend of the Bernsteins.

[9] The Aula Magna of Caracas University, built in 1952–3. The architect was Carlos Raúl Villanueva. Alexander Calder's magnificent "flying saucers" are memorable visually and useful acoustically.

baffles by [Alexander] Calder, what else? And both sold out to the rafters. In between we gave a special outdoor concert for 7,000 middle classers in an equally perfect Concha Acoustica: they ate up Copland and Roy Harris. So all is not lost. I'm the local hero, I'm loaded with presents; tons of records of folk music, [and] a liki-liki, which is a great beige linen national garment, very handsome with a high collar held by gold links.

I've met the new president of the Junta,[10] most charming, loved the Schuman 6th, fijate. Such houses, such jewels, such luxury I've never ever seen. And, again, of course, everyone knows you & loves you. The American Ambassador (at whose gorgeous residence I just had a party) is named Sparks; and his wife is a lovely lady who knows you of old – Andrée van der Brengen. Do you remember her? An angel. And dozens of others whose names go thru my ears like wind. They've all been expecting you, & are sorely disappointed. But we'll be back – I've become a national institution, & you'll even like it, you'll see.

Tomorrow ploughing on to Maracaibo, to conduct in my liki-liki, then on to Colombia, where I hear a big revolution is fermenting. Just in time for some fireworks. This should be a peppery tour. I hear Paraguay should just about be ready with their revolution when we arrive (May 1st was pretty tense here, too).

But it seems we're doing good – much more, according to all concerned, than Nifty Nixon, who has flubbed his whole mission in spades so far.[11] Can't wait to hole up with him in Quito.

So when are you coming already? You're missing a great trip – much fun; & I'm missing you. Try & come as early as you can. I hope you're resting, & that the back is a thing of the past. You must get all healthy again for the trip. So far, I've been well, though sleepless & oversmoked. But that's usual. Your Joan[12] still haunts me – how did you like *Time* on the subject?[13] I thought the picture was great. Brigitta[14] will *fry*.

Thanks for the cable. How long for those two guatoncitos!

Nicolas is not very bright, pobrecito, but he's trying hard, & he's very sweet. Things are never quite in order, & it always seems as though it was easier before when I knew where everything was. Trouble with a valet is that if he leaves you for a second you're lost & helpless. Also he's developing an old-maidish protectiveness

---

[10] The new President of Venezuela was Wolfgang Larrazábal, who was in office for less than a year, from 23 January to 14 November 1958.

[11] Vice-President Nixon's trip to South America (27 April–15 May) revealed to the US government just how bad relations were with Latin America, and reached its low point on 13 May when he was attacked by an angry mob in Caracas.

[12] Felicia had played Joan of Arc in Bernstein's New York Philharmonic performances of Honegger's *Jeanne d'Arc au bûcher* on 24, 25, and 27 April 1958.

[13] *Time* (5 May 1958) described the occasion as "a family triumph".

[14] Brigitta Lieberson, the wife of Goddard Lieberson, who performed as Vera Zorina. She played Joan in the first American performance of the work, given by the New York Philharmonic under Charles Munch on 1 January 1948.

worthy of la Belle.[15] He scolds people when something is not done for me that should have been done – like water in the dressing room, or whatever – & makes long, indignant Theta-ridden speeches about the great maestro, & how he should be treated. Ah well, it's all so familiar. Love to her, by the way, & to Mither [Mother] & to all the Kats. Do try to come early, like Quito, & let me hear *soon*!

All my love, dearest one.

L

416. David Oppenheim to Leonard Bernstein
Columbia Records, 799 Seventh Avenue, New York, NY
7 May 1958

Dear Lenny,

Believe it or not, I am still going to the office day after day even though you are not here, and so are a lot of other people. Life is tending to go on despite the wonderful reports we are getting back in the *New York Times* about your concerts.[16] I am delighted things are going so well and I suppose by now the Ravel Concerto must be almost ready to record. This is something we must consider when you return.

Also, while you were away, Felicia came to dinner with Glenn [Gould], Eugene I[stomin] and Vladimir Golschmann, and I am afraid it was not too stimulating an evening. To begin with, an enormous competition between the two young pianists corralled them out of the party, except for some horrendous noises they made on an untuned Baldwin in a room without a rug and without much furniture. Vladimir turned pages, I smiled encouragingly, and Ellen[17] and Felicia tried to communicate with each other by a combination of gestures and lip reading, which was not entirely successful I understand.

The evening ended when Glenn played his own cadenzas to Beethoven's First Concerto on a chair some inches too high, thereby ruining his left arm and impairing all his concerts from here to eternity.

Also, Van Cliburn was there in spirit – all things pianistic dimming in comparison with his coming ticker-tape parade. The pianists, especially the young ones, have a sort of haunted, old look, directly traceable to the affairs in Moscow.[18] We shall see just how long young Mr. Cliburn can sustain his glories, but if he can maintain his fees for a couple of years, I predict mass suicide involving quite a few of our friends.

---

[15] La Belle Hélène was the Bernsteins' nickname for Helen Coates.

[16] Between 29 April and 14 June 1958, Bernstein and the New York Philharmonic undertook an extensive tour of Central and South America, giving concerts in Panama, Venezuela, Colombia, Ecuador, Peru, Bolivia, Paraguay, Chile, Argentina, Uruguay, Brazil, and Mexico.

[17] Ellen Adler became Oppenheim's second wife in 1957.

[18] Van Cliburn had just won the first International Tchaikovsky Competition in Moscow.

If the above sounds like sour grapes, it is because Victor signed him over my dead body. But this we can discuss another time, too.

[...]

I saw your Bach program rerun Sunday and it was marvelous.

I hope this finds you as well as the press releases have described you and that you will find time to answer me quickly – always in the affirmative.

Love,

David O.

P.S. Incidentally, I see that you have returned the Duke Ellington scores. What is your impression? Can you use them? I think he is waiting to hear, or at least Irving Townsend in our Pop Department is. My impression is that these could be done in a recording session in addition to all of the others you and I are planning. Anyway, let me know.

417. Leonard Bernstein to William Schuman
Gran Hotel Bolivar, Lima, Peru
14 May 1958

Dear Bill,

It['s] so unbelievable to be in the lland of the llamas that I spend most of the day saying PERU over & over to myself, just for sanity. Peru?!? Auckland. Mozambique. And here it is, a nice normal warm capital like any other, beautiful, full of people and a number of things. Felicia has just arrived, making it all perfect.

The tour so far has been a smash; receptions such as I've never experienced, warmth & love from audience after audience, great reviews – & the orchestra playing like Gods. Every day they become more and more my orchestra, more than I could ever have expected. Your [Sixth] Symphony was remarked by a Caracas critic to be the most important offering we had, and the main feature of our *three* concerts there.[19] It's been great.

But now I find myself in a spot with our dear old Sixth [Symphony]: we can't play it except in the capitals, where there's a sophisticated audience of some sort; & the time lapse between capitals is such that the orchestra doesn't retain the piece. Last night, for example, it was really ragged and "forgotten" after more than a week; it's not a piece you can tour with; we've had to take it off the La Paz & Quito programs because the enormous altitude prevents the necessary blowing (almost *no* oxygen at all in La Paz – 13,000 feet up); & I'm scared of the next performance, 8 days away. I think we're going to have to take

---

[19] Schuman's Sixth Symphony (composed in 1948) was played in Caracas on 2 May, then on 13 May in Lima, the day before Bernstein wrote this letter.

it off the program for the rest of the tour, heartbreaking as it is; I know you'll understand. It's just plain murder to the players and to the piece. It's just one of those works that has to be hot off the griddle to be played at all well; otherwise it's a haphazard gamble.

We miss you both, & love you.

We also love the Sixth!

Lenny

418. Leonard Bernstein to David Diamond

Gran Hotel Bolivar, Lima, Peru

19 May 1958

Dear Dovidl,

Imagínate, here we are in Peru, lland of the llama, lland of llove. Felicia has just joined me (we've been two weeks touring South America already in Panamá, Venezuela, Colombia, Ecuador) & she'll be with me for the rest of the trip – Peru, Chile (at last!), Paraguay, Bolivia, Argentina, Uruguay, Brazil, Mexico – the works. Our reception everywhere has been magnificent – warm, thrilling, just the opposite of Nixon's, pobrecito. We think of you often, and miss you. I realize I have several letters from you as yet unanswered, & I beg forgiveness. These last months have been wild. But with beautiful, rewarding highlights: Felicia as Joan at the final concerts of the season, brave & inspiring & unforgettable (the whole orchestra in tears, Honegger notwithstanding); the television shows, especially those for the kids; the orchestra itself, which has become *my* orchestra to an astonishing degree of flexibility, warmth and respect; this exhausting but lovely trip. [. . .] We'll be home by June 15th. Hope to find a letter from you.

Love from us both.

Lenny

419. Rosamond Lehmann[20] to Felicia Bernstein

Flat F, 70 Eaton Square, London SW1, England

26 May 1958

My dear Mrs. Bernstein,

I meant to write this at once, but to my horror found I'd mislaid my address book when I left New York the morning after seeing *West Side Story* – and have

---

[20] Rosamond Lehmann (1901–90), British novelist. Her friends included many of the Bloomsbury Group, among them Lytton Strachey and his wife Dora Carrington, Vanessa Bell and Duncan Grant, and Leonard and Virginia Woolf. In the 1940s she had a ten-year affair with the poet Cecil Day Lewis. This warmly appreciative letter about *West Side Story* was written less than a month before the death of Lehmann's daughter Sally – a tragedy that virtually put an end to Lehmann's writing career and led her into Spiritualism.

only just re-discovered it in a folder stuffed with lecture notes etc. etc. I hope for your sake you are still away and will not have been conscious of my discourtesy. I *never* can thank you properly for your incredible generosity and kindness in enabling me not only to see the opera but to take my two dear far-from-wealthy spinster cousins who had been longing in vain to get tickets ever since the opening night. They are extremely earnest Educationalists, and got me down beforehand by spectacled conjectures about the Puerto Rican Problem being "too serious a subject for frivolous treatment" etc. etc. – but like myself were completely bowled over, breath-taken by the end of Act I. It was easily the most fascinating & exciting dramatic experience I've had for years, and I *still* feel exhilarated, amazed and heart-wrung by the whole affair. Would give anything to see it again! Words are quite inadequate to thank & congratulate your husband. I have the records – that's something. It *is* serious of course, and beautiful; also terrifying, moving, funny & disturbing. It was the high spot of my whole Marathon – and as I say I can never thank you adequately. I was very sorry indeed to miss you both – and thrilled to read of your husband's brilliantly successful S. American tour. I hope you are back safe and sound – & that he is able to have a rest. Or does he never?! I'm only just back, & still semi-prostrate from too many thousands of miles of flying – but I did enjoy a lot of it & confess I miss being spoilt & made much of! – as I was, everywhere. Martha [Gellhorn] is still abroad.

Again, so many thanks.

Affectionately,

Rosamond Lehmann

420. Martha Gellhorn[21] to Leonard Bernstein

Mexico

July 4 [1958] – Independence now from what?

Lennypot my dearie one,

I waited for the right time to write about *West Side Story* but probably the exact right time will never come, so now on a rainy (can you beat it?) Cuernavaca

---

[21] Martha Gellhorn (1908–98), American journalist and author. Gellhorn's work as a war correspondent started with the Spanish Civil War, which she witnessed with Ernest Hemingway (he dedicated *For Whom the Bell Tolls* to her, and they married in 1940). She covered Hitler's rise to power, and was one of the first journalists to report on the concentration camp at Dachau. She later covered the war in Vietnam, the Six-Day War in 1967, and numerous other international conflicts. She divorced Hemingway in 1945, and in 1954 she married Tom Matthews, editor of *Time* magazine. The Martha Gellhorn Prize for Journalism was established in her memory. Her friendship with Bernstein was a curious one. Though both were politically liberal, there were few other obvious connections between the two of them aside from being tennis partners when they were both at Cuernavaca in Mexico; Gellhorn was not musical, but she clearly liked Bernstein. For Gellhorn's remarks on Hemingway, see Letter 427.

morning, my fourth here, and my first not spent jumping with rage and activity against this house, I shall begin. But I know I am not going to do it well enough.

How can it be called a "musical comedy"? It is a musical tragedy, and were it not for the most beautiful music, and the dancing which is like flying, people would not be able to bear to look and see and understand. Certainly they would not pile into that giant stadium, paying huge sums, in order to be wracked by fear and a pity which is useless because how can help be offered, how can a whole world be changed? Tom and I found it beautiful and terrifying. But then he and Omi[22] must speak for themselves. Omi had seen it before, found it more enthralling the second time. Enough about their feelings.

I was literally frozen with fear. Do you realize there is no laughter in it, no gayety that comes from delight, from joy, from being young? You do, of course, and all of you knew what you were writing about. The immensely funny song, "Please Officer Krupke" (I will get these titles wrong, but near enough), is not laughter, but the most biting, ironic and contemptuous satire. And I felt it to be absolutely accurate – not the perfection of the wit, in music and words – but accurate as describing the state of mind of those young. Again, the Puerto Rican girls' song, when one longs for the beauty of home and the other mocks ["America"], is not laughter; but the hardness of life, the rock of life, a dream of something softer (softer inside, where it counts) as against the icy measuring rod of modern big city young. The love songs made me cry (they had before, when I heard the whole show twice in one day, listening to [Irwin] Shaw's record in Switzerland).[23] But this time, with the visual picture there, and the murderous city outside, and in America, where *West Side Story* becomes a sociological document turned into art, they made me cry like a sieve, from heartbroken pity.

But what stays in my mind, as the very picture of terror, is the scene in the drug store, when the Jets sing a song called "Keep Cool, Man." I think I have never heard or seen anything more frightening. (It goes without saying that I think the music so brilliant I have no words to use for it.) I found that a sort of indicator of madness: the mad obsession with nothing, the nerves insanely and constantly stretched – with no way to rest, no place to go; the emptiness of the undirected minds, whose only occupation could be violence and a terrible macabre playacting. If a man can be nothing, he can pretend to be a hoodlum and feel like somebody. I couldn't breathe, watching and hearing that; it looks to me like doom, as much as these repeated H-bomb tests, with the atmosphere of the world steadily more and more and irrevocably poisoned. I think that drug store and the H-Bomb tests are of the same family.

---

[22] "Omi" was Martha Gellhorn's mother, Edna Gellhorn, née Fischel.
[23] Gellhorn had already written to Bernstein about hearing the cast recording at Klosters, Switzerland, earlier in the year. In a letter dated 18 March 1958, Gellhorn told Bernstein that she "wept at parts, and roared with laughter at others. It is almost tangible music."

What now baffles me is that all the reviews, and everyone who has seen the show, has not talked of this and this only: the mirror held up to nature, and what nature. I do not feel anything to be exaggerated or falsified; we accept that art renders beautiful, and refines the shapeless raw material of life. The music and the dancing, the plan, the allegory of the story do that; but nature is there, in strength; and surely this musical tragedy is a warning?

It shames me to speak of music to anyone, owing to my hopeless ignorance and to the fact that I do not hear it, only feel it. I love your music – everything you wrote (much more than I like anything you conduct). It may be part of my loving you, but it wouldn't work entirely. I love some people whose writing and painting I deplore. No, it isn't that personal at all. I think I love it because it seems to me real. You'll have to figure that out for yourself.

Thank you for giving us perfect tickets, where Tom[24] could hear – you can imagine my anxiety about that, in advance – thank you very much, darling pie.

I think you must write music, more and more, and I think you will. My theory about this is that what one does and is and how one lives, grows and changes. Americans are fools to fear age. It is needed and proper; all one must certainly do is change with one's age, live one's own age, let one's shape (inside and out) alter as it should. I think that, being you, you had to have the great hectic period of doing everything, being everyone and going everywhere. I think that's raw material; and you had to swallow it all, for you will need it. But I also think you will chuck it, without effort or regret, in time; because that will be the time to work on the raw material yourself, draw your conclusions, make your own private gift out of all you saw, did, heard, felt. I think you will really write music, and be concentrated and used by that, in perhaps eight years from now. All you have to do is not ruin your health before that long slow hard second work-period of your life begins.

You must try to get a book called *Brighter than a Thousand Suns* by Dr. Robert Jungk. It was published in Germany, translated and published in England. The first part is slow and tedious going, and one sees how necessary it is, later. It is the story of the atomic scientists; it is the human side of how we have launched ourselves (and how accidental and ignorant and pitiful it all is) into doom. I find it needed reading, and too fascinating to stop. Now I must find some nuclear physicist, who is an honest man, to check with. But it is specially a book for us, who have no part in that world – and that world this very minute rules us. We must know; we may be ineffective to control our destinies, but we cannot ever be sheep. I do not believe in an atomic-hydrogen war, I don't think it is necessary or will happen. I believe the world is going to be poisoned

---

[24] Tom Matthews, former editor of *Time* Magazine and Martha Gellhorn's second husband. They married in 1954.

(literally, physically) without that. It might be that if people realized they were daily and invisibly being led to the slaughter, they would not go in silence. If they knew that right now the entire population of the world is infected, and that growing children are most susceptible to this kind of infection, there would be revolt. Anyhow, you read it. It is certainly the other side of the coin of the mad children, living in the streets and dreaming sick dreams.

Omi and I are here preparing this pleasure dome. We were robbed of course. It is not as bad as the house you and Feli had, but I must say I preferred your wide range of Navajo-Mexican striped rugs to the false pretensions of this house. I have removed every movable object and most of the furniture; the clothes cupboards seem to have been built for 1920 type movie stars and are useful warehouses. The servants are charming and pea-brained. The roof leaks like a faucet and is covered with slender brown boys gently and imperceptibly laying back broken tiles. The view would be perfection, a wide sweep from the black range of the mountains that rise towards the Mexico plateau, the Chinese follies of the Tepoztlan hills, the volcanoes behind them, and to the west the beginnings of the blue Taxco range. The idiot owners have elected to plant mingy palms and other uncertified trees in such a way that the only manner to see the whole view is to lie on one's stomach at certain points in the garden, or climb to the top of the wall. The doom of everyone is to have to walk with fools nor lose the common touch; but how many and heavy the fools, and maybe the touch is not worth keeping.

When in N.Y., I seem to have gone mad. Within a week (thinking that I knew what I was doing) I arranged four book contracts, two for Tom, two for me, and five articles for me. People leapt to offer me these contracts, paying more money than I have ever before received. The reason for this is that I really do not want to do any of the work, and I certainly do not want a cent more money than I have. The result is that I have to finish my book of collected war reporting by September 1. Beginning in October, and going through until April, I have to do two articles on England, one each on Poland, Hungary and Czecho. My only hope is that I won't be able to get into the last two countries. On April 15, Tom and I return and drive about this benighted land (not this one, the Estados Unidos) for three months, leaving presumably more dead than alive for some quiet spot where we have agreed to grind out a book on the subject in four months. I am surely mad. The only good I can see in it is that it forces me back to work habits, which I have lost, and will be a long dismal training for my muscles. There isn't a ray of light until a year from this coming Xmas. I also have to deliver a short story to the *Atlantic*. I wrote it years ago but in my usual way, I do not feel I have tinkered enough. (I never believe the thing is ready until I can recite every word of it by heart, and go on changing "a" to "the" with a maniacal desire for exactitude.) Well. That's what going to America does for one. I have already warned Tom that next spring's three months' jaunt may be the last visit of my life. I know I don't believe in progress. I want to live quietly and harmlessly and perhaps do one or two things right, if possible.

But on the other hand, I have grown lazy and I need to get back into that awful discipline of three hours a day at the typewriter and nothing at all else happening in the day, so as not to get cluttered in the noggin. So here and now we start. I have seen no one in Cuernavaca yet, and only been busy buying out the grocery stores; but in any case we live so far from the center, and have no car, that I think perhaps I'll only have an occasional loving chat on the Buena Vista terrace. Dread seeing Vera. What can I say to her? It appears that slob Ross [Evans] returned for a visit (sponge on Vera for a change?) last February and again departed "to look for a job in the north." And she loves him. Mr. [Somerset] Maugham is not the only one who knows about human bondage.

I hope little Feli is getting some rest on the Cape. You don't know how to, I think, and perhaps don't really want or need it. But do remember she weighs less than you. I find her always more beautiful, and more miraculous. Alexander has my vote for President right now. I trust you will not ruin Jamie by spoiling (Feli will not help you in that ruin) but I see it will be hard to avoid.

You know how I love you –

M.

421. Leonard Bernstein to David Diamond
Vineyard Haven, MA
16 August 1958

Dear Dovidl,

My 40th birthday approaches, and that makes me sentimental and pseudo-philosophical, and I also think of you when I get that way. I'm going through the usual fortyish motions of stocktaking, examination of life-purposes, re-examination of motives and drives, efforts at great self-knowing – and that's been my summer. My first free summer in twenty years: and it's been so shocking to have it that I've literally done nothing: not a note, imagine, not a bar, no letters written, only programs planned, sailing, and most important of all, spending huge gobs of time with my children. What splendid companions they are!

But not a note written: and I wonder, as I study my hairline in the mirror and pray desperately against baldness, whether any composer who is *really* a composer could go for two months without composing, and doing nothing else either. Where will it all lead? Baldness, I expect.

The Philharmonic season looms large and exciting and frightening. There will be much more television, more difficult programs, more "point" being made, more Handel, more Vivaldi. [Varèse's] Arcanes [*Arcana*],[25] at last, and all

---

[25] Bernstein's broadcast performance of *Arcana* was released on CD in *Bernstein Live* (NYP 2003).

kinds of Ruggles and Riegger, & the Sessions Vln. Concerto, and Ives #2 and Aaron Variations & Ned Rorem #3 & Bill Russo & Ken Gaburo and and and. A sort of overall look at the whole picture. Not the *whole* picture, of course: that's impossible, and I have to leave out all kinds of important fellers like Virgil and you and Marc and [Norman] Dello Joio (important?) and [Paul] Creston (ugh) and Ben Weber and [Andrew] Imbrie and [Leon] Kirchner. The Klee[26] arrived, & believe it or not, I haven't had a chance to look at it yet! That's my summer.

I haven't heard your 4th [Symphony] yet on records: I will when I get back to town in the fall.

I hope Goldoni[27] is fun, & rewarding on several levels. Felicia's Joan is never to be forgotten. She joins me in

Love,

L

I'll be in Milan for a few days in Nov (10–15 or so). Will I see you?

422. Jerome Robbins to Leonard Bernstein
154 East 74th Street, New York, NY
13 October 1958

Dear Lenny,

A deep bow of thanks for your wonderful letter. I'm so glad you liked it and I'm so sorry you didn't get to see the Chopin. I think you would have had a ball.[28]

Tomorrow starts rehearsals of *West Side Story*. You've *got* to come in and take them musically over their material, at least once, so they know what you're about, especially while the European conductor is here. We'll prepare them all and get them ready for you, but you *must* (IT'S IMPERATIVE) do this for the sake of the success of the show.[29]

---

[26] Diamond's *The World of Paul Klee* for orchestra.

[27] Diamond was working on a musical comedy based on *Mirandolina* by Carlo Goldoni.

[28] Bernstein had been to see the Broadway run of Robbins' *Ballets USA*, which included *New York Export: Opus Jazz* (music by Robert Prince and sets by Ben Shahn), Debussy's *Afternoon of a Faun*, *3x3* (with a score by Georges Auric), and *The Concert*, the first of Robbins' ballets to music by Chopin. *New York Export: Opus Jazz* was performed again at President Kennedy's 45th birthday party in the old Madison Square Garden – the occasion when Marilyn Monroe sang "Happy Birthday, Mr. President."

[29] These rehearsals were for the cast that was about to take the show to England (including George Chakiris as Riff, Marlys Watters as Maria, Don McKay as Tony, and Chita Rivera as Anita), and the "European conductor," Lawrence Leonard. It was first seen at Manchester Opera House on 14 November 1958, before heading to London where it opened at Her Majesty's Theatre on 12 December and ran for 1,039 performances.

Dybbuk Dybbuk Dybbuk.[30] I'm sending over an unseen but continually haunting prodder who will creep into your sleep and into your spare moments and will say the words Dybbuk Dybbuk Dybbuk. With this ghost's effort I know that suddenly something will be on paper that will get us all started. I've heard from [Ben] Shahn who is wonderfully enthusiastic and excited about the idea of working with you, so please keep haunted and jot down a few of those scribbles that turn out to be the basis, theme and dramatic motifs for the whole ballet.

Love,

Jerry

423. Thornton Wilder[31] to Leonard Bernstein

50 Deepwood Drive, Hamden, CT

27 October 1958

Dear Lennie,

Mrs. Alma Mahler-Werfel has chosen some words of mine as the title of her new volume of memoirs[32] and I wish to give a small party for her on the publication of the book. I am asking about twenty friends to meet her at the Algonquin Hotel – reception room 306 – on November 11 – Tuesday – between 5 and 7.30. She tells me her daughter – the sculptor – Gustav Mahler's daughter – will be there.

Don't trouble to answer this. But it would be a great pleasure if you and Mrs. Bernstein could come.

Cordially yours,

Thornton (Wilder)

---

[30] The paragraph about *Dybbuk* is a reminder of how long Robbins and Bernstein spent contemplating this project. The ballet was completed in 1974, but they had first considered the story soon after collaborating on *Fancy Free*, three decades earlier, and Robbins was eager to make progress straight after *West Side Story*. The proposed collaboration with the artist Ben Shahn never came about because he died in 1969. (When *Dybbuk* was presented by New York City Ballet in 1974, the designs were by Rouben Ter-Arutunian.)

[31] Thornton Wilder (1897–1975), American playwright and novelist, author of two of the most celebrated plays written for the American stage – *Our Town* and *The Skin of Our Teeth* – and the novel *The Bridge of San Luis Rey*. All three won Pulitzer Prizes for Wilder.

[32] Alma Mahler (née Schindler, 1879–1964) was married in turn to Gustav Mahler, Walter Gropius, and Franz Werfel. Her memoirs were published in 1958 with the title *And the Bridge is Love*, a quotation from Thornton Wilder's 1927 novel *The Bridge of San Luis Rey* ("There is a land of the living and a land of the dead and the bridge is love, the only survival, the only meaning"). The sculptor Anna Mahler (1904–88) was the second daughter of Mahler and Alma. Like her mother she married several times, including the composer Ernst Krenek, the publisher Paul Zsolnay, and the conductor Anatole Fistoulari.

424. Larry Adler[33] to Leonard Bernstein

[London, England]
24 December 1958

Dear Leonard,

It being impossible to keep a secret these days, you will no doubt have heard that a certain show whose title contains that part of New York where nobody, but nobody ever goes, opened in London and was not unfavorably received.

I took 2/3 of my children to see it last night, despite a darkling article in the *Telegraph* – "Should children be *allowed* to see W[est] S[ide] S[tory]?" They got it all, loved it all and in their comments were far more perceptive than those of several adults around us during interval.

I think your score is historic. Only in *Porgy and Bess* have I heard music become both words and plot and character, and it happens again with your music. (I might add a footnote here; in 1954 your score for *Waterfront* and mine for *Genevieve* were both nominated for an Oscar and I can tell you that had Dmitri – tote dat corn, lift dat theme – Tiomkin not edged us both out, this letter might not have been so easily forthcoming.)[34]

Further along in the true confessions hour, I am, or at least was, about to start work on a musical myself. But after that score of yours, where does one go except to say, "Face facts, Wotan, you ain't ready yet."

So, my heartfelt congratulations. You, as a musician, know how another musician feels when he hears something that says something new, different and honest.

Regards to Arthur Laurents, who got me my tickets. Also, if you see him, from [i.e. to?] the boychick of the fiddle, Isaac Stern.

Sincerely,
Larry Adler

---

[33] Larry Adler (1914–2001), American harmonica player for whom Vaughan Williams and Milhaud composed pieces. Adler was blacklisted in Hollywood and moved to London in 1949.

[34] Adler's name was not credited because of his blacklisting; instead the arranger and conductor Muir Mathieson was named as the composer of the score for *Genevieve* – an error that was only rectified officially in 1986. The nominations for Best Music Score at the 27th Academy Awards were: *The Caine Mutiny* (Max Steiner); *Genevieve* (Larry Adler); *The High and the Mighty* (Dimitri Tiomkin); *On the Waterfront* (Leonard Bernstein); and *The Silver Chalice* (Franz Waxman).

425. Louis Armstrong[35] to Leonard Bernstein
CBS Television Network, New York, NY
5 January 1959

Dear Daddy Bernstein,
    Man. I sitting in your office rehearsing my lines, and it is *knocking* me out. You're *My Man* and that's for sure. From your Swiss Kriss[36] Trumpet Player.
    Regards,
    Louis Armstrong
    Satchmo

426. Leonard Bernstein to Martha Gellhorn
Arizona Biltmore, Phoenix, AZ
7 January 1959

Dearest Marthy,
    Happy New Year. At long last, a rest – although God knows it takes fully as much energy to unwind and force the inactivity as it does to be active. But at least they're not all pushing from all sides: I have only my own sick silly psyche pushing from inside.
    I'm not staying at the above – just using the luxuriousissimo facilities & living with friends. Burtie has been with me, left yesterday, all is calm. We started out last week in Sun Valley. Skied three days on the daisies (and a bit of snow) and then left for the hot glorious desert, horses, tennis, swimming. Lord, if I only had a bit of peace in me – a bit only, is that too much? – how I could be enjoying all this! And Poland? And Alaska? And is here next? Did you do the hols in London? Are you as petrified as I of the lunik lunacy?[37] What the hell are we fiddling with? When do you arrive in this favorite land of yours for your Okie junket?
    I met Ernest Hemingway at Sun Valley last week, and was taken totally by surprise. I had not been prepared by talk, photos, or interviews for a) that charm, and b) that beauty. God, what goes on there under his eyes? What's that lovely adolescent tenderness? And the voice and the memory, & the apparently genuine interest in every living soul: fantastic. We spoke tenderly of you: he said you were brave.[38] His present wife seems to be a professional Ja-sayer, though simpatico enough. The question is not How could you have married him, but How could you have done anything else?

---

[35] Louis Armstrong (1901–71), jazz trumpeter and singer. In 1956, he appeared on Bernstein's album *What is Jazz?*
[36] Swiss Kriss was a herbal laxative that Armstrong used and promoted.
[37] A reference to the early years of the Space Race, starting with the launch of Sputnik 1 in 1957.
[38] Gellhorn was married to Hemingway from 1940 to 1945. See Letter 427.

Dearest love to you, every day, always, dearest potato-pipe. I played tennis today & almost wept with nostalgia for our version of tenny.

Write me –

L

427. Martha Gellhorn to Leonard Bernstein
20 Chester Square, London, England
postmark 14 January 1959

Dearest Lenushka,

I loved your Xmas card, both of you looking so beautiful and so tired and the children so beautiful and benign, like happy little dolls. I am saving my first-in-my-life vote for Alexander who will surely be President unless he decides it's all a silly joke and he'd rather live.

So much to say but I won't say it, probably. This is my last letter, anyhow, for some time, because now I am going to start on a novel and that means silence, fasting and prayer. A novel about Poland. Most daring. I was there 16 days; and learned more and felt more than I have, probably, since Spain. Terrifying and wonderful nourishing experience. I was also frightened the whole time, and I am not used to being; frightened for everyone because they are too brave. And all my desperate faith in the human spirit was revived and rewarded, because there they *are*. Proof.

Shall I say some ominous aunt-like words about peace? I think I will. It is a subject that I have really thought and worked on, you know. So: no one besides yourself will ever help you to get it; everyone, even with the best will in the world, will nibble and shred it. You have to fight for it, yourself, and it is perhaps that most essential fight there is. If you haven't got (and keep clinging to, through every reverse) a hard kernel of your own private peace, maybe no bigger than a pea, you cannot be, do or give any *real* thing. Practically, I find it works like this: one learns what conditions one needs, for oneself, to bring back or foster one's interior nugget of certainty and calm and happiness. For me, it's absolute solitude and silence, in the country; long walks, no timetable of any kind, no telephone, no mail, no newspapers. Long mooning walks, reading, sleeping a great deal. No booze, simply because booze makes me nervous. And then, after a longer or shorter cure of this (depending on how much my peace has been eaten away) I can start to work: and that sets it firmly. I have no idea what you need, but you must, by now, have learned for yourself. No other person gives it, you know, though anyone can take it away. Sex has nothing to do with it either.

The Xmas hols, just terminated, ruined me as usual. I cannot bear any season given over to organized official good cheer, and too many people, plans, parties. So, as soon as I'd put little Sandy on his plane for Switzerland, I rushed off to my usual country hotel for three days alone. Whereupon an old friend (known for

30 years, now aged 74) was in the hospital in London, and I had to take over everything by telephone. That fixed the peace allright. I'm hanging on however, and have now got the telephone here turned off all day, will not accept any invitations nor give any, and I mean by God to come back to myself and to where I really live. You see, I get physically sick when the peace all goes. I think you don't do that, though I am not sure. But I think you hardly know who you are, or why you are doing what you are doing.

Interested about Ernest [Hemingway]. Tenderness is a new quality in him; but people do luckily change all their lives and the luckiest ones get better as they grow older. His main appalling lack was tenderness for anyone. I longed for it in him, for myself and for others. I'd almost have settled for others. I do not remember his voice as being anything much, but I always was thrilled by his memory. He was interested in everyone but there was a bad side. It was like flirting. (Like you, in fact, he has the excessive need to be loved by everyone, and specially by all the strange passing people whom he ensnares with that interest, as do you with your charm, though in fact he didn't give a fart for them.) So he would take people into camp; they became his adoring slaves (he likes adoring slaves) and suddenly, without warning, he would turn on them. That was always terrible to see; it made me feel cold and sick and I wanted to warn each new conquest of what lay in wait for him. But one couldn't; they wouldn't believe; they were on the heights of joy – for he can be a great life-enhancer and great fun, and his attention is very flattering.

By the time I did marry him (driving home from Sun Valley) I did not want to, but it had gone too far in every way. I wept, secretly, silently, on the night before my wedding and my wedding night; I felt absolutely trapped. When I fell in love with him was in Spain, where for once he did have tenderness for others (not me, he was regularly bloody to me, lustful or possessive, and only nice when he was teaching me, as if I were a young man, the arts of self defense in war. And also he liked being the only man in Spain who took his woman around with him, and I was blonde, very helpful in brunette countries, raises one's value.) I loved him then for his generosity to others and for his selfless concern for the Cause. That was all gone by the time I married him. I think I was afraid of him though I certainly never admitted it to myself or showed it to him. You will also be surprised to hear that I have never been more bored in my life than during the long long months when we lived alone in Cuba. I thought I would die of boredom. But it was very good for me. I wrote more with him than ever before or since in my life, and read more. There were no distractions; I lived beside him and entirely and completely alone, as never before or since.

I am very glad he now speaks pleasantly of me. I never speak of him one way or the other with anyone. The whole thing is a distant dream, not very true and curiously embarrassing. It has almost nothing to do with me. What I write you here is, as you can understand, secret and between us only and forever.

He ought to be happy and he ought to be gentle; because life has showered gifts and blessings on him; and I hope he is.

Considering this was to be a quick letter, only saying that I love you and wish you well for 1959 and all years to follow, it has rather swelled, has it not.

My darling Lenny.

Marthy

P.S. Bertrand Russell uses the word "impiety" in relation to luniks and further attempts and he is right.

428. Darius Milhaud to Leonard Bernstein

Mills College, Oakland, CA

9 January 1959

My dear Lenny,

Everybody tells me that you made a magnificent performance of my old *Création du monde*. It is too bad I didn't hear it.[39] Generally I always listen on the radio to your programs which I love. They are full of miracles. For instance Schumann (Robert!) 4th Symphony sound[ed] like a transparent, light, tender orchestra.

Bravo, dear.

Best wishes for the New Year from both of us to your family.

Milhaud

429. Leonard Bernstein to Mary Rodgers[40]

22 January 1959

My dear little Miss Rodgers,

I am happy to inform you that you have won the contest for the best word to replace "classical". Your magnificent choice of EXACT will ring down through the centuries, and no doubt enter Webster's 567th edition, if only as a footnote.

Congratulations; and please accept the enclosed gift as a token of our esteem and gratitude for your fine thinking.

Faithfully yours,

Leonard Bernstein

---

[39] Clearly Milhaud had heard the performance by the time he wrote to Bernstein again three weeks later, on 29 January 1959.

[40] Mary Rodgers (b. 1931), American composer and author. She is the daughter of Richard Rodgers. A graduate of Wellesley College, where she majored in music, Rodgers had a Broadway hit in 1959 with *Once Upon a Mattress*. She worked as assistant to the producer of Bernstein's Young People's Concerts. In 1972 she published her first children's book, *Freaky Friday*.

430. Darius Milhaud to Leonard Bernstein
Mills College, Oakland, CA
29 January 1959

Lenny dear,

I was deeply touched by all the nice things you said about *Création du monde*, and you explained everything so *clearly*. You are just marvellous. The performance was *remarkable* too and you were so exciting in the Gershwin.

Lucky Philharmonic!

I hope it will not be years before we see you.

Most affectionately,

Milhaud

I should, I think, tell you that it is preferable not to use all the strings in *Création*. It's "sharper" with soli.

431. Joe Roddy[41] to Leonard Bernstein
Life, Time & Life Building, Rockefeller Center, New York, NY
24 February [1959]

Dear Leonard,

1. The *Leonore* [Overture No. 3] played Thursday night was the work of the best-sounding (that's a loathsome simplification) orchestra I have heard in years.

2. The television program Sunday was – again – the best one you have done. The pattern is set and you cannot allow a poor one. That's fine with me. But I defy you to improve on "How Dry I Am".[42]

3. Items 1 and 2 above are not set-ups for a complaint, but I have one. My children are pissed off, which is a concern of yours. They claim that at the last Saturday morning children's concert the TV strong-men blinded them by aiming great flood lights into the audience. Presumably the purpose of this was to make them – my spawn – look bright on television screens around the country. They don't give a good damn about being seen around the country because they came there to see you and the concert and they could not see

---

[41] Joe (Joseph) Roddy (1920–2002), American journalist. He worked on the staff of *Look* magazine and *Life* magazine as well as writing for *The New Yorker*, *The New York Times*, and *Harper's* magazine. A friend of Bernstein for many years, he was a passionate music-lover who regularly attended rehearsals at the New York Philharmonic.

[42] In *The Infinite Variety of Music*, broadcast on 22 February 1959, Bernstein took the four notes of Irving Berlin's "How Dry I Am" (G-C-D-E), showing how they were used by composers from Handel (*Water Music*) to Shostakovich (Fifth Symphony). The script was printed in Bernstein 1966, pp. 29–46.

either at times. They claim they cannot hear when they cannot see, but that's the exaggerated howling of the angry young men. I think they have a case.

And as for me, I think the picture of the Child Listening Fervently is a wearying cliché by now anyway. I strongly suspect you of being Christ (but hell, you know all that) and you of all people know perfectly well that "suffer little children to come unto me" is not to be understood this way. Even Kenneth Tynan knows that.

I have urged your appointment as Secretary of State and you will be hearing from the Feds about this suggestion any day now.

Highest regards,

Joe Roddy

432. Jule Styne to Leonard Bernstein

237 West 51st Street, New York, NY

20 March 1959

Dear Lenny,

As you know, I am devastated and shocked . . . as, no doubt, you were by Mr. Brooks Atkinson's and Mr. Walter Kerr's review of the show.[43]

I can understand them not liking the songs or a song; or not liking the book or direction; or not liking the performance or a performance . . . However, for Atkinson, a man of his high intellect, to write in his column his last line "a mongrel musical drama" about this show in this day and age, is shocking. This is unfair criticism.

Since you expressed yourself with great joy and thought the show was a beautiful musical and almost felt sure that it was a hit, I would appreciate your writing a letter to the *New York Times* Mail Bag immediately. I feel a letter coming from you, since they know how honest you are, would be of tremendous assistance to the show. I know you have the courage and honesty to consider writing this letter.[44]

Thanks again for your and Felicia's niceness and God Bless.

Love,

Jule

---

[43] The show was *First Impressions*, a musical based on Jane Austen's *Pride and Prejudice*, with music and lyrics by Robert Goldman, Glenn Paxton, and George Weiss, and a libretto by Abe Burrows (of *Guys and Dolls* fame), who also directed. *First Impressions* opened on 19 March 1959 and closed on 30 May, after just 92 performances. The production was under the overall supervision of the Jule Styne Organization, hence Styne's interest in it.

[44] Bernstein didn't write to *The New York Times* about Atkinson's acidic review. He wrote to Styne that he "would love to help out and did enjoy the show," but that he "makes it a rule not to do this kind of thing as so many people ask for it" (from the draft reply in Helen Coates' hand on Styne's letter).

433. Leonard Bernstein to David Diamond
23 May 1959

David, David, David,

(That's in answer to *three* letters of yours.)

The season is over: we've been to London and back in a week to see my *two* shows there (imagine that!), & it's as expected: *West Side* is booming, *Candide* is limping, & I guess always will. Since our return I've been doing mail mail mail with Helen – a whole season's worth, Lord – and spending days on the editing of my book that S[imon] & S[chuster] are bringing out in the fall (nothing new: just a collection of TV scripts & miscellaneous writings. But what time it takes to edit!)[45]

And so, finally, a minute to write you. And say how touched we both are by your wish to present us with the Trittico Dodecafonico! You are sweet. It's awfully hard to tell anything much from the photos: obviously color does a lot of the meaning; but what one can see is *fascinating*. I showed them to Danny S. [Saidenberg] & gave him a spiel, which I hope helps when he visits you this summer.

I've also talked twice to Oliver Daniel[46] based on a cooky notion I had that you might do well to just chuck ASCAP at this point & cross the stream. He looked into the story of you & BMI & couldn't learn enough to satisfy him. If you think it's a good idea, write Oliver (he has asked to have you do this: & it is promised to be kept confidential); & tell him the whole sordid tale. I sense an interest there. I wasn't up enough on the facts to give him the whole story. (I am also still trying to get in touch with Nissim.)

I saw David O[ppenheim] yesterday & reminded him about releasing the 4th Symph: he has promised it for the early fall.

And Tommy [Schippers] is apparently doing *Klee* in Russia! Isn't it wonderful? But, as you say, when on earth will he rehearse it? Strange, fancy type fellow, that. I suspect also, frightened to death.

Dear David, this time we *must* meet in Italy! We don't alas, come to Firenze, but we do go to Venice on 26th Sept, & thence to Milan (concerts on the 28th & 29th). Meanwhile, June & July on the delicious old Vineyard, where I hope to recoup some energy & sanity, & maybe even *write* something, please God!

---

[45] *The Joy of Music.*
[46] Oliver Daniel (1911–90) was an energetic promoter of new music. In 1954 he created the Concert Music Department at Broadcast Music Inc. (BMI), a rival to ASCAP. Daniel also helped to establish Composers' Recordings Inc. (CRI).

Bless you & love from us both

L

(& Best to Ciro!)

434. Leonard Bernstein to David Diamond
Vineyard Haven, MA
[Summer 1959]

Dear D,

The Vineyard is glorious, a blessing every day. I've decided that gratitude – rather, gratefulness – is the essence of joy, the basic emotion, what we feel when we hear music we love, or look at our loved ones, or simply breathe on this golden island; and growing old means only losing that emotion. The retention of gratefulness is the guarantee of continued youth, don't you think?

When I go into N.Y. to open the Stadium, I shall have a talk with Stanley Adams.[47] I've written him already & we have an appointment. I decided to go to the top, after failing with the underlings. We'll see. Meanwhile, write Oliver [Daniel].

As to the Ford grants, they were part of a special project for *performers*, who were asked to select composers they wanted concertos from. That's out. But I have a feeling Spivacke[48] could be in. Why not write him? I'll put in a blast too.

Very odd to think of you & Tommy S. [Schippers] together, I don't know why.

I know nothing of Marlon [Brando] or his whereabouts. Irene Lee[49] will be visiting you shortly – ask her.

I'll write after Stanley Adams.

До свидания [Dosvidaniya]

Lenny

(I'm studying Russian out of a little book, & I think of you every time I pronounce a hard L. What a delicious language!)

---

[47] Stanley Adams (1907–94), American songwriter probably best known for writing the English lyrics for *La Cucaracha*. He was President of the American Society, of Composers, Authors, and Publishers (ASCAP) 1953–6 and 1959–80.

[48] Harold Spivacke (1904–77), chief of the Music Division at the Library of Congress from 1947 to 1972.

[49] Irene Lee Diamond (1910–2003), Hollywood script editor and philanthropist. She was the Hollywood story editor who had recommended movie treatments for both *The Maltese Falcon* and *Everyone Comes to Rick's* (immortalized as *Casablanca*). In later life she became a generous patron of the arts and of AIDS research. She was unrelated to David Diamond.

435. Boris Pasternak[50] to Leonard Bernstein
[Peredelkino, near Moscow, Soviet Union]
1–3 September 1959

Dear Mr. Bernstein,

I am exceedingly touched and most thankfully surprised by your kind friendly wire. If other interjacent notes from me will not anticipate this my uttermost decision I hope to have the happiness to attend your concert on the eleventh. To that end, no daring or intending to trouble you to write anything, I shall by my own care look after four passes (for me and my family) to the performance. Only please indicate my name to the attendant before the door of your artistic room on the evening, that I may be admitted to you after the concert.

Besides that I shall try to get the luck the honour and the right to invite you to dinner at Peredelkino Wednesday the ninth at three o'clock.

I shall confirm it afterwards once more.

Obediently yours,

B. Pasternak

Sept 2nd 1959

No it will not go – I think it better to renounce to that great pleasure and not to meet apart from the concert evening (the 11) when I shall experience myself the delight and ecstasy all the town speaks of, & hereupon I am congratulating you fervently in advance.

Excuse my unexplainable discourtesy. My involuntary ungraciousness is my misfortune, not my fault. But I shall hear and see you.

With the same devotion,

Idem.

3 September 1959

Last note.

Please be welcome on the day and hour you dispose the best, except the intervals between 1–2½ and after 8 in the evening, when I can be about on

---

[50] Boris Pasternak (1890–1960), Russian poet and novelist most famous for *Doctor Zhivago*, for which he was awarded the Nobel Prize for literature in 1958. This caused a scandal in the Soviet Union, where the book had been refused for publication owing to its critical stance on Stalin and Socialist Realism (the manuscript was smuggled abroad so that the book could be published). Pasternak at first accepted the Nobel Prize, but after intolerable pressure from the Soviet government (including the KGB surrounding his house in Peredelkino), he was forced to decline it: "In view of the meaning given the award by the society in which I live, I must renounce this undeserved distinction which has been conferred on me."

walks. The best hour remains that of the dinner (3 o'clock). Come *as it were
unawaitedly*. Ask the guidance of the concert organisation to provide for
the return car. Agree with them upon my being admitted in the evening of the
concert in the entr'acte.

I wish you the renewal of your habitual triumphs I know of from hearsay.

Respectfully yours,

B. Pasternak

436. Boris Pasternak to Leonard Bernstein

Peredelkino, near Moscow, Soviet Union

9 September 1959

For Mr. Leonard Bernstein,

Paste this dedication in your copy of my novel. It was so fine and kind of you
to have wired to me from Leningrad, to have got the desire to find and to meet
me. After-tomorrow I shall attend to the marvel and triumph of art which are
your performances. In grateful presentiment of it.

B. Pasternak

437. Boris Pasternak to Leonard and Felicia Bernstein

Moscow, Soviet Union

12 September 1959

Dear friends,

In the morning of the next day Saturday – Fatigue, yearning, exhaustedness,
like after a sleepless night or a big command event, a great night fire in the town,
a conflagration, having devoured [a] lot of houses, or a mighty storm with a
powerful inundation.[51] So must be art. We must will its produced impression,
long, and pine for it. Art must leave us love-stricken and sorrow overcome, like

---

[51] Bernstein's concert on 11 September was Pasternak's first appearance in public after his denuncia-
tion following the *Doctor Zhivago* scandal. Bernstein was overwhelmed by his meeting at Pasternak's
dacha, but they never met again as the great writer died a few months later, on 30 May 1960. On 13
July 1960, Rabbi George Lieberman from Long Island, NY, wrote to Bernstein about his admiration
for the writer, and to ask whether, during their meeting, Bernstein had touched on Pasternak's
Jewish antecedents: "Was he a formal convert to Christianity? Now that he is no more, we may
never know whether he took the step. On the basis of your conversation with him, could you draw
any conclusions on this point? Were you in his home in Peredelkino and did you notice any icons in
it?" Bernstein's draft reply is written on the back of Rabbi Lieberman's letter: "My conversations
with P. never touched on this point. (They were in fact virtually monologues by him on aesthetic
matters.) But he conveyed the impression of a Tolstoyan Christian, a worshipper of nature and the
divine spark in man. I saw no icons at his home. I suspect that he felt little or nothing about
Jewishness, though he may have been deeply interested in *Judaism*. This is a guess."

a deep-felt parting or separation. Art is language of greatness, greatness is disclosure, its sight, its tragic and suffering *being exposed to view*.

Don't stand you both so often before my mental eyes, I will be along, don't hinder me to be diligent and working.

B. Pasternak

Hearty greetings to all yours; to Mr. St[even] Rosenfeld; to the whole orchestra, to the fiery, dear, expansive Mr. Zimmermann; to Goldstone and Varga.

Dear My Felicia, who was the lady you sent after me out of the lobby in the concert-room in the entr'acte? She wore a dark, straight, long dress, not girdled in the waist, that seems a sort of brocade. Her husband was dressed in a light brown suit.

They figure, they are present in my greetings, I am feelingly asking their names. Having spoken with them, I was so absent minded in the crowd, as to not have demanded to be presented to them. Write me be so kind about them, about her and him.

And forget I implore you, my stupid idiotic speeches when in commotion I employed one word instead of another (for instance I used the word "wife" for "woman" that in reality I intended to say), and gave occasion to think I have been foretelling incidents towards some certain future.

The Same, in the same state of affectionate devotion.

438. Leonard Bernstein to David Diamond
205 West 57th Street, New York, NY
19 October 1959

Dear David,

What a shock! The first I heard of Tommy [Schippers] taking off your Klee piece was *your* letter, which greeted my homecoming. I've thought hard; but there's nothing I can do about it. That he should replace it with yet *another* Barber piece is too silly, and that I will do something about.

Simultaneously, I heard two fine pieces of news: I ran into Stanley Adams in Washington, who said that all was *set* & definite for you to get a year's advance! Then Marc told me that the Minna C[urtiss] thing was in the bag for 4 thousand. Wonderful news, & congratulations.

But meanwhile you say you are broke; I hope the enclosed helps until the big money arrives, which should be soon.

We finally saw the paintings which are startling & fascinating! More about that later – I'm dashing off to Springfield & Boston with that goddamn Shosty #5!

Love, & don't despair,

L

439. Karlheinz Stockhausen[52] to Leonard Bernstein

Meister-Johann-Strasse 6, Köln-Braunsfeld, Germany
8 November 1959

Dear Mr. Bernstein,

How friendly you have written me! It is good that you understood my decision so well. I agree perfectly with your "postponement". That gives me an idea:

Should we not give Carnegie Hall the last lubrication before she will die? E.g. with *Kontra-Punkte* (instead of *Gruppen* 31st March), and David Tudor as pianist under your direction?

Carnegie Hall would be delighted by such a last honour: she would feel like Carnegie Walhalla, and then she will never be jealous of Lincoln Hall during her long death.

In the parcel (which I sent to you) you will find a tape 7½ inches/sec. with a copy of an old performance of *Kontra-Punkte* (1955) and copies of *Gruppen* performances in Köln and Donaueschingen (worse, but with corrections). You will find also a little score of *Kontra-Punkte* and a record with the electronic composition *Gesang der Jünglinge*.

A last word on your letter: you should never be sad. You are the only artist since long time ago who gave me the impression to be more than a "serious" one, who can fill a room with life, with Unbefangenheit, with Aufgeräumtheit just by his presence, just by speaking and laughing about everything. That's gold of endowment without any merit; and I wish with all my heart that nobody could ever ruin or distort your soul. We live for music – yes; but we can say as well that music exists for us. There is a secret relationship between your soul and Mozart's soul, perhaps you know it: brilliant seldom stars appearing from time to time at the sky of this earth, light and transparent like angels, making everybody happy for a little moment of this long serious history . . . homeless like only homeless ones can be.

I know what I say; one half of my soul is like you are, like Mozart's; but I am a strange mixture of heaven and hell.

Thanks for having met you, thanks for having heard you and seen you (during your concert I became so angry against you, that I could not stay: I listened too serious, too egoistic); but now, already soon after the concert, I discovered you in my own mind, in my own soul. I even don't think any more that something like this can be destroyed: misdeal yourselves without any limit, spread on this earth as much as possible, reserve nothing.

Yours,

Karlheinz Stockhausen

---

[52] Karlheinz Stockhausen (1928–2007), German composer, and a leading light of the post-war avant-garde.

440. Leonard Bernstein to Aaron Copland
Palm Springs, CA
12 November 1959

Dearest Aa,

Happy Birthday! I'm all alone, imagine, out in the desert, in a rented house (all Japonee, & ugly) & a wonderful pool, & a Baldwin, and big rocky desert hills, & sun & fine air, all alone thinking of you. How I miss seeing you, & have missed it for years; how much I was looking forward to visiting some Sundays ago, & couldn't because Felicia wasn't well; thinking about how we can splurge it up a year from now at the Philh. for your 60th; thinking about those inside wheels of me that compose music, and are so rusty now (I wrote a bar today!), and how long I can go on being an all-time maestro without writing; & thence to Mahler (I bought lots of albums of Mahler, & I've been listening & crying as I listen – *Das Lied* is still one in a million) – & thence to Bruckner (I bought some of his symphs too, having never heard #6, 8 or 9!!) & find him impossibly boring, without personality, awkward & dull, masked in solemnity.

But Mahler makes me think of you, hard, and of our music, which I don't think I really understand the direction of any more (or the purpose); & I long to talk to you & have you explain it to me, & reassure me that new music is just as exciting as it was when you showed me all about it 20 years ago.

And I long also to kiss you and wish you a very happy birthday –

Always,

Lenny

441. Fritz Reiner to Leonard Bernstein
1320 North State Parkway, Chicago, IL
14 November 1959

Dear Lenny,

Many thanks for sending me your book.[53] I shall look forward to enjoying it on my Christmas vacation at Rambleside.[54]

Meanwhile it is gratifying to read in the inscription that my teaching and ideas about music are remembered by my most brilliant and successful student.

Thanks again and arrivederci presto.

Your friend,

Fritz Reiner

---

[53] Bernstein's first book, *The Joy of Music*, was published in 1959.
[54] Reiner's home in Connecticut.

442. Lukas Foss to Leonard Bernstein
11 December 1959

Dear L,

Have you answered Stockhausen yet?

"None of your business Lukas" – Right. I am trespassing. But since you showed me his letter,[55] forgive my thinking about it. I just thought of the perfect answer. Allow me:

> Dear Mr. Stockhausen,
> I am of course the most gifted man of music in the USA but I have as much in common with W.A.M. as the man in the moon. *And you know it.*
> Sincerely,
> Leonard Bernstein

Who is that man who dares out-flatter the flatterers, who dares manipulate you as if you were vain and childish (like the great S[erge] K[oussevitzky])? He is a man who built an international reputation not on a composition but on promises and promises, on a *platform.* "I will lead music to . . ." Dictators promise and dictators flatter potential enemies into temporary allies, pulling the wool over their eyes. Did not Hitler once call the Italians "Aryans among Latins"? Ludicrous flattering which made the recipient quiver with joy. "Look here, everybody, the man whom I expected to hate me, whom everyone fears, he praises me, he wants to do business with me, he sent me a gift . . ."

What floors me is: it works. It's so ludicrous that it works. It worked on Stravinsky and it probably works on you.

But Lenny, suppose for a moment that Mozart were reborn, and that we'd all know: it's Mozart. What kind of a letter would a composer, would Stravinsky, would Stockhausen, would I write to him? Surely not: "I who am suspended between heaven and hell found you in my soul" but simply:

"Dear W.A.M. please allow me to show you my music. I need your advice, your criticism, and I hope you'll like me and the music. Yours . . ."

When I admire someone I do not "bestow" praise. Genuine admiration makes one modest, humble – in fact – a beggar.

Lukas

P.S. There is no possible apology for this letter of mine. Though I speak the truth it is quite obvious that I wrote it out of jealousy.

---

[55] See Letter 439.

443. Francis Poulenc to Leonard Bernstein
13 December [1959]

Dear Bernstein,

Forgive my late reply to your kind message. I accept very happily your commission for 61–62, very flattered to be numbered among the ten eminent composers. Since I will be going to New York in February, we can talk about that. As I am not a man of symphonies *alla Brahms* or Shosta[kovich], we'll see what I could write, because I want to do a good job. I've just finished my *Gloria* for Boston (60–61), so you don't need to fear a choral work. That said, I thank you and embrace you, hoping to see you soon.

Francis Poulenc[56]

444. Joe Roddy to Leonard Bernstein
Life, Time & Life Building, Rockefeller Center, New York, NY
13 February 1960

Dear Leonard,

The Mahler-mania in me is getting out of control and I cannot suppress an urge to sing the Second Symphony this week. I remind you, with good cause, that I am a survivor of City Center performances of the *Symphony of Psalms* and the *Airborne* [Symphony] conducted by you, Ninth Symphonys of Toscanini and Koussevitzky, Berlioz Requiem of Munch, and about one thousand ditties ranging from Ives to Byrd led by Robert Shaw when I was a Collegiate Chorale kid.

The best and worst that can be said of my voice is that it is harmless. It is white. I too am white.

I have crashed many a chorus in recent years, but this time the idea of legality pleases me. This morning I called one F. Austin Walker at Rutgers who said he would be pleased to have me – the flu and all that having decimated his mankind. If it's all right with you, it's all right with him.

I will call Helen Coates Tuesday for the news of Resurrection or Rejection.[57] Because the programs are printed and all that sort of thing, I will not insist on special billing, advance payment or the services of a claque.

Best,

Joe Roddy

---

[56] Written in French; English translation by the editor.
[57] Bernstein's performances of Mahler's *Resurrection* Symphony in which Roddy sang (as a member of Rutgers University Choir) were given in Carnegie Hall on 18, 19, 20, and 21 February 1960, with Phyllis Curtin and Regina Resnik as the vocal soloists.

445. William Schuman to Leonard Bernstein
130 Claremont Avenue, New York, NY
21 March 1960

Dear Lenny,

I was so pleasantly surprised by your charming and thoughtful call that I didn't tell you how touched I was that you should want to celebrate my 50th birthday. And I am delighted that you will celebrate it along with Barber's 50th and the 150th of R[obert] S[chumann], not to mention the Dean's (A[aron] C[opland]) 60th. You set me thinking about the program and I greatly appreciate your having consulted me. Actually, of course, any work of mine that you perform would afford me great pleasure. However, since this is a special occasion, I would like very much to be represented by a work with which I feel a close identification with you and one which will be having its own birthday next season too.

It will be 20 years next season that you and I first went over my Third Symphony with Kouss. But it is not just for sentimental reasons that this would be my choice for the program. On this occasion I would love to be represented by a piece of some weight and one that has been widely accepted. If you prefer No. IV (a tape of this will be sent to you tomorrow or Wednesday), fine. My idea for the program would be as follows:

1. W[illiam] S[chuman] Symphony No. III
2. Barber Violin Concerto
Intermission
3. Robert Schumann Symphony No. IV

In my view the order could also be 1, 3, 2, or 3, 2, 1. This is the closest I will probably ever come to making up a Philharmonic program. But I won't be the least bit insulted if you cannot carry out my suggestion.[58]

Once again, thank you for your vote of confidence. I told Frankie that Felicia will be calling and we will look forward very much to seeing you – it has been too long.

Affectionately,
Bill

---

[58] Bernstein played most of Schuman's suggested program. The only change was to end with Robert Schumann's Third ("Rhenish") Symphony instead of the Fourth. The concerts were given on 13, 14, and 16 October 1960 with Aaron Rosand as the soloist in Barber's Violin Concerto.

446. Larry Kert[59] to Leonard Bernstein
6 April 1960

Dear Lenny,

How excited I am at the thought of you in the pit for the overture. And Carol [Lawrence] coming back next week – well I am flying.[60]

Secco Records called me yesterday. I told them to add "some additions". Is there anything from *Peter Pan* I could do? Also what would you say if the album said "Leonard Bernstein presents Larry Kert"?[61] There would be no extra work involved for you, just your permission I guess. They want me to start on the album around the first of May. I sure hope it's a good one.

Can't wait to see you on April 27th. Nope I'm not bugging you.

Sincerely with love,

Larry K.

447. Aaron Copland to Leonard Bernstein
Green Park Hotel, Half Moon Street, London, England
1 May 1960

Dear Lensk,

Everyone's been writing me how wonderfully you did the *2nd H[urricane]*.

Also, was sent the write-ups. Naturally I'm tickled pink. Now I hear you're recording it – so I can hear it, and maybe CB[S]-TV will screen it for me when I get back end of June. Anyho this is just to say denks and denks again. (Did you get my wire? I really *was* all agog.)

When you get this I'll be in Tokio! (care Amer. Embassy.)

Had a nice concert here with the London Symphony Orch – big house and lots of enthusiasm. The English – of all ages – tend to spoil me anyhow, so I like it here.

I imagine Lukas has given you an earful about the Russkys. (Some nice lady piano teacher at the Leningrad Cons. asked after you most warmly.) It was an experience I wouldn't have wanted to miss.

Have fun with your new house. And love to you and Felicia.

Aaron

---

[59] Larry Kert (1930–91), American actor and singer who created the role of Tony in *West Side Story*.
[60] A reference to the only time Bernstein conducted any of *West Side Story* in the theater: the Overture at the opening night of the Broadway revival on 27 April 1960 (at the Alvin Theatre).
[61] Bernstein did not agree to Kert's proposal about the title of his album (a note typed by Helen Coates at the top of the letter says "cannot use L's name on Album"). It was released by Secco Records as *Larry Kert Sings Leonard Bernstein* (CELP 4670). At Bernstein's suggestion (jotted down by Helen Coates at the foot of the letter) the record included "Build My House" from *Peter Pan* as well as songs from *West Side Story*, *On the Town*, and *Wonderful Town*.

448. Jerome Robbins to Leonard Bernstein
916 North Foothill Road, Beverly Hills, CA
3 June 1960

Dear Lenny,

Thank you so much for your letter. It came almost in an ESP way, arriving after I had just had a meeting with [David] Selznick telling him that if he went to New York and enlisted you that then I would be interested in the project, otherwise not. I must have heard you writing a letter a few days before.

The opera idea about the Chassidic ghetto sounds really exciting. Sure I'd love to work on it.

Our Chino has been set for four weeks now, so unfortunately I won't be able to see Nikiforos. I'll keep him in mind if anything changes or turns up for him.

The garage idea is a good one, but true to Hollywood standards turns out to be a super garage and I seem to be spending most of my energy in pushing walls closer to each other, washing colors out of the sets, and acting like a sheep dog in trying to keep the script in a nice well directed herd aimed for the success it was in New York. I run from side to side barking warning noises about strayed lines, changed lyrics and cut choruses.[62] My they're getting tired of me.

Keep well, rest well and I promise not to pluck you out of your island repose unless I know that only you can do what has to be done.

All love as always.

Jerry

449. Jerome Robbins to Leonard Bernstein
916 North Foothill Road, Beverly Hills, CA
16 June 1960

Dear Lenny,

This just got to me. If this is *your* version of what happened about "Somewhere", it's news to me. Sure, we differed on it – but nothing was played by any orchestra that you did not know of. Nor would I ever be destructive to your music – I have too much respect for your taste and talent.[63] If it *is* your

---

[62] Robbins' entertaining description of his time in Hollywood working on the early stages of the film version of *West Side Story* shows just how tenacious he needed to be ("like a sheep dog") and shows the obvious concern he had for the way the show was being treated. However, a sharply contrasting account can be found in the long letter from Saul Chaplin to Bernstein about Robbins' work on the film (see Letter 462).

[63] Robbins was angered by an unidentified newspaper report about his treatment of "Somewhere" in *West Side Story*. It is likely that he is referring to Bernstein's comments (hitherto kept private) about Robbins changing the orchestration of "Somewhere" at the 1957 dress rehearsal of the show in Washington, DC. Amanda Vaill summarized what happened at this rehearsal as follows: "As the orchestra swelled into the lush refrain of 'Somewhere' after the ballet's end, Jerry sprang out of his

version (which I doubt) you owe me an apology I think – and if it isn't, I think you ought to put it straight. I don't think, Lenny – if I *am* to be accused of fang and claw – that I ever used them on you. I fought *for* "Somewhere" – over Arthur and occasionally Steve's objections.

Maybe I'm jumping the gun, and if so, forgive me – I value our collaboration and friendship in spite of difficulties we have when working (I'm sure we both have moments of wanting to brain the other). I find it always the most stimulating and valuable of all I've ever had anywhere. Moreover I always felt from you an admiration for my musicality as I've had for your theatrical ideas – so the item came as a shock. If that bit came from Arthur or Steve – I can understand it – but I'd appreciate hearing from you, and getting me or the paper straight.

Signed – like in Dear Abby,

'Upset'

Jerry

450. Dimitri Mitropoulos to Leonard Bernstein
12 July 1960

Dear Lenny, Dearest Friend,

I really ask you to forgive me for my silence, especially after your so generous and wonderful visit to me at the hospital, followed by your nice thoughtful gift of Gauloises cigarettes, which, it goes without saying, I enjoyed to the utmost!

What made me especially happy was to think and see that I mean something to you. Besides that, I want to assure you that your wonderful and justified development in the artistic musical world is the best gratification for me since the time I first met you in Boston. I remember in one certain instance when I told you, just like a prophet, that you are the *élu*, and certainly at that time I could not even foresee what happened, today.

So God bless you, dear friend, and keep on progressing, without paying any attention to criticism – and certainly you know as well as I that the higher you go, the more you will be criticized.

With many affectionate regards,

Dimitri[64]

---

seat and ran down to the pit to demand that the conductor, Max Goberman, cut the orchestration and give the first bars to an unaccompanied flute. 'Take that Hollywood shit out!' he cried. Without a sound, Lenny Bernstein got up and went to a bar across the street where Steve Sondheim found him staring at a row of neat Scotches lined up in front of him. Jerry later said he didn't realize Lenny was even in the theatre at the time and thought he'd understand that to make the 'extremely sensitive transition' into the duet work right, 'the song should start simply, purely.' [. . .] Jerry also admitted that 'my tactics were not of the best'" (Vaill 2007, p. 287). Evidently, some version of this story had got out and Robbins was irritated. This letter is of more general interest for Robbins' very positive view of their collaborations and their friendship.

[64] Mitropoulos died of heart failure on 2 November 1960, a few months after sending this letter.

451. Leonard Bernstein to Saul Chaplin[65]

Vineyard Haven, MA

18 July 1960

Dear Solly,

The three scores I've received look lovely (though I'm in no shape this summer to look at them microscopically). I wait in dread for the new version of the Prologue![66]

I hear it's all getting VERY expensive. That's life in Hollyburg. If it's not expensive, how can it be good? [. . .]

Much love,

Lenny

452. Leonard Bernstein to Aaron Copland

Vineyard Haven, MA

[July 1960]

Dearest A,

A greatly belated welcome home! And the fact that I think of you every day, and often twice a day, does not compensate for not having written you. But then, you haven't written me either (except: loved your cable about the *Hurricane*).

But today I must write, because last night I heard the test-pressing of the *2nd Hurricane* recording which will be out in time for your birthday. It's badly engineered in places, especially when there is choral complexity (the voices are too distant and unclear, the orch. is too present) – but in general I think you'll be delighted. Of course, it's similar to the TV version, with me narrating, preserving a line or two of dialogue here & there, & cutting Fat's Song plus 2 other small cuts. But mainly I'm writing because I'm so impressed all over again with the music. It is lovely & endlessly fresh: neither the simplicity nor the grandeur stales. Felicia loves it; Jamie & Alexander sing it marvelously by the yard. I hope you like it; it will be our November release on Columbia, along with *Billy* & *Rodeo*, making a delightful, gay (though costly) birthday package!

And à propos birthday. The Pension Fund concert I had planned for your birthday in Carnegie Hall is off, alas; too complicated to get all the participants I wanted (Ormandy, etc.), & perhaps not the right note for Pension Fund events. *But*, I have a better idea, which is something nobody else can do for your

---

[65] Saul Chaplin (1912–97), American composer and film-music supervisor. He first met Bernstein in 1944 and saw him conduct *Fancy Free* at the Hollywood Bowl in August that year. Chaplin was Music Supervisor and Associate Producer for the film version of *West Side Story*.

[66] The Prologue of *West Side Story*, which was extensively reworked for the film.

60th, and that is to make a whole TV show for the kids (the Shell series, originating in Carnegie) on the subject of the Venerable Giggling Dean.

Imagine, Judge-Nose for one hour, coast-to-coast! This will happen on the 12th November (Sat.) at noon in Carnegie Hall, & probably be telecast the following day, Sunday afternoon. I want you to participate, do you hear?! Either to conduct a piece, or play the piano, or maybe narrate the Lincoln piece, or maybe conduct same with me narrating. In any case it should be fun. Please say you'll do it, & that there aren't sixty other conflicting homages on the same day.

A couple of weeks ago I watched & heard you conduct the BSO for 90 minutes on WGBH-TV, and it was a joy. Man, you've improved incredibly! Clarity, meaningfulness of beat, ass not extruding. Only problem: die head too much in die score. You must to know die Musik better (or at least trust yourself more). But the big thrill was hearing the Symph #1 again – what a scherzo! And I had real pleasure out of your colloquy with Walter P[iston]. Even the Diamond *Rounds* sounded good! Want to succeed me at the Philh.?

I long to see you, & hear about your phenomenal travels. Any significant liaisons? When will we ever meet again?

I sorely miss T'wood also. My love to it, & its inmates. Me, I haven't written a note.

Much love,

L

453. Aaron Copland to Leonard Bernstein
Berkshire Music Center, Tanglewood, MA
28 July 1960

Dear Lensk,

A big pleasure to get your letter. On my one day in N.Y. before coming here I had Roger Englander show me the *2nd H[urricane]*. That was a big pleasure too – a revival only you could have made so moving. I hope the recording is as good. (Only one reproach: you didn't mention Edwin [Denby]'s name as collaborator.) Goddard had written me about the birthday package and I'm pleased as punch about that *too*. (He's also bringing out [William] Masselos' performance of the *Piano Fantasy* which I want you to hear – performance is *superb*, I think.)

About the TV – Nov. 12; of course I'll do anything you like. Whatever else happens it will give us a reason to "confer", i.e., see each other for a change! The only thing I don't want is to be presented as "grandpa for the kiddies." One item you might consider is a selection of songs from the *Old American Songs*. I did them with The Little Orchestra and W[illia]m Warfield 2 years ago. Warfield does them wonderfully and the orchestral versions are fun-things. (You might show the kids the original versions of the songs I worked with.) If you have a quintet of singers the "Promise of Living" from *The Tender Land* works fine. (Or

that and the Square Dance can be performed in the choral version with orch.)
Etc. Etc ... The hard thing will be to illustrate my "tougher" side, no?

The idea of *you* watching me conduct for 90 min. struck terror ... After
8 performances of the Symph #1 on tour I think I can trust myself to peek
outside "die score"! Anyway I've been getting lots of conducting practice: in
3 months I've had concerts with 7 different orchestras.

We need you in Tanglewood – but badly. That's a whole chapter by itself.
Our summer is enlivened by Luciano Berio who is guest composer and has
stirred things up considerably. But otherwise, routine reigns. Too bad ...

Aside from music, I had a lovely time in London and in Tokio. The only
thing I didn't do was write music, hélas!

Love to you always,

Aaron

454. Leonard Bernstein to Felicia Bernstein
The Faculty Club, University of British Columbia, Vancouver, Canada
[14 August 1960]

Darling,

Just a quickie:

We've arrived[67] into a glorious kind of Pacific autumn here, with marvelous
light over the sound, snow-capped peaks all around, and really *cool* air. I'm
ensconced in this palatial suite at the University, where it is said Queen Eliz. was
impregnated. Probably a canard.[68] Anyway I'm sleeping in her bed.

Denver was marvelous.[69] Now begins the piano nightmare. (You told me so,
I know.)[70] And I still can't memorize the Bartók or *Daphnis*.[71] Paresis.

All is well, the back is great so far, and the press conferences are enormous &
ghastly. I've just written David K[eiser][72] at length, offering myself for a long
period on the opening–closing basis of the coming season. OK? Call you from
Seattle.

All my love, my darling,

L

---

[67] Bernstein and the New York Philharmonic arrived in Vancouver on 14 August, and gave concerts
in the city on 15 and 16 August.
[68] Queen Elizabeth II and Prince Philip stayed at the newly opened Faculty Club in July 1959, a year
before Bernstein's visit. Prince Andrew was born on 19 February 1960 (so the story is, indeed, a
canard).
[69] The New York Philharmonic gave a concert in Denver, CO, on 13 August.
[70] Bernstein appeared as soloist in Beethoven's Piano Concerto No. 1 in one of the Vancouver
concerts.
[71] Bartók's *Concerto for Orchestra* and the Second Suite from Ravel's *Daphnis and Chloe* were on the
Vancouver programs.
[72] David Keiser was President of the Board of the New York Philharmonic.

455. Leonard Bernstein to Aaron Copland
Mark Hopkins Hotel, San Francisco, CA
26 August 1960

Dear Aa,

Loved your letter. First instant to catch up: two weeks gone out of seven, seems like two years – much work, but also glorious fun. All record-breaking crowds, and screaming ones at that. Like Russia. And Hawaii – now there's a chapter. Just arrived from there last night, utterly spent. Mon dieu, quelle beauté!

San Fran is all gold and blue, & teeming.

I think your idea of the *American Songs* is great. But we must be careful not to do too much stuff out of repertoire: there's so little rehearsal time, and you know how it's jammed into the busy week. But I'm sure we can swing some of the songs (& maybe an Emily [Dickinson] one too – hein?) and mebbe your tougher side through the Variations, which I could show at the piano first. Then perhaps the scherzo of the 3rd Symph, and finally a pop thing like *Rodeo* or *Lincoln*. How would you like to participate – that is, in what capacity? Conductor or speaker in *Lincoln* or pianist or speechifier? Don't bother answering; just mull, & we'll confer when I get home. There's time.

Much love, I miss you.

Lenny

26 Aug 60 (I'm 42!!!)

PS. About Edwin:[73] There were supposed to be big credits on the screen about his authorship, which were cut for time reasons. I couldn't really mention him, since we didn't do the play. But I had him invited to the event, in the hopes that I could have him stand up for a bow, but he didn't show. In any case, I had a sweet & very thankful telegram from him after the show. (The recording is poorly engineered – diction, etc. obscure. Alas.)

456. Marni Nixon[74] to Leonard Bernstein
The Mayfair Hotel, London, England
28 August 1960

Dear Mr. Bernstein,

Just saw *West Side Story* for the first time – here in London – and it's a tremendous show! I am "up" for the voice dubbing for the picture they

---

[73] Edwin Denby, librettist of *The Second Hurricane*.

[74] Marni Nixon (b. 1930), American soprano whose concert repertoire includes works by Schoenberg, Webern, Ives, and Boulez, and whose parallel career has been as the dubbed singing voice of several screen legends in film musicals, including Marilyn Monroe (the high notes in "Diamonds Are A Girl's Best Friend"), Deborah Kerr (*The King and I*), Audrey Hepburn (*My Fair Lady*), and Natalie Wood (*West Side Story*).

are making at Goldwyn – for Maria's singing voice. Can you help me in any way there? Would certainly appreciate anything you think you can do to help.[75]

Hoping you are well, and I understand we might get together for another fling at Pierre Boulez next March. Hope so!

I'm at present vacationing with my husband [Ernest Gold] – who just completed the score for *Exodus* and we've been in London for a while & now we will travel on the continent for a while before going back to Hollywood.

Ah – have you ever been on vacation? I suspect you haven't found the time for years now. It's wonderful!

Sincerely,

Marni Nixon

457. Leonard Bernstein to Saul Chaplin
20 September 1960
[Telegram]

Dear Solly,

Between Dixie and Berlin I send urgent pleas to consider rerecording some of the tracks I heard in Hollywood. Cool, Mambo and Jet Song are OK although slowish but America is much too slow and Rumble dies of Adagio. Also rhythms wrong at end of Something's Coming. Prologue of course is impossible and embarrassing. Johnny [Green] know[s] of feelings. Please try to redo and correct as much as possible.

Love,

Lenny

---

[75] On Bernstein's recommendation, Marni Nixon was chosen to dub Natalie Wood's singing voice as Maria, and she was in Hollywood less than a month after sending this letter. She was widely experienced in contemporary classical repertoire (on 31 March 1960 she had given the first American performance of Boulez's *Improvisation sur Mallarmé I* with Bernstein and the New York Philharmonic), and was already familiar to film studios as the singing voice of Deborah Kerr in *The King and I*. She arrived in Hollywood in late September 1960 to work on *West Side Story* for $300 a day, and had to tread a delicate path, since Natalie Wood was convinced she could do her own singing. Nixon's own account of the recording deserves quoting at length: "The sessions were set up so that Natalie would first record a song on her own and then I would get up and record the whole song again. I knew that this was going to be embarrassing and traumatic for her, but I was just an employee and went along with it. Musicians, especially ones this good, are noted for their disdain of mediocrity [...] As Natalie sang, they showed their displeasure by playing poorly. They kind of sawed away at the notes instead of playing with the sensitivity of which they were more than capable. Then, when I got up to sing the identical song, the same musicians would sit up in their seats and play with renewed vigor and passion. When I finished a take they would even applaud. I was both very embarrassed and disgusted at their rudeness to poor Natalie who was, after all, doing her best" (Nixon 2006, pp. 133–4).

458. Leonard Bernstein to Nadia Boulanger
New York, NY
22 December 1960

My dearly beloved Nadia,

I am so happy that you have accepted our invitation![76] Not only will your visit give great musical joy to a large public, but enormous personal joy to all of us who for so long have regarded you as the unique and adorable person you are.

Don't you think it would be marvelous to play something of one or two of your former pupils?

I look forward to seeing you with keen anticipation; and I was deeply moved by your beautiful letter.

Always,

Lenny (Bernstein)

Joyeux Noël!

459. Lukas Foss to Leonard Bernstein
University of California, Los Angeles, CA
[?December 1960 or January 1961]

Carissimo,

West Side Story score arrived and I am having a great time with it. Love it more and more. I am *proud* to do it!! But *when* can I get the definitive (final) version? And when is that one and only rehearsal?[77]

I am anticipating yet another Bernstein feast – on Saturday eve. May 20th. Ojai Festival.[78] Don't know if you know about the Festival. It's famous around here. Stravinsky did *Les Noces* and other works one spring, Copland conducted it another. This year it's mine. I am doing away with the large orchestra which makes for too skimpy rehearsal time, on the meager budget. I am using never more than 30 players, but the best in Los Angeles. Anyway, on that Saturday, the program – my pride and joy – will be:

---

[76] Nadia Boulanger conducted a series of concerts with the New York Philharmonic in February 1962 (see Letter 472).

[77] This concerns the first performance of the *Symphonic Dances from West Side Story*, which Foss conducted with the New York Philharmonic in Carnegie Hall on 13 February 1961 at the *Valentine For Leonard Bernstein*, a Pension Fund Benefit Concert, concluding a first half that had opened with Aaron Copland conducting the *Candide* Overture followed by the *Jeremiah* Symphony conducted by Vladimir Golschmann, with Jennie Tourel as the soloist. The second half of the programme, produced by David Oppenheim and presented by Betty Comden and Adolph Green, was a series of "Valentine Surprises" of music from Bernstein's Broadway shows and *Fancy Free*.

[78] The Ojai Festival, in California, was directed by Foss in 1961, the occasion on which the programme he outlines was given with André Previn, Shelly Manne, and others.

Anniversaries (Me at the piano)
Rondo for Lifey (Divace + Me)
West Side Story jazzed up (Previn and [Shelly] Manne and . . . the bass)
Masque from *Age of Anxiety* (with fade out on pianino)
(André plays, I conduct – or vice versa)
20 minutes of non-jazz improv. (my improv. Chamber ensemble)
Mozart C major 4 hand Sonata (André & Me)

I think that's a gem of a program. The shift from non-jazz to jazz back to non-jazz is subtle and meaningful thanks to your music and its enormous jazz–non-jazz range. Incidentally André and Shelly offered to donate their services and seem as pleased with the whole thing as I am.

Love to Felicia. *Did* you get the record, notes, charts – that messy little package? Until February, cher ami

Luke McLuke

460. Leonard Bernstein to Sid Ramin
[January 1961]

Sid,

Make it for tpts and tbns (4 each available) and percussion, but if you have time, add optional parts for horns and winds.[79]

Blessings and luck!

Lenny

If you're rushed, first make it for *brass*.

461. Frank Sinatra[80] to Leonard and Felicia Bernstein
Washington, D.C.
12 January 1961
[Telegram]

Greetings,

I thought I'd better send you a rundown of activities along the Potomac. First of all, the workaday side of it, I must ask you not to make any outside

---

[79] Given the scoring (including 4 trumpets and trombones), this note is almost certainly in connection with Ramin's orchestration of the *Fanfare for the Inauguration of John F. Kennedy*, first performed in January 1961, which Ramin orchestrated for 1 piccolo, 2 flutes (ad lib.), 2 oboes, 2 clarinets, 3 horns, 4 trumpets, 4 trombones, timpani, and percussion.

[80] Frank Sinatra (1915–98), American singer, actor, and entertainment legend. He had known Bernstein since the early 1940s when they had both worked in New York nightclubs such as the Riobamba (see Letter 115).

appointments for the entire day of the eighteenth which is Wednesday if you remember. This will be a tough day of rehearsal and as it behooves us all to put on a really slick show the next night[81] I think we should devote this entire day and night to rehearsals. And you know how much I like rehearsals. The morning of the nineteenth will be final orchestra rehearsals and we will start the dress rehearsal at noon.

Now for the social side of this hoedown. Exhibit A will be a supper party that Ambassador Kennedy is giving in honor of the entire cast immediately after our gala performance. This will be black tie for the fellows and something dazzling for the girls. Exhibit B is the inaugural ceremony itself at noon of the twentieth and the parade which follows. Sections of seats have been allotted for us for both events, for those who want to attend. I must ask you to please tell Miss Lovell in my office at the Statler Hilton Hotel whether or not you want to attend these two functions. Exhibit C is the little wing-ding dinner which I am tossing for all of us at seven thirty on the evening of the twentieth. We will also go *en masse* from this dinner to the Inaugural Ball at the Mayflower, which is pretty dressy for boys and girls. Black tie or white tie diamond and emeralds and all that jazz. Everything is shaping up for something that we all will be remembering for a long time and believe you me I don't think I have ever been so excited.

Love and kisses and I'll be waiting for you.

Frank Sinatra

462. Saul Chaplin to Leonard Bernstein
11 April 1961

Dear Lenny,

After much discussion with Bob Wise, it was decided that the opening of the picture would be handled in the following manner: the helicopter shots would be kept the way they are now except for the "motto" whistles which will precede the long orchestral note. Also, we *will* add the finger-snaps during the long note. The general feeling here is that the helicopter shots are very unusual and dramatic, and not at all travelogue-y. It is felt that they do progress the audience to the locale of the picture in a most effective manner. In any event, the opening will be kept this way for the preview. If, at that time, anyone feels that the high shots slow the opening of the picture, or interfere with the dramatic content of the "Prologue", the proper changes will be made.

---

[81] Sinatra is confirming arrangements for the Inaugural Ball for President Kennedy at which Bernstein conducted his *Fanfare for the Inauguration of John F. Kennedy*.

Your recital of Jerry's report to you concerning the picture has been on my mind constantly. He has, conveniently, omitted a significant amount of information in his usual vaguely dishonest manner.[82] Isn't it interesting that he didn't think it important to mention various large mistakes in the numbers he shot? Isn't it curious that he didn't mention that the Jets are out of sync during a section of "The Jet Song"; or that there's half a bar of music missing during the fugue of "Cool"; or how I pleaded with him to just "try" the faster version of "Cool" and how he refused; or how several sections of "America" and "I Feel Pretty" wouldn't cut together except through Bob Wise's ingenuity; or how he staged "One Hand" and was always aware that we were going to use just one chorus and had no *objection* whatever? I could further mention how he kept encouraging Natalie Wood to sing her own track so that as late as last Friday I was still having trouble from that quarter. I could go on endlessly reciting blunders, which he neglected to mention to you. But, I assure you, we've corrected, and are correcting, all of his mistakes without talking about them. I hope on the other hand, he mentioned how exciting the "Quintet" turned out; or how wonderful the "Taunting" is; or how touching "Somewhere" is; or many other facets of the picture which, I'm sure, slipped his mind since we managed to muddle through without him.

The reason for this diatribe is quite simple: the fact that Jerry is going to derogate all of us concerns me not at all; the fact that many people will believe what he tells them, since it's fashionable to regard us all out here as sun-loving, bungling, no-talents, also doesn't concern me. What *you* believe, however, concerns me deeply. I can only reiterate that never in my experience has so much money and care been expended in the making of a movie. If it is not perfect in every detail, my only answer is – what is? It isn't because we didn't try like Hell. Jerry, of course, is wildly talented. He is also wildly destructive of people and relationships. For me, one doesn't compensate for the other. He is easily the most reprehensible person I've ever known. And so, when the golden day dawns when I will, at last, be freed from *West Side Story*, I will make it a life's work never again to mention his name or think of him. That, indeed, will be a time for wild celebration.

---

[82] This brutally frank account of Jerome Robbins' work on the movie of *West Side Story* was intended for Bernstein's eyes only, but it conveys something of the profound frustration felt by the producers – Robert Wise (also the movie's co-director), Walter Mirisch, and Saul Chaplin – about what they felt to be Robbins' high-handed and unreasonable behavior on the set, as well as Chaplin's concern that Robbins was giving a very selective account of the movie's problems in his reports back to Bernstein.

I'm sorry to have kept you this long at a time when I know how busy you are. I wish you great success with your tour and I'm sure you'll have much better luck with Alaska than I did. (Remember *Bonanza Bound*?).[83]

Love and sholom,

Sol

463. Leonard Bernstein to Felicia Bernstein

Hotel New Nagoya, Nagoya, Japan

30 April 1961

Darling,

How can I describe the last two days? Paradise. At last, really Japan – once we got out of mad gay Tokyo. About 16 of us were put up at that famous Japanese inn called Minaguchi-ya, where I think I had the most beautiful day and night anyone has ever had. The gardens – the beauty – the sea – the quiet – the deep charm of Japanese rooms, the smell of new tatami (the straw mats used for carpeting) – the elegance of simple flower arrangements – the marvelous food – and oh, the girls. We were welcomed in a way that made me feel I'd never been really welcomed before. The girls crowd around, laughing, attending, bubbling, dressing & undressing you, preparing your kimono, your bath (oh that wonderful bath of old scoured wood) – and with none of the artificial gaiety of the Geisha (who embarrass the wits out of me) but with a natural spontaneous joie de vivre & delight in making you happy. I had the Emperor's suite, mind you, & slept in his bed, & had his breakfast (about 17 courses) and it was coincidentally the Emperor's birthday, so Lennuhtt was the Emperor (which is *Tenno* in Japanese, so now you can call me Tennuhtt). The morning after we visited the famous nearby temple Shuken-ji, a terribly moving Zen sanctuary with the most overwhelming gardens I have ever seen. The entire side of a mountain covered in every green imaginable, spotted with huge red azalea, & pierced by a long, narrow graceful waterfall from top to bottom. I shall never forget the sound of that silence, or the odors, the color, the peace.

All this is really to say that in two days you would change your whole mind about things Japanese. I know you would. You would adore the food (most of it anyway), the sense of beauty, the natural grace of people and houses. You'd even change your mind about paper windows & walls & screens & doors & mats & sitting on the floor. It is the way to live. I insist on bringing you here some time, without the orchestra and la Belle and Tourel.

---

[83] *Bonanza Bound* was a 1947 musical set in Alaska in 1898, with a score by Saul Chaplin, book and lyrics by Betty Comden and Adolph Green, sets by Oliver Smith, and musical direction by Lehman Engel. Try-outs opened at the Shubert Theatre in Philadelphia on 26 December 1947, but despite the talent involved in the show, it closed there a week later, never reaching Broadway. Bernstein toured to Alaska with the New York Philharmonic in 1961.

Now today that Paradise is all over, as we've moved into another noisy characterless big city, which doesn't even have the fun of Tokyo, but only the ugliness. But from here on it gets good again – more Japanese style inns, & Kyoto, which I can't wait to see, & Kobe, & *pearls*. I bought me two black kimonos today – one silk, one wool: something for you, don't dare really. Bought Axel a great boy-doll in honor of Boys' Day which is the big festival tomorrow. It's a Samurai-boy on a horse, in a glass case, & featuring a huge phallus, which I don't know how I'll explain to him. Then visited Nagoya Castle, a breathtaking piece of architecture, and a museum reminiscent of the Hermitage in terms of costumes, prints, & paintings. Now sleep. Then a koto-player is coming for to play the koto. Then sleep. Day off. Thank God. My big nose is still sick, & needs a big rest. All else is great, concerts et al. are smashes. Minimum of Saudeks [Robert and Elizabeth], etc. All under control. Only I miss you terribly.

My love, my little maid of Orleans, my swan, I miss you. My dearest love to the littles.

L

O, that inn! I had always thought the idea that Japanese made men happy was a commercial notion from Brando movies: but it's true!

464. Felicia Bernstein to Leonard Bernstein
1 May [1961]

Ha-ha Rennuhtt (or is it Chi-Chi),

Hip! Hip! Your letter arrived and not so chop-chop either – but then who can figure it out? I feel I cannot waste a minute if this is to reach you at all.

It was so wonderful to hear from you – sort of unbelievable since I confess that I still have the childish notion that the Orient is never-never land – it's hard to picture you all there. I mean like Helen Coates painted on a kaki-mono or Jack Fishburg[84] meditating at a Buddhist Temple, or you for that matter being fed by some dainty geisha – anyway Tokyo sounds disastrous and shatters all my childhood dreams.

New York, however, is exactly the same as you left it – the same set, the same cast of characters. There is *nothing* new on *any* front. Alexander is in bed with a cough (not serious). Henry is fine and looks beautiful. He was not allowed by the doctor to go to the country since he's still convalescing – so I took BB & Ellen instead. I've been with the "liver pip" for about a week so I was afraid to go by myself. It was to *die* there – no dogwood yet, but forsythia, daffodils, jonquils, pinks, blues – dreamy! I can't bear that you're missing it – still, I guess you're

---

[84] Jack [Joachim] Fishberg (1904–70) was a violinist in the New York Philharmonic for forty-four years.

getting spring in spades there! But somehow it's not the same when it doesn't belong to you.

I'm off to Rochester in a few days – I've worked hard and feel secure – I wonder if they are?

Don't buy me a "simple" pearl – I've decided I don't want rings any more! Kiss you long with all my love,

F

465. Nadia Boulanger to Leonard Bernstein

Écoles d'Art Américaines, Fontainebleau, France
5 May 1961

Dear Lenny,

Just receive[d] the score of *West Side Story* "at the request of the composer". Well – it sounds rather miraculous as I had just ordered it! Too beautiful – not to be true!

Merci – I am enchanted by its dazzling nature – perhaps facility is a danger, but it is enough to be aware of that and follow it.

Until soon. I often think of you, of the problems and temptations that your gifts give you – divergent and convergent.

With my greatest affection to all of you.

NB[85]

466. Felicia Bernstein to Leonard Bernstein

8 May [1961]

My darling,

Your wonderful beautiful letter from Nagoya followed me to Rochester – it arrived just in time for the concert and inspired me to new heights – in other words it went tickety-boo to the races! Hollenbach[86] turned out to be a jolly good conductor, the chorus was wonderful and your old Maid of Orleans did you proud. And here I am back at the store covered with laurels, my ego in top form for at least six months!

We are all counting the days to your arrival – such an enormity of events have taken place since you left that I feel it should all somehow quiet down once you are home safe and sound – so did it!

Love to all – kisses to you from the littles – I love you,

F

---

[85] The first paragraph of this letter is in English. The remainder is in French, translated by the editor.
[86] Theodore Hollenbach, conductor of the Rochester Oratorio Society from 1945 to 1986. Felicia was performing Honegger's *Joan of Arc at the Stake* in Rochester.

467. Leonard Bernstein: Stephen Sondheim Acrostic
5 July 1961

S tephen Sondheim is a maker and solver of puzzles:
T he mind's jig-saw, creativity's crossword, and
E specially the heart's cryptologies.
P uzzler-poet of word and note, now puzzled, now puzzling,
H e may on occasion inch apart
E nough to reveal the delicate cracks between;
N ext moment the pieces are magnetized, spring together with a

J olt of rightness: himself a puzzle, self devised, self-soluble.

S tephen Sondheim loves Christmas: not
O nly for the riddle of giving the precisely definitive gift;
N ot, surely, for the getting of it; but for the warm
D ecembral restatement of remembrance.
H e is compulsively loyal,
E ven to friends disloyal to each other. Finally,
I f you like his words, wait til you hear his
M usic, *qua solutum acrosticon est.*

Leonard Bernstein
July 5, 1961[87]

468. Leonard Bernstein to Arthur Laurents
31 October 1961

Dear Arthur,
    I've been meaning to tell you, ever since I saw the W[*est*] S[*ide*] S[*tory*] film,[88] that I had never realized until that moment how much I admired and, yes, even revered your work on the show, and how much we all owe to you. It becomes all too painfully obvious as one sees the line-by-shot destruction of the book by the H'wood exegists (there's no such word!), and the clearest of all is the line, however fine, between whatever art is, and non-art. I just wanted to say a personal Thank you.
    Lenny

---

[87] An earlier version of this acrostic, dated 22 March 1957, is printed in Bernstein 1982, p. 136. It contains several differences from the text printed here.
[88] The film version of *West Side Story* had its premiere in New York on 18 October 1961.

469. Francis Poulenc to Leonard Bernstein
Le Beau Rivage, Lausanne–Ouchy, Switzerland
1 November 1961

Dear Bernstein,

Great news!! The *Répons des Ténèbres* are finished. I hope that you will like them. It's very simple (because of the children) but also, I believe, very moving, with nothing decorative like the *Gloria* and completely internal. It's penitence, but "poverty is not a vice" as Markevitch put it in his *Rebus*. For a long time I've wanted to tell you that I went *twice in five days* to see *West Side Story* in Paris. I was *fascinated*, that's the exact word, by everything that you have expressed and suggested. For someone who loves the interval of a sixth

you'll know how much I liked the big love duet. Bravo!

The boys have told me that they played the Double Concerto, and recorded it, with you. What a joy! I cannot wait to hear it.

Thank you for remaining a faithful friend.

I embrace you, dear Bernstein

Fr. Poulenc[89]

470. Leonard Bernstein to Igor Stravinsky[90]
5 January 1962

Dear Maître,

It is our pleasure to hope to make a double celebration of your coming birthday. First we want to devote a special Pension Fund program to your works; this would

---

[89] Written in French; English translation by the editor.

[90] Igor Stravinsky (1882–1971), Russian-born composer; a dominant figure in twentieth-century music. His professional relationship with Bernstein was always friendly, but as Charles M. Joseph writes: "although his correspondence with Bernstein was cordial enough, the [Stravinsky] archives disclose some hostility in Stravinsky and his circle of friends. Bernstein's *The Age of Anxiety*, Symphony No. 2 of 1949, was inspired by W. H. Auden's book of the same name. Auden was not pleased and quickly distanced himself from any association with the work. He gave Stravinsky a copy of the book in which he wrote on the title page, 'Leonard Bernstein is a shit.' Stravinsky himself, Craft told me, walked out of a performance of the same symphony and wanted to leave *West Side Story* as well. [. . .] Perhaps at the root of this reprobation was an envy of Bernstein's public appeal, as well as an aversion to the charismatic conductor's mission to catechize about music, to convince people 'what to feel', as Stravinsky described it." (Joseph 2001, pp. 226–7). Joseph also points out that "Commercial record sales were another target of Stravinsky's annoyance. Bernstein was a major competitor for recording royalties, hitting home in a way that Stravinsky could not fail to notice. John McClure of Columbia Masterworks recalled that Stravinsky never accepted the fact that other conductors, especially dynamic ones like Bernstein, could steal the composer's thunder" (Joseph 2001, p. 229).

occur on the 21st of March and be a gala celebration. Then, on the following Saturday, the 24th, we are planning to play another program of your music for a Young People's Concert, and this one would be nationally televised a month or so later.

Remembering your charming cooperation with us on a previous television program, and recalling your kind telegram last season after our *Oedipus Rex* program, I am encouraged to ask you again if you would not join us on this television show as well. Perhaps you could say a word of greeting to the young people (who, as you have said, understand your music better than anyone!) – and then, if you wish, conduct the orchestra in some final work, like part of *Petrouchka*, or whatever you would like.

I don't have to tell you what an honor it would be for us all to have you present (at both occasions, preferably, since they are so close together), besides helping us, reciprocally, to honor you in the way we would like to. To say nothing of my personal delight.

Yours always,

LB[91]

471. Igor Stravinsky to Leonard Bernstein

1260 North Wetherly Drive, Hollywood, CA
11 January 1962

My dear Leonard,

I was delighted to receive your letter of January 4. I was also pleased to hear of your plans to perform my music during the spring season.

Alas, I cannot appear on television myself before I complete *Noah*[92] (when will that be?): on this point my television contract is very strict. And, two times also, I can't be in New York in March. The best I can do is send you my fondest greetings and to hope that all goes well. Perhaps, too, you would be kind enough to greet the children from me.[93]

Cordially,

Igor Stravinsky

---

[91] Pencil draft of the letter Bernstein sent.

[92] An earlier title for *The Flood*, commissioned by CBS Television and first broadcast on 14 June 1962.

[93] Stravinsky was eager to see the broadcast of "Happy Birthday Igor Stravinsky," Bernstein's *Young People's Concert* first relayed on 26 March 1962. He sent a telegram to Bernstein on 6 April: "Please tell Roger Englander Saturday May 5 is ideal for me. Many thanks. Would you lunch with me before or after the screening? Another great favor I have to ask is could you please record the three snippets John McClure has from *The Flood*. Cordially, Stravinsky." A draft reply is written below, partly by Bernstein and partly by Helen Coates: "Everything set for screening Sat. May 5 at 1 p.m. Delighted to have lunch with you afterwards. Will make every effort to accommodate you on *The Flood* snippets. Warmest greetings." Bernstein did in fact record part of the soundtrack for the CBS television relay of *The Flood*. According to Charles M. Joseph's *Stravinsky Inside Out*: "The work was finally recorded at the CBS studios in Hollywood on 31 March. [Robert] Craft led the orchestra for the audio taping (although the televised program led the audience to believe that Stravinsky himself was on the podium), and

P.S. Franz Waxman has urged me to try to persuade you to conduct a concert of my music in his (mid-June) Los Angeles Music Festival. I would be very happy if you would accept, of course, though I know you must be busy at that time (as I am; I can't participate myself).

472. Nadia Boulanger to Leonard Bernstein
1 Sutton Place South, New York, NY
20 February 1962

Dear Lenny,

What can I say to you? Words seem feeble [...] and I don't know how to tell you how grateful I am, but that must not prevent me from trying. Your spontaneity, your affection touch me deeply – and after this very moving week, for so many reasons, passed so quickly, alas.[94] I drown – yes, I drown in the memory of *ma Petite*,[95] hoping for you to receive a little of all that you give – and a little of the indefinable joy which gives peace to the heart, to life and to the spirit. And at the moment when this mystery is about to bring a new life into your existence I pray to God for [her] and for both of you.[96]

Read what isn't written, and feel all that goes to you, from the bottom of my heart.

Nadia[97]

Leonard Bernstein helped as well. A week later the composer wrote to McClure in New York, providing specific instructions for a passage to be recorded by Leonard Bernstein" (Joseph 2001, p. 152). Joseph goes on to quote from Stravinsky's 6 April letter to McClure, is which the composer raises the question of how the credits should read for the shared conducting duties: "It seems to me you invite speculation and call undue attention to a problem by saying two people conducted and not saying who conducted what. Therefore, leave out the word 'conductor' *entirely*. Say 'recording supervised by the composer' " (Joseph 2001, p. 152). Bernstein himself believed that Stravinsky's coolness towards him near the end of the composer's life was down to Robert Craft: "I could *kill* him – I mean, he spoiled such a lovely relationship between Stravinsky and myself" (Cott 2013, p. 31).
[94] Nadia Boulanger conducted four concerts with the New York Philharmonic on 15, 16, 17, and 18 February 1962. The program comprised Fauré's Requiem, the premiere of a specially made orchestral version of Virgil Thomson's *A Solemn Music*, and three Psalms by Lili Boulanger. There was another, more somber reason for this being a "moving week": the Fauré Requiem on 17 February was dedicated to the memory of Bruno Walter, who had died that day. Bernstein addressed the audience before the performance:

> My dear friends, I bring you the heartbreaking news that Bruno Walter died this morning. It is almost too much to bear. Last year our beloved Mitropoulos – and now this great genius, who for forty years has been so close to us here at the Philharmonic – who has guided us so wisely, and so generously brightened and enriched our lives. Like Mitropoulos, he was one of the saints of music – a man all kindness and warmth, goodness and devotion. We can only mourn, and pay tribute. I would like to add that the Philharmonic and Mlle Boulanger will perform the Requiem of Fauré in memory of Bruno Walter.

[95] Presumably Boulanger's sister, Lili (1893–1918).
[96] Nina Maria Felicia Bernstein was born on 28 February 1962.
[97] Written in French; English translation by the editor.

473. Fritz Reiner to Leonard Bernstein

Rambleside, Weston, CT
5 March 1962

Dear Lenny,

Carlotta & I are very happy over the safe arrival of Nina Maria and hope that we shall have the opportunity of seeing her – as well as the rest of the family.

I felt most unhappy at missing my concerts with the Philharmonic but was forced to give in to the doctor.

We are being very quiet and getting a good rest before leaving for Chicago on the 16th. Will be back for the rites of spring in Connecticut and hope that your plans are going to include Redding plus a visit to Rambleside.

Affectionate greetings to all and a welcoming kiss to the new Princesa.[98]
Faithfully,
Fritz

474. Rudolf Bing[99] to Leonard Bernstein

Hotel Sacher, Vienna, Austria
18 June 1962

Dear Lennie,

Apparently we cannot come to an agreement with your lawyer's requests which I consider totally unreasonable.

I *have* fulfilled my promise – I *have* a signed agreement with Zeffirelli! It is unfair and unreasonable to expect me to release you if Zeffirelli dies or breaches his contract (both of which I hope and trust are only remote possibilities). In such case I gladly agree to *consult* with you on a substitute but the decision must remain the Management's – unless you agree to run the Met! Really I feel this has now gone on long enough – even beyond contract there should remain an ounce of mutual trust and confidence – so please sign now and I won't worry. I have no intention of killing Zeffirelli and substituting Karajan as Director! You got all you want – so now please give me what I want: Bernstein!

Thanks and regards,
Rudolf Bing

No further "clause" is needed – attach this note to the contract! Bing[100]

---

[98] Nina Bernstein.

[99] Rudolf Bing (1902–97) was General Manager of the Metropolitan Opera from 1950 to 1972.

[100] A draft of Bernstein's reply (in Helen Coates' hand) is attached: "Whole starting point of this venture was the prospect of collaboration with Z[effirelli] & without that collab. the whole project loses its orig. meaning. It was not simply a case of finding a suitable opera to conduct at the Met, but rather to make my first appear. at the Met in this specific collaborative enterprise. I must therefore insist on collaborating with Z. or have approval of a substitute."

475. Louise Talma[101] to Leonard Bernstein

MacDowell Colony, Peterborough, NH

4 July 1962

Dear Lenny,

We miss you just terribly. There's been no real gaiety since you left. We've had a couple of games of anagrams, but without you there's no excitement. You're one of the blessed ones who make everything they encounter come alive. It's a rare and precious gift, and I wish you a long enjoyment of it.

A letter from Thornton [Wilder] contains a message for you: "Tell Lennie I know all about the Kaddish because it's in *Finnegan's Wake*, and give him my uproarious regards." He also says: "It sounds as tho' you were a congenial crowd – the 'Round' gives earnest of that. Anyway, with you and Lenny there the tone is set is How to be civilized though an artist." I quote the sentence exactly, punctuation, or rather the lack of it, capitalization and all.

Have a wonderful and refreshing time in Spain.

Love from all of us,

Louise

476. Leonard Bernstein to Adolph Green and Phyllis Newman

Barcelona [written on the headed paper of the ocean liner *Leonardo da Vinci* of the Italia Line]

3 August 1962

Darling Greens,

Does this notepaper look familiar? Do you suddenly feel queasy at the sight of it? Does it bring back gorgeous salons filled with square brown chairs, Doman & Pythias, Fancy Hat balls, ping-pong, the Lido Bar? Ah, the beautiful past we have shared!

And then, & then, you did Capri, which I trust was heavenly. And I did the highlife of all time – two weeks of Princesses & Maharanees & phony Barons, parties without end, villas to make you gasp. I was the kid of the moment: it was all insane, ignoble, absurd, & vastly entertaining. But I wouldn't want to live there.

I drove here yesterday, through Provence. God, what charm and beauty! Felicia has been in Paris for a week buying out Chanel: she & Mike join me here any minute now, & then we tootle off as tourists in this wild heat. I'm tired but

---

[101] Louise Talma (1906–96), American composer. She was a pupil of Nadia Boulanger and a regular at the MacDowell Colony, along with composer friends of Bernstein such as Irving Fine, Lukas Foss, Harold Shapero, and Arthur Berger. In her will, Talma left a bequest of one million dollars to the MacDowell Colony. Talma's letter refers to Bernstein's first visit to the Colony, in 1962, when he went there to work on the *Kaddish* Symphony.

strangely exhilarated by this feeling of holiday, and I'll be home the 15th to rest and to hug you both. A big kiss to Adam and God bless your new home.

Un abrazo fuerte,

Lenny

477. Karl Böhm[102] to Leonard Bernstein

Hotel Alden, New York, NY

30 November 1962

My dear friend Bernstein,

At the conclusion of my guest appearances at the Philharmonic Hall with your magnificent orchestra,[103] I am sending you my heartfelt thanks for your wonderful cooperation and for making it possible for me to be the first "foreign" conductor to appear at the new hall with the New York Philharmonic.

Everything was just perfect, and the members of your orchestra are musicians of the highest caliber. I felt at home with them right from the start of the first rehearsal, and I am very grateful to every one of them for their assistance, help and attitude.

My thanks also go to you personally for your sentiments, and I shall never forget the way in which you behaved when I was very sick in Vienna, after a dangerous eye operation. Then I experienced that you are a real and great human being.

With best wishes to you, Mrs. Bernstein and your children from Mrs. Böhm and

Yours very sincerely,

Karl Böhm

478. Morton Feldman[104] to Leonard Bernstein

337 Lexington Avenue, New York

7 January 1963

Dear Lenny,

The score you have of *Structures* underwent surgery last summer. C. F. Peters will send you the new version later in the week.

---

[102] Karl Böhm (1894–1981), Austrian conductor. He established a warm friendship with Bernstein. The two conductors admired each other greatly.

[103] Böhm conducted a month of concerts with the New York Philharmonic in November 1962, sixteen in all between 1 and 25 November.

[104] Morton Feldman (1926–87), American composer. A leading figure of the musical avant-garde and a pioneer of Indeterminate music.

At the Stockhausens New Year's Eve. After drinking in the new year he announced "and now we will have some music." Most of the guests' eyes lit up. They thought they were going to twist. He then went to the phono[graph] and played two hours of Stockhausen, Foss and Feldman.

Fondest regards from your non analytic

Morton

479. Leonard Bernstein to David Diamond
10 January 1963

Dear D,

This isn't exactly the moment for catching up on ages, literally, of Riverflow, but I have to write you today to say that Lina A[barbanell] died on Monday (or rather Sunday, I think, the 6th). We were all shocked: she had gone into hospital for removal of a tumor, and couldn't take it. Poor great gallant lady. 84 years old! Of course Marc is all but destroyed, and I think he'd deeply appreciate some word from you.[105]

A is born, B dies, C is in agony, D has some joy, E is humdrum, & we are all of them. I have not yet finished my 3rd Symphony (*Kaddish*) which will be *something* when and if it gets written. I had hoped by now to have it complete. Alas. Once I have finished it, I can rest in peace: it is my Kaddish for everybody. Last week had joy in it: Mahler #5. Glorious. This week, R[oberto] Gerhard's #1. Next week, East Lynne. Ça continue. Newspaper strike. Jamie has chicken pox. Alexander is a sensitive dream; Nina is funny & bright. Felicia is brave and a little tired. I am exhausted, and off to bed.

Love to you all, and a very happy '63.

L

480. Leonard Bernstein to Olivier Messiaen
New York, NY
18 March 1963

Cher Maître,

It is curious to be writing to you after some *thirteen* years – the year of the first performance of *Turangalîla*. But I think of you very often, and I keep up to

---

[105] Lina Abarbanell (1879–1963) was an opera singer and casting director. She was Marc Blitzstein's mother-in-law. As a singer, her debut at the Metropolitan Opera on 25 November 1905 was as Gretel in the Met premiere of Humperdinck's *Hansel and Gretel*, given in the presence of the composer. She later became a successful casting director (including *Street Scene* and the movie version of *Carmen Jones*). Though her daughter Eva died in 1936, she remained close friends with Blitzstein. Bernstein included Lina Abarbanell's name in the opening scat trio of *Trouble in Tahiti* ("Who but Abarbanel[l] buys a visa").

date with your music. Last season we had the great joy of presenting the *Trois Petites Liturgies* of which we have made a record for Columbia to be released next year. I hope that you will be pleased with it.

Today I am writing to you on the subject of your impressive work *Chronochromie*.[106] Despite my best intentions, it will not be possible to give this enormous work with the rehearsals that are allowed in a typical week of the season; but I believe that it would be possible to perform just the final part on its own, separately (i.e. the Épôde and Coda). Would that be blasphemous and meddlesome? It seems to me that this part, on its own, would be very effective in a concert, and very moving. If you have objections to this, do not hesitate to let me know. My address: 895 Park Avenue, New York, 21.

With my warmest good wishes,

Leonard Bernstein[107]

481. Olivier Messiaen to Leonard Bernstein
230 rue Marcadet, Paris, France
26 March 1963

Cher Ami,

I was extremely touched by your letter, and thank you with all my heart for it. I, too, think of you often, and – if you remember – I have applauded you several times after your marvelous concerts in Paris.

Thank you a thousand times for the *Trois Petites Liturgies* on record for Columbia. Who are the solo Ondiste and pianist? And who is conducting? Is it *you*? (During my trip to Japan, Seiji Ozawa also spoke to me of a performance of the *Trois Petites Liturgies*. Was that the same or another one?)

Your *name* and the first performance at Boston in 1949 are at the head of the magnificent edition that Durand has given the *Turangalîla-Symphonie*.

Now let me reply on the subject of *Chronochromie*.

The division of the work into seven sections (Introduction – Strophe I – Antistrophe I – Strophe II – Antistrophe II – Épôde – Coda) is a formal division. But there is no break between these sections, and the work forms *a whole, without interruption*. The Épôde uses only 18 solo string instruments, in 18 real parts, namely 6 1st violins, 6 2nd violins, 4 violas, 2 cellos. That's not interesting

---

[106] *Chronochromie* was composed in 1959–60 and first performed on 16 October 1960 by the Orchestra of South-West German Radio conducted by Hans Rosbaud. The New York Philharmonic performed two movements ("Strophe" and "Antistrophe") at a concert on 24 July 1965 conducted by Lukas Foss.

[107] Written in French; English translation by the editor.

except by contrast with the rest of the work. The rest is written for a very large orchestra, with a solo xylophone and marimba (plus a set of 25 tubular bells for which the part is rhythmically difficult). Finally, all of the work, and above all the two Strophes (where the harmonies of the strings and the wood-wind counterpoints of birdsong must underline the *rhythms* and the *durations* of the metallic percussion instruments by *coloring* them) justify the title: *Chronochromie*, that is to say: *Color of Time*.

Would you like to wait a little while? *Chronochromie* is entirely engraved, the plates are at the printer at this moment – and the work will appear in large score and pocket score here in two months, around 15 June, from Leduc, publisher, 175 rue Saint Honoré, Paris (1er), France.

I will send you a score at that time, and you will see the music for yourself.

Thank you again for your letter, and all my best wishes.

Olivier Messiaen[108]

482. Leonard Bernstein to David Diamond
2 May 1963

Dear David,

As usual, these words are penned in haste. Will there ever be no haste? I'm coming to think that only children, who believe themselves immortal, are blessed with time.

I've been working on Brandeis for you. (California is out.) I suspect that [Arthur] Berger still harbors some ancient grudges; but I approached President Sacher directly, and he informs me that he would like you to come for an interview when you are here. At least it's a step.

Deaths are frequent. Felicia's mother died 2 days ago in Chile, & poor F. has been there for an agonizing week, watching her mother die. A nightmare. And yesterday we lost that angelic Nat Prager, our 2nd trumpet player – after 34 years of glorious and uncomplaining service.

Death and spring. I am back with the orchestra again, and love it. The *Kaddish* is still unfinished, and its premiere is now set for December in Israel. I don't know if it'll ever be ready.

I must fly now to conduct. Bless you, & let me know how spring is in Florence.

Lenny

---

[108] Written in French; English translation by the editor.

483. Morton Feldman to Leonard Bernstein
337 Lexington Avenue, New York, NY
19 June 1963

Dear Lenny,

I had a talk with Jack Gottlieb on the phone this evening, and he gave me some of your thoughts on *Structures*. I was struck by the fact that you felt a lack of "rhythmic interest" in this piece, because what I was actually after was an atonal rhythm, or, more precisely, no rhythm.[109] It is the juxtaposing of various weights of sound which make for the movement, rather than any rhythmic design. This is equally true of *Out of Last Pieces* and is in fact one of the basic ideas throughout my work.

The key to my music is that I want to resolve each piece into one overall color (regardless of how the piece is notated). Because of this, what makes for an "interesting" composition for someone else has no place in my thinking.

That's that – and what are *you* doing these days?

Morty

484. Leonard Bernstein to Louis [?]
25 June 1963

Dear Louis,

I have finally listened to the recordings of ancient pianists & composers that you so kindly sent me. It has been a ball! Grieg performing his *Papillon* like a young lady just out of conservatory, Busoni stuttering his octaves, Ravel heavy and rhythmically obscure, [Teresa] Carreño running out of gas in the Liszt Rhapsody, [Vladimir] de Pachmann setting an all-time record for ritards at the end of Chopin's C# minor waltz, et al, et al – and all marvelously authentic, surprising, other-planetary, incredible. It is a thrill to hear these records: we not only extend our knowledge of past pianistic styles, but we gain a fresh view of our own age. And not only pianistically; this glimpse into the past, to the thoughtful observer,

---

[109] In a marginal note, Bernstein has written: "Jack [Gottlieb] misrepresented my reaction." Bernstein performed (and recorded) Feldman's *Out of Last Pieces* with David Tudor and the New York Philharmonic in February 1964 as part of an extraordinary programme that included "Autumn" from Vivaldi's *Four Seasons* and Tchaikovsky's *Pathétique* Symphony in the first half, and music by Cage (*Atlas Eclipticalis with Winter Music*), Earle Brown (*Available Forms II*) and Feldman's *Out of Last Pieces*. Bernstein was fascinated by Feldman's music even if he wasn't particularly sympathetic towards it.

becomes nothing less than a revelation of the present![110] I thank you for sending it to me.

Affectionately

[Pencil draft, unsigned]

P.S. Congratulations on the new baby.

485. Leonard Bernstein to David Diamond
24 August 1963

Dear DD,

Welcome! I had no idea you were already here: not a word have I had, or Aaron, or anyone. Your birthday card was the first modest sign. You were sweet to send it, to remember. How goes it? Plans? Medical matters?

I am at this second in the hurried grip of time, for a change: my last day in the country. Tomorrow (my birthday!) I rehearse the ork all day for the tour, which starts on Tue[sday]. Gone for 4 weeks to H'wood & back. But I wanted at least to say hello-&-have-a-good-visit-and-a-successful-one before I vanish for a month.

Best news is that I have finished *Kaddish* this summer. That's all I did. I had virtually no vacation. My text still needs cleaning up – and a short section or two remains undecided; but actually it's a piece! My first in 6 years – my first *concert* piece in 9 years! I can't wait for you to see it. Will you be in town late Sept? (when I return?) Let Helen know: on me – she can send you my itinerary.

Good health, love to you and Sabina.

L

486. John Cage[111] to Leonard Bernstein
Stony Point, NY
17 October 1963

Dear Lenny,

Two points. First, I am very grateful to you for having decided to present my work and that of [Morton] Feldman and [Earle] Brown before your audiences.

---

[110] Though the recipient of this letter has not been identified, this pencil draft of Bernstein's letter has been included because of his interesting comments on some of the legendary pianists of the past.

[111] John Cage (1912–92), American composer and musical pioneer.

We all admire your courage in doing this at the present time, for actual hostility toward our work is still felt by many people.

Second, I ask you to reconsider your plan to conduct the orchestra in an improvisation. Improvisation is not related to what the three of us are doing in our works. It gives free play to the exercise of taste and memory, and it is exactly this that we, in differing ways, are not doing in our music.

Since, as far as I know, you are not dedicated in your own work to improvisation, I can only imagine that your plan is a comment on our work. Our music is still little understood and your audiences, for the most part, will be hearing it for the first time. It would seem best if they could do so without being prejudiced. I admired Aaron when he presented my work at Tanglewood, letting the audience know beforehand that, though he didn't share my views, he felt the music, since it was seriously written and had found a following among composers, performers and audiences around the world, had a right to be heard attentively. I feel the opposite way about Smallens who, I am told, after conducting a first performance of Webern for the League here in New York, turned toward the audience and joined them in derisive laughter.

Surely there must be some less provocative way to conclude the program, one which will leave no doubt as to your courage in giving your audiences the music which you have chosen to present.

With best wishes and friendliest greetings,

John Cage

487. Leonard Bernstein to John Cage
[October 1963]

Dear John,

Your letter astonishes me. What, for example, makes you think that our orchestral improvisations should in any way constitute a "comment" on your work and that of your colleagues? What, again, gives you the idea that everything in this part of the program must be confined to the realm in which you work? The overall idea is *Music of Chance* and there are chances and chances in your work as well as that of Brown and Feldman and *as well* in total improvisation. We are trying to have as comprehensive a look at the aleatory world as is possible in half a complete program; and it seems clear to me that improvisation is an essential part of such a look. And, finally, how can you deny that your music enlists "free play of taste and memory" when you write for an orchestra that may or may not play at any given time, and if it *does* play, render approximations?

If it will make you feel any better, I shall be happy to play the improvisation *before* your work, thus avoiding the tendentious notion of its being a final comment on the preceding music. I hope that this will alleviate your concern, and prove to you the integrity of my intentions.[112] Most cordially.[113]

488. Claudio Abbado[114] to Leonard Bernstein
Berlin
28 October 1963

Dear Maestro,

I want to thank you by heart for everything I learnt by you during the weeks that I spent in New York with the Philharmonic. What I learnt from your rehearsing, from the musical and human point of view, I tried now to actuate in the rehearsals of my last concerts. So I succeeded in finding always a human contact with the orchestra, forgetting everything of the dictatorial way that I had in past years. The results have been wonderful, and I could musizieren in a

---

[112] Bernstein did place the orchestral improvisation at the start of the second half of this programme, which was given on 6, 7, 8, and 9 February 1964. The first half included "Autumn" from Vivaldi's *Four Seasons* and Tchaikovsky's *Pathétique* Symphony. According to Harold Schonberg's review in *The New York Times* (7 February 1964) it was an unusually long evening, ending at around 11.05 p.m. Of the second half, Schonberg wrote: "these pieces, with their new sounds, apparent chaos and weird textures, shook the audience quite a bit. Not unexpectedly, the most unconventional was Mr. Cage's [*Atlas Eclipticalis*]. He used an orchestra of more than 80 players, and each instrument was equipped with a contact microphone that led into a little preamplifier on the floor. This preamplifier led into an electronic mixer, which fed into six amplifiers, which went to six loudspeakers scattered through the hall. The piano was amplified, and on the podium was, instead of a conductor, a mechanical affair with a spoke that slowly revolved. When eight minutes were up, the piece was over. In the Brown piece, though, two live conductors were needed –Mr. Bernstein and the composer. One might think that Mr. Cage's piece, and the others, would have caused some kind of demonstration. What happened was that during the progress of the work, people walked out. When it was over, there was a more general exodus. There were a few lusty boos, a few countercheers, but on the whole the music fell flat. So did the music of Mr. Feldman [*Out of Last Pieces*] and Mr. Brown [*Available Forms II*]. The audience, the part that remained, seemed more amused than anything else. Its amusement had started with a demonstration of IBM music, and an improvisation by full orchestra that lasted a minute and a half."
[113] Draft reply written in pencil on the verso of Cage's letter.
[114] Claudio Abbado (b. 1933), Italian conductor. In 1963 he won the Dimitri Mitropoulos Prize, which enabled him to work for several months with the New York Philharmonic. Abbado has kindly supplied this reminiscence: "For the 1963–64 season, I was assistant conductor at the New York Philharmonic, an opportunity given me by the Mitropoulos Prize, which I won that year. So I had the opportunity to watch and conduct major concerts, working with George Szell, Josef Krips and soloists such as Arthur Rubinstein and David Oistrakh, as well as with Bernstein. Just to mention one episode, I remember very well during the rehearsal of Mahler's Second Symphony that Bernstein went to sit in the hall and asked me to get on the podium. He wanted to hear the very complex part, in the finale, where the principal ideas are played by the small orchestra offstage. Bernstein was surprised and very happy that I was aware of how difficult this passage was, though he didn't know that I had actually already done that symphony in Europe" (Claudio Abbado, personal communication).

completely new way in the last concerts in Rome, Venezia and Berlin. For all here in Berlin, also because the orchestra is better, I have been particularly happy. With this orchestra, with whom I will conduct also tonight and tomorrow, I have been invited for a European tournée.

Coming back to New York, I should be very happy to have the opportunity to speak with you about your music and about your wonderful interpretation of II [Symphony of] Mahler.

Grazie ancora ed arrivederci presto!

Claudio Abbado

489. Mary Rodgers to Leonard Bernstein
24 November 1963

For many years – six to be exact – I've been your highly expendable "children's expert." We all know you don't need a children's expert, and you don't need me for early morning joke telling either. But for me, it's a nice job. I love it. I love you.

It's occurred to me that I've never bothered to mention this before – and now seems a good moment.

What Kennedy[115] did for the affairs of the world, you do for the heart of the world. It seemed to me, tonight, that you two are not (were not) unalike – in courage, in conscience, in warmth and in purpose.

I'm grateful, *very* grateful, that there is one of you left.

Bless,

Mary

490. Leonard Bernstein: Talk given at the "Night of Stars" Memorial to President Kennedy at Madison Square Garden
New York, NY
25 November 1963

My dear friends,

Last night the New York Philharmonic and I performed Mahler's Second Symphony – the *Resurrection* – in tribute to the memory of our beloved late President. There were those who asked: Why the *Resurrection* Symphony, with its visionary concept of hope and triumph over worldly pain, instead of a Requiem, or the customary Funeral March from the *Eroica*? Why, indeed. We played the Mahler Symphony not only in terms of resurrection for the soul of

---

[115] President Kennedy was assassinated on 22 November 1963.

one we love, but also for the resurrection of hope in all of us who mourn him. In spite of our shock, our shame, and our despair at the diminution of man that followed from this death, we must somehow gather strength for the increase of man, strength to go on striving for those goals he cherished. In mourning him, we must be worthy of him.

I know of no musician in this country who did not love John F. Kennedy. American artists have for three years looked to the White House with unaccustomed confidence and warmth. We loved him for the honor in which he held art, in which he held every creative impulse of the human mind, whether it was expressed in words, or notes, or paints, or mathematical symbols. This reverence for the life of the mind was apparent even in his last speech, which he was to have made a few hours *after* his death. He was to have said: "America's leadership must be guided by learning and reason." Learning and reason: precisely the two elements that were necessarily missing from the mind of anyone who could have fired that impossible bullet. *Learning and reason*: the two basic precepts of all Judaistic tradition, the twin sources from which every Jewish mind from Abraham and Moses to Freud and Einstein has drawn its living power. Learning and reason: the motto we here tonight must continue to uphold with redoubled tenacity, and must continue, at any price, to make the basis of all our actions.

It is obvious that the grievous nature of our loss is immensely aggravated by the element of violence involved in it. And where does this violence spring from? From *ignorance* and *hatred*, the exact antonyms of learning and reason: those two words of John Kennedy's were not uttered in time to save his own life; but every man can pick them up where they fell, and make them part of himself, the seed of that rational intelligence without which our world can no longer survive. This must become the mission of every artist, of every Jew, and of every man of good will: to *insist, unflaggingly*, at the risk of becoming a repetitive bore, but to *insist* on the achievement of a world in which the mind will have triumphed over violence.

We musicians, like everyone else, are numb with sorrow at this murder, and with rage at the senselessness of the crime. But this sorrow and rage will not inflame us to seek retribution; rather it will inflame our art. Our music will never again be quite the same. This will be our reply to violence: to make music more intensely, more beautifully, more devotedly, than ever before. And with each note we will honor the spirit of John Kennedy, commemorate his courage, and reaffirm his faith in the Triumph of the Mind.

491. Walter Hussey[116] to Leonard Bernstein
The Deanery, Chichester, England
10 December 1963

Dear Mr. Bernstein,

I hope you will forgive me for writing to you and will not think me presumptuous. I did have the pleasure of meeting you briefly in New York when you kindly allowed me to attend one of your rehearsals, at the request of my friend, Dr. Chuck Solomon. But you will not remember this.

The choirs of Chichester, Salisbury and Winchester Cathedrals combine for a short festival each year which takes place in the three Cathedrals in turn. I enclose copies of the programmes for the last two years to give you some idea of the sort of thing it is. It has proved extraordinarily successful and I think it will be fair to say that it reaches a very good musical standard. Naturally, it is concerned to a great extent with the wealth of music written for such choirs over the centuries, but I am most anxious that this should not be regarded as a tradition which has finished, and that we should be very much concerned with music written today.

The Chichester Organist and Choirmaster, John Birch, and I, are very anxious to have written some piece of music which the combined choirs could sing at the Festival to be held in Chichester in August, 1965, and we wondered if you would be willing to write something for us. I do realize how enormously busy you are, but if you could manage to do this we should be tremendously honoured and grateful. The sort of thing that we had in mind was perhaps, say, a setting of the Psalm 2, or some part of it, either unaccompanied or accompanied by orchestra or organ, or both. I only mention this to give you some idea as to what was in our minds.

I have always been most eager to do anything I possibly can to foster the ancient links between the church and the arts. Before I came to Chichester when I was in Northampton, I got Henry Moore to carve a Madonna and Child, and Benjamin Britten to write a cantata. I am most eager to carry on this work and it would be a great pleasure and encouragement if you felt you could help us. Please do. We would of course be only too happy to pay a fee to the best of our resources.

---

[116] Walter Hussey (1909–85) was Dean of Chichester Cathedral from 1955 to 1977, and before that was vicar of St. Matthew's, Northampton. In both these posts he commissioned an extraordinary range of new music, literature, and works of art for the Church. In Northampton these commissions included Benjamin Britten's *Rejoice in the Lamb*, Gerald Finzi's *Lo, the full, final sacrifice*, W. H. Auden's *Litany and Anthem for S. Matthew's Day*, Graham Sutherland's *Crucifixion*, and Henry Moore's *Madonna and Child*. At Chichester, he continued his commissions, notably stained-glass windows by Marc Chagall, a magnificent tapestry by John Piper – and Bernstein's *Chichester Psalms*.

I shall be of course delighted to give you any further help I can or information you may require, and again may I express the hope that you will forgive me approaching you.

Yours sincerely,

Walter Hussey

492. Iannis Xenakis[117] to Leonard Bernstein
Berlin, Germany
7 January 1964

Dear Mr. Bernstein,

I want to thank you very much for including me in your concerts in New York. It made me very happy and proud. I think that the piece except its creation by H[ermann] Scherchen had its first real performance on January 64 by you![118]

Under your impulse the series of these concerts brings New York at the head of the cities who care for new music, because of the real popular character you give to them and because of the first quality of the orchestra and of the performers.

I wanted to write you one month ago, but I fell ill and had to support a heavy and painful operation in Paris. Now I can write you, being back in Berlin (I have received a Ford Foundation award and I am an artist in residence of Berlin for one year).

I wish you all the most brilliant success for your effort and that other concert organizations take you as a model.

Thanking you again.

Yours sincerely,

Xenakis

P.S. If there is any time left to you, I would appreciate very much to have your opinion on my piece. I'll send you my book *Musiques formelles* in French[119] (Mr. Karl Haas told me that you speak French) hoping that you'll enjoy it.

---

[117] Iannis Xenakis (1922–2001), Greek composer and architect.

[118] On 2 January 1964 (repeated on 3, 4, and 5 January), Bernstein conducted the first US performances of *Pithoprakta* by Xenakis and *Atmosphères* by Ligeti.

[119] *Musiques formelles* was published in Paris in 1963.

493. Harpo Marx[120] to Leonard Bernstein

15 January 1964

Leonard,

On one of your children's concerts I would love to conduct my version of the Haydn Toy Symphony which runs seven minutes. My salary to go to Musicians Aid Soc of N.Y. I have done the symphony on several occasions & most recently with the Philadelphia Symphony using little children to play the toy instruments in the last part. I will be in New York February 14 for two weeks – do you think you could set it up for that time?

As I don't read music, in order to stay in good standing with Local 47 I do all my corresponding on score-paper.[121]

494. Leonard Bernstein to Shirley Bernstein

[New York]
25 January 1964

Darling Hilee,

This is the first second I've had to write in months. I've been trying to call you for days to "be" with you at the death of Marc:[122] but no answer, no answer. I called you from Paris (en route home from Israel, having just been told that our plane *would* stop in London) and then again from the London airport, but no answer, no for an answer. And the wretched luck was that my plane *to* Israel decided *not* to stop in London. And so on, for bad communications.

It's an open season on Kaddish, all right. The President. Marc. I take it you've read substantially what we've read: first an auto accident; then a new story about being beaten by three sailors; then the blessed word *robbery* reiterated by the Consul in Martinique, & now by the police.

We pray the story gets no murkier – or should I say clearer? We are all shocked and miserable, as you must be, & I wish we could be together, at last, at last.

---

[120] Harpo Marx (1888–1964; born Adolph Marx), American comedian and actor, the second-oldest of the Marx Brothers (Chico, Harpo, Groucho, Gummo, and Zeppo). He was famous for never talking during performances or on screen (though in fact he had a deep, rich speaking voice). Harpo was also a regular of the Algonquin Round Table (with the likes of Dorothy Parker, Alexander Woolcott, George S. Kaufman, and Robert Benchley). He wrote this letter just before his decision to retire from public life, and he died on 28 September 1964.

[121] This letter is written on a sheet of manuscript paper, decorated with treble and bass clefs, rests, a fermata, and a double bar at the end of the last sentence. The titles at the head of the sheet have been filled in by Harpo Marx as follows: Prod.: "Maybe", Title: "Letter to Maestro Bernstein", Page: "3,472", Arranger: "Harpo Marx".

[122] Marc Blitzstein was murdered in Martinique by three Portuguese sailors on 22 January 1964.

The *Kaddish* itself gets its comeuppance in Boston this week, Friday the 31st. I wish you could be there. It will be a regular reunion: B[urton] B[ernstein]'s birthday and all. Felicia is there already, rehearsing. I'm staying out of it 'til the last minute: Münch is in love with the piece, but scared witless, & can't beat it (7/8, etc.) the chorus . . . Jenny T. . . . oy. Maybe you're wise to miss it.

Marc is dead, & I've lost an arm. Felicia can't stop crying. Come home, darling Shirley – we want you with us! It's been far too long, too many distances, interruptions, silences. Please come home.

I love you as always –

L

Do you realize we have loved Marc for 25 years?

Kaddish: they loved it in Tel-Aviv, but it may never go in English. I'm nervous.

495. William Schuman to Leonard Bernstein
27 January 1964

Dear Lennie,

I couldn't get you by phone to tell you several things.

In the first place, yesterday's performance of the *Eroica* was undoubtedly the best, the most exciting and the most moving that I have ever heard. Frankly I had not expected to stay tuned in after the Varèse. You wouldn't let me get back to work.

I wanted to speak to you about Marc. Actually, you two were so close, I felt the need of making a condolence call. Schuyler Chapin tells me that you and Dave Oppenheim are planning a memorial program this spring. Of course this is wonderful, and I am wondering whether you could consider doing one or two pieces from *Sacco-Vanzetti*.[123] And here, I keep wondering whether Marc finished the vocal score. In my last conversation with him – just one year ago this month – I gathered that mostly it was done. If this is the case, could not the work be completed and orchestrated by another? If this is a possibility, I am very much afraid that you are the only one who can do it. It's a thought.

And mostly, I called to wish you with all affection a stunning success with the new work this week.[124]

Yours,

Bill

---

[123] The Blitzstein Memorial Concert took place at Philharmonic Hall on 19 April 1964. Bernstein included "With a Woman to Be" from *Sacco and Vanzetti*, extracts from *Regina* and other songs, and a complete performance of *The Cradle Will Rock* narrated by Bernstein and directed by him from the piano.

[124] A reference to the Boston premiere of *Kaddish*, conducted by Charles Munch on 31 January 1964, the first performance of the work in the United States.

496. Walter Hussey to Leonard Bernstein

The Deanery, Chichester, England
10 February 1964

Dear Dr. Bernstein,

This is splendid news! I am indeed delighted to hear that you will write something for our Festival. It will be a great privilege for us all and I can assure you that everyone will do their utmost to do justice to the work.

Yes, by all means change from the second Psalm to something more familiar if you wish. We shall be very happy to leave it to you. And as regards the time, of course, we must leave this also to you: but the joint Festival with Winchester and Salisbury goes in rotation and so is only held here once in three years. It is to be held here at the end of July, 1965, and so as you can well imagine we are very much hoping that it may be possible to perform the work then. I shall be sad for it to receive its premier[e] elsewhere! However, I am so proud and pleased that you will write something for us that it would be unfair and presumptuous to try and press further.

I will try to send you within a few days particulars as to the sort of numbers that will be available in the combined choirs, in case this should be of any assistance to you. Please let me know if there is anything further I can do.

Again, my warmest thanks,
Yours sincerely,
Walter Hussey

497. Walter Hussey to Leonard Bernstein

The Deanery, Chichester, England
14 August 1964

Dear Dr. Bernstein,

We are all tremendously looking forward to the setting of the second Psalm which you kindly said you would write for us for our three Choirs Festival next year.

This year's festival has just taken place at Salisbury and I thought perhaps you would be interested to see what has been happening, so I am sending you a copy of the programme. A tremendous lot of people turned up and it proved very successful – I think the performance of Britten's *Cantata Misericordium* was quite outstanding.

Our Choirmaster and Organist has given me one or two particulars which he thinks might be helpful to you. The string orchestra will probably be the Philomusica of London, a first rate group. In addition, there could be a piano, chamber organ, harpsichord and, if desired, a brass consort (three trumpets, three trombones). It is not really possible to have a full symphony orchestra for reasons of space and expense and the fact that the combined strength of the three cathedral choirs is about 70 to 74 (all boys and men).

The Festival was founded a good while ago, but then lapsed for about thirty years and has recently been re-started with great success. I think it has throughout its time been of great value to English church music as a means of hearing works of large scale, impossible for any single Cathedral choir, but I am certain it must also provide new works in new idioms to keep the tradition really alive. I hope you will feel quite free to write as you wish and will in no way feel inhibited by circumstances. I think many of us would be very delighted if there was a hint of *West Side Story* about the music. I hope you will not mind my writing like this, but I talked of it with Chuck Solomon[125] when he was here recently, and he said I was certainly to say it to you.

Once again let me say how enormously grateful I am to you for saying that you will help us in this way. It will be exactly what I should wish for when the Festival is here at Chichester next year.

Yours sincerely,
Walter Hussey

498. Leonard Bernstein to Aaron Copland
19 September 1964

Sonnet on receiving an honorary doctorate with Aaron Copland[126]

This day, my will demurring, I grew old.
I could have written memoirs on that stage
For the first time. A long wave had unrolled,
And beached me, spent with swimming and with age.

Doctor honoris causa. First for him,
A craggy cedar planted by the sea
Since Adam. Then they called on me to swim
Ashore, and simulate that salty tree.

A poor impostor, I, Not even brave,
A plotter with no plan, and less than bold.
They fished me, red-eyed flounder, from the wave,

---

[125] Dr. Cyril [Chuck] Solomon was Bernstein's doctor for many years and a personal friend.
[126] Bernstein and Copland were both awarded honorary doctorates of music by the University of Michigan, conferred on 19 September 1964 (the date of Bernstein's sonnet), as recorded in *The Proceedings of the Board of Regents (1963–1966)*, University of Michigan, p. 577 (electronic edition: Ann Arbor, MI:University of Michigan, Digital Library Production Service, 2000).

Wounded, rigid, open-mouthed, and cold.
With velvet bait they plucked me from the sea
And dropped me, panting, near a cedar tree.

Much love,
L

499. Walter Hussey to Leonard Bernstein
The Deanery, Chichester, England
22 December 1964

Dear Dr. Bernstein,

I do apologize for burdening you with another letter. I have a horrid fear that you will be regarding me as an arch nuisance but I am most eager that we should have the work which you promised for our combined Choirs in time to learn it and rehearse it properly before the Festival. May I say again that I hope you will feel entirely free to write your setting exactly as you wish to. I hope you would not, at any rate on our behalf, feel any restrictions from the point of view of tradition or convention. The work would not be performed during any sort of religious service and I firmly believe that any work which is sincere can suitably be given in a cathedral and to the glory of God. No one feels more proud and grateful than I do of the tremendous value of the tradition of English Cathedral music, but I am sure that it is a very good thing for something like our Three Cathedrals Festival to have a sharp and vigorous push into the middle of the 20th century, and if you should feel inclined to write something that would do this I am sure nobody could do it better and we should be most happy and grateful.

It would be a great help if I could know the title and description of the work within the next six weeks as our preliminary announcements and publications will be appearing very soon after that.

Again, do let me apologize if I seem tiresomely importunate, but Chuck Solomon assures me that we shall get the work and I am most anxious that we should have it in time to prepare it properly. The prospect is a tremendous thrill to us all. I can assure you that the musicians will do their utmost to do [it] full justice, and I do not believe they will fail. I am more grateful to you than I can possibly say.

I do not suppose there is any chance of your being in England at the end of July? We should of course be delighted to welcome you to Chichester and I believe that in the place itself and the Festival Theatre as well as the Music Festival you would find much to enjoy.

With all good wishes,
Yours sincerely,
Walter Hussey

500. Leonard Bernstein to Mary Rodgers

[New York, NY]
[1964]

Dear Mary,

I just found a most moving note from you, dated a year ago, apropos the assassination [Letter 489]. In all the grief of those days a lot of mail went unanswered. But this one cannot go unanswered. Thank you, you dear girl, and irreplaceable assistant!

Love,

L

(If you haven't been a "children's expert" heretofore, you sure will be after the new one. Have a good one!)

501. Leonard Bernstein to David Diamond

28 January 1965

Dear Dd,

Finally the date is settled for your celebration – the week of 25 April, '66, concerts on 28th, 29th, 30th and 2 May. I had planned for you to conduct the *Rounds* and the Piano Concerto (for which Schumacher is already engaged); but having since received the 5th Symphony, which I find your absolute *best* to date, I will take the occasion to open the program with it myself (sorry to do you out of one conducting stint) – and then you can conduct the concerto with T[homas] S[chumacher]. I'm delighted and hope that you are. (The program will probably close with a staple – Sibelius #1 or something.[127] The whole year is devoted to a survey of the symphony in the 20th century, including all 7 of Sibelius, owing to his centenary. And that's another reason for doing your 5th instead of the *Rounds*. There'll also be some others you'll love – Vaughan Williams #4, Aaron #3, Nielsen #3, Bartók 2-pno Concerto, & Webern Op. 20, Mahler #7, #8 & #9! A big year, a lot of work: I look forward to it.)

What are you doing in Florence? What has happened to the Iron Curtain trip? Last I heard, you were in Copenhagen.

You've probably heard about the collapse of *Skin of Our Teeth*: a dreadful experience, the wounds still smarting. I am suddenly a composer without a

---

[127] The concerts of Diamond's music took place along the lines discussed here: Bernstein conducting the world premiere of Diamond's Fifth Symphony followed by Diamond conducting his Piano Concerto with Thomas Schumacher as the soloist. In the second half, the eventual choice was Sibelius' Second Symphony.

project, with half of that golden sabbatical down the drain. Never mind, I'll survive.[128]

----

[128] The saga of *The Skin of Our Teeth* is an unhappy one, though it did eventually provide some of the musical material used in the *Chichester Psalms*. As long ago as 12 September 1962, Sam Zolotow reported in *The New York Times* that "the Broadway association of Leonard Bernstein, Jerome Robbins, Adolph Green and Betty Comden will be renewed with the song and dance version of Thornton Wilder's fantastic comedy, *The Skin of Our Teeth*, winner of the 1943 Pulitzer Prize" and announced that everything would be "ready for a Broadway presentation during the 1964–65 season. [. . .] As explained yesterday by Mr. Bernstein, the reason for the long-range project is that 'we haven't started work on it yet.' Miss Comden said: 'We have been meeting on and off whenvever we can. Intensive work, however, will be done during the 1963-4 season.'" A year later, on 29 August 1963, Zolotow wrote of it as "an early 1965 entry," to which Robbins would turn his attention after the upcoming "Tevye" – not yet called *Fiddler on the Roof*. Another year later, on 4 September 1964, Zolotow wrote of the $400,000 investment in the project from CBS (following the success of their backing of *My Fair Lady* and *Camelot*) and promising that Columbia Records would be making the cast recording of *The Skin of Our Teeth*. But by the New Year, the whole project had fallen apart and the persistent Zolotow delivered the bad news on 5 January: "Leonard Bernstein, Jerome Robbins, Adolph Green and Betty Comden have cancelled their plans to do a musical version of Thornton Wilder's Pulitzer Prize play, *The Skin of Our Teeth*," adding that Bernstein "had told a friend that six months of work had gone in the wastebasket due to a dispute with his colleagues."

Bernstein himself wrote about this project in the poem he composed for *The New York Times* as a report on his sabbatical in 1964–5, published on 24 October 1965:

> Since June of nineteen-sixty-four
> I've been officially free of chore
> And duty to the N. Y. Phil. –
> Fifteen beautiful months to kill!
> But not to waste: there was a plan,
> For as long as my sabbatical ran,
> To write a new theatre piece.
> (A theatre composer needs release,
> And *West Side Story* is eight years old!)
> And so a few of us got hold
> Of the rights to Wilder's play *The Skin of Our Teeth*.
> This is a play I've often thought was made
> For singing, and for dance. It celebrates
> The wonder of life, of human survival, told
> In pity and terror and mad hilarity.
> Six months we labored, June to bleak December.
> And bleak was our reward, when Christmas came,
> To find ourselves uneasy with our work.
> We gave it up, and went our several ways,
> Still loving friends; but still there was the pain
> Of seeing six months of work go down the drain.

The "loving friends," Comden, Green, Robbins and Bernstein – who remained the closest of friends even after this harrowing project – had a tough time trying to recapture the success of earlier collaborations such as *On the Town* (1944) and *Wonderful Town* (1953). The surviving musical material is fairly desultory: a couple of numbers that were reworked for the *Chichester Psalms*, and Sabina's opening aria ("Oh! Oh! Oh!"), which survives in a pencil sketch.

Good news about Aspen. But the best news is the 5th Symphony. I have the "waves" in the first part, and the end particularly. The fugue is a killer. I hereby accept the dedication with due formal ceremony and much affection.

L

502. Walter Hussey to Leonard Bernstein
The Deanery, Chichester, England
5 February 1965

Dear Dr. Bernstein,

I am very sorry to bother you with another letter and I do not want to seem impatient, but I am constantly being pressed by the Organist and Choirmaster for particulars as to title etc. of the work which you most kindly said you would write for us. He is directing the Three Choirs Festival and has got to get his publicity out and tells me that it cannot be held up any longer. I am sure you will understand.

He also tells me that the music has to be printed and then circulated to the three choirs to practice individually before they come together for common rehearsals. I am sure you are conscious of all this and please do not think me impatient; but your work would of course be the highlight of the Festival and all of us are most anxious that it should be done as well as we can possibly manage.

Again, my apologies for bothering you with a tiresome letter.

Yours sincerely,

Walter Hussey

503. Leonard Bernstein to Walter Hussey
New York, NY
24 February 1965

My dear Dean Hussey,

I was on the verge of writing you a sad letter saying that I could not find in me the work for your Festival when suddenly a conception occurred to me that I find exciting. It would be a suite of Psalms, or selected verses from Psalms, and would have a general title like *Psalms of Youth*. The music is all very forthright, songful, rhythmic, youthful. The only hitch is this: I can think of these Psalms only in the original Hebrew. I realize that this may present extra difficulties of preparation; but more important, does it present difficulties of an ecclesiastical nature? That is, are there no objections, in principle, to Hebrew being sung in your Cathedral? If not, do let me know soon, so that I may plunge ahead, and have a working score for you by early April. The orchestration would follow a month or so thereafter.

If there *are* objections I should also know soon, for obvious reasons. I would be sad, but I would understand.

Faithfully yours,
Leonard Bernstein
P.S. The Psalms involved would be:
Nos. 23, 100 and 131, complete;
No. 2, vs. 1–4; No. 108, vs. 3; No. 133, vs. 1.[129]

504. Walter Hussey to Leonard Bernstein
The Deanery, Chichester, England

2 March 1965
Dear Mr. Bernstein,

Thank you very much for your letter. I was delighted to receive it and am indeed grateful for all the good news it contains.

I do not think that there is any ecclesiastical objection to the use of Hebrew. The meaning of the words could always be supplied by a translation in the programme. It will of course, as you say, present a little problem in the preparation of the work, but no doubt it will be possible for the Hebrew to be printed phonetically as in Bloch's *Sacred Service*.

I will write to you again shortly giving you the numbers in the choir etc. In the meanwhile let me say again how pleased and excited I am at the splendid news of your letter – and in this the Choirmaster and Organist joins me.

Yours sincerely,
Walter Hussey

505. Solomon Braslavsky to Leonard Bernstein
Temple Mishkan Tefila, Boston, MA
16 March 1965

My dearest Lennie,

Last Friday I received your record of the *Kaddish* Symphony.

I immediately opened the wrapping and looked for a bill, but instead I found a very "long letter" from you consisting of *four* priceless words. Last Saturday morning I saw your father in the Temple and I told him that I just got a priceless *Purim* present from Lennie.

Well, needless to say how happy I am to be able to play the Symphony again and again in search for some more jewels of liturgical value which only you are capable of working in such an artistic manner, and for this I am very much indebted to you.

---

[129] Printed in Hussey 1985, p. 113.

I shall also like to listen again to the recitations so beautifully done by Felicia and evaluate it from its philosophical as well as its artistic point of view. I only regret that I am at present extremely busy with my duties in the Temple and I shall have to wait for a while before I will be able to put aside a few hours for a thorough consideration of this beautiful music.

With many thanks and all of my best wishes to you and your dear family, for good health and lots of happiness.

Your devoted,

Solomon

P.S. I shall write to you after my first hearing of the records in the near future [. . .]

506. Walter Hussey to Leonard Bernstein
The Deanery, Chichester, England
14 April 1965

Dear Dr. Bernstein,

I promised to let you have the particulars as regards the choir and the orchestra for the Festival in July. I have now got these from John Birch.

There are 46 boys, 8 male altos, 9 tenors and 12 basses. All the adults are professional singers and the boys are all members of our three Choir Schools, and I think really very competent.

The orchestra is the Philomusica of London and the players required for the rest of the programme are strings – 3.2.2.2 (3 players), 1 (1 player) – 18 players in all plus a chamber organ. Other players could be provided if you wished, for example trumpets and trombones, percussion, piano and harpsichord. I dare say you know of the orchestra but I think it is fair to say that they are highly competent players and perhaps the best chamber orchestra in London.

We are all tremendously excited about *The Psalms of Youth*. I do hope all goes well. I cannot tell you how grateful I am to you.

Please let me know if there is any further help or information I can give you.

Yours sincerely,

Walter Hussey

507. Leonard Bernstein to Walter Hussey
11 May 1965

Dear Dr. Hussey,

The psalms are finished, Laus Deo, are being copied, and should arrive in England next week. They are not yet orchestrated, but should be by June, and you should receive full score and parts in ample time for rehearsal. Meanwhile the choral preparation can start forthwith.

I am pleased with the work, and hope you will be, too; it is quite popular in feeling (even a hint, as you suggested, of *West Side Story*),[130] and it has an old-fashioned sweetness along with its more violent moments. The title has now been changed to *Chichester Psalms* ("Youth" was a wrong steer; the piece is far too difficult). The work is in three movements lasting about eighteen and a half minutes, and each movement contains one complete psalm plus one or more versions from another complementary psalm, by way of contrast or amplification. Thus:

I. Opens with a chorale (Ps 108, vs. 3) evoking praise; and then swings into Ps. 100, complete, a wild and joyful dance, in the Davidic spirit.

II. Consists mainly of Ps. 23, complete, featuring a boy solo and his harp, but interrupted savagely by the men with threats of war and violence (Ps. 2, vs. 1–4). This movement ends in unresolved fashion, with both elements, faith and fear, interlocked.

III. Begins with an orchestral prelude based on the opening chorale, whose assertive harmonies have now turned to painful ones. There is a crisis; the tension is suddenly relieved, and the choir enters humbly and peacefully singing Ps. 131 complete, in what is almost a popular song (although in 10/4 time!). It is something like a love-duet between the men and the boys. In this atmosphere of humility, there is a final chorale coda (Ps. 133, vs. 1) – a prayer for peace.

I hope my score is legible. In order to help with the Hebrew text, I shall enclose a typewritten copy of the words (the Hebrew words of Ps. 2 are a tongue-breaker!). The score contains exact notes on the pronunciation.

As to the orchestra, I have kept to the prescribed forces, except that there will be a large percussion group necessary (xylophone, glockenspiel, bongos, chimes, etc., in addition to the usual timpani, drums, cymbals, etc.). Also, I am sure more strings will be necessary than the number you list – especially the low ones. Certainly *one* bass will not do the trick. One of the three trumpets must be very good indeed, in order to perform several difficult solo passages. There is also an extensive harp part.

One last matter; I am conducting a program of my own music with the New York Philharmonic in *early* July, and I have been asked if I could include the

---

[130] Never one to waste a good idea, Bernstein used almost all of "Mix!," a cut number from *West Side Story*, in the second movement of the *Chichester Psalms*. His recycling of the music originally written for "Mix!" had uncanny parallels with the idea of conflict in the original song: "Lamah rag'shu goyim" ("Why do the nations rage"), a passage from Psalm 2 about the futility of nation fighting nation. Hussey's "hint" of *West Side Story* (see Letter 497) turned out to be a very apt choice.

Chichester Psalms. I realize that this would deprive you of the world premiere by a couple of weeks; do you have any serious objections?

In any case I wish you well with the piece; and I may even take your performance as an excuse to visit Sussex in late July. I should dearly love to hear this music in your cathedral.

Faithfully yours,

Leonard Bernstein

508. Walter Hussey to Leonard Bernstein
The Deanery, Chichester, England
11 June 1965

Dear Dr. Bernstein,

I have just returned after being away for five weeks as a result of a tiny cerebral thrombosis. In due course the doctors assure me that I shall be quite fit again and need take no notice of it, but just at present I feel slightly old and tired!

The *Chichester Psalms* arrived yesterday and I do indeed thank you for them. They are splendid and exactly the sort of thing that I was hoping for. So far as I can judge they seem to be admirable and I thank you most warmly for them.

If it is at all possible for you to come over and hear them in late July we shall be delighted for you to do so. In this case please come and stay at the Deanery. Would you like to conduct them?

As to the orchestra, Mr. Birch has got this in hand and will I am sure follow your wishes.

Yours sincerely,

Walter Hussey

509. Walter Hussey to Leonard Bernstein
The Deanery, Chichester, England

8 July 1965

Dear Mr. Bernstein,

Thank you very much for your letter.

I expect by this time you will have heard from Mr. Robert Lantz giving you a formal invitation to come for the Music Festival, and the final rehearsal and the first performance of the *Chichester Psalms*. It is unfortunately impossible to get lodgings anywhere in this part of the world at the time, they are all booked up eight or nine months ahead for the Goodwood Race Meeting which takes place on the Monday to Saturday of that week. This is most unfortunate for us because it does make it frightfully hard for any people to get accommodation for the Music Festival within a fifteen to twenty mile range. I have had a word with numbers of hotels and they all tell me the same. However, I shall indeed be delighted for you and Mrs. Bernstein to come here and Mr. and Mrs. Robert Elwes, who live just a mile or two from the Cathedral in a very lovely house, will be delighted for the children to go there. They have two children aged 13 and 10 of their own, and a swimming pool, if only the weather will allow them to use it! They are very nice people indeed and I am sure you could feel absolutely happy for them to be there. If this would be satisfactory for you Mrs. Elwes says she would be delighted for them to be there from Thursday until Monday, and of course I shall be only too glad for you to be here.

I am delighted to hear that Chuck Solomon hopes to be in Chichester for the Psalms and I have written to tell him so, but my only fear is that if he had not made the arrangements already he may well find it impossible to get anywhere. It would be great to see him again.

Please tell me if there is any way in which I can help you further.

Yours sincerely,

Walter Hussey

510. Leonard Bernstein to Walter Hussey

17 July 1965

My dear Dean Hussey,

Our Psalms had their "creation" last night, to a standing ovation, and I was overjoyed for you as well as for myself. I enclose this morning's *Times* review, which pays you just credit for your kindness. Even juster credit is paid you by the program notes. I'm having them sent you: won't you need them for your own use?

I have your last letter, and am most grateful for your solicitude. Mrs. Bernstein and I will be most happy to stay at the Deanery; and my children are terribly excited at the prospect of living with an English family, and making British friends of their own age. Please tell Mr. and Mrs. Elwes how very grateful we are. The only minor hitch is that our visit is planned one day earlier; we should arrive on the 28th and leave on Sunday, 1st August. I hope this does not complicate your and the Elwes' lives.

We are leaving here the 27th, arriving in London that night, which we shall spend at the Savoy Hotel. We have covering bookings at the Savoy for the whole 10-day period, so don't hesitate to evict us if you would have to; in any emergency there will be a roof over our heads.

Looking forward with immense pleasure –

Yours,

Leonard Bernstein[131]

---

[131] Printed in Hussey 1985, p. 116.

511. Walter Hussey to Leonard Bernstein

The Deanery, Chichester, England
22 July 1965[132]

Dear Mr. Bernstein,

I am *delighted* you & Mrs. Bernstein & the children can come over to England for the first performance of the Psalms. All is ready – except the weather! Miss Chavez[133] of CBS records will meet you at London Air Port and has laid on a car, if you should require it, to bring you to Chichester the next day.

I am very glad that the Psalms have met with such a warm reception – I'm sure they entirely deserve it.

I wrote to Chuck a while back, but have not heard. Still, he may well turn up when the time comes!

There was an excellent article about the *Chichester Psalms* in the *Times* (of London), but I'm afraid I haven't got a copy now. However, I'll have one when you come.

Looking forward to seeing you with great pleasure – & some little apprehension!

Yours ever,
Walter Hussey

512. Walter Hussey to Leonard Bernstein

The Deanery, Chichester, England
1 August 1965

Dear Lenny,

I hope you arrived safely back at the Savoy last night – with no breakdowns!

I cannot begin to tell you how grateful I am for the *Chichester Psalms*. This morning the Bishop of Chichester said to the Archdeacon – they were a new revelation to him & brought home afresh the meaning of them, joyous & ecstatic & calm & poetic – he said you could imagine "David dancing before the ark".

We were *all* thrilled with them. I was specially excited that they came into being at all as a statement of praise that is oecumenical. I shall be tremendously proud for them to go around the world bearing the name of Chichester.

I hope the family are enjoying their brief stay in London. They won the hearts of all who met them! But especially Felicia, who has gone straight to the number 1 place of the most charming & attractive of wives.

---

[132] Hussey has written "1963" but this is an error. The *Times* article to which Hussey refers appeared on 19 July 1965, three days before he wrote this letter.
[133] Quita Chavez was classical promotions manager for CBS Records in London.

Please come again any time you can. You will always be welcome & it will be an honour to have you here.

Bless you indeed for everything.

Walter

P.S. I wonder if there is *any* chance of getting the MS – to go with those of Britten and others who have written things for us? It doesn't matter if it is terribly crossed out & untidy!

513. Felicia Bernstein to Walter Hussey

Savoy Hotel, London
3 August 1965

Dear Walter,

This is the first chance I've had to sit down in relative peace since our drive back from Chichester! As you can imagine it's been non-stop – finally today I asked for time off to see an old childhood friend and write to you.

We will all remember Chichester for many reasons but the main reason is you. We talk about you so much and miss you already; so you see, for all our sakes you simply must return the visit. Do come!

Bless you for all your kindness and hospitality, and think of us once in a while as you stare at the yellow carpet! A reference to the coffee disaster!

With best wishes from us all.

Felicia[134]

514. Leonard Bernstein to Walter Hussey

Savoy Hotel, London
6 August 1965

Dear Walter,

We are all about to leave London, and in this last hour I wanted somehow to talk to you again, to thank you, not only on a social level, but on the deepest personal one, for all the things you are, do, and stand for. I shall carry sweet memories of Chichester for a long time.

The Psalms are, of course, dedicated to you, and you should receive the very first published copy. Meanwhile I shall arrange to have a photocopy sent you.

Again, Felicia and I send you our most affectionate thanks.

Lenny B.[135]

---

[134] Printed in Hussey 1985, p. 118.
[135] Printed in Hussey 1985, pp. 118–19.

515. Leonard Bernstein to Walter Hussey
20 September 1965

My dear Walter,

Chichester seems awfully far away by now, but the memory of our days there is a glowing one, reinforced this week by the test pressing of the recording, which should be out within the month. I'll see that you get one of the first copies.

I have also been busy proofreading the vocal score, which is to appear at the same time as the record, and of course you'll get one of these too.

Apropos of the printed score, I must confess that I have yielded to a very human weakness. I could not resist sharing the dedication between you and Chuck Solomon. (You get the first credit, as having commissioned it, and there is then a line dedicating it to Chuck.) I happened to talk to him the other day, and he sounded very *down*; and in that instant it occurred to me that this dedication would set him up for at least a year. It's just what he needs – and I am sure that you, of all people, will understand the nature of this gesture, since you and Chuck are such good friends, and since he was the originator of our relationship, yours and mine. I somehow feel I owe this to him. I hope you agree.

Again, thanks from us all for your kindness and friendship.

Yours,

Lenny[136]

516. Walter Hussey to Leonard Bernstein
The Deanery, Chichester, England
16 October 1965

My dear Lenny,

I found your letter here when I returned from a fortnight's holiday, and that is the reason it has gone unanswered so long. I am very sorry.

Thank you indeed for writing it. I also carry with me the most happy memories of your visit – now we are having the most wonderful, cloudless weather that we should have had then!

Yes indeed, I entirely understand about Chuck and approve his sharing the dedication. I am sure he will, rightly, be as pleased as a dog with two tails. I sent him, some while ago, a letter thanking him for his part in the *Chichester Psalms* and telling him it would never have come about apart from him!

Of course I am only to pay the bill for the car-hire. I was only anxious that we should not *both* pay it.

---

[136] Printed in Hussey 1985, p. 119.

I am most anxious, and so are many other people, to hear the record. It will be very exciting. It is *most* good of you to say you will send me a copy of the score and the record. It's far more than I deserve. Have you the original score you wrote? I feel awful asking, but I should love to have it if you can spare it, to put with the others. It doesn't matter how rough it is – Britten's is in pencil & a mass of scratching out!

Give my love to Felicia and the children. I look back on your visit as a great time and a very happy one.

Yours ever,

Walter

P.S. I hear rumours that the BBC want to do the *Chichester Psalms* again from here, with a different orchestra. I do hope they are true!

517. John Cage to Leonard Bernstein

Stony Point, NY

28 October 1965

Dear Lenny,

Was very good to be with you, Felicia, and the Fosses. I'm now organizing a show and sale of 20th century music mss. (Stable Gallery April 1966) for the benefit of the Foundation for Contemporary Performance Arts, Inc. Gifts to the Foundation are tax-exempt. Will you give us a page of your work?[137] Wd. be very grateful.

As ever,

John (Cage)

518. Leonard Bernstein to Walter Hussey

29 October 1965

[Dear Walter,]

I can't describe to you the surprise and pleasure of receiving your gift. It is at least as extraordinary of you to remember my liking your pen as it is for you to have sent me one.

And, of course, the pen's first act-in-office is to write this note, sending thanks and affection.

The recording and the published score should be arriving any day now. Meanwhile I am sending you my original "fair copy" – though alas, only a

---

[137] A note in Helen Coates' hand at the top of the letter reads: "Sketch of Psalm XXIII (*Chichester Psalms*) sent to him Nov. 15th." This sketch was requested by Cage as part of his *Notations* project, started in 1965. Cage donated all the manuscripts he collected to Northwestern University (Evanston, IL) in 1973, where Bernstein's sketch now forms part of the John Cage Notations Project collection.

photostat of the manuscript, since the true-original is committed to the Library of Congress, as is the case with everything I write. This is the next-best; it is all in my own hand, and I hope it pleases you.

Bless you, your health, your work, and your touching generosity in sending me this treasureable pen.

Warmest greetings,

Lenny[138]

519. George Szell[139] to Leonard Bernstein

New York, NY

29 October 1965

Dear Lenny,

Many many thanks for your sweet note. Your wishes for pleasure with your orchestra have already come true: I am enjoying myself with them thoroughly and find them in better shape & spirits than I can remember.[140] The prospect to spend a little time with you after you return is positively *enticing*. I hope it *will* happen. Meanwhile, all good wishes for a pleasant & restful vacation.

Ever cordially,

George

520. Yo-Yo Ma[141] to Leonard Bernstein

138 East 94th Street, New York, NY

21 December 1965

Dear Mr. Bernstein,

Do you still remember me? Now I am ten years old. This year I learned with Prof. Leonard Rose three concertos: Saint-Saëns', Boccherini's and Lalo's. Last week my sister and I played in a Christmas Concert in Juilliard School. We are invited to give a joint recital in Brearley School on January 19, 1966 at 1:45 p.m.

If you have time, I would be glad to play for you.

Yo-Yo Ma

---

[138] Printed in Hussey 1985, pp. 119–20.

[139] George Szell (1897–1970), Hungarian-born conductor who was Music Director of the Cleveland Orchestra from 1946 until his death.

[140] The same day that Szell wrote this letter he conducted the first of four concerts with the New York Philharmonic (28, 29, 30 October, and 1 November 1965), which included Mussorgsky's Prelude to *Khovanshchina*, Prokofiev's Piano Concerto No. 3 (with Gary Graffman as the soloist), and Tchaikovsky's Fifth Symphony. He remained with the orchestra until 22 November, conducting three further weekly programs in the subscription series.

[141] Yo-Yo Ma (b. 1955), American cellist; he had already played for Presidents Eisenhower and Kennedy as a child prodigy by the time he wrote this letter to Bernstein.

521. Leonard Bernstein to John Adams[142]

[27 January 1966]

Dear Mr. Adams,

I am touched by your intelligent letter, but hard put to answer it. When you depict me as "turning my back" on "new" musical trends you do me a disservice, to say nothing of making an irrelevancy. One writes what one hears *within* one, not without. Lord knows I am sufficiently exposed to the "influences" of non-tonal music; but obviously I have not been conditioned by them. Mahler apart, I cannot conceive music (my own music) divorced from tonality. Whether this is good or bad is, again, irrelevant. The only meaningful thing is the truth of the creative act. The rest of the chips will fall where they may.

Good luck to you.[143]

522. Leonard Bernstein to Felicia Bernstein

Hotel Bristol, Vienna, Austria
2 March 1966

Fleshy darling,

It is a week to the hour that I am in Vienna, and this is literally the first moment free. It's been all rehearsals, 10 a.m. to 8 p.m. daily, studying at night, & trying (not too successfully) to get some sleep. The time-change threw me for a loop; I'm just now coming out of it.

But all goes well.[144] The orchestra is cheering, the directors are fawning, the press is voluminous and astonishingly sympathetic. Fischer-Dieskau is a dream-singer – I've never heard anyone better.[145] And the rest of the cast is superb, with a weakness here or there – but not important. Dr. Caius is a German with a frightful accent in Italian which will sound bad on the record, & Oncina's Fenton is not ideal. But you can't have everything. The Opera people have given me extra rehearsals; the orchestra goes overtime without a word of protest (never

---

[142] John Adams (b. 1947), American composer, who was a student at Harvard in 1966. Adams writes about the circumstances of this letter in *Hallelujah Junction*: "Despite my hunch that Boulez's was the wrong way to make art, I continued to try embracing the beast. Still in my freshman year, and by way of venting my frustration with the direction contemporary music was heading, I wrote a letter to Leonard Bernstein. I had never met him, but for some reason I felt the need to prick such a famous superstar to see if he might possibly bleed. I thought maybe that sharing my own frustration would perhaps sting him enough to elicit a response. Composed more in the negative spirit of a heckler at a baseball game than in any true seriousness [. . .] it was prompted by my hearing of his most recent piece, *Chichester Psalms*. [. . .] In my letter I chided him, asking 'What about Boulez?' A week later there in my mailbox at Wigglesworth Hall was a letter – from Leonard Bernstein" (Adams 2008, p. 32).
[143] Draft letter written in pencil, unsigned.
[144] Bernstein was in Vienna to conduct *Falstaff* at the Vienna State Opera.
[145] Dietrich Fischer-Dieskau sang Falstaff in this production. See Letter 546.

before, since Strauss himself, says Dr. Hilbert). In short, I'm a sort of Jewish hero who has replaced Karajan – and all this at the moment of the general elections which happen tomorrow, & are full of anti-Semitic issues & overtones. It's a strange feeling . . .

I've just come from a place in Nussberg – a suburb – an old palais devoted to vineyard activity, where some members of the orchestra took me to play for me "Schrammelmusik" – old, authentic, "kitsch" Viennese tunes arranged for 4 instruments – the original *Rosenkavalier* stage-music. Fantastic. Lots of glorious wine, platters of hot roast chickens, hams, Gott weiss was. Very touching, from orchestra men: toasts, good feeling. As I say, a very strange moment for me.

The Kripsies[146] have been here, & invited me daily to his performances & to dinner or lunch – I funked out ever time, being left with a bad conscience, especially since they sent me (us) huge lilies, & today, as a *farewell* gift (!) two boxes of Demel chocolates. They're in San Francisco now: and I've written a conscience-letter.

Maazel is also here doing *Carmen*. I heard 10 minutes & left: *bad*. But the musical life is wilder than Milan: everything seems to center around it, & *Falstaff* is the event everyone is waiting for.

Many of Willie Weissel's[147] friends have written or called – I don't dare to accept or answer: *què lata*. Luchino [Visconti] is tired & morose, at once doing *Falstaff* & preparing *Rosenkavalier* for London, & cutting a movie: he's insane, & surrounded by numerous young Italian assistants, which gives him pleasure. And now I go to be fed & fêted by Regina Resnick [Resnik], who lives across the square, & has been preparing a risotto for days.

As you can see, it's a fascinating, glorious life so far. The haut-monde is yet to come. Bet you can't wait! But I'll tell you one thing: I can't wait for you to come. You'll love Vienna, somehow I smell it.

Have a great Buffalo, love to Fossies, & come soon. I miss you!

Love,

L

I read a bad Kerr notice of Mendy's[148] play in the *Trib*. Are they all bad? Give him & Susan my love. And the kiddies: kiss them. And write me. And make the kiddies write me – xxx

---

[146] The conductor Josef Krips and his wife.

[147] William Weissel was the Viennese-born assistant manager of the New York Philharmonic.

[148] "Mendy" was the nickname of the actor Michael Wager (1925–2011). The play mentioned by Bernstein is *Where's Daddy?* by William Inge, produced by Wager and directed by Harold Clurman. It ran for just 22 performances in March 1966.

523. Leonard Bernstein to Sam and Jennie Bernstein

Hotel Bristol, Vienna, Austria
19 March 1966

Dear Folks,

At last I have a minute to write you. I am enjoying Vienna enormously – as much as a Jew can. There are so many sad memories here; one deals with so many ex-Nazis (and maybe still Nazis); and you never know if the public that is screaming *bravo* for you might contain someone who 25 years ago might have shot me dead. But it's better to forgive, and if possible, forget. The city is so beautiful, and so full of tradition. Everyone here lives for music, especially opera, and I seem to be the new hero. What they call the "Bernstein wave" that has swept Vienna has produced some strange results; all of a sudden it's fashionable to be Jewish.

But I work very hard, practicing & studying, recording (20 sessions!) and rehearsing. So far everything has gone brilliantly, but I'm tired – too many parties, also. Don't be upset by that bronchitis story: I had it for only two days. And I really feel very well.

This morning I went to *Shul*, imagine, with Regina Resnick [Resnik]. The old, famous Wiener Schul, restored as it used to be, on *Judengasse* (what a name for a street!). But it was warm and heartening. I ran into a Bar Mitzvah *and* a *Rosh Chodesh*, got a *Misheberach* & held the Torah for Rosh Chodesh, got a plug from the Rabbi & even attended the Kiddush afterwards. Very sweet. And tell Prof. Braslavsky that I met his old friend Rothenberg, who sends his greetings. They all remember him here.

Now I have a TV interview, a cocktail at Princess Hohenlohe, and then a dinner party with the recording people from London. So I'm off – and I send you much love. Soon you should receive some chocolates from Demel – the best on earth. Be well & take care of yourselves.

Your Wiener Schnitzel,

Lenny.

Shabbos, 19 March '66 after Havdala[h]

Jennie: Every morning I eat Vienna rolls – what you always used to call *Vianna* rolls. Remember?

524. Victor de Sabata[149] to Leonard Bernstein

Santa Margherita Ligure, Italy
28 June 1966

Dear Leonard,

In my purest and deeply felt joy I read this very morning that *at last* you plan to write an opera. Very seldom in my life I felt so thrilled and impatient! I wish to have your new score near my heart as soon as possibly! I am sure this will enable me to plunge into *real music*, a thing that – let us be sincere! – I am vainly longing for since centuries. Useless to tell you how often I think of you and your incandescent musical vitality. To know that a Bernstein does exist helps a lot. Ciao!

Tuo affezionatissimo,
Victor de Sabata

---

[149] Victor de Sabata (1892–1967), Italian conductor, renowned not only for his operatic conducting (especially at La Scala, Milan), but also for his performances of twentieth-century orchestral repertoire and for his phenomenal musical memory. When Bernstein first saw de Sabata conduct in London in 1946, he described him in a letter to his sister Shirley as "a wildman" (see Letter 225), but once Bernstein came to know him at La Scala in the 1950s he developed a warm admiration for de Sabata. In 1977, he wrote a short tribute entitled "Memories of Maestro de Sabata":

> The first word that comes to mind as I call up memories of de Sabata is *generosity*. It seemed to me to inform and characterize all his actions: his abundant love for music and for the colleagues with whom he produced it; the abundance of his passions and of his patience; his profound gratitude for his own gifts; his kindness to young performers like me; his devotion to his public, whether in Milan or Pittsburgh – all of it generous, generous. It was also in the music he composed: the spirit of *abbondanza*.
>
> It was because of his sudden illness in 1953 that I was called upon to open the Scala season with Cherubini's *Medea*, Callas and all. There were only six days for me to learn an unknown score, to make cuts and repairs, to meet and cope with Callas (which turned out to be pure joy), to make a difficult debut alla Scala, and all with severe bronchitis. In all this Maestro de Sabata was intensely helpful and encouraging; he gave me the extra measure of courage that I needed. And two years later, when I returned to conduct a new performance of *Sonnambula*, he virtually saved my life. "Too slow! Too slow!" I can still hear him chiding. "Bellini was Sicilian; and Sicilian blood runs hot! Run with it! Run!" Who knows what a boring disaster I might have made without that affectionate warning!
>
> There was much other good counsel besides; and of course he was equally generous with his praise. And this abundance of spirit flowed through all his conducting: one has only to listen to his old recording of *Tosca* with Callas. I still believe it to be the greatest recording of an Italian opera I have ever heard. I have only to listen to it – any dozen bars of it – and the spirit of de Sabata is in the room with me. Leonard Bernstein, May 1977.

525. Robert Russell Bennett[150] to Leonard Bernstein
150 East 50th Street, New York, NY
26 November 1966

Caro Maestro,

There is no reason why my opinion should be of especial value to you, but I can't resist sending you this note to voice my enthusiastic approval of your decision to give full time to music composition.

My opinion is not without substance because I once, when we were both much younger, tuned into a broadcast and hear a Sonata for clarinet and piano written by you, and as I turned away from the loudspeaker I said to Louise, "This is one of our big composers." As years have gone by I felt a certain reluctance to see you pursuing the conducting, and even the composing of Broadway music, as being a waste of that precious commodity, time, when so much is needed for the full realization I had in mind. I never saw Gustav Mahler conduct. If he was as great as I have been told, he is just about the one exception that proves the rule as far as I am concerned.

I leave you to comb through the history of our profound composers and see how they fared at strictly commercial roundelays. Of course, someone will answer this remark by bringing up that innocent era of Mozart and Haydn when "popular music" was the reaction of a whole era to the deep expression of Bach, for instance. Be that as it may, you have at least one enthusiastic vote for your career as a real composer.

All the best as always,
Russell

526. Georg Solti[151] to Leonard Bernstein
17 Woronzow Road, London, England
19 May 1967

Dear Mr. Bernstein,

I hope that you will not regard this letter as interference, but I felt that I had to write to you about Mr. Wobisch.

---

[150] Robert Russell Bennett (1894–1981), American composer and arranger. After studying with Nadia Boulanger in Paris, Bennett began working as an arranger and orchestrator on Broadway, collaborating with Kern (*Showboat*), Gershwin (*Girl Crazy, Of Thee I Sing*), Porter (*Anything Goes, Kiss Me, Kate*), Rodgers (*Oklahoma!, Carousel, South Pacific, The King and I, The Sound of Music*), and many others. He also composed extensively for symphony orchestra, concert band, and chamber ensembles.

[151] Georg Solti (1912–97), Hungarian conductor. This letter serves as a reminder of the dilemma that faced Jewish musicians working in Vienna during the 1960s. In dealing with anti-Semitism, Solti – himself a Jew – had an outlook that was a mixture of humanity and pragmatism: to look forward

I first heard from John Culshaw[152] about the reports in the Vienna Press concerning you and Wobisch. Two days later Wobisch telephoned me about another matter, at the end of the conversation he told me more about the reports and how very distressed he was about them. Afterwards, I felt that without wanting to interfere in a matter which does not concern me at all, I had to write to you for purely human reasons.

As another Jewish conductor, I understand your feelings surely better than anyone else. If somebody, after the Nazi horrors, does not want to work with a German or Austrian orchestra, as is the case with several Jewish artists, I understand only too well. I have been through great soul searching in the past about this, and several times have been on the verge of breaking contact with them. But finally I always had the conviction that one must forgive the past and try to work to help and educate the younger generation in these orchestras.

I am aware of Wobisch's political past, as surely you were before you went to Vienna. However, working with him and knowing him for the past ten years, I have come to the conviction that despite everything he is probably one of the few trustworthy members of that orchestra.

Wobisch worked very hard to bring you to Vienna and to prepare your appearances and successes there; I even heard from Mr. Rosengarten of Decca that Wobisch went as far as threatening to change the orchestra's contract from Decca to Deutsche Grammophon unless they were released to make *Rosenkavalier* with you. As you will know by now this involved the postponement of my own recording of the opera with the orchestra, which should be enough indication of my real neutrality in this issue.

---

rather than back, with the aim of rebuilding Europe after the ravages of war. He established a productive working relationship with the Vienna Philharmonic during the 1950s that grew into a warm and enduring association. The same was to happen with Bernstein, but not until he had come to terms with the fact that Helmut Wobisch, the orchestra's manager (and also one of its trumpeters), had been an active Nazi during the Second World War. Solti played a crucial role in this: his advice to Bernstein – to give Wobisch a chance rather than to condemn him out of hand – was both wise and realistic: he knew the Vienna Philharmonic very well by 1967, whereas Bernstein had made his debut with the orchestra only the year before; and Solti's letter is also written by someone who had clearly learned to rise above the gossip-mongering that was a constant feature of the city's musical life.

Bernstein quickly took his colleague's advice to heart. According to Humphrey Burton (1994, p. 354), Bernstein "brushed aside [Wobisch's] past: he would refer to him openly as 'his SS man.'" Wobisch's well-documented past was catalogued in detail in a letter to Joseph Wechsberg from Simon Wiesenthal on 3 February 1967 (a copy of which was sent by Wechsberg to Bernstein) confirming Wobisch's membership not only of the Nazi Party and the SS, but also of the SD (Sicherheitsdienst), the intelligence agency of the SS and the party. Despite these grim associations, both Solti and Bernstein found Wobisch friendly and supportive, and Bernstein was to spend much of the latter part of his career performing and recording the symphonic repertoire with the Vienna Philharmonic (including Mozart's late symphonies, Beethoven, Brahms, Schumann, Mahler, and Sibelius). Solti's letter was a timely and characteristic intervention, encouraging Bernstein to take a conciliatory approach.

[152] John Culshaw (1924–1980) was a producer for Decca. He is best remembered for producing the Solti *Ring* and for numerous recordings conducted by Benjamin Britten.

If Wobisch should have to resign as a result of this controversy with you, I am convinced that not only would this be bad for the orchestra, but that both you and I might well find any replacement totally unacceptable for political and human reasons.

I hope that these few lines may have helped in some way.

With kindest regards,

Yours sincerely,

Georg Solti

527. Janis Ian[153] to Leonard Bernstein

7 June 1967, "Evening tide"

Hello sir,

Excuse the formality of the address, but if you remember everyone was bopping about calling you "Lenny", and since I felt rather strange doing that we decided on sir.

I would have written sooner but... Well, no excuses. I didn't really have much to say except thank you, and I'd said that. But now I want to tell you what's happened.

If you didn't see, the biggest rock station in California wrote out a public apology for their recent timidity, and thanked you for showing the way. More stations on the West Coast went on "Society's Child", and now it's number one in California. I'm waiting for it to hit the top 20, so NY stations will be forced to play it. Except the station manager of WMCA or WABC said he'd *never* play it because he wanted to keep his children's ears free from the "objectionable" lyrics.

Anyway, this is just to say that you're lovely and thanks again for everything.

Janis Ian (me)

P.S. Is it okay if when a reporter asks what I think of you I just say that you're gorgeous and charming?

528. Leonard Bernstein to Lukas Foss

Casa Malone, Orbetello, Grosseto, Italy

8 August 1967

Poor, dear, blessed Luky-Puky!

A grief ago! I pray that period has lengthened to a vague unpleasantness ago. When I read the accounts in the paper I was sure something like what you

---

[153] Janis Ian (b. 1951), American songwriter, singer, and author. The CBS News Special, *Inside Pop –the Rock Revolution*, was broadcast on 27 April 1967, presented by Bernstein and produced by David Oppenheim. In this program, Janis Ian performed "Society's Child," which Bernstein discussed as a social protest song.

described had happened: I wanted to rush home and set things right. But I can't rush anywhere: the *dolce far niente* has taken over. I do nothing. No note written, no score studied, no idea thought out. I'm a fish, living with other fish under-water in my glorious diving gear. I have a rubber motorboat and a divine Maserati (my first & last pure playboy object); my summer romance & constant companion is Alexander; I read the mail & some newspapers; I fret from afar over race riots, Vietnam, tax hikes, bad N.Y. weather, increasing horror in the world from Cairo to Memphis, Tenn. I fret over Myrow's *Salome* libretto (lousy, pompous, meaningless, imitative in the worst way, and corruptive of youth). I fret over your neoclassicism & Philharmonic tragedy[154] (Oh, well; it gave Brigitta a chance for a big triumph, no?)

I don't sleep (it is now 4.30 a.m.). My back has been in agony for a month. Felicia can't take the sun. But the water and sky & air are divine, as is the weather and this house-&-garden; and you have a birthday in a week. Bless you. Time. . . I am tortured by the passing of time, to the point where I can hardly enjoy the passing of these beautiful days. Each day is a horror because it leads me one day closer to the end of summer; & the guilt of not working is intolerable. But my brain & crea-tive innerds are dormant, or dead. Why? I shriek inside. For what, for whom? Shall I leave music & enter politics? My tune of the summer, obsessive, is the Beatles'

> Will you still need me
> Will you still feed me
> When I'm sixty-four?

At least it's gay and simple and no trouble.

John Gruen[155] sits with me for hours, a tape-recorder between us, and I talk, talk, talk. I have been photographed to a crisp. Israel was astonishing and semi-sad and like a religious experience. The concerts there were my last conscious acts.

I have a gnawing feeling that David O[ppenheim] is still miffed at me. Ask him. I miss him a lot; if he can, would he write?

Rio → Warsaw → Buffalo! Only Luky could concoct that itinerary. But at least have fun, feel like Marco Polo, adventurize!

---

[154] Foss' "Philharmonic tragedy" was the cancellation at the last minute of the first performance of Foss' Variations. According to *The New York Times* (9 July 1967), this was because "the materials needed to perform the new work were not ready." The other work on the program was Honegger's *Joan of Arc at the Stake*, conducted by Seiji Ozawa, with Vera Zorina (whose real name, Brigitta, Bernstein uses) playing Joan. *The New York Times* review suggests that it was indeed the triumph Bernstein suggested: "Her diction was beautiful, her voice was musical, and her intensity was compelling."

[155] John Gruen's *The Private World of Leonard Bernstein* was published in 1968.

I long to see you in September. I rejoice in your "fan letter" and in the good news of the *Phorion* tape. I pray for you to write beautiful music. I love you.

L

Hugs to Corny & Chris-Andrew and L-Baby and the Opps. And the Rivers and rest. How did *Phorion* phare in Chicago? Phabulously, I hope.

Write again before you leave.

529. Leonard Bernstein to Stephen Sondheim
Casa Malone, Orbetello, Grosseto, Italy
19 August 1967

Dear SS,

The appearance on my desk, *faute de mieux*, of a pack of Winstons brings you instantly and clearly into the room. Besides I can't sleep o' nights, nor have I been able to for over a month. And these guilty sleepless hours, drugged yet jumpy, are my only epistolary moments. Reading H. P. Lovecraft this evening has also brought you to mind, as has Nina's incessant playing of the *WSS* album. In, out, let's get cracking. Neutral territory. One-handed catch. Then the Princes appeared for dinner, reporting you depressed at Merrick's failure to announce your work among his plans, or, indeed, to come up with a theatre. And beside these, I just happen to think of you often, apropos a thousand trivia, all warmly nostalgic.

A strange summer. Glorious weather, sea, boats, diving gear, skis, sun and air – all the goodies. But a fearsome back (how's your back, Lenny? And now I'm to be 49) prevents aquatic fun, and nameless anxieties (is that the word?) forbid work. Not a note, scores unstudied, books unread. Thoughts and ideas are absent, except for such stuff as *Improvised, eh? Garbled and poor!* Felicia sleeps badly too: only the children prosper. I teach Alexander Hebrew – my one real activity. I shudder at the heaps of unanswered mail. I itch.

There's my report. What's yours?

You should have come to this Eden-on-the-Sea; we could have moaned together.

If you see or talk to Jerry, please tell him I'm simply too guilty to write him, owing to the absence of a single idea. Total non-energy.

I hope your musical is ship-shape.[156] I read that *Lion in Winter* is to be cinematized. I hope you are loving somebody, regularly and in bed. I hope the soul-brothers haven't reached Turtle Bay yet. I hope the world can survive its awful weight a bit longer. I hope –

---

[156] The musical Bernstein hopes is "ship-shape" is *Follies* (information from Stephen Sondheim). Ted Chapin explains that: "In June of 1967 *The Girls Upstairs* [the original title for *Follies*] was scheduled for the coming Broadway season, to be produced by David Merrick and Leland Hayward. The plan ultimately fell through" (Chapin 2005, p. xxii). *Follies* eventually opened in 1971.

I send you wee-hour love and personalized sentiments. Be dour if you must, but be happy.

Lenny

530. Joe Roddy to Leonard Bernstein
25 October 1967

Dear Leonard,

Because you have one of the last grasps left of the human comedy, I am counting on you to see me into, and then out the other side, of this absurd fix I am in. For all the Mahler I never knew before, for Ives, for much Haydn, for an overwhelming *Missa Solemnis*, for the world's first *Falstaff*, for the *Chichester Psalms*, for *Candide*, for – well, Christ, for ninety percent of the music that matters to me nowadays, I am in debt to you. Clinking oceans of gold pieces would not repay all. So really, it cannot matter, can it?, that there is an ice cream stand at Expo 67 on which there is writ in chocolate sauce *L. B. OWES J. R. $100*. Debt for debt, mine is hardly worth mentioning.

Except that, weeks from now when you are savoring a distraction or two instead of settling down to write the next to last song for that Brecht show, into the mind of you will come the picture of me. I will be seen sitting, sitting and sitting at some many Philharmonic rehearsals, day after day after day. Why, you will then ask yourself, did he come round so often? Why, why, why? Then a terrible thought will come over you, a thought so disruptive that it may dislodge forever that shred of melody you were counting on to get you started again, the thought that I was sitting there not watching and listening to you work with the orchestra at all, but instead just waiting there like some mouse creep of a bail bondsman from Baxter Street worrying about his cheesy C-note.

But, my ever so dear friend, that is not why I was there, nor why I will be there tomorrow maybe. I like it there, but you know all that. I just want to protect you from that blinding light in which I might glow, though dully, like a mouse. I don't want you to lose that shred of tune, and surely you don't want me to sit there at rehearsals with these grotesque introspections.

Unless I know

That you know

About my dough

At Expo,

I can't show

At rehearsals any mo'

Bo!

Love,
Joe Roddy
. . . and I don't even know what present you bought for your sister.

531. Leonard Bernstein to Joe Roddy
27 October 1967

Dearest Joe,

Why, you will ask yourself, $112.49? Precise figures follow: $100, plus interest (at, I believe, the going rate of usury, 4%), making $104, plus interest compounded for compound guilt and shame, making $108.16, plus further compound interest for neglect and discourtesy.

My only redeeming feature for my life-long inability to remember debts owed is my concomitant inability to remember debts owed to me by others. In short, money is the thing that interests me least of all this world's wonders.

But:

Now that you know   But be my beau,
That I've eaten crow   Dear Joe,
Over the dough   Fo'-
You lent at Expo   ever. And FO'-
Never go   GIVE!
Away no mo',

Love,
Lenny

532. Leonard Bernstein to Aaron Copland
[New York, NY]
12 November 1967

Dear A,

It's two days before your birthday, but I'm already thinking hard and tenderly about you; and this note is your birthday present carrying with it such abiding love as I rarely if ever get to express to you in our occasional meetings. I don't know if you're aware of what you mean, have meant for 30 years, to me and my music and so many of my attitudes to life and to people. I suppose if there's one person on earth who is at the centre of my life, it's you; and day after day I recognize in my living your presence, your laugh, your peculiar mixture of intensity and calm . . . I hope you live forever.

A long strong hug.

Lenny

533. Janis Ian to Leonard Bernstein

Richard Armitage Management Corp., 130 East 57th Street, New York, NY
[November 1967]

Hello Sir,

("Sir" on account of "Lenny" sounds too presumptuous, and "Mr. Bernstein" too unpresumptuous)

I guess you know what happened by now, everyone calling up and apologizing for not playing "Society's Child", and then playing it and it turned into a top twenty record . . . and the album too . . . and the new record looks like it will . . .

Because of that, because you drilled me on Spanish, because you're a nice person, I'd like to invite you to my concert.

It's to be at Philharmonic Hall on December 8 (a Friday night). I'd really like to have you there, and though I can't quite explain why, I'm sure you understand.[157]

If you can come, would you please call Jean Powell who's my manager, and let her know how many tickets you'll want. Or ask David [Oppenheim] to call if he's around, as we're inviting him too and it'll be killing two birds with one stone.

I really hope you can come.

Yours for sunshine etc.

Janis

P.S. Passed my Spanish Regents with an 86.

534. Leonard Bernstein to Joe Roddy

[New York, NY]
7 January 1968

Dear Joe,

Your piece in *Look* was a fine Xmas present, in that it is always a gift to read something sanely considered and well told.[158] I have, naturally, a few objections (oh, two or three hundred) – nothing sensational, like what's so special about

---

[157] Bernstein has written a draft reply at the foot of this letter: "Dear Janis, I'd love to come but I can't and I'm flattered you asked me & thought of me. I wish you a *howling* success. LB"

[158] The 9 January 1968 edition of *Look* magazine (pp. 74–7) included an article by Joe Roddy entitled "How to Think about Leonard Bernstein," mostly about his tenure at the New York Philharmonic and his relationship with the orchestra.

sport-jackets (Dimitri [Mitropoulos] wore them constantly, as do you) and who ever lived like Scott Fitz[gerald] – anyone – who, me? – at 32 W. 10th? 40 W. 55th? The Chelsea? What else? Oh, *On the Town* is *not* in any sense a version of *Fancy Free*: there is not one note in common – only three sailors.

But all these I forgive easily; what may take a bit more time is your quoting a quote which is a misquote to begin with, and by Ned Rorem, at that! I never expected that you'd reach that far and that low, just for a kicker. But peace, I'll get over it. And I'll manage to survive not being loved by you, which should patently disprove Ned's quote.

This note was started as a thank-you, and so it should end, with the addition of a Happy New Year.

Lenny

535. Richard Rodney Bennett[159] to Leonard Bernstein

[Munich] *as from* 4 Rheidol Terrace, London, England
25 January 1968

Dear Mr. Bernstein,

I wanted to write as soon as I arrived here in Munich, but the time has been so taken up with rehearsals for my opera that this is the first moment I've had.

The performances of my symphony were, it seemed to me, absolutely perfect.[160] They had all the passion and excitement that I hoped I was writing into the work, plus a brilliance & power which I couldn't have imagined. It was a most thrilling time for me, and I am extremely grateful, both for the chance to write the work and for the marvellous performances. I was only sorry not to hear them all. Paul tells me the Saturday one was especially good.

I hated to leave N.Y. but there seem to be all sorts of things in the air & I rather feel I shall be back *quite* soon. So I hope to see you again before very long.

With many thanks,

Yours,

Richard

536. Leonard Bernstein to Stephen Sondheim

Hotel Sacher, Vienna, Austria
19 April 1968

Darling Steve,

Life is good, the gods are kind, *Rosenkavalier* is sensational, I've never worked so hard, etc. etc. My third act rehearsal was almost ruined by my staying up all

---

[159] Richard Rodney Bennett (1936–2012), English composer and pianist.
[160] Bennett's Symphony No. 2 was commissioned by the New York Philharmonic for its 125th anniversary and first performed on 18 January 1968, conducted by Bernstein.

night with your enthralling Dodecahedron.[161] Things like that. But why I'm *really* writing is, as they say here, *das volgendes*:

The Funke literary effort.[162] It was sent me by dozens of people and I never really read it to the end, what with all the hectic goings-on here, until yesterday, when I found myself shocked by the last line.[163] Shocked for you, that is – and I want you to know (as if I needed to tell you!) that, natch, I could never be the source of such a stupid and indelicate remark. But I have talked to Stu[art] O[strow] and told him so, that I will gladly write Funke if you'd like me to, that it's all too silly, life is too short, that I hope you've not been offended, that I love you.

And there you are. Tomorrow morning I get up and play a Mozart concerto for thousands of people and I haven't practiced a note. Tonight's *Rosenkavalier* boasted the presence of Strauss' son who made known that never before . . . but why go on. Fact is, I miss you and can't wait to get back and dig in.[164]

Love,
Lenny

537. Jacqueline Kennedy[165] to Leonard Bernstein
Washington D.C.
9 June 1968

Dear Lennie,

It's 4:00 in the morning – after this long, long day. We stayed in Washington, at my mother's house.

---

[161] Sondheim's "Dedicated Dodecahedron" puzzle was published in *New York Magazine* on 15 April 1968.

[162] "The Funke literary effort" refers to an article by Lewis B. Funke published in *The New York Times* on 8 April 1968, under the headline "*West Side Story* Collaborators Plan Musical of Brecht Play".

[163] Derived in part from comments made by Bernstein "speaking from Vienna," Funke ends with what seems like an unduly brusque comment: "Mr. Sondheim, who will do the lyrics, will have to wait until Mr. Bernstein completes some of the score." Understandably, Bernstein was keen to clear up any misunderstanding this remark might have caused.

[164] Bernstein's desire "get back and dig in" refers to the planned musical based on Brecht's *The Exception and the Rule* that he was working on with Sondheim and Jerome Robbins. Though several songs were written and there are a number of sketches in the Leonard Bernstein Collection, the project was abandoned.

[165] Jacqueline Kennedy (1929–94), First Lady of the United States during the presidency of John F. Kennedy, from 1961 until his assassination in 1963. She had come to know and like Bernstein during his frequent visits to the Kennedy White House.

Everyone has gone to bed but I just want to stay up by myself – to think about so many things – and about today.[166]

In awful times I think the only thing that comforts you is the goodness in people.

I want to write you that tonight – or this morning – whatever it is – because when I come home I will be so tired – and I may start thinking about the badness in people.

When your Mahler started to fill (but that is the wrong word – because it was more this sensitive trembling) the Cathedral today – I thought it the most beautiful music I had ever heard. I am so glad I didn't know it – it was this strange music of all the gods who were crying. And then – if only you could have seen it – it was the time when Ethel had thought of the most touching thing – having the littlest nephews and nieces, small children, before that terrifying array of Cardinals and gold and Gothic vaults, carry all the little vessels for Communion up to the high altar, so they could have some part in the farewell to the uncle they all loved so much. They were so vulnerable – and your music was every-thing in my heart, of peace and pain and such drowning beauty. You could just close your eyes and be lost in it forever. That is what I thought the whole service might be like – but as you and Monsignor Duffy and the Archbishop have found out, I don't know very much about liturgy and ritual.

So out of all the confusion – all your days of conferring, postponing, cance-ling, adding etc., etc., etc., – with every one under strain and out of control, I think something emerged that is as beautiful as your Mahler, and that is the way you have been, through all of this.

The only thing that mattered in the world was that Ethel should have what she wished as music for her husband.

All the music that meant so much to her – all the music the church could or couldn't play – all the intermediaries who cling to their old ways, even through

---

[166] Shortly after midnight on the morning of 6 June 1968, Jacqueline Kennedy's brother-in-law, Robert F. Kennedy, was assassinated in Los Angeles. The younger brother of President Kennedy, Robert had served in his brother's administration as Attorney General, then as Senator from New York. He had just won the California Democratic primary in the 1968 presidential campaign, running on a radical platform of social justice and racial equality. Jacqueline Kennedy phoned Bernstein later on the same day (6 June) to ask him to oversee the musical aspects of the funeral Mass at St Patrick's Cathedral, New York. The funeral took place on 8 June; Bernstein conducted the Adagietto from Mahler's Fifth Symphony with thirty members of the New York Philharmonic Orchestra, and part of the last movement of Verdi's Requiem. As reported in *The New York Times* (9 June 1968), "Mr. Bernstein's role in the Mass was specifically requested by the Kennedy family, with whom he has been friendly for several years." As Jacqueline Kennedy wrote in her letter, the Mahler was played at a particularly touching moment in the Mass, during the Offertory procession. *The New York Times* described this "procession by eight Kennedy children who marched in twos up the sanctuary behind two candle bearers to present the hosts and the wine used in the consecration of the Mass."

this. Now [we] have the most Ecumenical of Archbishops – through all that, dear Lennie – you were so tender and gentle and understanding – and tactful and self effacing – so she had *everything* she wanted, including the last solo that I didn't know of until I heard it – and that is what I mean by what I said in the beginning of this endless letter – it is the goodness of people that is the comfort.

I think your goodness and those few soaring moments of Mahler together are more beautiful than if you had played the most beautiful Requiem all the way through.

And it was so much more appropriate for this Kennedy – my Kaleidoscopic brother-in-law – and his wife who loved him mystically. If there had been anything organized or unified about it, it would not have been Bobby and Ethel!

And now we know they were something this world will never see again.

Will you tell your noble orchestra, drowning in heat and cables when I passed them – that so many people all this day have said: how beautiful you were – how many people cried – people who don't know music, and all the ones who were saying the day before, "You should have so-and-so's trumpets, Fourmier (or a name that sounds like that)[167] Requiem, a Beethoven quartet – a brass quartet?" etc. etc. all the people who really know music – which I don't – today, yours was the time when they wept.

Thank you dear Lennie – I had better not write any more – I could have spared 6 pages of my mother's writing paper and said all I mean and feel so much more coherently, but I wanted to thank you tonight.

With my love, and to Felicia

Jackie

538. Adolph Green to Leonard Bernstein
[August 1968][168]

Dear Lenny,

Not being one of the valiant ones (already, is this sentence defiantly grammatical???), I have tasted death on a considerable number of occasions (no, but it's certainly going to be haphazardly, helplessly, convolutedly kind of maybe Jamesian) – well, anyway, blackest despair – the dark night of the soul – the journey into cold sweatland 7 nights a week, the sprawling, crawling, pumping,

---

[167] Presumably one of the suggestions was Fauré's Requiem.

[168] This undated letter was sent on the occasion of Bernstein's 50th birthday in August 1968. It is particularly valuable for Green's recollections of their first meeting at Camp Onota in 1937. Bernstein and Green were near contemporaries, though not quite as near as Bernstein imagined when he responded a few months later (2 December 1968), with a poem to celebrate "Adolph, on his 50th(?) Birthday," actually his 54th.

exploding, expanding and contracting, 4 A.M. – Mippy-Bosch time – lost and screaming in the depths – the pits of hell. (Wow!!)

However – like others of my ilk who have descended whimpering into the maelstrom, I have from time to time been conversely blessed (this is not Jamesian at all, it turns out – rather Micawber-Dickensian), emerging suddenly from darkness to light, tasting unexpected moments of re-birth.

Most fortunately, in one or two of the instants that I have been re-born, I have known it and recognized it, not by hindsight, in a sad desperate, wandering through the jungles of Recherche à temps perdu (wow, wow!!) in search of a landmark that may never have been there – but known it and gloried in it, at the very moment of borning.

One such on-the-spot recognized re-birth occurred on a hot July night in 1937, when I, a sallow, bloated (195 lb.) unemployed Hungarian-American Pirate King-to-be, disembarked on the steps of the mess Hall of Camp Onota, to be greeted by my mentor, monitor, R[obert] Weil, counselor of Dramatics, who had loyally and rigorously and self-effacingly plotted and planned my engagement extraordinaire at Uncle Lou's Heavenly Haven for Healthily well-fed young Hebrews.

I was immediately introduced by Robert to you, a handsome lad of possibly 12 to 14, or so you appeared in the well-gathered post-dusk as you came down the steps to greet me and whisked me at once indoors, to the inner sanctum of the outer mess-hall – with piano, for our first music quiz. About 5 minutes after we had made our first tentative and mutually suspicious hellos and I had triumphantly *not* identified your Anna Sokolov music (??) as Shostakovitch (was this the future Miss Turnstiles??) and you had sprung up and thrown your arms about me for accomplishing this sensational-non-feat, I felt a sudden, complete exuberance, the fresh air of 1,000,000 windows opening simultaneously and a sense that my life had been building towards a turning point and that it had happened – now.

My sense of the "turning point" was as sure and conscious, as Judy H[olliday] knew and felt in her own more subterranean way about me when we met the following summer, and she took me up to her apartment and pressed my tattered trousers, on an ironing board with me standing around before the eyes of her horrified mother in my less than provocative jockey-shorts. She told her mother that this unappetizing young stranger and she were going to go places together and very soon (based on no knowledge, information or past association whatever).

But back to us (or have I left us at all?), since in not too long a time to come from *our* meeting, we were all 3 and 4 and more bound together with mysterious and continuing consequences that still continue, on and on.

We trouped the Onota Hills that night, for hours and hours up and down, to the dock and back to the camp gate and up and around the bunks and back and forth, and every moment was a new miracle. I knew I had been listening to music all these years and making my funny and odd full-orchestra phonograph sounds, with soloists thrown in simultaneously, in preparation for this meeting and that I had been carefully rehearsing Sibelius' 5th Symphony to give you its definitive performance that night. All those seemingly hopeless years that I wandered around NY in my sloppy shabbiness, conspicuously sporting rubbers over my shoes in every kind of weather, were not hopeless, were not wandering at all. I had always been on the road, leading straight to these hills, this night.

Have I ever told you that I often used to sing aloud to myself in those days as I stumbled around Times Square or Bryant Park – Brahms' First, the Sibelius 5, *Petrouchka*, or whatever, always hoping, some kindred spirit would perk up his or her ears and join me on the next phrase with arms thrown round me? I was looking for *you* to join me the whole time.

On and on we hiked that night, and the miracles kept exploding around me. Why had I treasured every word and measure and record scratch of [*I Wish That I Was Born In*] *Borneo*, all those years from my pre-historic childhood, if not to share them with you with that night? There was no other soul in the universe, besides you and me, to savor and bellow that Crumit masterpiece with every treasured nuance, into the starry midnight sky. Somehow, someway back in Sharon and the Bronx we had stored up *Borneo*, shored up our memories of it, for this night.

What am I wheezily, puffily, floridly trying to tell you??? The simple fact that suddenly there was meaning in my life. I felt *alive*. There was *Borneo*, Sibelius, T. S. Eliot, *Alice In Wonderland*, *L'Histoire du soldat*, *Of Thee I Sing*, with Auden and Spender, Gilbert and Sullivan, old old movies, Palestrina, Black Pete, eighteen million wires and associations I had been waiting all this time to connect with.

I knew as we walked and sang and talked, that you, the boy L. B., was nothing less than a genius, but this knowledge was only another comfortable fact to me, by now – part of the magic of our continuing dialogue.

Leonard, my friend, it seems that you are now 50 or about to be, and I am 50 and certainly have been (and never the twain shall meet, and that last phrase certainly means nothing, but my pen jes' wrote it down).

Whatever our ages, and until we stop all walking, we are still taking that walk in the night around the Onota hills. It seems haphazard, and unexplained as ever, but it goes on, and it is all still the same moment of re-birth of me.

How happy your friendship makes me. It fills me with the simple and complicated joy of knowing there can be a meaning to life – that our haphazard and rambling walk is filled with endless connections into the past and the future.

Hwhatt I'm saying is – I'm not writing – I'm only looking for a way to say I love you, my friend. Happy birthday.

Adolph

539. Harold Byrns[169] to Leonard Bernstein
Kudamm 50A, West Berlin, Germany
28 September 1968

My dear Leonard Bernstein,

It was more than a good deed (just here in Germany) to bring Mahler's Fifth. Since I have done this work innumerable times myself (as all other works by our beloved Gustav Mahler), I am in a position to really embrace you as a *Brüder in Apoll*, as Mahler called people (la Burlesca of the Ninth). Your insight into the "cookies" of Mahler's spiritual secrets touched me profoundly. You see, right after coming back from the USA in 1952, I started to re-introduce Mahler in many a European country. Your Mahler-cycle on records is one of the great achievements of our period, I mean also in a "missionary" way.

When Mrs. Byrns and I came backstage after your last concert, you asked me – after Shonah Tovah and before Leihitraoth[170] – if I played still under Mahler. Great Jove, no! I was not even 7 when he passed on.

But I wanted you to see a fagotto part retouched 3 times by Mahler's own hand. In fact, being a close friend of Alma Mahler and Franz Werfel, I studied most of Mahler's work anew with his *manuscripts*. Quite an exciting experience.

Perhaps, you do remember me, my name was, until 1939 *Bernstein* and it was our great late friend K[o]ussevitzki who suggested to me to change into Byrns. It was K[o]ussevitzki who gave me the first breaks in the USA.[171]

And more than that: some time ago, many European papers carried headlines in the music columns: "Two Bernsteins get the Mahler Medal" from the Bruckner Mahler Society of America, as some people still remember me under my real name (which is your name!).

From 1952 I conducted Mahler cycles in many European centers (Vienna, Roma, Torino), where I am for the past 17 years steady guest. Also I am steady guest conductor at the Norddeutsche Rundfunk Hamburg and Hanover (I was actually born in Hanover, where my father had one of Europe's leading concert managements – Gieseking, Erdmann, Hindemith, etc., etc.) [...]

---

[169] Harold Byrns (1903–77), German-born conductor (born Hans Bernstein) who studied with Erich Kleiber and Walter Gieseking at the Stern Conservatory in Berlin and became Kleiber's assistant. After moving to the United States, Byrns became known as a specialist in contemporary music. In October 1949, he conducted a concert for Schoenberg's 75th birthday in Los Angeles (attended by both Schoenberg and Stravinsky), including the First Chamber Symphony; the same year he made the first recording of Bartók's *Music for Strings, Percussion and Celesta* and gave one of the earliest performances of Stravinsky's Mass. Byrns was particularly devoted to Mahler's music, and was a friend of Alma Mahler.

[170] Hebrew greetings, meaning "a good year" and "see you soon."

[171] Bernstein has added two exclamation marks beside this paragraph: the remarkable coincidence of two conductors called Bernstein, both of whom Koussevitzky attempted to persuade to change their names. Byrns took his advice, whereas Bernstein didn't.

Mahler, my dear Leonard Bernstein, is the very backbone of my spiritual and human existence. I was 15 when I played (4-mains) the *Fifth* with a schoolmate, and I knew I would be a conductor and my life's main task would be to help Mahler. *His day*, indeed, *has come*!

I was interested to hear you went to [Walter] Felsenstein's *Traviata*. He is one of my oldest friends and I conducted *Entführung* and *Zauberflöte* and Mahler's 3rd and 4th at the Komische Oper 9 and 8 years ago! Yes, you are so right (and so said Klemperer): "the chorus is fabulous". [...]

And now let me sign off. I want to reassure you that this missive is a sign of my – how shall I say – inner relation, and *subsequently* friendship for another Bernstein.

Take good care of yourself and, when I come to New York again, I should very much like to just chatter with you. There are many things about Mahler's life and stories (true ones) that you may not know yet. Have you been to Toblach where I induced the mayor of the town (with the Wiener Mahler Gesellschaft) to have the plaquettes on the tiny cottage and the Bauernhaus (where I stay frequently)?

Again, lehitraoth, mazal tov,

Harold Byrns

540. Leonard Bernstein to Adolph Green
2 December 1968

To Adolph, on his 50th(?)[172] Birthday

ROUND NUMBERS ...

Are misery to escape from:
They're so round.
The roundest is O,
Next roundest 100,
And neither experienceable.
Which leaves 50,
Round enough, God knows,
A hollow glob
Within which
We skitter and slide
Like a doomed bug.
Huis clos.

---

[172] In fact, Adolph Green's 54th birthday.

There is, however,
Comfort, however freezing cold.
Tomorrow, yeah, tomorrow,
We are in our Fifty-First Year,
And the perfect N-dimensional circle
Is busted.
So live for tomorrow (song title).
I did, and am still alive, barely.
So I clasp you
In my freezing cold embrace,
And comfort you with refrigerated love.

As the Romans would say,
L

541. Leonard Bernstein to Alan Fluck[173]

Hotel de Paris, Monte Carlo, Monaco
11 September 1968

Dear Alan,

For the puzzle, for your warmth and ingenuity, for all these dear signatures, for the beauty of the idea, for the drawing, for . . . well for all the love contained in that charming packet, I send my sincerest thanks. It makes me want to sit down immediately and write the Youth Orchestra an overture. Alas, there is hardly even time to write this letter. It was only last night, after a concert and much grisly socializing with princely royalty and TWA officialdom, that I attacked your puzzle, and regained some cheerfulness and faith in what has seemed to me these last weeks a fairly hopeless world. Thank you for that. And today, owing to a sudden bad cold-cum-cough-cum-you name it, I am in the enviable position of being able to cancel lunches, etc, and spend my one free day of the tour in bed, and writing you this letter. I don't mind the work, you understand (although the programs are very heavy) but the "official" part of it – receptions, press conferences, etc. – have felled me. And so I cough my fare-well to you, sneeze a kiss to all the Farnham youth, and thank you rheumily again for the brilliant puzzle. Hope to see you in London.

---

[173] Alan Fluck (1928–97) was Director of Music at Farnham Grammar School and the moving force of the Farnham Festival with its numerous commissions of pieces for young musicians. Fluck had a warm friendship with Bernstein. He commented on this letter that for Bernstein's 50th birthday he "made a gigantic crossword puzzle, 50 words across and down. Clues and answers were all based on the life and works of LB. I sent it to him in Brussels and received this [letter] a month later."

Affectionately,

Lenny B

P.S. Why was the *Candide* mss. clue (65 across) inverted? Some subtle meaning I've failed to catch?

542. Randall Thompson to Leonard Bernstein

22 Larch Road, Cambridge, MA

27 October 1968

Dear Lenny,

I felt grateful to you when I heard that you and the Philharmonic were to play my Second Symphony – "our symphony".[174] Now that you have done so and I have heard the way you did it, I have no words worthy to express my gratitude and admiration. At a rough guess this must have been about the six-hundredth performance. I have never heard a more beautiful one, or one that expressed so fully and so lovingly what I wanted to say. My hearty congratulations and thanks to each and everyone concerned. You have given me a joyous experience.

Gratefully & devotedly, your old friend

Randall

543. Leonard Bernstein to Alan Fluck

17 September 1969

Dear Alan,

I have just listened to young Overbury[175] playing the *Anniversaries.*

Reactions:

a) You are an angel to have sent the tape. A perfect birthday present.

b) The boy is marvelous. A natural. One reservation: a feeling of dynamic sameness, lack of contrast. But this may well be due to tape difficulties. The whole tape came over very distantly on my machine, necessitating full volume turn-up.

c) I am moved to write a hundred more *Anniversaries.*

d) I love you for being so good to Helen.

---

[174] "Our symphony" given Bernstein's long history conducting the work, as well as the enduring friendship between the two men. Bernstein conducted Thompson's Second Symphony at Tanglewood in 1940, and later with the New York Philharmonic in 1959 and 1968 (followed by the recording praised in Thompson's letter of 16 January 1970, Letter 545).

[175] Michael Overbury (b. 1953), English organist. After his youthful success as a pianist, he was organ scholar at Corpus Christi College, Cambridge, and subsequently held positions at New College, Oxford, St. Alban's Cathedral, and Newark Parish Church, before being appointed Director of Music at Worksop Priory in 1999.

Summation: Thank you, bless you, more power to you.

Always,

Lenny B

544. Elliott Carter[176] to Leonard Bernstein

Mead Street, Waccabuc, NY

24 October 1969

Dear Lennie,

Here is a great deal of the *Concerto for Orchestra* we spoke about.[177] I appreciate your interest and am sending a copy which is still somewhat in the state of a sketch: i.e. the percussion part throughout will probably be revised somewhat in order to scale it up or down in the light of the entire work – the third movement – 287–419 – may be slightly revised, and the fourth movement I am still in the state of writing out in score having about 100 measures more to do, which I hope to finish in the next two weeks.

The score you are receiving is not to be used for conducting (if it could with its crazy binding) *because a number of details* (mistakes and changes) will be different in the final score.

The work was originally suggested to me by St. John Perse's long poem about America *Vents* which has a rather large Whitmanesque vision of winds blowing over our continent, changing everything, wiping away the old world, bringing in the new, and of the poet stating:

O vous que rafraîchit l'orage ... Fraîcheur et gage de fraîcheur.

... Et vous avez si peu de temps pour naître à cet instant.

Such lines as the opening of the poem:

C'étaient de très grands vents sur toutes faces de ce monde

De très grands vents en liesse par le monde, qui n'avaient ni d'aire ni de gîte,

Qui n'avaient garde ni mesure, et nous laissaient, hommes de paille

En l'an de paille sur leur erre ... Ah oui, de très grands

vents sur toutes faces de vivants!

Or

(Ces grands vents)

Sur toutes choses périssables, sur toutes choses saisissables, parmi le monde entier des choses ...

---

[176] Elliott Carter (1908–2012), American composer. He studied with Walter Piston at Harvard and later with Nadia Boulanger. Stravinsky called Carter's *Double Concerto* (1961) "the first American masterpiece."

[177] Carter's *Concerto for Orchestra* was commissioned by the New York Philharmonic for its 125th anniversary. Bernstein conducted the world premiere performances at Lincoln Center on 5, 6, 8, and 9 February 1970, and recorded it on 11 February.

Et d'éventer l'usure et la sécheresse au coeur des hommes investis,

Car tout un siècle s'ébruitait dans la sécheresse de sa paille, parmi
d'étranges désinences: à bout de cosses, de siliques, à bout de choses
frémissantes.
[...]
(The poem ends:)
Quand la violence eut renouvelé le lit des hommes sur la terre,
Un très vieil arbre, à sec de feuilles, reprit le fil de ses maximes ...
Et un autre arbre de haut rang montait déjà des grandes Indes
souterraines,
Avec sa feuille magnétique et son chargement de fruits nouveaux.[178]

As soon as the piece began to take shape, however, I forgot about the poem
and find its false epic tone a little too bombastic for my taste. I have quoted it at
length because [it] gave me the overall mood of an idea of the work, which was
finally reformulated into my own, human and musical terms.

Technically this is a work built on four main strata of chords, with different
interval structures. The normal state of these are five note chords and their complementary seven note chords (of which pairs there are 38, all of which are used).

The five note chords are associated with the four movements of the work
[...] Each of the movements is embedded in the others – movement I contains
elements of II, III, IV etc. as on page 1 of analysis, and emerges and disappears
throughout the work.

The opening and some of the important climaxes (138–140, 285–6 and the
coda) combine elements of all four movements simultaneously, as indicated at
the top of p. 1 of the analysis.

Each of the movements has a characteristic tessitura, as the analysis shows, and
a characteristic temporal behavior. Movement II appears in a fast version at the
beginning, and during its long statement gradually slows down, a pattern it

---

[178] The following is an English version of the quoted passages, in the translation by Hugh Chisholm:

These were very great winds over all the faces of this world, great winds rejoicing over the
world, having neither eyrie nor resting-place,
Having neither care nor caution, and leaving us, in their wake,
Men of straw in the year of straw ... Ah, yes, very great winds over all the faces of the living!
Over all things perishable, over all things graspable, throughout the entire world of things. . . .
And airing out the attrition and drought in the heart of men in office,

For a whole century was rustling in the dry sound of its straw, amid strange terminations at the
tips of husks of pods, at the tips of trembling things.
When violence had remade the bed of men on the earth,
A very old tree, barren of leaves, resumed the thread of its maxims ...
And another tree of high degree was already rising from the great subterranean Indies,
With its magnetic leaf and its burden of new fruits.

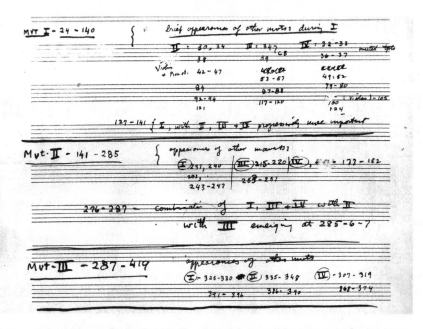

continues at each secondary appearance. The reverse is true of mvt IV. Movements I and III combine ritardation and acceleration: mvt 1 tends to start each successive pattern of ritardation at a faster point, and mvt III starts each successive pattern of acceleration at a slower point. All of this is not carried out too schematically.

As for the many "metrical modulations" which occur in the work: the tempi of this work should be somewhat flexible since it deals primarily in written out rubati, but the carry-over of note values from one tempo to another should be quite exact so as not to break the continuity. For instance, from 26–27 the septuplet of 8th notes of the piano should be exactly the same speeds as the regular 8th notes in 27; in 40 to 41, the piano's triplets in 40 should flow evenly into the septuplet under the triplet, the beats in the piano's left hand in 40 state the tempo of 41, as I have indicated in red pencil [...] The same applies to all other "metric modulations" which I think are clearly marked.

These changes should be fairly accurate as the whole pacing of the work depends on progressive reappearances of materials coming in at different tempi, i.e. mvt IV material comes in bit by bit faster over the entire work, and this will not come out if the tempo changes are not reasonably accurate.

As you can see, while the work has an underlying structure of chords and tempi, it should be played in a way that gives the impression [of] freedom almost abandon.

If I can clarify anything please feel free to call on me – we shall be returning to 31 W 12th St, WA-9-1618, in a week or so, and hope to get in touch with you and see you quite soon after.

With kindest regards to Felicia,

Elliott

7

Triumphs, Controversies, Catastrophe
1970–78

Bernstein relinquished his post as Music Director of the New York Philharmonic in 1969, but he remained firmly in the public gaze. Two events stirred up controversy – both of them for questionable reasons. When Felicia hosted a reception (at the behest of the American Civil Liberties Union) to raise funds for the legal costs of thirteen members of the Black Panthers, this was seized upon gleefully by the press and widely misreported. Declassified files reveal that it gave the FBI yet another excuse to take an interest in Bernstein's allegedly suspicious activities. "Radical chic," the phrase coined by Tom Wolfe to describe the event, is a resonant one, and doubtless contributed to sustaining the widely reported but largely mythical version of the story – that Bernstein gave a party for the Black Panthers. As Bernstein told Jonathan Cott in 1989, "It's a legend and it dies hard. It *wasn't* a party and *I* didn't give it. [. . .] So what am I to do? You can't beat the legends . . . except by telling the truth. And ultimately, maybe, legends die."

In 1971, Bernstein caused controversy again, this time at the highest levels of government – in this case the paranoid and criminal administration of Richard Nixon. The problem was a rumor, investigated by the FBI, that Bernstein's newly finished *Mass* was intended to embarrass the President by promoting an agenda of peace. Nixon detested Bernstein, and when the FBI passed the investigation back to the White House, what ensued was something close to black comedy. So convinced were Nixon's aides that Bernstein was out to cause trouble that they lost any kind of grip on common sense. Pat Buchanan – then an advisor to Nixon, later a conservative pundit – wrote this memorandum on 28 July 1971:

> My view is that we ought to find someone who can definitely translate that Latin Mass Bernstein is working on – to make sure this is accurate. Then, we might want to sand-bag him; i.e. wait until it is too late for him to change his format – and then unload on him. Another course would be to have this released to front-page and force him to back down. However, we should be able to get a copy of what he is preparing – as there will have to be rehearsals – and once we get that, get us a good Jesuit to translate, maybe Father McLaughlin

will do and once translated – leak the thing. But we ought to move rapidly lest the President be tied into attending and forced to back down.[1]

Mass was Bernstein's first work to be written in the 1970s, much of it conceived during a stay at the MacDowell Colony. It was followed by three other large-scale pieces. The ballet Dybbuk – which Jerome Robbins had been urging him to write since the 1940s – finally saw the light of day at New York City Ballet in 1974: it turned out to be the last of their collaborations. It is a very demanding score, making use of some twelve-tone techniques, about which Oliver Knussen wrote as follows: "After the militant anti-atonal statements which abounded in his Norton Lectures at Harvard, it is surprising to find Bernstein making use of numerical formulas derived from the Kabbalah [...] and producing his most austerely contemporary-sounding score to date."[2]

The Norton Lectures, given on six consecutive Tuesday evenings in October and November 1973 and published as The Unanswered Question, were the most fully developed expression of Bernstein's thoughts on music, and his attempt to apply Noam Chomsky's theories of linguistics to it. Bernstein's work was criticized by some academics as unsystematic – but surely the important point is that his conclusions are so often inherently musical. Virgil Thomson and Bernstein had known each other for thirty years, and Thomson was sometimes a harsh critic of Bernstein's music; but he was impressed by the lectures. He praised Bernstein's "skill in explaining music" and went on: "Myself I find nothing reprehensible about your bringing in linguistics. You needed an authority to support an 'innate musical grammar' and Chomsky's heavy artillery is surely that."

The musical 1600 Pennsylvania Avenue turned out to be an unhappy experience. It was overlong when it was tried out in Philadelphia, but the score includes a great deal of music that is beautiful (some of the best numbers were later salvaged by Charles Harmon and Sid Ramin for A White House Cantata). Written by Bernstein and Alan Jay Lerner as a celebration of the United States Bicentennial, by the time the show opened on Broadway it was doomed – especially as it had been cut to shreds, against Bernstein's wishes. Friends were well aware of the trials and tribulations, and rallied round: during the try-out in Philadelphia, Robbins did his best to encourage his old friend ("Take care of your house. You can do it. Come on kid, get

---

[1] Published by Alex Ross in The New Yorker online: http://www.newyorker.com/online/blogs/newsdesk/2009/08/the-bernstein-files.html (accessed 26 February 2013). It would be reassuring to think that this bizarre episode was the only time that the words of the Latin Mass came under suspicion from a Presidential aide. Presumably, Buchanan's main cause for alarm might have been the last line of the Agnus Dei: "Dona nobis pacem" ("Grant us peace"). It's surprising that Buchanan felt the need to "get us a good Jesuit" to provide a translation, since he had himself been educated at Jesuit-run institutions: Gonzaga College High School and Georgetown University, and English translations of the Mass were so readily available.

[2] Oliver Knussen, "Bernstein: Dybbuk," Tempo, No. 119 (December 1976), p. 34.

the spirit up again. No limp cocks!"), while Sondheim sent a telegram saying "you're still the only artist writing musicals with one exception that is." The great photographer Richard Avedon was (understandably) overcome by the beauty of the music. But it was to no avail. Despite the wonderful score, and clever lyrics by Lerner, *1600 Pennsylvania Avenue* was a failure. Another commission intended for the Bicentennial (finished a year too late) was *Songfest*, an anthology of thirteen poems for solo voices and orchestra. Completed in 1977, it was much admired by Bernstein's old friend and collaborator Oliver Smith, and was praised by others: Oliver Knussen pointed out the lessons Bernstein appeared to have learned from Britten, especially the *Spring Symphony* (which Bernstein knew well, having conducted it in 1963), but he also valued the originality of the score: "I can't think of another living composer who could approach Bernstein's complete involvement with and response to such varied texts."[3] Despite the quality of the music (and the sensitivity of Bernstein's settings), *Songfest* is hardly ever performed. It deserves better.

From a creative point of view, the 1970s must have been rather disheartening for Bernstein: of four major works, only *Mass* could be counted a success, and even that was the focus of some very hostile criticism. But the musical disappointments were as nothing to the turmoil in Bernstein's personal life. In 1974, Felicia was diagnosed with cancer – Bernstein's letter to her from New Zealand is full of reminders to see her doctor. But things quickly got even worse. By 1976 their marriage was in tatters: *Newsweek* announced a "trial separation" – Felicia was increasingly disturbed by what Humphrey Burton has described as "intimations that her husband was abandoning the discretion that was part of their unspoken covenant" (Burton 1994, p. 414). Burton's evidence is pretty damning: Bernstein was having affairs with at least two men, one of them Tom Cothran, a young musician Bernstein had met in 1973. Felicia was not prepared to see their family life put in peril and gave him an ultimatum: either he must stop seeing Cothran alone, or he need not come home. Bernstein's daughter Nina – who was 13 at the time – recalled some difficult family scenes in an interview with Ginny Dougary in 2010: "My mother was a fairly conventional lady and so she expected to be treated like one. The deal was that he would be discreet and that she would maintain her dignity. And then he was not discreet, and so that was that."[4] Bernstein and Cothran set up in a new apartment for a few months, but then Felicia was diagnosed with lung cancer, and Bernstein begged to be allowed back. Nina recalls that "The whole thing was terribly awkward and painful," and, of course, matters were made worse by the intrusive glare of publicity. When Felicia died on 16 June 1978, Bernstein blamed himself. Humphrey Burton writes about this with harrowing honesty: "The crushing impact on Leonard Bernstein was that he believed himself responsible for his wife's death, and his sense of guilt never left him. Felicia was the greatest love of his life. He never recovered

---

[3] Oliver Knussen, "Bernstein: *Songfest*," *Tempo*, No. 128 (March 1979), pp. 21–2.
[4] Dougary 2010.

from her loss, and he never forgot the curse she uttered when he told her he was leaving her for Cothran. She had pointed her finger at him in fury and predicted, in a harsh whisper: 'You're going to die a bitter and lonely old man.'"[5]

545. Randall Thompson to Leonard Bernstein
22 Larch Road, Cambridge, MA
16 January 1970

Dear Leonard,

What a glorious recording of my Second Symphony![6] What can I say to express my appreciation and my happiness? The whole interpretation is perfect – and inspired. The orchestra is superb and seems to be breathing with you all the way through. The engineering is both sensitive and powerful, refined in solo passages and rich in the *tutti*. And throughout, the rhythm is so vital that the whole work throbs with life. I wrote it exactly forty years ago, in this very village, for Koussy. It's yours now, and I see him smiling.

Thank you from the bottom of my heart.

Ti abbraccio.

Randall

546. Dietrich Fischer-Dieskau[7] to Leonard Bernstein
Baur au Lac, Zurich, Switzerland
9 February 1970

Dear Lennie,

Just because I don't want to miss a chance of making music with you please give me a hint whether you would like me as Kurwenal in the Bayreuth *Tristan* production of which I heard.[8] You know how opera houses are in their short notice planning.

In case of "yes" it would be a great thrill. Should you already have made an agreement with somebody else, I am still your greatest admirer. Only – I am dying to sing with you again. So please let me know.

Ever,

Sir Dieter Falstaff

---

[5] Burton 1994, pp. 446–7.

[6] Bernstein and the New York Philharmonic recorded Thompson's Second Symphony for Columbia Records on 22 October 1968, straight after four concert performances. It is difficult to argue with the composer's delighted response to Bernstein's magnificent recording of the work, which has been reissued on CD by Sony Classical (SMK 60594).

[7] Dietrich Fischer-Dieskau (1925–2012), German baritone who had sung the title role in Bernstein's Vienna production and recording of Verdi's *Falstaff* in 1966, the reason he signs himself "Sir Dieter Falstaff" here.

[8] See Letter 548.

547. Rabbi Judah Cahn[9] to Leonard Bernstein
10 Park Avenue, New York, NY
28 February 1970

Dear Lenny,

I received the copy of Rabbi Schindler's letter addressed to you and the note which you added to it.

Lenny, since 1934, I have been deeply involved in inter-racial affairs. I believe my credentials are quite adequate to demonstrate that for thirty-six years I have put my physical being, my professional standing, and my financial means on the line any number of times when the struggle for civil rights demanded it, and you know this.

When Felicia spoke to me, I suggested that the best way to handle the situation was to drop it.[10] Your friends will never question your motives, even if they do not agree with you. To defend yourself is totally unnecessary. Frankly, as your friend for all these years, and one who loves you deeply, I needed no letter explaining why you called a meeting in support of the Black Panthers. I know that you were motivated by the highest ethical imperatives, and you acted in a way that you thought just and right. I do believe, however, that you must give me equal credit for ethics and motivation.

I believe that the need to defend oneself is a necessity, if we are going to defend others. If those I personally defend would, in turn, defend me, then such a defense has a top priority in my scale of values. If, on the other hand, those who seek my assistance would, if they could, destroy me, then logically it would be a mistake to give such a group my special, personal assistance.

However, in order not to neglect out concern for all groups who are struggling to achieve civil rights, whether or not we agree with the philosophies of those groups, we should continue to support the American Civil Liberties Union, whose purpose it is to defend the rights of those who espouse unpopular causes.

At no time, since the Hitler holocaust, has the Jewish people been faced with the complexity of problems which now confront us. Both of us are wholly committed to the future and safety of our people, and I will not, under any circumstances, give special time and energy to strengthening those who are

---

[9] Rabbi Judah Cahn (1912-84) was the founding Rabbi of the Metropolitan Synagogue of New York, which has always had a reputation as an informal and liberal Reformed synagogue. Cahn was a family friend of the Bernsteins, and he was also passionate about music (he appears as a speaker on Bernstein's recording of Bloch's *Sacred Service*).

[10] A reference to the fundraiser for the legal defense of the Black Panthers held in Bernstein's apartment. On a number of occasions Bernstein explained that the event had not been intended to endorse the radical (armed) agenda of the Black Panthers. But Tom Wolfe's description of the event as "radical chic" (in *New York Magazine*, 8 June 1970) has refused to go away.

outspoken in their avowed attempt to destroy me. Since Hitler, I take such "forthrightness" very seriously.

I will fight for the right of the Panthers to a just trial. I will fight to secure justice for them, as I would for any other group, but I will do so through channels which are already established for such purposes. Frankly, I would not open my home and ask my friends to make special contributions to their cause. This constitutes a difference of opinion. I honor you for your position, and I ask you to honor me for mine.

As for "lessons," Lenny, as you know, it is not the lessons but the practicing that makes the artist. I have been practicing a long, long time, and I took my lessons when it was not so fashionable.

With my best wishes and kindest regards to your family.

As ever,

Judah

548. Leonard Bernstein to Ingmar Bergman[11]

11 August 1970

Dear Ingmar Bergman,

I have just talked with my good friend Humphrey Burton in England who tells me that he spoke to you about the possibility of our working together on a production of *Tristan und Isolde*. Even though Humphrey reported that you had misgivings I want to tell you personally how very much I would love the opportunity of our working together, particularly on a project as fascinating and challenging as *Tristan*.

The *Tristan* idea has been growing in my mind ever since Wieland Wagner asked me to do a production at Bayreuth, but there never was time during the years I was with the New York Philharmonic. Now that my time has become more flexible, I return to *Tristan* as one of the major projects I want to achieve in the near future. The idea would be to produce it at the Bayreuth Festival in 1973 and to record and film it thereafter. I realize that you may not be interested in staging the opera at Bayreuth but I can think of no one on Earth better suited for a free, fresh and "inner-directed" film version.

Could we talk about this? I will be going to Japan next month, then back in New York from mid-September through January '71. In early February I go to Paris for concerts and then generally around Europe and Israel until the end of April.

---

[11] Ingmar Bergman (1918–2007), Swedish film and theater director, described by Woody Allen (in a TV interview with Mark Kermode) as "probably the greatest film artist, all things considered, since the invention of the motion picture camera." Unfortunately, the plan outlined by Bernstein for a filmed production of Wagner's *Tristan und Isolde* came to nothing.

I am your profound admirer, and want to work with you!

In friendship.

Leonard Bernstein

P.S. Of course, if you were interested in the Bayreuth staging as well, that would be a more than welcome bonus.

549. Leonard Bernstein to Stephen Sondheim

[Christmas 1970]

Dear Steve,

These balls are not meant to symbolize any contribution to your testicular powers. They are simply beautiful carpet-balls (*bocci*, I believe), and when I saw them I knew they had to be for you. So Merry Xmas!

As for your gifts, I bless you for the *Listener* book, thank you for the *Company* record, and adore you for the gum-machine.

Happy 1971, and have a glorious *Follies*!

Love,

Lenny

550. Leonard Bernstein to Helen Coates

Hotel Sacher, Vienna, Austria

18 February 1971

Dear H,

The Paris concerts went gloriously, finally, in spite of all kinds of problems: 1) my usual Parisian diarrhea, really bad this time, 2) a cut thumb, 3) a bad back, 4) the failure of the Berlioz material to arrive until the last day of rehearsal (sent to wrong address!) so that I had to use *their* material which was full of errors, had no rehearsal numbers or markings or anything. A nightmare, necessitating hours of extra work & fatigue for orchestra & conductor. But finally all was well, with audiences screaming & happy.[12]

Rehearsals here go beautifully: I seem to be playing most of the notes of the Ravel,[13] & my stomach, back, thumb, etc. are very well indeed. Tonight I'm even going to the Opera Ball!

---

[12] Bernstein's concerts with the Orchestre de Paris at the Théâtre des Champs-Élysées in February 1971 included Ravel's *Tombeau de Couperin* and the G major Piano Concerto (directed from the piano), and Berlioz's *Roméo et Juliette*.

[13] Bernstein's concerts with the Vienna Philharmonic on 20 and 21 Februrary 1971 included Haydn's Symphony No. 102, Ravel's G major Piano Concerto (directed from the piano), and Schumann's Fourth Symphony.

I've received both your letters, with enclosures (sad about Ethel L[inder] R[einer],[14] horrid and shocking about Debs Myers!).[15] Very pleased at your progress report on the dictaphone – brava!

I'm feeling better than I had expected – all is well.

Love to all, & to you,

L

551. Leonard Bernstein to Shirley Bernstein

Hotel Sacher, Vienna, Austria

25 February 1971

Mine Hilee,

Strange, but everything seems to be going well, & better. Or, as they say here (pure Annie M), *es geht gü-at*. Paris (as always) was a bit of a trial – the trots in spades, the back, the cut thumb, the usual list. But great concerts, and now Vienna – why, I even drink the tap water! Back great, thumb prima, stomach glorious (or as glorious as my Tumburger can be). *And* the concerts are, so far, tops. Sunday I think I conducted one of the really best ones of my life – including playing the Ravel. It was fleed, my dear, *fleed*.

But you, mine ape, have you vot to do, vot to eat? I worry about you. How about a letter telling all. Find out my tour schedule from Felicia, & send me a letter. Simple. A.B.C. We leave on tour Sat. a.m. for Munich. Back in Vienna 13th March for a Unicef benefit, then off for another week, then back here for three more weeks. Schreib!

And love to Mither when you talk to her.

I hug it upon you.

L

I do a March [?] every day, *plus* the London Times, *plus* an occasional Telegraph, etc.[16] So you see, my time is well spent, intellectually.

552. Leonard Bernstein to Helen Coates

Dan Hotel, Tel Aviv, Israel

16 April 1971

Dear Helen,

Life is not too kind to me at the moment: I left Vienna a wreck and went straight to Eilat for some days of sun and sea – my first four free days in months.

---

[14] Ethel Linder Reiner was a Broadway producer whose credits included *Candide* in 1956. Her death was announced in *The New York Times* on 11 February 1971.

[15] Debs Myers was described in his *New York Times* obituary as a "political press aide." He worked on Senator Bobby Kennedy's Senate campaign and on both of Adlai Stevenson's presidential campaigns. He died on 2 February 1971 at the age of 59.

[16] Cryptic crossword puzzles.

Well, there was no sun, no sea – only stormy weather, nothing to do but watch the mindless hippies on the beach. Very lonely. I came back to Tel Aviv early – same bad winter weather. We had our first rehearsals yesterday – the orchestra is in fine form, but I'm not. I'm depressed most of the time, and longing to get home.

I've been worried at not finding any mail from you here. I hope you're all right, and that your brother is not causing you too much anxiety. My mother seems to be enjoying herself, although her activities are necessarily limited.

Today is again a free day, and I'm spending it mostly in bed. It's storming outside. What a non-holiday! People here can't remember such weather at Pesach-time in years.

Please call Dr Gaylin[17] and ask him if he can reserve some time for me the week of May 3rd. I should be back on the 3rd. I have a dentist appointment that day which will have to be cancelled. [...]

Everyone asks for you – with affection – Katia, etc.

Be well, and let me hear from you.

Much love,

L

553. Jamie Bernstein[18] to Leonard Bernstein
Cambridge, MA
Sunday 18 April [1971]

Hey, Dadz!

A quiet, pleasant Sunday eve in rainy Cambratch ... I stayed here this weekend, cause I've been in New York over Spring break for a week and a half. This was my first week back, in which I had a paper due Monday, a paper due Tuesday, and a paper due Wednesday, for God's sake. So this past week has been an incredible hassle, and this weekend was blissfully uncluttered. Friday night: two girlfriends and I went out and had a deliciously sickenening (whoops!) Italian dinner, after which we played gin rummy and watched C movies on television. Saturday: zero. Slept till twelve (for the first time in months), ate, had a nap, ate, did some leisurely reading. *Then* Jane Weeks, some other people and I decided to go and see the Russian Easter service, cause we'd always heard how beautiful it was, and Mummy had just given us a big pep talk about it, so we decided to go to the Russian Orthodox Cathedral on the Fenway. Well ... it sounded good. We got there, and damned if it wasn't a *modern* church! Oh, God, were we disappointed! Where were the onion domes, the gold? Just wood and plaster and a gold-plated gaudy chandelier with flickering red electric

---

[17] Bernstein consulted the psychiatrist Willard Gaylin regularly in the early 1970s.
[18] Jamie Bernstein (b. 1952), the eldest child of Leonard and Felicia Bernstein.

"candles". [. . .] *No seats*! Hundreds of *ugly* people, badly dressed, very upper middle, very reformed Jewish in a funny way. So okay, there we all were, waiting for the fireworks, and out comes this little dumpy priest in an ugly ill-fitting robe, and starts mumbling most unmusically.

And then the chorus opened their mouths. AAAAAAUUGGHHH!!!! Good *God*! That poor chorus must have been made up of volunteers out of the congregation, I guess, because it really was indescribable. I never did figure out what key they were in.

So we split. No offense to the Russians, *but*, as Nina would say, but gee whiz . . .

We dropped someone off in Harvard Yard, got back on to Mass. Ave., and *the car stalled*. So we all have to get out and push the car down Massachusetts Avenue at one thirty in the morning like a bunch of Keystone Cops! Oh, God, it was funny. Anyhow, that was Saturday. Today I got up at one, ate, read the paper, went to the library for a while, ate, watched *The Wizard of Oz* on TV, and now here I sit, tapping away and watching a Diana Ross (of Supremes fame) special. As I said, a quiet, pleasant Sunday eve.

Bruce couldn't come up this weekend; he had to go down to Etlontik City to visit his dying grandfather. Oh, dear God, I know what he's going through. Otherwise Bruce is in pretty fine shape. [. . .] I've been going through some strange changes lately, and I've been a big pain in the ass some of the time, and boy, Bruce was so patient. He has his bad days too, God knows, and then I have to be patient. And sometimes we both run out of patience, but love ain't a bowl of latkes.

Bruce leaves on June 3 for his summer job in England. And guess what?! Mummy said I could travel this summer, and stay with Anya, and the Smiths, and stuff like that. OBOY!!! SUMMER!!!!!!! I can't wait. And the bestest part of all is going to be those few weeks when I don't have to do *anything* but sit in the country and swim and play tennis and read what I *want* to read, and lie in the sun and see my friends in New York . . . oboy, is that ever going to be loads of fun. And then when I get to England, I can see Bruce, and I even got invited to West Pakistan by Pinkie Bhutto,[19] and if you've been keeping up on your current events, you'll know that Pinkie's father[20] is the Alessandri of West Pakistan. Far out! I'd *really* like to go, and see what the vestiges of the Arabian Nights look like. Hey Daddy . . . you think you can get yourself invited to Red China to conduct? Boy, that's the place I want to go to more than anywhere else.

Well, it being eleven and all, I think I'll get a head start on this week and go to bed early. Say a big *Hello, Grandma* to Grandma. I hope she's grooving on her

---

[19] Benazir Bhutto (1953–2007), the first woman in modern history to lead a Muslim state, attended Harvard (Radcliffe College) from 1969 to 1973. Her nickname at Harvard was "Pinkie".
[20] Zulfikar Ali Bhutto.

trip, man, and I sure hope you feel better yourself. Anyhows, see you soon. Hurry back; I can't remember what you look like already!

Love and kisses,

Jamie.

P.S. I got into Adams House, in case I lived here next year. Eliot House is a most unpopular house these days: all preppies and jocks. Were you one of those? I think if you were going here now, you'd be in Lowell House. Adams House is where all the hippies are. Birds of a feather spoil the broth, I always say . . . J

554. Oliver Smith to Leonard Bernstein

The Watergate Hotel, Washington, D.C.

8 September 1971[21]

Dearest Lenny,

What can I say? Nothing but to hug and embrace you to express my feelings concerning *your* superb *Mass*. You are such a genius that with you I am speechless with admiration and humility.

To work on this project was a rare privilege.[22] Thank you deeply for making this possible.

All my love,

Oliver

555. Christa Ludwig[23] to Leonard Bernstein

Paris

13 November 1971

Dear Maestro,

I want to say thank you for the recital! I loved so much, no: I *love* so much to make music with you! I heard the tape and I think we shall do it again. My voice is sometimes unsteady and breathless. And I also think that the placement of the microphone is too close. So, let's do it in Vienna.

Best regards.

Yours,

Christa

---

[21] 8 September was the opening night of *Mass* at the Kennedy Center in Washington, D.C.

[22] Oliver Smith designed the sets for *Mass*.

[23] Christa Ludwig (b. 1928), German mezzo-soprano with whom Bernstein collaborated on numerous occasions from the late 1960s onwards, notably in Mahler (Symphonies Nos. 2 and 3, *Das Lied von der Erde, Des Knaben Wunderhorn*), Brahms (lieder), and in Bernstein's own work: the *Jeremiah* and *Kaddish* symphonies, and, in December 1989, as the Old Lady in *Candide*.

556. David Charles Abell[24] to Leonard Bernstein

466 Poplar Street, Winnetka, IL
21 November 1971

Dear Mr. Bernstein,

I would like to thank you very much for the fantastic time I had in Washington D.C. in September. It was thrilling to be in as big and important a production as your *Mass*. I think it is a great piece of music, and my favorite parts are the Epistle, and from the "Agnus Dei" to the end. I was an alternate in the Berkshire Boy Choir and I was in over half the performances and all of the recording (the two easiest sessions I have ever seen or been in).

Recently, I heard the piece on radio and was so excited about it that I didn't do my homework so I could listen to it! I can't wait until I can get the record, but the stores around here are slow getting it in. Wasn't the recording changed a little from the performances? (Ron Young singing the first "I don't know").

Is *Mass* going on Broadway or to Los Angeles or any place like that? I'm sure if you took it around to different cities, the crowds would be miles long.

I wish I could re-live the fantastic experience I had in Washington, but anyway it will benefit me in many ways all my life.

Sincerely,
Your friend and admirer,
David Abell
Berkshire Choirboy

557. Richard Rodney Bennett to Leonard Bernstein

4 Lonsdale Square, London, England
[1971]

Dear Mr. Bernstein,

This is a big thankyou letter. I gather from Sam Spiegel that you put in a very kind word for me over *Nicholas and Alexandra*, and I am very grateful indeed. It was a very happy and I think successful job altogether, and both Sam and the director, Franklin Schaffner, were splendid to work for, considerate and helpful. So altogether I feel pleased and satisfied and without your kindness it would not have happened. There will be a sound-track album very soon and I will make sure they send you a copy.

---

[24] David Charles Abell (b. 1958) is now a successful conductor. At the time of writing this letter, he was a member of the Berkshire Boy Choir and had performed in the original production of Bernstein's *Mass*. At the time he conducted Stephen Sondheim's 80th birthday concert at the 2010 BBC Proms, he wrote: "None of that would probably have happened if I hadn't been in *Mass* at age 13" (David Charles Abell, personal communication).

I was hoping that André Previn would be conducting it, and I know he wanted to do it, but there were contractual problems. The man who always does my films for me[25] – I have a mortal dread of conducting – did it, and did a very good job.

Congratulations, very late in the day, on the huge success of the Kennedy *Mass*. I have been reading avidly about it, and long to hear an English performance. I'm sure plans for it are well under way.

Now I think of it, I hope you won't be *dismayed* when you hear the *Nicholas* score . . . It's rather a curious mixture stylistically.

Excuse frightful typing.

Yours ever,

Richard Bennett

558. Leonard Bernstein to Felicia Bernstein
6 February 1972

> F ifty is nothing but twice twenty-five:
> L et me take over one half of the weight,
> E xtending my years to seventy-eight –
> S eventy-eight – still here, and alive!
> H appy birthday, dear Child-Bride,
> Y outhful always, at my side.

> All my love,
> Ben

559. Richard Rodgers to Leonard Bernstein
598 Madison Avenue, New York, NY
27 March 1972

Dear Leonard,

Is there anything you don't do better than anyone else? Your playing last night was so simple and pure that it gave a grace that little song never had before.[26] Your words were kind, too, but taking the trouble to be there was the kindest of all. I appreciate it tremendously.

Fondly,

Dick

---

[25] Marcus Dods (1918–84), British conductor. He was music director for all of Richard Rodney Bennett's major film scores: *Billion Dollar Brain* (1967), *Far From the Madding Crowd* (1967), *Nicholas and Alexandra* (1971), *Lady Caroline Lamb* (1972), and *Murder on the Orient Express* (1974).

[26] Bernstein played his own arrangement of Rodgers' "Nobody's Heart Belongs to Me" from *By Jupiter* as part of the "Celebration of Richard Rodgers" held at the Imperial Theatre on 26 March 1972 in honour of Rodgers' forthcoming 70th birthday (28 June 1972).

560. Leonard Bernstein to Helen Coates

Hotel Sacher, Vienna, Austria

14 April 1972

Dear H,

This is a brief moment grabbed out of a monstrous schedule just to send love and say that all is well with health – though not with the schedule. There's been some poor planning (too much at once) and the Vienna Philharmonic simply doesn't know Mahler[27] – so it's all from scratch. Besides, I don't feel like performing much these days: I'd rather be quietly composing. But I'll get through it, somehow – and there is the compensation of beautiful music.

The sun is just beginning to show itself for the first time since I arrived here.

I hope all is well with you, and thanks for all the envelopes filled with goodies.

Love,

Lenny.

Felicia is in Venice for a few days, returning on the weekend. Then, I guess, she'll return to NYC on Monday.

561. Leonard Bernstein to Shirley Bernstein

Hotel Sacher, Vienna, Austria

21 April 1972

Dearest Hilee,

I think of you with every puzzle (and in Europe that's 2 or 3 a day). But when a *Nation* puzzle arrived from la Belle with a *whole wrong diagram* then I had to write. It's not enough to think: one must share. What is happening to our world?

What indeed?

I want to write music.

I've had Vienna.

I think I've had performing.

Spring is *not* here, and all is somewhat sad, foolish, exaggerated. Very tiring indeed.

Why don't you ever write me, you thriving, prosperous, presidential wonder?

Please call BB & Ellen & send my love. I can't write any more – Mahler calls.

And special hugs for Ofra.

And mostly to mein Schwest –

L

21 Ape, '72

---

[27] On 15 and 16 April 1971, Bernstein conducted performances of Mahler's Fifth Symphony with the Vienna Philharmonic. A few weeks later (6 and 7 May) he conducted Mahler's Fourth Symphony.

562. Luciano Berio[28] to Leonard Bernstein
Villa della Mendola 131, Rome, Italy
28 April 1972

Caro Leonardo,

I want to thank you once more for your precious contribution to *C'è musica e musica*.[29] The 9th program, where you led the way deeply into yourself and through American music, was certainly one of the best. I hope you will be able to see it soon. In 10 days this incredible TV adventure will be finally over – and now, because of these 12 TV hours on music I have more "enemies" in Italy than I ever had (mainly singers and conservatory professors and one music critic wrote that I have prostituted music).

I will be in NY very soon and I hope to see you.

Love, as ever,

Luciano

P.S. Maybe a correspondent of an Italian newspaper ("Messaggero") will call you for a short interview. Please give him a few minutes – even on the phone. I promised him that you will not push him away.

563. Leonard Bernstein to Shirley Bernstein
3 October 1972

For Mine Schwestöahs

"Nothing Could Be Finer Than to Be a Forty-Niner"
I thought of finding you a gift
Of cashmere, silk or leather;
But nothing seems so precious as
October's Bright Blue Weather.

When H. H. Jackson thought it up
She had her head together,
And Hilee in mind, as high she penned
"October's Bright Blue Weather."[30]

---

[28] Luciano Berio (1925–2003), Italian composer. Bernstein commissioned Berio's *Sinfonia*, which was first performed by the New York Philharmonic on 10 October 1968.

[29] This innovative television series, presented by Berio and broadcast in 1972, included an episode entitled "Nuovo mondo" in which Bernstein appeared.

[30] "October's Bright Blue Weather" by Helen Hunt Jackson (1830–85) was first published in her *Verses* (Boston, 1870). Her poetry was admired by Ralph Waldo Emerson, and she was a lifelong friend of Emily Dickinson. As well as poetry, Jackson also wrote a popular novel (*Ramona*) about the government's mistreatment of Native Americans.

So may it be for all your life
And when your birthdays trouble you
Remember you are shone upon
By high O. B–B–W.

Love moöahs,
L

564. Jerome Robbins to Leonard Bernstein
7 October 1972

Len,

Tried to reach you before departing.

If the ballet isn't working out (I think it *is*, and is mostly there) then we'll do it next year when you are less pressured.[31] I'll tell the N[ew] Y[ork] C[ity] B[allet] *not* to count on it for their Gala of June 7th – that way they don't get fucked up on their money raising – and if by chance something breaks there for you, and you feel more optimistic – or one of your miracles occurs – we can always do it in June with less commotion around it. Anyway, write me in London, care of Royal Ballet, Covent Garden Opera House.

Love to all,

J.

(*Interplay*[32] went very well!)

565. Benjamin Britten to Leonard Bernstein
The Red House, Aldeburgh, England
[Spring 1973]

My dear Lenny,

Please forgive p. c. (I'm not supposed to write!) – but I was very touched by your wire. The present little medical blow is maddening, boring & v. painful! I am just coming up to one of these miracle modern operations and shall be

---

[31] *Dybbuk* was slowly taking shape when Robbins wrote this letter, but there was still much to be done. *The New York Times* reported (12 July 1972) that Bernstein was planning to take "nearly a year off from public performing to give his undivided attention to writing music" and as a result he did get the score finished. The ballet was first performed by New York City Ballet at Lincoln Center, New York, on 16 May 1974.

[32] *Interplay* was Robbins' second ballet (after *Fancy Free*). It was set to a score by Morton Gould and first performed at Billy Rose's Concert Varieties on 1 June 1945. It was subsequently taken into the repertoire of the New York City Ballet. In October 1972, the Joffrey Ballet gave a successful revival, the one referred to in this letter.

inactive for several months – which means I'll miss *Owen Wingrave* (first time on stage)[33] & *Death in Venice* (first time ever!).[34] But they must look after themselves. It was so good of you to think of me with the 1001 things you have to do.

> Yours ever,
> Ben

566. Jennie Bernstein to Leonard Bernstein
21 March 1973

Birthday reflections.

This seventy five year *young* mother and grandmother is counting her blessings, moments filled with joy and pleasure. I am indeed blessed to have such precious children and grandchildren. All these wonderful things in my life will keep me happy and young. How do I love you all, let me count the ways?

> With all my love,
> Jennie (Elizabeth Browning)
> Circa 1898.

567. Benjamin Britten to Leonard Bernstein
The Red House, Aldeburgh, England
[?December 1973 or 1974][35]

My dear Lenny,

I am so sorry I haven't answered your last letter – but writing is still very difficult for me. I do want to write a proper letter to you, & to say how touched both P. & I are that you have come on to the board of the Maltings Friends, how deeply I have been touched personally by your concern about me, & several other things too! Can I have your address to write to, please?

> With much Xmas love from
> Ben

---

[33] *Owen Wingrave* was originally composed as an opera for television, first broadcast on 16 May 1971. In this letter Britten is referring to the work's stage premiere, at the Royal Opera House, Covent Garden, on 10 May 1973.

[34] The world premiere of *Death in Venice* was given at Snape Maltings on 16 June 1973.

[35] Undated, written inside a Christmas card from Britten and Pears.

568. Virgil Thomson[36] to Leonard Bernstein

222 West 23rd Street, New York, NY
14 March 1974

Dear Lennie,

My warm congratulations on the success of *Candide*.[37] Way back in 1945, when I used to help out the French radio with broadcasts of American music from discs available through U.S. Information Service, by far the most popular with the public were excerpts from *On the Town*. And the French musicians around simply could not get over their astonishment that in New York an *opérette* composed in so advanced a musical style could be successful.

So still, with *West Side Story* and *Candide* you remain world master of the "musical". All honor to you!

Now that I have been through the Norton lectures (three by video, all six by reading) it is clear that your skill in explaining music is also tops, as indeed it was when you used to do it at Carnegie Hall.

Myself I find nothing reprehensible about your bringing in linguistics. You needed an authority to support an "innate musical grammar" and Chomsky's heavy artillery is surely that. Especially since post-war researches in the physiology of hearing, though they do support a syntax based on the harmonic series as unquestionably built into the human ear, are being treated by both the Germanic twelve-tone world and the French-based solfeggio world as "controversial".

So the linguistic argument, though merely an analogy, as you pointed out, does carry weight. And it enables you to by-pass vested musical interests.

I am sure your conclusions are valid, and I see no reason why you should not have used any material conveniently to hand for expounding them. All the more so since that material is relatively familiar and hence easily acceptable. I enjoyed everything.

Many thanks for the courtesies of your office.

I am returning the borrowed scripts with gratitude.

Ever warmly your admirer,

Virgil

---

[36] Virgil Thomson (1896–1989), American composer and critic. Thomson had known Bernstein since the 1940s, when he encouraged Bernstein, Paul Bowles, and others to develop as tonal composers. As a critic, he always took Bernstein's music seriously. In John Rockwell's obituary of Thomson in *The New York Times* (1 October 1989), Bernstein was quoted as follows: "The death of Virgil T is like the death of an American city: it is intolerable. Virgil was loving and harsh, generous and mordant, simple but cynical, son of the hymnal yet highly sophisticated. He will always remain brightly alive in the history of music, if only for the extraordinary influence his witty and simplistic music had on his colleagues. I know that I am one twig on that tree, and I will always cherish and revere Virgil, the source."
[37] The 1974 Broadway revival of *Candide* opened at the Broadway Theatre on 10 March and ran for 740 performances.

569. Alan Jay Lerner[38] to Leonard Bernstein
15 May 1974

Dear Lenny,

Blessings tonight. I can't wait to see it and hear it.[39]

If Jerry wants any more changes after tonight I'll put a contract out on him.

I'm starting the second act[40] and waiting for you like Duse for D'Annunzio. The room is ready, the piano has been tuned, the plane is revved up and I have fired my children.

Hurry,

Always,

Alan

570. Maurice Abravanel[41] to Leonard Bernstein
Utah Symphony, Salt Lake City, UT
4 June 1974

Dear Lennie,

Please accept my apologies for having taken so long to thank you for your lovely telegram. I passed it on to all the participants who thank you for your kind message.

The two performances went exceedingly well and were highly successful, and your *Mass* was exceedingly impressive and moving even in the very large auditorium. We had in excess of 12,000 attending between the two consecutive nights.

In addition to the fact that I felt it essential to present *Mass* in our city, I felt very gratified that it was only possible through cooperation among our orchestra, Repertory Dance Theatre, some people from Ballet West, the Music and Theatre Departments of the University of Utah, in addition to three other

---

[38] Alan Jay Lerner (1918–86), American lyricist and librettist who was a contemporary of Bernstein's at Harvard. A plan to work together on a show in 1949 came to nothing (see Letter 288), but in 1957 Lerner and Bernstein wrote two choruses for the Harvard Glee Club. In 1976 they collaborated on *1600 Pennsylvania Avenue* – a work that has, alas, become more famous for its catastrophic failure on Broadway than for the beauty of Bernstein's score and the brilliance of Lerner's lyrics (both heard to advantage in *A White House Cantata*, arranged from the show by Charlie Harmon and Sid Ramin after Bernstein's death). Lerner's most productive collaborations were with Frederick Loewe: *Brigadoon, Paint Your Wagon, My Fair Lady, Gigi*, and *Camelot*; he also worked with Kurt Weill (*Love Life*) and Burton Lane (*On A Clear Day You Can See Forever*).

[39] The first performance of *Dybbuk* took place the day after this letter was written.

[40] Presumably the second act of *1600 Pennsylvania Avenue*.

[41] Maurice Abravanel (1903–93), Greek-born American conductor. He was a pupil and friend of Kurt Weill and conducted the original productions of several of Weill's Broadway shows, including *Knickerbocker Holiday, Lady in the Dark, One Touch of Venus, The Firebrand of Florence*, and *Street Scene*. In 1949 he was conductor for the Broadway run of Blitzstein's *Regina*. Abravanel was Music Director of the Utah Symphony Orchestra from 1947 to 1979, leaving an extensive legacy of recordings. The orchestra's home was renamed Abravanel Hall in 1993.

universities in the state from which we borrowed sound equipment and robes. As far as I know, it is the first time so many organizations worked together for the common goal. 6,195 University of Utah students attended, which is almost one-third of the total enrolment.

I discovered that you and I are part of the establishment and were therefore (especially!) outrageously censured by a small but very vocal group. Also, our top Roman Catholic personage was personally against *Mass*, but even though quite a few of his people prompted him to do something about it, he refused to take any stand against it.

My associate conductor, Ardean Watts, did a fantastic job of organization and conducting. He used our entire orchestra plus a dozen extras, 185 singers and 10 dancers. The set was terrific, and I think that you would have been very happy with the whole thing. Of course I knew that you were working on *Dybbuk* which is a much more important thing.

I was putting in a strong pitch for asking you to serve again on the National Council on the Arts. I realize that right now, as I was told, it would be hopeless to expect President Nixon to appoint you, but I would like to know whether you would be ready to again serve. Even if you could attend meetings but rarely, your name alone would mean a great deal to the Endowment and in particular to its music component.

I am not quite sure that you yourself know how much your name means and how much more it could mean for us, the hewers of wood, who have to confront day in and day out the unrelenting putdown of the symphony orchestra in America.

Forgive me for having written such a long letter. Again, many thanks for having written *Mass* and so much other beautiful music, and for having done so much for music in our nation.

With best wishes always.

Affectionately yours,

Maurice

571. Leonard Bernstein to Felicia Bernstein

Clarendon Hotel, Christchurch, New Zealand

[August 1974]

Dearest F,

This letter has been a-borning for days, ever since arriving in Auckland, but there was always a reason to postpone – until we'd seen something to write about, until the first concert was over, until the first Mozart Trial by Fire[42] was

---

[42] In August–September 1974, Bernstein was on tour with the New York Philharmonic to New Zealand, Australia, and Japan. Bernstein's concerts began in Auckland on 16 August, and ended in Nagoya, Japan, on 6 September. In Wellington (17 August) and Christchurch (18 August) the programme was Mozart's Piano Concerto K503 (with Bernstein as the soloist) and Mahler's Fifth Symphony.

over, etc. Well, they're all over now, and all is more than well – triumphant concerts, orchestra in top form, even the Mozart last night in Wellington was a joy, with only a moment here and there of Frozen Fingers, and no Heart Attacks to speak of. Mozart again tonight here, and *Steinways* all the way, which is 50% of the joy. (And I can't tell you the joy of having Axel[43] along, he's a glorious companion.)

Interruption: the "Physiotherapist" has just arrived for massage purposes. Be back in a flash.

An hour later:

Terrific treatment – all those neck and shoulder pains gone. A genius; he brought along his 2-year-old daughter Katie, who "helped". The aches aren't serious – just this sudden spate of thick schedule – much rehearsing in Auckland, then nightly concerts in a row, all in different cities. Tonight is Christchurch (where I was greeted at the airport this morning by, natch, the Christchurch Hebrew Youth Group or something, with flowers and planted trees in Israel) – and they have a gorgeous new concert hall where I've just been trying out the piano: I'm really looking forward to this concert.

Don't forget Dr. Clarke check-up.[44]

Tomorrow is a free day, and Alexander and I are going skiing in the nearby Alps. Yesterday in Wellington we spent the afternoon sailing in the harbor: glorious it was, with buckets of beer and a jolly crew of real leathery mates. The city is a beauty – all great green hills around a huge harbor, and the cleanest air in the world. Architecture abysmal, however. Auckland even worse: it's all so new, just a century old, that everything is either the worst Victorian or plastic office buildings. The houses are sort of seaside shacks with a curiously familiar Oaf Gloves look.

But oh, the country around Auckland – that whole north tip! You would adore it: all rolling Scottish hills and Scandinavian fjords, massive firs, etc. – and anoma-lously, mitten drinnen, *palms* and other tropicalia. Rain forests. Monster fern-trees, vines. And around it all, the green hills with the millions of little sheep grazing peacefully. I don't know anything quite like it. Also, in that region, we discovered some thermal pools, hot mineral baths, and we became addicted: we went out there twice, and whiled away two mindless afternoons soaking in these pools while it rained on us, shone on us, and rainbows adorned the Hobbema skies.

Aside from a bit of a dust-up with the press on first arrival from Hawaii, we've found the people warm and simple and delightful – sort of provincial British midlands mixed with beautiful Maoris (Tahitians who came over in the 14th century) plus all kinds of other Islanders – Fijians, Samoans, etc., who keep

---

[43] Alexander, their son.
[44] In June 1974, Felicia had mastectomy surgery.

arriving owing to the population explosion back home. It's all a beautiful mixture.

And the milk! The best on earth.

Interruption: concert time – (to be continued).

It's now two days later; it's all one can do to find ten minutes to write a letter. So much activity! First the concert itself, Mozart & Mahler, in the great new concert hall here – and I mean *great*. I've never played the piano so well – really deep Mozart, and no nerves. You'd have been proud of the Town Hall.

And yesterday, a free day. Axel and Paul and I were taken skiing by some charming local ladies & small son – it was bliss. A perfect day, cool, brisk mountain air and a hot sun – dream Chilean weather. We came back last night in rapturous exhaustion, Axel and I both with banged-up knees & Paul with torn Pectorals. We're all limping around today, happy as clams.

Axel is actually doing a local crossword (in the authentic British style)[45] while I finish this letter, and then we're off to mad gay Brisbane, & the Australian leg commences – probably all downhill from here on. New Zealand was climactic, and those who say it's a final refuge when the crunch comes are probably right.

We miss you terribly; it seems incredible that ten days ago I had a last glimpse of you standing in the airport being abandoned by your males. I hope you're not too lonely, that there are all kinds of cheery *visitors* and chums, and that Nina is also not lonely. I miss her so. And Jamie, of course, would have gone bonkers over all this; it's a pity for her to miss it, and that Axel doesn't have her to share so many things with. But he's having a great time: he even acquired a cute dimply girlfriend of 17 in Auckland.

Well, the siren blows for Australia, and we're off, as Shirley would say, across the straits of Magellan. Take care of yourself, rest, have fun, and I fervently hope to find a letter from you waiting in Brisbane, full of news about the Dakota and Dixie's love life and the great Sublime Kitchen of Life.

Hugs and kisses to all, and so much love to you, my angel.

Ben

P.S. Don't forget to see Dr. Clarke. Or have I already mentioned that?

xxx

572. Lukas Foss to Leonard Bernstein
12 September 1974

Dearest Lenny,

Welcome back. I know you could not care less, but I do: ages ago a Mr. Buketof[f] sent me a form (the 111st of the year) to fill out: the 15 best

---

[45] A "British-style" cryptic crossword.

American orchestral pieces – for some European library. I sent him my choices. 2 Sundays ago I open the N.Y. *Times*, find an asinine list of 11 pieces, find myself listed, also among the jurors who "deliberated" to arrive at their idiotic choices.[46] I called Buketof[f], asked him to fish out *my* list: sure enough, it has little in common with the published one. Mine starts with *Age of Anxiety*, proceeds to Aaron's *Variations* etc. No Harris, no Brown. So I wrote to the *Times* a small note of protest for publication, calling their list: "conspicuous for the absence of America's best composers." (So far not publ. to my knowledge). You can laugh it off; but I can't write about my frustration to all the colleagues. In fact I won't write to any but you. Basta.

I'm off for 7 long weeks, 3 to Jerusalem, 4 with the Jerusalem Symphony all over Europe. Also trying to write a string quartet. There must be a saner way of life. What is it? How was Kyoto without me and my Buddhist nuns? Congrats!!!

Write the flute piece.

Arigato.

Love to Felicia, Nina, Jamie, Alexander [and] you.

Lukas

573. Christa Ludwig to Leonard Bernstein

Vienna, Austria
1 February 1975

Dear Maestro,

You are so famous, but in N.Y. the telegram office doesn't know your address! When your wishes for New Year arrived I learned that you have a new home. So I am really very sorry that when I came back from holidays and I saw your cable, my answer couldn't reach you. But I do hope that things will go better for Israel, but: oil! It is a terrible world. But we can hide ourselves a little bit in the music. I am glad that you come back to Salzburg. Why don't we make music together any more?!

The best to you and your family.

Love,

Christa

I think it is wonderful that our *Lied* [*von der Erde*] and Brahms Lieder are now on records!

---

[46] This article appeared in *The New York Times* on 25 August 1974. Written by Raymond Ericson and headed "The Pick of Modern American Music," it included no work by Bernstein. According to the report, Igor Buketoff collated the list in *The New York Times* from the responses of a jury of nine experts. Foss (like Diamond) was one of the American composers who actively supported Bernstein's music from the 1940s onwards. Foss was understandably hurt that his choice of Bernstein's *Age of Anxiety* had been ignored by *The New York Times*.

574. Thornton Wilder to Leonard Bernstein

Edgartown, MA

20 July 1975

Dear Leonard Bernstein,

As I told you on the phone:

I did not want an opera to be made of *The Skin of our Teeth*.

But I admired and trusted you, and was persuaded. I trusted you and the fellow-worker you would select.[47]

When your fellow-work fell apart – who was left to write the book? – I felt relieved of my commitment to you.

Hereafter, while I'm alive no one will write or compose an opera based on that play.

Torn from its context, Sabina's opening aria "Oh! Oh! Oh!" sounds awful, unmotivated, synthetic vivacity.

The nearest thing to it would be Zerbinetta's aria (or rondo). Who cares what her words are, except as are implied somewhat in Ariadne's abandonment? *These* words bear the weight of a crowded historical story of many facets.

I'm sorry to disappoint you, but my mistake was to have said "yes" in the first place; yours, to have not followed through with the original plan offered me.

Always with much regard.

Ever,

Thornton

575. Stephen Sondheim to Leonard Bernstein

[New York, NY]

23 July 1975

Dear Lenny,

I encountered the enclosed when I was organizing my files (well, it's better than working). I thought you might like to have them for future archivists, as your corrections are on them in your inimitable handwriting.

Love from Kanagawa,[48]

Steve

---

[47] Thornton Wilder died in December 1975, a few months after writing this letter, but the story of Bernstein's attempt to set *The Skin of Our Teeth* went back more than a dozen years (see note to letter 500). Why was Bernstein in contact with Wilder about this project as late as 1975? Perhaps it was because the revue *By Bernstein* that opened on 23 November 1975 at the Chelsea Theater Center, New York, included "Here Comes the Sun" and "Spring Will Come Again," both originally written for *The Skin of Our Teeth* in 1964, before being recycled in the *Chichester Psalms* the following year. Perhaps Bernstein also contemplated including Sabina's opening aria ("Oh! Oh! Oh!"), described by Wilder in unflattering terms in this letter. Sketches for this survive in the Leonard Bernstein Collection.

[48] "Kanagawa" is a reference to *Pacific Overtures*. Tryouts for this show started at the Shubert Theatre, Boston (8–29 November 1975), and then the Kennedy Center Opera House, Washington, D.C. (4–27 December 1975), before opening on Broadway at the Winter Garden Theatre on 11 January 1976.

576. Stephen Sondheim to Leonard Bernstein
15 November 1975

Dear Lennie,

Thanks for the good wishes. We got one terrible review (from Kevin Kelly, very bitchy) and one mixed (Eliot Norton, heavy on the good side), the rest raves.[49] The show needs an enormous amount of work on details: clarity, making the numbers land (the "button" problem again,[50] God save us), timing, etc. But the structure is sound and the production startling and terrific. Keep your fingers crossed.

Hope things have taken an upturn on your show and your spirits.

Back to rewriting the opening number.

Love to Felicia,

Steve

577. Stephen Sondheim to Leonard and Felicia Bernstein
16 January 1976

Dear Lenny and Felicia,

Just a note to thank you for the tree – I've discovered that it thrives if you keep yelling 'Bonsai!' triumphantly at it. It's easily fooled.

Love,

Steve

578. Stephen Sondheim to Leonard Bernstein
26 January 1976

Dear Lenny,

I've responded to the Societi Musiki Shiki as per your request. I sent them my collection of Bernstein birthday and Christmas compositions and advised them to make their own choice. I also offered to conduct for them, since I figure that the placement of downbeats is irrelevant in Japan.

Love,

Steve

P.S. Your letter arrived with no postage and came from the Dead Letter Office. Should I read anything into this? S.S.

---

[49] The reviews for the Boston tryout of *Pacific Overtures*.
[50] The "button problem" refers to finding the most effective way to end a song.

579. Jerome Robbins to Leonard Bernstein

The Barclay, Rittenhouse Square, Philadelphia, PA
[February 1976]

Dear Lenny,
    Good Morning!
    I wanted to talk to you last night just for a moment. I understood your black moment of despair – but for God's sake, you are a big, capable, enormously talented man – with tons of energy – and so is Allan [*recte* Alan Jay Lerner] and *don't* sink (like that down moment). It's understandable; but now is the time to muster up all your wonderful optimism and get it still moving, come to the aid etc., and above all – as in the show, *keep it going!* You *are* rehearsing in public, you are in *some* chaos, but as in our democracy, you must believe your system will work, which I *know* you do, in order to move it. Your show now is exactly like the one you are writing about.[51] Now you *can* make it work much *much much* better. Take care of your house. You can do it. Come on kid, get the spirit up again. No limp cocks!
    Ole Coach Jer[ry]
    See you about 1.
    LOVE

580. Stephen Sondheim to Leonard Bernstein

New York, NY
4 May 1976[52]
[Telegram]

    The point is it's over and you're still the only artist writing musicals with one exception that is.
    Love
    Steve

581. Sid Ramin to Leonard Bernstein

8 May 1976

Dear Lenny,
    Just a note to thank you again for your marvelous gift. Not only is it lavish but the inscription on the inside of the beautiful Gucci leather case is something I will always remember and treasure.

---

[51] The tryouts of *1600 Pennsylvania Avenue* were in Philadelphia: it was proving to be an exceptionally troublesome show. Jerome Robbins was not only Bernstein's most regular theatrical collaborator and a trusted friend, but he was also a brilliant "show doctor." Despite a score that is often very beautiful, *1600 Pennsylvania Avenue* failed when it moved to Broadway.
[52] 4 May 1976 was the opening night of the troubled *1600 Pennsylvania Avenue* on Broadway, where it ran for just seven performances.

As you may know, Lenny, I'm always on cloud nine when I'm in the same room with you. The show made it possible for us to spend some time together and I savoured every minute.

From our pre-orchestration meetings to our post-orchestration meetings to our Fine and Schapiro[53] festivities, I look back at the last three months with great affection.[54] Especially, one very long and late meeting (in [Apartment] 92 [in the Dakota]) when we talked into the dawn. I'll never forget it.

I'm sorry the show didn't work out for you (for us!) but I will be eternally grateful for the wonderful moments I've had (including that great night at the Variety Club) in just being with you.

Gloria joins me in sending you much love.

Always,

Sid

582. Richard Avedon[55] to Leonard Bernstein
407 East 75th Street, New York, NY
[May 1976]

Dear Lenny,

I know it isn't what you dreamt it would be,[56] but you can *not* be responsible for anything but your music which is *superb!* I wept during "Take Care of This House" as I haven't since ". . . and make our garden grow!"

And:

Rehearse

Seena

The dirge during the second act funeral –

The Red, White, and Blues

and much more. It's just beautiful, Lenny, and everyone near me was moved, and happy, and so was I, and it was because of your music.

You stand alone. Terrifying, but true.

Love always,

Dick

---

[53] Fine and Schapiro is a famous Kosher restaurant and delicatessen in New York.

[54] Ramin (and Hershy Kay) orchestrated *1600 Pennsylvania Avenue*.

[55] Richard Avedon (1923–2004), American photographer who helped to "define America's image of style, beauty and culture for the last half-century," according to his obituary in *The New York Times* (1 October 2004). Avedon and his wife Evelyn were close friends of the Bernsteins, and he loved Bernstein's music (a few years earlier, on 3 January 1972, he had written to Bernstein and Felicia about *Mass*: "I play it over and over (not while I'm photographing), and when I'm not listening, I sing 'I Go On' and cry a lot. How can I thank you?").

[56] *1600 Pennsylvania Avenue*.

583. Leonard Bernstein to Helen Coates
"Xmas 1976" [December 1976]

Dearest Helen,

At this very crucial turning-point[57] in both our lives my annual wishes for a happy new year carry very special weight. So: a very Happy '77, with all my love.

As always,

Lenny

584. Leonard Bernstein to Irwin Kostal[58]
17 June 1977

Dear Irwin,

I've just heard the Fiedler–Pops recording of my *Mass* music, and I am so pleased that I must write you. What a job of sound-making you did! I almost don't miss the voices . . .[59]

I hope all is going well with you. My warmest thanks for *Mass* –

and my affection,

Lenny B

585. Oliver Smith to Leonard Bernstein
70 Willow Street, Brooklyn, NY
18 December 1977

My dear friend,

Your *Songfest*[60] is a composition of such emotional variety and richness, it is difficult to be articulate about it after one hearing except to express to you the tremendous emotional effect it had on me. It contains ravishing sound, humor, tenderness, strident joy and anger, and sweet melancholy. Whatever I say to you is inadequate in expressing the joy your beautiful music gave me.

---

[57] One of the very few allusions in Bernstein's correspondence to his separation from Felicia in 1976–7. The story of this traumatic episode is eloquently told by Humphrey Burton (1994, pp. 426–41). Felicia and Leonard were reconciled by the summer of 1977, but she was already suffering from the lung cancer that would kill her a year later.

[58] Irwin Kostal (1911–94), American orchestrator and arranger. One of the original orchestrators of *West Side Story* with Sid Ramin. His Hollywood credits included *West Side Story* (again with Sid Ramin) and *The Sound of Music* (conductor and music supervisor), winning Oscars for both. He also conducted the 1982 digital re-recording of the soundtrack to Disney's *Fantasia*.

[59] The album *Music from Mass – Overture to Candide* by Arthur Fiedler and the Boston Pops Orchestra was issued by Deutsche Grammophon. It included nine movements from *Mass* arranged for orchestra by Irwin Kostal.

[60] The first complete performance of *Songfest* took place in Washington, D.C., on 11 October 1977.

You are such a dear, great artist, and I hug you again with great love and thankfulness.

Oliver

586. Leonard Bernstein to Helen Coates

Hotel Sacher, Vienna, Austria
28 January 1978

Dear Helen,

I haven't written in all these three weeks (this pen is finished!) because I've been spending all my time between rehearsals in bed, sleeping and trying to regain my strength. It's a long, slow haul, and I still don't feel quite up to snuff. The doctor says that I don't need medicine, but a vacation in the sun, and that's just not possible for many weeks to come. So I muddle through, and *Fidelio* goes surprisingly well (tremendous reaction & critics) considering that I don't feel my full powers, and that I had to cancel so many rehearsals. Tomorrow is the live TV broadcast – I pray it will go well.[61]

So you too have had the flu! Isn't it ghastly? It's as though one's whole body had been attacked, ear-lobes, toe-nails & all. I also have no appetite & have lost weight: I hope yours is restored to normal.

I'm expecting Felicia on the 3rd of February & I hope you can give her a pleasant birthday party. She sounds splendid on the phone.

Do take care of yourself, & write – I love hearing from you.

Always,
Lenny

587. Betty Comden to Leonard Bernstein

117 East 95th Street, New York, NY
2 July 1978[62]

Dearest Lenny,

The impossible letter must be written. I have seen you, and we have talked, and I have felt close to you, and it is hard to write when you are close, and you know that so much is both expressed and understood without the need for the written word. Yet I think of you and feel for you, and I think of Felicia, and what this last year must have been like for you, and the void that is now, and I wish I could write something to lessen the pain so visible in your eyes.

---

[61] The live performance of *Fidelio* from the Vienna State Opera on 29 January 1978 was released on DVD (Deutsche Grammophon 073 4159) in 2006. It's a magnificent performance that has been widely praised, not least by John Steane in *Gramophone* who said that it constituted "one of the great artistic experiences of a lifetime."

[62] Felicia Bernstein died on 16 June 1978, having been ill with cancer for several years.

That Felicia was an extraordinary person, we all know. She impressed me the moment you brought her to our green living room on 55th Street. Her patrician beauty and her cool sparkle awed me a bit. I later came to enjoy her great earthy streak, crazy sense of humor, and her many sudden radiant bursts of warmth, and I wish I could have gotten closer than I did. I was close enough to feel totally bereft now.

You must not blame yourself for not coming through this as a kind of patri-archal leader and rock of ages. If I am bereft, what must you be? You are entitled to full grief, and floundering, and, yes, weakness. These are the feelings you expressed to me. This is a deep tragedy you are experiencing. You are so much, Lenny – so many qualities and gifts and inner voices not given to many human beings. You will find your strength somehow in them – and in the beautiful elements added to them by the co-mingling of your life and Felicia's.

Much love, always, from Steve and from me.

Betty

588. Nadia Boulanger to Leonard Bernstein
Écoles d'Art Américacies, Fontainebleau, France
7 August 1978

Dear Lenny,

To try to be with you in your commensurable distress.

And you knew so well, and for so long. Hope she did not suffer too terribly. Life sometimes is so difficult to stand. May your courage be as great as your sorrow.

Forgive these poor lines, I feel myself so sick and miserable.

With love,

NB

589. André Previn[63] to Leonard Bernstein
The Watergate Hotel, Washington D.C.
28 August 1978

Dear Lennie,

It bothered me a lot to hear you sounding so depressed when I spoke to you the day after the concert. I thought about it quite a lot. At first I came to the naive conclusion that writing to you about it was none of my business, but then,

---

[63] André Previn (b. 1930), German-born American conductor, pianist, and composer. Previn was the piano soloist in Beethoven's Triple Concerto (with Yehudi Menuhin and Mstislav Rostropovich) in the gala concert conducted by Bernstein on 25 August 1978. This was a celebration of his 60th birthday with the National Symphony Orchestra, at its summer home, Wolf Trap in Virginia.

the more I gave it thought, the more I realized that both as an old friend and as a musician, it *was*. I've been an admirer and a follower and, in a more remote way, a disciple since I first heard you make music in San Francisco in 1950 with the Israel Philharmonic. You've touched, directly or circuitously, a great many musical decisions of mine, but what's more important, the lives and ambitions of every conductor in this country. That's the kind of statement usually found on the scrolls of Doctorates, but for all its grandiloquence it happens to be true. Therefore, if you were to succumb to a depression, however temporary, that would keep you from your usual frighteningly energetic achievements, you'd be letting down an amazing number of musicians. You've kept those of us who grew up in the same years as you feeling young; you've kept those older than you correctly infuriated, and you've been a lighthouse of constancy to all those 20-year-old current phenomena. As a friend, I can see that this is a burden you might not want right now, but as a member of that weird band who feel that a day without music is an irresponsible waste, I have to tell you that you're stuck with it. I'm certainly not entitled to be a spokesman, and all this sounds terrifyingly pompous, but we depend on you and love you and trust you.

When I celebrate my 60th birthday, you will be a hell of a lot younger than [...] Karl Böhm is right now, and I will expect you to play the Triple Concerto while I conduct.

See you soon.

André

590. Aaron Copland to Leonard Bernstein
Peekskill, NY
5 September 1978

Dear, dear Lenny,

That was a *beautiful* note you sent me. I was so pleased that you were pleased with the *Jeremiah* movement.[64] It sure is a beauty!

And now the sad part. I'm not going to be present at the "Remembrance" for Felicia on the 18th because I am under contract to conduct the same day in Virginia (Norfolk). But my thoughts will be with you and the family that day.

As ever,

Aaron

---

[64] Copland conducted the Lamentation from Bernstein's *Jeremiah* Symphony (with Christa Ludwig as the soloist) at the gala concert for Bernstein's 60th birthday at Wolf Trap, on 25 August 1978.

591. Leonard Bernstein to Burton Bernstein

"Sharm-el-Skeikh, Tiran Straits, Sinai, Israel (or, by the time you get this, Egypt?)"
[October 1978]

Dearest BB,

I've thought of you all day, driving down the old S[inai] Peninsula (with the McClures and Tommy C.) and hearing your voice from Eilat to Sharm, Bedouin by Bedouin, camel by camel (one dead by the road in rigor mortis) & glorious geological grandeur by g. g. g. But the climax came tonight, walking up the beach from our Tunisian shrimp dinner, as we were confronted by one of the truly great signs of my experience, repeated at intervals along the strand, in the usual 3 languages. The English reads (and this may well merit a *New Yorker* appearance):

SECURITY WELL DESTINED
FOR ABSORPTION SUSPICIOUS
OBJECTS ONLY.

I cannot get it out of my mind: it defies all intelligibility. "Only"!

Aside from this I've thought of you often this month (Holidays *very* late this year) climaxed by *Shmini Hatzsreth*[65] (gasp! of childhood total recall) only yesterday. Rosh, Kol, Yom, Succoth, etc. have come and gone in a welter of rehearsals & concerts & much sleeping in between. Very difficult to resume the old schedules, but God knows I've tried, acquitted myself passably, & have these 4 days of desert holiday before attacking the even more rigorous set-up in Vienna. I'll make it . . .

This great wonderful Sinai . . . give it back?!

Not one word have I received from anyone all month. I have phoned & written: not been answered. What is happening to the loving old family? Do call Mamma (if that is indeed her name) & give her my love. Tell Horse she's a cad not to have called or written.

And much love to all, & to you, – mine Brothoass,

Ben

Best from Moish [Moshe Pearlman].

I hope the book goes apace.

---

[65] Often given as Shemini Atzeret, the "Eighth Day of Assembly," a Jewish holiday sometimes combined with Simchat Torah.

8

Final Years
1979–90

There was no lack of glory in the last decade of Bernstein's life – nor any shortage of love – but Felicia's furious prediction doesn't feel too wide of the mark either. In terms of composition, the last ten years are difficult to assess: there are some fine pieces, of which *Halil* for flute and orchestra is certainly among the best. Typically for Bernstein the inveterate self-borrower, the fast section of *Halil* (starting at p. 15 of the published full score) was derived from an occasional piece: the music he wrote in October 1979 for the 50th Anniversary of CBS in 1978 (the main notes of the theme, C–B flat–E flat, spell out C–B–Es [S] in German). But with the opera *A Quiet Place*, there's an inevitable sense of declining powers – made manifest by its integration of *Trouble in Tahiti*, which emerges as much the strongest part of the work. Bernstein longed to write the Great American Opera, and had done for decades, but while he made some glorious contributions to American musical theater – *On the Town* and *West Side Story* are unquestionably two of the greatest scores ever written for Broadway – Bernstein felt he should push himself further, and in a more "serious" direction. But this was not something he could do by himself. Perhaps if Jerome Robbins had wanted to write an opera, it might have happened, since Robbins was one of the very few people from whom Bernstein took criticism and who had superb theatrical instincts. John McClure, Bernstein's long-time record producer, surely put his finger on the problem of the late years: "Felicia was vital to his stability as was Jerry Robbins, the only two people who could make Lenny sweat."[1] It's very hard to escape the feeling that he was right.

The letters from the 1980s are less substantial – above all because Bernstein no longer had Felicia to confide in when he was away, but also because of an increasing reliance on phone calls and faxes. Even so, there were still faithful letter-writers, Stephen Sondheim and Jerome Robbins among them, and there are interesting – often touching – letters to and from other musicians, especially conductors. Bernstein's profound admiration for Karl Böhm is apparent from the letter that he sent in 1981 to his ailing colleague on his deathbed. There are

---

[1] John McClure, personal communication, 20 February 2013.

delightful letters from Carlos Kleiber (requesting an autograph for his son, but in a way that is full of humor and charm), from Yehudi Menuhin praising Bernstein's controversial performance with the BBC Symphony Orchestra of Elgar's *Enigma Variations*, and from Marin Alsop early in her conducting career. She wrote to send heartfelt thanks to Bernstein for his inspiration, and for the opportunity to work with him in Japan. It's well known how warmly Alsop admires her mentor, but Jonathan Cott's 1989 interview reveals just how highly Bernstein also thought of her: "There's a young woman named Marin Alsop. She was a student of mine at Tanglewood – she did Hindemith's *Mathis der Maler* and Roy Harris' Third Symphony under me, and she's fabulous, she is simply wonderful" (Cott 2013, p. 125).

Bernstein's 70th birthday brought tributes from friends, celebrities, and even politicians. Ronald Reagan wrote to congratulate him, as did Frank Sinatra (an old friend – they'd worked together in nightclubs in the early 1940s), Miles Davis, and Claudio Arrau, who recalled fondly the first meeting of Bernstein and Felicia at his party in 1946. But there's a feeling of nostalgia about many of these greetings – celebrating great times that have, to a large extent, been and gone. In terms of Bernstein's compositions, it certainly seemed to be the case: *A Quiet Place* (1983, revised in 1984 and 1986) was his last large-scale work.

And yet in the concert hall he continued to give triumphant performances with orchestras in New York, Vienna, Amsterdam, Munich, London, and else-where: these were not just huge public successes, but inspiring accounts of Schubert and Schumann, or of Copland, Harris, and Ives. There were extraordinary and daring concerts of Tchaikovsky in New York and Sibelius in Vienna, and Mahler performances that it seems too easy to describe as "revelatory" – but Bernstein's understanding of Mahler grew ever deeper, and his interpretations evolved as a consequence: the thrilling drive and drama of his earlier Mahler gave way to a kind of visionary splendor. It's as if Bernstein's frustration about his inability to compose with any consistency over these last few years found a more positive counterpart in his conducting of music by others. After Felicia, he didn't – indeed, he couldn't – find any lasting personal relationships. There were some passionate affairs, there was infinite love poured out on his children, but there was a certain loneliness: as a musician, Bernstein's interpretative insights grew deeper and richer, and yet at the same time his extreme celebrity carried with it the inevi-table problems of having less time to spend with people he loved and cared about, or even to be alone. He fell out with David Diamond in a viscious exchange of letters, after half a century of friendship – and the publication of Joan Peyser's tell-all biography hurt him (even though he claimed never to have read it). What disturbed him was probably not so much what it said, but the people who said it: friends and colleagues who Bernstein felt had been disloyal by sharing secrets that should have remained private. But there were still faithful friends, and Bernstein took great pleasure in their company, as they did in his – for instance, he took Sid and Gloria Ramin to Israel in 1986. His devoted secretary Helen Coates died in 1989, and by the start of 1990 concerns about his own health started to preoccupy him. A malignant tumor was diagnosed and in great secrecy he was given a course of radiation therapy. Still, he managed a trip to Prague to conduct Beethoven's Ninth Symphony (and to spend time talking with President Václav Havel). After a few days delayed convalescence, he set off for the first Pacific Music Festival in Sapporo, Japan (where Marin Alsop worked as his assistant), but it quickly became apparent that his condition was worsening. He struggled through the concerts there and in Tokyo. Humphrey Burton quotes an anguished diary entry made by Craig Urquhart[2] about Bernstein's dependency on massive doses of painkillers: "The real question is why he bothers at all. Here is a very sick man who knows he is doing his *danse macabre*" (Burton 1994, p. 519). Bernstein had to withdraw at very short notice from his last engagement in Japan – a big outdoor concert – earning some criticism in the Japanese press, who were unaware of the seriousness of his condition. He returned to New York and was soon on the road again, for concerts at Tanglewood. The major event was the 50th anniversary concert of Tanglewood and – on a more personal note – the 50th anniversary of Bernstein first conducting there. The Bernstein family was out in force for the occasion, including his mother, Jennie. Heavily medicated and fighting for breath, he conducted the "Four Sea Interludes" from Britten's *Peter Grimes*, and the concert ended with Beethoven's Seventh Symphony. Listening to the published recording of this concert, it's immediately apparent that Bernstein was uncomfortable, but in the Scherzo third movement he succumbed to a coughing fit that prevented him conducting for several minutes. The Boston Symphony Orchestra kept playing, and Bernstein was able to resume conducting for the last movement, but only with the greatest difficulty. It was his last concert – and he knew it. Back in New York he told Craig Urquhart: "You know it's incredible how I did my first concert at Tanglewood and I did my last concert at Tanglewood. There's a real sense of closure" (Burton 1994, p. 524). On 5 September his mother Jennie, then in her nineties, wrote: "You are surrounded by a beautiful family, your children and grandchildren. That in itself should be good medicine for you." But by then it was far too late. His apartment in the Dakota began to resemble a hospital ward, and on 9 October a statement was issued announcing his retirement from conducting. Five days later, at 6:15 p.m. on 14 October in his apartment at the Dakota, Leonard Bernstein died.

---

[2] Craig Urquhart was Bernstein's assistant from January 1986 until 1990. He is a vice-president of the Leonard Bernstein Office, and founded the Bernstein newsletter *Prelude, Fugue & Riffs*.

592. Oliver Smith to Leonard Bernstein

70 Willow Street, Brooklyn, NY

23 July 1979

Dearest Lenny,

Yesterday I had the enormous pleasure of hearing you conduct at Tanglewood.[3] You were simply wonderful. I felt so proud of you. I made a darting trip up to "welcome" you back along with the enthusiastic thousands to whom you bring inspiration and joy and so much of your innermost being. Unfortunately I had to rush back and didn't have the opportunity to go back stage, see those eyes open very wide with delight and give you a great hug. I do so now.

You were simply magnificent. The Haydn Mass in B flat was so joyous I was ready to embrace the church, something I am sure would horrify you. I heard the chorus rehearsing as I came on the grounds, only one half hour before the performance! I thought: just like Lenny.

I was a little apprehensive about the Shostakovich on such a steaming afternoon. You made it absolutely riveting, with all its prolix fascination and strangeness as well as introspective qualities. I was as thrilled as the audience and found a joyous release in joining in the ovation.

It is wonderful we are finally again doing *West Side Story*.[4] It is my favorite theatrical effort. This week I take off to England for a few weeks to rest up for the battles to follow, to which I am looking forward.

Meanwhile I send you my love and a tender embrace of thanks.

Oliver

P.S. I am very sorry to miss the Mahler 9th.[5] It is something very special to you and your interpretation is the greatest. I shall never forget that great performance in Vienna several years ago at the Musikverein.

Love,

O

---

[3] The program on 22 July consisted of Haydn's *Thereisenmesse* and Shostakovich's Fifth Symphony.

[4] This important (and acclaimed) revival of *West Side Story* opened at Broadway's Minskoff Theatre in February 1980 and ran for 333 performances. It was directed by Robbins – his first work on Broadway for sixteen years – with the close involvement of several people involved in the original 1957 production, including sets by Oliver Smith, costumes by Irene Sharaff, and lighting by Jean Rosenthal. The Musical Director was John DeMain, who went on to conduct the world premiere of Bernstein's *A Quiet Place* at Houston in 1983.

[5] Bernstein conducted Mahler's Ninth Symphony at Tanglewood a week later, on 29 July.

593. Leonard Bernstein on Aaron Copland
Tribute delivered at the Kennedy Center Honors, Washington, D.C.[6]
2 December 1979

Last month Aaron Copland celebrated his 79th birthday, out of which evolved a plethora of toasts, lunches, speeches, tributes and honors, of which tonight's honor is certainly the grandest. But if all this happens when he is 79, what volcanoes will erupt when he hits 80 a year from now? I can't begin to imagine; but whatever monster celebrations, fireworks and celebrations may take place, they will never suffice to honor in proper degree this great gentleman of American music. Never have we had a composer of his superb lyric and symphonic quality who has been personally so admired, respected and – let's say it – *loved* by so many people as Aaron. I speak not only of the music but also of the man. Ask anyone who knows him: "What is Aaron like?" And they will surely respond by describing the Copland grin, the Copland giggle, the Copland wit and warmth, and width of his embrace.

He has always had time for everyone – especially the young (that is the mark of a great man: time for *people*); and his unmistakeable sharp "judge-nose", as he once described it, has always been sniffing out new talent, in whatever hamlet or continent it might be hiding, to encourage with praise, to nurture with criticism, and to help on its way to public exposure.

And yet he is also the most moderate, balanced, objective, sane and non-melodramatic man I have ever known. When he exaggerates, it's to make us laugh; when he understates, it's to point up an irony. Everything else is plain truth – "plain" is one of his favorite words – and "truth" is the very essence of the man.

All of these qualities – the generosity, the wit, the quirkiness, the compassion and tenderness and plainness – all of these inhabit his music with a mirror-like truth. But there are other qualities in the music which reflect aspects of the man he never allows us to see. The music can have an extraordinary grandeur, an exquisite delicacy, a prophetic severity, a ferocious rage, a sharp bite, a prickly snap, a mystical suspension, a wounding stab, an agonizing howl – none of which corresponds with the Aaron we loving friends know – but comes from some deep, mysterious place he never reveals to us except in his music.

I have known Aaron intimately for 42 years, and I have only once seen him in a state of anger. Once. And I recall a luncheon date in which he was uncharacteristically quiet, mentioning only that he had a headache. I learned much later that day that his father had died on the previous night. And once – again only

---

[6] Bernstein delivered this speech at the second annual Kennedy Center Honors gala on 2 December 1979. Copland, Henry Fonda, Martha Graham, Tennessee Williams, and Ella Fitzgerald were the five artists honored with lifetime achievement awards. The *Washington Post* (9 December) described Bernstein's tribute to Copland as "a piece of magic."

once – have I seen him weep when, at a Bette Davis movie that caused me to oo and ah and marvel and groan "NO, NO, NO" at the unbearable climax (I am always very vocal at the end of Bette Davis movies), he turned to me, his cheeks awash with tears, and sobbed, "Can't you shut up?"

Now usually men of such restraint and moderation, who also harbor such tumultuous inner passions and rages, are sick men, psychotics who are prone to unpredictable and irrational explosions. Not so Aaron. The unpredictability is all in the music, which is why that music is so constantly fresh and surprising, as is the music of Beethoven. The man himself is sanity itself – and that is why the first moment I met him – on his 37th birthday – I trust[ed] him instantly and relied completely on his judgment as gospel and have done so ever since. It is my honor to present him to you, my first friend in New York, my master, my idol, my sage, my shrink, the closest thing to a composition teacher I ever had, my guide, my counselor, my elder brother, my beloved friend – Aaron Copland.

Leonard Bernstein
30 November 1979

594. Aaron Copland to Leonard Bernstein
Peekskill, NY
4 December 1979

Dear Lensk,

How to thank you for that *splendiferous* talk at the Kennedy Center Sunday night. (Not to mention the special effort needed to be in 2 cities almost simultaneously!)

And everyone around me seemed to be enjoying the talk as much as I did (including Mrs. Carter,[7] who was seated next to me).

It was truly a night to be remembered – thanks a million!

Love,

A

595. Francis Ford Coppola[8] to Leonard Bernstein
The Sentinel Building, 916 Kearney Street, San Francisco, CA
7 March 1980

My most respected Maestro Bernstein,

Certainly the telephone conversation that my assistant Tess related to me broke my heart. The confusion that comes when four different artists attempt

---

[7] Rosalynn Carter, wife of President Carter and First Lady.
[8] Francis Ford Coppola (b. 1939), film director whose screen credits include *The Godfather* and *Apocalypse Now*.

to assemble a collaboration; the complexity of each individual's time, place and temperament – the more difficult areas of lawyers, agents and deals – is the reason very often that desirable collaborations never happen at all.

I'm sure you can understand how hard it must be on me, who essentially must be the pivot-point for the project – and also work as writer and director, when it's quite obvious to me that my ideas are being auditioned by you, and I can plainly see that every so often those with whom I wish to collaborate are obliged to talk to their agents to see whether or not a deal has been struck.

So that, as I understand it, the collaboration hinged on whether in fact you were committed and approved the project as it had been (however vaguely) outlined by me to you, Betty [Comden] and Adolph [Green].

I didn't know I was expected to call you or that you were waiting to hear from me, as of course I had just assumed that we were all friends enough that if you or anyone wished to talk to me, you would simply call, and not stand on ceremony.

In short, as I see the entire situation, it is as follows:

My ideas and concept for this kind of musical–opera–film are too embryonic in form to really be presented to collaborators who must have something defined and specific so that they can do their work. I guess I had hoped that the discovery of this kind of unprecedented film would be made together, on a slow, arduous hit or miss kind of artistic exploration. But I realize now that this process is too difficult to put together between three different groups of artists, who are also all working on other things and have a tight schedule. I also understand, Maestro, that your own composition schedule is heartbreakingly short, and that you can ill afford to waste your time.

I have personal opinions also, about this matter, which I have never mentioned because it would have been rude to you, whom I have always admired. My opinion is that for a composer of your scale and stature to limit his composition, which is the flower of his work, to take a second chair to certain other of the performing arts of which others are perfectly capable, is wrong. But no one can *write* music like Bernstein. And Bernstein's theatrical music is as good as any that has *ever* been written.

And so I came to say . . . "Here, let me give you musical cinema. Take theatrical music to its next step, in a medium that the whole world will see and respond to." Well, that is my dream, and I know as sure as I know anything that it is your dream too. Please bear with me – maybe we'll work more informally, over the next six months or even year.

But then when we put these sketches together, it would be a pleasure to fully collaborate with you and Adolph and Betty.

Excuse me for the ownership and the beginning of a new movie studio, Zoetrope Studio, which makes you want to say that I have gone from being an artist to a "mogul". Zoetrope Studios will create the most modern, electronic studio in the world, and its first work will be TUCKER by Leonard Bernstein,

Betty Comden and Adolph Green – who knows, maybe even Jerome Robbins, and Francis Coppola. I'd sure want to see that film.[9]

Maybe someday you'll say: "I didn't know he was going to be Francis Coppola".

With sincere love,

Francis

596. Leonard Bernstein to Stephen Sondheim
16 March 1980

Dearest Steve

This Es/la[10] tritone comes with warmest memories of work and play and friendship. S–L is almost a quarter of a century old, and it seems all wrong that I should not be in attendance on your glorious 50th. But I'll be down in the Caribbean with my children on that date, and will be thinking strongly and affectionately of you. More power to you and much merriment.

L = 50 = Love = Lenny

---

[9] Coppola's *Tucker: The Man and his Dream* was eventually released in 1988, but as a biographical film rather than the "musical–opera–film" outlined to Bernstein in this letter. The genesis and tribulations of this project are described in detail by Gene D. Phillips in *Godfather: The Intimate Francis Ford Coppola* (Lexington: Kentucky University Press), pp. 261–78.

[10] "Es" (E flat) is normal German spelling for "S," while "La" is solfège for A and can be used to spell "L"; by a neat coincidence these musical spellings for Stephen and Leonard form a tritone (augmented fourth) – an interval that is of particular significance in *West Side Story*. Sondheim was born on 22 March 1930 and started working with Bernstein on *West Side Story* in October 1955.

LEONARD BERNSTEIN

Dearest Steve:

[musical notation drawn inside a heart shape]

This Eb/A tritone comes with warmest memories of work and play and friendship. S-L is almost a quarter-century old, and it seems all wrong that I should not be in attendance on your glorious 50th. But I'll be down in the Caribbean with my children on that date, and will be thinking strongly and affectionately of you. Mon power to you, and much Merriment…

L = 50 = Love = Lenny
16 March '80

597. Stephen Sondheim to Leonard Bernstein
New York, NY
19 March 1980

Dear Lenny,

As usual, clever, appropriate, poetic and touching. Thank you for this one, and the others, and what's behind them.[11]

I am sorry you won't be here, but I suspect you'll have a better time anyway among the natives.

Love,
Steve

---

[11] A reference to the piano pieces that Bernstein often sent Sondheim as birthday gifts (Stephen Sondheim, personal communication).

598. Jennie Bernstein to Leonard Bernstein
[August 1980][12]

I remember saying, "Dear son, some day you will have it all." Your Dad of blessed memory objected to your career out of his love for you.

You write and think young. Stay that way my dear, for many more healthy musical years.

With much love and good wishes,

Your ever loving,

Mom

599. Jerome Robbins to Leonard Bernstein
12 November 1980

Dear Lenny,

Thank you for sending me the tape and score of your latest work.[13] I really like it very, very much, and I'm in love with so many of the middle movements. I'd love to do it, but I worry about it because, as you know, music tends to shrink when you add dancing to it, and the pieces themselves are so short to start with that I don't know how it would avoid resulting in broken, tiny pieces. At least, that's my reaction now. Let me know if you have any suggestions, and we'll get together. But I do love the work.

Sorry that I've only gotten to this now. I just finished the Mozart Rondo in A minor, and I like it, although like the music, it is a fairly quiet work. If you want to come see it, let me know.

All my love,

Jerry

---

[12] An inscription written inside a birthday card.

[13] The *Divertimento for Orchestra* first performed by the Boston Symphony Orchestra under Seiji Ozawa on 25 September 1980. Bernstein has written a note at the top of this letter outlining ideas (perhaps the result of a discussion with Robbins) for a ballet treatment:

Fanfare	1 – Tutti
Waltz	2 – Diminished corps (girls?)
Mazurka	3 – Pas de 6
Samba	4 – Pas de 4: Kay Thompson & Boys
Turkey	5 – Pas de 2 (Castles)
Sphinxes	6 – Solo: joke on [Martha] Graham vs. ballet on cadences
Blues	7 – Solo blues
[March]	8 – a) Adding company gradually during flutes
	b) Tutti march.

600. Doriot Anthony Dwyer[14] to Leonard Bernstein

3 Cleveland Road, Brookline, MA

25 July 1981

Dear Lenny,

Just a note to tell you, in writing, that it was an enormous pleasure you gave me this year, to play your *Halil* with you. It is rare one flutist plays a solo with a great conductor who is *that* involved in the same work. I suspected as much and the anticipation nearly tore me apart, and I loved *Halil* right from the start. Still it was more than that: even if it had *not* been your composition, I knew once you decided to perform it you were giving it your creative attention & delivery. *That* is what was added to make this time a magical, great adventure for me.

I *hope* we can work together again in some similar capacity. I don't expect, exactly. But I will keep on with this stimulus, this gift of your composition & performing with such as you & I *do* thank you for it – a lot!

Doriot

601. Leonard Bernstein to Karl Böhm

13 August 1981[15]

Dear Maestro Karl,

They tell me you are now very ill, worse than our last time in Munich. Some people even imply that you feel your life coming to a close – for me, an inadmissible thought. The years of physical age have mounted close to 90, and even I, on the eve of my 63rd birthday, can feel their weight and the concomitant panic at time running out before all our works can be finished.

I have always been somewhat amazed at the warmth and musical closeness of our relationship. After all, you were born in the lap of Mozart, Wagner and Strauss, with full title to their domain; whereas I was born in the lap of Gershwin and Copland, and my title in the kingdom of European music was, so to speak, that of an adopted son. That is why I was so surprised to receive your message, some months ago, when you were stopped by illness from completing your *Elektra* recording, that if you should in time not recover to finish the missing central love scene, I, of all people, must be the one to complete it for you. You can imagine the honor I felt at this request and, also, my sense of inadequacy at the prospect of replacing so great a master.

---

[14] Doriot Anthony Dwyer (b. 1922) was principal flute of the Boston Symphony Orchestra from 1952 until 1990. She gave the American premiere of *Halil* with the Boston Symphony conducted by Bernstein in a Fourth of July concert of Bernstein's music given at Tanglewood. Bernstein inscribed her copy: "For my beautiful colleague Doriot, with all the old affection and a brand new admiration, Lenny – 4 July '81".

[15] Bernstein received word on 13 August that Karl Böhm was gravely ill, and immediately wrote to him. It is unlikely Böhm ever saw this letter as he died in Salzburg the next day, 14 August.

But you *must* recover; I know what your recuperative powers can be. You are resilience itself. I have observed it in brilliant action last January in Munich when I watched and heard your last *Entführung*. It was charming and subtle as ever, but I did notice the difficulty you were having in moving, the extra long time it took you to reach the podium, and the extra effort the singers on stage had to make in order to follow your beat, usually small, but always so clear. Backstage, in the interval, you asked me if you might attend one of my *Tristan* rehearsals for only 20 minutes – all you thought your body could bear. Remember that you stayed for all of it – all 91 minutes of Act I (in a not very well polished first run-through). Remember, if you can, that you came bounding down the aisle to my podium, when orchestra and singers had left, your eyes aflame, and your cheeks ablaze. "Na Bernstein," you said looking up (up!) at me from floor to stage, "jetztz hab' ich endlich zum ersten Mal im Leben *Tristan* gehört." You looked like a young man, burning, radiant. I was in heaven, not only because of this unbelievable *imprimatur* from the Wagnerian pope himself, but also because I was watching a mystical, quasi-Faustian rejuvenation. "Auch das Vorspiel?", I asked timorously, knowing that there was at least a five-minute difference between your timing of the Prelude and mine. "Überhaupt das Vorspiel," you answered, and began to give me an extraordinary analysis of what I had just done in terms of phrasing, tempo relationships, etc. You *taught* me, in wisdom, what I had been performing by intuition. You were a young, strong man.

You are young. Please stay so, for me, for my colleagues, for the holy art. What you have done in music has already made you immortal; does that not encourage you to remain with us, and teach us forever?

I pray for you, as does the whole world of music.

With devotion,

Bernstein

602. Leonard Bernstein to Richard Horowitz[16]
August 1981

For Dick H,

Dear friend, and cherished colleague, Dick:

Bless you for each and every stick,

---

[16] Richard Horowitz (b. 1924), American percussionist and baton maker. He joined the Metropolitan Opera Orchestra in 1946 and played with it for 66 years, retiring as principal timpanist in 2012. He made his first baton in 1964 for Karl Böhm and subsequently made batons for many of the world's leading conductors, including Riccardo Chailly, Carlos Kleiber, James Levine, Charles Mackerras, and Klaus Tennstedt, among others. In 2008 he was interviewed in *The New York Times*: "I made Bernstein's batons. He's buried with one of my batons. I think he gave them away more than anything else, gave them to his students. [...] Bernstein's, I made out of corks from Champagne bottles."

Especially these new birthday sticks
Which are delicate, strong, and *free*, and six!
 Loving thanks,
 Lenny

603. Lukas Foss to Leonard Bernstein
1 September 1981

Hi Lenny,

 Halil arrived this morn. What a moving piece. As an x-flutist (I used to play well at 15) I enjoy the flute writing, and I love the Alto Flute's role. The end reminds me of the 1st version of the *Age of Anxiety* with that reentry for one chord; here it is reentry for 2 notes. It works though and if I can't get Rampal or Galway to play it with me, I'll have my 1st flute in Milwaukee learn it (she is wonderful).

 Sometime can I hear a tape or will the record be out soon?

 Love

 Ever

 Lukas

604. David Charles Abell to Leonard Bernstein
Hotel Schweizerhof, Berlin, Germany
30 April 1982

Dear Lenny,

 I want to thank you from my heart for having made possible my debut with *Mass* in Berlin. When I stepped off the podium last night, I felt so wonderful, I could have conducted the whole piece through right there again. Had I planned it all when I was twelve years old sitting backstage at the Kennedy Center listening to *Mass*, I could not have done better than the reality. It gives me so much joy to conduct your music. I know it so well and I love it so much and believe in it and understand what it has to say – it makes me very happy that *Mass* is the first piece I have conducted professionally. I grew up with *Mass*, and I hope God will permit me to grow old and die with it too.

 There are some things about this production which would please you very much. I think that the space it is in, an enormous arena, is better for the work than an opera house. The Deutschlandhalle, however, is just *too* big.[17] I would like to see *Mass* done in a smaller arena in three-quarter round as it is here.

---

[17] Built in 1935 for the 1936 Berlin Olympic Games, the Deutschlandhalle has a seating capacity for concerts of about 10,000.

When we see each other next, I'd like to discuss this production and what should be done in the future.

Everyone here working on the show – the cast, the staff, singers, players and dancers – send their love and gratitude. It is really wonderful working with this Czech orchestra, all very fine musicians, who consider it such an honor to be invited to the West to play an American piece. They understand the music quite well and find a lot of joy in it. As with every production of *Mass* that I know, the piece has brought the cast together as a family. It is an experience which everyone comes away from a little bit changed. I am always in awe of its power.

I wish you joy with your tours and hope that you are having time to work on your new opera. I have a feeling that "Tahiti Two" is a very important work for you and for all of us who know and love you. I am looking forward to hearing it and seeing it and studying it.

I hope to see you in Milano at the end of the month. If not, until July.

Shalom,

David Abell

P.S. And the flowers! I'm having them framed – will you sign them? Thanks so much.

605. Yehudi Menuhin to Leonard Bernstein

15 Pond Square, Highgate Village, London, England

[1982]

Dear Lennie,

I asked a friend to send me a tape of your *Enigma Variations* in London recently.

I have just listened to it and it is the most moving performance of the work I have ever heard.

I just wanted you to know how much I admire your interpretation and how I felt it revered Elgar's every indication.

Love,

Yehudi

606. Leonard Bernstein to Helen Coates

19 July 1983

Dearest Helen,

I want you to have this *in writing* on your birthday, since flowers can wilt and the telephone-voice is ephemeral. This is only to say, once again and for always, this I cannot imagine my life without you, not one year of it out of the soon-to-be-three decades.[18] My admiration, gratitude and deep *respect* are matched only by the intensity of my prayers for your health and happiness.

Love,

Lenny

607. Leonard Bernstein to Stephen Sondheim
28 July 1983

Dear SS,

Saw [*Sunday in the Park with*] *George* Tues eve (but not you). It (and you) is brilliant, deeply conceived, canny, magisterial, and by far the most *personal* statement I've heard from you. Bravo.

Love,

L

608. Kristin Braly[19] to Leonard Bernstein
10 January 1984

Dear Man,

Somehow, in the midst of clicking cameras and microphone-bearing reporters, mystified onlookers and frantic volunteers, conducting students, my buzzing musician colleagues [. . .] the wires, lights, echoes and occasional blurt-ings of babies, I discovered that Leonard Bernstein was not just an image on a screen, a part of the title on a page of sheet music, a dusty recording on my shelf. What had been a name to me became a heart. His heart was in my heart, and I warmed myself by the fire of his affection. I wanted to hold him in silence. But so many needed him, his touch, his smile, that I became very small.

At home, after the concert, I found myself alone, surprised and shaken. From all those hands and faces, would he remember mine?

If only I were a cat needing a fish, how simple life would be! But here I am, traveling the human road, and needing Leonard Bernstein.

Kris Braly, viola,

Baltimore Symphony

---

[18] Bernstein's arithmetic is shaky here: he first met Helen Coates in October 1932, almost fifty-one years before writing this letter. If he was counting back to his New York Philharmonic debut, that had taken place almost forty years earlier, in November 1943. Miss Coates began working as Bernstein's secretary in 1944.

[19] Kristin Braly (b. 1948), was a violist in the Baltimore Symphony Orchestra until 2005. She wrote this letter two days after playing in the performance of Mahler's *Resurrection* Symphony given in aid of Musicians Against Nuclear Arms that Bernstein conducted in the National Cathedral in Washington, DC, with an orchestra drawn from members of the National Symphony and the Baltimore Symphony.

609. Christa Ludwig to Leonard Bernstein

Vienna, Austria

8 March 1984

Dear Lenny–Maestro,

In the last weeks I worked on the *Wunderhorn-Lieder* and found out that my voice isn't suitable any more to these songs and I don't want to be my own competition to the wonderful records we made – 18 years ago!

So, I am really very sorry, but wise enough not to sing with you in the coming summer!

I hope I am not making you and Harry [Kraut] too many problems with my cancellation, but *please* understand my point of view.

Love,

Christa

610. Mary Rodgers to Leonard Bernstein

The Watergate Hotel, Washington, D.C.

received 24 July 1984

Dearest Lennie,

The last time I had as glorious a time in DC was '57 – *West Side* – you asked me if I'd like to work on the Y[oung] P[eople's] C[oncert]s – and you've been making me happy – musically, personally, too, ever since.

With deepest love and praise and delight. *A Quiet Place* is not uncomplex but boy is it worth it. It's truly wonderful.[20]

Love you,

Mary

611. Oliver Smith to Leonard Bernstein

Box 184, Yellowgate, North Salem, NY

4 August 1984

Dearest Lenny,

It was a wonderful occasion to attend your opera *A Quiet Place* at the Kennedy Center. The work is very moving, absorbing and complex. All is held together by the wrenching beauty and intensity of the score, which as I told you at the party gave me the good "old goose pimples" of emotional involvement. I especially loved the trio at the end of Act I, and all the third act. That does not mean I did not appreciate the second act, which is full of its special delights.

---

[20] The first Washington performance of *A Quiet Place* was given at the Kennedy Center Opera House on 22 July 1984.

While melding the two operas may make for a better balanced evening, I still feel the two operas have very separate emotional values. The performances were superb and could not have been better. It was also beautifully directed and simply, but very effectively designed.

I can think of no modern opera of such intensity or in a sense generosity. By letting it all "hang out", you have bared your soul, which few modern composers are prepared to do. Thank you for your beautiful music.

I do love you.

Oliver

612. Alan Jay Lerner to Leonard Bernstein
21 Bramerton Street, London, England
16 April 1985

My dear old chum,

Bobby passed on to me your interest in trying to reshape and make something out of *1600* [*Pennsylvania Avenue*]. I gather that although there is no schedule you would like to get it done some time before the *tri*-centennial.

To get to the point: *of course* a fresh pair of eyes is needed. Even though I've had an eye implant and don't wear glasses any more (can you believe it?) I don't think this brand new one will be sufficient, and I would welcome a writer with ideas on how to reorganise and rewrite.

As far as the lyrics are concerned, I suddenly seem to have taken on a new lease of life and am scribbling away like fury. I have a musical in rehearsal here in July which John Dexter is directing,[21] and am two-thirds through the score of another that Allan Carr plans to put into rehearsal sometime in the autumn. Besides that I am just completing a huge tome for Collins on a history of the musical theatre since Offenbach. So if the right time for you should be impossible for me, and time adjustments cannot be arranged, as much as I would dislike it I would understand if you had to turn to someone else for any additional lyrics. But I truly hope that will be only the last resort. I would love to have another crack at it.

It is very interesting how *1600* started because Robby[22] remembers its inception one way and I have a clear memory of it in another. Originally I wanted to do five episodes which were critical in the history of the White House. I remember that I thought the entire production would look like a rehearsal, on the theory that democracy is still rehearsing. Robby, on the other hand, is convinced that the original intention was to write a sort of "Upstairs Downstairs"

---

[21] The stage version of *Gigi*, directed by John Dexter, opened at the Lyric Theatre, Shaftesbury Avenue, London, on 17 September 1985.
[22] Possibly Robert Whitehead, one of the producers of *1600 Pennsylvania Avenue*.

history of the White House – without the upstairs. In other words, it would be told strictly through the eyes of a multi-generational servant family. What I think we got was a mixture of both with moments of the black experience thrown in, all of which added up to a horse with three heads. I still vote for the "upstairs" story – perhaps now even more than ever because the upstairs material is fresher and we have been surfeited with the history of the blacks in America. Another reason is because I don't – and didn't – do that sort of thing very well. But, I am open to any and all approaches.

In any event, I have some two thousand books and crates of pre-play material that are finally about to be shipped over to me and I will be able to examine all those early versions.

I am, at long last, not happily married but ecstatically so to a smashing lady[23] – we've been together for five years and married for four, a track record for me. We bought a house too quickly that was and is too small, but we have finally got around to looking for a place large enough to accommodate all that I left in storage. I adore living in London and I've had the most wonderful five years of my life here. So whenever we meet – which I hope will be soon, somewhere – prepare yourself for a bubbling version of your old Virgo friend.

I hear the new *West Side Story* album is terrific. We have been in Spain for a few days on hol and this is our first day back, but I've already ordered a copy.

I think of you often. And always with love.

Aye,

Alan

613. Stephen Sondheim to Leonard Bernstein
[April 1985]

Dear Lenny,

Thanks for the album – very impressive – but I wish you'd have asked me before restoring that first (and not-my-favorite) Jets quatrain.[24]

Love,

Steve

---

[23] Liz Robertson married Alan Jay Lerner in 1981.

[24] The "Jets Quatrain" refers to the passage beginning "Oh, when the Jets fall in at the cornball dance" in the "Jet Song," included on Bernstein's recording of *West Side Story* made in September 1984. This passage is not in the first piano-vocal score, nor on the original cast recording. It is printed in the 1994 full score (pp. 43–4) and the revised 2000 piano-vocal score, marked in both editions with an optional cut.

614. Leonard Bernstein to Stephen Sondheim
25 April 1985

Dear Steve,

It's particularly hard to apologize to today's Pulitzer Winner for a bit of thoughtlessness (or perhaps it's easier: you might understandably be in a euphoric and forgiving mood). In any case, I *was* thoughtless, so carried away by the fun of presaging the Gym-swing-music that I neglected to consult you for approval. I am sorry, but also (forgive me) singing and leaping about in celebration of your new glory. And does your show deserve it![25]

Congrats
Blessings
Love
Lenny

615. Leonard Bernstein to Helen Coates
Ben-Gurion Airport, Tel Aviv, Israel
27 August 1985

Dearest Helen,

A quick note from Ben-Gurion Airport, en route to Munich & Japan and . . .

The last two nights have made concert history here (Mahler #9).[26] I don't think I've ever heard it played with quite so much passion and tenderness. The orchestra is transformed, the newspapers ecstatic. I'm enclosing the one *non-*ecstatic review, at least of *Halil*; the rest is the usual rave. I personally, on the other hand, have fallen in love all over again with *Halil*, and Ransom W[ilson] is playing it like a god.

I think of you so often, and send you love from so many friends – especially the Lishanskys, who gave me a great fish-festival dinner-party after our Haifa concert.

Keep well, and cool. I'm managing to do so, although I frankly don't understand how, given this formidable schedule of rehearsals, travel, concerts, receptions, parties, time-changes . . . But I've survived my birthday, and feel younger than ever.

A big hug & kiss,
Lenny

---

[25] *Sunday in the Park with George* won the 1985 Pulitzer Prize for Drama for Sondheim and James Lapine.
[26] The performance of Mahler's Ninth Symphony given in Tel Aviv on 25 August 1985 (Bernstein's 67th birthday) has been released on CD by Helicon Classics (HEL029656).

616. Jerome Robbins to Leonard Bernstein
9 December 1985

Lenny,

What a *good* concert![27] Especially the Copland & the last movement of it. Thank you! It was good to see you working again, and so finely. Sorry I couldn't get back stage to say hello & thanks in person.

Have a good holiday season – & all love.

Jerry

617. Leonard Bernstein to Helen Coates
19 July 1986

For HGC
[Echo from Haydn's *Creation*]

The Heavens are tellin'
The glory of Helen!
And me too, I'm yellin'
HOORAY FOR HELEN!

And *I'm* tellin' Heaven:
She's now eight-seven;
So you better keep her well 'n'
Happy! PRAISE HELEN!

All love, as always,
Lenny

---

[27] On 5, 6, and 10 December 1985, Bernstein conducted an unusual program comprising the Third Symphonies of Roy Harris, William Schuman, and Aaron Copland.

618. Yevgeny Yevtushenko[28] to Leonard Bernstein

Peredlikino, near Moscow, Russia
[?September 1986]

My dear Lenny!

I haven't seen you for ages. I send you with a kind help of Sarah Caldwell my script *The End of [the] Musketeers*. In my immodest opinion it could be very easily transformed into kind of "sparkling tragedy", full of joy and bitterness, strange mixture of French champagne with a womit [vomit]. Probably, only composer who could create music for such kind of theme are you, because you are all of my musketeers and it could be your own confession, like it was mine. Of course it needs a lot of work if you'll like it in collaboration with me and one American poet. I am waiting for your answer. I was hopelessly trying to find you in USA.

My love and respect,
Yevgeny Yevtushenko

619. Leonard Bernstein to Yevgeny Yevtushenko

"Napoli – Paris – Zurich – Jerusalem" [sent from Jerusalem]
27 September 1986

My dearest poet-friend Yevgeny,

I have just tried to telephone you to Peredelkino; I *think* I got through to someone who understood. In case not, the message was: I finished yesterday reading the *Musketeers* script. I loved it; I love you.

Further, I am moved and excited and want to work with you (and, of course, an English or American lyricist, although you are already a great lyricist).

Further: I believe this will be a great musical work – *not* an opera in an opera house, but directly for *film*. It is a natural film, "cast of thousands" as they used to say in the great old days of Eisenstein and Cecil B. de Mille – a wildly funny epic that tears out your heart even while you laugh. I don't know exactly how this film should be made, or where; perhaps it is all *animated*, like Disney cartoons, or played by robots (they make fantastic ones now in California) or eventually by *real* actors and singers, or all together. Maybe someone like Fellini should direct it; it should be a *major international project*.

What is the next step? I don't know now, but I will soon. I will be in Wien, Hotel Bristol, this next week, then back in New York on 8th October. Then I become

---

[28] Yevgeny Yevtushenko (b. 1933), Russian poet. This was a project that clearly excited Bernstein (see Letter 619), but nothing came of it. Among Yevtushenko's earlier poems, the most famous – and the one that caused controversy with the Soviet authorities – was *Babi Yar* which provided the inspiration for Shostakovich's Symphony No. 13.

composer for five months! In this period we can decide many things. Where and when can we meet? Can you call me in Vienna, or if too late, in New York?

Beginning of *big* song: music already shouting in my head!:

Live before you die!

Don't die until your death!

(in Eb)

Call me, write me, come to me, or all three . . . we have a lot of work to do, and play . . .

Much love,

Lenny

620. Sid Ramin to Leonard Bernstein
6 October 1986

Dear Lenny,

What an experience![29] The Via Dolorosa, The Masada, wading in the Dead Sea, peering into Lebanon, exploring Jerusalem, meeting new friends, hearing and seeing you conduct in Tel Aviv and Jerusalem, and so much more.

There is no way I can express my feelings towards you and to you when I think of our magnificent trip to Israel. A first visit would always be exciting but the circumstances that permitted me (and Gloria) to share with you, be part of your routine, to be included in your success and adulation, to listen to you, to learn (!) from you, and, most important, to *be* with you – is something I will never forget.

It's incredible for me to realize that we spent so much time together in Israel (and in Fairfield) and the thrill of being with you will never diminish. It seems you are a bit biased. Whatever I do, right or wrong, you always justify my mistakes or ignorance with a kindness and warm admonition that I am grateful for and love.

And so, Lenny, I thank you again for a "dream trip" and my gratitude for including me in your life knows no bounds.

Imagine, from Roxbury to Jerusalem!

Where next?

With love, from your devoted and oldest,

Sid

---

[29] In Autumn 1986, Bernstein conducted a series of concerts with the Israel Philharmonic to celebrate its fiftieth anniversary. The first performance of *Jubilee Games* was given in Avery Fisher Hall, New York, on 13 September, and Bernstein then went to Israel to conduct the work in the opening concerts of the 1986–7 season. Sid Ramin (who had helped with the orchestration of *Jubilee Games*) and his wife Gloria went with Bernstein on this trip – their first visit to Israel.

621. Sid Ramin to Leonard Bernstein

[New York, NY]
15 October 1986

Dear Lenny,

After spending so many wonderful hours with you in Israel, I thought you'd like to have something to remind you of the many wonderful hours we spent together over a half-century ago. God, that sounds ancient!

The first few letters were written in the summer of 1933, when you were in Sharon and I was at Revere.[30] Luckily you numbered your pages so that you can now better follow the order in which they were originally written.

In 1937, when you were at Harvard, I began to "seriously" study with you ... no more governing chords, finishing chords, pre-finishing chords, etc. Your notes to me show that we really started with the basics ... and we're still at it!

Now on to the next fifty!

With love as always,

Sid

622. Leonard Bernstein to Stephen Sondheim

[1986]

Sorrowful Song
Last night
I sat down and wrote a poem.

This morning
I looked at it and didn't like it much.
So I started
All over again,
Making (major and minor but) significant
Changes.

This evening
I looked again and didn't like it much better.
So I changed it back
To Version One
Which I wrote last night,
And this is it.

Love,

L

---

[30] These are Bernstein's letters to Ramin printed in Chapter I.

623. Leonard Bernstein to Harry Kraut[31]
7 April 1987

Dear Harry,

Having just finished Martin Gardner's brilliant/hateful wipe-out of occultism (in the *N.Y. Review of Books,* a propos the collected *oeuvre* of Shirley MacLaine) I find myself beset by feelings of paradox – and thinking of *you.* I guess your paradoxical duality is one of the things I most like in you (and, for that matter, in any thinking–feeling person – including myself, in those ever-decreasing moments when I like myself).

Which of us worth his salt is not a paradoxnick? There's something in the Bible we all believe, even if not literally; and there's also something in Darwin and Freud that grabs us equally. Wm. Blake vs. Martin Gardner, X vs. Y, and on down the list of all the antitheses that engender free inquiry and democracy.

I like to think of myself, and of you, as primarily rational humanists, but then, there I go inhaling cosmic energies via Aaron Stern.[32] And then, there *you* go, so movingly, pursuing your profound and loving experiment with Patrick Porter.[33] I can't tell you how touching I find it.

This is not a sketch for some future lecture, but a spontaneous love-letter on your birthday. Have a happy one and many more.

Lenny

624. Maureen Lipman[34] to Leonard Bernstein
London
[April 1987]

Dear Mr. Bernstein,

The show is off and the star is off-colour, but the memory is just the grandest. *Wonderful Town* ended in triumph, with a dynamic show, encores and bravos, a weeping star, the weeping star's children in *Wonderful Town* T-shirts, coming on stage bearing flowers – the whole audience on its feet and a mass "Conga" round the stage and auditorium.[35] The rafters sang with your wonderful music and I

---

[31] Harry Kraut (1933–2007) was Bernstein's business manager from 1971, and became a valued confidant.

[32] Aaron Stern was a close friend of Bernstein's in the 1980s. He believed that the arts could be used as a way to greater self-knowledge and cultural transformation. With Bernstein's support he established an institution, the Academy for the Love of Learning.

[33] Probably Patrick K. Porter, who founded Positive Changes in 1987 to help people bring about lifestyle changes through hypnosis and counseling.

[34] Maureen Lipman (b. 1946), English actress and writer.

[35] The London revival of *Wonderful Town* opened at the Queen's Theatre in August 1986 and ran until April 1987, with Maureen Lipman as Ruth and Emily Morgan as Eileen. She recalled the occasion of her meeting with Bernstein: "The memory lingers of our meeting: him in tan leather trousers and a bright turquoise macramé pullover, hugging me and telling me I was a wonderful Ruth

hope it continues to do so right through the next production (which should never have been allowed in!)

Looking back, we had just the best notices we could have wished for, but no advertising, no record – no hype! You can't exist without it now in the West End. We had "a perfect gem" as the *Punch* critic said – but we needed a master jeweler – Van Cleef & Arpels even! – to set us, invisibly, into the bracelet of Shaftesbury Avenue! I wish I had hot latkes [potato pancakes] for every person who came to the dressing room glowing with the pleasure of seeing a *real* show with a book, lyrics, music and a HEART. After being disappointed by the Phantom of the Chessboard school of musical theatre.

Enough. Onwards. I know you are working on a new project with Stephen Sondheim and I wish you huge success. I'm taking three months off to do a second book and I hope it will be OK to include a wonderful picture of you and I – me kissing you on the nose, taken by Christina Burton of Watford.

Meanwhile – this really is the point of this rambling missive – *Thank you*, for the privilege of your music in *Wonderful Town* and for the joy of translating it, through Ruth, for the last year. God bless and take care of you.

Love,

Maureen (Lipman)

625. Leonard Marcus[36] to Leonard Bernstein
299 Under Mountain Road, Lenox, MA
20 September 1987

Dear Lenny,

Merely a line to tell you that 1) you nearly caused me to have an accident and 2) I heard a performance of the Mahler Second that was more overwhelming than anything I remembered even you ever having done – and that goes back to my unforgettable first encounter with the work, singing it as a teenager under you at Tanglewood.

Earlier today I drove down to NYC from Lenox. When I got close enough to catch a City station worthwhile fielding, the radio was in the middle of the Mahler. Almost immediately, even with the lo-fi of car radio, I realized I was

---

and my brain saying 'take a mental picture of this moment! It'll never come again!' " (Maureen Lipman, personal communication).

[36] Leonard Marcus, a Harvard music graduate, was appointed editor-in-chief of *High Fidelity and Musical America* in 1968, a post he held until 1980. Before then he had worked in Minneapolis, had studied conducting with Bernstein and composition with Copland, and was assistant manager of the classical department of London Records from 1959 to 1961. He subsequently worked at Columbia Records and as editor of the Carnegie Hall programs. He became conductor of the Stockbridge Chamber Orchestra (later the Stockbridge Sinfonia) in 1975 and later became the orchestra's conductor emeritus.

surrounded by an extraordinary performance. By the middle of the last movement, I concluded that a new champion of the work had succeeded in snatching from you the belt reading "Most in Tune with Mahler's Soul."

I anticipated the penultimate choral chord – and what genius did it take to bring this epic to its perfect climax simply by expanding a dominant from closed to open position? – but what I heard so overpowered my expectations that I did something I haven't done in a couple of years.

I cried.

It only lasted a moment, but in that moment, I nearly swerved into another car as we came to the 59th Street exit of the West Side Highway.

You needn't worry. By 42nd Street I had already forgiven you. During the interim, Marty Bookspan had announced which Philharmonic concert had just been rebroadcast.

Does anyone realize how dangerous great music can be? I mean, Plato's dead and all that, but even he could only have had a more formal, Dionysian version of Rock in mind, and everybody knows to complain about *that*. No, I'm referring to the perils of the classics. I hope Surgeon General Koop doesn't find out.

As always, with love.

Lenny

626. Leonard Bernstein to Claudio Arrau[37]
20 December 1987

Dear Claudio,

I am at this moment remembering, with deep emotion, our Brahms D minor in 1946. It was your birthday; and besides playing like a god, you had a post-concert birthday party at your house. It was at this party that I met a ravishing girl called Felicia Montealegre, who was not only a fellow-Chilean of yours and your one-time pupil, but who also shared your birthday, *and* for three decades thereafter shared my life.

So you see, my dear Claudio, how closely intertwined our lives have been, with Music playing the rôle of Destiny. May we long continue this closeness.

A very happy birthday, and may you go from strength to strength.

Love,

Lenny[38]

---

[37] Claudio Arrau (1903–91), Chilean pianist.
[38] Written for a published tribute to Arrau on his 85th birthday on 6 February 1988.

627. Claudio Arrau to Leonard Bernstein
29 February 1988

Dear Lenny,

I cannot thank you enough for your beautiful words of good wishes on the occasion of my 85th birthday. Imagine, 85, hard to believe.

As I sat holding the Festschrift on my lap, we all remembered our dear Felicia. Your words have special meaning for us and always will.

Now that you yourself are getting to be a grand old man, don't let the thought of age bother you. It really is not so bad. Some of us get better and stronger and I hear that is what is happening to you. So God bless you because nothing is more wonderful than fulfillment in later life.

All our love.

As ever,

Claudio

628. Jerome Robbins to Leonard Bernstein
19 April 1988

Dear Lenushka,

Sorry we didn't meet yesterday. It was *Fancy Free*'s 44th birthday – and I was looking forward to giving and getting a big hug!

But, I was very happy to know you were working hard on your new piece – and I know how much that means to you, *and* all of us.

We do have some things to solve, not much, but things we can settle so we can move ahead.[39] W[est] S[ide] S[tory] is in pretty good shape as we outlined it with only one spot a bit bumpy. [*On the*] *Town* needs some talking about. I've a few ideas. So let's get it done & out of the way.

I look forward to Tuesday (and the hug) and any other time you can manage to make for us.

Love,

Jerry

629. Jerome Robbins to Leonard Bernstein
117 East 81st Street, New York, NY
10 June 1988

[Note at top:] Lenny: *First, play the tape!* Then read this.

---

[39] For the forthcoming *Jerome Robbins' Broadway*.

Dear Lenny,

Here's a tape of the *On the Town* Ballet such as we have put together musically and I have choreographed. It combines the elements we talked about and where I had some problems we made some temporary fill-ins and adjustments. I know there will be places which you think are over-extended musically, such as in the Penny Arcade and in the Dance Hall section which follows it, but they don't seem over-extended when you watch it with dancing. However, I'm certainly looking forward to your reactions and help.[40]

Scott, the pianist, did a wonderful job and I like the total buoyancy of the piece. It still is episodic which curtails a dynamic flow-through feeling. But, I like the little reprise of the fugato leading back into the finale material very much. I know you will love what I have choreographed for the fugato and the music that comes after it. It's all joyous and now that I've completed sketching it, I'll do better by it when I get back to it. But I'm most anxious to get your reaction.

Sorry I can't be there to dance it for you. You know how much respect I have for the music and anything we have to add has been an imperative necessity to make the logic and the story work out.

So how are you? I miss you and hope you're not too tired and that the tour has been wonderful. I cannot come to Chicago but I hope to see you on the 26th of June.

I send you a big hug and await your response.

Love,

Jerry

P.S. I've started finding out about the *Dance in America* tape rights. Of course if I can manage to help, I will.

630. Miles Davis[41] to Leonard Bernstein

c/o Shukat & Hafer, 111 West 57th Street, New York, NY

28 June 1988

Dear Leonard,

Having received the Son[n]ing Award in Copenhagen which only Isaac Stern, Stravinsky, you and I have received[42] I am reminded of what an honor it is to be in your and their company.

---

[40] Like Robbins' letter of 19 April, this concerns the preparations for *Jerome Robbins' Broadway* which opened in February 1989. The show included sequences from *On the Town* and *West Side Story*, and early versions of the extracts from *On the Town* were filmed at piano rehearsals in April and May 1988. This, or something very similar, must be the tape that Robbins describes (copies of these rehearsal tapes are in the New York Public Library of the Performing Arts).

[41] Miles Davis (1926–91), jazz musician.

[42] The Léonie Sonning Music Prize is Denmark's highest musical honour. The first recipient, in 1959, was Stravinsky, and the second was Bernstein (1965). Other winners included Lutosławski

I also think about the time when my wife,[43] who was the lead dancer in *West Side Story*, said to me: "Leonard wants you to think about playing this music", and I replied "how am I going to play this corny shit". Needless to say it turned out to be a classic.

You are one of America's true geniuses along with [Thelonius] Monk, [Dizzy] Gillespie, [Charles] Mingus and [Charlie] Parker. You are a true musician and if you chose to be you could be a great pianist in addition to being a great composer and conductor.

On this your 70th birthday, I wish you all the best and wish you many more productive years in pleasing the world with your music.

Sincerely yours,

Miles Davis

631. Gerald Levinson[44] to Leonard Bernstein
Swarthmore College, Swarthmore, PA
9 July 1988

Dear Mr. Bernstein,

I send greetings and wishes for much nachas, as well as "harmony and grace," on your birthday. After having made so much great music as composer, conductor, and teacher over the past seven decades, I'm sure you won't be content to rest on your laurels now.

I'll always be grateful for the Leonard Bernstein Fellowship that allowed me to spend an inspiring summer at Tanglewood in '71 – not least for the unforgettable *Missa Solemnis* you conducted that season. Hanging around the B.S.O. all summer certainly contributed to my appetite for the big orchestra, of which you've heard some of the fruits. And fellow TMC Fellows of the time are now friends and colleagues. The ties that keep bringing me back to that wonderful place formed then and keep growing.

(1967), Britten (1968), Shostakovich (1973), Messiaen (1977), Stern (1982), Boulez (1985), and Miles Davis himself (1984).

[43] Frances Elizabeth Taylor married Miles Davis in 1958; they divorced in 1968. In the original production of *West Side Story* she played Francisca (credited as Elizabeth Taylor).

[44] Gerald Levinson (b. 1951), American composer, a pupil of George Crumb, George Rochberg, and Olivier Messiaen. Levinson met Bernstein on a few occasions, notably at Tanglewood in 1987 when Levinson's first symphony, *Anāhata*, was performed. Levinson recalls: "In '87 when Oliver Knussen conducted a spectacular orchestra concert which concluded with my *Anāhata* (and included Peter Serkin playing Stravinsky's *Movements*), Lenny and Seiji Ozawa followed my piece with the score, and both – but Lenny in particular – were very enthusiastic. Backstage afterward he said it brought him to tears ('That bad, eh?' I stupidly responded). I asked if he'd like to keep the score (my publisher, standing beside me, nodded vigorously); he said, 'I don't think I'd ever conduct it, but I'd love to possess it' " (Gerald Levinson, personal communication, 23 March 2013).

Finally, here's a coded message for your seventieth. A key is included for the lower stave;[45] you're on your own for the upper stave.

Many happy returns – from Ari, too.

Jerry Levinson

---

[45] The lower stave is written using Messiaen's *langage communicable*, an alphabetical code for musical spelling (the decoded message is "Mazel Tov and Gesundheit on your Seventieth"). The upper stave includes a Bernstein-ish version of "Happy Birthday," followed by references to several Bernstein tunes, described by Levinson as follows: "Once Happy Birthday is done it keeps on going through a medley of bits of Bernstein tunes: 'Maria,' 'New York New York,' and 'Trouble in Tahiti.' And the durations of the rests, carefully counted out in numbers in parentheses, add up to 70" (Gerald Levinson, personal communication, 23 March 2013).

632. Ronald Reagan[46] to Leonard Bernstein
The White House, Washington, D.C.
5 August 1988

Dear Mr. Bernstein,

Nancy and I are delighted to join with your many friends and admirers gathered in Tanglewood to extend warmest congratulations to you on your 70th birthday.

Your remarkable career as a conductor, pianist, and composer has greatly enriched American culture. Your memorable compositions during a long and prolific career have captured the hearts and dreams of generations of your countrymen.

From *West Side Story* to *On the Waterfront*, your music has cheered us, thrilled us, rallied us, and gladdened us. Today, we salute you for your rare gift for music and your outstanding contribution to the artistic life of our Nation.

Happy Birthday and God bless you.

Sincerely,

Ronald Reagan

633. Leonard Bernstein to David Diamond
[postmark Stamford, CT]
8 August 1988

Dear DD,

Thank you for the birthday wishes, but how dare you talk of no communication from me when the last I've seen or heard from you was after I'd lost five years of my life learning & teaching & performing your 9th Symphony and you walked off with your 75,000 bucks and little or no thanks and remained unheard from except via certain people who read your weighty input to a Peyser book which I have promised my children on my honor never to read.

... and I think that after decades of saving you from suicide, mental collapse, poverty, public fantasizing, and generally spoiling other people's lives you may owe me a bit more than a green, posterity-oriented birthday greeting, but never mind ...

---

[46] Ronald Reagan (1911–2004), fortieth President of the United States. Reagan was not known for his interest in music, and his conservative political outlook was diametrically opposed to Bernstein's. One of Bernstein's kinder assessments of Reagan's presidency is to be found in his November 1989 interview with Jonathan Cott: "The last time I went to the White House was during the last days of Jimmy Carter's administration. [...] I love the White House more than any other house in the world – after all, I'm a musician and a citizen of my country – but since 1980 I haven't gone back there because it's had such sloppy housekeepers and caretakers. [...] We had eight lovely, passive, on-our-backs, status quo, don't-make-waves years with Ronald Reagan. The *fights* I had with my mother! 'Don't you dare say a word against our president!' she'd say to me." (Cott 2013, pp. 81, 82, and 83).

... (as always, ungenerous to my colleagues)

Goodbye & good luck.

L[47]

634. Claudio Arrau to Leonard Bernstein

18 August 1988

Dear Lenny,

I salute you on the wonderful occasion of your 70th birthday and wish you many more years of success, happiness and fulfillment.

I cannot believe that so many years have gone by since we first met and first performed together and Ruth and I introduced you to Felicia, your beautiful bride to be. Then, I felt like an older brother full of admiration for your God-gifts. Today, I feel more like a loving uncle delighting in your enormous growth and achievements. May the gods continue to carry you to the ultimate portals of your deepest hopes and wishes.

Yours ever,

Claudio

635. Frank Sinatra to Leonard Bernstein

[Reno, NV]

25 August 1988

Dear Genius,

Happy Birthday!

You are one of the few who deserves everything warm and wonderful that will be said about you on this marvelous occasion of reaching what Abe Lincoln would have called 3 score and ten.

And I think it's sensational this big bash in your honor is being held at your beloved Tanglewood in the shade of the Boston Symphony Orchestra.

Be assured, Lenny, that between songs here in Reno, where I am performing tonight, I raise a toast in your honor, in gratitude for all you have done for the musical world which bows towards you in appreciation this day, and for all you

---

[47] The real source of Bernstein's rage was almost certainly Diamond's contribution to Joan Peyser's book, in which, among other things, he was quoted as saying that Bernstein "often hurt him very much." Diamond replied to Bernstein's furious letter on 26 August 1988 with a long, 12-page diatribe in which he challenged Bernstein's claims, made some harsh comments about the effect of fame on his old friend, defended his own cooperation with Peyser, and ended with a plea: "Lenny – don't make our friendship a poisoned one. Make it instead as rich as it once was. Take me out of this horrible depression your letter has caused me. No matter what I will be at your concerts this fall." After returning from concerts in Europe, Bernstein replied on 24 October (see Letter 637). But it was too late: after almost fifty years, their friendship was over.

have done for the personal world I alone inhabit and which is a far better place because of your friendship, which I will always cherish.

Happy Birthday, young man. I can hardly wait for your next seventy.

Warmest hugs,

Francis Albert

636. David Del Tredici[48] to Leonard Bernstein

1 September 1988

Dear Lenny,

Among all the wonderful things, I was most moved by *Mass*.[49] It is way out there (a place I, too, inhabit), takes every kind of chance, and succeeds wonderfully. The pacing of the whole musical, dramatic unfolding is so skilful!

Thoughts of the moment and thanks for the never-to-be-forgotten music.

David

P.S. Look forward too, to Fall![50]

637. Leonard Bernstein to David Diamond

[postmark New York, NY]

24 October 1988

Dear old Dovidl,

I've just returned from Europe and discovered your letter of two months ago. I don't want to discuss details, but I do want to say that I'm sorry I wrote you in the way I did. I should never have sent that letter in such a burst of anger (I can't remember ever having written such a letter to anyone, and besides, the anger was probably related to something else and only triggered by you).

So, I'm sorry; but I must say I meant every word of it.

Shalom uv'rachah [peace and blessings to you]

Lenny[51]

---

[48] David Del Tredici (b. 1937), American composer.

[49] *Mass* was performed at Tanglewood on 27 August 1988 by the Opera Theater of the Indiana School of Music to celebrate Bernstein's 70th birthday.

[50] When Bernstein was to conduct Del Tredici's *Tattoo*.

[51] This is the last letter Bernstein wrote to Diamond. See note 47 to Bernstein's letter (Letter 633) of 8 August 1988.

638. David Del Tredici to Leonard Bernstein

28 November [1988]

Lenny,

You were every bit as terrific as I thought you'd be. *Tattoo*[52] came to life like I'd dreamed and in 4 different ways, too. I love your Rubens, Van Gogh, Vermeer, Rembrandt versions of the piece!

And most of all I love you.

All my gratitude, love, and envy.

David

639. Leonard Bernstein to Charles Harmon[53]

[New York, NY, with hand-drawn postage stamp "Namibia State Prison"]
"New Year's", 1989

Dear Lito,

Overleaf, behold my refuge from ragweed,[54] 1941, and the garret where I wrote my Clarinet Sonata, and started a ballet called *Conch Town* (bits to be found in *Fancy Free*, all the shows, including the whole tune of "America" in *West Side*). The house was dark brown then, and all I could afford.[55]

Love,

LB

---

[52] Bernstein conducted the US premiere of *Tattoo* with the New York Philharmonic at concerts on 17, 18, 19, and 22 November 1988.

[53] Charles (Charlie) Harmon joined Amberson (Bernstein's publishing company) as his personal assistant in 1982. After Bernstein's death, Harmon contacted many of the people who had been close to Bernstein, requesting photocopies of letters. These are an invaluable addition to the Leonard Bernstein Collection in the Library of Congress. Harmon also edited several Bernstein works for publication, including the full orchestral scores of *West Side Story* and *Candide*, and the definitive piano-vocal scores of *On The Town* and *Wonderful Town*.

[54] Bernstein suffered from acute hay-fever all his life.

[55] Written on a postcard on the verso of which is a picture of the house in Key West, Florida, where Bernstein stayed in the summer of 1941. An arrow points to the right-hand window on the top floor and reads "This was my first abode. Cattie room in KW, 1941." Another postcard from Bernstein to Charles Harmon (undated, but with the same image of the house in Key West, with an arrow pointing to the same top-floor window) reads: "This room is where I worked on my Clarinet Sonata, late *August '41*, when I was fleeing from Ragweed & total hayfever (2 nights & days by train from Boston). LB. P.S. The house was then a drab dark grey-brown."

640. Stephen Sondheim to Leonard Bernstein
22 March 1989

Dear Lenny,

Thanks for the telegram, and for the quick glimpses of your face on Sunday night's broadcast when you were listening to the song.[56] I empathized with your apprehension at the start of it and was therefore doubly pleased at your relief when you realized that it was going to be affectionate (as well as brilliant, of course).

As you may have gathered, I called you when you were on vacation – it was just to give a nostalgic Christmas hello. I was about to do so again two weeks ago but Harry [Kraut] said you were in the slough of despond and it was not a good time. I'll try again. It would be nice to see you. Or at least talk.

Love,

Steve

641. Leonard Bernstein to Marin Alsop[57]
20 August 1989

My Marvelous Marin,

The bronchitis has finally felled me, and I've cancelled everything for this Sunday (a *necessary* Sabbath!) Forgive me, and do understand that I'm with you, every 16th-note.

Be glorious.

Love

LB

642. Leonard Bernstein to Doriot Anthony Dwyer
20 August 1989

Dear Darling Doriot,

Forgive & forget! I am in temporary collapse, abed, and have cancelled all activities for the day (including my own kiddies' concert) so that I can do this coming week with full powers. I know you'll understand.

---

[56] Sondheim's reference to "the song" concerns his affectionate spoof "The Saga of Lenny" (based on the "Saga of Jenny" by Kurt Weill and Ira Gershwin) written for Bernstein's 70th birthday gala concert at Tanglewood in August 1988, when it was sung by Lauren Bacall. This was broadcast in the *Great Performances* series on 19 March 1989, the Sunday night mentioned by Sondheim.

[57] Marin Alsop (b. 1956), American conductor, who became Music Director of the Baltimore Symphony Orchestra in 2007. As an undergrautate at Yale, she played with Steve Reich and Philip Glass, developing a passionate interest in new music. A decade earlier, when she was nine years old, Alsop's father had taken her to one of Bernstein's *Young People's Concerts*: "I immediately knew that I wanted to become a conductor. Becoming his student at Tanglewood in 1988 was a dream come true. To have a hero exceed my expectations was too much to hope for, but Leonard Bernstein certainly did that and more. I loved being around him, soaking in his way of looking at the world and connecting the dots in life. His encouragement and support were invaluable on every level" (interview for National Public Radio, 12 October 2012).

Have a great party – and I do so look forward to our Shosty!
Love,
Lenny

643. Yo-Yo Ma to Leonard Bernstein
[No place]
31 October 1989

Dear Mr. Bernstein,

It was so wonderful to have the chance to see you in New York last week. Thank you for your time and for the lunch. My only regret is that I did not get to see the letters that you received from Boris Pasternak with his comments on the meaning of art.

I am very excited that you are willing to write a trio for Mr. Stern, Manny [Emanuel Ax], and me; I can't tell you what a thrill it is. Although you must hear this from so many people, I would just like to add that those of us who have the privilege of coming in contact with you do feel truly blessed.

Warmest wishes,

Yo-Yo Ma

644. Carlos Kleiber[58] to Leonard Bernstein
The Carlyle, New York, NY
[October 1989]

Dear Maestro, Dear Lennie!

"Non per me, ma per altri", "che voi dire, per altri"?[59] It's my son: he has become a fan of yours. (This is an understatement.) He is working at Unitel in Munich, translating your Salzau *Romeo und Julia* tapes–commentaries into German. He "schwärms" about you on the phone and I hear about Romeo sitting in the garden, the triangle that shouldn't sound like a doorbell – in short (he is 24) you seem to have revived his interest in music (something I haven't managed to do) and he is pestering me for the following:

Here is a CD of *West Side Story*. Do you by any means think it *possible* for you to sign the first CD of the set (on the label-side with an indelible thingamajig) with a "dedication" to *Marko* (with a K) *Kleiber*? and leave it (have it left) at the Met or the Carlyle?[60]

---

[58] Carlos Kleiber (1930–2004), conductor. Famously elusive, his performances were legendary for their unique combination of blazing intensity and attention to detail.

[59] This near-quotation comes – aptly enough – from Act II scene 6 of Verdi's *Don Carlos*.

[60] This letter was probably written while Carlos Kleiber was in New York to conduct Franco Zeffirelli's production of *La Traviata* at the Metropolitan Opera.

This would make him the happiest person in the world, renew his respect for me (cause I know you personally) and generally improve the morale all round.

Kindest greetings and best wishes from your old

Carlos

645. Stephen Sondheim to Leonard Bernstein
6 November 1989

Dear Lenny,

I was playing over my "Anniversary"[61] and noticed an error, which you might want to correct in future (let's hope) editions: namely: in the third bar of the fifth system, the soprano note on the second beat should be a G, not an A. And why did you change the final cadence from a G major chord to an E major chord? Is there a runic significance I missed?[62]

Love,

Steve

646. Lukas Foss to Leonard Bernstein
19 November 1989

Hi Lenny,

Must write to you because these San Francisco Symphony days you are *with* me: 2nd half of program: "Masque"[63] and [*On the*] *Waterfront*. 4 evenings in a row at Davies Hall. It's great. 1st half is [Copland's] *Billy the Kid* and *Time Cycle*.[64] Practicising "Masque" again is always a revelation; every note so right, so inventive (what I used to love in Stravinsky). Have to practice a lot to get my fingers to do it and my brain to memorize it all, but it worked. 2 evenings behind me, 2 more to go.

---

[61] The third of Bernstein's *Thirteen Anniversaries*, published in 1989, is "For Stephen Sondheim (b. March 22, 1930)" dated at the end of the piece "20 March 1965".

[62] Bernstein's annotations on this letter include "Right?" beside the "G, not an A" (it is corrected to G in the 1990 revised edition); Bernstein has written "Beats me" next to Sondheim's question about "runic significance" of the final cadence that ends in D major in the 1990 edition.

[63] "Masque" is the Scherzo from *The Age of Anxiety* Symphony, a movement described by Bernstein in 1949 as "a kind of fantastic piano-jazz [. . .], by turns nervous, sentimental, self-satisfied, vociferous." Foss specialized in playing the solo piano part of *The Age of Anxiety*: he was the soloist in the first New York performance (26 February 1950; see Letter 295), and he recorded it twice with Bernstein conducting (in 1950 and 1977).

[64] Foss composed *Time Cycle* (for soprano and orchestra) in 1959–60. The first performances were given on 20, 21, and 23 October 1960 by Adele Addison with the New York Philharmonic conducted by Bernstein.

Doing *Waterfront* without cuts (there is a cut suggested in print[ed score] from 32 to 33 which I really thinks makes for a lot less drama). Enough! Don't want to bore you.

Hope you are doing what I *should* be doing – composing.

Love,

Lukas

647. Stephen Sondheim to Leonard Bernstein
20 December 1989

Dear Lenny,

What a terrific letter – thank you! You'll be interested to know that the rhyme you particularly liked ("He goes . . ., etc.")[65] was the rhyme that Cole Porter liked when Jule [Styne] and I played a few songs for him. I always detected his influence on your work.

And thanks for the advance birthday present. It's indeed tempting to set – maybe for your 75th. I'm still a slow writer.

If you have the time and inclination when you get back from tanning your-self, give me a call and let's have our semi-annual evening alone.*

Love,

Steve

*I'll even play you the new score[66] SS

648. Marin Alsop to Leonard Bernstein
14 July 1990

Dearest Maestro,

I wanted to telephone you, but didn't want to disturb your rest.

Thank you for introducing me to Japan – and vice versa!

The greatest enticement (if it can be called that) to come on this trip was the opportunity to work with you once again.[67]

---

[65] A reference to lyrics from *Gypsy*:

Wherever I go, I know he goes
Wherever I go, I know she goes
No fits, no fights, no feuds and no egos
Amigos
Together!

[66] The "new score" was *Assassins*, which opened Off-Broadway at Playwrights Horizons on 18 December 1990. It includes a crazed and darkly amusing monologue addressed to Leonard Bernstein by Samuel Byck (1930–74), a psychopath who attempted to hijack a plane in order to crash it into the White House and kill President Richard Nixon.

[67] In June 1990, Marin Alsop traveled with Bernstein to the Pacific Music Festival in Sapporo, Japan.

And, once again, it was an inspiration. You haven't ever let me down since I first wanted to become a conductor when I was 11 and saw one of your NY Phil concerts! But more than that, you've been a constant source of energy and integrity and leadership and innovation to our world.

I hope only that I can make a small contribution and always make you proud of me.

I love you – and thank you for helping *all* of us.

Marin

649. Jennie Bernstein to Leonard Bernstein
5 September 1990

Dearest Son,

I have confidence in you, that you are on the right track. I know you are watching out for yourself. No one can do it for you, but you and you alone.

I feel a lot better now because I am looking towards your quick recovery. As you know dear, if you stay well, I will stay well.[68] You are surrounded by a beautiful family, your children and grandchildren. That in itself should be good medicine for you.

Looking forward to a Happy (Jewish) New Year for you, and your dear family.

I want to wish you happy composing and so much love.

Your one and only

Mother xxx

650. Georg Solti to Leonard Bernstein
Chicago Symphony Orchestra, 220 South Michigan Avenue, Chicago, IL
10 October 1990

My dear Lenny,

I was more than sorry to learn of the announcement you have made yesterday and I would just like to send these few lines, to let you have my warmest thoughts and support, both now and in the future.

It is wonderful that you will continue to write and teach; do keep in touch and let me know if we can meet when I am in New York next, in April.[69]

As ever,

Georg

---

[68] Jennie Bernstein outlived Leonard. She died in December 1992 at the age of 94.
[69] This letter was written a few days before Leonard Bernstein's death on 14 October 1990.

Appendix One

Arthur Laurents (with Leonard Bernstein): Outline for *Romeo* sent to Jerome Robbins

[New York, undated, shortly before 18 October 1955]

ROMEO

Act One
Scene One: Back Alley – Nightfall.
Against music, we see two or three shadowy figures beating up a boy. A lookout signals, the assailants flee. Their clothes are different from the "cool" outfits of the boys who stroll on: Mercutio and members of his gang including Romeo and Benvolio. Their exaggerated talk is interrupted by the discovery of a kid who was beaten up: A-rab. Baby, the youngest member of the gang, is shocked by what has been done to A-rab and by the "Puerto Rican mark" left on him. The others are enraged, want to have a rumble with the Puerto Rican gang because there have been too many of these raids (by both sides). It is up to Mercutio to decide – and he does in a "Let's Have A Rumble" song with the gang. During this, the formalized ritual of sending scouts to summon the PR gang leader, Bernardo, to a War Council is done. Benvolio, the best fighter, is to be one scout. Romeo – much to Mercutio's pleasure for M is Romeo's protector and Romeo doesn't partake too much of gang activities – volunteers to be the second scout. But Romeo's real reason is to see Rosalind who loves dancing and will probably be at the Crystal Cave, the dancehall where Bernardo is and which is neutral territory. The "Rumble" song comes back as the scouts start off on their mission.

Scene Two: Crystal Cave – Later.
A wild mambo is in progress with the kids doing all the violent improvisation of jitterbugging. Benvolio and Romeo enter, searching for Bernardo. Benny (Benvolio) has to keep Romeo's mind on their mission, for the latter thinks only of Rosalind who snubs R as she whirls by. They find Bernardo and start negotiations. Romeo keeps looking around for Rosalind. (All this in pantomime.) Then

Romeo sees a lovely young girl, dressed more simply, more innocently than the others; obviously a newcomer being shown around by an older, more experienced girl: Juliet and Anita. Romeo goes to Juliet and, as they meet, the music goes into half-time, the dancers keep going but as in a dream state, the lights change. Now there is dialogue – between the two. It is finally interrupted by Bernardo who pulls Juliet away. The music goes back to tempo and the number finishes and the lights go back to normal. Bernardo is Juliet's brother and Romeo's opponent. Thus, the two lovers learn, to their mutual dismay, that they belong to opposing factions. Benny takes Romeo off to report the results of their meeting with Bernardo to Mercutio; and Bernardo, despite the pleading of Anita, sends Juliet home with one of his Lieutenants as escort.

Scene Three: Gang Hangout – Later.
A shack of some sort, depending on the designer. Mercutio and the gang are horsing around when Benny and Romeo enter, to report. Romeo, his mind on Juliet, gets the facts wrong so Benny takes over: War Chieftains from the two gangs (Mercutio and Bernardo and aides) are to meet in Doc's Drugstore at midnight. Then Mercutio, in song, proceeds to give Romeo some advice about love: the older bon vivant (probably just old enough to vote if that) to the neophyte. The gang joins in a razzing, possibly they chase Romeo – who tries to duck them – in a number which overflows out of the set. And at the end, he does elude them.

Scene Four: Tenement – Later.
This is in the Puerto Rican area and shows the scrabbly building Juliet lives in, with a fire escape. Puerto Rican music from the unseen interior of the flat as Romeo moves in the shadows looking for her house. Then she comes out on the fire escape and the "balcony" scene begins. This should go from dialogue to song and back, ending in song. In it, these facts: Romeo works for Doc as drugstore delivery boy and general helper; Juliet sews in the bridal shop and has not been long in this country (let us take the dramatic license of eliminating all accents) and Anita is her confidante and adviser. Plus, of course, R and J's mutual lack of caring about prejudice, gangs, hostility, etc. It might end with "Good night" and "Buenos noches", the latter repeated lovingly by Romeo.

Scene Five: Street or outside Crystal Cave.
Bernardo taking his girl, Anita, home, before he goes to the Rumble meeting. Various points can come up here: Bernardo's hatred of the "American" gang and thus his hate for Romeo as beau for his sister (as opposed to Anita's feeling that love is love and it all ends anyway); note of future disaster, heightened by Anita's plea to B not to get into bloody rumble. She is probably a little older than Bernardo and tho she has been kicked by love before, is still in love with Bernardo – but

expects the worst. Her attitude is explained in a torch version of Mercutio's song after Bernardo has gone off to the rumble.

Scene Six: Drugstore – Midnight.
Mercutio and his aides impatiently awaiting Bernardo. Doc (possibly a Jew) tries vainly to stop the coming rumble. Here the violence, restlessness, lost feeling of these strange kids should be explored. The bursting inside then which needs a release should build and build until it explodes into a violent cold jitterbug number kicked off by a record on the jukebox. First the boys dance by themselves. But, as the set should show both inside and outside the drugstore, as gang girls come along the street, they grab them as partners, though still maintaining that frozen-faced solo quality such jitterbugging has. At the peak, Bernardo and aides enter; the dance continues to its finish, though the attitude of Mercutio and his gang changes subtly. They are aware of Bernardo but will not, deliberately, stop for him. At the conclusion, silence: the girls go, the boys line up in formalized gang positions. Mercutio, as "host", offers cokes; negotiations on the rumble begin. Time: sundown; place: Central Park. But the type of rumble is argued over as Romeo – who has arrived with a happy "Buenos noches" – argues for the simplest and least bloody kind: a "fair fight" between the two best fighters from each side. Romeo, who seems to have grown, to have become stronger as a result of his love, manages to prevail. Partly because, however, of Mercutio's fondness for him and happiness that Romeo is finally interested in the gang. Bernardo wants to fight Romeo at the rumble but Benny is the best fighter for Mercutio's gang. At this point, Shrank the policeman enters. He is suspicious because the boys are so quiet: he is their common enemy and this is the one time all are allied against the same thing. He suspects they are planning a rumble. No one says a word but Shrank, starting quietly, builds himself up to a frustrated frenzy which makes him throw everybody out of the store except Romeo since he works for Doc. Shrank makes a crack against both sides and goes. Romeo and Doc are alone. There must be some sharp note to underline the prejudice that stands between Romeo and Juliet, then Doc goes (his closeness to Romeo must emerge here, too) leaving Romeo to close up, turn out the lights as he sings softly of his love.

Act Two
Scene One: The Neighbourhood.
This is a musical quintet which covers various parts of the neighbourhood in space and the whole day in time. Its theme is "Can't Wait for The Night"; its mood is impatience of different kinds, exemplified by five of the principals: Mercutio (with humor) and Bernardo (with anger) can't wait for the rumble; Romeo can't wait to see Juliet; Juliet, at her bridal shop sewing machine, can't wait to see Romeo. Only Anita strikes a different note: she is afraid of the night because of what the rumble may bring. It should end with Juliet and thus go directly into:

Scene Two: The Bridal Shop – Late Afternoon.
Everyone has gone except Juliet who has pretended she has to finish up a wedding veil needed for the next morning. Romeo comes in and they arrange the mannequins as a bridal party, almost like children playing a game, and marry themselves. Here again, dialogue goes in and out of song. The entrance to the shop is at the rear of the stage and as they leave at the end, the curtain closes for:

Scene Three: Outside the Park.
Bernardo and his aides come from one side and, after a moment, Juliet and Romeo from the other. Bernardo is furious that his sister is with a member of the other gang. He wants to provoke a fight but Romeo won't be provoked and Juliet becomes surprisingly strong. Romeo is going to take her home and no one is going to stop that – and no one does. Alone with his aides, Bernardo says the hell with a fair fight: get ready for a real rumble.

Scene Four: Central Park – Sundown.
Mercutio and his gang are waiting for Bernardo and his. They, too, are actually prepared in the event that the "fair fight" should bust into a bloody rumble. Romeo enters on this and tries to talk them out of it. Bernardo and gang arrive. Romeo tries to prevent any rumble. Bernardo accuses him of stalling and really tries to make Romeo fight, finally spitting at him. Romeo almost lunges, but won't fight. This enrages Mercutio who slams Romeo out of the way, leaps at Bernardo and the fight is on. The scene is probably underscored and, here, breaks out into a stylized gang canon as both gangs take up positions for the fight. It does break out into a fracas when Bernardo, almost beaten, whips out a knife and stabs Mercutio. Romeo, horrified at what has been done to his protector, grabs a broken bottle from A-rab and plunges it into Bernardo. There is a wild moment of melée – then everybody clears because of the two still bodies on the ground. Both Bernardo and Mercutio are dead. This is horrifying even to the kids. A clock begins to chime as they slowly leave the scene. Romeo stares at the bodies. A police whistle, a siren, the roving light of a police car picks over the ground; the whistles, the sirens louder, music – the chase is on and Romeo runs as:

CURTAIN.

Act Three
Scene One: Juliet's Apartment – Sundown.
This is a very crowded place: room made into rooms for all purposes: a curtained corner for Juliet who is dressing up happily as her family sings a gay street song in Spanish (mother, father, uncle). During this, the clock strikes the same hour as in the previous scene. And, after a time, faint police whistles, sirens. But the song goes gaily on until Shrank comes in. Juliet's family's English is too poor to

understand what he says, so she must translate the terrible news: their son has been murdered by Romeo. Shrank goes, and the family goes to claim the body. Juliet starts to go with them when Romeo appears on the fire escape which is right outside her little corner. His one drive has been to find her and tell her it was a horrible mistake. But her first reaction is: you killed my brother. He tries to explain but there is a police whistle and shouts: they are after him. Juliet doesn't call to the police. She stands, confused, as Romeo whispers "meet me at the hangout" and disappears. As he goes, Anita comes into the flat and sees him. She would call the police but Juliet stops her. Anita's attitude has changed. Bitter, angry over the death of her lover, Bernardo, she tells Juliet to stick to "your own kind". This is a duet for both girls. But Juliet's confusion resolves itself during the duet: Romeo is her own kind, for she loves him. And at the end, she starts down the fire escape to meet him. Immediately the apartment moves off (as it did in the balcony scene) and three other fire escapes appear behind it for:

Scene Two: Love Ballet.
As Juliet shins down the fire escape, other girls wind down the other fire escapes, all going to meet lovers representing Romeo. The dance goes from forgiveness to love to passion to actual sex. It ends with:

Scene Three: The Hangout.
Romeo and Juliet are in the positions the dancers were at the end. Romeo sings a happy song to Juliet about what their world will be and, in dialogue, they agree to run away together and be safe with each other. This dream-plan is broken by the arrival of Benny. The police have found out where the hangout is (the gang is constantly moving from one shack to another) and are on their way. Benny is furious with Juliet: a lousy Puerto Rican, in his mind, has prevented Romeo from making a safe getaway. Romeo kicks him out, tells Juliet Doc will know where to find him and runs.

Scene Four: Streets.
Romeo running from the police who fire at him and wound him. He escapes.

Scene Five: The Drugstore.
The same jitterbugging tune is being played in a muted way and the gang is going thru the motions of dancing to avert suspicion from the police. Doc comes up from the cellar to get more bandages and medicine. Romeo is down there: he has been hit badly. Doc goes down again and the gang vents its bitterness against Puerto Ricans, now specifically for murdering their leader and for causing one of their good men to be shot by the police. Juliet comes in, seeking Doc, and all the hatred is turned against her. The kids tell her Romeo is dead and jeer at her extreme reaction. She almost faints and instead of offering her water etc., they

hideously offer her all kinds of poison so she can kill herself for love and pay for the evil she has done. This is done with macabre humor. All their prejudice and hate and violence comes out in the taunting until, able to bear no more, she grabs the bottle Benny holds and runs out of the store. Doc returns to see her run out. He doesn't know what the gang has done but realizes they have driven her away. He tells them off for what they really are – and yet winds himself down because, somehow, what they are is not their fault. He goes to tell Romeo and the kids' reaction is: all that because of a dirty Puerto Rican.

Scene Six: The Bridal Shop.
This scene is almost completely in song. Juliet has put on the wedding veil, is arranging the mannequins as she sings. Her strangeness is explained by the empty bottle of poison which she addresses for a moment. She is becoming more and more delirious when Romeo comes in. He is very weak but so happy to see her. She is so happy to see him: in her delirium, she thinks they are at least in their own world which has been transported to heaven. He doesn't realize at first that she has taken poison. But when he does discover the truth, it is too late. She sinks to the floor, he cradles her in his arms, they both start a reprise of their balcony song but they never quite finish. The lights change, the walls disappear, the music soars upward and the audience swoons.

THE END

Appendix Two

Bernstein's Letters and Postcards to Mildred Spiegel

In December 1991, Mildred Zucker (formerly Mildred Spiegel) sent details to the Leonard Bernstein Office of all the letters and postcards she had received from Bernstein. Her annotated list was divided into two sections ("Contents of Letters" and "Contents of L.B. Post Cards"). The following includes the most significant items, which have been amalgamated into a single chronological sequence.

The additional indented comments are taken from a long letter of 23 July 1978 that Mildred Zucker wrote to Jack Gottlieb, full of information ("I have been continuing my homework about Lenny and came across a few more facts"), and ending as follows: "I consider it a great privilege to have been a close friend of Lenny's. It was thrilling for me to watch him grow and reach such great heights. Lenny was and still is a great source of inspiration to me. Give him our love."

29 December 1935, Boston, MA: Lenny asked me to turn his pages at a lecture.
2 January 1936, New York, NY: Has a lot to tell me. Reminds me to turn his pages.
24 June 1936, Philadelphia, PA: Description of Curtis Institute audition/judges' reaction. They thought he should be at Curtis.
29 June 1936, Philadelphia, PA: Attended Robin Hood Dell concert – writes his reaction upon hearing *Romeo and Juliet* Overture of Tchaikovsky. Appointment with [José] Iturbi.

> "In June 1936 in Philadephia, Lenny had an audition with Merrs. Simpkin and Lorenz (arranged by Don, his Harvard roommate). They were greatly taken with his playing. Among other things they said: 1) The boy is an artist. 2) He has stage personality. 3) Interpretation a little youthful and immature. 4) He ought to be at Curtis – not for what they could teach him but for what contacts he could make. 5) Mr. Lorenz confided to a girl, 'You see a great boy – you'll see a greater man'. They also arranged an interview with Iturbi. While visiting Don at 2008 N. Park Aven., Lenny attended a Robin Hood Dell concert where he heard Spalding play the Mendelssohn Violin Concerto under Alexander Smallens, also the *Romeo and Juliet* Overture of Tchaikovsky and a rehearsal of Harold Bauer playing the Schumann."

3 August 1936, Sharon, MA: Wrote me about an eleven-page letter which he will show me. He has grippe and asked me to visit him.

4 August 1936, Sharon, MA: Invites me to Sharon for lunch.

August 1936, Sharon, MA: Eleven-page letter written in the blackest of moods describing a clash with his father who did not want Lenny's friends visiting. He also poured his heart out about his friends.

13 September 1936, Alfred, ME: He is staying at a farm. Will come to visit me at York Harbor, where I am playing with a trio.

"In September 1936, he wound up at Elm Top Farm in Alfred, Maine for a short vacation. He borrowed the farmer's truck and drove to the Emerson House at York Harbor, Maine, where I was playing with my trio. I was delightfully surprised to see him."

9 July 1937, Pittsfield, MA: His activities at Camp Onota as a music counselor – casting for *The Pirates of Penzance*, first month, then *Of Thee I Sing*, second month.

"In July 1937, on his night off from Camp Onota, he went to Cap Allegro and was in the clutches of a million women, playing all evening – Lecuona, Ravel and de Falla etc."

21 January 1938, Cambridge, MA: Announcement – he's soloist in Ravel Concerto. He changes the printing and writes Boston Symphony and not State Symphony. [See Letter 18].

6 April 1938, Minneapolis, MN: Describes visit to Mitropoulos – quiet, interesting week.

2 May 1938, Cambridge, MA: He wrote out two measures of a theme.

7 July 1938, Sharon, MA: Thinking of putting on *Cradle Will Rock*. Rehearsal with Forum Quartet, and off to a publicity tea in Scituate, MA.

"In July 1938, Lenny was at the Sharon summer home (17 Lake Ave) and entertaining persuasive notions of putting on *Cradle Will Rock* that summer. He returned my copy of the Bach *Well-Tempered Clavichord* Vol. I which he had borrowed and marked up for his Harmonic Analysis class at Harvard."

25 July 1938, Sharon, MA: Audience reaction to his Newport concerto where he earned $50.00 playing in a home and made many friends. Summer plans.

15 August 1938, Sharon, MA: Describes trip home in the fog – from the Berkshires, Massachusetts.

25 August 1938, Chicago, IL: En route to the West. Bus driver would not stop at Pittsfield, where Lenny wanted to visit me.

18 September 1938, California: En route home from trip out West. "Glorious trip. We live in a great country."

29 December 1938, New York, NY: Staying in New York for the New [Year] – work to do – wishes me a happy New Year.

30 December 1938, Maywood, NJ: Saw *On Your Toes*. Will let me know of his arrival. It may be by plane.

7 July 1939, New York, NY: Having a terrible time with his nerves. No future. Staying with Adolph Green. Looking around for work.

3 October 1939, Woodstock, NY: Went to see [Léon] Barzin about a conducting class. Out of the question. Lenny's plans depend on Curtis examination.

"In early October 1939, he went to Woodstock to see Barzin who was doubtful as to whether he'd have a conducting class that year."

20 October 1939, Philadelphia, PA: Curtis Institute – Fierce desire to work hard – helpful, considerate faculty – lists subjects and teachers – majoring in piano and conducting – practices three hours a day.

9 November 1939, Philadelphia, PA: Studying *Tristan* – found a deli that sells Halvah – more in accompanying letter.

9 November 1939, Philadelphia, PA: Description of piano lesson with Vengerova. Offers to teach me when he returns home. Made friends with Mme Miquelle.

20 January 1940, Philadelphia, PA: Curtis Institute – Hard work – one tremendous piece of news – will tell me when he returns home.

1 February 1940, Philadelphia, PA: Mitropoulos has plans for him to come to Minneapolis and be official assistant conductor and pianist for the orchestra – be at every rehearsal and ready to take over – will be presented as soloist with orchestra – also as a composer.

28 February 1940, Philadelphia, PA: Curtis Institute – He was the only conducting student to get an A from Reiner. Helen Coates sent him brownies.

29 March 1940, Philadelphia, PA: Writes that my letter was the most wonderful letter he ever had. Heard Cleveland Orchestra and Rodzinski in Wilmington, Delaware. Koussy came to Curtis and remembered him.

10 April 1940, Philadephia, PA: Writing vocal quartets, settings of poems by Kenneath Fearing. No contract from Minneapolis and no confirmation about the Berkshires. Going to Washington with Mme Miquelle for the weekend.

23 April 1940, Philadelphia, PA: Letter explaining why Mitropoulos cannot import him. The union claims that Lenny is not a necessary function that cannot be filled by local people. Manager did not want Lenny because he was a student.

3 May 1940, Philadelphia, PA: Coming home on weekend. Writes me to cultivate my left dimple for the occasion. Sings "Love in May".

22 June 1940, New York, NY: Leaving for telecast. Will write from New Hampshire. Writes card in Aaron [Copland]'s studio using his card. I asked him what score he would like. He suggested Schumann's 4th Symphony, *Petrouchka*, Debussy *Nocturnes*, *Firebird*, *Don Juan*, *Till Eulenspiegel*.

27 June 1940, Hanover, NH: Kenny Erhman looking for him. Leaving for Cranwell School for Boys, Lenox, Massachusetts.

"In June 1940 he did a television show in Hanover, NH, while staying with Raphael Silverman (Hillyer)."

15 July 1940, Lenox, MA: Made an auspicious conducting debut. Lenny writes it was terrific, thrilling, awe shedding. Letter to follow.

16 July 1940, Lenox, MA: Conducted his own first concert at Tanglewood – Randall Thompson's Second Symphony – marvelous time – Koussy and orchestra like him. Plans to conduct *Scheherazade*, Copland's *Music for the Theatre*.

24 October 1940, Philadelphia, PA: Reiner is furious at Koussy for stealing his pupil. Never feels wholly alive in Philadelphia.

13 December, 1940, Philadelphia, PA: Practices four hours at the piano – Mozart Concerto, restudying Chopin Études in 3rds and 6ths. Teaching "rich brats" at the Meadowbrook School on Wednesdays.

18 January 1941, Philadelphia, PA: Life is dull and lonely, but very active. He is broadcasting the Stravinsky two-piano concerto on February 1st, 5:30 p.m. on NBC. He will imagine me at the other piano.

7 February 1941, Philadelphia, PA: Vengerova wants to make a two-piano team with him and another student. She was swept off her feet with their Stravinsky. Feels like he is finishing up a jail sentence and can't wait to get away from there fast enough. *Bored.*

12 March 1941, Philadelphia, PA: Next broadcast April 26th.

21 April 1941, Philadelphia, PA: Plans to be home May 4th. Will be on the air.

21 July 1941, Lenox, MA: Big success conducting William Schuman *American Festival Overture* on the same program with Koussy conducting the *Faust Symphony*. Lenny got two more bows than Koussy. Lenny got a screaming ovation. Conducted *Mastersingers* Prelude at Esplanade – 22,000 people in audience – $150.00.

2 December 1941, Boston, MA: Theme from Schumann Symphony.

5 December 1941, Boston, MA: Card announcing opening of his studio for the teaching of piano and musical analysis at 295 Huntington Avenue, Boston.

20 December 1941, Boston, MA: Christmas card and invitation to see his new studio.

6 October 1942, New York, NY: No real secure job yet. Doing odd jobs.

23 June 1943, New York, NY: One week late for my birthday. Wishes me success and happiness.

12 July 1943, New York, NY: Will conduct Goldman Band concerts. Leaving for Hollywood in August for a month vacation. Will conduct Boston Symphony concerts in Boston on August 1st and 2nd before leaving.

11 August 1943, Brookline, MA: Rehearsals for Tanglewood – will be back at end of month for Army induction.

22 October 1943, New York, NY: Written on Philharmonic Symphony of New York stationery. Wonderful and exciting.

15 December 1943, New York, NY: Thanks me for the "glorious Halvah". Do I ever get to New York?

26 June 1944, New York, NY: My wonderful cards delight him. Was in the hospital having his septum out. Leaving for Chicago to begin his summer season. Will conduct at Stadium in New York.

20 September 1944, New York, NY: Wants to know how I am. Will conduct *Fancy Free* in Boston on October 2nd and we will get together. Some day we will play the Saint-Saëns 5th Concerto together.

19 February 1945, St. Louis, MO: Conducting was wonderful, responsive orchestra, audiences wild. Middle of a huge tour across the continent through Canada and back.

4 September 1945, New York, NY: Thanks me for my most touching card. He asked if I heard of his acquisition of the New York City Center Orchestra. It was a thrilling birthday gift.

11 December 1945, New York, NY: Came home from a two-week bout in St. Louis and found my heavenly Halvah – beautiful surprise.

24 December 1945, en route from Minneapolis to New York: He talked of me with mutual friends, and loved me very much.

1 February 1946, New York, NY: Coming in March to Boston and wants to spend some time together. He is redoing the Beethoven 1st Concerto. It is full of me.

9 April 1947, New York, NY: Am I coming to Tanglefoot?

15 April 1948, New York, NY: Off to Europe to conduct in Munich, Budapest, Vienna and Milan.

29 November 1951, Cuernavaca, Mexico: Encouraging me to teach in Israel. He is composing, sunning, swimming. Opera progresses slowly – throws away more than he keeps.

3 January 1952, Cuernavaca, Mexico: Wishing me happiness for my marriage. He feels lazy.

4 December 1961, New York, NY: He is sick in bed. The Halvah is like Manna from Heaven. It cheered his ailing days.

9 February 1962, New York, NY: He was overcome with nostalgia when he met a mutual friend in Aspen, Colorado. Memories of my Madison Trio, joyful early days.

3 June 1970, Paris, France: Conducted Mahler 3rd in Paris, Verdi Requiem in London, *Fidelio* in Rome. He can hardly keep up with himself.

10 January 1972, New York, NY: While he was in Vienna, he recalled meeting "under Beethoven" when we met for two pianos [under the Beethoven statue] at the New England Conservatory.

Bibliography

Archives

The vast majority of the letters published in this book are in the Leonard Bernstein Collection, Music Division, Library of Congress, Washington, D.C. Thanks to the work of Charlie Harmon and others in the Leonard Bernstein Office, the Bernstein Collection also includes many photocopies of letters from Bernstein as well as those written to him.

Other collections in the Library of Congress containing letters from Bernstein include those of Aaron Copland, David Diamond, Hans Heinsheimer, Serge Koussevitzky, and Helen Coates, as well as the papers of other members of the Bernstein family, notably Leonard's sister Shirley, his brother Burton, and his wife Felicia.

Bernstein's letters to Jerome Robbins about *Fancy Free* are in the Robbins Papers at the New York Public Library of the Performing Arts, and other letters from Bernstein are drawn from the institutions and private individuals listed below:

> Leonard Bernstein Collection, Music Division, Library of Congress, Washington, D.C.
> Aaron Copland Collection, Music Division, Library of Congress, Washington, D.C.
> David Diamond Collection, Music Division, Library of Congress, Washington, D.C.
> Hans Heinsheimer Collection, Music Division, Library of Congress, Washington, D.C.
> Serge Koussevitzky Collection, Music Division, Library of Congress, Washington, D.C.
> Jerome Robbins Papers, New York Public Library for the Performing Arts, New York, NY.
> Richard Adams Romney Letters, Beinecke Rare Book and Manuscript Library, Yale University, New Haven, CT.
> Yevgeny Yevtushenko Papers, Manuscripts Division, Special Collections, Stanford University Library, Stanford, CA.
> Pat Jaffe, New York, NY.
> Phyllis Newman, New York, NY.
> Shirley Gabis Rhoads Perle, New York, NY.
> Sid Ramin, New York, NY.

Books and Articles

Adams, John (2008): *Hallelujah Junction: Composing an American Life*. New York: Farrar, Straus, and Giroux.

Barnouw, Erik (1990): *Tube of Plenty: The Evolution of American Television*. New York and Oxford: Oxford University Press.

Bernstein, Burton (1982): *Family Matters: Sam, Jennie, and the Kids*. New York: Summit Books.

Bernstein, Leonard (1957): "Excerpts from a West Side Log," *Playbill*, 30 September, pp. 47–8; repr. in Bernstein 1982, pp. 144–7.

—— (1959): *The Joy of Music*. New York: Simon and Schuster.

—— (1966): *The Infinite Variety of Music*. New York: Simon and Schuster.

—— (1982): *Findings*. New York: Simon and Schuster.

Bernstein Live at the New York Philharmonic (2000): Disc notes for NYP 2003, New York: Philharmonic-Symphony Society of New York.

Burlingame, Jon (2003): "Leonard Bernstein and *On the Waterfront*: Tragic Nobility, a Lyrical Song, and Music of Violence," in Joanne E. Rapf, ed.: *On the Waterfront*. Cambridge: Cambridge University Press, pp. 124–47.

Burton, Humphrey (1994): *Leonard Bernstein*. London: Faber and Faber.

Chapin, Ted (2005): *Everything Was Possible: The Birth of the Musical Follies*. New York: Applause Books.

Chaplin, Saul (1994): *The Golden Age of Movie Musicals and Me*. Norman, OK: University of Oklahoma Press.

Cooke, Mervyn, ed. (2010): *The Hollywood Film Music Reader*. New York and Oxford: Oxford University Press.

Copland, Aaron, and Vivian Perlis (1984): *Copland: 1900 Through 1942*. London: Faber and Faber.

—— (1992): *Copland Since 1943*. London: Marion Boyars.

Cott, Jonathan (2013): *Dinner with Lenny: The Last Long Interview with Leonard Bernstein*. New York: Oxford University Press.

Crist, Elizabeth B., and Wayne Shirley, ed. (2006): *The Selected Correspondence of Aaron Copland*. New Haven and London: Yale University Press.

Dougary, Ginny (2010): "Leonard Bernstein: Charismatic, Pompous – and a Great Father," *The Times* (London), 13 March. Online version at www.ginnydougary.co.uk, accessed 19 March 2013.

Dunning, John (1998): *On the Air: The Encyclopedia of Old-time Radio*. New York: Oxford University Press.

Gordon, Eric A. (1989): *Mark the Music: The Life and Work of Marc Blitzstein*. New York: St Martin's Press.

Gottlieb, Jack, ed. (1998): *Leonard Bernstein […] A Complete Catalog of His Works. Volume 1: Life, Musical Compositions & Writings*. [New York:] Leonard Bernstein Music Publishing Company.

Hoopes, Roy (1982): *Cain*. New York: Holt, Reinhart, and Winston.

Houseman, John (1972): *Run-Through: A Memoir*. New York: Simon and Schuster.

Hussey, Walter (1985): *Patron of Art*. London: Weidenfeld and Nicolson.

Joseph, Charles M. (2001): *Stravinsky Inside Out*. New Haven and London: Yale University Press.

Jowett, Deborah (2004): *Jerome Robbins: His Life, his Theater, his Dance*. New York: Simon and Schuster.

Kimberling, Victoria J. (1987): *David Diamond: A Bio-Bibliography*. Lanhau, MD: Scarecrow Press.

Laurents, Arthur (2000): *Original Story By: A Memoir of Broadway and Hollywood*. New York: Alfred A. Knopf.

Mangan, Timothy, and Irene Herrmann: *Paul Bowles on Music*. Berkeley, CA: University of California Press.

Massey, Drew (2009): "Leonard Bernstein and the Harvard Student Union: In Search of Political Origins," *Journal of the Society for American Music*, vol. 3, no. 1, pp. 67–84.

Milhaud, Darius (1995): *My Happy Life* (trans. Donald Evans, George Hall, and Christopher Palmer). London: Marion Boyars.

Moorehead, Caroline, ed. (2006): *The Letters of Martha Gellhorn*. London: Chatto and Windus.

Nixon, Marni (2006): *I Could Have Sung All Night: My Story*. New York: Billboard Books.

Oja, Carol J., and Kay Kaufman Shelemay (2009): "Leonard Bernstein's Jewish Boston: Cross-Disciplinary Research in the Classroom," *Journal of the Society of American Music*, vol. 3, no. 1, pp. 3–33.

Pollack, Howard (1999): *Aaron Copland: The Life of an Uncommon Man*. London: Faber and Faber.

Sarna, Jonathan D. (2009): "Leonard Bernstein and the Boston Jewish Community of His Youth: The Influence of Solomon Braslavsky, Herman Rubenovitz, and Congregation Mishkan Tefila," *Journal of the Society of American Music*, vol. 3, no. 1, pp. 35–46.

Seldes, Barry (2009): *Leonard Bernstein: The Political Life of an American Musician*. Berkeley, Los Angeles, and London: University of California Press.

Simeone, Nigel (2009): *Leonard Bernstein: West Side Story*. Farnham: Ashgate.

Swayne, Steve (2011): *Orpheus in Manhattan: William Schuman and the Shaping of American Music*. Oxford and New York: Oxford University Press.

Vaill, Amanda (2007): *Somewhere: The Life of Jerome Robbins*. London: Weidenfeld and Nicolson.

Zadan, Craig (1974): *Sondheim & Co*. New York: Macmillan.

Websites (selective list)

Leonard Bernstein Collection, Library of Congress: http://memory.loc.gov/ammem/collections/bernstein

Official Leonard Bernstein website: www.leonardbernstein.com

Leonard Bernstein's Boston Years: Team Research in a Harvard Classroom [includes interviews with Lukas Foss, Raphael Hillyer, Sid Ramin, and Harold Shapero]: http://isites.harvard.edu/icb/icb.do?keyword=bernstein

FBI Records: The Vault (online archive): http://vault.fbi.gov

The Harvard Crimson: www.thecrimson.com

Internet Broadway database: www.ibdb.com

New York Philharmonic Digital Archives: http://archives.nyphil.org

The New York Times: www.nytimes.com

Time Magazine: www.time.com

Index of Compositions by Bernstein

Note: this is an index of works mentioned in the present book. For a complete catalogue of Bernstein's compositions, see Gottlieb 1998.

Missa brevis (1988) 349 n24
First performance: 21 April 1988, Atlanta,
GA, Symphony Hall, Derek Lee Ragin
(counter-ten.), Atlanta Symphony
Chorus, Robert Shaw (cond.)
Dedication: For Robert Shaw
Derived from music for *The Lark*, 1955

Nicest Time of Year, The (by 12 July 1943,
see Letter 148) 133
Probably unperformed at the time. The
melody used the following year for
"Lucky To Be Me" in *On The Town*

On the Town (1944; book and lyrics by Betty
Comden and Adolph Green, on an idea
by Jerome Robbins) 2, 30 n43, 41 n60, 51
n75, 70 n104, 76, 167, 168, 169, 170, 171,
173 n9, 196, 221, 222 n90, 265 n173,
307, 311–12, 329, 345, 395, 426 n61, 465
n128, 489, 519, 534, 561
First performance: 13 December 1944,
Boston, Colonial Theatre, cast incl. Betty
Comden (Claire DeLoone), Nancy
Walker (Hildy Esterhazy), Sono Osato
(Ivy Smith), Adolph Green (Ozzie), Cris
Alexander (Chip), John Battles (Gabey);
Jerome Robbins (choreo.), George
Abbott (dir.), Max Goberman (cond.)
First New York Performance: 28 December
1944, Adelphi Theatre, cast as above
Orchestrations by Bernstein and Hershy Kay,
Don Walker, Elliott Jacoby and Ted Royal
Dedication: none, but the *Three Dance
Episodes from "On the Town"* are dedicated
to Sono Osato (I), Betty Comden (II)
and Nancy Walker (III)
On the Waterfront (1954; film score) 299,
317–18, 333, 564
Sound recording: 25–8 April 1954,
Hollywood, CA, Columbia Pictures
Studio, North Gower Street, orchestra,
Morris Stoloff (cond.), supervised by
Leonard Bernstein
Bernstein also played the piano for part of
this recording: he performed the solo in
saloon scene, approx. 37 minutes into the
film (the manuscript of the music for this
scene is headed "4C – Juke Box")

Peace, The (1941, incid. music for play by
Aristophanes) 3, 73, 75
First Performance: 23 May 1941,
Cambridge, MA, Sanders Theatre,
Harvard Student Union Theatre, Robert
Nichols (dir.), Leonard Bernstein (cond.)

Peter Pan (1950, incid. music for play by
J.M. Barrie) 263, 266, 268, 269, 270, 273,
274, 275, 276, 291, 316, 329, 426
First performance: 24 April 1950, New
York, Imperial Theatre, cast incl. Jean
Arthur (Peter Pan) and Boris Karloff
(Captain Hook); John Burrell (dir.),
Trude Rittmann (music coordinator),
Ben Steinberg (cond.)
Orchestrations by Hershy Kay
Piano Trio (1937) 16 n18
First performance: 1937, Madison Trio:
Mildred Spiegel (piano), Dorothy
Rosenberg (violin), Sarah Kruskall (cello)
Later performance: 1939?, Harvard
University, Paine Hall, Raphael Silverman
[Hillyer] (violin), Jesse Ehrlich (cello),
Mildred Spiegel (piano) [according to
Raphael Hillyer]
Dedication: For the Madison Trio: M.S.,
D.R., S.K.
On the last page of the autograph score,
Bernstein has written "Revised Apr.
1937"; Bernstein's movement listing on
the inside front cover of this manuscript
calls the work "Pianoforte Trio, op. 2", as
do the autograph parts

Quiet Place, A (1983, rev. 1984; libretto by
Stephen Wadsworth) 31 n46, 534, 535,
537 n4, 549
First performance of original version (in one
act; the second work on a double bill with
Trouble in Tahiti): 17 June 1983, Houston
Grand Opera, John DeMain (cond.)
First performance of the revised version (in
three acts, incorporating *Trouble in
Tahiti*): 19 June 1984, La Scala, Milan,
John Mauceri (cond.)
First U.S. performance of the revised
version: 22 July 1984, Washington, D.C.,
Kennedy Center for the Performing Arts,
John Mauceri (cond.)

Riobamba, The (1942) 89, 435 n80
First performance: 10 December 1942, New
York, Riobamba Club, 151 East 57th
Street (*see* Letter 115), possibly Jane
Froman (singer), who headed the bill on
the club's opening night
Derived from music in *Conch Town* and later
reworked as the "Danzón" in *Fancy Free*

Serenade (1947–8; 1955) 236–9; 334, 336
Planned musical setting of James M. Cain's
Serenade, not composed

General Index